BACKING HITLER

CONSENT AND COERCION
IN NAZI GERMANY

Robert Gellately

OXFORD
UNIVERSITY PRESS

OXFORD
UNIVERSITY PRESS

Great Clarendon Street, Oxford OX2 6DP

Oxford University Press is a department of the University of Oxford.
It furthers the University's objective of excellence in research, scholarship,
and education by publishing worldwide in

Oxford New York

Auckland Bangkok Buenos Aires Cape Town Chennai
Dar es Salaam Delhi Hong Kong Istanbul Karachi Kolkata
Kuala Lumpur Madrid Melbourne Mexico City Mumbai Nairobi
São Paulo Shanghai Taipei Tokyo Toronto

and an associated company in Berlin

Oxford is a registered trade mark of Oxford University Press
in the UK and in certain other countries

Published in the United States
by Oxford University Press Inc., New York

First published 2001
First published as an Oxford University Press paperback, 2002

British Library Cataloguing in Publication Data
Data available

Library of Congress Cataloging in Publication Data
Data available

ISBN-13: 978-0-19-280291-0
ISBN-10: 0-19-280291-7

5 7 9 10 8 6

Typeset by Graphicraft Limited, Hong Kong
Printed in Great Britain
on acid-free paper by
Biddles Ltd
King's Lynn, Norfolk

For Marie

PREFACE

This book began to take shape one day as I was reading through the dossiers of the Secret Police (Gestapo) in an archive in Germany. I was struck by the story of an unfortunate woman who had been reported to the police. Her accuser, in an anonymous letter, said that she 'looked Jewish' and was supposedly having a sexual relationship with a neighbour. The dossier also included a press clipping about the subsequent court case. The newspaper report was distorted and hate-filled, but I found it remarkable that the press, apparently as a matter of course, was publicizing the fate of the woman and her partner. After all, for decades I and others of my generation had been told by our teachers that so much of the terror in Nazi Germany had been carried out in complete secrecy. Upon reading the newspaper clipping, I began to wonder how much and what kind of information the press conveyed to the German public in the Third Reich. What did the Germans know about the 'secret' police, the persecutions, and the concentration camps? I began looking into German newspapers from the Nazi period, and at the same time, I continued to work on the dossiers of men and women who became entangled in the webs of the Secret Police, the Criminal Police (Kripo), and the Nazi Party. The results of this research are in this book, and they will be surprising to many people.

Germans were in fact meant to know that their country had a Secret Police and a concentration camp system. Contrary to what has been passed down, the Germans did not just accept the 'good' that Nazism brought (the economy, for example), and reject the evil institutions. Instead, Hitler was largely successful in getting the backing, one way or another, of the great majority of citizens. The consensus formed quickly, but was and remained pluralistic, differentiated, and at times inconsistent. However, as I show in this book, the Germans generally turned out to be proud and pleased that Hitler and his henchmen were putting away certain kinds of people who did not fit in, or who were regarded as 'outsiders', 'asocials', 'useless eaters', or 'criminals'. Although the Nazis certainly aimed their venom at people drawn from the ranks of such 'enemies', Hitler and his henchmen did not want to cower the German people as a whole into submission, but to win them over by building on popular images, cherished ideals, and long-held phobias in the country. Even as the Nazis 'cleansed' the body politic in the name of the future and a perfect race, even as they grew more radical and brutal in the war years, they also aimed to create and maintain the broadest possible level of popular backing. They expended an enormous amount of energy and resources to track public opinion and to win over the people.

In the book I trace the story from the beginning of the new Reich in 1933, into the war years, and down to its last desperate months. Whereas most books on Nazi terror devote considerable attention to the foundation years, many of them often neglect the radical changes that began with the coming of the war, when everything about Hitler's revolution was revolutionized. I show what happened on the ground, and follow the story during the stormy last months of Hitler's dictatorship.

I have attempted to give voice to the victims of oppression, particularly by using diaries and other testimony, and to include a wide range of men, women, and children who suffered at the hands of the Nazis. I focus attention on the Jews, and in addition I spend a good deal of time on the slave workers, particularly those forced from their homes in eastern Europe. Not only the German state, but also thousands of private ventures and hundreds of thousands of individual farmers and small businesses, became involved in the subjugation and exploitation of these people.

The book concludes with a brief account of the apocalyptic end of the Third Reich. For the first time German-on-German terror really grew widespread, directed as it was at anyone who dared to contemplate resistance. Terror grew more open and pronounced against foreign workers, and especially against the millions of prisoners in the camps. Even as the country spiralled toward defeat, for the most part Germans held on stubbornly, and did so for a wide range of reasons.

This is also the place to thank all those who have helped me in the course of research and writing. A number of historians and scholars from other fields have pointed me in the direction of important documents, offered useful advice along the way, or answered my questions. I can only mention some of them here: Omer Bartov, Volker Berghahn, Peter Black, George Browder, Christopher Browning, Ludwig Eiber, Richard Evans, Jürgen Falter, Gerald Feldman, Marie Fleming, John Fout, Norbert Frei, Henry Friedlander, Peter Fritzsche, Michael Geyer, Geoffrey Giles, Peter Hayes, Ulrich Herbert, Susannah Heschel, Peter Hoffmann, Eric Johnson, Marion Kaplan, Michael Kater, Sybil Milton, Jeremy Noakes, Gerhard Paul, Hans-Dieter Schmidt, Peter Steinbach, and Gerhard Weinberg. I received assistance over the years in many archives and libraries, and I want particularly to mention Anselm Faust (Düsseldorf) and Wilhelm Lenz (Berlin). Julia Torrie, my former student and research assistant, was enormously helpful.

I learned a great deal through discussions at a conference I organized with Sheila Fitzpatrick on denunciations in European history. My understanding of the wide range and the fates of the victims was influenced by discussions we had at a conference I organized with Nathan Stoltzfus and supported by the Harry Frank Guggenheim Foundation. My warm thanks go to all participants, and to Karen Colvard of the Guggenheim.

The book could not have been written without funds made available by the Social Sciences and Humanities Research Council of Canada and the Alexander von Humboldt-Foundation in Germany. I gratefully acknowledge the generous support of the Strassler family, and I thank David Strassler and Clark University for fostering my work.

CONTENTS

LIST OF ILLUSTRATIONS

(between pages 78 and 79)

LIST OF TABLES

Introduction

The steps in the establishment of Hitler's dictatorship followed quickly on his appointment as Chancellor at the end of January 1933. He began as merely the head of a coalition government in a country riddled with political, economic, and social problems, and on top of that he immediately had to prepare for an election that was in the offing. None of this distracted his attention from ambitious plans, and only days after his appointment he was already talking to military leaders about how he wanted to end the 'cancer of democracy', to install the 'tightest authoritarian state leadership', and even to embark on the 'conquest of new living space in the east and its ruthless Germanization'.[1] At the end of February he took advantage of an arsonist's attack on the Reichstag to obtain an emergency measures act in the name of stopping an alleged Communist coup. Less than a month later, he secured the mandatory two-thirds majority in the Reichstag he needed for a constitutional change and an Enabling Law that in effect made it possible for him to become a law-giving dictator.[2] Although Hitler and the Nazis could not win the support of the majority of Germans in free elections, within a matter of months after his appointment as Chancellor, most citizens came to accept and then firmly to back him.

Hitler wanted to create a dictatorship, but he also wanted the support of the people. The most important thing he could do to win them over was to solve the massive unemployment problem. Although it is clear that his regime beat the Great Depression faster than any of the Western democracies, it still took time. In the short term, Hitler conveyed a sense of the strong leader who was in charge, and after the years of upheaval that marked the Weimar Republic, the German state took on an aura of 'normality' that harked back to the days prior to World War I. Weimar was identified with the lost war, humiliating peace, economic turmoil, and social chaos, and had been loved by almost no one in Germany. This attempt to establish democracy did not sink deep social roots, and it became relatively easy for people to turn away from it.

Hitler not only filled a power vacuum, but soon won patriotic acclaim for systematically tearing up the humiliating peace settlement of 1919 and for restoring, almost overnight, what many Germans felt was their 'rightful' place as the dominant power on the continent. He managed to do so almost without an army. As a reward for such accomplishments, and even though there were persistent pockets of negative opinion, rejection of Nazism, and even examples of resistance, the great majority of the German people soon became devoted to Hitler and they supported him to the bitter end in 1945.[3]

The new regime made no bones about using coercion in many forms against its declared enemies, but it also sought the consent and support of the people at every turn. As I try to show in the book, consent and coercion were inextricably entwined throughout the history of the Third Reich, partly because most of the coercion and terror was used against specific individuals, minorities, and social groups for whom the people had little sympathy.[4] Coercion and terror were highly selective, and certainly did not rain down universally on the heads of the German people. Beginning in early 1933, the police and Nazi Storm Troopers started cracking heads, and new concentration camps were established, but not much more than a mini-wave of terror swept Germany. By and large, terror was not needed to force the majority or even significant minorities into line. By mid-1933, or the end of that year at the latest, power was already secured, and the brutalities and violence that are identified with the so-called Nazi 'seizure of power', began to wane.[5] Terror itself does not adequately explain how the Third Reich came to be, nor account for its considerable staying power.[6] As I will show, the regime continued to elicit popular support well into the war years.

The Nazis initially built on the popular mood in the country in early 1933. Most solid citizens, and not just the Nazis, were fed up with the failed Weimar experiment. They were also outraged by what they saw as evidence all around them of decadence, decay, and crime.[7] Under the circumstances, there was an obvious political incentive for Hitler's regime to act decisively against democratic and liberal activities of all kinds, to outlaw opposition parties beginning with the Communists, and to combine that with a crackdown in the name of law and order. In March 1933 Hitler called for the 'moral purification' of the body politic. Whatever that might be taken to mean, it is clear that his personal convictions, Nazi ideology, and what he deemed to be the wishes and hopes of many people, came together in deciding where it would be politically most advantageous to begin creating what the Nazis termed a racially-based 'community of the people'.

The book begins in 1933 and traces the story to 1945, with the emphasis on what happened inside Nazi Germany. I show how and why a social consensus emerged in favour of Hitler and Nazism within months of Hitler's appointment as Chancellor. This consensus took many forms, and was fluid rather than firm, active rather than passive, differently constituted according to context and theme, and constantly in the process of being formed. I argue, however, that from 1933, consensus in favour of Hitler and increasingly also Nazism, was virtually never in doubt.

Although historians have tended to pay more attention to the first phase of the dictatorship, especially its foundation years, I trace how that system, including the new police and concentration camps, went through two additional and quite distinct phases. The first of these began with the coming of the war in 1938–9, and I argue that the war revolutionized the revolution. Nearly everything about the dictatorship changed, with the police becoming more invasive, arbitrary, and murderous, and the system as a whole turning far more radically against its declared enemies at home and abroad. The final phase in the history of Hitler's dictatorship began as the prospects of invasion and defeat grew, so that the revolution was revolutionized once more. At the end of 1944 and into 1945, the dictatorship became more openly terroristic in an effort to stave off the inevitable. I try to show how the consensus broadly held through all three phases, what changed, and why some people began to seek a way out. As the home front also became the battlefront, for the first time, German-on-German terror became the order of the day.[8]

It is worth drawing attention to several other historians who have studied aspects of social consensus in the Third Reich, although they have adopted other perspectives and used different sources. I share some of the views expressed by Ian Kershaw and Detlev Peukert, who suggest that Hitler's own popularity provided one of the main foundations on which the regime was founded and built. Moreover, as Peukert has put it, popular acclaim for the Führer really 'articulated a certain basic consensus of the majority of the population for the system, a consensus that remained unaffected by outspoken expressions of criticisms on points of detail'.[9] Workers were often thought immune to the appeals of Nazism, but Alf Lüdtke's recent study shows on the basis of soldiers' letters sent to their families back home, that in fact most people in the country 'readily accepted' Hitler, and they widely cheered the goals of ' "restoring" the grandeur of the Reich and "cleaning out" alleged "aliens" in politics and society'.[10] As a matter of fact, even to this day, when Germans look back they have fond memories of the dictatorship's 'accomplishments' in restoring social values, bringing back order, and instituting social harmony.[11]

Women also were won over, and according to Ute Frevert most of them did not experience the Nazi era (even in comparison to the liberal Weimar years) as some kind of 'regression' into the dark days of discrimination. The 'relative rarity of deliberate acts of political resistance', Frevert suggests, can be taken to mean 'that women who satisfied the political, racial and social requirements—and the vast majority did—did not perceive the Third Reich as a woman's hell. Much of what it introduced was doubtless appealing, the rest one learned to accept.'[12] One well-spoken middle-class woman, wife of a prominent historian of Germany, neither of whom incidentally were Nazi Party members, stated in a recent interview how 'on the whole, everyone felt well'. She remembers how she '*wanted* only to see the good' and the rest she 'simply shoved aside'. She feels even now that most Germans 'tried at the very least, even when they didn't agree one hundred per cent with the Third Reich or with National Socialism, to adapt themselves. And there were certainly eighty per cent who lived productively and positively throughout the time. . . . We also had good years. We had *wonderful* years.'[13]

The most controversial recent study of social consensus in the Third Reich, is Daniel Goldhagen's lengthy book, a popular success, but much criticized by professional historians. Unlike most historians, he emphasizes the role of long-term, and pre-Hitler 'eliminationist' antisemitism as the basic and essential element in the consensus. He claims that the murderous potential of this phobia was already there before 1933, and so tends to underestimate what changed beginning in 1933. Given this framework, he necessarily plays down Hitler's role, and concludes among other things that 'what Hitler and the Nazis actually did was to unshackle and thereby activate Germans' pre-existing, pent-up antisemitism'. What he calls the 'great success' in persecuting the Jews, resulted 'in the main' from 'the preexisting, demonological, racially based, eliminationist antisemitism of the German people, which Hitler essentially unleashed'.[14]

Daniel Goldhagen's study, for all of its problems brought a number of important issues up for debate and called out for investigation.[15] However, I am inclined to the view that monocausal explanations of the kind he employs, do not hold up to scrutiny and that social agreement with or merely popular toleration of Hitler and the dictatorship was attained for many reasons, some of the most important of which had little or nothing to do with the persecution of the Jews.

Antisemitism was initially soft-pedalled, not only because depriving the Jews of making a living would hurt the economic recovery, but as I show in the book, also because most Germans in 1933 did not feel as strongly and as negatively about the Jews as did Hitler and the Nazis. Therefore, the first targets were not the Jews, but individuals and groups long regarded as threats to the social order (like the Communists) or to the moral universe, like criminals, 'asocials', and other 'problem cases'. As I make clear, during the first years of the new Reich, racist policies in general were formulated and implemented quite cautiously.

Thus, the Nazis did not act out of delusional or blind fanaticism in the beginning, but with their eyes wide open to the social and political realities around them. They developed their racist and repressive campaigns, by looking at German society, history, and traditions. The identification and treatment of political opponents and the persecution of social and racial outsiders illustrated the kind of populist dictatorship that developed under Hitler.

The book shows how antisemitism changed and slowly spread after 1933. Indeed, until the late 1930s, as many Jews who lived through those times have testified, antisemitism was not the primary concern of the public, most Germans were not rabidly antisemitic, and pushing out the Jews was not the top priority of the German state.[16] At the start of the Third Reich, as many Jews who lived there have testified for years on end, they were not social outsiders, certainly not in comparison with pre-emancipation times, and things changed slowly for many of them.[17] Jews in Germany were almost universally envied by the Jews in central and eastern Europe, and throughout the Weimar years, and to some extent even earlier, they had more social opportunities (as judges and professors, for example) than most Jews enjoyed even in the United States. Since the legal emancipation of Germany's Jews in 1871, they had become increasingly well integrated as law-abiding citizens who adopted middle-class values of hard work, clean living, and solid family values. In the German context in which such behaviour was lauded, their way of life made it initially more difficult for the antisemitic Nazis to go after them. As the regime promulgated one discriminatory measure after the next, or turned a blind eye to radical Nazis at the grass roots, Jews were slowly transformed into social outsiders, but even that happened gradually for most of them.

I suggest that it is important to show how antisemitism spread after 1933, and what changed and why, and especially how and why citizens began collaborating in the police and Nazi Party harassment and persecution of the Jews. As we will see in the book, the public inexorably became entangled in the discriminatory side of the dictatorship, including in the persecution of the Jews, and they did so for reasons that did not always include being explicitly racist. They went to the authorities and denounced the Jews and those who did not share official antisemitism. At times they were motivated by selfish reasons, often linked to active hatred and the profit motive. One effect of the persecution was to drive many Jews from the country, while those who remained were faced with the growing hostility of the authorities and what Ulrich Herbert has called the 'escalating indifference' of their fellow citizens.[18]

I began research for this book by addressing one of the major questions that has been raised since 1945, when we became aware of the concentration camps, namely, 'what did they know and when did they know it?' Did the Germans know about the secret police and the camps, the persecutions, the murders, and so on, and did they go along? Germans have defended themselves by saying they were unaware of, or poorly informed about, the camps, and were surprised by the revelations at the war's end. There was close to general agreement among historians for a long time, that the Nazis deliberately and systematically hid what they were doing, so it was possible that ordinary people really did not know.

This book challenges these views. It shows that a vast array of material on the police and the camps and various discriminatory campaigns was published in the media of the day. In the 1930s the regime made sure the concentration camps were reported in the press, held them up for praise, and proudly let it be known that the men and women in the camps were confined without trial on the orders of the police. The regime boasted openly of its new system of 'police justice' by which the Secret Police (Gestapo) and the Criminal Police (Kripo) could decide for themselves what the law was, and send people to the camps at will. The Nazis celebrated the police in week-long annual festivals across the country, and proudly chalked up their many successes in the war on crime, immorality, and pornography. Judges also got into the act. They meted out harsh justice and used the death penalty on an unprecedented scale. Far from clothing such practices in secrecy, the regime played them up in the press and lauded the modernity and superiority of the Nazi system over all others.

I make extensive use of newspapers in this book, but what about censorship? The novelist Christa Wolf indicated some years ago, that anyone in Nazi Germany who wanted to find out about the Gestapo, concentration camps, and the campaigns of discrimination and persecution, need only read the newspapers.[19] Nazi Germany was in fact a modern mass media society, and for its day was in the vanguard of modernity. Germans were both highly literate and voracious readers of newspapers, and moreover Hitler's regime did everything possible to put a radio in every home, and used newsreels and movies to get across their messages.[20] Movie-making was soon transformed into a system-friendly industry, and it proved remarkably easy to win over journalists. Even renowned middle-class and conservative newspapers demonstrated their agreement with Hitler's appointment or asked readers to give him a chance.[21] Thereafter, the regime guided the press mainly by holding owners, editors, and journalists politically responsible for what they published. In time more formal methods, like press conferences and directives were used. Reporters and editors colluded with Hitler by virtue of what they wrote, and reached a point where they simply chose not to follow up leads about the murder of the Jews, and numerous other atrocities.[22] Even when newspapers published death notices about the victims of euthanasia, reporters apparently made no enquiries.[23]

Readers of the press in dictatorships do not read less because they know it is censored.[24] If anything, they read more attentively because it is so important to figure out what is going on. The emphasis in the book, at any rate, is not what the Nazis wanted to keep out of the media, but what they wanted to put in, and how they crafted their stories to appeal to the minds and hearts of the German people. I surveyed a number of German newspapers, and consulted several important collections of newspaper clippings.

I try to show that media reports and press stories were an essential dimension of life and death in Hitler's dictatorship. Not only did citizens pay avid attention, but most of them 'experienced' the Gestapo, the courts, and the camps via the media.[25] These media representations need to be taken seriously and studied from various angles in order to bring out the theme of coercion and publicity.[26] Not only did the Nazis publish many 'crime and punishment' stories, but they worked out a coherent, rational, and 'scientific' police and confinement theory. They put forward the idea of the boot-camp for delinquents, and a 'lock 'em up and throw away the key' approach to repeat offenders. Preventive arrests and the use of 'work therapy' on criminals, drunks, and layabouts, supposedly led to crime-free streets, a return to good order, and restoration of tried-and-true German values. All these matters were played up in the press.

I argue that the rationalizations the Nazis provided the German public about why new forms of coercion and new laws were needed were an integral and essential part of the discrimination and persecution. Germans were informed of the new approach to crime that overcame the scruples of 'bleeding-heart' liberals and 'weak-willed' democrats. Brutal language in the press that described anyone deemed to be 'undesirable', became a characteristic feature of the era, and 'had a considerable impact upon the majority of the population'.[27] I have tried to decipher the glowing self-descriptions of Nazism as founded on a new theory of 'law and order' and as practising superior 'justice' against the social background of what was really happening in society at large as well as before the courts, in the prisons and concentration camps.

What about Hitler's role? This book in not a biography of Hitler, nor does it attempt to cover the entire history of the Third Reich. However, I have been struck by how often Hitler played a hands-on and a key role in the creation and operation of the coercive apparatus of the Third Reich. Where he did not give specific orders or instructions, his ideas, hate-filled speeches, and 'wishes' inspired police, justice, and SS leaders all along the line.[28]

Readers interested in more details of Hitler's life and role in all spheres of domestic and foreign policy can now turn to Ian Kershaw's masterful new biography, the first volume of which covers the period from 1889 to 1936. It marks an important turning point in the study of Hitler and the Third Reich. In the last chapters, Kershaw skilfully studies Hitler's interventions in domestic and foreign policies, and shows how other leaders often 'carried the ball' because Hitler's unique decision-making style left them plenty of room to do so.[29] When his second volume is completed, this biography will become the new standard work on Hitler.

At relevant points, I will discuss Hitler's decision-making, but the main focus of this book is on the social and public sides of the dictatorship rather than what went on behind closed doors and in secret. Hitler and those who worked closely with him in the police establishment consistently favoured police prerogatives over the regular court system. The Gestapo employed these new powers to track down all kinds of (vaguely defined) political foes, while the Kripo used them to end what was perceived as a crime wave when the Nazis came to power. Both police forces were no longer hampered by traditional legal constraints. It was easy to lock up suspects, without even a hearing before a judge, never mind a trial. Soon the Gestapo took on a mission to stop all 'political criminality', and to harass the Jews, while the Kripo obtained extraordinary powers to deal with criminality as it had been traditionally defined. In time the distinctions between political and non-political crimes grew blurred. I study these developments, including how the courts became entangled in a murderous competition with the police, and deal with the echoes heard in the public sphere.

A sense of how Germans responded positively to various waves of persecution and even to the spirit of Nazi 'justice', is conveyed on almost every page of Professor Victor Klemperer's recently published diary.[30] It represents the most detailed chronicle we have of the implementation of the repression, especially the measures aimed at the Jews. Klemperer recorded one telling conversation he had in late February 1935 with his last two students, whom he said were 'completely anti-Nazi'. The fact that they persisted in studying with this Jewish professor showed they had some civil courage. However, when their discussion turned to a recent newspaper story about the trial and execution of two young aristocratic women in Berlin, the students said they found the court's verdict 'totally appropriate'. They saw no fault in the procedures of the secret trial, nor were they troubled in the least that the accused had been denied essential legal rights. Klemperer concluded sadly that 'the sense of justice is being lost everywhere in Germany, is being systematically destroyed'.[31] In this book I examine the background of such stories, explore how coercion and consent were entwined, and finally how and why the German people backed the Nazi dictatorship.

1
Turning Away from Weimar

The years leading up to 1933 were difficult ones for Germany. The Weimar Republic's parliament was divided into more than a dozen political parties, and from the onset of the Great Depression in 1929, German Chancellors had to rely increasingly on the President's emergency powers to pass legislation.[1] At the end of 1932, when the crisis facing the country deepened and government ground to a standstill, a group of influential conservatives advised President Paul von Hindenburg that Adolf Hitler's leadership would be a way to deal with mounting social, economic, and political crisis.[2] Hitler was appointed on 30 January 1933. At 43 years of age, he was relatively young for the post, and beyond leading his own party since 1920, had not previously held a position of political responsibility.

Those men around the President and the social elites with whom they had contact, favoured Hitler as an interim leader, or at least saw him as a necessary evil. They no doubt believed that, lacking political experience, he would not be able to assert himself too much, and that they would retain ultimate control. In fact, men like ex-Chancellor Franz von Papen, considered that Hitler's limited background in politics, when combined with his unusual ability to connect with the masses, presented a unique opportunity. Hitler had other advantages, including a passion to revise the Peace Treaty of 1919 and to build up the military, and he was a staunch opponent of Communism, who could provide the government with the kind of popular backing it needed.[3] By January 1933 even some of the more reserved big businessmen came to see wisdom in Papen's project of 'yoking the Nazis to a conservative-dominated government'.[4] The well-connected and experienced non-Nazis with whom the President stacked Hitler's own cabinet, would supposedly ensure that he was more a figurehead than a real leader with effective ideas and a programme of his own. They badly misjudged the situation. In less than six months the Nazis undermined the parliamentary system and had begun the destruction of justice by suspending civil and legal rights, which in turn opened the way for the creation of the Gestapo (Secret State Police) and the establishment of the first concentration camps.

Signs of Crisis and Support for Hitler

Hitler was able to make the transition from rabble-rousing political speaker, into the deeply beloved Führer of the German people in a remarkably short time. He recognized that most men and women wanted radical steps taken to deal with the wide-ranging crisis facing the country, and even if not everyone yearned for a specifically Nazi leader, most were weary of the Weimar experiment in democracy, with the endless elections, the countless demonstrations and lawlessness in the streets, the long lines before the welfare offices, and the scale of the social chaos.[5] The German people, despising Weimar politicians who had utterly failed to reach out to them, found themselves ready to place their trust and understanding in someone who could re-connect them to what they felt were the sounder elements of German traditions. Hitler was able to scheme behind the scenes, and to manoeuvre himself into that position of trust and understanding.

There was a sense of hopelessness in the country on the eve of Hitler's appointment, and it was reflected in suicide rates for 1932 that were more than four times higher than those in Britain at the time, and nearly double what they were in the United States.[6] There was a broad perception that the country was experiencing a breakdown of cultural and moral values. Large families were becoming a thing of the past and more women were going to work; abortions were thought to be reaching alarming proportions; and prostitution, sexual deviancy, and venereal diseases were presumed to be spreading.[7]

Women had the vote and equality in law since 1919, but once the Depression hit, the virtues of the modern 'new woman' and emancipation were questioned, especially when issues arose about abortion, working wives (the so-called double-earners), and the falling birth rate. Although historians do not agree that the 'new woman' really existed in Weimar and tend to think she was an alarming myth constructed in the mass media of the time, Cornelie Usborne, for one, shows convincingly that there were enough such people to cause anxieties among social conservatives, who worried about upholding traditional marriage, gender roles, and morality. Many contemporaries saw the young, mainly middle- and lower middle-class 'new women' as sexual anarchists out to destroy social order, and threatening nothing less than 'racial suicide' by refusing to perform what traditionalists regarded as their 'biological duty'.[8]

Women on the left of the political spectrum no doubt were appalled at the prospect of a Hitler government, but there were many others, including even politically active women, who were not at all displeased. One of them remarked in mid-1932, that the social trend was 'away from liberalism, toward obligations; away from the career woman, toward the housewife and mother'.[9] Conservative, Catholic, and even liberal women by and large shared the point of view advocated by the Nazis, as to a 'naturally' determined sexual division of labour, and that it was important to reconstruct a 'community of the people' in which they would be involved primarily as wives and mothers, and 'not be forced to compete with men for scarce jobs and political influence'.[10] Not surprisingly, therefore, women voted almost at the same rate as men for Hitler and his party, and for its promise to restore some semblance of the 'normality' for which they longed.[11] The general sense of crisis was reinforced by massive unemployment, which in turn fuelled discontent in all social classes, even those not threatened directly. When Hitler came to power, six million were officially unemployed, but in addition as many as two million more were the 'hidden' unemployed, people who gave up even registering for a job. With a corrected total of up to eight million unemployed, nearly 40 per cent of Germany's blue- and white-collar workers were without work, and in addition, an estimated three million more were underemployed. In the face of these numbers, the state clawed back social welfare measures, like the unemployment insurance that was granted in July 1927 when Weimar was at the height of its 'stable' period.[12] There were three categories of state assistance for the unemployed, and the trend was for them all to decline into the lowest level, where bare survival was an issue.[13]

Political violence in the streets literally became an everyday experience in many parts of the country.[14] Most of the fighting was among the paramilitary organizations associated with various political parties, and involving millions of men, but the Nazis and the Communists were the most active.[15] Pitched battles broke out and innocent passers-by were killed when caught in the cross fire, as happened when sixteen people were killed on 'Bloody Sunday' (17 July 1932) in Hamburg-Altona: two more died later. The police intervened to break up the fighting, but as often happened, they came down in favour of the Nazis. Although most fatalities were non-Nazis, apparently shot by the police and security forces, such events were given an anti-Red interpretation in official reports and in the press with claims that Communist snipers were on the roofs.[16]

The anti-Communist tendencies of the German police were well known elsewhere. For example, eight days before Hitler was appointed, Berlin police shot several demonstrators and arrested nearly seventy more in the name of stopping a Communist demonstration against the Nazis.[17]

What made the general situation grave in the eyes of many middle-class Germans, was that support for the Communist Party (KPD) grew once the Depression hit. Indeed, in all three of the elections before Hitler's appointment, the KPD invariably came third, and its vote kept on rising.[18] The more moderate Social Democrats (SPD) usually came second, so that from a liberal or conservative perspective, a majority of people were voting for Marxist parties. Conservative newspapers asked: 'Who could effectively counter the Marxist threat?'[19] Alongside other factors, the growing sympathy in the extensive right-wing press helped Hitler into power.[20]

In the last elections before 1933, the Nazi vote also rose, but it dropped slightly in November 1932. However, there was no viable right-wing alternative to Hitler, with most middle-class parties already gone, so that for many property owners in Germany, the relentless rise of unemployment and the KPD would most likely have soon led them back to Hitler, even if he had not been appointed Chancellor in January 1933.[21] By the time Hitler became Chancellor, his support was far from unravelling, because 'the Nazis were the only acceptable party for the non-Marxist and non-Catholic voters who constituted the majority of German voters'.[22] There was no obvious alternative by 1933, and soon many Catholic voters would come into the fold.

Even at the time of Hitler's appointment, the Nazis were not doing as poorly in the elections as some historians have suggested. In the last two elections before 1933 they were denied a majority, but still won more votes than any party had received in any federal election since 1920. Hitler even challenged Hindenburg in the presidential elections of 1932, and though he did not win, this young 'corporal' took 37 per cent of the vote in the second round against the distinguished old Field Marshal's 53 per cent. The anti-democratic mood in the country can be gathered from the fact that the other candidate in the run-off presidential election was the Communist Ernst Thälmann, who won 10 per cent. The last pre-dictatorship elections showed that a majority of voters (men and women) supported the anti-Republican parties (namely, the Nazis, the Communists, and the Nationalists), all of whom wanted to get rid of parliamentary democracy.[23]

Hitler's appointment as Chancellor on 30 January 1933 was followed next day by the dissolution of the Reichstag. His slogan for the elections called for 5 March, 'Attack on Marxism', was bound to appeal to solid citizens and property owners. Hermann Göring, one of the few Nazis in Hitler's Cabinet, took immediate steps to introduce emergency police measures.[24] Over the next weeks the Nazis did not need to use the kind of massive violence associated with modern takeovers like the Russian Revolution. There was little or no organized opposition, and historian Golo Mann said of those times that 'it was the feeling that Hitler was historically right which made a large part of the nation ignore the horrors of the Nazi takeover. . . . People were ready for it.'[25] To the extent that terror was used, it was selective, and it was initially aimed mainly at Communists and other (loosely defined) opposition individuals who were portrayed as the 'enemies of the people'.

Hitler certainly was interested in more than just solving a momentary crisis, even one he could drag out as a continuing Communist plot. He wanted to formalize his position as law-giving dictator, and to outlaw all political parties but his own. During the stormy days of February and March 1933, a federal election campaign was under way in which the Nazis pulled out all the stops, trashed their opponents without mercy, and won tremendous support. For all that, in the elections of 11 March, Hitler was denied an outright majority. We should not exaggerate the significance of that fact, as he got the vote of just over seventeen million people (or 43.9 per cent of the votes cast). The outcome gave the Nazis a slim majority of seats in the Reichstag when combined with those of their

Nationalist partners. Hitler proved a master of the situation, and just as importantly, over the next months, the majority of Germans quickly made clear that they supported him.

Hitler convened the newly elected Reichstag in the famous Potsdam Church on 21 March, the first day of Spring, to signal a new beginning. On 'Potsdam Day', several innovations were introduced on the initiative of the Justice Ministry to show that the courts and judges would play their part. The vain hope of some of the 'legalists' was that if new Special Courts and a new decree against 'malicious attacks' on the government, could protect the regime from any criticism, and judges would mete out swift justice, then the dictatorship would return to the rule of law. Hitler took these concessions, but wanted much more. He needed two-thirds of the Reichstag to vote for a constitutional change that would enable him to pass laws through the Cabinet, and not just through the Reichstag. Hitler got this constitutional change on 23 March, when the deputies—except for the Socialists (and Communists who were not allowed to take their seats)—obliged him by voting for the so-called Enabling Law. Prior to the vote, Hitler gave a government declaration in which he signalled that he had a social and political agenda that went beyond suppressing Communism, getting people back to work, and restoring Germany's position in Europe. His stated goals now included creating a 'real community of the people' and he alluded to the need for 'the moral purification of the body politic'.[26]

The combination of Reichstag Fire Decree and Enabling Act gave the Nazi Revolution a veneer of legality and made it easier for citizens to accept the dictatorship. Hitler could claim to be the lawful head of government (by mid-1934 he was also the head of state), and anyone who wanted to resist was in the difficult position of having to act illegally. Soon even verbal criticism of the government was criminalized.[27]

Hitler's fate initially was tied to dealing with Communism and unemployment. The first part was easy, given the kinds of forces the Nazis could mobilize, the extent of popular anti-Communism, and the small numbers of militant Communists. But curing Germany's massive economic problems represented a formidable challenge. The 'Battle for Jobs' in time showed victories, and these were played up in the media for all they were worth. The 'war' on unemployment was hard-won, but even so, by 1936 reached a point where labour shortages were reported. The return to full employment was not the overnight 'miracle' some Germans remembered who lived through these times, but was more like a knock-down dragged-out struggle.[28]

Jobs and incomes bounced back and hope was restored, especially among the young men and women, who were also offered shiny state-sponsored programmes (like 'Landhelp', 'Landyear', and 'Labour Service'), that provided work experience in the countryside. Such projects were also designed to cement the 'community of the people' by bringing together youths with diverse backgrounds. The reintroduction of conscription in 1935, drew off large numbers of working-age men from the labour market, and so helped reduce the unemployment rolls.[29] Other government measures combined economics and ideology, like the introduction of marriage loans for medically fit and 'racially correct' couples. The loans were offered as part of a law on the reduction of unemployment (1 June 1933). Women were of central interest to the regime, not merely as potential mothers as they were in Fascist Italy, but as mothers of the race. Thus, not only was a fairly generous marriage loan provided on condition that the female spouse leave her job, but she also had to pass medical tests. To encourage her also to have children, the regime almost immediately decreed that repayments would be reduced by one-quarter on the birth of each new child.[30]

In Alison Owings's oral history of women in the Third Reich, nearly all of them point to Hitler's success in curing unemployment. It does not matter that the work creation programmes were the initiatives of leaders out in the provinces. Even some opponents of Nazism remembered the sources of Hitler's popularity to be the work creation programme; getting the drunks off the street and the youth in order again; introducing a 'work duty' programme and new road construction. The daughter of a nobleman, who was anything but sympathetic to Nazism, remembered that even her father was impressed by the 'accomplishments' of the regime. 'He was satisfied that order reigned again, that people had work, that the economy was going forward, and that Germany again enjoyed a certain respect.'[31]

Where persuasion failed, coercion was used to get the unwilling to take up low-paying jobs they did not want.[32] Grumbling did not go away, of course, and working-class family consumption in 1937 was lower than it had been in 1927; they drank less than half as much beer as they had a decade earlier. They also ate less meat, fish, tropical fruit, bacon and eggs, and wheat bread.[33]

Hitler also reached out to opponents, like the Catholics, by signing a Concordat with the Vatican on 8 July 1933. Until then, Catholic voters were loyal to their Centre Party, and it was they who were mainly responsible for denying the Nazis their electoral majorities. Catholics soon adjusted to the dictatorship. Protestants, however, were more sympathetic to Nazism all along. In their church elections of 1933, two-thirds of the voters supported the German Christian sect that wanted to integrate Nazism and Christianity, and to expel Jews who had converted to Protestantism.[34] Hitler made a brief radio appeal to Protestants on the eve of these church elections, and asked them to show their support for Nazi policies. He could not have been disappointed by the pro-Nazi results.[35]

Although the Communist and Socialist working class had been firmly against the Nazis up to 1933, in the Third Reich activists who were willing and able to resist were soon overwhelmed. The Communists were more active and held out longest, but even so, at the outside no more than 150,000 of them were touched directly by some form of persecution. If we presume they were all 'resisting', some more than others, we are left to conclude that Communist resisters, among a population of between sixty and seventy million, represented a small minority, and we know that even fewer members of the other working-class party were 'persecuted'.³⁶ It is clear that large sections of the working class were won over, especially by the return of full employment, so that by the mid-1930s they, too, contributed to the formation of a 'pro-National Socialist consensus'.³⁷ Even when workers were less than overwhelmed by appeals to become part of the 'community of the people', they nevertheless were impressed that the Nazis took seriously their everyday concerns on the shop floor. Workers 'did not keep their distance from the cheering masses' on occasions like the Nazi May Day of 'national labour', nor when Hitler spoke on the radio and especially when he gained one success after the next on the foreign policy front.³⁸

We are used to ignoring the subsequent elections and plebiscites under Hitler's dictatorship, but they tend to show that a pro-Nazi consensus formed and grew. In October 1933 Hitler withdrew Germany from the League of Nations and called a national plebiscite to ask Germans if they agreed. The results were 95 per cent in favour. Hardly less spectacular were the results of the election he called for November, held along with the plebiscite. The results were that Hitler and his party received almost forty million votes (92.2 per cent of the total). Hardly less remarkable was the turnout of 95.2 per cent of those eligible.³⁹ We can hardly take the election at face value, because all other political parties were outlawed. Nearly three and a half million people spoiled their ballot, presumably to show their opposition. Still, the vast majority voted in favour of Nazism, and in spite of what they could read in the press and hear by word of mouth about the secret police, the concentration camps, official antisemitism, and so on. The plebiscite and election have rightly been called 'a genuine triumph for Hitler', and 'even allowing for manipulation and lack of freedom', there is no getting away from the fact that at that moment 'the vast majority of the German people backed him'.⁴⁰

Citizens were asked to express themselves once more on 19 August 1934 in a plebiscite on the issue of uniting the offices of head of state (after President Hindenburg died), with that of the head of government (Chancellor Hitler). Again around 90 per cent supported Hitler. These results disappointed opponents, who kept waiting for the people to see the light.⁴¹ The Nazis were clear in their own minds about their popular backing, and Hitler was fond of saying that henceforth the struggle was for the support of the last 10 per cent.⁴² According to the Reichstag elections held on 29 March 1936, the Nazis were well on the way to getting that support, because they received no less than 99.9 per cent of the vote. Certainly, by then the elections were heavily tilted in favour of the government, which counted spoiled ballots or those left blank, as a 'yes'. At times entire communities were reported to have voted 100 per cent for Hitler, when that clearly was not the case. There is little doubt, however, that an overwhelming majority of the German people did vote 'yes'. The government obtained the same outcome on 10 April 1938 in a plebiscite when Germans and Austrians were asked whether they agreed with what was called the 'reunification' of Austria and Germany. Even the Socialists in exile noted that 'the great majority' of the people agreed with the question put to them.[43]

The undoubted swing of Germans towards support for Hitler's dictatorship can be illustrated in many other ways, such as how many rushed to join the Nazi movement. Whereas in 1930 there were 129,583 members in the Nazi Party, the registration jumped in early 1933 to 849,009. In order to control the influx, the Party itself called a (temporary) halt in May 1933 and would accept no new members. Once the ban was lifted a stream of people from all classes signed on, and by the early war years, there were more than five million card-carrying members.[44] There was a flood of joiners to the other Nazi mass organizations, such as to the ranks of the brown-shirted Storm Troopers (SA). In early 1931 there were around 77,000 members in the organization, and that increased to nearly half a million in August 1932; exactly two years later membership approached three million.[45]

Women also became part of the movement, and joined the Party's organization for them, the 'National Socialist Womanhood' (NS-Frauenschaft, NSF). At the end of 1932, the NSF as a kind of elite group for Nazi women already boasted a membership of 110,000. It grew to almost 850,000 a year later, and increased to over 1.5 million in the course of 1934. In addition, the mass-oriented 'German Women's Enterprise' (Deutsches Frauenwerk, DFW), founded in September 1933 as an umbrella organization to take the place of women's organizations that had been 'coordinated' or eliminated by the Nazis, gained a membership of 2.7 million by 1935, and that number grew by 1938 to 'around four million' and thereby became the largest non-compulsory organization in the country.[46] Several scholars have suggested, as does Adelheid von Saldern, that 'by and large, these women, and especially those who were leaders, accepted the role allotted to them by the Nazi system. Many were more or less positively inclined to National Socialism. Although there was some grumbling and criticism in certain areas, this did not usually amount to serious (political) opposition.'[47] Tim Mason concluded that 'a variety of different sources convey the impression that in the later 1930s the Third Reich enjoyed a large measure of active and passive support among women, a larger measure than it gained from among men'.[48]

The ease of the Nazi takeover and the emergence of a pro-Hitler and pro-Nazi consensus suggests that the majority had abandoned any hopes they might have had for democracy, and especially with the recovery from the Great Depression, they found it easy to support an authoritarian dictatorship.

Practising 'German Law'

Immediately on the heels of Hitler's appointment, Nazi newspapers made it seem that bloodthirsty Communists were fomenting revolution in the streets.[49] As early as 4 February 1933, in the name of stopping such activities, a presidential decree was promulgated 'for the protection of the German people'. Although mild by later standards, it restricted freedom of expression, permitted certain forms of censorship, banned publications, and outlawed meetings and demonstrations when the police judged that they constituted a 'direct danger to public security'.[50]

These measures were heralded in press reports as showing that Hitler was providing police with 'extensive powers to carry out the work of construction'.[51] Newspapers were full of stories of the ongoing battle in the streets between Nazis and Communists.[52] Placed alongside these accounts were reports that some local heads of police were cracking down on the Reds and purging the police of anyone accused of being a Marxist or Marxist sympathizer.[53]

Newspapers reported, without blinking an eye, that a number of senior police officials in Prussia were dismissed as unreliable.[54] By mid-February 1933, Göring gave numerous chiefs of police across Prussia their 'leave' merely because they belonged to the SPD or Catholic Centre Party.[55] Replacements were applauded for saying they would 'practise German law', and do 'everything for Germany'.[56]

On 17 February 1933, Göring, who was Hitler's right-hand man in the National Cabinet and also the new Prussian Minister of the Interior, issued a decree to all Prussian police. Published to make his intentions perfectly clear, he instructed police to avoid the impression they were ill-disposed towards 'national organizations', that is, especially the Nazis, but to use their 'sharpest methods' against 'treasonous organizations' and 'Communistic acts of terror and violence'.[57]

Göring cooperated with Dr Rudolf Diels, a career policeman, to get rid of politically unreliable officials, and Diels stated in one story that he wanted only those policemen to stay who could devote 'body and soul' to their work. As for Diels himself, the public was told of his experience in 'the struggle against, and observation of, the Communist movement'.[58] The announcement of changes to Prussia's political police, out of which the Gestapo was created, emphasized that the new police was designed mainly to eliminate Bolshevism and to deal with treasonous activities.[59]

During February 1933, the atmosphere in Germany was at fever pitch. To capitalize on the situation, deputy police were created, with men drawn from organizations like the Nazi Storm Troopers (SA) and Himmler's SS. News stories said that steps had to be taken to protect public security and private property against Communism.[60] The deputized SA took the law into their own hands and carried off helpless victims who were beaten in temporary prisons and private torture chambers. The novelist Georg Glaser, a Communist milit-ant, recalled that after Hitler was named Chancellor, soon 'dead bodies were found in the surrounding forests, and no one dared to know anything about them. People disappeared without a sound, and their best friends did not have the courage to ask where they had gone. Only very rarely did a scream, a gruesome rumour . . . make itself heard; they were paid less notice than every-day traffic accidents.'[61]

There was no need for the Nazis to 'purge' the police, because most police found it easy to adjust. Reports submitted to Hitler in early 1934 showed that more than 98 per cent of Prussia's uniformed police, and more than 90 per cent of its officers, were allowed to stay on.[62] In places such as Leipzig, where some members of the old political police were not up to Nazi expectations, they were transferred out and replaced by trained policemen, none of whom were in the Nazi movement before 1933.[63] Not just the little guys in uniform were allowed to stay, but so were most of the detectives in the Criminal Police (Kripo). The Nazis purged only 1.5 per cent of the Prussian Kripo in 1933 and more than 11,500 detectives across Germany kept their jobs.[64] The number of detectives in the Kripo was reduced in the early years of the dictatorship, but only because they were transferred to the Gestapo where their professional training and experi-ence counted more than their past politics. The limited 'purge' of the police as a whole, such as it was, focused on the senior ranks and more public figures, such as the Police Presidents in the big cities. Many in the police and justice establish-ment favoured the Nazi approach and were pleased to be part of a regime that wanted to fight crime and give the police more power to operate as they saw fit.[65]

Nothing short of an anti-Communist hysteria was in swing during February 1933, and it was given a shot in the arm on the night of 27 February, when a lone arsonist tried to burn down the Reichstag. Even though Marinus van der Lubbe, a Dutchman with no particular ties to the Communists, was caught, Hitler immediately blamed all Communists, and demanded that KPD members of parliament be hanged that very night. Rudolf Diels recorded the outburst and further quoted Hitler as shouting in the glow of the fire, that of course the Marxists had miscalculated: 'These sub-humans do not understand how the people stand at our side. In their mouse-holes, out of which they now want to come, of course they hear nothing of the cheering from the masses.'[66]

Göring ordered the arrest of leading Communists, and Hitler prevailed upon President Hindenburg the next day on 28 February, to declare a state of emer-gency. Hitler insisted on 'the presidential decree for the protection of people and state', or the so-called Reichstag Fire Decree, the opening lines of which were phrased to appeal to the anti-Communist majority in Germany. It claimed that measures were needed 'in defence against Communistic violence endan-gering the state'.[67] The decree suspended 'until further notice' the constitutional guarantees of personal liberty; made it possible for police to arrest and detain anyone they saw fit; and to impose restrictions on freedom of expression, assembly, and association. Police were allowed to exceed all previous legal limits on house searches and could intercept mail and tap telephones. Anyone found guilty of crimes relating to attempts at revolution or social unrest would be subject to heavy prison sentences and even the death penalty. The Reichstag Fire Decree also made it possible for the federal government to extend its authority over the individual states.[68]

In the name of stopping 'bloody red terror', police actions were mounted against the KPD, with thousands arrested.[69] Round-ups of Communists swept the country, at times on the basis of lists prepared by the Weimar police before Hitler's appointment.[70] Throughout March, the public was informed of one police success after the next, with no attempt to hide the fact that those arrested were sent without trial to concentration camps.[71] Reports in the non-Nazi press emphasized that the main prisoners in camps like the one that opened in Dachau, were Communist and other Marxist leaders who temporarily were held in the camp because regular prisons were filled to overflowing.[72]

Most Germans, especially anyone close to the Nazi Party, accepted the official version of events about the attempted Communist insurrection and the need to take radical measures.[73] Ian Kershaw concludes that the violence and repression that took place, far from damaging Hitler's reputation 'were widely popular'.[74] More than 200 telegrams were sent to the Ministry of Justice demanding the death penalty for the culprit who burnt down the Reichstag, and many volunteered for the position of executioner.[75]

By early May Göring was boasting that the number of people killed during political battles in the street was down from what it had been, but he made no mention of those killed inside the new camps. Nevertheless, the obvious intention of such stories was to play on citizens' desire for the pacification of the streets.[76]

Whole groups of Communists were tried and sentenced to death, as happened to four men in Altona in August 1933; nine more met the same fate in Düsseldorf in September, when four others were put on trial for their lives in Hagen; and six people were sentenced to death in Cologne in December. The sensationalized stories of these events and the background to them in the press, above and beyond news published about the stream of people sent to concentration camps, provided an obvious lesson to any potential opponents. For good citizens, of course, these stories showed the new regime in the best light.[77] Jews were disturbed by all the talk about the death penalty,[78] and already were vulnerable to dismissal as judges, attorneys general, and so on.[79]

The inequality before the law that was an essential feature of justice under Hitler's dictatorship was made clear when Special Courts, created on 21 March 1933, were justified in the name of the anti-Communist crusade.[80] Soon, however, anyone suspected of widely defined political crimes was brought before them.[81] A new measure outlawed all (vaguely defined) 'malicious gossip', that is, it criminalized all criticism. Justice officials offered it to Hitler originally for what it really was, namely an 'ordinance against discrediting the national government'.[82] The accused were tried before the Special Courts, where their rights, including the right to appeal a verdict, were reduced or eliminated.[83] Another new law (29 March 1933) retroactively made crimes such as the attempt to burn down the Reichstag into a capital offence and broadened the applicability of the death penalty to cover other crimes.[84] Just over a year later (on 24 April 1934) more laws expanded the meaning of treason and set up a People's Court to mete out justice to offenders.[85]

The government insisted it was responding to a revolutionary threat that called for emergency measures on a short-term basis. It kept assuring the public that, once the crisis passed, Germany's rule of law and all freedoms would be restored. It was obvious, however, even at the time when such vague promises were made, that the innovations introduced were going to be permanent features of Hitler's dictatorship.

Political Police

When Germans voted increasingly for Hitler, and especially when they voiced their support for the dictatorship, they accepted that their country would have a secret police. The process of creating this kind of political police, by no means new in Germany, but going back well before 1914, was bound to be accelerated in a country run by a man like Hitler, who left no doubt about his ideas on law and order before he was appointed. Germany was quickly transformed from a liberal state ruled by law, into what has been termed a 'prerogative state', that is, one regulated increasingly by arbitrary measures.[86] The new regime shifted the scales of justice away from the rights of citizens, in favour of the powers of the police in one German state after the next.

The Nazis informed Prussians that establishing the secret police or Gestapo, was part of the programme to reorganize the police, and its mission was defined 'to track down and to combat all political efforts to destroy the state'.[87] In order to fulfil its tasks, the new organization set up regional offices. Personnel were recruited not from loyal Nazis, but from the professionally trained police with the necessary expertise. Men who claimed to be 'idealists' relished the thought of working for the new Gestapo and hurried to join in hopes of helping to restore 'law and order' as they understood it at the time.[88]

A law of 30 November 1933 effectively freed the Gestapo from all outside interference. As needed, they could call on the cooperation of all other police, including the local uniformed city police and rural gendarmerie.[89] The Gestapo was also given a preventive mission, charged with stopping political crime before it took place, and permitted to detain suspects in a concentration camp or elsewhere without a hearing before a judge.

Gestapo-like police were soon established in all other German states. It is not necessary here to examine each in detail, but what happened in Bavaria under Heinrich Himmler deserves attention, as he was head of the SS and became Chief of the German police. In an interview on 14 March 1933, after he was appointed provisional head of the Munich Metropolitan Police, Himmler was asked if a purge of the police was in the offing. He answered that it was not, and said that henceforth it would be easier for them to do their duty. He was pleased that the police were functioning smoothly with the assistance of the SA and SS as deputy police, and together they were tracking down many Communists and other Marxists. House searches turned up numerous weapons, illegal printing presses, and large quantities of suspicious writings. He also offered one of the first justifications for the new concentration camps. The reasoning behind the camps was meant to appeal to traditional German social values, as well as antisemitism:

The state protects the life of all citizens. Unfortunately, it is only possible to provide such protection for certain individuals, and those involved have to be taken into protective custody under the direct protection of the police. The individuals involved, who are often of the Jewish faith, have through behaviour towards the national Germany, such as through offending nationalist feelings, and so on, made themselves so unloved among the people, that they would be exposed to the anger of the people unless the police stepped in.[90]

Less than a week later, Himmler gave instructions to open a concentration camp at Dachau.[91] In claiming that 'protective custody' was designed to protect individuals from the wrath of the mob, he made it easy for Germans to construct stories of their own in which supposedly endangered persons were picked up for their own good. Not only that, but according to Himmler 'often' the alleged culprits who outraged the national feelings of citizens were Jews, a statement which opened the possibility for citizens, even those who were not antisemitic, to conclude that it was good to have such 'enemies' off the streets. The comforting thought was that most prisoners in concentration camps were not at all like 'good citizens'.

The Jews were not the main Nazi targets during 1933, when the camps were created, but some were attacked because they were in the Communist Party, or belonged to opposition groups.[92] For the most part during the early days, the new police, like the old one, was against illegal 'excesses', including actions of Nazi hotheads against the Jews. Once the regime was established, however, the Gestapo became the most determined enforcers of officially condoned and inspired antisemitism.[93]

Himmler ended his first major interview by assuring citizens that there were proper guidelines for the future work of the police, and said that good citizens had nothing to worry about. He expressed determination to 'eliminate all criminals', and talked of the need to re-educate, strengthen, and support the people as a whole to a German way of thinking, because, so he claimed, many people had lost sight of these values during the previous years of an allegedly corrupt democratic system. He said that when and where necessary 'police measures' would be 'hard, just, and without any sentimentality'.[94]

By 15 March 1933 Himmler was in charge of a new Bavarian Political Police (BPP) that formed the basis of a Gestapo-like organization there. He chose as his key assistant, the young and ambitious Reinhard Heydrich. On 1 April 1933, Himmler became Political Police Commander (BPP) for all of Bavaria, and he also had control of the concentration camps, which were still in their infancy.[95] The BPP immediately used new powers granted under the Reichstag Fire Decree to destroy all left-wing groups. It is no accident that some Weimar police officials, like Heinrich Müller, with experience in tracking Communists, were in demand by the new police bosses. Such men were particularly anxious to please once it became clear they were not going to lose their prized jobs to Nazi Party or SS 'amateurs'.[96]

The police and judicial authorities, frustrated by Weimar's rule of law, soon introduced policies and plans formulated well before 1933 to deal with all kinds of criminals. Those plans had been left on the drawing board, but now police were allowed to use methods that diverged sharply from anything permitted in Germany before.[97] Serving the dictatorship 'came naturally to conservative-nationalist detectives'.[98]

Throughout 1933, the political police, backed by armed bands of Nazis, did what they could to repress the KPD. Although some Communists were released from the camps, the press stated that it was 'obvious' some would be kept under arrest.[99] Members of the Socialist Party (SPD) also were picked up, and in May and June they were followed by selected members of liberal, conservative, and, especially in Bavaria, Catholic parties.[100] Press reports said that while many were released, others would be kept in the camps.[101]

Even as Himmler created a police empire, he also was head of the black-shirts, the notorious SS.[102] Most of the men in the SS, as well as those in the Nazi Party and the SA, were civilians; most did not become state employees during the period down to the war. However, opportunities were given members of both the Gestapo and Kripo to join the SS.[103] Even so, according to historian Robert Koehl, at the outbreak of war 'the SS and Police were still two very separate entities' and the bulk of the members in the Gestapo and Kripo remained 'professional police officials'.[104] The fusion of the police into the SS was underway in the late 1930s, but as Himmler explained to the regular police (Orpo) at meetings in May 1937, only in the future would leaders of the police be recruited exclusively from the leadership schools of the SS.[105]

The influence of the SS on Hitler's dictatorship in the early years was summed up in a published article by Werner Best in 1936, shortly before Himmler was named Chief of the German Police. According to Best, by attaining that appointment Himmler would finally connect the 'unified ability of the German police with the unbending fighting will and the ideological consistency of the SS'.[106] For Reinhard Heydrich, writing at the same time, the hope was to have the Gestapo trained as police specialists who were imbued with National Socialist ideas.[107]

What filtered down to Gestapo officials over time, regardless of whether they formally joined the SS or some other Party organization, were Nazi teachings on law and order. Nazi ideology (of which there were many variants) could readily be grafted onto traditional demands of police for more power to fight criminals; for a reduction of the rights of the accused; and for a campaign to clean up the country from what many in the police regarded as criminal, or just immoral practices. From the early years of Hitler's dictatorship, there was a systematic and sustained effort 'to school' all police in Nazi teachings, and by the mid-1930s, a branch of the SS provided the leaders and the lecturers. Himmler issued detailed orders on how to spread Nazi propaganda through weekly and monthly sessions, and in June 1940, the 'educational' sessions were sometimes carried out on a daily basis.[108] This 'schooling', in case any policemen needed it, was intended to turn them into good Nazis, and appears to have been carried out on a regular basis from the beginning to the end of the regime.[109] Nazi ideology also was reinforced by everyday experiences during which the police were empowered as never before.[110]

Alongside 'cool' police actions, the Nazi revolution was carried forward by an army of 'hot' activists, especially those in the paramilitary SA. Beginning in February 1933 the millions-strong organization indulged in vigilante acts of violence that totally ignored the law. Across many parts of the country they let loose an 'elemental, increasingly uncontrollable outbreak of violence'.[111] By early March a social upheaval of sorts was under way in Germany, unlike anything seen since the revolutionary days of 1918.[112] In April, Bavarian Minister of Justice Hans Frank listed other complaints that arose in the course of taking some 5,000 people into 'protective custody'. He said he wanted to put a stop to the unacceptable practices whereby 'simple denunciations and arbitrary arrests of subordinate organizations' landed people in custody. He felt that real opponents should be charged or released; their security should be guaranteed; they should be given an opportunity to lodge complaints about their treatment; and their claims should be investigated.[113] In addition to Justice Minister Frank, other Bavarian Nazi leaders tried to insist on proper procedures, but like most such efforts, this one had no lasting effect.

Removing Legal Protections from the Jews

Part of what happened when Germans turned away from Weimar and embraced or accepted dictatorship, was that they left themselves open to the influences of Hitler's ideas, one of the most important of which was his virulent hatred of the Jews. In early 1933 it was unclear what the Nazis would do to implement their antisemitism. German Jews, who were better integrated in Germany than anywhere in Europe, were proud of their country, and many were staunch nationalists. The Jews were a small minority in Germany and in January 1933, statisticians reported that only approximately 525,000 'believing Jews' lived in the country.[114] These Jews were less than 1 per cent of the German population, and had been declining well before Hitler came to power. More vigilant racists, like those in the German Christian movement, a new religious organization that strove to unite Christianity and Nazism, noticed that the published statistics missed 300,000 or more 'Jews' who did not practise their faith, and who were not counted as Jews by the statisticians. At the very least, the German Christians wanted to expel them from Protestantism. The Ministry of the Interior's document from April 1935 to which the German Christians alluded with alarm, also recorded that there were an additional 750,000 'Jewish-Germans' of mixed race in the country.[115] The latter figure was in fact exaggerated, for in 1939—even allowing that emigration had reduced their number—there were just under 85,000 people who were officially classified as 'mixed race' in Germany.[116] Although such people were not subjected to the full scope of Nazi antisemitism, many suffered discrimination and lived in fear.[117] When they applied for and were granted special legal and racial certification to show they were not 'Jews' as defined in the laws, it often entailed the destruction of their family or at least of their relationship to their Jewish parent. Regardless of the outcome of their quest, their lives remained precarious, not least because decisions about ancestry could always be reversed.[118]

Antisemitism had not been a top priority issue for the Nazis in the last elections of the Weimar Republic. On propaganda posters used in the various elections leading up to 1933, the main 'enemy groups' were political parties identified with defeat and revolution in 1918, and with the Weimar system. Only 6 of the 124 Nazi posters from these elections pointed to the Jews as the main enemy.[119] On the other hand, in the presidential elections of 1932, the Nazis used posters to suggest that 'good Germans' should support Hitler, because Hindenburg was the candidate of the Jews.[120]

The Nazis did not need to make much of their antisemitism in those last elections, as by then their stance was already well known, and they could emphasize other aspects of the platform to win respectability and votes.[121] At the local level, the Nazis used violence against the Jews and anyone who they thought even 'looked Jewish', and these actions continued well into 1933.

Even during 1933 and 1934, Hitler's public statements on the Jews were if anything notable by their absence.[122] After his appointment, government-ordered steps against the Jews moved forward slowly, because the priority was to solve the unemployment problem. The Nazis even backed away from one of their oldest election promises, namely to close the department stores owned by the Jews, because it might increase unemployment when the 'Aryan' employees lost their jobs. Initially, anti-Jewish actions that could disrupt the economy were avoided, and there was concern about international public opinion, and the potential of an anti-German boycott in countries like the United States.

Nonetheless, antisemitism was important for Hitler and other Nazis, and in 1933 and 1934 'quiet' persecutions took place, as well as so-called 'individual actions', all of them officially disavowed and discouraged by leaders in Berlin.[123] This first wave of antisemitism came as an enormous shock to German Jews. After the March 1933 elections, the Nazi Party organized attacks against the Jews, such as boycotting or damaging their shops and businesses. On occasion Jews were openly assaulted, but that was more the exception than the rule.[124]

The first step taken by the German government to put legal pressure on the Jews as a group was a law of 7 April 1933, which made it possible to purge Jews and others from the civil service. Cleverly called the 'Law for the Restoration of a Professional Civil Service' to avoid the impression that the Nazis were tampering, this law had enormous implications.[125] It applied not just to the federal civil service, but to the entire corps of officials all the way down to the village level, including judges, the police, university professors, and school-teachers. The public was told that the law aimed at 'the elimination of Jewish and Marxist elements'.[126]

Millions of people were affected by the notorious questionnaires that were part of the law, and when follow-up investigations dragged on, they guaranteed lots of snooping. Informers rushed in to settle old scores or to gain personal advantages from the process.[127] Above and beyond the considerable direct effects these proceedings had on Jews and/or on people with some association with 'Marxism', the process undoubtedly made the entire civil service aware of the new rules of the game, and, in case anyone did not yet know, it was guaranteed to spread the word that official antisemitism was now government policy.

The subsequent purges of the Jews took their cue from this law, and, for example, led to the dismissal of Jews from the arts and the press, and even from the free professions. Such steps were justified as necessary—according to press reports—to placate the 'outrage of the entire German-blooded population'.[128] The announcement about what would happen to Jews in the Prussian justice system in the hitherto liberal and quite famous *Berliner Morgenpost* of 1 April

1933, dripped with antisemitism. The Prussian Ministry of Justice stated that during 'the great defensive struggle of the German people against the all-Jewish atrocity propaganda', all Jewish judges and other court officials should either leave or be forced out.[129]

Nazi hotheads out in the provinces continued their uncoordinated, and often violent attacks against the Jews and their property, kept up unofficial boycotts of businesses and so on. In the weeks following Hitler's appointment, leaders in Berlin tried to get a hold on the situation and to coordinate what was happening as best they could. Having fanned the flames of antisemitism for so long, and being radically antisemitic himself, Hitler could hardly back away from a confrontation with the Jews. However, German public opinion was not happy with violence in the streets, and there was a threat from the USA to carry out a boycott of German goods in response to the Nazis' violent attacks on the Jews. On 26 March Hitler, whose hand was to some extent forced by radical Nazis 'from below', opted for a national boycott of all Jewish businesses.[130]

Although Hitler just had been given dictatorial powers by way of an Enabling Law, he did not use the powers of the state or the police to enforce the boycott, but gave that mission to a Central Committee of the Nazi Party led by the notorious Julius Streicher. Local action committees were created 'for the practical, systematic implementation of the boycott of Jewish businesses, goods, doctors, lawyers'. The boycott was supposed to reach beyond the cities, into the countryside and 'down to the smallest village'.[131] Nothing like it had happened before and it heralded the waves of discrimination, violence, and terror to come.

The boycott was called for Saturday, 1 April, and the major theme in the press leading up to it was that it was a 'counter-measure' of the Party against the 'atrocity propaganda' allegedly spread by Jews abroad, including those in the Socialist and Communist movements.[132] Nazi organizations mobilized women to discourage others from buying from Jews.[133] The boycott was justified in a radio speech by Goebbels on Friday evening, and heavily publicized to begin promptly at 10:00 a.m. on 1 April and to continue until the Nazi Party leaders called it off.[134] Hitler gave his blessing, and remarked in an interview that the action must avoid taking 'undesired forms'.[135]

During the week leading up to the event, newspapers were full of stories about the activities of Jews at home and abroad as a build-up to Saturday. Detailed guidelines were issued about how to proceed against Jewish businesses and professionals, including even the kinds of signs and the slogans that should be used on the banners across the streets and held in front of stores.[136] In the big cities, the boycott was directed particularly at department stores, many of them owned by Jews. In Stuttgart, as elsewhere, the SA already had the names and addresses of Jewish firms and the buildings containing the offices of Jewish professionals and others, and within minutes of the beginning of the action, they plastered the word 'Jew' to the name signs of the entrances.[137]

The SA, some of them armed, stood at the doorways of shops, and tried, not always successfully, to discourage anyone from entering. The boycott was carried into smaller towns and out into the countryside, at least where Jews could be found and be demonstrably boycotted. Accounts in the press played up the success of the actions and made much of the evidence that could be found when non-Nazis also showed signs of agreement with what was happening.[138]

In addition to slogans for the boycott, such as 'Don't buy in Jewish department stores' or 'Avoid Jewish doctors', far cruder ones were used. A stranger from another country walking the streets would have concluded that the Jews were not just hated, but in danger for their lives.

In fact violence was used on a wide scale, several Jews were murdered, and some Jews fought back. Hans Schumm, a Jewish lawyer in Kiel, shot one of the Nazis trying to break up his sister's wedding. He was arrested and when rumours spread (as it turned out they were false) that the Nazi had died of his wounds, comrades broke into the prison—which is to say, they were allowed in by the police—and murdered Schumm in his prison cell.[139] In Chemnitz, another lawyer and head of the Jewish Veterans' Association there, was carried off to a nearby forest and shot by members of the SS; in Plauen a Jewish merchant was killed.[140] Jews were also taken into 'protective custody' with great public fanfare and shipped to concentration camps.

In most areas, people did not respond as positively as the Nazis hoped, and in bigger cities there were those who made a point of shopping at Jewish stores. In Frankfurt am Main, most of the larger stores did not open and so robbed the Nazis of the chance to make a big fuss. Soon even the smaller ones closed.[141] All in all, most historians argue that the boycott failed as a public relations event with ordinary Germans, and have suggested that behind the scenes the Nazis themselves considered it a propaganda failure because of the public's aversion to such methods.[142] At least on the day of the boycott, most citizens certainly did not demonstrate anything like the antisemitic zeal of their leaders. Germany had an antisemitic tradition, but it would take some time for the Nazis to radicalize it.

Already on the afternoon of the boycott a temporary 'pause' was ordered by Goebbels until the following Wednesday to see, as he put it, if the 'atrocity propaganda' against Germany would cease.[143] Of course, the tactic was a way of avoiding a political defeat if, as happened, the boycott won less than wholehearted popular support.[144] What the event did, was to present the regime's stand on the Jews. The hate-filled message was that Jews were over-represented in certain professions and trades and their influence had to be broken.[145] No one could doubt that, whether or not antisemitism was soft-pedalled by the Nazis before, now it was clearly of central importance.

Jews who loved Germany felt they were being turned into social outsiders. Many German Jews were proudly nationalistic, and for that reason were more than cool to the appeals of the early Zionist movement. Some now began to think that a violent pogrom was in the offing and for the first time in their lives started to feel more like hostages than equal citizens.[146] The boycott was the first nationally organized and condoned antisemitic event, and it forced even staunchly nationalistic Jews to conclude that they had been sadly mistaken about their beloved Germany.

Some Jews fought back as much as they could under the circumstances. Edwin Landau, at the time of the boycott a store owner in a small West Prussian town, refused to give in. He donned his war medals, visited other Jewish shops, and confronted the Nazis posted at his shop door. Customers (particularly Catholics) came to offer sympathy and, as in other places in Germany, showed their disapproval of the action. The overall effect of everything Landau experienced on that day—particularly the crude expressions of young Nazis—left him 'inwardly broken'. He soon joined the Zionist movement and by November 1934 had left Germany for Palestine.[147] The Nazis hoped for such a turn of events, and what they called a 'joyous rise' in Jewish emigration.[148] Evidently showing their devotion to Germany by displaying their war medals represented a form of resistance used by many Jewish shopkeepers across Germany, with some in Berlin even painting their distinguished war records on the shop windows.[149]

Professor Victor Klemperer, soon forced out of his university post because of his Jewish background, recorded in his diary on 25 April 1933 that he considered Germans as a whole to be not particularly antisemitic. He felt the Nazis were making a mistake in the early days by raising the issue so high on the banner. Klemperer was not merely a witness, but a self-conscious and critical one. He confided in his diary 'that the fate of the Hitler Movement unquestionably lies in the Jewish thing. I do not understand why they have made this point of the programme so central. It will go to ruin on that. We likely along with it.'[150]

Historian Richard Bessel maintains that the early antisemitism and the boycott, unlike the campaign against the Left, 'appears to have aroused widespread misgivings among the public and created difficulties for the Nazi leadership without offering compensating political dividends'.[151] Perhaps so, but one can find plenty of evidence that at least non-violent forms of antisemitism gained Hitler's dictatorship more support than it lost.[152]

The Jews were turned into social outsiders and their legal emancipation was slowly reversed. They were pressured in business, but soon driven from the professions, and it appears beyond doubt that their expulsion was popular. In March 1933 the SA invaded courts and took out their spite on Jewish judges and attorneys. Some of the Jews were marched through the streets, like the one in Munich who was trying to get his client released from 'protective custody'. He was dragged into the street and, with his trouser legs cut above the knee for comic effect, paraded through the streets with a sign around his neck which said, 'I am an insolent Jew and I will never complain again.' In another city (Breslau) at about the same time, the SA forced their way into the court buildin while shouting 'Jews out!', chased and beat Jewish judges, lawyers, and a they even thought might be a Jew. The Higher Court President informea judges and attorneys that it was necessary to curtail the activities of Jewish lawyers in order to bring about what he called 'a calming of the population and an easing of the general situation'.[153]

The response of local police, otherwise prone to being supersensitive about any public disturbance, was to do nothing about the violence, as happened when 500 to 600 demonstrators entered the higher court building in Frankfurt am Main in June, and when 200 students forced their way into the courts in the same city in July. The attitude of judicial authorities on the spot was that it would be better if Jewish lawyers simply ceased to appear, and that Jewish judges retire to avoid provocation. However, if the Jews did not leave on their own, it was made clear they would be forbidden to practise law in the courts.[154]

The universities dismissed nearly all Jewish professors in one fell swoop thanks to the Civil Service Law of 7 April. German university students, long prone to antisemitism and needing little prompting from above, pushed ahead with various actions against both Jewish students and professors.[155] The government introduced a 'numbers clause' on 25 April—a long-time demand of the Nazis—to restrict the percentage of Jewish students who could attend university. On some local campuses, students demonstrated against Jewish professors or took advantage of the situation to make mischief by writing letters of complaint against those to whom they bore a grudge.[156] These acts opened up places for students and jobs for professors, and was popular at a time of high academic unemployment.[157]

In March and April 1933, Jewish professionals not already affected by discrimination were pressured, for instance by leaders of German medicine. In early April Hitler promised nothing less than 'purging of the nation and particularly of the intellectual classes of influences of foreign origin and racially foreign infiltration'. He stated before representatives of the educated German elite 'that immediate eradication of the majority of Jewish intellectuals from the cultural and intellectual life of Germany had to be carried out to assure Germany's obvious right to the intellectual leadership of it own kind'. He was fully aware of problems faced by young doctors in an overcrowded profession, he said, and reassured them that 'precisely for this German youth, living space and employment opportunities must be created by thoroughly repulsing racially foreign elements'.[158]

With Chancellor Hitler setting this tone, national and local medical associations felt comfortable in compelling Jews to resign. Some municipalities and regional administrations, acting illegally and anticipating anti-Jewish legislation yet to come, barred Jewish physicians who were in public employ.[159] Physicians' organizations were Nazified by dissolving them and putting a

Nazi-dominated one in their place. Although doctors may have found themselves more regimented than they might have wished in the new Germany, there was virtually no opposition to what happened. Doctor-patient confidentiality was routinely compromised as doctors were given the opportunity (already by the Sterilization Law of 14 July 1933) to report evidence of hereditary diseases and their suspicions about illegal acts (like abortions). There was no mention that doctors were forced to inform on a patient in the original law, but a supplementary decree of 5 December 1933 stated that when physicians learned that patients suffered from what were termed hereditary diseases or chronic alcoholism, the doctor had a duty to inform the medical authorities.[160] A new Physicians' Ordinance in 1935, while claiming to protect the Hippocratic Oath, stated that all medical secrets could be revealed if doctors thought that 'wholesome popular sentiment'—an obviously subjective criterion—demanded that they do so.[161] Soon statutes with the force of law were issued by a new Reich Physicians' Chamber, in place by 6 April 1936, that helped to infuse the medical profession with Nazi ideology. Many sections of the profession already were prone to racial thinking, and the more radical Nazi doctors were not only antisemitic, but demanded that medicine work in the service of purifying Germans' own racial stock by weeding out impurities.[162]

Doctors were told to report genetic illnesses, just as they would births and deaths, and patients as a result were sterilized, usually against their will. In that sense many doctors were instrumental in extending the eyes and ears of the dictatorship into their own practices.[163] They did so also in new roles in the much expanded and reorganized public health system. For example, doctors played a crucial part as examiners and counsellors at what has been sarcastically called the new 'biological headquarters', that is, the 739 public health offices the Nazis established across the country by 1939.[164]

The new antisemitism had particularly devastating effects on Jewish schoolteachers and pupils. Jewish children were picked on by students or teachers, some were paraded before school assembly and used as models to demonstrate how students should be able to recognize Jews.[165] Teachers were obliged to open classes with the Hitler greeting, a salutation that was bound to bring home their precarious situation to Jewish students. If not all teachers and students jumped on the bandwagon, the negative psychological effects on Jewish children can easily be imagined.

In the event that Germans did not witness antisemitism personally, they could read a great deal about it in any newspaper. All of Germany's papers, and not just the Nazi ones, were full of negatives stories about the Jews, and there were too many to be missed.[166]

Worries about disrupting the economy and international opinion gave Hitler's government pause about proceeding against the Jews. In the wake of the boycott in 1933, Nazi radicals out in the provinces continued their 'individual actions' against the Jews on an uncoordinated basis. The SA were particularly active, and on 2 August 1933, in an effort to clip the wings of the SA and to exert some control, Prussia dissolved the 'deputy police', and thereby put an end to the SA's role in the police. The same step was soon taken elsewhere.[167] Some local SA leaders, however, persisted in their attacks on Jews, as happened in March 1934 in Gunzhausen. That town, in Middle Franconia, Bavaria, had a history of antisemitism, so that when a mob of between 1,000 and 1,500 gathered on Palm Sunday and set upon the Jews, it included not just Nazis, but non-Nazi townspeople as well. Several Jews were severely mistreated, and two of them died as a result. Instructively for the way 'law and order' changed and how Jews could no longer look to the law for protection, the main culprits were charged and brought to court, but their sentences were quashed on appeal. Only one of them, Kurt Bär, got 10 months, and even he does not seem to have served time in prison.[168] But unlike what we might expect from a dictatorship, such violence was not ordered from on high.

According to Marion Kaplan, on the whole, Jewish women seemed to sense the danger signals first, or at least were more inclined to leave Germany than were their menfolk.[169] All Jews watched the situation closely, and many no doubt hoped the storm would pass. In addition, precisely because Hitler's new government did not act across the board, many Jews decided to stay on, also because in an era marked by antisemitism internationally, not many countries were prepared to accept Jewish refugees. Their hopes in Germany were fuelled because there was no definitive 'law' or decree that regulated the 'Jewish question'. Instead literally thousands of separate 'measures' were brought in to govern their every move. Jews like Peter Gay and his family in Berlin concluded from the mixed messages sent by the dictatorship, that it was safe enough for them to remain.[170]

'Germany Prefers Hitler to the Communists'

By the end of 1933, there was so much support for the dictatorship, and so few enemies left, that the Nazis toyed with the idea of getting rid of the Gestapo.[171] Some newspaper accounts hinted that the concentration camps and a secret police were becoming superfluous.[172] Instead, Göring's new law on the Prussian Gestapo (30 November 1933) and follow-up instructions (in March 1934) established the autonomy of the Gestapo, made it free of all outside administrative tampering, and brought it under his authority as Prime Minister of Prussia.[173] To some extent, this move was an attempt to hold on to the Gestapo in Prussia, which was Göring's only power base, and to resist the centralization trend. The inexorable rise of Heinrich Himmler could not be stopped, and the justification given to the public for his taking over as head of the police in one state after the next was the persistent need to fight the Communists.[174] Himmler's new role was said to be 'in the interests of the unified work of the entire political police of the German Reich'.[175] Perhaps recognizing the inevitability of Himmler's ascendancy, Göring soon said that he 'saw himself compelled for organizational reasons' to ask Himmler to take over.[176]

Such vague phrases have led to debate about why Himmler emerged as Germany's supreme political policeman.[177] Was he merely a better schemer? Perhaps, but there is no question he had Hitler's implicit or explicit support, and in late 1933 and into 1934, he ploughed ahead, taking over the political police in one German state after the next. He did this at a time when the press was reporting that there was growing political tranquillity everywhere in Germany.

Given the authoritarian tendencies that Hitler frequently expressed, and his desire to centralize the country and to undermine states' rights, the chances of success were good for anyone like Himmler who was a keen centralizer. That the police should be removed from the jurisdiction of the individual German states was only a matter of time in a Hitlerian dictatorial system. The trend towards centralizing the political police took a major step forward on 20 April 1934, when Himmler was made head of the Prussian Gestapo. At that moment, the leadership of the political police in Germany was, in a much used phrase of the time, 'unified in one hand'.

At the ceremony where Göring passed over leadership and gave his blessing, he made the point that the change was welcomed by Hitler. Himmler's remarks were intended not only to lift the spirits of the police he addressed directly, but were part of his continuing effort to provide information out of which loyal citizens were supposed to figure out what the Gestapo was all about. He mentioned his favourite theme about the new Nazi police, whose officials, he remarked, took up their duties with the dedication of soldiers. He appealed to the hatred of everything the Weimar Republic stood for, by charging that 'the police suffered a terrible reputation during the 14 years of the Marxist system because the officials were misused'. He insisted that would change, and that 'in Germany, it must again become the highest honour and distinction to be allowed to belong to the political police'.

Why the need for such a police when, as Himmler himself made clear, 'millions of people with good heart' had come to support the new system? The reason was, he claimed, that there were 'still thousands, even tens of thousands' who remained enemies 'even when they raise their arm' in the Hitler salute. Appearances could be deceiving, and enemies were organizing worldwide. Even so, he expressed confidence in the ability of the new police to master the difficult mission.[178]

Himmler's appointment as head of the (Prussian) Gestapo came on Hitler's birthday in 1934, and we can surmise that this step happened on that day as a sign, either that it was done at Hitler's express wish, or to please him as a kind of birthday present. Himmler became Germany's most important policeman at the age of 34; at that time he also was head of the SS and was busily organizing a concentration camp system. Whether or not there was social peace in the country, it was clear that the foundations of the new system were in place.

The autonomy of the constituent German states themselves was undermined through a series of new laws in 1933 and 1934 in favour of rule from Berlin. As one of these laws put it, the elections of 12 November 1933 'have proven that the German people have overcome all domestic boundaries and conflicts, and have united in an indissoluble inner unity'.[179] It was reported that 'on Hitler's insistence', and in order to avoid the 'dangers of a particularistic power build-up' in the provinces, the new position of the Reich Governor for each state was created already on 7 April 1933.[180] Hitler thus extended Berlin's domination over the individual German states whose parliaments were abolished.[181]

By 1 January 1935 the administration of justice was made uniform across Germany, and the Ministries of Justice of the individual states were brought under central control.[182] Thus, Himmler's drive to strengthen and centralize the police, with its headquarters in Berlin, was completely in keeping with Hitler's wishes and with the entire spirit of the Nazi revolution. The trend was especially pronounced with regard to the police. On 17 June 1936 Himmler was made Chief of the German Police, and was thereby head of the newly nationalized Gestapo as well as the Kripo and regular uniformed police.

As Germans watched these events unfold, they believed that the Communists had attempted to seize power illegally and were grateful the Nazis stopped them. Victor Klemperer noted in his diary about the elections of late 1933, that an overwhelming majority voted in favour of the Nazis, because in the final analysis 'all Germany prefers Hitler to the Communists'.[183] In spite or rather because of all the changes wrought by Hitler or by others in his name, he was more popular than ever, and support for his dictatorship was growing by the minute. We move now to examine other parts of Hitler's 'experiment' in popular dictatorship.

2

Police Justice

The perception that Germany was falling apart during the Great Depression was reinforced by what seemed like a crime wave. Such perceptions were fuelled by the media, but the feeling that crime was increasing was not entirely without basis, for all across Germany, there was a steady climb for most years from 1927 to 1932 in thefts of all kinds, as well as in armed robbery and fraud. The rise was continuous in large cities (with 50,000 or more inhabitants), and some crimes nearly doubled between 1927 and 1932.[1] In the last years of the Weimar Republic, newspapers were full of stories about crime, drugs, and murder, including the activities of organized gangs. There were many accounts of finance scandals, sexual predators, serial murderers, and even cannibalism. The emergence of gays and the growth of pornography were held up as evidence of depravity. The blossoming of unconventional styles in art and music made Berlin famous and drew freedom-loving souls from all around the world, where they celebrated their emancipation. It was just this kind of 'un-German' behaviour that many good citizens despised.[2]

The open society and democratic freedoms were new to Germany, and many people longed nostalgically for a more disciplined society of the kind they identified in their minds with the era before 1914.[3] Many Germans, and not just those in the conservative, religious, or Nazi camps believed that the liberal Weimar Republic was a degenerate society, and that their country was on the road to ruin.[4]

'The Fist Comes Down!'

Christopher Isherwood, the English novelist, wrote in 1933 just before leaving the free and easy Berlin he loved in the 1920s, that the newspapers were 'becoming more and more like copies of a school magazine. There is nothing in them but new rules, new punishments, and lists of people who have been "kept in" '.[5] Law-abiding citizens, of course, saw matters differently, and could hardly fail to be pleased that police began to take seriously their concerns about crime and loose morals. One woman fondly recalled long after the Third Reich was gone, that even during the early years of the new regime, the laws were stiffened and supposedly even thieves were shot, so that thereafter 'nobody took anything that belonged to anyone else'.[6]

The Nazi approach to crime was not to search out its deeper social causes, but to enforce existing laws far more vigorously. The Nazi motto was summed up in a front-page story of their leading newspaper in the phrase 'the fist comes down'.[7] They adopted this stance even before the Reichstag fire at the end of February 1933. They appointed new Police Presidents for a number of major cities, including Berlin, where hardliners promptly declared war on crime. The impression conveyed in the press was that the Nazi Party and the German police had a lot in common, as both hated Communism and were determined to stamp out crime.[8]

Admiral von Levetzow, new head of the Berlin police, said he wanted to restore the tried-and-true German values embodied in his old-fashioned sounding name. In his address to uniformed police in mid-February 1933, he called on them to fight for 'law and order, for decency, for discipline and morality'.[9] These were the mythical values associated with the strict Prussian past.[10] At the end of March, Hitler demanded the 'purification of the body politic', and whatever that was supposed to mean in practical terms, the Nazis translated it into threats that criminals would now be treated with 'utmost severity'.[11] The public was assured, as one headline put it, that prisoners behind bars would 'not continue to have it better than the unemployed'.[12]

In the early months of 1933, the police got temporary 'preventive' arrest powers to fight the Communists. These powers enabled the police to dispense with hearings before a judge and to hold Communists in what was called 'protective custody'. Until the Third Reich, protective custody was used in Germany to shield untried people from the wrath of the mob and keep them out of harm's way. Beginning in 1933, the meaning of 'protective custody' was turned on its head. It became a weapon in the hands of the Gestapo, a euphemism for their regular arrest and confinement practices. They could pick up men and women, send them to a concentration camp without trial, and keep them there indefinitely.

The Gestapo systematized their use of 'protective custody', anchored it in the exceptional measures decree at the end of February 1933, and never looked back. The system of 'police justice' was established at the expense of citizens' legal rights, and at first it existed alongside, and to some extent in conflict with, the regular justice system. With Hitler's backing, however, police prerogatives soon got the upper hand.[13] The Gestapo used their new powers to track widely defined political crimes, and the Kripo obtained similar 'preventive arrest' powers to pursue other types of crimes.

As the 'emergency' began to fade in 1933, some of Hitler's Cabinet colleagues were ambivalent about the apparent ascendancy of the police and the sweeping arrests. However, their objections were half-hearted and in any case were directed 'against neither the principle nor the practice of protective custody as such, nor opposed to its complete arbitrariness and lawlessness'.[14] The Ministers of Justice and Interior were unwilling or unable to control the social dynamics of the situation.[15] Interior Minister Wilhelm Frick was more concerned about procedures, than substance, but if anything he favoured the police over Nazi Party hooligans.[16]

Law and order stories became constituent parts of Nazi mythology and were exaggerated. Nevertheless, the police were quick to use their new powers, even against petty thieves like exploiters and swindlers, who were packed off (without trials) to concentration camps.[17] The same thing happened to butchers and cattle dealers who took advantage of the Depression to force farmers to sell livestock at low prices. Newspapers self-righteously declared that these criminals would now 'have an opportunity to discover through manual labour, how difficult the work of a farmer is and how much sweat and work it takes in these hard times to hold on to a bit of soil'.[18] These stories about swift justice, undoubtedly fuelled populist myths about the regime as a crime fighter, and thus earned it considerable support.

In September 1933, using imagery drawn from the military, the police declared open war on the beggars and vagrants. Citizens were discouraged from showing false pity, and asked to give their money instead to charities. A police sweep across the country picked up as many as 100,000, and as a recent study puts it, 'never before had the police in Germany taken in so many people by way of a single police action'.[19]

In the days and weeks that followed, the press was full of glowing stories about the event, like one that proudly proclaimed 'Berlin, a City without beggars'. In December another featured a 'Report on the Cleansing of Berlin', stating that 'the measures of the Berlin police and their results find the support of everyone. The capital city is freed within a few months from an evil whose scale represented an unacceptable annoyance to Berliners and to visitors in the city'.[20]

The beginning of better times and diminished crime was signalled in a Christmas-time story that ran under the headline, 'Insecurity Diminished: there is work again for the people; now we can go home again at night in peace.'[21] Although some of the beggars who were arrested were soon released, the no-nonsense image of the new system was hammered home in the press. In Hamburg the police took the opportunity not only to arrest beggars, but to force unemployed single men and others to work for any welfare support they received.[22] There was a crackdown on petty criminals, like those who lived from the avails of prostitution. On 24 November 1933, the penalty for this crime was drastically increased, from a minimum of one month (in less onerous-style prison or workhouse), to a minimum of five years in the hardest form of it.[23]

Almost immediately after Hitler's appointment, the impression in the press was that at the very least, more use would be made of the death penalty and it would be carried out sooner after sentencing than in the past.[24] There were also menacing announcements that capital punishment could be used for 'violations' of measures adopted by the new government.[25]

New Criminal Code

Discussions about making the method of execution uniform across Germany —whether it should be hanging, shooting, the executioner's axe, or the guillotine—were taken up by a commission formed to give Germany a new Criminal Code.[26] Hitler considered the idea of changing the Criminal Code, whose weaknesses he never tired of pointing out. His wishes took concrete shape soon after the elections of March 1933. Already at a Cabinet meeting on 22 April 1933, Minister of Justice Franz Gürtner suggested a commission of jurists work on a new code that reflected the spirit of Nazism and its philosophy of law. During 1933, the commission took shape under Gürtner's chairmanship. Some members, like the Prussian Minister of Justice Hanns Kerrl, suggested in a news story that the code should reject individualistic and liberal legal principles, and that priority be given to the protection of the community. Without specifying what he meant, Kerrl said that the new code should work as a defence 'against the undermining of the German race'.[27]

The stream of press releases from the commission kept reporting that its work was nearly finished, and over the years, it completed several drafts. Hitler would not accept them, as he and other Nazis ultimately preferred a system in which the police not only enforced existing or written law, but decided what the law was. Those who favoured 'police justice' did not want the police restricted in any way, even by a legal code that embodied many of the harshest ideas and suggestions espoused by the most radical Nazi jurists on the commission like Hans Frank, Roland Freisler, and Georg Thierack. Although the code was never passed, some of the more radical and far-reaching principles put forward by judges and politicians who held senior positions in the new regime came to inform new laws and changes in court procedures. Not only that, but the many reports over the years, even if unwittingly, suggested to the public that the liberal legal system was hopelessly weak on crime. In place of the outmoded Weimar system, commissioners favoured one that reflected 'racial values' and fostered the 'community of the people'. They wanted to demolish equality before the law, the essence of the liberal legal order, and in its place make legal rights contingent on the extent to which the accused person was a useful member of the community. They favoured speedier trials and the reduction of legal protections for the accused, and they wanted to count an attempted (but failed) crime as equivalent to one that succeeded. They also wanted to Nazify certain old crimes, for example, by supplementing the traditional concept of 'treason against the state' by adding 'treason against the race'.[28] They wanted to make it possible for judges to punish someone who offended 'wholesome popular sentiment', even though they might not have broken a law.[29] Whereas the old law code supposedly favoured the 'security of the criminal', the new one aimed at 'securing the community of the people'.[30]

Citizens were told that the liberal principle of 'no crime without a law' (*nullum crimen sine lege*), was changed into 'no crime without a punishment' (*nullum crimen sine poena*). This slogan was meant to appeal to those fed up that the justice system gave too many rights to perpetrators of crime and ignored the social costs. The catchy Latin phrase was translated and popularized in the press, and as early as mid-1934 was even reprinted on small postage-stamp posters that were glued to the covers of court dossiers. Presumably the little stamp would inspire the everyday activities of lawyers and judges in the courts, and it read as follows: 'Then: [that is, before 1933] No punishment without law. Now: No crime without punishment.'[31]

Hitler's statement on such legal changes was very simple. He said on the fourth anniversary of his appointment, noticeably leaving out any mention of the emergency that was supposedly justified by a Communist threat, that 'the mission of the justice system is to contribute to the preservation and the securing of the volk in the face of certain elements who, as asocials, strive to avoid common duties or who sin against these common interests. Thus, the volk takes precedence over persons and property, also in German law.'[32]

Once Hitler's new police got a taste for speedy measures, however, by which they could bypass time-consuming legal procedures, there was no chance they were ever really going to dispense with them. In mid-1934 they got an opportunity to bid for public support, when they finally came down on the Storm Troopers (SA). On 30 June 1934, the leaders of the SA were killed on Hitler's orders. During this so-called 'night of the long knives' the radical ambitions of the SA, who kept longing for a real social revolution, were brought to a halt once and for all. The event was presented to the German public as an attempted coup by SA leader Ernst Röhm, but no effort was made to hide the fact that Röhm was executed without a semblance of a trial.[33] Most people accepted that Hitler (not the courts) 'sentenced' the 100 or so culprits to death.[34] Far from causing Germans to have second thoughts, by all accounts this first mass murder of the Third Reich paid positive political dividends for Hitler, because it gave many citizens the opportunity to accept the new 'normality' and the coercive side of the dictatorship.[35] The police wanted the government to be more trusting than to censor news and to be upfront about what happened to those killed during the purge.[36] They felt it was impossible to stop citizens from listening to foreign radio, and suggested it would be best to publish 'authentic explanations to remove the basis of wild rumours'.[37]

Hitler signalled that political stabilization had arrived by granting a selective amnesty on 10 August 1934. He used the occasion of President Hindenburg's death and the opportunity to publicize the 'unification of the office of Reich President with that of the Reich Chancellor'.[38] The amnesty was supposed to still the worries of top civil servants and to assure the general population that all was well, in spite of what was called the Röhm 'revolt'. According to press reports, as many as one-third of those in 'protective custody' were released in some places, and more concentration camps were dissolved. The reports stated that 'deadly enemies' who prepared and carried out acts of treason were not included in the amnesty, but that many already had left the country.[39]

Hitler was not interested in legal niceties, so it was characteristic that he did not disband the Gestapo, nor curtail its powers, even though most of those considered real enemies were by that time already gone. On the contrary, on 20 June 1935, he gave Himmler his blessing to expand the concentration camps, which had been closing down everywhere.[40] Himmler also obtained Hitler's support on 18 October 1935 to broaden the powers of the police. A meeting between them took place shortly after the infamous Nuremberg Party rally in September at which Hitler announced discriminatory laws against the Jews.

The Nuremberg rally in 1935, heralded as the 'National Party Meeting of Freedom', represented a milestone in the establishment of the dictatorship's system of racial discrimination and persecution. Of three new laws passed on 15 September by the Reichstag which met in Nuremberg, the most important turned out to be the 'law for the protection of German blood and German honour'. The law forbad further marriages and extramarital sexual relations between Jews and 'Germans' and people of 'associated or similar blood'.

Another part of the Nuremberg event, one frequently overlooked, took place on 11 September, when Hitler announced by proclamation what he termed a 'struggle against the internal enemies of the nation'. These 'enemies' were vaguely defined as 'Jewish Marxism and the parliamentary democracy associated with it'; 'the politically and morally depraved Catholic Centre Party'; and 'certain elements of an unteachable, dumb and reactionary bourgeoisie'. The proclamation did not say what steps would be taken, but it sounded like the beginning of a social war. The speech was all the more curious in that it went on to underline how Germany enjoyed greater security and tranquillity than at any time in the recent past. Hitler contrasted the situation in 1935 with the 'ferment of decomposition' and 'signs of decay' that existed at the time of his appointment.[41]

A little over a month after the Nuremberg rally, on 18 October 1935 Hitler and Himmler broadened the concepts of 'enemy' and 'crime' the new police were supposed to fight. The Gestapo was not going to vanish after all, nor were the camps. The number of camp prisoners had been falling since mid-1933, but promptly began to grow again.[42]

By mid-1935 the new police were getting the upper hand. At this time the dictatorship had to respond to the issue of whether suspects in protective custody should be allowed legal counsel. The argument as stated by Dr Werner Best, a key figure behind the creation of the new system, was simple. The main consideration 'from the point of view of the leadership of the state', he said, was whether or not giving lawyers access to clients would help in the battle against the state's 'deadly enemies'. Lawyers' questions were inevitable, but were incompatible with the state leadership's 'trust in the organizations given the mission to defend against the attacks of enemies'. Best said that because the Gestapo regarded protective custody as its 'most important weapon' against enemies of state, any weakening of that weapon was the equivalent of strengthening the dangers threatening the state. Therefore, he concluded, no lawyers should be allowed as the usual 'procedural forms of the judiciary were totally inapplicable for the struggle against the enemies of state under the present circumstances'. That argument was met by a minor quibble from the Ministry of Justice, which was silenced when Himmler informed officials on 6 November 1935 of a Hitler order barring lawyers access to anyone held in protective custody.[43]

The Völkisch Police

The creation of the new Gestapo system culminated with a Prussian law of 10 February 1936. According to this law virtually any actions taken by the Gestapo were no longer subject to court review, not even in the event of wrongful arrest, and no one could sue for damages.[44] In other words, if the Gestapo was above the law even earlier, by early 1936 that situation was formalized. Henceforth, the only route open for any complaints was to appeal to the Gestapo head office (Gestapa).[45] Far from being hushed up, the full implications of these developments were spelled out to the public in the press, so that no doubt could exist that citizens' basic legal rights were all but ended.[46] Gestapo headquarters in Berlin simply wished to ensure that local officials did not overuse their powers of arrest and bring discredit on the police.[47] Although in theory the legal immunity enjoyed by the Gestapo did not apply to the rest of the police, if and when they acted on behalf of the Gestapo, what they did could not be challenged either.[48]

　　The Nazis worked out a clearly articulated *völkisch* or Fascist theory of the police by the mid-1930s, and proudly presented it for the edification and enlightenment of the public. The most succinct statement of this new theory was by Werner Best, the legal expert at Gestapo headquarters. Although his remarks were published in a specialist journal, summaries of them made their way into the popular press.[49] Germans could now read that the police powers justified initially to fight Communism had a new rationale. Best stated flatly that the new police regarded 'every attempt' to realize or to maintain any political theory besides National Socialism 'as a symptom of sickness, which threatens the healthy unity of the indivisible volk organism'. All such efforts would be 'eliminated regardless of the subjective intentions of their proponents'. He now said that the new police watched over the 'health of the German body politic', recognized 'every system of sickness', and destroyed all 'destructive cells'. He summed up the mission of the Gestapo as follows:

> The preventive police mission of a political police is to search out the enemies of state, to watch them and at the right moment to destroy them. In order to fulfil this mission the political police must be free to use every means required to achieve the necessary goal. In the National Socialist leader state it is the case, that those institutions called upon to protect state and people to carry out the will of the state, possess as of right the complete authority required to fulfil their task, an authority that derives solely from the new conception of the state and one that requires no special legal legitimization.[50]

Best used the comparison between the Gestapo and the army at war, when he wrote that the Gestapo 'in its struggle against clever, determined and ruthless enemies must claim the same trust and the same powers as an army, which in fulfilment of its task—to destroy an enemy whose behaviour cannot be predicted—also cannot be bound by the letter of the law'. What had to be recognized about the police and the law, according to Best, was that above all 'for the fulfilment of its tasks, which could not be mastered according to fixed norms, the police must be given the same authority to take the necessary measures on the basis of its own knowledge and own responsibility so as to ensure the security of the people and state'.[51]

This kind of *völkisch* or biological theory of the police was presented to the German people as the rational basis for what the new police did. Himmler reported calmly in March 1937 that the tradition of the nightwatchman state was dead, and so was the old liberal order in which, theoretically at least, the police were neutral. Whereas the old police watched but did not interfere to fulfil agendas of their own, the new police, he said, were no longer subject to any formal restrictions in carrying out their mission, which included enforcing the will of the leadership and creating and defending the kind of social order it desired.[52]

According to Reichsminister Hans Frank, it was unthinkable for police to be restricted merely to maintaining law and order. He said that these concepts used to be considered value-free and neutral, but in Hitler's dictatorship, 'philosophical neutrality no longer exists', that is, supporting or embracing any other political view besides Nazism was a crime. For the new police, the priority was 'the protection and advancement of the community of the people', and police counter-measures were justified against every 'agitation' opposed to the people, and had to 'smother' them. The police could take whatever steps were necessary, including the invasion of house and home, 'because there exists no private sphere any more, in which the individual is permitted to work unmolested at the destruction of the basis of the National Socialist community's life'.[53]

'Law is what serves the people and unlawful is what hurts it.'[54] Hans Frank was fond of that motto, which was often conveyed to the public. Werner Best's typically more legalistic formulation ran as follows:

Law in a völkisch-authoritarian state is established by those organs of the people's order, which on behalf of the highest authority—that of the Führer—has the functions of regulating a specific area of social life. In what form this regulation is pursued, whether by an order from the Führer, by law, by ordinance, by decree or by an organized regulation, is not important when the enforcement agency [the police] acts within the bounds of its mission.[55]

These arguments were meant to appeal to citizens, even though they advocated nothing less than an unchecked authoritarianism, unrestricted police interventionism, and also the end of all pretences about the neutrality of the state. Citizens were asked to consent, to give up the sanctity of the private sphere, and to accept the new police and the order of things for which they were even given 'philosophical' explanations.

In keeping with these mission statements, the Gestapo began 'correcting' court decisions. The issue arose in an acute form in early 1937. At that time the chief judge of the notorious People's Court objected when Gestapo officials arrived in court to arrest a woman. The judge told the surprised policemen that the People's Court was sovereign and police had no business there. In the short run, the judge got his way, but two days later the Gestapo arrested the woman on the grounds that it was in keeping with their mission. On 21 April 1937, in order to avoid further public conflict between the Gestapo and the courts, the Minister of Justice informed the President of the People's Court—the most radical and Nazified of all the courts—that the actions of the Gestapo were valid and the judge was out of line. As his note stated, 'the character of protective custody as a preventive police measure that was to circumvent a threat to public order and security' was such that it could be requested and used in exceptional circumstances against 'enemies of state', even when such people were found not guilty by the courts for want of evidence. In effect this decision gave the Gestapo a kind of 'blank cheque', and the police sent word of the decision to the Gestapo across Germany because of its 'fundamental importance'.[56]

This resolution of the issue between the regular court system (*Justiz*) and what was termed 'police justice' (*Polizeijustiz*) did not settle the matter. On 25 January 1938, Interior Minister Frick (still officially Himmler's boss) tried to establish new guidelines for the uses of 'protective custody' by the Gestapo. He repeated many of the worn-out phrases, but did not question the fact that protective custody was 'a coercive measure of the Gestapo', nor that only its Berlin headquarters could issue arrest warrants. He wanted the measure used only 'against persons whose behaviour endangers the existence and security of the people and the state', but acknowledged that 'protective custody' was long-term incarceration, and for the first time, that the place of confinement was the concentration camp. Technically speaking, detained persons were supposed to be informed of the grounds for their arrest, and, on paper, the Gestapo had to apply for the renewal of the detention orders every three months. However, such minimum safeguards were robbed of any meaning by the fact that Gestapo headquarters in Berlin, that is, the police itself, had the exclusive power to decide whether confinement was to continue. Decisions were made in secret, no defence counsel was permitted, and the imprisoned person was not even allowed to appear.[57]

The Gestapo exercised the power to decide when, or if, a case involving Jews or anyone else would be dealt with through 'preventive police measures' or handed over to the courts, so that the police were operating in what has been well described as 'a sphere completely apart from the regular justice system'.[58] They could dispense with procedures, more or less as they saw fit, especially if Jews were involved.[59] The Gestapo could re-arrest men and women released after serving their court-ordered sentences.[60] Just as in the final analysis, the Gestapo decided what was gossip and what was dissent or resistance, so too they could attribute a 'political' dimension to 'ordinary' crime.[61] If an accused person was found not guilty in court, or if the verdicts did not meet police expectations, the Gestapo could administer a 'corrective', and during the war simply inform the press that a 'violent criminal had been shot while resisting arrest'.[62]

The 'Day of the German Police'

The Nazi effort to foster the relationship between the police and society took many forms, including a new public relations event, the 'Day of the German Police'. It was held for the first time just before Christmas in 1934, and every year across Germany thereafter around that time to show the gentler and social side of the police, who collected money for the charity 'Winter Help Works'. In some places the methods police used annoyed citizens, but on balance the big day—which also featured parades and bands, tried to change old images.[63] Himmler, ever conscious of public relations, put the matter succinctly: 'The police in National Socialist Germany has set as an aim for itself, to be seen as the best friend and helper of the German people, and as the worst enemy of criminals and enemies of state.'[64]

Year in and year out, these events proved so popular, that by 1937 the 'Day' of the German Police, became a week-long event.[65] Reinhard Heydrich boasted that even though the Security Police (the Gestapo and Kripo) of which he was head, had 'the best experts', the police needed people to 'offer themselves as helpers'.[66] Minister of the Interior Frick said cooperation with police was 'essential for the protection of the people from asocial elements'.[67] Himmler added that the new police was 'not a police of the state against the people, but the Führer's police that grew out of the people and for the people'.[68]

By the late 1930s, Nazis celebrated the idea that the police no longer played the role of the hands-off 'nightwatchmen'. Himmler asserted that such a liberal approach permitted nothing less than the 'self-destruction of the *volk*'. He said the new police had two essential tasks, one positive and the other negative. First of all they had 'to carry out the will of the state's leadership and to maintain the kind of order it wished'. At the same time they had 'to secure the vitality and institutions of the German *volk* as an organic unity against destruction and subversion'. The negative or defensive mission was to fight dangers that imperilled the 'health, vitality, and ability to act of the *volk* and the state'. Both missions were given the police by the state's leadership, so that it followed for Himmler, that the powers of the police were no longer subject to any 'formal restrictions'.[69] The police were still distinct from the SS, but they were supposed to merge, a point subtly mentioned in the press as part of other stories.[70]

Fighting crime and stifling conflict was celebrated as worth giving up one's civil and legal rights for. Citizens were asked not to worry about the letter of the law, but to trust the police. Speeches and newspaper articles on the occasion of the last 'Day of the German Police' before the war showed further signs of radicalization. Heydrich and others long emphasized the 'preventive' tasks of the police.[71] When it came to 'degenerate' criminals, and 'the wilful enemies of the German community of the people and of the German Reich', he now said it would be 'senseless to wait' until after they had committed their deeds or repeated their crimes. 'It is much more the duty of institutions called to secure the *volk* and the Reich, that such deeds threatening the *volk* be hindered in good time in the first place.'[72]

The 'Day of the German Police' for 1940 was used to highlight the actions of the German police in the east, where a front-page story said, they were re-establishing a 'clear legal order'. Playing on well-entrenched anti-Polish sentiment in Germany, Polish criminality was described as 'unimaginable'. Rumours that German police used 'torture methods' were denied. One claim was that before constructive work could succeed in Poland, the Jews would have to be removed from the economy and their influence 'ended'. Just how that might happen was left to the imagination, although given that Jews in some cities mentioned made up half the population, readers would have had to wonder where they might be sent.[73] One long story was followed up with a national radio broadcast that featured police and SS leaders reporting on their 'mopping up operations to destroy the hard-nosed resistance of bandits and criminal riffraff'.[74]

Everywhere in conquered Europe the German police went, at least so readers were told in many stories during the first years of the war, they stopped the starvation of prisoners and ended the days of the dark cells: the Germans were presented as introducing better order and more humane methods.[75] Even the establishment of the Warsaw ghetto in late 1940 for Jews was shown in terms of how it would prevent crime and the spread of disease.[76] The 'positive' slant to such stories and radio broadcasts conveyed images that were designed to appeal to those people in Germany who lauded what was happening on the 'law and order' front there. One image was that the relatively few men guarding the backs of the armed forces in the east could only keep the peace by using an 'iron hand'.[77] The 'accomplishments' of the German police in Poland, from the Gestapo to the regular police (Orpo), were paraded for the greater glory of the police back home, where day in day out, people could read of death penalties and heavy prison sentences that would hardly have been possible for such infractions even in Nazi Germany during the years of peace.[78]

The Kripo

During the celebratory 'Days of the German Police', police leaders invariably pointed with pride to the Kripo. Arthur Nebe, first head of the Kripo, wrote a reflective essay at the end of the 1930s about how it took shape, in which he noted that because Hitler's dictatorship almost immediately set out to fight both 'enemies of state' and asocial elements, it was logical that soon after the Gestapo was set up to fight the former, the Kripo would be empowered to deal with the latter. Nebe repeated the much-used phrase that 'the struggle against the political enemy of state and against the asocial criminal must logically be led by one hand'. He said that both Kripo and Gestapo, were given the mission to protect the community not just by pursuing enemies of the people after they acted, but by working preventively to hinder misdeeds in the first place.[79]

Until 1933, the Kripo was the detective force of the regular police, and worked as the police enforcement arm of the State Attorney. The Kripo's powers grew in the emergency situation, and like the Gestapo, it came to adopt a preventive role, by which they meant arbitrarily arresting people who police thought might commit a crime. The announcement on 17 June 1936 of Heinrich Himmler's appointment as Chief of the German police by Hitler, was a front-page story. Within days, the population was informed that to carry out Hitler's mandate to unify the German police, a new Main Office of the Security Police, or Sipo was created. The Sipo combined under a single umbrella, both the Gestapo and Kripo, with Reinhard Heydrich in charge. At the same time Kurt Daluege was put in command of the newly centralized uniformed police in the Main Office of the Regular Police or Orpo.[80] Just over a year later, the Kripo was set up in central offices in a new Reich Criminal Police Office (RKPA).[81]

The police as a whole, including the Kripo, adopted methods and missions that were inspired by Nazi ideology.[82] Paul Werner, who between 1937 and 1945 was head of 'prevention' desks at Kripo headquarters in Berlin, stated in 1941, that the preventive mission of the Kripo was 'to exterminate' criminality and to work for the 'lasting and complete annihilation' of the 'criminal enemy of the people'.[83] Arthur Nebe and Kurt Daluege shared this view, along with virulent racism and antisemitism, and they fostered Nazi ideology in the police establishment. They pushed for the same kind of independence from the justice system and courts as enjoyed by the Gestapo, and for the same kinds of preventive powers of arrest.[84]

Historian Martin Broszat rightly noted

that there was a tendency to solve the problem of criminality in the Third Reich in the last analysis in the same way as in dealing with something like hereditary disease, namely with the radical approach of 'neutralization', 'disposal', or 'eradication'. People who were accused of a crime, were no longer regarded as human beings with legal protections, but simply as parasites against whom it made no sense to open legal proceedings, but who were simply neutralized and eliminated.[85]

As frequently happened on the 'Day of the German Police', the one in 1937 was taken as an opportunity to boast about how modern the police had become. Heydrich conducted a press tour of the Police Institute in Berlin and pointed out some of the new scientific methods used by the Kripo to catch criminals. He said the 'highest guiding principle' even of the Kripo was 'in maintaining the good order of the race', and stated as if it were a fact, that 'criminals frequently develop out of inherited predispositions'. He claimed that the police were there to prevent crime and to act as a warning, and were trained in criminological techniques and schooled in National Socialist teachings.[86]

Himmler and Heydrich issued invitations to police from around the world to visit Kripo headquarters in Berlin, as a way of showing off the modernity of the German police. Among those who took up the invitation was Edmund Patrick Coffey, who came on behalf of J. Edgar Hoover of the FBI. The news report of the visit in January 1938 carried the headline, 'German Security Police as Model'. During his stay, Coffey visited the Kripo's technical facilities, and expressed his 'great pleasure' about the Kripo, and the rest of the police. He hoped that Hoover would visit during the summer after the new Kripo headquarters was finished. We can only speculate as to how German readers would respond to such stories, but most likely many of them were impressed that after five years of Hitler's dictatorship, the Nazi police had won the FBI's seal of approval.[87]

Numerous other stories reinforced the image of German police as in the vanguard of science, and as new specialized police facilities were created, what they did was written up in the press in the best possible light.[88] According to one story, the Kripo 'would lead the battle against criminality by using the most modern methods, no longer hindered by any jurisdictional restrictions'.[89] The Kripo developed fifteen different 'special branches', each focusing on specific forms of criminality, like one that aimed at homosexuality and abortion, another at drugs, and so on.[90] The reporter for one long-established newspaper, after examining the work at headquarters, with its central offices dealing with matters like drug smuggling, and especially noting its new fingerprint catalogue, shared his admiration with readers. The reporter was assured in all seriousness by one detective, that given modern methods, 'it was as good as certain, that every crime can be solved within a given period of time'. The story concluded that the net effect of changes was that the Kripo reverted to the 'real and original function' of police, namely, 'defence against dangers and protection of the public from the lawbreaker'.[91]

The Kripo may or may not have used the kinds of third-degree methods as much as the Gestapo, but recent research strongly suggests that members of the Kripo were not above using strong-arm tactics.[92] Although we can find evidence of rivalry between the Gestapo and Kripo, for example, on the question of which of them had jurisdiction in certain cases, the importance of such conflicts should not be exaggerated. In spite, or even because of a certain amount of overlap between the two (for instance, each of them had special sections to deal with homosexuals and with illicit extramarital relations between Jews and non-Jews) the general impression is hard to avoid that the police functioned well together, and competition between the two does not seem to have operated to the benefit of those who fell into their grasp.

The Courts

The courts were the source of many more stories about the dictatorship's approach to law and order. New 'emergency' Special Courts were created by decree of 21 March 1933 in each of the twenty-six higher court districts across the country. These courts, as well as the 'malicious gossip' decree, came into force on the famous 'Day at Potsdam', and were meant by judicial officials to show that the courts could be counted on to shield the new regime from criticism. The hope was that the regime would return to the rule of law, and that these 'emergency' courts would fade away. Quite to the contrary, they became permanent, and by February 1941, there would be sixty-three of them, with some higher court districts having as many as four. They were initially responsible for trying two political offences, particularly those accused of posing a political threat to the 'people and state'—as that broad notion was embodied in the so-called Reichstag Fire Decree of 28 February 1933. They tried 'malicious gossip' cases and verbal attacks on the government.[93] The latter was broadened further in a new law of 20 December 1934 which, among other things, made public criticism not just of the government, but of the Nazi Party, into a crime. Such a 'malicious' attack was unlawful even if the remarks were made in private, at least if it could be shown that the person responsible knew or should have known that the statements might be repeated in public.[94]

These courts reached into the private lives of citizens, as nearly all such 'crimes' were verbal exchanges among the people, and they were discovered only when one person denounced someone they knew to the police. Some of these cases ended tragically, and might well have been thrown out except that the courts treated remarks as having been made 'in public' even when some were uttered among a small circle of friends or even privately.[95] The business of the Special Courts increased more than ever during the war because they were responsible for trying offences against the War Measures Acts.

A new People's Court was established in Berlin on 24 April 1934 to try cases of what was broadly defined as treason, but might well concern a minor verbal criticism of the government or of Hitler.[96] After a relatively slow start, the People's Court, especially under the leadership of Georg Thierack and later Roland Freisler, attained a bloody reputation because of its frequent use of the death penalty.

Each Special Court was assigned three professional judges who utilized new procedures to speed up trials without worrying about the rights of the accused. As of 1 September 1939 this model was introduced in the County Courts as well, as part of what was referred to as the judiciary's 'Simplification Decree'.[97] The decree also stated that if and when an attorney general felt that 'public security and order was seriously endangered', the case could be brought before a Special Court. The activities of the County Courts were also affected by a law to 'modify criminal proceedings' (16 September 1939) which gave justice authorities the right to intervene when they felt a verdict was too mild.[98]

By the war years, Special Courts dealt not only with 'political' matters, but increasingly also with 'criminal' cases that would ordinarily have gone to the regular courts. If and when the local attorney general decided that the 'deed was so reprehensible' or caused such 'public agitation' that it needed an 'immediate verdict', he could send the case to the Special Courts.[99] Within weeks of the outbreak of war, the Special Courts were referred to in the press, and quite favourably at that, as the equivalent of a military 'drumhead court martial of the home front'.[100] According to one Ministry of Justice official, citizens ought to see in these courts 'the swiftest and mightiest weapon for eliminating gangster elements from the community of the people at one stroke, either permanently or temporarily'.[101]

During the war, the criminalization of social life spread, as more aspects of daily life came under regulation. In an overlapping process, all crime was politicized in that even minor (and non-violent) theft or fraud could be interpreted as undermining the nation's will to win.[102] Either way, more offenders found themselves facing Special Courts. In Hamburg, for example, in 1943 at the height of the war, the Special Courts tried 73 per cent of all court cases.[103]

All these courts adopted a simple rule of thumb, as one newspaper story put it: 'Anyone who offends against the community of the people, must fall.' In this particular account, stealing rationing cards or accepting bribes for such cards qualified a person for the label of 'parasite', and they were sentenced to death. The term 'parasite on the body politic', used from the beginning of the Third Reich as a term of abuse, became a common label for anyone capitalizing on the war for personal gain, but also continued to be used to condemn behaviour (such as homosexuality) that apparently did not fit the norms of the 'community of the people'.[104]

What role did the press play in making Nazi courts and police come to life? In terms of the court system, which was very much efficiency-oriented in the Third Reich, newspaper stories were extremely important, and arguably were as decisive in terrorizing 'enemies' and winning 'friends' as what actually took place in the courtrooms.[105] A never-ending series of crime and punishment stories was published during the Nazi era. These morality tales were supposed to be crafted according to specific guidelines laid down by the Propaganda Ministry and press officers attached to the police and the courts in order to obtain the maximum public relations effect. Instructions to the press on 24 February 1934 said that stories must avoid describing how a certain worker or carpenter was sentenced to death, but instead tell of how a murderer or arsonist was executed.[106]

The police also used newspapers to fulfil their political and racist missions. For example, Berlin headquarters issued orders to local Gestapo very early in the regime to ensure that press notices were written up in such a way that they would 'awaken in the impartial reader the feeling for the necessity and internal justification' for such actions.[107] Such stories were designed to fulfil the dual function of legitimating the new system and deterring 'criminality'. The Gestapo made use of the newspapers to which stories were systematically given with the expectation they would help police fulfil their mandate to stigmatize 'enemies' (especially the Communists, Jews, even Catholic priests, and others). A concerted effort was made by police to show the alleged connections of Jews to treasonous activities like Communism.[108] Another way to spread hatred of the Jews was to link them to crime, and that became a common theme in the Nazi press.[109] There were countless stories about Jews who were accused of being 'profiteers'.[110] The press ran accounts of any Jews who were accused of crimes, from embezzling, to swindling and smuggling, to others involving sex, money, and drugs.[111] The Gestapo was an openly politicized police force and was active well beyond the usual bounds of these sterile-sounding phrases. Thus, as part of its political task, Gestapo headquarters in Berlin ordered local and regional Gestapo offices to turn over certain kinds of information to *Der Stürmer*, the notorious antisemitic rag. In a communication from headquarters, police were told to support the 'educative work' of this newspaper by letting its editors view and use 'official material on criminal and other kinds of misdeeds of the Jews'.[112]

By the end of the pre-war era, if not before, the Nazi police (especially the Gestapo and Kripo) began to take very seriously their new mission to cleanse the body politic of 'harmful', or 'degenerative elements'. In that sense they took on wholly unprecedented, racist-informed, preventive tasks as they moved into the field of social biology. The vision the police adopted was of a conflict-free society from which would be eliminated all social and biological carriers of 'harmful' behaviour.[113] As we have seen, these changing missions were not merely worked out behind the scenes, and put into practice in secret, but by and large they were explained in the German press to win support for the dictatorship. For the same reason, as we will see next, Nazi officials informed the public about concentration camps, and provided rationalizations for them.

3
Concentration Camps and Media Reports

The first concentration camps were hardly 'camps' at all, but temporary places the Nazis used to hold their political enemies soon after Hitler's appointment. These camps resulted from local initiatives, and did not stem from a 'centrally guided action' by Hitler's government.[1] In the beginning, no one seems to have thought that the camps would become a permanent part of the dictatorship, and they were set up in buildings like old military barracks and castles, or were merely special sections in a workhouse or a prison. Regional authorities created such 'camps' to cope with the flood of prisoners, but the SA and Nazi hotheads used them to beat up Communists and other enemies. Like the torture cellars of the SA in many cities, none were designed to last.[2]

After 1945, Rudolf Diels of the Gestapo used the term 'wild concentration camps' to suggest that Nazi radicals, not the police, created them all. As historian Johannes Tuchel has pointed out, however, most of these camps were linked to the police or to the regular state administration.[3] Columbia House in Berlin, for example, was established as a concentration camp in an old military prison in the middle of the capital city. From late June 1933, it held prisoners, but it was not the 'independent domain' of the SS that Diels later claimed it was, but under the control of the Gestapo main office (Gestapa) from its headquarters at Prinz-Albrecht-Strasse 8, with only the guards supplied by the SS.[4]

How citizens were informed about the foundation of the camps can be seen in the case of Dachau, the site of the infamous camp on the outskirts of Munich. On 21 March 1933, Himmler announced its opening in his capacity as Police President of Munich, under the headline 'concentration camp for political prisoners'. It was supposed to hold up to 5,000 prisoners who were described as primarily Communist Party functionaries. Himmler said it was out of the question to release such prisoners from the overcrowded jails, because they would take up their subversive activities again. Thus, both the temporary and the preventive nature of the camps was made explicit from the start. An additional rationalization was that they were needed to quiet the anxieties of the 'national population' who allegedly felt threatened by a left-wing revolution. News stories assured citizens that, contrary to rumours, no one was mistreated and none would be incarcerated longer than necessary. Although townspeople in Dachau itself were warned to keep away, a newspaper story reported that 'numerous curious onlookers' were on hand to see the first group of 200 Communists arrive.[5]

The simple appeal was that the camps were mainly for Communists.[6] Press reports from across the country repeated that story-line, under headings like 'concentration camp for Marxists'.[7] During the first half of 1933 the 'successes' against the Communists, the arrests of thousands of them in police 'actions', and the discoveries of alleged conspiracies were paraded in the press.[8] There was a flood of reports about the camps in virtually every town and city in Germany, so they were anything but secret. Stories often mentioned that members of the press visited the facilities.[9] One Attorney General who in May 1933 led reporters through the prison at Sonnenburg assured them that prisoners, including famous Communists like Erich Mühsam, did not live much differently than they would in a military barracks.[10]

A key point in the media was that the camps were needed to uphold 'law and order', but their pedagogical side was played up from the beginning. Stories referred to the 'educative factor' that the 'appropriate work' would have on prisoners. There were rare hints that some Germans were not pleased about camps like Dachau, and unhappy about detaining people without a proper trial. Munich's Cardinal Faulhaber, for example, asked the authorities in mid-April 1933 to speed up hearings, so that by Easter family fathers would be released. The request was granted up to a point and the Nazis promised that 1,000 prisoners would be allowed to spend the holidays at home.[11] The camps, however, were not fading away, but justified as providing prisoners an 'opportunity to reflect on their shameful deeds'.[12]

The press in Dachau greeted the foundation of the camp as bringing new 'hope for the Dachau business world'. It was hailed as an 'economic turning point' and beginning of 'happier days' for the small town, population 8,234 in 1933.[13] On the day the camp opened one local paper spoke of the economic advantages of setting up a 'state-run camp' in a depressed part of town. There was local unemployment, and the camp, the guards, and civil servants would bring new income and help businesses recover.[14] Although there was temporary employment in constructing the camp, expectations about its economic advantages were short-lived, as the camp was run on an autarkic basis. It met most of its own needs and had plenty of its own low-cost labour.[15]

In the short term, however, citizens were proud of having a camp in town. Indeed on 23 May 1933, one newspaper shouted that Dachau was Germany's 'most famous place', and boasted that the 'model concentration camp' in town 'makes Dachau known well beyond the borders of the Fatherland'.[16] Alas, this 'fame' was based on what happened in the camp whose reputation was well summed up in the saying of the time: 'Dear God, make me mum so that I don't to Dachau come.'

Newspaper editor Hermann Larcher visited the camp in late June 1933 and repeated how it was needed to relieve overcrowding of the regular prisons, and to hold Communists in 'protective custody'. Larcher asserted that prisoners would be 're-educated to practical, honest work, and that was ultimately the aim of their arrest'. Prisoners restored the run-down property on which the camp was situated, and Larcher reported, 'they work cheerfully and willingly and, probably most of them are happy that they now have a regular life, good food and a roof over their heads.'[17]

In the first six months of the Dachau camp, the three local newspapers kept citizens up to date, including justifying how guards shot prisoners in 'self-defence'. Those in the camp were invariably described as Communists who needed to be re-educated but who, it was reported, were well treated. A long article on 1 February 1934 on life in the camp by another local writer who was allowed inside to see for himself was full of uncritical praise for everything he saw, from the singing in work columns to the positive effect that discipline was having.[18]

As the city tried to make itself more attractive to tourists, and especially for the build-up to the Olympics, the newspapers grew silent on the camp. By 1936 the mayor and some councillors were having second thoughts about the reputation of Dachau as the 'KZ-city'. In May that year one notable suggested changing the camp's name, which he no longer wanted associated with the town. According to historian Sybille Steinbacher, by then the local population, influenced by Nazi ideology and press coverage, had come to regard the camp 'as a legitimate, necessary institution, in which aliens of the community would have to be re-educated. For a long while the dominant opinion was that it was quite proper that "enemies of state" be confined in a concentration camp.'[19]

The creation of other camps in Germany was reported along similar lines. For example, on 14 March 1933 the Nazi press in Württemberg mentioned hopes for a new concentration camp to hold 500 or so Communists in 'protective custody'. Before the end of the month it reported on the creation of a camp at Heuberg, and provided both a story and photograph of the facility.[20] The camp in fact merely took over some of the buildings of what was until then an independently run home for orphaned, neglected, and sick children. The buildings in Heuberg, originally built by the military in 1910 for troops during military exercises, fell into disuse after the lost war until some were taken over for the children. The creation of the concentration camp was initially greeted by locals who wanted to be rid of the children's home and hoped that the camp would mean a return of prosperity. During the year the camp existed, local merchants gained little, however, and were pleased when the military returned at the beginning of 1934, and camp prisoners were transferred elsewhere. In the meantime, Heuberg was the object of considerable press attention. Over the course of the year, the camp was written up in most newspapers of the area, and it was frequently visited by public figures, including, in late March 1933, the American General Consul from Stuttgart. Newspaper reporters were often given access to the camp, and many used such opportunities to publish accounts of life on the inside. The theme in a story in the *Stuttgarter Süddeutsche Zeitung* in early April was that the camp was for Communists, who had to be incarcerated until they came to their senses. The story emphasized the military-style training and concluded that sending these men to a place like Heuberg was 'probably the most humane way in which one can deal with such subversive elements'.[21] Journalists were on one occasion bussed in from Stuttgart for a tour, and their accounts as well as others in the regional press were enthusiastic, or at least uniformly positive about everything in the camp. They conveyed the impression that prisoners (in Heuberg, dressed in their own street clothing) lived amid pleasant rural surroundings and enjoyed the clean air. One report in an article that was widely reprinted expressed satisfaction that prisoners were not treated as 'criminals', but as 'seduced' by Communism, so that their stay in camp was not designed to be a 'punishment', but an 'education' that would bring a 'change of opinion'.[22] However, none of the stories questioned the legitimacy of the camps, and all of them insisted that the prisoners deserved what they got. Whatever else readers of the press might conclude, they could be in little doubt that prisoners were in the camp because they did not agree with the Nazis.

Another such small camp was established at Breitenau near Kassel in June 1933, which lasted only until March the next year, and was covered by many newspapers. It was described in the regional press as necessary to relieve pressure on the prison in Kassel, and supposedly would be used as a 'place of education'. That description was in keeping with usages of the time which tended to portray prisons as both places of punishment and correction.[23] A week after the camp was founded, no less than seventeen daily newspapers from the region and one national, published accounts of it, often simply repeating verbatim the official news release. Some papers, like the *Kasseler Neuesten Nachrichten* (*KNN*) sent reporters. The *KNN* not only had the largest circulation, but was not associated with Nazism before 1933. Its lengthy story no doubt carried considerable weight in forming the image of the camp in the public eye. It described the facilities and pointed to the usefulness of prisoners' work, such as land reclamation. The story closed with the assertion that 'all in all the prisoners in protective custody at Breitenau lead a quite acceptable existence that in part is actually above the level to which they were accustomed from earlier times'.[24]

On the negative side, the story admitted that no one liked to be deprived of their freedom. However, those responsible for 'poisoning the atmosphere' in Germany had to be stopped. Readers could rest assured that prisoners were not kept in dark cells, but on the contrary, in the phrase that headed the story, 'they can't complain'. Indeed, with the help of what the story called 'work as therapy', prisoners would be rehabilitated, become useful citizens again, and be released. The story noted that even 'for the political police, the camp represents an unhappy necessity, and the state would be satisfied when it could dissolve the last concentration camp'.[25]

Foundation of a camp at Oranienburg, just to the north of Berlin, also was widely covered by the press. Within a week of its opening, the *Oranienburger Generalanzeiger* (*OGA*) noted rumours about mistreatment of prisoners, and supposedly to get to the bottom of the story, sent reporters to investigate. What they wrote was a cover-up, but one that used the catalogue of phrases that was already standard fare. The reporter for the *OGA* likened it to a military training camp, an oft-used analogy from those times. He informed readers that prisoners got mail, plenty of exercise, and lots of wholesome work in the fresh air. Provisions for them were as good as for the guards. This on-the-spot account made the overriding point that persistent rumours of mistreatment were propaganda spread by foreign countries.[26]

A reporter who also visited Oranienburg at this time on behalf of one of the main Nazi newspapers rejected what he labelled as Marxist 'nonsensical fairy tales in the foreign press'. He pointed to camp discipline and work, and lauded both as the only way to bring prisoners back to their senses. The wholly positive slant of the reporter, who did not fail to mention prisoners' leisure activities like sport and chess, ended with quotes from an inmate who shakes a sentry's hand at the gate. As he was leaving he said that Nazi guards 'were upstanding guys. We thought you would deal mercilessly with us. But you treated us, your enemies, as human beings. And we thank you!'[27]

The distinguished *Berliner Morgenpost* published what it said were the first pictures from what it termed the Oranienburg 'collection camp' on 7 April 1933. The caption stated without comment, presumably because none was necessary, that the pictures showed 'protective custody prisoners and politically suspicious persons'.[28] A visitor to Oranienburg from still another newspaper at about this time reiterated that the 'atrocity stories' were untrue. The combination of military-style training, exercise, and sport was supposed to have an educative effect on rank-and-file Marxists who for years were misled, corrupted, and incited to misdeeds by their leaders. The story stated that once prisoners saw the light, as they certainly would, they could be released. Although the camps might not be able to turn die-hard Communists into reliable people, the article concluded that daily routines got these men again used to order, discipline, and obedience. The story emphasized that the camps represented the clearest sign that the state was no longer prepared to see the streets terrorized.[29]

'Obviously', according to still another story, Communist and pacifist agitators and certain left-wing members of parliament would be kept on in the camps.[30] In order to refute the atrocity tales, photos were taken in Oranienburg and published widely, including by the *OGA* on 27 April 1933. These images made the camp look peaceful and settled, and anything but the terrorizing institution reported in the foreign press or whispered about in Germany.[31]

Germany's largest illustrated newspaper, the *Berliner Illustrierte Zeitung*, carried similar pictures in its edition of 30 April 1933. Like other photographs from the early camps published all over the country, these visual 'refutations' showed idyllic scenes of healthy, suntanned, muscular men doing useful work and learning basic skills under open skies in the countryside. The photo-essays from the times, pictured prisoners during leisure activities (one showed them playing chess) or otherwise involved in sports. There was usually a communal scene as the men gathered for a hearty meal.[32] Another illustrated newspaper from Berlin carried such pictures on 28 May 1933, under the headline, that in the camp 'climbing over the wooden horse is a favoured sport exercise'.[33] Although early photo-essays from the camps varied in accent, the same themes were generally repeated about all of them.[34]

The German press dismissed as anti-German propaganda, the *Brown Book about the Reichstag Fire and Hitler's Terror*, published in 1933 in Switzerland.[35] Camp Commandant Werner Schäfer of Oranienburg wrote a book-length refutation.[36] Where the *Brown Book* spoke of terror and murder, Schäfer said SA guards were 'educators' who had to deal with hardened Communists, whose twisted faces mirrored their souls, so corrupted by the teachings of Marxist class struggle that they were unrecognizable as German 'racial comrades'.[37]

Schäfer pointed to other accounts based on visits to Oranienburg, to back up his refutations about allegations spread abroad. One described the camp as a 'place of education' for 'enemies of state', and for bigwigs who misused their positions and lived high on the hog. In the camp they would get a chance to experience humbler conditions. The reporter recited the camp's virtues as being 'military order, discipline and neatness'.[38] Schäfer published these stories in his book, along with photographs, some of them later reprinted in German newspapers.[39]

Pictures from the camps invariably played up their healthy and 'civilized' character. They usually show men reading or involved in other uplifting activities, and one story noted that Communist prisoners who had been in the Soviet Union said life was better in Dachau than it was for the 'free' workers under Stalin's regime.[40] In keeping with Hitler's own thinking, newspaper stories favourably compared Nazi concentration camps with more terroristic images from the French and Russian Revolutions.[41]

There were some pictures of the prisoners, however, that hinted how there was something biologically amiss with them, so that their 'cure' might be more complicated. Some close-up pictures of the prisoners in Dachau from mid-July 1933, for example, created the impression that there was a racial-biological basis to their pathological behaviour. The photographs, including one on the front page of an illustrated newspaper, showed a close-up of less than cheery men standing at morning roll-call. The accompanying text claimed the pictures provided 'a vivid indication' that some prisoners were biologically determined to such an extent, that they could never be improved or released. The story said that these men would be kept apart from the others and given special jobs to do.

In word and picture these articles invoked a standard set of motifs, of hard but healthy work, good and plentiful food, and leisure time for sport, reading, and relaxation. The camps were portrayed as places of resocialization for the men, described as 'racial comrades', who fell victim to (foreign) Bolshevik Communism. 'The healing effect of productive work and firm discipline,' as the caption under one picture of men going off to work stated, 'would educate them to be productive members of the Nazi state'.[42] There was an underlying nationalist appeal, whereby Germans were invited to ignore even persistent charges about the camps when they originated from foreigners (who were ignorant by definition), or anti-Nazis in exile, whose prejudices were too well known to need refuting.

The 'educative' role of the camps was mentioned repeatedly, as in one story about the Emsland camps from June 1933. It stated as a given, that 'a very large number of these prisoners' only needed a limited stay and they would be won back to the community.[43] The work of prisoners on land reclamation projects in the Emsland was praised for turning the moor into fruitful land that could be settled.[44]

Some praise for the camps came from unexpected quarters, like Osnabrück's Catholic Bishop Berning, who paid an official visit to the Emsland camps in the summer of 1936. He was quoted in a press story as saying that 'those who still doubt the constructive work of the Third Reich should be led here. What was earlier neglected is today being undertaken.' Berning used the poetic image of the Emsland as a Sleeping Beauty that long awaited a prince to awaken it, and, he concluded breathlessly, the prince was 'our Führer Adolf Hitler'.[45] Surely the Bishop must have thought that all or most citizens agreed with the establishment of these camps.

At precisely this time, the Council of the German Evangelical Church wrote to Hitler to express reservations about the new Germany. Although the Council emphasized worries about how the country was moving away from Christianity, they also mentioned that their conscience was burdened by the continued existence of the concentration camps and the Gestapo. Alas, nothing came of this mild protest.[46]

There were enough voices in the press singing the praises of the camps to offset occasional complaints. Foreign notables and pro-Germans like Sven Hedin, the Swedish explorer, were invited in late 1936 to visit the camp at Sachsenburg. Although he admitted that 'cruelties' might have been committed in some camps early on, he echoed Hitler's words that the worst was now over. Hedin suggested that the camps were on the way out.[47] His book, laced with racism and antisemitism, was full of admiration for everything he saw, and it was promptly translated into German and English. Along with other such accounts, his book reinforced the public images presented by the Nazis themselves.

Some Camp Realities

Behind the bucolic images, the apologies, rationalizations, and cover-ups, how much terror do we find in the early camps? Because of poor record-keeping and because much of the documentation was destroyed, we do not know all the details about the prisoners in the first camps. If we include temporary sites where victims of the Nazis were held and tortured, such as in schools, factories, castles, fortresses, and prisons, the number of such 'camps' was quite large. One recent account lists over 160 places used in 1933 alone, some for only a short time before they were dissolved.[48] It is more difficult to ascertain the exact number of men and women taken into 'protective custody' at one time or another in 1933. In the first wave of arrests in March and April 1933, an estimated 25,000 people, mainly Communists, were picked up in Prussia alone.[49] There are grounds for suggesting that perhaps as many again were picked up in the rest of Germany during those months.[50]

Women were also sent to concentration camps, beginning at Gotteszell (Baden), established in March 1933. It is usually considered the first designated as a concentration camp for women, and around 50 of them were sent there, mostly Communists in early 1933. A second camp for women at Moringen (near Göttingen) received its first two women prisoners, both Communists, on 3 June 1933. By the autumn, Moringen had 75 women prisoners, and in general those numbers remained in that range over the next several years.[51] The press especially played up the stories of prisoners held for a short time and released.[52]

Another wave of arrests took place in the summer of 1933; this time the victims were the leaders of virtually all other political parties, right down to the local level. The national figures we have for 31 July 1933, put the number in 'protective custody'—that is, formally speaking under the control of the Gestapo and in concentration camps—at 26,789.[53] That figure was not much higher than the one in the press.[54] The impression that the camps were meant to be temporary could be deduced from these stories and also from the fact that already by August 1933, according to one press account, while the 'big fish', that is, the leaders of left-wing parties, were going to be kept in custody, the 'seduced workers' already were being released.[55] Less mention was made in the press of prisoners who were not Communists or other left-wingers.

Accused people were picked up, sent for a stint to a camp, and released. They were then replaced by new prisoners. For example, at the Dachau camp from June to December 1933, there were usually around 3,800 prisoners at any one time, of whom between as many as 2,000 and as few as 600 were released each month, with about the same number rearrested.[56] For all of 1933, a total of about 100,000 people spent time in a concentration camp; an estimated 500 to 600 were killed.[57] However, not included in this substantial number were many who were beaten by the SA and let go. The estimates of the latter illegal 'arrests' for Prussia alone range up to 30,000 for the period up to the end of April 1933. In Berlin there were more than 100 temporary torture chambers in working-class districts of the Communists and Socialists.[58] The total number of those mistreated and terrorized in this way in 1933, even without being formally or semi-legally arrested, or sent to one of the concentration camps, certainly exceeded 100,000.[59] Most of these, like the 100,000 or so who were sent to the concentration camps, had been involved in the Communist Party in some way.

These numbers are horrific when set against what happened in German history before 1933, but in comparison to major revolutions, like the one in France in 1789, or the Russian Revolution, when opposition grew and led to civil war, the Nazi revolution appears almost consensual.

After 1933 the Communists continued to be over-represented in the camps. A list from 10 April 1934, for example, shows that of the 2,405 people in concentration camps in Bavaria, 1,531 of them (62.5 per cent) were accused of being in Communist activities; another 222 people (9.1 per cent) were in for 'high treason' and another 33 (or 1.3 per cent) for less serious forms of treason. Some of the latter might also have been Communists, as perhaps were another 98 prisoners (4 per cent) accused of 'Marxist activities'. The only other politicals mentioned were 24 Socialist functionaries, who made up less than 1 per cent of the prisoners. Jews were not listed separately, and it is unlikely that many were in Dachau or the other camps in Germany at that time. [60]

The End of the Camps in Sight?

Public knowledge of the camps was coloured by the media. Newspapers frankly blamed the victims, even those who were killed. One death in Dachau was reported in August 1933 as marking 'the end of one of the most dangerous Communists', who was shot allegedly 'while trying to escape'.[61] The town press in Dachau reported the violent deaths of a dozen prisoners during 1933, and claimed both that guards acted in 'self-defence', and that the victims were 'in any case sadistically inclined'.[62]

How did Germans react to the creation of the first camps? We have already seen that very few critical voices were raised. In the detailed underground reports the Socialists wrote beginning in early 1934, it is clear that they objected most of all to the Gestapo and camp system. No doubt, there were many other people in Germany, perhaps even some who supported Nazism, who would have liked to see the end of these two new institutions of the dictatorship.

The beautified photographs of the camps carried in the German press of the time, with their idyllic scenes and uplifting stories were important, but not necessarily because they were accepted at face value by everyone. Germans knew only too well that the news was censored, and some of the circulation of the Nazi Party press even fell for a time in 1933 before it picked up again.[63] The first images of the camps, constituted for most people their formative or first impressions and were the only real 'experience' most people had of the camps. This is not to say that the representations of the camps and the terror had uniform effects on the population. The social reception of the images that were projected no doubt varied enormously. At one end of the scale these published accounts had a terrorizing or deterrent effect on potential opponents of Nazism and those who were officially stigmatized. Many people, like the Socialist underground, rejected everything about the terror, kept waiting for the dictatorship to crumble, and eagerly pointed to any sign that the end was near. At the other end of the scale there can be no doubt that the same images won support and helped to ease the acceptance of the regime. 'Good citizens' were tired of lawlessness, and wanted a crackdown on 'law and order', and were unlikely to be faced by the prospect of a stay in a concentration camp. The camps were presented as educative institutions that provided a 'correction and a warning' for Communists and those described as 'social rabble', that is, outsiders like habitual criminals, the chronically unemployed, beggars, alcoholics, homosexuals, and repeat sex offenders, all of whom would be rehabilitated by military-like camps and at least kept off the streets.[64]

If we take a broader view, one sign that the German people accepted or were willing to tolerate the camps and the new police can be seen in the plebiscite and election of 1933, and the plebiscite of August 1934. The vast majority of Germans had dropped their reservations about Hitler, and it would be surprising if many were outraged by the camps or the Gestapo.[65]

For a brief moment at the end of 1933, especially after the November elections, the new regime was so firmly in control, that the Nazis considered getting rid of both the Gestapo and the camps. In early December, Hermann Göring in his role as the Prime Minister of Prussia and head of the Gestapo, announced the release of large groups from the camps. Göring said a Christmas amnesty would release 5,000 prisoners and in a simultaneous announcement, the Bavarian political police (under Himmler) said that over 500 would be set free there.[66] It was Göring's publicly stated view, one that was fairly accurate, that Hitler's government no longer had many enemies.[67] The hope was prisoners had learned their lesson and would find their way back into society and 'again prove to be useful members of the community of the people'.[68] Hitler was quoted in a front-page story at the end of 1933 as saying (prematurely as it turned out) that 'at least we have not set up a Guillotine'; even the 'worst elements', he said, 'had been only separated from the nation'.[69] In an interview (reprinted 19 February 1934) Hitler played down the excesses of the Nazi revolution and the stories about the camps. He was quoted as saying that 'enemies' were interned 'because these enemies ought not to disturb the rebirth of Germany's political health'. A stay in the camps gave them time to change their point of view and to give up their 'negative attitude' towards the new regime. When they did so they would be released.[70]

In 1934 reports continued about the release of prisoners and the closing or reduction in size of many camps.[71] In an interview on 21 April 1934, Göring boasted that there was 'security in Germany', and said there were only between 4,000 and 5,000 prisoners in the Prussian camps, and a total of between 6,000 and 7,000 in all of Germany, most of whom (he said) were Communists. Although these figures, especially for those outside Prussia have been questioned, there is no doubt that eliminating the camps was the trend at the time.[72] Throughout 1934 more camps closed, like the one at Oranienburg in September, because it was no longer needed. The announcement said that in future 'protective custody' would be used more sparingly and only when state security was in imminent danger; otherwise, anyone in conflict with the law would be sent without delay to the courts.[73]

There were 'at most' only 3,000 prisoners in the camps by the end of 1934 and that was the lowest point they ever reached in the Third Reich.[74] The decline was accelerated by a Hitler amnesty of 7 August 1934. Shortly thereafter there were less than 500 prisoners in all the Prussian camps and by year's end only around 1,600 in Bavaria.[75] It made perfect sense to close the camps, because by 1934–5 the country was positively inclined towards Hitler's dictatorship. Organized opposition was silent or as good as dead. The surprise was that for all Hitler's popularity and the social consensus that supported the new regime, the camps did not disappear.

Expanding Rather than Dissolving the Camps and the Gestapo

Just as Himmler made the Gestapo independent of the courts, so he also made concentration camps separate from the traditional places of incarceration, like prisons and workhouses. It took time to set up such an entirely new system, which had to be paid for, especially when the country still had to master the economic situation. Himmler wanted funding to flow to him as the head of SS and not as head of the Gestapo, presumably because he was the supreme leader of the SS and had greater freedom of action.[76] Himmler won Hitler's support for the retention of the camps at a meeting on 20 June 1935 and at the same time got agreement that by 1 April 1936 the camps and the guards would be funded under the federal budget, which was important to the future of the camps.[77] On 18 October 1935, Hitler met again with Himmler for a discussion of a number of questions, including the camp guards, and the definition (which was broadened) of enemies to include the vague category of the 'asocials'.[78]

That Hitler was aware of what was going on in the camps can be seen from the note of a conversation he had with Himmler, the gist of which was communicated to the Minister of Justice on 6 November 1935. Justice officials continued to be concerned about the deaths of prisoners in the camps. Hitler's response was that they should pay them no attention.[79] The number of prisoners in all the camps, which hit an all-time low of 3,000 at the end of 1934, began to increase again, and by the summer of 1935 stood at around 3,500.[80]

Himmler already had taken steps to set the camps on firm organizational foundations. In April 1934, he appointed the commandant of Dachau, Theodor Eicke as the 'Inspector of concentration camps' and SS guards, that is, the SS Death's Head formations.[81] Eicke organized and systematized the camps. By March 1935 he consolidated those still operating into seven camps, and by August 1937 reduced them further to four main ones.[82] He also developed a code of conduct for the guards, and a minutely detailed set of rules to govern life and death in the camps, down to precise corporal punishments for various infractions.[83] It is partly because of these features of the 'model camp' he developed in Dachau, and also because many future camp commandants and guards were trained there, that Dachau has been called the 'school of brutality'. Inside the camp was a world apart, with command structures, symbols, and obscure meanings all their own that are well described by camp survivor Eugen Kogon, as 'the theory and practice of hell'.[84]

Eicke also created (from 1936) the administrative set-up of the camp, divided into five sections, beginning with the management of the camp; a political department—run either by a member of the Gestapo or Kripo; a section dealing directly with the prisoners; an administrative branch; and finally the camp doctor.[85] Eicke was in charge of SS concentration camp guard formations and on 2 August 1936 moved into new headquarters at Oranienburg, close to the new camp at Sachsenhausen; it remained there until the end of the war.[86]

By 20 March 1936 Hitler agreed to a longer-range plan for the camps prepared by Eicke, who saw them mainly from the point of view of national security, and as places to hold real threats to the regime. The strategy was to cover Germany from north to south with five large camps in order to deal efficiently with 'enemies of state'. Presumably, having a concentration camp close by would be convenient for the Gestapo and have a deterrent effect on anyone thinking about opposition. Another factor was that at the time, Hitler was actively preparing for war, and given his fears about security on the home front, he readily agreed to the suggestion put to him for a chain of camps into which a variety of 'enemies' could be dumped.[87]

Himmler and Oswald Pohl, chief of SS administration, took advantage of Hitler's approval of the camps and how to finance them and they also began to see the economic advantages for the SS of cheap camp labour. By 1938 they founded the first of what would be many SS-owned companies, the German

Earth and Stone Works. It set up rock quarries and brickworks, and economic considerations partly determined the locations of new camps built in 1937–8. It was at this time that Flossenbürg came into being, along with camps at Buchenwald (near Weimar) and Mauthausen (in newly annexed Austria). Two more major camps at Gross-Rosen (Lower Silesia) and Natzweiler (in Alsace) were built in 1940 and all of them were constructed at locations where there was an abundance of raw materials.

As the realities of the camps began to change, so did images of them presented to the public. Newspaper stories said nothing in detail about long-term plans, but informed readers in typically prejudicial ways about the social types and wayward individuals allegedly interned. If the initial function was to confine 'political' enemies, above all the Communists, all along other kinds of social outsiders were imprisoned, and this point was mentioned in the press.[88] Over the course of 1935, actions against the Communists and other leftists continued, but newspapers featured stories about a wider range of 'political criminality', including especially cases involving Jews.[89]

In September 1935 and again at the beginning of 1936, the police were told that henceforth there was a publication ban on anyone taken into 'protective custody'. The police would determine when or if a case was reported in the press, for example, in order to make a special point. Permission to publish was required in writing from Gestapo headquarters. The Gestapo seemed to be as interested in the public relations side of their operations as they were in other aspects of the terror.

Changes in the accentuation of the image of the camps can be seen quite graphically in a photo-essay of 13 February 1936 in the journal of the SS, whose popularity in Germany went well beyond members of the SS. Among the pictures published was one showing, as usual, prisoners doing useful work. However, this time the photographs of 'typical camp prisoners' included a downtrodden alcoholic, several unsavoury-looking criminals covered in tattoos, and Jews who were accused of 'race defilement'. Communists were not mentioned in the story and the camps were shown as places for 'race defilers, rapists, sexual degenerates and habitual criminals'.[90] According to official but unpublished documents, by 1 November 1936 there was a total of 4,761 prisoners in the camps, of whom most (3,694) were there because of alleged political crimes, while the rest were branded as 'professional criminals and assorted asocial elements'.[91]

In late 1936 the broadening mission of the camps was made clearer in another photo-essay, published in the main Nazi illustrated newspaper. The photographs built on the images that had circulated in the press since 1933, but pointed in new directions. As usual, the camp was made to look spotlessly clean, with pictures from inside the barracks offering a vision of good order. There were scenes of prisoners marching off like soldiers to work, and one of a park-like setting where they supposedly took their leisure. The Nazi theory of the criminal was illustrated by close-up pictures. Race-tinged theories of the criminal had circulated widely in Europe since the mid-nineteenth century. The Nazis accepted as given the 'self-evident' connections between racial or biological defects and crime, and that theory began to be used as part of the justification for the camps, as well as for other measures, like sterilizing those known to be habitual 'criminal' and welfare cases.[92]

In close-ups of what were described as 'typical representatives of the sub-humans' in the camp, there was not just a Communist, but also a 'work-shy' person, a 'parasite on the body politic', and a professional criminal. The caption under one picture asked readers to notice the deformed head shape by which such people allegedly could be recognized and another photo drew attention to the facial features of a 'political criminal'. In the caption alongside another picture, there was the casual statement that 'in order to protect the community of the people, the German state permanently removed types of this sort from association with the rest of the nation'. The conclusion to be drawn was that some kinds of people belonged in camps and should never be allowed out. Also included in the close-ups were pictures of two Jews, one said to be guilty of 'race defilement', as if to convey the point that Jews in the camps were there because of sex crimes.

The text told readers that in contrast to 1933, when most prisoners were political prisoners, now the majority were 'asocial elements'. The camp's 'virtues' were said to be its military discipline, punctuality, scrupulously observed cleanliness, and the work ethic. The stated aim was to protect the state and the community from implacable enemies and those who had shown they were 'parasites on the body politic'. Secondly, the camp aimed to win them back to the community by reawakening their social instincts through work. It was clear that the camps would never disappear entirely because their educative purpose could never be a complete success. The article ended by saying that 'discipline was tough', but it was a battle of 'hard against hard' for the camps to fulfil their primary mission to serve as 'a place of education in the simplest principles of human social life'.[93]

Hitler used part of his speech to the Reichstag on 30 January 1937, the fourth anniversary of his takeover of power, to say of the camps, that they were used 'only for the few, whose political activity was merely a cover for a criminal attitude, as proven by numerous criminal convictions'. In keeping them in the camps, he declared, 'we hinder the continuation of their ruinous work of destruction in so far as, likely for the first time in their life, we hold them to useful tasks.' He rejected international protests about German camps, and described them as a means of defending the Nazi revolution against the 'criminal subjects of Moscow'. He also claimed that the Nazi revolution cost fewer lives than the Nazis themselves suffered at the hands of Communists in the year 1932 alone. As well, Hitler wondered aloud whether any other revolution had permitted so many of its earlier political opponents to have their freedom and be allowed to take up their old jobs. However, for Hitler, toleration stopped when it came to other races. Only those who belonged to the German *volk* could be included in the community and he completely rejected the view that an (unnamed) 'foreign race', by which he doubtlessly meant the Jews, should be allowed to influence Germany's political, intellectual, or cultural life in future. He offered a benign picture of the camps at the moment when, behind the scenes, he was taking steps to make them permanent.[94]

Himmler reflected in public on the police and the camps at almost the same time. In an address from January 1937 which gives us clues about his thinking, he said he was pressured after 1933 'by the Ministries' to release prisoners from the camps. He now said that with 'the agreement of the Führer', the number of prisoners was rising again and already had reached 8,000. He wanted to explain 'why we must have so many, why we must have still more'. First, Communist functionaries had to be rearrested, given the growing international tension, so that internal security could be ensured. He said the camps were also the proper place for social outcasts, professional criminals, and problem cases, and made no secret of his disdain by saying that 'none of that lot sits without justification; they are the remnants of the criminal class, of ne'er-do-wells. There is no more lively demonstration of the laws of heredity and race than such a concentration camp. There are those with hydrocephalus, cross-eyed, deformed, half-Jews, and a whole series of racially inferior types. The whole lot is there together.'

Germany was intensively preparing for war at the time, and Himmler insisted on the importance of the home front. 'We have to be absolutely clear in our own minds, that the enemy in a war will be in the military sense an enemy, but also in the ideological sense an enemy.' Whenever war came—he speculated that it would be best if that were generations in the future—then there would be war not just on the land, on the sea, and in the air, but also in 'a fourth arena of war: inside Germany'.[95] In the meantime, 'if we want to be immune against the poison of destruction in our people, we must support our life through social prosperity, social order and good discipline.' Hitler echoed these sentiments, including preparation of the home front, in a January 1937 speech and again at the Nuremberg Party rally in September that year.[96]

Presenting the concentration camps to the public was important to Himmler, and in early March 1938, as if to show the press what was 'really' going on in the camps, he approved a long list of 46 journalists (by no means only those writing for Party newspapers or journals) to visit Sachsenhausen, where they were to be shown around and addressed by Himmler himself.[97] The camp visit by journalists was a tried and trusted method used to refute 'distortions' spread about them. Because Germany soon annexed Austria (taking it over on 11 March), and because the SS and German police were sent there in force, it is not certain that the visit to Sachsenhausen took place. The intention of showing so many around suggests the continuing concern attached to the public relations side of the camps.[98]

The public image of the camps and the police was buffed up again at the national 'Day of the German Police' in January 1939. According to a news story and radio address by Himmler, contrary to the 'tales of horror of some foreign newspaper or other', if Germans were to visit places like Oranienburg near Berlin, they could expect to be disappointed. Contrary to a concentration camp as many people might imagine it, they would come upon 'bright, and in their own way, architecturally model buildings' surrounded by 'friendly, small villages'.

Himmler lauded the service of the concentration camp guards (the SS Death's Head Brigades), and sketched the history of the camps, tracing them from the Dachau model to 1939. He pointed to the decisive year of 1936 when, among other things, the guards and the camps were put on the state's payroll. He said the number of political prisoners was declining, but they were being replaced 'primarily by asocial elements and those organized sub-human types of the street who had been in the earlier Bolshevik groups'.[99] These people were, as Heydrich pointed out on this occasion, precisely the sort who should be arrested before they acted, as they would never be deterred by the criminal code nor by the courts.[100]

Himmler repeated the message, that in 'combating criminal deeds' the new system no longer waited until a 'criminal' acted, but instead 'isolated the well-known and often convicted criminal on a far greater scale than ever and protected humanity from him'. In the last years, he continued, those sent to the concentration camps 'were all asocial elements, who one way or another came in conflict with the law, yet again committed the same crimes, those who out of habit avoided all work and, in a state in which everyone can have work, lay about and beg.'

Himmler said he wanted to speak 'candidly' about the camps, and once again used the tactic of pointing to lies and exaggerations in the foreign press. Of course, he said, like any deprivation of freedom, the concentration camp was a 'sharp and severe measure'. The object was to teach 'hard, new values created through work, a regulated daily routine, an unheard of cleanliness both in general living and in bodily care, decent food, a strict but fair handling'. In this manner, work and rudimentary skills would be learned again. The mottoes at the gates of these camps say: 'There is a way to freedom. The milestones are: obedience, hard work, honesty, good order, discipline, cleanliness, sobriety, truthfulness, self-sacrifice, and love for the Fatherland.'

Ending on a somewhat defensive note, Himmler said he found it remarkable that the Western democracies worried so much about German camps, when, he alleged, these democracies used concentration camps as 'time-honoured institutions'. In any case, he credited 'the rigorous approach' to criminals with the continuing decline of all crime in Germany. Although he underlined the importance of removing the 'worse elements' and 'hard-nosed' criminals from German society, he insisted that this task was only a small part of ongoing police work. Their broad new mission was of 'positive education' and to win people 'to cooperation'.[101]

A Camp at Flossenbürg

An illustration of what the Nazis did not make explicit in the stories they published about the camps can be seen by looking at relatively little-known Flossenbürg. Situated in north-eastern Bavaria, a short drive from Nuremberg and Regensburg, the camp was founded in late April/early May 1938, when the Gestapo and Kripo picked up many thousands of the so-called asocials. (More on this later in the book.) Like other camps created that year, it was supposed to generate funds to finance further SS endeavours, and also like them, it was one of a new generation of camps located near the German border and looking east. Such camps would be used to terrorize conquered populations and to exploit foreign labour.[102] It was initially designed for 'non-political' prisoners, that is, for conventionally defined criminals like repeat offenders and for certain social outsiders, like pimps, tramps, beggars, 'Gypsies', and alcoholics. Physically fit males, removed from one institution or another, or arrested on the street, were supposed to be sent there, and forced to work.[103]

The village of Flossenbürg, population just over 1,200 in 1933, was out of the way and in an economically depressed area of north-eastern Bavaria in the Upper Palatinate. The village initially benefited economically, civilians found work in the camp, retail trade improved, the tax base of the community grew, and especially when the SS brought their wives and children, the population increased. Soon, however, the existence of the camp began to have a negative impact on the tourist trade just getting off the ground. The SS forbad anyone from climbing to the top of the local castle, the main tourist attraction on the hill above the town, because with binoculars it was possible to see into the camp. Soon the economic gains began to fade.[104]

The population of the camp was initially made up mainly of so-called asocials, but it became far more heterogeneous over time.[105] At the start of the war there were around 1,500 in the camp, but from April 1940, the Gestapo began sending non-Germans there as well. Foreign workers who would not follow the strict rules of their slave-like existence, those who dared to entertain forbidden social contact with Germans, or merely tried to flee from their place of work, were sent to the camp. By mid-1941, 700 Poles made up the largest non-German nationality. With the opening of the war against the Soviet Union, increasing numbers of Soviet prisoners of war and civilians began to arrive.

A survey of 8 February 1943—the last one before the camp was inundated with evacuees from camps to the east—showed just over 4,000 prisoners (an estimated one-third of whom were Germans), while most of the rest were made up mainly of Polish foreign workers, followed by those from the Soviet Union. Included in the survey were 782 held as 'preventive detainees', that is, they were sent there by the Kripo, as more than likely were also 66 'work-shy' and 105 (German) homosexuals.[106] There were small numbers of Jews in this camp in mid-1940, and most Jews came later, between August 1944 and January 1945, when at least 10,000 arrived from Poland and Hungary. They went primarily to the subcamps of Flossenbürg where thousands perished.[107] By the end of 1944 the inmate population at Flossenbürg doubled to 8,000 and in February 1945 stood at 11,000.[108]

Like the other main camps in the empire of the SS, a whole series of subcamps was created under Flossenbürg's authority. The subcamps spread far and wide, often situated on the sites of factories involved in war-related production, but they might be in the centre of some small village or town or next to the railway station. Some of Flossenbürg's subcamps quickly grew to be larger than any of Germany's pre-war main camps. Two of the more infamous ones at Hersbruck and Leitmeritz, for example, each held 6,000 prisoners in 1944. The death rate at Hersbruck and Leitmeritz was staggering and, although both existed for less than a year, 6,000 victims lost their lives in them.[109] Flossenbürg's own empire of subcamps grew each year from 6 in 1942; 17 in 1943; 75 in 1944; until in 1945 there were 92 subcamps linked to the main camp.[110]

A survey of the Flossenbürg system from 28 February 1945 shows how the camp population had grown and become internationalized. The Poles made up the largest contingent (38.2 per cent) of the 22,000 prisoners, followed by Soviets (23.2 per cent). Among the 30 nationalities in the camp, there were many Hungarians, especially Hungarian Jews (9 per cent), but also many French (6.7 per cent), Italians and Germans (each with 5.5 per cent), and Czechs (with 4.8 per cent). The Flossenbürg system alone contained 40,000 prisoners, of whom 29,000 were male; and by the time it collapsed in 1945, the estimated population had grown to 52,000.[111]

What happened at Flossenbürg and in its subcamps reflected what took place in many other camps in Germany. While these camps were nothing like the death camps in the eastern occupied territories, the suffering, death, and outright murder in them was staggering. Additionally, the main camp at Flossenbürg was used as a place of execution by the Gestapo and Kripo. There were 1,500 recorded executions in the year covering April 1944 to April 1945; at times, up to 90 executions were carried out per day, including many Germans involved in resistance activities like Pastor Dietrich Bonhoeffer and General Hans Oster.[112] There were no gas chambers at this camp, no assembly-line killing, yet even so, in little-known Flossenbürg and its subcamps, at one time or another no less than 100,000 people were incarcerated, of whom at least 30,000 died.[113]

The number of prisoners who were executed, who were killed in other ways, and/or who died from various forms of malnutrition and abuse that verged on murder in the tiny world of Flossenbürg alone was greater than the number of people killed during the bloodiest period of terror in the French Revolution. (Common estimates for the latter range between 11,000 and 18,000.)[114] If Hitler's dictatorship had produced only Flossenbürg, it already would have gained the Third Reich a place of infamy in European history. Of course there was not one Flossenbürg in Germany, but many of them, some of them worse, with death tolls well into six digits. It is with Flossenbürg in mind, however, that I would like to suggest that much less is known about the camps than we might assume, and that the memory of the murders committed in and around such facilities has faded over time.

The images of the camps in Germany were powerful enough to make their way into annexed territories where they found fertile soil in the minds and hearts of Germany's new citizens. For example, the camp at Mauthausen in Austria, created in 1938, situated near a rock quarry, was designed to exploit the cheap labour of prisoners. Far from being secret, it was intended that Austrians know about the camp.[115] Perhaps anyone with resistance on their mind might have seen the camp as a warning. However, most Austrians seem to have welcomed the camp, more or less for the same reasons that such places were applauded in Germany. For example, in an enthusiastically received speech in March 1938 to the people in Gmunden, Upper Austria, the local Nazi Party boss said the region was to have the distinction of a camp into which all the 'traitors' of Austria were to be thrown.[116] Civilians working in the camp or living near it, regarded its existence and the often unruly behaviour of off-duty SS guards, as a mixed blessing and some were disturbed at the murders of prisoners that took place on occasion outside the camp gates in public view.[117]

On the other hand, many Austrians accepted the 'need' for Mauthausen. Evidently the officially propagated image of the concentration camp spread in Austria, and was essentially the one publicized in Germany, namely, that camps were dangerous places for 'hardened criminals'.[118] In time, some 200,000 people were sent to Mauthausen, of whom half died or were killed.[119]

We return to the history of the concentration camps in the latter part of the book, but in the next chapters we study what happened to the men and women who faced the coercive machinery of Hitler's dictatorship.

4

Shadows of War

From the earliest days of the Third Reich, Hitler's dictatorship was over-shadowed by thoughts and plans for the war that he and his collaborators regarded as inevitable. Almost immediately in 1933, Hitler forged ahead on the diplomatic and military front—winning accolades from the people at every turn, especially as he tore up the hated peace treaty forced on Germany in 1919. His aim was not peace, but war, and as he prepared for it, he thought in terms of a total war in which a trustworthy home front stood firm behind the soldiers on the battlefront. One way of interpreting why Hitler encouraged Himmler to create a new police and camp system was that he saw the elimination of all internal 'enemies' as preparation for the coming war.

A recurrent theme in Hitler's thinking was that in the event of war, the home front would not fall prey to saboteurs, that is, anyone vaguely considered to be 'criminals', 'pimps', or 'deserters', as supposedly happened in 1918, and he promised that the next time, accounts would be settled with the Jews.[1] He told Himmler early in the war on more than one occasion, that should there be any reason to fear troubles breaking out at home, all opponents should be killed and everyone in the concentration camps executed, so that a revolution would be deprived of its leaders at one stroke.[2] In his view it was bad enough to preserve criminals in peacetime, but war made it imperative to shoot anyone who sinned against the people, for otherwise 'the inferior' would get the upper hand as the best people were killed on the battlefront.[3] For Germany's leaders, the defeat in 1918 'proved' that not enough attention had been devoted to the home front, and internal enemies were allowed to stab the soldiers in the back. Many Germans and not just Hitler and the Nazis accepted this mythical version of why they lost World War I.[4] Indeed, British war planners in the 1930s apparently also believed the myth of 1918, and took steps to uphold their home front in World War II in fear of their own 'stab in the back'.[5]

As the Nazis took steps to purify the 'community of the people', they thus did so with their eyes fixed on war. They worked out their schemes in the shadow of 1918 and the alleged 'stab in the back', and at the same time, they operated as if the next war already was under way. The coercive measures used inside Germany were dramatically radicalized with the coming of the war, as this chapter shows.

The Enemy Within

Initially, the German people did not greet the coming of the war with anything close to enthusiasm, and many were as shocked as Hitler and the Nazis that Britain and France opted for war in the face of Germany's invasion of Poland. In Berlin American journalist William Shirer was with some 250 or so people who had gathered to follow developments on the radio via public loudspeakers. When word came that Britain had declared war, the crowd reacted in stunned silence, 'there was not a murmur.'[6] To be sure, most people in every other European and world capital were also shocked, and certainly no one anywhere welcomed the war as they had done in 1914. Whereas in 1914 the crowds cheered, in expectation of a short and victorious war, and certainly little knowing the death and destruction to come, in 1939 there was general awareness of the murderous potential of modern warfare and that civilians would very likely become involved because of the much discussed potential of long-range bombing. The British government and its experts, to mention an illustrative example, wildly exaggerated the potential of death from the skies, and planned on the fact that in the first two weeks of the war, there would be 900,000 casualties, at least one-third of them fatal, and another three million psychological casualties.[7] These figures and the projected effects of bombing on morale in Britain proved to be far wrong, but recalling them today should remind us that no one greeted the war in 1939, and most people were horrified at the thought. However, back in Germany William Shirer noted even before the end of September how ordinary people, whom he thought generally very patriotic, began to back Hitler, and he found no one, 'even among those who don't like the regime, who sees anything wrong in the German destruction of Poland'. For days on end 'people of all classes, women as well as men', gathered in front of windows in Berlin and 'approvingly gazed at the maps in which little red pins showed the victorious advance of the German troops into Poland. As long as the Germans are successful and do not have to pull in their belts too much, this will not be an unpopular war.'[8]

Initially, the reserved and in some cases negative attitudes inclined Hitler to soft-pedal or postpone potentially unpopular policies, like mobilizing women for the war effort.[9] The employment of women, however, was already much more widespread in Germany in 1939 than in Britain or the United States, so that in effect large numbers of them were already mobilized for war.[10] Even if not all members of the German working class were swept away by the social appeals of Nazism, and some grumbling continued on the shop floor, state control of wages and prices was such that inflation barely existed, even with growing labour shortages at the end of the 1930s. Most people had it better in the 1930s than any time since the Depression, more people were working, and 'real earnings' increased every year from 1933 to 1938 (the last year when figures were available).[11] Few workers extended their criticisms to the political regime or social order, and 'after 1939 notions of the Germans at war and their "people's community" tended to absorb the remnants of skepticism that remained'.[12]

The war depleted the number of police, including the Gestapo, available for duty inside Germany. A memorandum of 31 August 1939 sent to the Gestapo across the country, put them on a war footing, and reorganized personnel.[13] There were only around 7,000 officials in the Gestapo in the last pre-war years, and that number stagnated during the war.[14] The number of men available to the police as a whole in Germany was reduced by the war, so the police needed the active cooperation of good citizens more than ever in order to keep the country under surveillance, especially because the war was used as an excuse to attack old enemies, like clericals in the Catholic Church.[15]

As the crisis that led to war heated up at the end of August 1939, in spite of the calm in the country, general directives were issued to arrest specified groups and individuals. A circular from 28 August to the heads of penitentiaries requested that they make room for 'many persons' about to be picked up.[16] In order to nip any resistance in the bud, a whole series of arrest sweeps took place in and around September 1939. Early that month a special Gestapo 'action' arrested between 2,000 and 4,000 Communist Party functionaries, a number of Social Democrats, and some foreign nationals. On 7 September the Kripo rearrested some Jews who had been released from the camps on condition that they leave the country, but who had not done so. On 12 September 'psychopaths' were arrested because they might create 'unrest in the population'. On 18 October it was the turn of people who tried to avoid regular work, who were sent to a concentration camp if they had a prior conviction. Jews in Germany were surprised there were no pogroms when the war came in 1939. Victor Klemperer noted in his diary on 3 September 1939 that he fully expected to be shot or sent to a concentration camp at any moment. A week later he recorded that the 'Jewbaiting' had passed.[17]

One effect of all these arrests was that the number of prisoners in the camps increased from 21,400 in August 1939 to 32,120 by October.[18] The transformation of the camp system, which eventually held hundreds of thousands of prisoners, was well under way. The Gestapo was soon permitted to hold suspects in so-called 'educative work camps' (AEL), which 'officially' were created by decree of 28 May 1941, but already were operating in some places as early as August 1940.[19] These camps quickly spread and came close to being the Gestapo's own concentration camps.

Gestapo arrests at the outbreak of war took place on the basis of a card-index system in preparation from as far back as December 1935. In a note to the Gestapo on 5 February 1936, Heydrich had explained the need to be informed of the whereabouts of 'enemies of state' especially in the event of war. Creating such an index proved difficult, but at the beginning of 1939, the Gestapo had cards on nearly two million 'suspects' and the relevant files on more than a half million of them.[20] In the last month before the war, problems with the system were hastily ironed out and pre-emptive arrests followed.[21]

Less than 48 hours after the opening of the war against Poland, and just before he left for the front, Hitler ordered Himmler to take 'all necessary measures' to maintain and uphold Germany's domestic order.[22] Forwarded to Reinhard Heydrich, Chief of the Security Police, this order was implemented in several ways. First of all, Heydrich translated it into a general decree which, on 3 September he immediately sent to Gestapo regional and local headquarters. These 'principles for domestic security of state during the war' laid down the basis upon which the organs of state security would operate. Heydrich insisted that 'in order to realize the aims of the Führer', it was necessary to mobilize 'all the powers of the people against any disturbance and subversion', for only in this way would it be possible for state security to fulfil its new and numerous enforcement tasks.

The participation of ordinary citizens as informers who would tip off the authorities was recognized as essential to safeguard the home front. However, since 1933 such informing had been often misused for selfish reasons that were at odds with what the regime wanted. Heydrich's 'principles' recognized that without the help of citizen informers the Gestapo could not function, but he demanded that local police 'take steps' against those who came forward with information out of selfish motives or who made exaggerated claims. This demand did not solve the problem and within weeks Heydrich presented further proposals to deal with it. For example, on 18 September he brought a proposal for a 'citizens' reporting service' to the newly created Ministerial Council for the Defence of the Reich, with the idea that this new system would control the 'the total mobilization of the political attentiveness of the people'. Heydrich floated the idea earlier that the police only use the eyes and ears of politically reliable people, but the proposal was rejected by the Ministerial Council, because several members considered it would do more harm than good by fostering a denunciatory atmosphere.[23] The upshot was that the Gestapo continued to rely on volunteer denouncers as before.

The Gestapo was ordered to suppress 'every attempt to subvert the determination and will to fight of the German people'. Anyone who voiced doubts about victory or questioned the justification for the war was to be arrested. Attention was focused on public places like pubs, restaurants, and elsewhere, and Heydrich was to be kept fully informed if anything turned up 'in order to request a decision of what should be done next with the arrested persons, because where appropriate the brutal liquidation of such elements' might prove necessary. He ended his September orders by reminding all local Gestapo leaders that they were 'personally responsible' for the suppression of defeatist agitation.[24]

On 20 and 26 September 1939 Heydrich issued follow-up instructions to clarify any 'misunderstandings' about the 'principles' to be applied during the war. He reiterated that 'every attempt' to subvert the war and the will to victory was to be suppressed with 'ruthless harshness and severity'. Saboteurs, agitators, Communists or Marxist activists, and even thieves who hoarded large quantities, would be eliminated. Heydrich told the Gestapo to insist to local police that henceforth serious cases should be sent directly to the Gestapo to avoid time-consuming judicial procedures. It was up to the Gestapo itself to decide when and if a case should be dealt with by 'special handling', that is, by an execution, and/or whether the case should be sent to court.[25]

Gestapo arrest procedures were streamlined during the war, as they increasingly dispensed with formalities. The last pre-war regulations (from 1938) on 'protective custody' said that within ten days a suspect should either be released or placed in protective custody. That decision would be made by Gestapo headquarters in Berlin, not the courts. Soon after the war began, the old deadline became impossible to keep because of 'increased arrest activities', and on 4 October 1939 it was extended to 21 days.[26] A more fateful decision was communicated to the Gestapo not quite three weeks later which flatly stated a new rule of thumb: the 'release of prisoners from protective custody will in general not take place during the war'. The justification for this step was that it was easier to watch enemies of state, 'asocial elements', and others by keeping them in camps than it was to set any of them free—especially because many police officials were drafted for special tasks and could not keep an eye on released prisoners.[27] Similar orders were issued to the Kripo on 20 March and 18 June 1940. A sign of the brutalities brought on or permitted by the war was signalled by a Himmler note to regional Gestapo headquarters on 23 November 1939. He said that henceforth it was no longer necessary even to notify the relatives of executed 'Polish-Jewish Camp Prisoners'.[28]

Still more Gestapo 'simplification' procedures were introduced in 1941 after the beginning of the invasion of the Soviet Union. In June of that year, in a repeat of what happened in 1939, many 'enemies of state' were picked up and sent to concentration camps. These arrests were based on a decision reached about 'all subversive pastors, anti-German Czechs and Poles, as well as Communists and similar riffraff, who in principle ought to be sent for an indefinite period to a concentration camp'.[29] More streamlining followed in 1941, and more again in 1943. Beginning in May 1943, local and regional Gestapo could dispense their own 'justice' when Poles were involved, and did not have to bother getting authorization from Berlin.[30] Hated minorities inside Germany, especially the Jews and the Poles were essentially removed from the jurisdiction of the courts, and subjected to 'police justice'.[31]

The institutional structure of the police, whose centralization was favoured by Hitler, and which had been under way since 1933, also reached a milestone

with the outbreak of war in 1939. On 27 September Himmler ordered the creation of the Reich Security Main Office (RSHA) under Heydrich's leadership.
A new organization resulted that included all security police, divided into main
offices beneath which were countless sub-branches. The significance of the
RSHA was that it represented a further attempt to systematize social control and
surveillance within the jurisdiction of the police and the SD in Germany, and it
also established the foundations of a system that could be extended into the
occupied and annexed territories abroad.[32]

Executions and Hints of Genocide

The first news report of an execution in the war was published on 8 September
1939. The story was that Johann Heinen was shot in the concentration camp
at Sachsenhausen the day before because he refused to work on a construction site, vaguely described as part of a national security project. The only
additional detail was that Heinen was a previously convicted thief.[33] On 11
and 15 September, newspapers carried the stories of two more executions, the
first of a man found guilty of arson and sabotage, the second a member of the
Jehovah's Witnesses who refused to serve in the military.[34]

The 'threat' posed by the Jehovah's Witnesses was insignificant. Their persecution suggests how the war was used as an opportunity to sharpen the battle
against all 'political' enemies, and to hammer the German 'community of the
people' into an indivisible whole. Jehovah's Witnesses were estimated to have
between 25,000 and 30,000 members at the beginning of 1933. In April/May
1933, the organization was forbidden in one state after the next, but not until
1 April 1935 was it banned everywhere. They offended the Nazis on a number of
grounds, particularly in that they refused to give the Hitler greeting and to serve
in the armed forces after the draft was reintroduced. The Gestapo created a special commando in June 1936 to track down anyone who would not give up their
beliefs, and, according to survivors of the persecutions, they were often informed
upon by ordinary citizens. One of the first wartime executions in Sachsenhausen
concentration camp happened only days after the beginning of the war. The
Gestapo ordered the execution of August Dickmann in order to set an example.
Dickmann's 'crime' was that he would not sign a loyalty oath, and so was regarded
as opening the door to anyone who would refuse to serve in the military. The
execution on 15 September was promptly reported in the press and on the radio
to deter others.[35] Over the course of the dictatorship, as many as 10,000 members
of the community were arrested, with 2,000 sent to concentration camps, where
they were treated dreadfully and as many as 1,200 died or were murdered there.[36]

There is an abundance of evidence that in Hitler's mind, the coming of war
marked an ideological turning point. He was fond of saying he was a prophet,

and on more than one occasion he 'prophesied' what would happen to the Jews should 'they' cause another war. The first time he announced such a prophecy was in 1939, on the anniversary of his appointment on 30 January. Over the next several years, when he repeated this prophecy, he invariably misdated it to 1 September 1939 as if in his own mind the coming of war—for which he blamed the Jews—'justified' the Holocaust. The charges were believed by many citizens. We know that when Victor Klemperer's Jewish star was spotted during the war, he was confronted by Germans who repeated Hitler's accusation that the Jews caused the war, and that Germany was only defending itself against Jewish aggression. Klemperer even found non-Nazis who did not think past such propaganda.[37]

Hitler took specific steps to begin genocidal politics with the approach of the war. On 22 August and again on 7 September 1939, he mentioned (and soon reiterated) to the heads of the army his wish for the 'ethnic cleansing' of Poland, a wish that was transmitted by Heydrich immediately to subordinates, and full of genocidal implications for Jews and Poles in the soon-to-be conquered east.[38] By 29 September Hitler spoke again among Nazi leaders of his plans for dividing Poland into three zones. All non-Germanic nationalities would be removed from the old German area, which would be resettled by 'proper German peasant families'. Another area would be left to 'good Polish elements', and a third zone would be used for 'bad' Poles, who would be joined by the Jews, including those from Germany. Orders for mass murder, however, were not given. According to Goebbels's diary on the meeting, the issue was whether these people could survive.[39]

In an address to the Reichstag on 6 October, Hitler spoke openly of his intentions for the east in terms such as bringing about 'law and order' and security to the area, and above all as establishing a 'new order of ethnographic relations'.[40] What was really happening, as reported by German authorities on the spot, was that in the first months of the war 'tens of thousands' of civilian Jews and Poles were murdered.[41] There were immediate forced population movements, with indications about the great mass murders to come.

The conquest of Poland awakened radical thoughts among other Nazi leaders besides Hitler and Himmler. Goebbels thought the German administration in Poland was too soft. At lunch with Hitler on 31 October 1939, he suggested that instead of trying to set things right in Poland, the Germans should do everything to help the Poles self-destruct.[42] As for the Jews, Goebbels said after a brief visit in early November when he saw the misery of the people in the Lodz Ghetto, that these were not people 'but animals', so that Germany faced 'not a humanitarian, but a surgical task'. He promptly passed on these views to Hitler, who agreed with them.[43] Hitler shied away from publicizing anything about the killing behind the lines in Poland, but he responded positively to broadening the scope of antisemitic discrimination once the war began. For example, he agreed to the proposal put to him by Goebbels in December 1939, that so-called half-Jews be dismissed from the Wehrmacht, supposedly because they might cause trouble.[44]

The first stages of serial genocides began in the autumn of 1939 in Poland, aimed at Jews and Poles. In addition to outright murders, thinly veiled ones were ordered by police regiment courts, as for example on 11 November 1939 when such a court near Warsaw collectively tried Jews for a minor case of arson, and ordered the execution of 159 Jewish men who were found guilty; after an inquiry to headquarters, an additional 196 Jewish women and children were executed.[45]

The war also radicalized popular expectations that courts would act more firmly in Germany. When in September 1939 a Special Court gave several bank robbers heavy jail sentences, German citizens who were expecting the death penalty criticized the sentences as too mild. The Nazi opinion surveys turned up a positive response to news whenever robbers were executed. The Minister of Justice responded on 16 September 1939 by creating a department to oversee Special Courts, and to ensure that the new 'measure against parasites on the body politic' was enforced to the fullest.[46]

Stories in the press about police-ordered executions made clear that the war represented a new chapter in Hitler's dictatorship. From the beginning of the war up to 20 January 1940, the Ministry of Justice noted rumours and stories about 18 such executions, and half of these cases never went to trial.[47] Even so, many citizens seemed to support what the regime was doing. After news of these executions was published, Minister of Justice Franz Gürtner, a 'traditionalist', was concerned that the courts were losing their authority and were being pushed aside in the competition with the Gestapo. In a note on 28 September he attempted to get a 'clarification of the situation' from the Reich Chancellery and wanted to know whether Hitler had really 'ordered or permitted' such executions.[48] Gürtner pointed out that the courts were perfectly capable of using the death penalty, as in a recent case where a farmer had torched his own farm and destroyed the grain. Instead of waiting for the course of justice to unfold, however, the Gestapo simply picked up the suspect and executed him. Gürtner said such arbitrariness was not needed, as the victim already had been sentenced to death by the court. He asked the Reich Chancellory to let him know 'according to what points of view the competition between the courts and the police in specific cases' should be decided in the future. Gürtner's plea was to maintain at least a semblance of the rule of law over such arbitrary 'police justice'.[49]

Hitler's answer was given orally, passed on by the head of the Reich Chancellery Hans Lammers, and was typically ambiguous in that he said he never gave a 'general instruction' for Himmler to order executions as he saw fit and without regard to the courts. Hitler himself took credit for ordering the first three executions of the war. He also said that when it came to specific cases in the future, he would not refrain from doing so again 'because the courts (military and civil) have shown themselves not to be up to the special conditions of the war'.[50] Apparently this response shocked Gürtner, but not enough for him to resign. Hitler's signal to the judiciary was impossible to overlook: the courts would either become more radical or they would simply be made superfluous.[51]

Not long after (13 October 1939) Hitler demanded executions as 'corrections' to Special Court verdicts on two Berlin bank robbers because he found their sentences too lenient. He intervened once more at almost the same time in another case, to 'correct' the Special Court in Munich which sentenced a man to ten years in prison for stealing a purse while taking advantage of the darkened streets (ordered to be kept dark to hinder Allied flyers). Even though no violence was used and the woman's purse only contained a few Marks, when Hitler read of the story in the newspaper, he was outraged and ordered that the man, convicted as a 'parasite on the body politic' or *Volksschädling*, be executed forthwith. If the first three executions of the war just mentioned pertained to broadly defined 'political' matters, these latter executions had little to do with conventionally understood notions of politics at all, but were petty thefts that were treated as high treason.

The death sentence—or simple execution by shooting—for these crimes demonstrated that there was no longer any clear-cut distinction between 'normal crimes' as defined in the criminal code, and 'political crimes'. The whole concept of 'crime' had become politicized and regarded as illegal 'opposition'. On the basis of Hitler's explicit orders and/or with the authority conferred by carrying out the Führer's will, the Gestapo could disregard the courts as they saw fit. Gestapo officials even suggested to the judiciary that if judges believed 'the demands of the people for the death penalty' in some case could not be satisfied because of a legal problem (such as lack of proof), then judges should hand over the accused to the police for execution. The argument for this change was that it would stop police 'corrections' to court verdicts, and avoid further damaging the credibility and public image of the courts.[52]

Hitler's interventions began as far back as 21 March 1933 when he amnestied some Nazis for crimes, including murder, they had committed in the course of the revolution. This intercession and similar ones that followed, struck directly at the very existence of the rule of law and as a consequence contributed both to the ascendancy of the police system of justice and to the growing radicalism of the courts.[53] More than one historian has concluded that even when judges and other judicial officials raised objections to thinly veiled and technically illegal executions from the start of the war, there was a widely shared consensus that such 'asocial elements' should be 'eradicated'.[54]

The stories in the press about the first executions of the war, and the occasional execution of a German without trial on Himmler's orders, were

1. Hitler greets the population from the window of the Reich Chancellery on the evening of his appointment as Chancellor (30 January 1933)

Berlin ißt heute fein Eintopfgericht

2. One-dish meals became a tradition, sometimes served in public kitchens across the country, as here, in front of Berlin's Kaiser Wilhelm Memorial Church in 1935

3. Enthusiasm of the workers is shown at the launching of the training ship *Horst Wessel* in 1936. In the top-right quarter of the picture one man, with folded arms, apparently refuses to go along with the 'German greeting'

4. A marching column of the Nazi Women's Association (NSF) in 1937 in Nuremberg

5. The 'Day of the German Police' became an annual week-long celebration across Germany to show the police as 'Friend and Helper'. Here the police perform in the event for 1939 in Berlin

6. On 12 January 1937 some leaders of the German police, led by Heinrich Himmler, convey their birthday greetings to Hermann Göring. Between both of them (in lighter brown uniform) is Head of the Order Police Kurt Daluege, to whose right is Reinhard Heydrich

7. By 1939 the cult of Hitler had reached enormous proportions. Here people waited until shortly after midnight on 20 April 1939, Hitler's birthday, to convey their good wishes to the Führer

8. After the incorporation of Austria into Germany, Hitler returned to a massive demonstration of support in a triumphal parade from the airport in Berlin to the Reich Chancellery on 16 March 1938

Konzentrationslager für Schutz= häftlinge in Bayern

München, 20. März.

Bezüglich der Dauer der Schutzhaft laufen fort= gesetzt zahllose Anfragen bei der Polizeidirektion ein. Polizeipräsident Himmler erklärte hierzu, es sei notwendig, das Material, das wir in un= geahnten Mengen beschlagnahmen konnten, zu sichten. Anfragen halten in der Sichtung dieses Materials nur auf und laufen praktisch darauf hinaus, daß j e d e A n f r a g e d e m S c h u t = h ä f t l i n g e i n e n T a g m e h r k o s t e t.

Bei dieser Gelegenheit trat Polizeipräsident Himmler den Gerüchten über eine schlechte Be= handlung der Schutzhäftlinge entschieden entgegen.

Aus zwingenden Gründen sind einige Ände= rungen in der Unterbringung der Schutzhäft= linge notwendig geworden.

Am Mittwoch wird in der Nähe von Dachau das erste Konzentrationslager mit einem Fas= sungsvermögen für 5000 Menschen errichtet wer= den. Hier werden die gesamten kommu= nistischen und soweit dies notwendig ist, Reichsbanner= und sozialdemokra= tischen Funktionäre, die die Sicherheit des Staates gefährden, zusammengezogen, da es auf die Dauer nicht möglich ist und den Staats= apparat zu sehr belastet, diese Funktionäre in den Gerichtsgefängnissen unterzubringen. Es hat sich gezeigt, daß es nicht angängig ist, diese Leute in die Freiheit zu lassen, da sie weiter hetzen und Unruhe stiften. Im Interesse der Sicherheit des Staates müssen wir diese Maßnahme treffen ohne Rücksicht auf kleinliche Bedenken. Polizei und Innenministerium sind überzeugt, daß sie damit zur Beruhigung der gesamten nationa= len Bevölkerung und in ihren Sinne handeln.

9. The announcement of the first concentration camp in the *Völkischer Beobachter* on 21 March 1933 at Dachau was carried in many other local and national newspapers

10. New prisoners arrive at the Dachau camp in May 1933

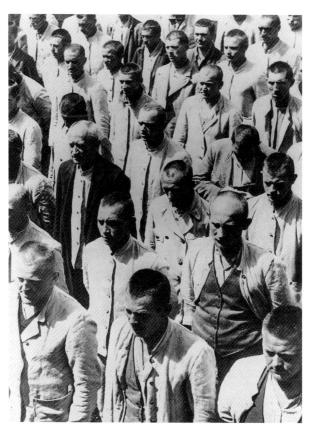

11. Title-page of an illustrated story 'The Truth about Dachau' as carried in the *Münchner Illustrierte Presse* (16 July 1933)

Preis: 20 Pfennig

Elsass und Memelgebiet 20 Pfg
Ausland mit ermäß. Porto 30 Pfg
Danzig 20 Guldenpfennig

11. JAHRGANG / FOLGE 49 / DONNERSTAG, 3. DEZEMBER 1936

VERLAG FRANZ EHER NACHF. G.M.B.H. MÜNCHEN 2 NO

In diesem Heft:
KONZENTRATIONS-
LAGER
DACHAU

12. Title picture for the detailed and illustrated account of Dachau, as published in the *Illustrierter Beobachter* (3 Dec. 1936)

important for setting a new tone.[55] That the example was not lost on judges became clear immediately, as they began imposing the death penalty for crimes committed by people who tried to take advantage of Germany's darkened streets. For example, 27-year-old Franz Blawak was sent to his death by the Berlin Special Court in early November 1939 for attempting a (non-violent) petty theft of a woman's purse. The prosecutor said the court 'had to set an example', because 'the Special Court was a kind of drum-head court on the home front, with responsibility to protect it from criminals. . . . The front soldier must absolutely be assured, that the solid wall of the inner front cannot be worn down by sub-humanity.'[56]

Hitler's expressed wishes were enough to inspire most judges, but when they seemed not to get the point, he intervened again, often merely on the basis of reading about a case in the press. Such stories could be incomplete or one-sided, but that did not stop him from demanding that the verdict be nullified, and the person involved handed over to the Gestapo for speedy execution. He continued to make such demands throughout the war.[57]

Hitler's first Minister of Justice, Franz Gürtner, though by any measure a hardliner, was a moderate by the standards of the Nazi era and he continued to fight for at least a semblance of the rule of law. Well before he died on 29 January 1941, he had encouraged judges to pass verdicts that met Hitler's wishes, and even to treat attempted crimes like successful ones. On Gürtner's death the leadership of the Justice Ministry went to its senior official, Franz Schlegelberger, who promptly assured Hitler that he would contact judges whose decisions 'were not in agreement with the will of the leadership of the state', and have such decisions overturned.[58] Schlegelberger did his best, for example, when Hitler said that the court in Lüneburg (26 March 1941) was wrong in the trial of a Polish worker to accept that the worker, 'as a Pole', should not be punished too severely, as he did not have the same reservations as a German. The Pole molested a female co-worker, and although the file does not say what happened to him, the chief judge in the case was removed and two fellow judges were replaced.[59] In fact, by that time judges were well aware that their authority was being undermined by the police, especially when it came to dealing with war-related crimes.[60] The Berlin judicial authorities could only guess how many people were executed by the Gestapo, but they were convinced such executions hurt 'the image of the justice system'.[61]

In spite of Schlegelberger's eagerness to run the ministry as Hitler wished, the situation called for a more radical Minister of Justice. By 1942, Hitler wanted someone more like himself in charge, and on 20 August, gave the position to Georg Thierack, President of the People's Court.[62] As we shall see later, Thierack contributed to the continuing transformation of Germany's judges into Hitler's loyal enforcers.

Executions Continue to Make News

Early in the war, even before the tide turned and the dictatorship became yet more radical, it took evident pride in being able to report speedy justice. For example, in September 1940 the Munich Special Court tried and sentenced a man to death for attempted (non-violent) theft of a woman's purse and was clearly pleased to report that the process from beginning to end was completed a mere six days after the crime.[63] Other petty thieves, and anyone else labelled a 'parasite on the body politic', were frequently mentioned victims of the death penalty.[64] The efforts against crime on the home front also were used to spread antisemitism. For example, at a 15 September 1939 press conference, instructions were given to newspapers to print that, as reported in the foreign press, Jews were not allowed on the streets after 8:00 p.m. The press was told that this measure was introduced on the grounds that Jews 'often' took advantage of the darkened streets to 'molest Aryan women'.[65]

My systematic survey of a major regional newspaper in the Rhineland reveals that during the war, hardly a week passed without the report of one or more death sentences. In the first week of 1940, there were reports of the death penalty issued by various courts across the country on almost every day the paper appeared; there was no paper on Monday, but there was one report of an execution on Tuesday. The Friday edition ran a story under the headline, 'No place in Germany for criminals', and Saturday's edition printed one on 'Parasites sentenced to death'. These stories involved the executions of four men.[66] Some of the victims were found guilty of murder, but others were arsonists and one attempted indecent assault and was found guilty of rape. The Sunday edition reported the execution of five men in a story with the headline, 'Death penalty for traitors'.[67] Most were guilty of civilian crimes, like arson or fraud, and all but one of them were not really traitors in the sense of working to overthrow the government. Numerous short reports simply bore the title 'Death penalty carried out' or 'Traitor executed'. Others involved what today would be called common criminals, most of whom did not even use violence, but who, because of their past record or for other reasons were considered by the courts to be deserving of the death penalty. Himmler occasionally reported in the press that a certain prisoner was 'shot while trying to escape' or 'shot while offering resistance'.[68] These were obviously executions.

Far from there being a news blackout on the death penalty during the war as sometimes suggested in the literature, the press office of the Gestapo and Ministry of Justice issued precise guidelines on how these punishments were to be written up. Press officers at local courts were reminded in a communication from the Ministry on 28 October 1942, that the procedure should continue whereby reports of the death penalty should be published only after executions.

The story should be clearly and forcefully written in one or two sentences so that the unbiased reader would conclude, even without knowing anything of the trial itself, that the execution was necessary and justified.[69] Not just national newspapers, but local and regional ones, were full of stories of trials and executions during the war, often for what until then would have been considered minor crimes. An indication of the radicalization on the 'law and order' front can be gathered from early 1942, when the death penalty was used against four men, each supposedly with criminal records, whose breaking-and-entering and theft did not involve violence.[70]

According to the Nazis' own opinion survey from March 1942, citizens during the war were decisively influenced by what they read in the press. They were keen and critical readers of crime and punishment stories, but the Nazis were concerned that unless reports of death penalties were written up properly, the social effects were counter-productive. Changes recommended included mentioning the full name of the person executed, instead of disguising their identity.[71]

A year or so later, after news of the decisive defeat suffered at Stalingrad, and at a time when Germans were increasingly sceptical about news reports, the opinion surveys continued to show that there was popular understanding for the harsh penalties, even as the war took a turn for the worse.[72] A report for 16 September 1943 noted with satisfaction that recent press reports of better-off 'defeatists' who were sentenced to death 'finds greater attention in all circles. It has been said, that it is a good thing that finally once and for all something is really being done and that not only "the little guy" gets punished.'[73]

Deeds punishable by death included stealing post packets or illegal dealings in foodstuffs. In early 1943, detailed stories 'from the courtroom' appeared in which crimes and the executions were described. One case pertained to a 75-year-old butcher, charged with, and found guilty of black-market dealings, whose execution was announced as 'already carried out'.[74]

The crimes of women were occasionally reported, especially for having illicit sexual relations, such as one woman who early in the war was given six years in prison for sleeping with a Polish prisoner of war.[75] Female criminals, even when found guilty as 'parasites on the body politic' were generally treated less severely than men and fewer of their cases were reported in the press. One 20-year-old Düsseldorf woman, found guilty in October 1943 of obtaining goods from well-meaning people after falsely claiming to have lost her parents and home in an air raid, met an understanding Special Court, and received the minimum sentence of a year in prison.[76] At that stage in the war such fraud would generally have cost a man his life.[77]

It would be remiss to leave the impression that all Germans accepted everything the police and the courts did. During the first days of the war, when the press reported Himmler's orders for police executions, there were even scattered rumours that some people were alarmed about the 'arbitrariness' and absence of proper procedures. The population saw through phrases used to mask executions, like 'shot while trying to escape' or 'while resisting' arrest. The Attorney General in Bamberg, for example, raised objections that were typical of many more that could be cited. On 30 April 1940 as part of his regular situation report, he stated that 'often in the last while' press announcements from Himmler, that 'persons, who had been duly found guilty and sentenced to prison by the regular courts, were shot by organizations of the police "while resisting" or "while trying to escape." ' These executions created the impression that the Gestapo, by way of 'corrections', superseded the courts, a fact 'that was not accepted' by many. At least from the point-of-view of judicial authorities in Bamberg, 'police justice' took away from the population's sense of 'legal security', and so was unlikely to stiffen their will to hold out in the war.[78]

And yet there were other reports that citizens praised the use of the death penalty, even to deal with crimes such as morals offences and homosexuality, that had never been capital offences.[79] Even when people began to doubt the outcome of the war, support persisted for Draconian punishments.[80] Again and again, as we will see later in the book, citizens on the spot at wartime executions right in their midst, favoured what happened, and at other times showed themselves to be more radical than the police.

After the Allied invasion of Normandy in June 1944, increased warnings were issued to citizens to guard their behaviour. In one of the last issues of the Düsseldorf newspaper, Himmler threatened the death penalty and other severe penalties for anyone forgetting their duty, like the Police President of Bromberg, whose execution by shooting was reported as an example.[81]

What about the many death sentences being issued by and reported from the notorious People's Court? In a 1940 interview, Georg Thierack, President of this court, and soon to become the most radical of all the Nazi Ministers of Justice, asserted that the People's Court, introduced in 1934 for speedy trials of people accused of treason, was a perfectly 'proper court' and no 'revolutionary tribunal'. He said the court's judges were fighting with the only weapon they had, the law, to protect the people from all attackers.[82] Although Thierack wanted to put the best face on the court, anyone reading the newspapers during the war, could easily deduce that the People's Court was extremely radical in the sense in which it handed out draconian punishments, often for the most trivial crimes.

Nonetheless, Thierack insisted that the courts were anything but a system of arbitrary coercion. In an interview in March 1944, he admitted that 'it was no secret that today in the war, the punishments being handed down are hard, at times very hard. Some people—and by no means always the enemies of our people—consider in fact, that very often the system of justice is too hard and particularly makes too frequent use of the hardest punishments.' Thierack defended such punishments, however, as necessary to maintain the home front against 'defeatists' and other such 'creatures'. There was no room for 'any false mercy' which would 'represent an unforgivable weakness'.[83]

Hitler Becomes 'Highest Judge' (Oberster Gerichtsherr)

Hitler showed his obvious preference for 'police justice' over even the Nazified court system, especially by his interventions. In 1942 he took time away from many pressing tasks, to formalize his position as Germany's 'Supreme Judicial Authority'. This was a curious move, because Hitler already had the powers to overturn court decisions and to order executions. In the early months of 1942, his anxiety about the war was reflected in private ruminations that the system of justice was 'too inflexible' and that judges did not recognize dangers that could be taken advantage of by 'criminal elements'. Harking back to supposed mild punishments given to civilian and military offenders in the last war, which allegedly embittered the troops, Hitler advocated more use of the 'ordinance against parasites on the body politic' and wanted more offenders sent to the concentration camps or executed. He complained that judges and jurists spent too much time fussing over their verdicts, as if it were peacetime.[84] Therefore, on 21 March 1942 he introduced more 'simplifications' to make the administration of justice 'frictionless and speedy work'. The effect of the decree was that the powers of judges increased at the expense of the accused.[85]

Hitler turned his attention to sharpening measures against those in the armed forces on 2 April 1942, and particularly to men who committed certain offences in the expectation that they would be caught and, instead of fighting, sent to prison. Hitler ordered that 'the probationary possibilities on the eastern front must in the future be used more fully than up to the present'.[86] Those who shirked their duty would be sent to serve in 'probationary battalions' in which they would be assigned to do the hardest work under dangerous conditions on the eastern front. Such 'probationary battalions' were mentioned first in a 'Führer order' as early as September 1940. Their purpose was to win back the offender for the 'community of the people' and to provide a deterrent to any disobedience. After the invasion of the Soviet Union, being sent to such a 'probationary' unit, given their extremely high casualty rates, became as good as a death sentence.[87]

Hitler's worries about maintaining discipline and order culminated in a major speech he delivered on 24 April 1942 in what was, perhaps fittingly enough, the Reichstag's last sitting. No one could have heard this speech and been in any doubt about Hitler's deep-seated and wholly delusional anti-semitism. Germany was presented as the innocent victim that made 'endless' peace initiatives, all subverted by 'the secret powers' behind the scenes who were the Jews.

Hitler offered less than a realistic assessment of the war and played up Germany's military achievements, but it was impossible to hide concern about the eastern front. He claimed that the Wehrmacht averted disaster, in part because of his leadership and because of the 'bravery' and the 'trust' of the average German soldier. He admitted that there were spots 'where the nerves broke, obedience failed' and the necessary sense of duty was missing, but on such occasions he 'made tough decisions and on the basis of the power of the sovereign law', a power he believed was conferred on him by the German people.

Hitler tried to justify asking that the German people grant him, through the Reichstag, the formal power as the country's Supreme Judge. First of all, he said he needed the 'express confirmation' to take steps against anyone who did 'not throw themselves totally into the service of the greater mission, which was to be or not to be'.[88] He spoke of the link between the 'front and home', and said he would lose no time worrying about legal rights and privileges: 'today there are only duties.' After threatening the civil service in general, Hitler turned to the judiciary, insisting it must serve the nation. He then used one of his favourite parables about the good and honest woman who needed to be protected. He could not, he said,

to mention one example, understand a court verdict in which a criminal—who married in 1937 and mistreated his wife until she was taken to a mental hospital where she died from the consequences of the last attack—could be sentenced to five years in prison when tens of thousands of brave German men must die to protect their homeland from destruction by Bolshevism. This means that, in order to protect their women and children, from now on I shall intervene in these cases and remove judges who are obviously not aware of the needs of the moment.[89]

Hitler's justification for the new powers reflected his sense of the perilous situation Germany faced in 1942, for the man who mistreated his wife had long since been retried, found guilty, and executed.[90] According to public opinion surveys at the time, Hitler, in demanding powers he was already exercising, was seen to be attacking the judiciary.[91] The speech sent messages to judges to be tougher, and to the people to stiffen their backbones or face the consequences. Opinion surveys said that Hitler's allegations about the Jews, were enthusiastically greeted 'especially in politically engaged circles'.[92]

Hitler repeated his thinking on justice issues in public on 30 January and 24 April 1942, and again later in the year. A September speech dealt at greater length with the situation in the war, and mentioned the infamous prophecy about what would happen to the Jews in the event of war. Hitler was proud of allegations printed by an English newspaper, that anyone who took advantage of the war in England was given merely a slap on the wrist, while such people were as good as dead in Germany. 'This English newspaper is right', he said, adding that 'at a time in which the best of our people have to be used on the front and there giving their lives, in such a time there is no place for criminals and unreliable types who destroy the nation.' The criminals who might try to take advantage of the situation would be treated without mercy. 'We will make sure, that not only the decent can die at the front as is fitting, but that under no circumstances will the criminals and the indecent at home survive this time.' To reinforce the point, he repeated his parable about the upright German woman who must be protected on her way home from work in the darkened streets. She was not going to have to worry about being accosted by 'criminals' while the men were off to war. Hitler stated in unambiguous terms, that 'we will annihilate these criminals, and we have annihilated them'. Men on the battlefront had the right to demand, he insisted, that while they risked their lives as soldiers, their families, wives and relatives should be protected at home. The speech ended with the motto: 'we stand behind our soldiers just as the soldiers stand up for us.'[93]

The Death Penalty

Hitler was a strong proponent of the death penalty, and its growing use was well advertised and generally applauded. Comparing the Third Reich to the Weimar Republic (1919 to 1932), which includes the stormy revolutionary years of the early Republic and the Depression years, we find that in Weimar of 1,141 people sentenced to death, 184 were executed. During the Depression years from 1929 onwards, even though there was a sense that Germany was in the midst of a crime wave, less than 10 per cent of all death sentences led to executions. As soon as the Nazis came to power, not only did the number of death sentences increase, but so did the percentage of executions, so that in the years for which we have records from 1933 to 1939—except 1934—more than 80 per cent of those sentenced to die were executed.[94]

Hitler insisted on many occasions that wartime conditions on the home front were unprecedented and called for greater use of the death penalty, even for crimes that he would have considered minor before the war. He observed, for example, on 20 August 1942 in conversations with newly named Minister of Justice Thierack, that wartime conditions demanded not only that a petty thief who stole a woman's purse should be executed, but that 'barbaric methods' were needed against all crimes to prevent them from becoming a plague or epidemic. Moreover, Hitler's vision of war as a Darwinian struggle in which the best were killed, posited that judges should redress the balance by sending ne'er-do-wells to their deaths instead of preserving them in relative security and comfort behind bars. He encouraged Thierack to guide judges and remind them to use methods that were appropriate to the times.[95]

Between 1933 and 1945, civil courts, that is, mostly the People's Court and the Special Courts, sentenced approximately 16,500 people to death inside

Germany, the vast majority of whom were not Jews. Some of them were 'ordinary Germans', but overall, most were foreign nationals (such as slave workers) brought to Germany during the war. An estimated three-quarters of these sentences were carried out.[96] Although many of the men and women who were sent to their deaths by German courts were foreigners, in some areas that have been studied lately, the majority of victims (male and female) were ordinary Germans.[97]

The revolutionary transformation of the entire system of justice in Hitler's dictatorship, and the marked effect of the war, can be suggested by looking at what happened to the death penalty. At the start of the war there were three offences punishable by death and by the end there were at least 46 of them. The number of the accused brought before the People's Court for 'serious' political crimes, such as treason, increased almost 10 times, from 470 cases in 1939 to 4,379 in 1944, but the death penalties meted out grew nearly 60 times, from 36 in 1939 to 2,097 in 1944. So not only did the activities of the People's Court increase dramatically, but it became more bloody-minded in the war years. By 1944, which is the last date for which we have statistics, nearly half of the accused brought before the court (2,097 of a total of 4,379) were sentenced to death.[98]

Above and beyond court-ordained executions, throughout the war, many others took place on the orders of the police, Himmler or Hitler himself. Not only were no trials held, but Ministry of Justice officials sometimes only learned of what happened by reading the stories in newspapers. Only half-hearted efforts were made to keep these thinly-veiled murders from the public.[99]

Germany's military courts, if anything were more brutal than the civilian ones. Apart from sentencing somewhere between 13,000 and 15,000 men to death (about 85 per cent of the sentences were carried out), the military courts habitually handed down very long prison terms. As the war proceeded the number of military trials per month more than tripled, from 12,853 in December 1939 to 44,955 in October 1944; the rate at which military courts handed down the death penalty increased by eight times: in 1939–40, there were 519 of them, but in 1943–4, there were 4,118 such cases.[100]

The brutality of these verdicts underlines the fact that in spite of some competition between the courts and the police we should not exaggerate them, nor conclude that judges somehow strove to uphold the traditional rule of law. At times, it is true, representatives of the Ministry of Justice, as well as local court officials, expressed reservations that the police acted outside the law. Historian Ralf Angermund points out, however, that the complaints were all too rare and pertained to isolated cases of particularly egregious police measures, and often arose because local judicial officials were not informed of prior agreements reached by leaders in Berlin.[101] In practice, after occasional and weak protests by judicial officials and judges, they all accepted the Third Reich and none of them, as far as we know, lifted a finger in defence of their Jewish colleagues, all of whom were dismissed from their posts.[102]

Judges aimed for frictionless collaboration with all the new police, and from 1933 onwards, judicial authorities at all levels offered the Gestapo many 'good will' gestures, such as letting the Gestapo know when political prisoners were about to be released from custody; when certain charges were withdrawn in a case; and even when release was called for because an accused person was found innocent, so that the police could check whether they wanted to place such persons in 'protective custody'.[103]

Judges worked for harsh verdicts in their own courts and in collaboration with the police, as loyal servants of the new system and did so not because they were forced, but rather because they evidently shared so many National Socialist convictions—including its racism—as well as broader general assumptions about 'law and order'.[104]

A small incident from May 1941 may suggest how much changed about 'law and order' during the war. The report we have was that a police official in SS uniform, probably a member of the Gestapo, turned up in a senior high-school class in the Stuttgart area. He was there to explain the background of 'shootings "because of resistance" one could read about from time to time in the press'. He said simply, that while courts worked well when hard evidence could be found, the police had to act when there was insufficient evidence. They knew how to recognize guilt and were not bound by rules of evidence as were judges, so that the police could become the proverbial judge, jury, and executioner. Lest students worry unduly, they were assured that the police did not execute anyone without 'previously thoroughly examining' the case.[105] How students might have reacted to this frank explanation of police justice is not mentioned by those who reported the event.

That the police could explain unlawful executions to the public and expect to quiet any public reservations on the subject, speaks volumes about how Germany had been transformed since 1933.

Crime Figures

Hitler's dictatorship repeatedly boasted about the success of sweeping new police powers in reducing crime. By early 1936 the authorities announced that the country had undergone 'a great cleaning up', crime was down, and citizens should be appreciative.[106] In early 1941, Reinhard Heydrich used the occasion of the Day of the German Police to remind people that the Kripo and other police had reduced crime by 40 per cent compared to 1932.[107] Over the years citizens heard many such stories, and no doubt some crime went down for reasons that had nothing to do with the new police and court system. For example, the return to full employment by 1936, got many potential offenders working again, and the build-up of the armed forces drew millions of young men off the streets and away from the opportunity to commit crimes.

Assessing the incidence of 'real' crime is difficult, but if we look at the statistics from 1933 to the war, we can see general decline.[108] However, crime was underestimated for a number of reasons. For one thing, the statisticians defined a crime as a breach of the criminal code that was found guilty by the courts. The many hundreds of thousands of cases tried by the Special Courts and the People's Court were excluded from the statistics. In addition, the police and even the Nazi Party handled many thousands of accusations and offences on their own authority, and never went to court.[109]

The number of accused persons before the courts also went down because of many Hitler amnesties. According to an undated report of the Minister of Justice from 1939, there had been ten amnesties since 1932, and an estimated 2.5 million persons benefited from them. Numerous pending cases were struck down, were dropped by the courts, or never went to court at all. These amnesties thus had the side-effect of exaggerating the reduction of 'crime', defined as a successfully prosecuted case.[110] Judicial officials themselves complained that wartime personnel shortages most likely meant that many crimes went undetected and untried.[111]

When all is said and done, there are good grounds for concluding that 'crime'—accepting the definitions of the Nazis themselves—as a whole probably increased over the years of the Third Reich, above all in the war years when many new crimes were invented. Whether crime was rising or falling was neither as straightforward nor as simple as police spokesmen would have German citizens believe.[112]

An analysis from 1944 by the German Statistical Office shows that the total number of German men and women (not just foreign nationals) who were tried and found guilty by the criminal courts, which fell at the beginning of the war because of an amnesty, began to rise again. The statisticians gave the following reasons for the initial decline in 1939 and into 1940: on top of Hitler's amnesty (9 September 1939), the draft called up many others whose trials were pending. The statisticians also pointed to the reluctance of the population to report less serious crimes, and to employers who grew reluctant to complain about workers for fear of being unable to replace them at a time of acute labour shortage. In addition, fewer policemen were available to carry out investigations, as many were drafted or sent on police missions outside Germany proper. Nevertheless, the number of men and women, and especially young people, who were sent to trial and found guilty began to increase once the effects of the amnesty began to fade. The rise in crime was reflected in the statistics from 1941 onwards. Indeed, new opportunities for criminal activity were offered with the darkening of the nation's streets, and more arose with the introduction of measures to feed, clothe, and shelter the population in war.[113]

Not mentioned in this statistical analysis was the effect on the number of cases that went untried before the courts, but were handled by the police on their own authority. An analysis of the Justice Ministry from late 1944, which does not count the latter, insists that in comparison with 1937 (the only year without an amnesty), the war years saw a modest decline in crime inside the borders of old Germany. Juvenile delinquency, however, was on the rise and, comparing 1937 with 1942, grew by 110 per cent.[114]

Isolated Kripo (pre-trial) records that survive for the period from 1938 to 1943 show a continuous rise in the cases they handled of 'serious theft'.[115] The number of thefts and extortions increased; and homicides grew most years between 1938 and 1943.[116] Although these figures pertain to the enlarged Reich (Austrian data are included from 1939, those of annexed Polish areas from 1940), the increase was significant each year after 1940 within this new Reich area. According to reports, only one type of crime fell, and that was fraud. However, the Kripo had turned its attention away from prosecuting fraud, and other offences like 'simple theft', in favour of crimes such as breaking-and-entering. As well, they were concerned with policing the many new war measures.

There is another side of criminality that we must take into account if we want to assess the crime rate in Nazi Germany at war, and that involves the millions of foreign workers and prisoners of war brought to Germany. Foreign workers became the number one preoccupation of the police in the war years. If we take the run-ins these foreigners had with the police—which became astronomical —then we would have to conclude there was nothing short of an explosion of 'crime' in Nazi Germany. Most of this latter crime was dealt with directly by police measures and the cases were never sent to court at all.

Nevertheless, the mythic crime-fighting statistics achieved by the Nazis were the biggest crime stories of all, and even if the successes were more apparent than real, we cannot underestimate the impact on the population of repeated announcements that the dictatorship was winning the war on crime. This propaganda left a big impression on many contemporaries, so much so, that the images of Nazi crime-fighting, however false, are still fondly recalled by contemporaries.[117] They were particularly struck by how the dictatorship cleaned up the streets of the misfits and the social outsiders, which is, as we see in the next chapter, a tragic story in its own right.

5

Social Outsiders

The Nazis offered the Gestapo enormous new powers to track down political opponents and those deemed to be 'race enemies'. At almost the same time, the Kripo was given a mission to find and eliminate a wide variety of social outsiders, from criminals, to beggars, and even the homeless. The police in general, as well as a host of other authorities, were part of a much larger effort to restore the mythical purity of the racially based 'community of the people' that supposedly existed in the past. In this chapter the emphasis is on the Kripo and its campaigns to deal with variously defined social outsiders. We need to be aware of the larger context, however, in which a whole array of biomedical experts were engaged in efforts to cleanse the body politic. As we will see, the police, medical experts, and other authorities often worked hand in glove in eliminating people deemed 'unfit for community life' (*gemeinschaftsunfähig*).

Well before 1933, certain individuals and groups lived on—or had been driven to—the margins of society because they would not, or could not, live according to dominant social values, such as hard work, cleanliness, and sobriety. These values and norms, and the negative attitudes towards those who did not conform to them, carried over into the Third Reich, but were magnified many times. The Nazi vision of a harmonious, healthy, hard-working, and politically committed 'community of the people', was not new, but what set Hitler's dictatorship apart was its determination to make things happen.[1] Anyone who did not fit the pure white 'Aryan' nation was not only subjected to an increasing array of discriminatory measures, but was threatened with being sent to camps, worked to death, or killed out of hand.[2]

Before 1933 Hitler showed nothing but contempt for those whom he called 'degenerates' and 'parasites', and once in power he became a radical proponent of cleaning up the streets, banishing offenders, and purifying the race.[3] He despised the kind of liberal world associated with the Weimar Republic, and like other Nazi leaders, he preferred the no-nonsense actions of the police. He also scorned lenient judges and reviled not only convicted criminals, but anyone who seemed not to fit his social and racial vision.

However, although Hitler and to some extent other leaders like Heinrich Himmler determined the specifics as to steps taken to deal with social outsiders, they did not draw up their far-reaching goals and tactical plans in a social vacuum. Not only was the social identity of the persecuted outsiders largely determined by German traditions, but dealing more radically with them was meant to appeal to good citizens and win them over. Thus, Nazi plans and policies towards social outsiders combined ideological convictions with political calculations as to what German citizens would support, or at least tolerate. Many authorities out in the provinces, recognizing the new possibilities of dealing with their 'problem cases' not only followed their leaders, but exceeded orders and often suggested initiatives of their own.

Repeat Offenders

The Nazi version of a preventive approach to crime was for the police to identify likely criminals and arrest them before they did anything. Himmler stated the obvious in newspaper articles and in speeches, that it was difficult and expensive to keep track of repeat offenders, and like Hitler, he wanted to send anyone who committed three or four crimes to a concentration camp for good.[4] Underlying these views was the conviction that criminals were born, not made.

For decades, a wide range of European and American scientists had been propagating the idea that hard-core criminals and those described as the 'asocials'—a term going back generations before the Nazi era—were biologically or even genetically determined. The search for the magic key to crime and social deviancy went back before 1914 when theorists like Cesare Lombroso attempted to construct a 'criminal science' by which one could improve the state's capacity 'to anticipate delinquency by revealing the true criminal in advance of any particular action and thus extend the possibility of preventive detention'.[5] Nazi criminologists like Robert Ritter built on Lombroso's work.[6] Hitler made the point, often quoted by police experts, as follows: 'the born criminal will be and remain a criminal; but numerous people, in whom a certain inclination towards crime exists, can through proper education still become valuable members of the community of the people'.[7] In time, however, more kinds of offenders and 'deviants' were added to the list of people in the vague category of 'the born criminal'.

Leaders of the Nazi police besides Himmler also shared these views. Kurt Daluege, in charge of uniformed police (Orpo), and Arthur Nebe of the detective branch (Kripo), consistently argued for 'preventive custody' to nip crime in the bud. A Prussian decree (13 November 1933) and a federal law (24 November 1933) dealt with what were called 'dangerous habitual offenders'. The Prussian decree stated that police could place someone in preventive custody if they committed premeditated crimes or misdemeanours and were sentenced to at least six months in prison on three different occasions. The decree also set quotas for the 'preventive police arrest' of criminals known to police in each district, more or less following the pattern by which the Gestapo frequently arrested political opponents.[8] Soon the police could detain those with no convictions at all, if they had grounds for concluding such persons had a 'criminal will' and might endanger security in the future.[9]

The commission on the Criminal Code that began meeting in 1933 also discussed what to do about such offenders. Minister of Justice Gürtner stated in one story, that the laws should be changed to protect the community, if need be by curtailing individual rights. He claimed that the community would not wait for such criminals to commit yet another crime, but must stop them before they acted and would regard them as 'parasites who had to be eradicated for the people'.[10] At the end of 1933, in anticipation of the more radical approach to repeat offenders that was supposed to be contained in the new Criminal Code, justice officials singled out for immediate attention those termed 'criminals undermining of the community'. Gürtner stated that under the old liberal system it was impossible to deal with such offenders, but that the new German criminal code would change that.[11]

Kurt Daluege, the man who began his career in the Third Reich in charge of the police desk in the Prussian Ministry of the Interior, was a strong proponent of the Nazi approach to crime. He offered a public account of the new law against 'dangerous habitual offenders', and explained in a radio address how the new regime, no friend of half measures, would use 'pitiless severity' against these criminals, whom he defined as 'consciously asocial elements with long prison records'. He said the new law was a good example of the National Socialist administration of justice, because repeat offenders would be kept under lock and key, and thus spared society a 'superfluous, difficult, involved and expensive investigation'.

Daluege reported even before the law came into force, that the Kripo already sent many such persons to a special concentration camp where they 'ought to learn to work again'. Anyone deemed by police to be a repeat offender could be arrested without having committed a fresh deed and sent to such a camp. Daluege told the public that the Kripo took such preventive actions without any reference to the courts, and concluded his radio talk with the kind of fable that was repeated often in the Third Reich. He said the aim of police was to achieve a society 'in which every racial comrade could also walk through lonely streets in the evening with complete security. He [sic] ought to be able to leave the windows open without having to worry about a break-in and above all ought to be able to sleep peacefully again with the feeling that we are watching out for him.'[12]

Other officials also emphasized that the new regime counted successes in the war on crime, even before the new measure on repeat offenders came into effect. The newly appointed head of the Berlin Kripo, Friedrich Schneider said in November 1933 that criminality in the capital city, especially theft and breaking-and-entering, had declined dramatically, and he explained it by pointing to the preventive detention of professional criminals.[13] Others underlined that in the new Germany, the return of full employment helped to get the beggars and criminal elements off the streets. They all proclaimed the days were over when 'unaccompanied women had to worry about getting home safely at night'.[14]

After 1 January 1934, as explained in the press, anyone deemed a 'dangerous habitual criminal', even after serving their full sentence, would not be released any more. To protect the community, they would be held in 'preventive detention'.[15] To add to the no-nonsense image of the dictatorship, the public was informed that life behind bars was going to be an unpleasant experience. Time in prison was not only punishment for a crime, but it was meant to have an educative effect on criminals.[16] The Nazis insisted that stiffer penalties and harder punishments also worked as a deterrent, and rushed to proclaim their successes before the end of the first year of Hitler's dictatorship.

Police spokesmen, like Daluege, explained the unchecked prerogatives of police with the same kinds of arguments used to justify the new powers of the Gestapo. In late 1934, he hailed preventive custody as having 'proved itself already successful', because it gave police a means to stop professional criminals before they reoffended. The new operating principle was 'prevention is better than reacting' to crime.[17] He asserted that fear of preventive detention had broken the (mythical) solidarity of criminals, who were not as bold as they used to be.[18]

Judges soon got into the act, because the federal law gave them new powers to order the 'preventive detention' of persons deemed likely to reoffend. The 'criminals' could be sent to the state's own facilities, like a prison, workhouse, or mental institution, and judges could order the sterilization of those defined as 'dangerous habitual offenders'.[19]

Hitler long held that sterilization should be used to restore the 'racial purity' of the community, but it had been illegal in Germany until 1933.[20] One of the first sweeping measures introduced in the Third Reich was a 'Law for the Prevention of Offspring with Hereditary Diseases' of 14 July 1933, which made possible compulsory sterilization. Initially the law was aimed at those suffering various mental and physical problems, such as congenital feeble-mindedness, schizophrenia, inherited blindness, deafness, and epilepsy.[21] This sterilization law has been called 'the model for all eugenic legislation' in Nazi Germany.[22] New hereditary health courts, attached to lower courts, were made up of a judge and two doctors as experts. Seventy-five per cent of all the cases were denounced to the courts by the medical profession, and of the approximately 200,000 women and the 200,000 men who were sterilized in the course of the programme, nearly all were sterilized against their will.[23] Approximately 5,000 people died as a result of the procedures, most of them women, but invariably the result had devastating psychological effects. Not only medical, but social criteria were used in the decisions, so that undesired behaviour, like severe alcoholism, or even unruliness, could lead to sterilization. The same could happen to women who changed sexual partners too frequently or had more than one illegitimate child.[24]

Far from being secret, the massive sterilization campaign was played up in the press; there were more than 50,000 public meetings and assemblies to discuss *Erb- und Rassenpflege* (genetic and racial hygiene) in the period down to the war; schools introduced the topic in the curriculum; and there were endless books, literally millions of pamphlets and articles, and even some movies devoted to the topic.[25] Although the Catholic Church had reservations, it did not act on them, and there were no protests about sterilizations in Germany. It is very likely that the idea of a sterilization law was quite popular, certainly when it came to dealing with criminals. Even in the United States at about this time, *Fortune Magazine* reported that 66 per cent of those surveyed in 1937 favoured the compulsory sterilization of habitual criminals.[26]

The American experiences were considered quite positively by German advocates of compulsory sterilization who pointed out that it had been widely practised in the United States since before World War I, and compulsory sterilization was upheld by the Supreme Court in 1927. Justice Oliver Wendell Holmes said, 'it is better for all the world, if instead of waiting to execute the degenerate offspring for crime, or to let them starve for their imbecility, society can prevent those who are manifestly unfit from continuing their kind.'[27] The annual rate of compulsory sterilizations in America down to 1930 was between 200 and 600 per year, but increased in the 1930s, when there were between 2,000 and 4,000 sterilizations per year.[28]

The November 1933 law in Germany against 'dangerous habitual offenders' gave judges of the regular courts options such as ordering 'preventive detention', but also opened the possibility for courts to recommend the compulsory sterilization of 'dangerous morals offenders'. Judges were quick to take advantage of their new powers, and in 1934 they ordered the 'preventive detention' of 3,723 'habitual criminals'. The numbers fell slowly after that until 1938 when they picked up again.[29] The courts also sent others to hospitals, and prescribed sterilizations, and between 1934 and 1939, judges alone used their new power to incarcerate 26,346 people (without trials).[30]

There was tension and obvious overlap between the Kripo's right to order 'preventive custody' and the power of courts to hold someone in 'preventive detention'. The two concepts sound much alike. Given Hitler's hostility to written law, it should not surprise that the prerogatives of the Kripo prevailed. The Ministry of Justice eventually advised judges to place more people in 'preventive detention', and in that way avoid being outdone by police. In March 1938 the Ministry reminded judges that the law against habitual criminals put a powerful weapon in their hands, and they ought to use it 'relentlessly'.[31]

From the beginning of the regime, however, Daluege and other police leaders echoed Hitler by proudly claiming that the police were no longer bound by 'the dead letter' of the law, but acted out of 'the spirit of the law, the spirit of the people, and the spirit of the Führer'. They promoted the idea that it was proper for all police, not just the Gestapo, to push aside legal issues to restore security and order, two old and treasured German values. They insisted that the days were gone when police only arrived after a crime was committed.[32] Thanks to arresting and sending criminals to what were called 'educative camps', the boast by early 1935 in the press was that crime was cut by half.[33] These kinds of successes tempted citizens to overlook excesses in the name of putting the rights of the community before individual rights.

Liebermann von Sonnenberg, head of the Berlin Kripo, explained in August 1935, that professional criminals sitting in concentration camps like Esterwegen, could not commit crimes. By way of illustration, he observed that whereas for Berlin in March 1932 there were 67 serious armed robberies, the number fell to 14 in March 1934, and there were only 12 of them in March 1935.[34] Officials explained that now 'the first attack is the task of the police', and criminals no longer had a head start. The police would not wait for the attorney general or the courts to start the process, nor sit and hope that courts would find the accused guilty and give them a stiff sentence.[35]

The German police pointed to what happened in the United States and how the liberal approach to crime was a failure there. The Kripo summed up the essence of the Nazi alternative in 1936 in phrases that could have been taken from a Hitler speech: 'prevention through education with the educable [criminals], and removal [from society] of the ineducable'. It was up to the police to decide into which of these categories they would place their suspects.[36] The 'community of the people', and hence police considerations to protect it, took precedence over the rule of law and individual rights, so that judges were not supposed to release anyone from preventive detention without checking with the Kripo.[37] An effort was made to keep a place for the courts by changing the penal code on 4 September 1941, to make it possible for them to apply the death penalty to 'dangerous repeat offenders'. The operative word was 'repeat' and not 'dangerous', since the measure was explicitly aimed at even petty offenders, who would be eliminated in the name of a racial biological cleansing of the body politic.[38]

'Asocials'

Nazi theory and practice towards habitual and professional criminals shaded into what happened to the asocials, a loosely defined group that was much discussed in welfare and police circles well before the Nazi era. The concept was used to describe anyone who did not participate as a good citizen and accept their social responsibilities. Apart from convicted criminals, the Nazis wanted to rid society of all asocials, that is, people whose way of life did not conform to the new ideals, or accord with what the Nazis called 'wholesome popular sentiment'.[39] In a more general sense, the Nazis claimed to be offended by life on the wrong side of the tracks, and in 1933 made noises about chasing away street prostitutes, pimps, and abortionists. They threatened anyone who would not take up a regular job, and over the summer, various authorities went after 'Gypsies', the 'work-shy', and tramps (in the instructive phrase from a local ordinance) for 'bothering the population'.[40] In mid-September 1933, the Nazis ordered a nationwide round-up to end what they called the 'plague of the beggars' in the streets. Citizens were asked to cooperate by holding back their funds for proper charities and reminded that Germany was too poor to afford 'full-time beggars, work-shy, drinkers, and fraud artists'.[41] Supposedly, the round-up also would prevent crime because it would eliminate the environment that bred deviance.

Himmler ordered numerous other arrest 'sweeps', such as one that began less than a year after his appointment as Chief of the German Police. Early in 1937 the Kripo was told to prepare lists of 'professional and habitual criminals'. A second note explained that in spite of the reduction of crime, certain criminals continued to operate whose deeds indicated an asocial attitude, and even opposition to the state.[42] Himmler ordered a 'special action' for 9 March 1937 to arrest 2,000 people out of work. The instruction was to send to concentration camps, those who *'in the opinion of the Criminal Police'* (emphasis in the original) were professional criminals, repeat offenders, or habitual sex offenders.[43] The enthusiasm of the police was such that they arrested not 2,000, but 2,752 people, only 171 of whom had broken their probation. Police used the event as a pretext to get rid of 'problem cases'. Those arrested were described as break-in specialists (938), thieves (741), sex offenders (495), swindlers (436), robbers (56), and dealers in stolen goods (86). Only 85 of them were women. Some Jews were arrested, but the precise number is not known. By the end of the year, only 372 were released and 68 died in custody.[44] None were to be released unless there was a genuine prospect they would take up work and keep their job.[45]

Given that the 1937 'action' was carried out by police without any reference to the courts, it constituted another step in the rise of the police at the expense of the rule of law. Authorization for the 'special action' was issued through the Ministry of the Interior without even discussing it with the Ministry of Justice, whose officials—like other citizens—learned about it a month later in the newspapers.[46]

On 14 December 1937 the Ministry of the Interior issued a 'fundamental decree on the preventive police battle against criminality'. The recent reorganization of the Kripo, it said, made it important to unify preventive arrest practices. The decree was based on the Reichstag Fire Decree (28 February 1933) that justified the creation of the Gestapo, and permitted the Kripo to deal with criminals to protect the community 'from all parasites'. Two approaches were prescribed, the most radical being the arrest of those who, because of their police records, were defined as 'professional or habitual criminals'.[47] At the discretion of the police, such persons could be placed in 'preventive custody', and that mandate also could be extended to the vague category of the asocials. The second method available was 'police-ordered planned supervision', which made it possible for the Kripo to keep ex-prisoners under surveillance, and entailed much more than simple parole. Nazi police were given complete control over the everyday lives of released prisoners, and for an indefinite period could impose 20 different restrictions on them. The police could determine place of residence and leisure activities, forbid alcohol consumption, certain social company, and visits to a wide assortment of public places. Ex-prisoners could be kept under house arrest, not allowed to drive, own pets or any weapons.[48] Kripo headquarters wanted to be certain that the police, and not the courts, made the final decision about whether 'dangerous habitual criminals' were released after they served their time and lived up to their probation.[49]

In early 1938 the Kripo moved towards complete independence from the courts, and claimed that in so far as they dealt preventively with 'criminal enemies of state' they could claim to be carrying out the mandate of the Führer, and needed no authorization from the courts. The German public was informed about the nature and extent of these new powers, although specific police 'actions' that followed were not publicized.[50] That same year, the Kripo even tried to get their hands on asocials with prior convictions who were sitting in regular prisons, to have them sent to concentration camps, instead of being released when their prison term was up.[51] There was no place for 'loose people' with 'no fixed abode' in the Third Reich.[52]

Himmler's instructions to the Kripo on 4 April 1938 defined the asocials as those 'who demonstrate through behaviour which is inimical to the community, but which need not be criminal, that they will not adapt themselves to the community'. The list of the asocials who fit this vague definition, included anyone 'who through minor, but oft-repeated, infractions of the law demonstrate that they will not comply with the social order that is a fundamental condition of a National Socialist state, e.g. beggars, vagrants, (Gypsies), prostitutes, drunkards, those with contagious diseases, particularly sexually transmitted diseases, who evade the measures taken by the public health authorities'. Also considered asocial by this point was anyone who avoided work, which is to say, 'persons, regardless of any previous conviction, who evade the obligation to work and are dependent on the public for their maintenance (e.g. the work-shy, work evaders, drunkards)'. The Kripo was empowered to arrest anyone who fell into these broad categories, and selectively was doing so already. In order to protect citizens and their property, the Kripo was given still 'greater freedom of action' to deal with all 'lawbreakers and all asocial persons'. The Kripo could extend planned surveillance or order preventive custody, which was defined as the 'sharpest method' against criminals and asocials. 'In the first instance' the decree was aimed at people with no fixed abode. At the discretion of the police, such people could be sent to a concentration camp.[53] At the same time that the Nazi police, especially the Kripo, claimed new powers, they hatched plans for further 'actions'. On 26 January 1938 Himmler informed Kripo and Gestapo of his wish for a nationwide sweep against the 'work-shy', who were more difficult to catch than other problem cases. For Himmler, the 'work-shy' were males medically fit to work, but who (without good reason) refused jobs on two occasions, or quit after a short time. He contended that if word leaked out about a police action, such people would find a job, but with no real intention of reforming. Therefore, 'to attain a complete removal' of these asocial elements, Himmler called for a 'one-time, comprehensive and surprise attack'.[54]

Himmler put the Gestapo in charge of the first 'asocial action' set for early March 1938, but carried out only at the end of April. The Gestapo were told not to worry about defining the concept of asocial too narrowly. Those picked up were kept in 'protective custody', held for two to three weeks in local police prisons, after which they were to be sent to Buchenwald for a minimum of three months. Because the Gestapo had few files on the 'work-shy', Himmler asked labour exchanges, state and Nazi welfare offices to provide information.[55] A recent estimate puts the number arrested at around 2,000, all sent to Buchenwald.[56]

On 1 June 1938 the Kripo was told to arrest a minimum of 200 unemployed asocials in each police district. Between 13 and 18 June 1938 they arrested asocials that included tramps, beggars, Gypsies, and pimps. Anyone who used hostels was investigated to see if they might be 'work-shy', and such checks continued later.[57] The Kripo threw themselves into the task and exceeded orders. Instead of arresting a total of around 3,000, in Berlin alone the Kripo and Orpo picked up an estimated 2,000 persons. To judge by statistics mentioned by a member of Himmler's personal staff, the Kripo came up with more than 8,000 people who were sent to concentration camps. At the beginning of 1939, 'well over 10,000' of those taken into custody were still in the camps.[58] Contrary to express orders, the Kripo even arrested men who were no longer 'work-shy' at all, but were gainfully employed.[59]

Some information was provided in the Nazi press about the Kripo's use of preventive detention, but it gave few details. One instructive story appeared during an earlier visit of Italian Fascist officials. Giovanni Novelli, from the Justice Ministry in Rome, said that detention proved effective because it removed direct and indirect influences that induced people to crime, and made it easier to control their behaviour. Nazi jurist Roland Freisler agreed and long had thought that preventive detention should be a 'permanent feature' of the judicial system.[60] He noted that, just as in Italy, the German Reich prevented the criminal carriers of degeneration from propagating. He attributed Germany's decline in crime to the way the regime protected the race and insured its well-being. Freisler ended by lauding the educative role of work in reforming prisoners.[61]

Another ideological justification for arresting the 'work-shy' and assorted asocials, and forcing them to work, was that it fitted the mandate of police, often mentioned in the press, to cleanse the body politic by wiping out all criminals. Above and beyond that, the aim of the police was to discipline and punish anyone who did not fit the image of the hard-working citizen and committed racial comrade. Some mayors got into the spirit and asked the Kripo to arrest well-known drinkers, as asocials, in order to get rid of them; the mayors were told this was the job of welfare organizations, not the police.[62]

Economic considerations also played a role in the large number of arrests in 1938, when Germany was preparing for war and suffering a labour shortage. Once social misfits were sent to concentration camps, often referred to in official directives as work camps, their labour could be put to use. While in detention, they were exploited to finance the burgeoning SS empire.[63] The camps were sarcastically portrayed by the SS in early 1939 as places that were 'excellently suited' to provide an 'educative cure through work' for the asocials.[64]

As we have seen, concentration camps in the last pre-war years were used not only for political 'enemies of state', but also for those who were undesired socially. Any persons checked by police and found to be 'work-shy' during the war, at least if they had a previous conviction, were sent to a concentration camp.[65] Even before the war, however, concentration camps increasingly confined social outsiders. By the end of October 1938, for instance, if we take the camp at Buchenwald as an example, its 10,188 prisoners included 1,007 'professional criminals' and 4,341 picked up as 'asocials'. Together they constituted over half the camp population and outnumbered those held under the Gestapo's 'protective custody' orders (3,982). Even the Gestapo arrested many kinds of 'offenders', including asocials, so it is unlikely that all the Gestapo prisoners in the camp were 'politicals'.[66]

Camps like Buchenwald, therefore, incarcerated as many or more social outsiders as it did political foes like the Communists. This point holds also for the concentration camp north of Berlin at Sachsenhausen. The total camp population between June 1938 and September 1939 fluctuated between a low of just under 6,000 to a high of around 9,000. The main exception was December 1938 when the number of prisoners was reported at 12,622, which included many Jews sent there as part of the November pogrom.[67] The figures show that more than half the prisoners at any one time in this period were 'asocials'. No complete figures have survived for all of Germany of those who were held in preventive detention in subsequent 'actions'. A partial reconstruction shows that there were 12,921 at the end of 1938; 12,221 at the end of 1939; and 13,354 at the end of 1940.[68]

The effect of the war on the powers of the Kripo relative to those of the courts can be seen in what happened to the asocials. In a note from the Reich Security Main Office to the Kripo on 20 March 1940, the Kripo was told to ensure that anyone whom judges released from (court-ordered) 'preventive detention' would in fact not go free. If judicial authorities insisted on trying to do so in spite of Kripo objections, then the police should use 'preventive arrest' to send such persons to a concentration camp. The wartime principle was the same as the one for prisoners held on Gestapo orders: no one was to be released for the duration.[69]

It was perhaps to avoid being overtaken any further by the police, that the Minister of Justice reminded judges on 4 May 1940, to take wartime conditions into account when considering the release of prisoners. He noted that changed social conditions, like Germany's darkened streets, might reawaken the criminal tendencies of those whom it might have been appropriate to set free during peacetime. Apparently at least some judges continued releasing prisoners from preventive detention in spite of the expressed wishes of the police, and the Minister urged them to cease.[70]

The Reich Security Main Office (RSHA) ordered the Kripo on 18 June 1940 not to agree to the release of any asocials or anyone with a criminal record beyond petty offences, and to keep behind bars beggars and tramps who were repeat offenders. All Jews in the camps, given the 'current impossibility to emigrate', like all Gypsies, were to remain.[71]

The radicalizing effect of the war is one of the themes of this book, and it was made abundantly clear to anyone considered by police to be asocial. A note (23 January 1941) from Heydrich to the Kripo spoke of the need to deal more 'rigorously' with criminals, and the maximum period (up to one year!) the Kripo was allowed to hold prisoners in preventive detention without reviewing their case was changed into a minimum, with police themselves making the final decision.[72] Victor Klemperer noted how Nazi justice officials were 'justifying' the brutal treatment of asocial 'elements' at a time when the 'best' were being destroyed in the war.[73]

'Lives Unworthy of Living'

Another side of the official campaign to deal with broadly defined asocials and social outsiders was constituted by the 'euthanasia' programme. It involved medical specialists, nurses, and many others beyond the police. The concept of asociality had long included disabled hospital patients and handicapped children, and on more than one occasion from 1933 onwards, Hitler told confidants that he favoured 'euthanasia'. He mentioned to Hans Lammers of the Reich Chancellery in 1933, that he would like to have seen 'euthanasia' included in the sterilization laws, and said to Reich Doctors' Leader Wagner in 1935, that he would use wartime conditions to introduce some kind of programme, when it would be easier and smoother to do so, as less resistance from the churches could be expected then.[74] The decision to begin with children seems to have come about by a chance petition to Hitler in the autumn of 1938 from a father of a newly-born, but severely retarded child who additionally was blind and without an arm and a leg. The father with the family name Knauer asked permission for the child to be granted a 'mercy death'. The plea was brought to Hitler's attention by Philipp Bouhler, leader of the Chancellery of the Führer (KdF), perhaps in hopes of finding a new mission and certainly to gain favour.[75] Hitler took the time to order an investigation by his own physician, Dr Karl Brandt, and soon granted Knauer's wish.

In May 1939 Hitler ordered the creation of what became the secretive 'Reich Committee for the Scientific Registration of Serious Hereditarily- and Congenitally-based Illnesses', usually shortened to the Reich Committee. Hitler seems then also to have been strengthened in his resolve by advice from his personal physician Theo Morell, whose investigations in the summer of 1939 of public attitudes led him to conclude that few parents would be totally opposed to the 'mercy killing' of their chronically ill children, and would like to free themselves and perhaps their malformed children from suffering, but wanted to do so with a clear conscience.[76] By 18 August the Reich Committee had prepared circulars and began sending them to regional governments in search of information on 'deformed births etc.'[77] Those children were then transferred to one of thirty or so special clinics, where they were starved to death, given lethal injections, or murdered in some way. Altogether, more than 5,000 children were killed using various methods in the first phase of the programme.[78]

In June or July 1939 Hitler gave instructions to introduce 'euthanasia' for adults in an operation that eventually bore the code name T-4, a name taken from the address of headquarters in Berlin at Tiergarten Strasse 4. Sometime in October 1939 Hitler issued a specific authorization to Bouhler and Brandt to empower certain doctors to give a 'mercy death' to those whom they regarded as incurably ill, and backdated it to the first day of the war in 1939. Together with other decisions we have already seen, this timing clearly suggests that the coming of the war represented a significant turning point in Hitler's mind. Some thought was given to making 'euthanasia' legal. For example, in August 1939, the commission drawing up a new criminal code drafted a proposal suggesting that someone suffering from an incurable or terminal illness could request a mercy death, and that the life of someone suffering from incurable mental illness could be terminated.[79] Nothing came of that proposal as a law, but the killing proceeded (apart from T-4 operations) particularly in the context of the war with Poland, where incurably ill patients were taken from hospitals and shot by the SS. The same happened in regions in the eastern part of the country, such as Pomerania, West Prussia, and East Prussia, where in May and June 1940 the notorious Herbert Lange Commando began using a gas van to kill patients.[80]

Meanwhile in Berlin, plans took shape for an adult 'euthanasia' programme under the secret auspices of the KdF. On 9 October 1939 Viktor Brack, one of the main leaders of the T-4 operation in the KdF, calmly told a meeting of the steering group (including medical doctors, professors, and a representative of the Kripo) that he had calculated how many should be killed by way of the formula 1,000:10:5:1. Thus, for every 1,000 people, 10 needed psychiatric care; of whom five would be hospitalized, and of those, one patient would be killed. Given the population of 65 to 70 million at that time, the result would be that between 65,000 and 70,000 should be killed. They opted for gassing as the method, because there were too many people to give them injections or overdoses of medicine.[81]

The business of managing the operation soon grew too big, and the organizers moved into new headquarters at Tiergarten Strasse 4—with T-4 as the codename for their programme. The scope of the killing became impossible to keep secret; for one thing, death notices were commonly published in newspapers by the families of the deceased.

When the public got wind of what was happening, some family members wanted to know what was going on and some even rushed to remove their kin from hospitals and asylums. One woman wrote the hospital where her two siblings reportedly died within a few days of each other. She claimed to accept the Third Reich, and hoped to 'find peace again' if doctors could assure her that her siblings had been killed by virtue of some law that made it possible to 'relieve people from their chronic suffering'.[82] The official thinking behind the programme was left vague, so that some people believed that it was the Gestapo, not physicians, who were the murderers. To judge by contemporary reports, such as one by American newspaperman William Shirer, people knew roughly how many were killed and that Hitler had provided an authorization, not passed a law, so that the programme was illegal.[83] Even some Nazi officials expressed concern about the killings, especially because the open secret about them fuelled fantastic rumours, such as that wounded soldiers would also be killed. For some people, 'mercy killing' ran up against their religious, ethical, and legal principles. Nazis out in the provinces (women and men) seemed to feel that if there was a law with proper criteria and procedures along the lines of the sterilization laws, then the unrest would go away.[84]

Indeed, Reinhard Heydrich and others in the police drew up a draft 'Law for the Killing of Unfit Life and the Asocial', circulated it in July 1940, and kept up discussions into 1941. Hitler eventually vetoed such a law, partly because it was thought that enemy propaganda would capitalize on it, and perhaps also because he preferred to dispense with any limitations on his powers, even of the most sweeping laws.[85] The Nazis proceeded with their 'euthanasia' project and killed (by their own accounting) 70,273 people (exactly 273 beyond the target figure as calculated by Brack for the programme), and only then did Hitler call what was merely a temporary halt on 24 August 1941.[86]

Hitler did so, in some accounts, supposedly because of the public disquiet and especially because of the condemnation of it by Catholic Bishop Clemens August von Galen, who spoke of it in his sermon on 3 August 1941.[87] Among other things, von Galen suggested that the murder would spread to include invalids, the incurably sick, injured soldiers, or merely the unproductive, and noted that the police and courts could certainly not be trusted to investigate the murders. Although that sermon and isolated, but undeniable pockets of negative public opinion, may have played some role in halting 'euthanasia', such reactions most likely did not initiate the decision to call a temporary halt. Von Galen's and other expressions of disagreement probably reinforced that decision, which was easier to take, in that the programme already had met its initial killing target of 70,000 that was set before it began. That is the impression conveyed by Goebbels's brief mention of the topic in his diary the day before Hitler's stop order. The Propaganda Minister expressed relief that the radical and somewhat untimely action was 'at an end'.[88] Another factor may have been that the T-4 personnel were needed in the east where their expertise would be used in the mass murder of the Jews.[89]

In spite of the temporary halt to the gassings, the killing of children did not stop, and a distinct second phase of killing began in places like Hadamar from August 1942 onwards, where the methods changed to lethal injections, overdoses of drugs, and starving patients to death.[90] Moreover, undesired social behaviour or lifestyle that was considered asocial by medical experts came to be used as justifying the clinical executions, as happened in 1942 to an unruly young woman (17 years old) with some long-term medical and mental problems. She had been able to finish school for the handicapped and was not confined to an institution, but was taken from her home when she grew difficult for her parents to handle. Although she may have needed some help, and before the war, would probably have been sterilized, in 1942 she was sent to a mental hospital where she was killed.[91]

When radical 'euthanasia' stopped in the asylums, it shifted almost immediately to the concentration camps in Germany. In early 1941, Himmler had approached Bouhler in hopes of using T-4 gassing facilities to free concentration camps of 'human ballast', including asocials, criminals, Jews, and others.[92] Presumably there were too many such people to be shot out of hand and disposed in the camps, and Himmler wanted them done away with more efficiently. He was thinking in radical terms at that point, for at almost the same time he asked Brack to investigate the technical feasibility of mass sterilization of the Jews, but did not take up the matter again until later.[93] In the meantime, in

September SS doctors and the Gestapo in camps such as Dachau, Mauthausen, Ravensbrück, Buchenwald, Flossenbürg, and Neuengamme made preliminary selections of prisoners, from whom panels of visiting T-4 physicians picked the victims for gassing in an operation with the code name 'Action 14f 13'. The number '14f' was used as code for all deaths in the camps, while other digits that followed it were a code for how the victim died: '13' stood for gassing. The first group selected to be killed were asocials, but any Jews in these camps were especially vulnerable. T-4 doctors used not only medical, but also social and racial criteria in their selections, and sealed the fate of individuals whose symptoms they described variously as 'fanatical German-hater and asocial psychopath'; or someone as having a 'long prison record'; or another for being 'habitually guilty of race defilement'.[94] Evidence of T-4 evaluations of female Jews justifying their murder included having an 'attitude hostile to the state', or merely suffering from a venereal disease.[95] Up to 20,000 such persons were gassed in T-4 facilities at Bernburg, Hartheim, and Sonnenstein in this action alone.[96] By 26 March 1942, as more people were needed to work, Himmler reminded camp authorities to pay attention to labour needs before they sent prisoners to their deaths, and on 27 April 1943, he restricted the killing further to those who were mentally ill and could not work.[97]

There was at best a muted public response to 'euthanasia', and according to more than one recent account, public opinion was 'quite divided'.[98] Historians continue to debate what citizens thought about this programme, with some suggesting that eliminating mentally ill adults 'was not entirely unpopular', and that killing handicapped children 'appears to have received a broad level of public support throughout the country'.[99] The regime itself provided remarkably little guidance to citizens, passed no laws, nor issued much more than a few statements, as if official silence rather than active propaganda would help to foster the public's physical and psychological distance from the victims. Not surprisingly, the regime registered at least some negative opinions and complaints. Hitler, ever wishing to be a popularly backed dictator, may have decided in August 1941, that the moment was right to end that phase of the operation, all the more as the (relatively few) negative remarks, some local unease, and von Galen's sermon showed that the social agreement and level of acceptance of the programme might not have been what he hoped it would be. The dissenting opinions, however, at most reinforced Hitler's decision.[100] Such disquiet 'lent added urgency to the regime's efforts to win, if not support, then collusive passivity' in face of the killings.[101] From the medical personnel involved, of course, the killing programme required and obtained more active support. As a recent study of nurses has shown, they went along—sometimes with reservations—and for a wide variety of reasons, not simply because they shared all the negative attitudes towards 'lives unworthy of living'.[102]

Although some Catholic leaders spoke out, at almost the same moment they openly welcomed the war against the USSR, and said next to nothing about the persecution of the Jews.[103]

We also have evidence that many ordinary citizens and even religious leaders of Catholic and Protestant faiths did not condemn 'mercy-killing' in principle, regarding it as justified under some circumstances, and some leaders of both faiths continued to think so even after 1945.[104] The organizers of the murders, when explaining their programme to a meeting of justice officials in April 1941, claimed that 80 per cent of the relatives of those killed 'agree' with what happened, 10 per cent 'protest', and the other 10 per cent were 'indifferent'.[105] Some individuals wrote letters of complaint, and we do have one case where townspeople blocked buses moving patients in a small Bavarian town (Absberg) on 21 February 1941, but that seems to have been one of the only exceptions to the rule of silence, indifference, toleration, and support.[106]

Judicial officials all across Germany reported that where there was some 'disquiet' among the people, the main cause of which was that they were not aware of any legal basis to the programme. Some areas of the country raised no objections at all, however, but most wanted to ensure proper safeguards and legal procedures.[107]

The Nazis' own public opinion surveys rarely dealt with 'euthanasia', but in early 1942, did so in the context of surveying responses to '*I accuse*', an enormously popular film—seen by over 15 million people—on the theme.[108] The report noted that 'almost without exception the *broad mass* of the German people has reacted favourably to the issues raised', but there were reservations that had more to do with procedures than the principle involved. Churches were generally against the practice, and most people wanted extensive medical consultation in the decision about whether a disease was incurable. The report concluded that 'all in all, from the wealth of material at hand, that in general the practice of euthanasia is approved when decided by a committee of several doctors with the agreement of the incurable patient and his [*sic*] relatives. The general approval culminates in the agreement with the words of the Major in the film: "The state demands from us the *duty* to die, then it should grant to us also the *right* to die." '[109]

Historian Götz Aly among others has wondered what would have happened if there had been more vocal protests, and suggests that negative responses might have slowed down 'euthanasia', and perhaps also hindered the genocide that began in 1941. He shows with considerable plausibility, that the secrecy surrounding the killings was never intended to keep all information from leaking out. That the programme was officially a 'secret Reich matter', however, 'gave the public and those who indirectly shared in the crime the opportunity to give their tacit consent'.[110] As it was, he continues, most relatives did not want to know too much, and numerous German families were prepared to accept the murder of their closest relatives without protest, even with approval. By so doing, they created the psychological conditions for the genocidal policies carried out in the years to come. If people did not protest even when their relatives were murdered, they could hardly be expected to object to the murder of Jews, Gypsies, Russians, and Poles.[111]

Sinti and Roma

The radicalizing effects of war had fateful consequences for all social outsiders, especially those known as the 'Gypsies'. Social prejudice and state policy against this group in Germany went back well before 1933, and both grew worse during the Nazi era. The Sinti and Roma, as they preferred to call themselves on the basis of their different languages and cultures, were a small minority in Europe and especially in Germany, where in 1933 there were an estimated 20,000 of them. There were many more in what would become the annexed or occupied areas of the Third Reich. Hitler himself said little about these people, so that their persecution in Germany and the murder of so many of them in the Third Reich suggests that the inspiration came from elsewhere.

Sinti and Roma were subjected to official harassment initially in Nazi Germany because they were stereotyped as an outsider racial group prone to criminality. They were unwilling or unable to hold a regular job, establish a fixed abode, so that they were seen as something of a social problem.[112] Local and regional (non-Nazi Party) authorities were quick to see the advantages of Hitler's regime to solve their own 'Gypsy problem'. The common denominator of many suggestions and/or demands for action from 1933 onwards that originated 'below', from mayors, county councillors, welfare officials, as well as the police and others, was that the Sinti and Roma should be confined to a camp, with or without barbed wire. Occasionally more radical proposals were made, as in Lower Franconia, a Catholic region in northern Bavaria, and an area not noted for its support of Nazism, where the demand was made in 1935 and 1936 by several local government authorities that all 'Gypsies' be sent to Dachau.[113]

However, the initial police approach was to enforce more vigorously the measures that were already on the books, and a limited number were sent to concentration camps. Between 1935 and 1939 specific camps were created in cities such as Cologne, Düsseldorf, Essen, Frankfurt, Hamburg, Magdeburg, and Berlin. The camps were less than concentration camps, but life in them was far more regimented than in traditional camping grounds, and soon barbed wire was added. After 1939 these camps were used for internment purposes where Sinti and Roma were kept until their deportation to the east.[114]

The dictatorship centralized the approach to the 'Gypsy problem', and created a 'Reich Central Headquarters to Combat the Gypsy Pest' under the authority of the Kripo in October 1938 with headquarters in Berlin. The significant powers already conferred on the Kripo to deal with groups like the asocials and 'work-shy' were also employed. Precisely how many were arrested and sent to concentration camps in the various police campaigns of 1938 has not been established, but isolated evidence suggests that police took the opportunity to arrest 'Gypsies' when they had the chance, such as when a police check revealed they had no regular work. Even so, it would seem that the number arrested in 1938 was generally small and a fraction of the minority living in Germany.[115]

The Nazis' main priority by 1938 with regard to 'Gypsy Research' was to determine exactly how many there were, and to register and supervise them more closely. Himmler issued fundamentally new guidelines to police on 8 December under the heading, the 'Battle Against the Gypsy Plague'. That term harked back to police usages in Germany even before the Nazis took over.[116] According to new guidelines, experience in this 'battle' and racial-biological research supposedly showed that a national approach was called for, one that considered the Gypsies as comprised of 'mixed race' and 'pure-breeds'. The 'eventual solution of the Gypsy question' would entail dealing with each separately.[117] Michael Zimmermann has recently shown that until that point none of the Nazi racial researchers considered Gypsies to be a 'race', so that formulation of the guidelines sent a signal that police persecution of Sinti and Roma would adopt an explicit racist approach, with predictable consequences.[118]

The Nazis wanted to register all members of this minority and establish their 'racial background'. Kripo headquarters in Berlin was put in charge, and specifically its new special branch that dealt with Gypsies. The Kripo's 'preventive campaign against crime', supported by its theory of social biology as put forward by Arthur Nebe, led to the confinement of many German and Austrian 'asocial Gypsies'. Local police were ordered to report anyone 'who by their appearance, their morals and habits can be regarded as Gypsies or Gypsies of mixed race, including also others who travel about like Gypsies'. The more numerous Sinti, the smaller number of Roma, and other related groups like the Lalleri in the incorporated areas were registered, and by 1 March 1939 most were forced to undergo a racial-biological examination.[119] A sign of things to come was that in early July the Kripo was told that, in the event of war mobilization, 'Gypsies' with no fixed abode were to be sent to a concentration camp, along with the vague category of social outsiders termed 'those considered unworthy of serving in the armed forces'.[120]

Dr Robert Ritter headed the race experts who began to work closely with the Kripo. He was in charge of a 'Racial Hygienic and Human Biological Research Centre' at the Reich Health Office. Although not a Nazi before 1933, Ritter soon adopted research interests that were considered very important by the Kripo, especially his work on the racial-biological make-up of criminals. That the Nazi regime was interested in this topic can be seen from the fact that already in October 1936 Justice Minister Gürtner ordered investigations into the background of criminals at the fifty examination stations he established across the country.[121]

In 1936 when Ritter was appointed as the head of the new Racial Hygiene Office, he had been working on various projects dealing with the relationship between heredity and crime by focusing on family histories. His theory was that there was a biological or genetic basis to criminal behaviour, and he noted that Gypsies of 'mixed race' were especially prone to crime.[122] Ritter wanted criminal biologists 'to discover whether or not certain signs can be found among men which would allow the early detection of criminal behaviour, signs which would allow the recognition of criminal tendencies *before* the actual onset of the criminal career'.[123] His institute worked closely with Kripo headquarters, and they shared the theory that biology was the key to understanding, fighting, and eliminating criminality, and it was no surprise that Ritter's ascent was crowned by his appointment in 1941 to head the Criminal Biological Institute of the Security Police. In 1939 Himmler ordered that henceforth an integral part of a criminal investigation would entail research into the racial-biological and family background of suspects.[124]

The campaign against the 'Gypsy plague' was stepped up first in Austria, when the Kripo was ordered to deal with the problem in 1938 and especially in June 1939. They were to arrest 2,000 or so men, and about 1,000 women, and send the men to Dachau, and the women to Ravensbrück.[125] September and October 1939 marked a turning point in both the police system and racial persecution. At a meeting on 21 September 1939 the first of several fateful decisions was taken that affected the German Jews and those in newly conquered Poland. Chaired by Reinhard Heydrich, the meeting took a number of important steps, such as ordering the creation of Jewish Councils in the occupied areas, whose members were '*fully responsible* (in the literal sense of the word) for the exact execution according to terms of all instructions released or yet to be released'.[126] The results included the decision to force Jews into the cities; to send Jews from the Reich to Poland; and also to send the remaining 'Gypsies' to Poland.[127]

The registration of the Sinti and Roma in Germany was completed before the war, and there were isolated attempts in October 1939, without much success, to ship them by attaching them to the trains of the first deportations of Jews to the Lublin region of Poland. Such haphazard efforts were soon halted by Himmler.[128] Head of the Kripo, Arthur Nebe wondered on 13 October 1939, whether it would be possible to send Berlin's Gypsies to the 'planned reservation' in the east for the Jews and others.[129] Days later Himmler told the Kripo that 'within a short time for the entire area of the Reich, the Gypsy question will be fundamentally regulated according to uniform standards'. The Kripo was ordered by Heydrich as head of the RSHA on 17 October 1939 to ensure, with the cooperation of local police and gendarmerie, that all Gypsies, including those of mixed race, should not be allowed to change their place of residence, and to send them to a concentration camp if they tried. Police were told that any Gypsies discovered later were 'to be kept in collective camps until their final deportation'.[130]

At the beginning of 1940 Ritter's Gypsy research concluded that about 90 per cent of all those in the German Reich were of mixed race, that is, they were prone to crime. Ritter flatly stated that the 'Gypsy question' would be solved 'if the bulk of the asocial and useless Gypsies of mixed race are assembled in large, migrating work camps and forced to work, and if the further propagation of this mixed-race population is finally hindered. Only then will the coming generations of the German people be really freed of this burden.'[131]

The Ministry of the Interior wrote to the Kripo and other police on 24 January 1940 earnestly suggesting the complete sterilization of all 'Gypsies' including those of mixed race, as the 'ultimate solution of the Gypsy problem'. The main question seemed to be whether they should all be sterilized before the date set for deportation, and if no longer a biological danger, whether they might be exploited as workers in Germany.[132] Nothing came of the suggestion, partly because the technical means of mass sterilization was not developed. On 27 April 1940 the Kripo was ordered to begin the 'resettlement' operation, starting with the western and north-western parts of Germany. The Kripo in Hamburg and Bremen were to collect 1,000 Gypsies from their area; the Kripo in Cologne, Düsseldorf, and Hanover were to add another 1,000; and from the Frankfurt and Stuttgart regions, a final 500 were to make up a 'first transport' of 2,500 to be sent to occupied Poland in mid-May.[133] Detailed 'guidelines for the resettlement' were issued to police, using language that became common in the later deportation of the Jews, especially as regards what each person could take with them.[134] Also a sign of things to come, those rounded up as Gypsies were strip-searched for valuables, and in public view, an experience they found deeply shaming.[135]

The hope expressed by the orders to the Kripo was that more deportations from Germany would follow, but the plan was opposed by Hans Frank, now in charge of the General Government, the district constructed out of parts of former Poland. Frank's jurisdiction was designated as the dumping grounds for the Gypsies and Jews, but he got a temporary cessation of the trains. The Sinti and Roma in Germany were stuck in no man's land, unable to carry on their lives as of old, but condemned to wait in camps for what might happen. The Kripo was informed on 22 June 1941, the day on which Germany opened war on the Soviet Union, that for the moment 'a general and definitive solution of the Gypsy question' could not be carried out.[136] However, behind the lines in the East, the death squads who began shooting Jews, also murdered many Sinti and Roma as well.

Police out in the provinces and security officials in Berlin were not alone in wanting to be rid of the Sinti and Roma. Local initiatives, originating in communities in which they were bound over, came from cities and towns, from local Nazi Party branches, businesses, mayors, and local dignitaries who wanted to make their village or city district 'totally free of Gypsies'. The motives behind these suggestions, ranged from social and racial prejudices to persistent concerns about crime, sex, and morality.[137]

In the period during which the Kripo awaited orders from Berlin to start deportations, conflicts festered among Nazi leaders and institutions about what should happen. In the camps in Germany and annexed Austria in the meantime, conditions were often as deadly as in concentration camps. The waiting period was used by Dr Ritter and the Kripo's Gypsy branch, to study them as if they were laboratory specimens.[138] Ritter's interest in 'family origins' later brought him to investigate female Jehovah's Witnesses in the Ravensbrück concentration camp, in order to evaluate their 'racial worth'.[139]

There were at least three different and competing schemes used to classify the 'Gypsies', all of them racist to the core. Unlike the Jews, the Gypsies of 'pure race' came to be regarded by Himmler as worth preserving, almost as exotic and romantic collector's items, on a 'reservation' in the east.[140] Himmler's orientalist point of view won the day, even though for a time Hitler, Bormann, and Minister of Justice Thierack wanted no exceptions to the deportations. Himmler finally issued orders on 16 December 1942 for the deportations to begin, and not just of Sinti and Roma from Germany, to Auschwitz-Birkenau. Hitler was informed and raised no objections.[141] The main deportations from Germany, based on Himmler's orders to the Kripo, began in early 1943.[142] Although Himmler left options open to local Kripo and other communal authorities to make choices about whom to include, they used the opportunity to make their communities totally 'free of Gypsies'. In areas where Sinti or Roma still lived—and where they were forced by police to stay—citizens had developed resentment towards their continuing presence, and those feelings hardened after the outbreak of the war, and in turn affected the behaviour of local authorities. In Germany the persecution was directed especially by the Kripo against the 'asocial Gypsies' and those of 'mixed race' who had settled down, left their old ways of life, but thereby grown closer to the majority society and supposedly threatened the purity of the 'body politic'. Most Germans did not notice the disappearance and deportation of this tiny minority, but those who did, turned away, were indifferent, or agreed with it.[143]

Outside Germany, the trend was to persecute and murder Sinti and Roma who wandered and who had kept to their traditions—partly because they were accused of being anti-German spies in the service of the 'Jewish-Bolshevik' enemy.[144] Michael Zimmermann's authoritative new study, concludes that around 15,000 persons who lived in Germany and were labelled as 'Gypsies or

Gypsies of mixed race' were murdered during the Nazi era.[145] However, many times that number were killed in other parts of Europe, either shot out of hand by the police, SS, or the army, often side by side with the Jews, or sent to camps like Auschwitz to be worked to death, used in human experiments, sterilized (inside the camps and in Germany), or gassed.[146] Sybil Milton suggests that between one-quarter and one-half million Roma and Sinti were murdered during the Holocaust years.[147]

Sexual Outsiders

The lives of women and men in the Third Reich were often deeply affected by official concerns about sex, reproduction, and race. A racist regime inevitably focuses an enormous amount of its resources in regulating and dealing with sex. In the first instance, the 'wrong' kind of sex had to be hindered, so it was not surprising that, as we will see in detail in the following chapters, Hitler and the Nazis were particularly keen to outlaw sexual relations between Jews, other race 'enemies', and Germans. The racial hygienic basis of the Third Reich virtually guaranteed that considerable efforts would be made to deal with prostitution and its part in spreading sexually transmitted diseases. As well, there was a crackdown on other sexual outsiders, particularly the homosexuals.

Hitler long regarded prostitution and the diseases that resulted, as typical symptoms of decay and degeneration.[148] One of the first steps of the new regime, was to issue orders for police to use measures on the books (such as laws on spreading venereal diseases) to eliminate street prostitution; to control brothels; and to charge prostitutes if and when they offered their services in public in a conspicuous way.[149] Local police enforcement of these measures varied greatly, but there certainly were round-ups in many cities during 1933. Hamburg was not typical in that it was well known for its large number of prostitutes, but there the police arrested some 3,201 women between March and the end of August 1933; most were let off with a warning and/or soon released, but 274 were forced to undergo treatment for venereal disease.[150] The scope of these arrests suggests that considerable numbers of women were involved in prostitution, but the full extent remains hidden, because much prostitution was carried out on an 'occasional' basis to supplement incomes.[151]

Not only the police, but health, welfare, and youth officials soon became involved in the campaign to deal with this group of asocials, and one trend was to seek the sterilization of repeat offenders. These authorities used the new system to deal with bothersome cases, like two young women who had been giving trouble in Reutlingen since at least 1929. By 1932, Anna and Klara (still in their teens) were reportedly engaged in prostitution in Stuttgart; along with their mother, they were considered by the authorities to be genetically inferior.

Beginning in 1933, the new dictatorship provided the Youth Office with more radical means to deal with the family. By November 1935, the youngest sister Elsa (born 1920) was sterilized, and the Youth Office, which also petitioned for the same thing for Anna and Klara (both of whom were by then married), in all likelihood was granted its wish. Evidently, the authorities regarded these women 'as threats to the genetic/racial purity of the *Volksgemeinschaft*'.[152] We know that similar events unfolded all across the country. In 1933, the Health Offices in Germany had 20,000 women like Anna and Klara on their books, women accused of 'frequently changing their sexual partners'.[153]

The war brought major changes in how prostitution would be dealt with for the duration. On 9 September 1939 the Reich Minister of the Interior ordered police to register all prostitutes, and to ensure their examination by health officials. Prostitution in public now was totally outlawed, but it was permitted in specific houses to meet local 'need', and, as required, the police were to oversee the establishment of such brothels.[154] As follow-up reminders suggested shortly after, the real worry was the spread of venereal disease.[155]

The Kripo had long used its powers to deal with prostitutes, but during the war they cracked down especially on those who tried to work on their own outside officially permitted brothels, and sent these offenders to concentration camps as asocials. Young women who went out alone or with different men, others who seemed to know many men, but had no regular work, all had to worry about accusations that they were secretly working as prostitutes. We certainly have cases from the wartime where health authorities turned in women when they suffered a repeated case of venereal disease, or were merely picked up as homeless after a marriage breakdown.

It was indicative of the official emphasis on race, sex, and health, that during the war the Health Offices informed the police and asked that an 'offender' be sent to a concentration camp. From cases that survive, we can see how the system worked. For example, on 14 August 1941 the Kripo in Essen ordered the 'preventive arrest' of a 38-year-old woman who had neglected her four children and her home, and had relationships with a number of men even before her stormy marriage finally collapsed. At some point the welfare office took away her children, and she was sterilized. She wandered the streets of Duisburg, had no fixed address, and apparently led a promiscuous life until the Kripo picked her up as constituting a danger to public health. The Kripo claimed that her immoral behaviour and asocial attitude justified their sending her to Ravensbrück, where she arrived on 13 September 1941. For reasons unknown in her file, she was sent on to Auschwitz on 25 March 1942, and died there on 23 July.[156]

If we can extrapolate from the small sample of Kripo files that survive for Duisburg, there seem to be indications that similar fates must have befallen many other women, such as one turned in by the Health Office in November 1941, among other things, for avoiding 'control measures' and an ordered medical examination. The Kripo concluded she was 'morally decadent and work-shy', so that she was arrested and sent via Ravensbrück to Auschwitz, where she died on 3 November 1942.[157] The general impression created by these files is that the Kripo used whatever accusations came to mind—whether prostitution, lesbianism, asociality, or being work-shy—to get rid of bothersome or unruly women. The Kripo used their new powers to dispatch women whose behaviour they found unbecoming in a German 'racial comrade' to a concentration camp without even a semblance of a hearing or court appearance.

During the war, the Kripo not only hounded suspicious women, but they also established large numbers of brothels, and by 1942 the Kripo had set up 28 such houses in Berlin alone. There are good grounds for concluding there were as many and more in port cities like Hamburg.[158] In addition, by the end of 1943, the regime had created as many as 60 brothels for foreign workers, with another 50 in preparation, in which foreign women worked as prostitutes. Brothels also were set up in many concentration camps. If we take the full range of all these establishments into account, state-sanctioned prostitution in the Third Reich reached considerable proportions.

The SD report of late November 1943 on the brothels or 'B' barracks for foreign workers noted that most Germans did not agree that the state should spend the considerable sums necessary to build them, and would have preferred the money used for sheltering homeless Germans. However, the priority for the regime, was 'maintaining the purity of the blood'. Citizens were told that the presence of foreign workers in the country 'ought under no circumstances to lead to a decline or even destruction of the German blood pool'. The report noted that the delicacy of the subject made discussions of it in public difficult, so that the Party should deal with it on an individual basis. If the consequences of 'race mixing' were forcefully explained, the report concluded, then citizens would recognize the need to avoid contacts with the foreign workers, and also that it was necessary to create these brothels for them.[159]

Homosexuals were also regarded as threats to the body politic by Hitler and many Nazi leaders, and those sentiments were not unpopular in Germany at the time. Hitler was reported as saying even before 1914, that homosexuality should be fought 'by any means possible', and said he turned 'against this and other sexual perversions in the big city with nausea and disgust'.[160] Police persecution of homosexuals in Germany was not new, but beginning in 1933 they stepped up enforcement of laws on the books since the nineteenth century that criminalized homosexuality. The Nazi police began to deal with 'public immorality', and outlawed trashy publications and pornography.[161] Local police, also created special branches to arrest traders in obscene literature or pictures.[162] Although lesbianism also offended what the Nazis called 'wholesome popular sentiment', there was no systematic campaign, partly because lesbianism was not regarded as a serious 'danger to the nation's survival'.[163]

At the end of October 1934 a special branch to fight homosexuality was created at Gestapo headquarters in Berlin to coordinate activities against gay men. On 28 June 1935 the regime sharpened the criminal code. Arrests were carried out in the summer of 1936, such as in Hamburg, where a Special Section of the Gestapo was formed. These and other such actions revealed that an alleged 'epidemic' of homosexuality had spread to all professional groups and social classes.[164] Himmler encouraged Gestapo and Kripo to do their bit, and in 1936 a new 'Reich Central Office for Combating Homosexuality and Abortion' was created to register all homosexuals investigated by police.

The press pilloried homosexuals tried before the courts, especially in 1936 and 1937, with many stories of the alleged homosexual activities of religious orders.[165] These accounts of the clergy in court formed part of the effort to discredit the Catholic Church and to stop all sexual deviancy. Stories were published about abortionists, and there was a steady diet of gruesome accounts of paedophiles, some of whom were involved in the serial murders of young boys.[166]

The persecution of homosexuals was reflected in court verdicts on men charged and convicted for breaking the provisions of the Criminal Code. In 1933 there was a small increase in the number of gay men who were convicted in comparison to the last Weimar years (853 convictions, up slightly from 801 in 1932). Arrests rose in each of the following years as follows: 1934 (948); 1935 (2,106); 1936 (5,320); 1937 (8,271); 1938 (8,562). Amnesties had the effect of underestimating the extent of all crimes, and the one at the beginning of the war reduced convictions for 1939—falling to 7,614. During the war, the numbers declined further, to 3,773 in 1940; 3,739 in 1941; 2,678 in 1942; 2,218 in 1943, which was the last year for which we have figures.[167]

Gestapo records on homosexual suspects survive for three areas in Germany centred around the cities of Düsseldorf, Würzburg, and in the Palatinate. They show that the largest numbers were brought in between 1936 and 1938.[168] Many arrested in smaller cities and rural locations were not caught by the police, but denounced by citizens. In larger cities like Düsseldorf, however, which had something of a gay sub-culture and well-known hangouts, surprise police raids took place. Even there, the police relied on collaboration from the population.[169]

The Nazis criminalized mere expressions of sexual interest, not just consummated homosexual acts, and thus opened the door for denunciations from the public. The motives behind these denunciations, in so far as they can be identified at all, varied from wishes to support official policies on gays, to take advantage of the situation, or merely to gain in some way personally.[170] Under police pressure, many 'confessed', as did 47 per cent of all those arrested by the Gestapo in Würzburg; 37 per cent in the Palatinate; and 10 per cent in Düsseldorf.[171]

The Kripo also dealt with homosexuality, and because of competition with the Gestapo, officials working for both seemed to double their efforts. In the years after 1935, the Kripo arrested large numbers of gays. For example, between April and December 1936, the Kripo alone investigated 6,260 men for suspicion of homosexual activities, and in the same period a year later, the number rose to 12,356. In order to appreciate the fear behind the statistics, we have to recall that Germany then had a system of 'police justice', and any brush with the police could have disastrous consequences.

Kripo investigations show an upward trend until statistics stopped in the early war period. Some of the increase resulted because the Gestapo got out of the business of harassing the homosexuals and the Kripo picked up the slack.[172] Kripo enforcement methods, like those of the Gestapo, ranged from entrapment to planting evidence. If and when the accused happened also to be Jewish and/or was considered objectionable for other reasons, then persecution might not relent until the man was sent to a concentration camp and hounded to death.[173]

Once in a police cell, gays were put under such pressure that some took their own lives as a way out.[174] Men known to police because they had been convicted as homosexuals were singled out in the guidelines of the Kripo on preventive custody.[175] Homosexuals could also be placed under 'planned surveillance' and, if they were repeat offenders, held in preventive custody. They were vulnerable to indignities, coerced into self-incrimination, and even into agreeing to being castrated. Although it was officially forbidden by a joint decree (23 January 1936) of the Ministries of the Interior and Justice to pressure homosexuals into castration, a communication from Himmler to the Kripo of 20 May 1939 said that it could be suggested to homosexuals in preventive custody that their 'probable' release would follow if they agreed to castration.[176] Another communication to the Kripo (12 July 1940) ordered that henceforth any homosexual who 'seduced' more than one partner was, on their release from prison, to be placed in preventive custody, unless and until a medical examination could prove there was no fear of a relapse into 'homosexual failings'.[177] Medical examinations were to follow after the first month, then after one-, three-, and five-year intervals to check on the 'success' of the castration. The men were also kept under 'close supervision' by police.[178]

We know much less about what happened to gays in the military during World War II. Some preliminary findings suggest that, at least compared to what happened in World War I, there were in all probability 25 times as many convicted by military courts.[179] Whether or not the total number of convictions went on rising, or even declined somewhat after 1939, we should not lose sight of the fact that anyone picked up by the Gestapo or Kripo could end up dead. At Himmler's request, on 15 November 1941 Hitler approved the use of the death penalty for anyone guilty of homosexual activities in the SS and police.[180] As

Himmler put it in follow-up instructions, the SS and police had to be kept free of the 'parasites' because they themselves were leading 'the struggle for the complete elimination of homosexuality among the German people'.[181]

In principle there remained an important difference between the police persecution of homosexuals (and most criminals), and what happened to 'race enemies' like the Jews. When it came to homosexuals, as well as most others deemed criminals, the object was not so much their physical annihilation, but instead it was, as far as possible, to rehabilitate and re-educate them.[182] In principle, nothing could rescue Jews. Nevertheless, many gays ended up in a concentration camp, and a shockingly high number of them, estimated at somewhere between 5,000 and 15,000, died there.[183] To that number must be added those killed in action when, given something of a choice between sitting out the rest of their prison sentence or serving in what was euphemistically called a 'probationary battalion' at the front, they opted for the latter when often that was as good as a death sentence. That the number of homosexuals who died in the camps (or at the front in these battalions) might appear to be relatively 'modest' is only in comparison to the massive numbers of others killed by the Nazis as 'enemies'.

Juvenile Delinquents

Young people were among Hitler's strongest supporters, and oral history projects and the autobiographies of young people who experienced these times, testify that the appeals to youth were remarkably successful.[184] Melita Maschmann, as a young woman in the girls' branch of the Hitler Youth, was swept away by antisemitism as well as new teachings that awakened in her a sense of idealism and spirit of self-sacrifice based on the theory of being part of the 'master race'.[185] On the other hand, juvenile delinquency was a problem at the beginning of Hitler's regime, and it did not go away.[186] Although down to the war years, youth crime grew, the figures would have shown even more growth, but for the amnesties that annulled many cases.[187] Also the Hitler Youth (HJ), which by March 1939 was compulsory, had its own Foot Patrol and dealt with petty crimes and rowdy behaviour on their own.[188]

The Gestapo became involved in dealing with juvenile delinquency, particularly when the activities involved so-called 'bands, cliques, and gangs' whose activities were criminalized.[189] In fact, these young people wanted to avoid the regimentation of the Hitler Youth, to enjoy jazz music, dancing, and unsupervised outings in the countryside. By 1936 most youth organizations, especially those linked to the Communist, Socialist, and Catholic parties, were destroyed. Working-class youth who were individualistic enough to reject the uniformities demanded by the Hitler Youth, gravitated into informal groups or cliques and often dressed or wore their hair in such a way as to make a statement. The Gestapo was uncertain about what to call these 'wild' or disorganized groups and opted for labelling them as part of the 'Bundisch' youth, thereby attributing more of an organizational status than these loose groupings really possessed. The label harked back to the youth movement at the turn of the century and the Weimar years, but most of those picked up by the Gestapo were too young to have had links either with those pre-Nazi movements or with those of the working class.

Along with outlawing these 'organizations' in 1936, the Gestapo established a 'Special Commando for Combating the Bundisch Youth in the West' in Düsseldorf. A recent study of the Gestapo's activities against these ill-organized youth bands turned up 1,441 police files, most based on tips from civilians. The informants, some of whom simply invented charges, were mostly members or functionaries of the Hitler Youth or Nazi Party. The Commando's busiest time was during the war, when 80 per cent of the interrogations of suspected clique members took place.[190]

The Kripo established a Special Branch for Combating Youth Crime at its Berlin headquarters on 1 July 1939, and it focused on youth who 'appear by heredity as prone to criminality', like the children of professional and habitual criminals. It adopted measures like finding foster homes or welfare institutions, but if all else failed the police were given the option of using preventive detention.[191]

The Reich Security Main Office offered the Kripo reasons to adopt a new approach to juvenile delinquency, in a follow-up instruction on 1 December 1939. It reported the signs that youth criminality was growing, and that wartime conditions fostered crime, and spread prostitution and homosexuality. In spite of a shortage of officials, the Kripo should investigate all cases, and when they discovered repeat offenders or others whose upbringing was neglected, they should consider whether 'special educative measures' were called for. Young girls should be warned away from sexual activities that could spread sexually transmitted diseases.[192]

The Kripo was informed on 1 April 1940 that a special place of confinement for 'criminally endangered and asocials', was under consideration. Within two weeks the police were to contact welfare institutions to determine the numerical dimension of the problem.[193] On 26 June the Kripo was told it would soon be possible to accommodate these minors in a 'police camp for the protection of youth'. Such a camp was set up at Moringen, designed to hold young males, such as those who outgrew welfare institutions (because of their age), or for whom welfare training had proven pointless. At the same time, there was a plan to establish a similar camp for young females at Uckermark, but it only became operational two years later.[194] Kripo headquarters in Berlin asked for 'suggestions' from regional offices by 20 July 1940, to be forwarded to the new 'Reich

Central for the Battle Against Youth Criminality'. Confinement in the camp could follow a trial, or simply on the orders of the police.[195]

Paul Werner of the Kripo published accounts of the camp to put it in the best possible light, many visitors were permitted, and stories about it appeared elsewhere.[196] One of the most detailed explained that it was established in the context of the 'police-preventive work in the battle against the criminality of youth'. Young men would be sent there, only after all 'the usual social-pedagogical methods' failed to influence them. The aim was not punishment, but a 'timely protection of the community from asocials and criminals', who had shown their 'deviant disposition' and 'false way of life'. The camp was described as part of a long-term plan for youth and by no means merely a temporary expedient.[197] It was located in the village of Moringen, not far from Göttingen and Nordheim.[198] Prisoners were marched out daily in work details, and the population, in keeping with the usual approach used to explain the presence of concentration camps, was warned that prisoners were 'murderers, dangerous criminals, and street robbers'.[199] Age limits for prisoners at Moringen were raised to the end of 21 years and, under exceptional circumstances, boys younger than 16 could be confined there.[200]

It was not so much that youth criminality became a major problem in Nazi Germany, and that sheer numbers of delinquents forced their attention on the Kripo. In fact the police sought out these people and asked youth offices across the country to check their files to see if they had problem cases who could be sent to the camp.[201] The creation of Moringen, and especially the message conveyed to the many visitors from the courts and the Nazi Party, indicated that the police wanted to expand their mission to include welfare and educative tasks. Visitors were assured that the camp experience would transform this 'negative human material', and that they could be 'won back for the community of the people'.[202] A report from July 1944 noted that half the 'pupils' sent to the camp until then had criminal records and others were welfare cases. They were regarded as worthy specimens for research purposes, and it was little wonder that Director Dr Ritter from the Criminal Biological Institute was a frequent visitor.[203] In fact, the prisoners were problem cases that various localities wanted to be rid of, and plenty of 'suggestions' flooded in, so much so that officials called a halt soon after the camp opened. The camp's initial capacity of 150 was expanded to hold an additional 400 delinquents. The inmate population rose to 620 by 1942 and 674 the next year. The camp for young girls at Uckermark was filled to a capacity of 200 within months of opening in June 1942.[204]

The same 'paternalistic' approach led in March 1940 to the proclamation of measures that criminalized many aspects of social life and youthful leisure time activities. Thereafter, anyone under 18 years of age was not allowed to smoke in public or to loiter after dark; they were forbidden to enter bars, or to visit entertainment places like movies, or go to dances, unless accompanied by an adult;

and even then they could not stay later than 11:00 p.m.[205] Stories in the press lauded the Kripo for carrying out systematic checks, taking young people to task, and even warning parents to take responsibility for their young.[206] Another invention of the war years was 'youth arrest'. Introduced in October 1940, partly to deal with minor offences, it was a measure by which the courts and the police (also the Hitler Youth) could order minors confined at justice facilities. They would not have a criminal record and to the extent they were employed, they could keep their job and serve their time on weekends. The aim was that arrest would be a 'serious shock' and 'genuine warning' for youthful offenders, who would not come into contact with regular prisoners, and thus avoid becoming corrupted.[207] After its introduction, 'youth arrest' was heavily used by the courts. Police also made extensive use of 'youth arrest', at least according to the complaint of one judge in 1942, and there was a tendency for police to seek control of all 'youth matters'.[208] In the last years of the war, police brutality towards young people reached a point where, as in the Ehrenfeld district of Cologne on 10 November 1944, six youths, almost certainly not the resistance fighters they were painted by the Gestapo, were executed in public without trial.[209]

The growing scope of the police at the expense of the court system, was aided and abetted by Minister of Justice, Georg Thierack. It was clear to insiders at the time that Hitler favoured Thierack both because he was a radical and already had numerous conflicts with judicial officials. Hans Frank, at one time a chief spokesman for Nazi legal theory, saw the new Minister's appointment in August 1942 as the final victory of the 'arbitrary police state'. Frank regretted that Hitler and others had concluded that their own authority was fortified by removing what remained of citizens' legal security. Hitler not only firmly backed Thierack, but forbad Frank from speaking in public and thus stifled his mild criticism.[210] At any rate, less than a month after Thierack's appointment and in order to justify Hitler's faith in him—soon after a visit to Hitler's headquarters—he proposed to Himmler that inmates in German prisons held in 'preventive detention' be sent to concentration camps or used for labour purposes else-where in the east. At one fell swoop, 12,658 Germans held in court-ordered preventive detention were sent to concentration camps, and already by April of the next year, nearly half of them were dead.[211]

A recent estimate suggests that more than 20,000 male and female state prisoners were handed over to the police, of whom a minimum of two-thirds died in the camps.[212] Thierack and other officials in his Ministry made it clear in public, as he did at a mass propaganda meeting in Breslau on 5 January 1943, that penitentiary inmates were being put to work in such a way, that they would inevitably die.[213] Other 'criminals' were arrested under what were termed 'simplified proceedings' and sent straight to the concentration camps, and orders were given to find more.[214] It was in fact in the context of the September

1942 conversation between Thierack and Himmler, as well as another between Thierack and Goebbels that the concept of 'destruction through labour' was mentioned for the first time.[215]

Historian Detlev Peukert believes that the German population generally agreed with the more radical approach taken to all crime.[216] The general impression conveyed by public opinion surveys was that Germans reacted on a case-by-case basis, that is, they did not favour everything the police and the courts did, but went along with the harshest punishment when they felt it fitted the crime, and was consistent with their own values, expectations, and the personal experiences they drew on. Thus, while they heartily welcomed that a business manager should be executed in early 1942 for cheating some of his workers out of their ration cards, at least some citizens did not agree with reports of executions for listening to forbidden foreign radio.[217] The Nazi surveyors of public opinion showed that, to put it mildly, the population attentively read newspaper stories of 'crime and punishment'. During the war, people favoured severe punishments for anything that might hinder victory, and were critical if courts went easy on the better off or well connected.[218] Many citizens wanted a harsh approach to repeat offenders, and by the war years were not unhappy to see the death penalty used for non-capital crimes like morals offences and homosexuality.[219]

Some people calmly accepted that the Special Courts used the death penalty as never before during the war, but others were sceptical and not always convinced by the news story as to the justice of the case. When that happened, the Nazi opinion surveyors suggested, not that the police or the courts should relent, but rather that more attention should be paid to writing up the story.[220] When it came to 'plunderers', that is, those who stole something from a bombed out home, the people were one with the police in wanting the culprits executed.[221] The police and court systems did not simply ignore public opinion, but kept on trying to win it over through the media. Their attention was focused especially on 'race enemies' and it is their story we now take up.

6

Injustice and the Jews

As we have already seen, antisemitism was pushed from the beginning of Hitler's dictatorship, but in the first two and a half years, more cautiously than often supposed. From May 1935, however, actions aimed at Jews accelerated, and by mid-July vandals were hitting stores on the best streets in downtown Berlin.[1] Antisemitism of one kind or another was reported from all over the country. One account from Osnabrück in August 1935, noted 'massive demonstrations' against Jewish businesses in that city and the surrounding countryside. Not only were the businesses marked with crude slogans and signs, but customers were photographed and their pictures were displayed in public. The police noted that the 'high point of the struggle against the Jews' was a meeting of 25,000 people who gathered to hear the local Nazi Party leader on the theme 'Osnabrück and the Jewish Question'. We can see in the records of many localities out in the countryside, that various kinds of intimidation continued.[2] The Party insisted that its members boycott the Jews, with the obvious implication that all citizens should do so as well.[3]

The Gestapo was in the contradictory position of being the chief enforcer of anti-Jewish policies, but also responsible for keeping law and order. In some locations the Gestapo (as in Stettin) suggested in late summer 1935 that the Party should be told more forcefully to cease and desist.[4] A similar report was penned at about the same time by the Gestapo in Münster to the effect that boycotts of the Jews were inappropriate, given recent orders.[5] However, that the Gestapo was generally interested in more rather than less antisemitism, at least if it was officially condoned by political leaders in Berlin, can be seen from a Hanover report from September 1935, in which the Gestapo noted that more should be done in rural parts to step up the struggle against the Jews, particularly because many farmers still preferred commerce with Jewish cattle dealers.[6]

Although Hitler issued no specific orders for these attacks, his speeches encouraged them. Local Nazis pressured Jews to give up their way of life, and interpreted Hitler's vague remarks as support for what they already wanted to do.[7] In some areas the Party openly assaulted individuals who did commerce with the Jews, or demonstrated in front of their homes. To be sure, some people continued to deal with the Jews, and a few (identified in one case as having been in the Communist or Socialist movement) actually began to shop at Jewish-owned stores in September 1935 to show their opposition to antisemitism.[8] Even into the mid-1930s, most citizens still clearly did not endorse lawless excesses aimed at the Jews.[9] Nevertheless, such violence became widespread, and the underground Socialists considered they were almost like pogroms. If the population did not openly embrace what happened, the events, as even the ever optimistic Socialists admitted, 'definitely left an impression'.[10]

Nuremberg Laws

One of Hitler's longest-held convictions was that any nation that allowed 'blood mixing' was bound to decline, so it was only a matter of time before he would criminalize sexual relations between Jews and non-Jews, and outlaw intermarriage. Other top Nazi leaders shared these views. In September 1935, having directly or indirectly fostered limited antisemitic violence, Hitler decided the time was ripe to announce new laws at the Nuremberg Party rally. Although the laws themselves were hastily put together at the last minute on Hitler's orders, it was indicative that he opted for the less far-reaching versions put to him, no doubt because he took German public opinion into account.[11]

The promulgation of the Nuremberg laws gave Hitler the opportunity to appear as the sovereign statesman, and for the time being the worst excesses subsided.[12] The 'Law for the Protection of German Blood and German Honour', as it was called, outlawed new marriages between Jews and non-Jews; forbad extramarital sexual relations between them; made it illegal for Jews to employ non-Jewish women under 45 as servants; and illegal for Jews to raise the German flag. There was a lack of clarity on key points, however, especially on the definition of who was a Jew and who was a person of 'mixed race' (*Mischling*). At the last minute, Hitler considered a broader version of these laws, one that would have applied to more people of 'mixed race', but backtracked when the German public thought them too sweeping in their potential applicability.[13]

Hitler insisted that lingering violence stop, and tried to appear reasonable by saying the laws opened new opportunities for Jews to develop their 'own ethnic ways of life in all social areas'.[14] In fact, the Jews were at once transformed into social outsiders, and their legal status reverted to pre-emancipation days. The definition of who counted as Jewish, included those with three Jewish grandparents.[15] Those with two Jewish grandparents were considered Jews only if they practised the Jewish faith, were married to a Jew, or the legitimate or illegitimate offspring of at least one Jewish parent.[16] Confusion at the grassroots continued, however, about people of 'mixed race'.[17]

The Times of London recognized that the Nuremberg laws were a kind of 'cold pogrom'. The police and other officials could capitalize on the vague laws, and 'any individual can report his Jewish enemy or competitor as having been seen in the company of an "Aryan" woman, or trump up alleged business obligations from the past.'[18] The complicated follow-up regulations did not settle the issues.[19]

Historians who have studied public opinion have reached different conclusions about the extent to which the German people agreed with these laws.
Israeli historian David Bankier underlines the agreement between the people
and the regime.[20] Otto Dov Kulka, another Israeli, suggests that most Germans
were probably pleased to see these laws with the hope they would put an end
to lawlessness and violence.[21] More recently, Peter Longerich maintains that
some may have disagreed with what was happening, but in public they dared
object only on pragmatic grounds about the violence or the destruction of
property.[22]

Victor Klemperer, who lived through the events, asked non-Jews he met what
they thought about the Nuremberg laws and he concluded that 'all go back
and forth or have contradictory opinions'. He and other Jews kept expecting a
pogrom, but that did not materialize.[23] One man who wrote to Klemperer of his
decision to emigrate, said that living in Germany for Jews was like living 'under
the guillotine'.[24] Klemperer tried but failed to leave as well. When he experienced an insult or rejection by Germans, he tended to think that most people
supported Hitler, but as soon as someone showed a small kindness, he would
revise his opinions. He kept searching for an answer to the question: 'What
is the real opinion of the German people?' The evidence remains mixed, but
historian Marion Kaplan is correct to note, that long before the Holocaust
began, 'the regime transformed Jews into the object of a general, hateful taboo'.[25]

David Bankier examines how Hitler's dictatorship tailored its antisemitism
to fit public opinion. He concludes that by the mid-1930s 'the prosecution of
anti-Jewish policy depended, to a large extent, on the public's reaction. There is
conclusive evidence', he continues, 'that on the whole the population consented
to attacks on Jews as long as these neither damaged non-Jews nor harmed the
interests of the country, particularly its reputation abroad'.[26] From 1935 onwards,
Nazis out in the provinces used the new laws to harass the Jews. A momentary
respite was called in the first half of 1936 because of the Olympics held in Germany. The underground Socialists noted at the time that as soon as the games
ended, however, verbal and physical assaults on the Jews picked up again.[27]

The Acceleration of Discrimination

The Socialists called what the Nazis did to the Jews after 1935 'Judicial Terror'.
The Socialists drew up long lists from newspapers of the Jews caught and sentenced for 'race defilement' to show how the police and/or the courts 'legally'
pushed antisemitism. The full names of Jews, unlike other citizens, also were
published in the press.[28] The police were told in June 1937 to rearrest anyone
who served their time for breaking the Nuremberg laws, and send them to a
concentration camp.[29]

The Kripo was involved in enforcing anti-Jewish measures, and all the police discriminated against the Jews more than any other group. For example, in the June 1938 campaign against 'asocials', Jews qualified for that dubious status if they had served a minor prison sentence of one month and it did not matter if they were gainfully employed. Approximately 1,500 Jews were arrested in the June 1938 'asocial action'.[30] That was the first time a large group of Jews was systematically rounded up and sent to a concentration camp.[31] The Nazis were willing to release the Jews, if and when they agreed to leave Germany.[32] In the meantime, one exclusionary measure after the next made it difficult for them to earn a living, while other policies made it hard to leave.

Jews who lived through the era remembered the complete lack of clarity and inconsistency of Nazi policies.[33] Living in a country that officially endorsed antisemitism had a devastating social and psychological effect on many German Jews. Peter Gay recalled of his Berlin youth, that in spite of how tough it was, the Jews got mixed signals. He was spared antisemitism at his school, and even in June 1935, only days after attacks on Jewish stores took place on the famous Kurfürstendamm, his uncle, who was a Jewish war veteran, was awarded an honorary Cross of Honour. The certificate was signed by Berlin's police commissioner in Hitler's name.[34] Until 1938, it was still possible for Jews to appeal for help from the uniformed police or other local authorities if they were bothered by the rowdies, after which they were often left alone.[35]

Official and unofficial antisemitism led many Jews to give up their business activities.[36] That trend was encouraged by the Nazi Party's regional economic staff from the autumn of 1936, and by the summer of 1938 an estimated 75 to 80 per cent of all Jewish businesses that existed in 1933 had been liquidated.[37] Over the years many firms were ruined when customers began to avoid Jewish-owned stores out of fear they would be denounced for shopping there. For the same reason suppliers grew reluctant to trade with Jews. The slightest misstep by a Jewish firm could bring reminders of their precarious legal position in the new Reich, and the Gestapo used house searches to harass individual business families.[38]

In 1938 there was a transition from haphazard practices, when a special decree of 26 April made it mandatory for all Jews (and their non-Jewish spouses, if they were in a mixed marriage), to register all their worldly wealth.[39] Between April and November alone more than 4,000 businesses were taken from Jews.[40] Front-page stories explaining the mechanics of the decree, and the law that made the registration of all Jewish businesses mandatory, had a terrorizing effect on all Jews.[41] Goebbels announced proudly at the time, that Jewish influence on the economy would be broken within a short time 'by legal measures'.[42]

During the summer of 1938 the persecution of the Jews went much farther than the more publicized boycott of April 1933. Even so, the underground

Socialists generally continued to be optimistic, kept waiting for the people to see through the Nazi lies, and so held on to their conviction that most Germans did not support what the Nazis were doing. There were some Socialists, however, who noted, as one did from Berlin, that 'as a result of the long antisemitic campaign many people had themselves become antisemitic'.[43]

Besides excluding the Jews from the economy, which was welcomed by many people, the Nazis used propaganda to foster their exclusionary policies. One major theme in the mid-1930s emphasized the alleged criminality of certain Jews and, especially after the Nuremberg laws, the charges of 'race defilement'.[44] Articles on antisemitic events and speeches from around the world, made it appear that the Third Reich was in the vanguard of a broader movement against the Jews, and that other countries (including the United States) were also, not unlike Germany, dealing with race issues.[45]

The Nazis said that to stop the Jews was to stop Communism, and so used one of its foundational appeals to spread antisemitism.[46] In the press, Jews were linked to Bolshevism, Stalin, and the Soviet Union.[47] A preview of the notorious exhibition that travelled across Germany in late 1937, 'The Eternal Jew', was reviewed under the heading, 'Domination of the Jews is Domination by Bolshevism'.[48] Antisemitism also was linked to anti-Americanism when Americans began questioning what was happening in Europe and Germany. The Nazis took particular exception to what they considered the decay and degeneracy of American lifestyles, and Hitler among others fondly pointed to the racial and social problems in the country.[49] Soon the Jews were said to dominate the United States, including its government, cultural life, and the press.[50] Just before and into the war years, the anti-American speeches of Hitler and others played up anti-Jewish themes, and won many converts.[51]

There was a dynamic interaction between propaganda and the people. Films and documentaries with themes that were negative towards Jews did not automatically succeed just because they were shown. Bad films or tasteless ones made bad propaganda, a fact clearly recognized at the time when the 1940 documentary film on 'The Eternal Jew'—which replayed the themes of the popular exhibition—was not well received.[52] By any standards the film was distasteful, but its failure was not due to its obvious antisemitism. 'Jew Süss', an equally racist film the same year, which is regarded as having worked aesthetically, is usually taken to be the most successful propaganda film of the Third Reich, and not merely because it was seen by 20 million people. It conveyed, to general acclaim, Nazi distortions of the historical role of the Jews, including how they victimized the people and preyed on young women.[53] Another production that was almost as successful (viewed by 15 million people) dealt with the touchy issue of 'mercy killing', a topic about which Germans had more reservations. As art, it was able to find a way to speak to the German people, and thus generated support for the policy.[54] By the end of the 1930s, the incessant propaganda and the numerous measures taken against the Jews convinced increasing numbers of Germans, that at the very least there was a 'Jewish question', and that it might be best if the Jews just left the country.[55]

Pogrom and War

All the legal and semi-legal steps taken against Jews in Germany in the pre-war period paled in comparison to the pogrom aimed at them in early November 1938. As contemporary witnesses, the observers in the Socialist underground, considered the events were so significant, that their long reports of what happened began with the chilling phrase, 'the campaign of annihilation of the German Jews is by all appearances entering its final stage'.[56]

The nationwide attack on the Jews, labelled the 'night of broken glass' on 9/10 November 1938 began in Paris on 7 November when a 17-year-old Polish Jew, Herschel Grynszpan shot a minor official (Ernst vom Rath) in the German Embassy. Part of the motive was that his parents, once resident in Germany, were deported from Germany. The deportation of Jews of Polish nationality was provoked when the Polish government invalidated the passports of Polish citizens living abroad if passports had not been given a new stamp. In response, on 26 and 27 October 1938, Himmler issued instructions to arrest and deport all Polish Jews. The Nazis used those deportations to get rid of Jews who had lived in the country for years but never obtained citizenship, and on 7 November young Grynszpan took his revenge.[57]

Even though vom Rath did not die immediately, a number of influential Nazis wanted to take advantage of the shooting. In some areas of Germany like Hesse, known for its antisemitic tradition, actions against the Jews, including the arson of synagogues, broke out on 8 November. More such events followed in Kassel and Dessau early on 9 November. There were other signs that a national response of some kind would follow. The editorial in the leading Nazi newspaper, spoke of 'the beginning of a new German attitude on the Jewish question'.[58]

Nazi leaders were in Munich to celebrate the anniversary of the Beer Hall Putsch of 1923 when news arrived that vom Rath had died of his wounds. Hitler spoke with Goebbels in private and said he wanted demonstrations 'to be allowed to continue', a wish Goebbels took as authorization for giving 'appropriate directions' to Party leaders, who rushed to the telephones to send out orders.[59]

Berlin headquarters of the Gestapo, which was informed of the impending 'actions' against the Jews and especially the synagogues, passed word to local Gestapo offices at 11.55 p.m. on 9 November. The telegram signed by Heinrich Müller stated that the Gestapo was not to disturb these 'actions', but 'in agreement with the regular police' were to stop 'plundering, thefts', and so on. The Gestapo was told to prepare the arrest of somewhere between 20,000 and 30,000 Jews.[60] At 1:20 a.m. next morning further orders, signed by Heydrich, were sent out to the Gestapo to coordinate local 'actions'. Perhaps the most remarkable instruction given to the police was that, far from stopping the destruction of property, they were to allow the businesses and homes of Jews to be destroyed.[61] Kurt Daluege, head of the uniformed police, ordered them to check for instructions with the Gestapo, and if the police appeared at all, they were not to do so in uniform but in civilian clothes.[62]

Hitler and Goebbels discussed whether or not to let the pogrom run on, but Goebbels said they decided to stop it as the action might get out of hand. Goebbels recorded that Hitler wanted more 'sharp measures' against the Jews, including driving them from commercial life.[63] Follow-up instructions to the Gestapo for the arrest of the Jews, specified that they be male and 'especially the better off'. Judicial authorities were told not to investigate these 'actions', nor to issue any warrants against anyone arrested for something they did during the events.[64]

Detailed local studies have shown that the anti-Jewish riots not only swept through the streets of the big cities, but went all the way down to the smallest villages.[65] Not a single place where Jews lived remained untouched, and often travelling squads of Nazis arrived by truck, inflicted incredible damage on Jewish property, paraded Jews through the streets, and left as quickly as they came. Although we have some scattered records that Germans hid Jews from the pogrom or helped them secretly, few dared even to criticize what happened. In the days that followed it was indicative of the status of the Jews that any who appeared in public were attacked by children, who threw stones, harassed, and insulted them.[66]

The events were written up in the press across the country as if the perpetrators were somehow 'heroic', when in fact the reality was that the Jews were socially isolated, unarmed, and easy targets.[67] A brief statement by Goebbels to the press on 10 November, said that German 'acts of retaliation' were understandable, but they must end. He gave notice that 'the final answer' to the Jews, who were held collectively responsible for vom Rath's assassination, would follow 'by way of new legislation and government decree'.[68] The front-page news stories added the disinformation that 'not a hair was touched on a Jew's head', and congratulated the German people for showing discipline. On the same page, as if to justify the reality of the danger posed by Jews, Himmler issued a special order forbidding Jews from owning guns, and threatened transgressors with 20 years in a concentration camp.[69]

Heydrich's report of the events to Göring on 11 November 1938, admittedly based on incomplete information, stated that 20,000 Jews were arrested, 36

128 *Injustice and the Jews*

killed, and 36 seriously injured, and it said that 'most' of their businesses were destroyed and their homes were damaged. Historians have set the final figure of those arrested at closer to 30,000 and the number killed was certainly in excess of 100.[70] Some Jews responded to the terror by committing suicide and somewhere between 300 and 500 of them took that way out. (Their suicides rose during the war, and by 1945 an estimated minimum of 3,000 had taken their own lives.)[71]

In November 1938 approximately 10,000 Jews were sent to each of three main camps at Dachau, Buchenwald, and Sachsenhausen; most were released within several weeks.[72] There was considerable variation in the local extent of the arrests, and more Jews tended to be taken into custody where police and Nazis were keen, and when the area was known for being hostile towards the Jews.[73] These arrests represented the largest single Gestapo 'action' ever carried out inside Nazi Germany.[74]

Although there were Jews among those who were arrested during the first years of the camps, they were not the primary targets until the end of the 1930s.[75] Most of the Jews who were singled out between 1933 and 1936 by the Gestapo or other police were members of opposition parties or well-known public figures. In the camps, the Jews were subjected to the worst treatment, but initially they were not segregated.[76] As antisemitism grew, it was reflected in the camps, and even before the pogrom in 1938, 500 Jews were sent to Buchenwald as alleged asocials in June, and were 'packed into a sheep barn' so that within two months 150 of them were dead. Survivors also reported that in September 1938 around 2,000 Jews arrived in Buchenwald as Austrian political prisoners.[77] After the pogrom they were segregated from the rest of the camp population and mistreated.

Although there was brief mention in the press about the destructive aspects of the pogrom, there was not a word about murder, and only hints that some were sent to the camps.[78] Many people exaggerated the number of victims, and one sympathetic witness who was generally well informed, wrote in his diary that he heard that 'hundreds of thousands had been arrested'.[79] A Jewish diarist thought that between 50,000 and 80,000 men were taken into custody.[80] The press reported, with the obvious intent of gaining popular support, that the Jewish community was 'fined' one billion marks to pay for the damage, but even so, Germans thought the pogrom was wasteful.[81] The one-sidedness of that response has been interpreted by many historians as evidence that most people worried less about the morality of what happened to the Jews, and most likely shared the official antisemitism.[82] However, evidence can be found in the private diaries of non-Nazis, that the riots and the arrests that followed really were disturbing.[83]

It is of course difficult to generalize about the German population whose reactions were often mixed and whose real opinions, at least if they were negative, could not be freely expressed. David Bankier, who has provided a full-scale study of public opinion on the issue of antisemitism in Nazi Germany, suggests that the anti-Jewish riots even 'aroused disapproval among many who had hitherto endorsed "moderate antisemitic measures"'. He concludes that one reaction to these riots was that 'for the first time, non-Jews sensed a *real* danger of being the next victim of Nazi terror'.[84] The reporters to the Socialist underground noted that opinions were divided, and that in some places, anyone wishing to talk about the negative aspects of the pogrom had a hard time making their point.[85]

On 12 November a meeting chaired by Hermann Göring, levied a collective fine on the Jews to pay for the damages, and all were forced to contribute.[86] Other politicians were at this meeting, such as Goebbels, as were leading police officials like Reinhard Heydrich.[87] According to Heydrich, Adolf Eichmann (also at this meeting) had forced the emigration of 50,000 Jews in the short time Germany was in Austria, while in the same period only 10,000 left 'old' Germany. Heydrich wanted to adopt the 'Vienna model'. He said he did not want to create ghettos in Germany because he thought they would breed crime and disease and would be 'impossible to place under surveillance'. He favoured a kind of invisible ghetto, with the Jews marked by a yellow star on their clothing. They would then be 'controlled by way of the watchful eye of the entire population'.[88]

Within days, Jews were forbidden to go to movies or visit theatres, and soon were barred from schools and universities. These steps constituted what Goebbels said in a front-page story on 13 November 1938, was the 'definitive solution of the Jewish question'.[89] He said Germany's only interest was 'that the Jews leave the country'.[90] Internal government documents continued to talk about various methods of dealing with them.[91] Goebbels thought Germans were 'totally in agreement' with the approach of harassing the Jews into leaving.[92]

The Socialists saw that Nazi policy aimed at genocide. In their underground report of February 1939, they brought up the comparison with the genocide of the Armenians carried out by the Turks during the last war, and saw that the main difference was that in Germany the process was slower and better planned. The Socialists felt that 'the overwhelming majority' of the people 'abhorred' the excesses of November and the 'continuous pogrom' since then, but the ever-optimistic Socialists, almost certainly underestimated how far antisemitism had spread.[93]

Antisemitic propaganda picked up with the outbreak of war, for which the Jews were repeatedly blamed. Although there was no replay of the pogrom, many things were done to make their existence miserable, such as cutting their food, coal, and other rations. Whenever the occasion arose, Jews were accused of being the hidden wire-pullers. For example, the press said they were behind the attempt to assassinate Hitler in November 1939 at the annual meeting in Munich. Georg Elser planted a bomb in the Bürgerbräukeller, the beer hall where the event was held. He came closer than anyone to succeeding, by secretly working away for many nights to hollow out a stone pillar, in which he planted a bomb timed to go off at 9:20 p.m., in the middle of Hitler's speech which usually ran from 8:30 to 10 o'clock. Because of poor weather, Hitler left early and narrowly missed the explosion that killed eight and injured 60 more.[94] Newspapers promptly spoke of the 'spiritual' links to the event of both England and the Jews, although as it turned out Elser worked alone and was not Jewish.[95]

The echo of this assassination attempt was heard in the Buchenwald concentration camp. The morning after, 21 Jews were selected, marched to a nearby rock quarry and executed. Although many Jews died in the camps as a result of their arrests during the 1938 pogrom, this mass execution was new. Apparently the SS leaders in the camp regarded the killings as their own private reprisal, and they hinted of things to come.[96]

After the pogrom of November 1938, the 'Aryanization' process, which until then was pushed mainly by the Party at the local level, was turned into an accelerated national campaign to force Jews to give up their businesses, and eventually to hand over their wealth and all other valuables. Much of the money went to the German state, but many individual Party members and ordinary citizens also profited. Even in places where we can find evidence of sympathy for the Jews, there were citizens who bought the furniture, personal effects, and businesses of the Jews who finally decided after the pogrom that emigration was their only option.[97]

In the war years the circle of people who gained materially from the persecution of the Jews expanded yet again when confiscated properties and goods were offered at public auctions. When Jews were forced from their apartments in Würzburg to the Jewish communal home and later to the 'east', everything they could not take with them was auctioned off, all of it according to strict Gestapo guidelines.[98] The same happened everywhere. In the port city of Hamburg, between early 1941 and the end of the war, hardly a day passed without Jewish property being offered at auction. The goods were stolen from the Jews of that city and/or from other parts of Europe and sent back to Hamburg to be put under the hammer. At least 100,000 citizens purchased these wares, and gained from the persecutions.[99] Even more people learned what was going on at the auctions, and could read about them in the press.[100] After individual Jewish citizens were deported, their apartments were opened, sometimes to find half-filled tea cups still on the table. All such private possessions were then auctioned off to the public amid scenes that have been described by an American observer as 'ugly spectacles, with ill-tempered citizens crying curses at one another and at the auctioneer, threatening with all the standard threats to have one another arrested and to call friends "high in the party" into their squabbles'.[101]

Emigration, forced and otherwise, remained official policy towards the Jews in Germany even after outbreak of the war, but the international hostilities made emigration increasingly difficult. Between the end of the pogrom and the eventual deportation of the Jews who remained, many Jews were selectively forced to work. Various public authorities and institutions, as well as private firms, employed these Jews. By the summer of 1941, just over 50,000 of the 167,245 Jews remaining in Germany were so employed in the public sphere, and many had to live and/or work in various kinds of camps inside Germany. There is evidence of 125 such small camps for German Jews at that time, in which over 5,000 Jews were forced to live, quite apart from concentration camps.[102] By the beginning of 1943, 20,406 male and female Jews in thirteen different cities in Germany, 15,100 of them in Berlin, were compelled to work.[103]

There were some local initiatives to force deportations, such as one that began on 16 July 1940 when 22,000 Jews of French nationality were sent from the newly incorporated area of Alsace-Lorraine to the unoccupied part of France controlled by Vichy. Again in October about 6,300 Jews were deported to France, apparently on the orders of the local Nazi Party Gauleiter in Baden, and another 1,150 were deported on orders of the Gauleiter in Saarpfalz.[104] A more concerted effort to deal with the German Jews began in the autumn of 1941 when the Gestapo began a series of systematic deportations with the aim of eventually removing all Jews.[105]

Jews (aged 7 and older) were forced to wear the yellow star (from 15 September 1941), and a follow-up decree of 24 October 1941 made it a crime for non-Jews to appear in public with them. Henceforth, both were to be placed in 'protective custody'. In serious cases, non-Jewish offenders were to be sent for up to three months to a concentration camp, but all Jews were to be sent there.[106] The reaction of the public to the star decree was described initially by Nazi opinion surveyors as being 'greeted' by the population. In Catholic and middle-class areas, however, there were expressions of pity and some people spoke of 'methods out of the middle ages'.[107]

On the other hand, some citizens said they were unpleasantly 'surprised' to see how many Jews were still around. In some parts of the country, Protestant churchgoers were displeased to note how many (converted) Jews went to church, and demanded of their ministers that they should not be asked to take communion next to these Jews, whom they wanted forbidden to attend common services. Although there were Protestant ministers, such as one in Breslau, who rejected this anti-Christian attitude and the star decree, regional church leaders distanced themselves from his suggestions to find ways of extending a warm hand to these 'Jewish Christians' because of the negative opinion of the population and the position of the local Nazi Party.

Catholic responses to the issue were not much more comforting, and there were suggestions to give 'Catholic Jews' separate services, to avoid contact with the rest of the community. Catholic leaders, like Fulda's Cardinal Bertram, disagreed, and he sent instructions to his flock on how to behave when converted Jews went to church. Everything was to be avoided, he said, that might hurt their feelings. He insisted that the star decree was against the teachings of Christian love, and all churchgoers were to be reminded of that fact. Nevertheless, Bertram said that if 'great difficulties' arose, such as a boycott of mass by civil servants and Nazi Party members, or if others ostentatiously marched out, then it might prove necessary, in consultation with the Jews themselves, to find a gentle way to hold separate services for Jewish Catholics. Even then, priests were told to remind all, that once men and women believed in Christ and were baptized, they were no longer Jews, but were equal in the eyes of God and must be treated accordingly. Cardinal Innitzer in Vienna also rejected the star decree and went further than Bertram by insisting that no special services would be held for Jewish Catholics as that would amount to a concession to Nazi racism. These responses were duly noted by Nazi public opinion surveyors in late 1941, who concluded with resignation that, given the attitude of both Cardinals, Jews would not be singled out at mass in the foreseeable future.[108]

Not long after, however, another survey noted with more satisfaction, that within a few months the star decree had a 'generally positive effect'. It mentioned criticisms, but said most were because the decree did not go far enough. The decree 'went a long way to meeting a long-desired wish of broad circles of the population, especially in places with still relatively large numbers of Jews', even if some people objected that there were a number of Jews, like those living in 'mixed marriages' and others of 'mixed race', who did not have to wear the star. The opinion survey said that there was 'in general more understanding for a radical solution of the Jewish problem rather than for any compromise, and that among many people there exists a widespread wish for a clear, obvious, separation of the Jews from German racial comrades'. The claim was that many people wanted 'an immediate deportation of all the Jews out of Germany'.[109]

Citizen Participation in the Persecution of the Jews

Another way of studying what happened to the Jews, and the non-Jews who resisted antisemitism or offered Jews comfort and support, is to examine how the Nazis enforced antisemitic polices, and how they caught anyone who dared to defy the letter or the spirit of the laws. The best sources for the study of the police activities and of the role played by ordinary citizens, are the original police dossiers that were drawn up whenever an arrest or an accusation was made or when information about suspicious behaviour was offered to the authorities. These kinds of files, based on named individual men and women, grew to be enormously extensive in the Third Reich. The files were destroyed everywhere, with only three exceptions, including Lower Franconia, in Bavaria.

The region had a large Jewish community that could trace its roots back for 1,000 years. It was a very Catholic area, and that fact carried over into politics. In the last four national elections before Hitler took over, Catholics remained loyal to their own party, as did the smaller number of voters who opted for the Socialist and Communist parties.[110] At the beginning of 1933, Lower Franconia had the dubious distinction from the Nazi point of view, of having the lowest proportion of its population enlisted as members of the party in all of Germany's 32 districts.[111] The Nazi vote there was the lowest in Bavaria and was even smaller than in other districts with a higher percentage of Catholics, so that not only the religious factor put the brakes on the Nazi movement in the area, but so did culture, which was known for its resistance to extremist points of view.[112] Turning Lower Franconians into supporters of the Gestapo's enforcement activities, therefore, was a challenge for Hitler's dictatorship. That the population, even of this area, came to collaborate with the Gestapo hints at the more troubling national pattern.

The Jews in Würzburg and Lower Franconia rightly regarded Hitler's appointment with trepidation.[113] The Nazis used selective terror against them, as during the boycott of 1 April 1933, but the shock deepened when mayor and council of several villages in the area voted to forbid the Jews even from travelling through.[114] Even before there were laws on the books, Nazis and non-Nazis began to volunteer information to the authorities about Jews whom they suspected of having affairs with non-Jews. For example, on 20 August 1933, neighbours of Karolina Mengerst in Würzburg complained about her to local Nazi district boss Hermann Voll. They said the 35-year-old widow and mother of two was having an intimate relationship with a Jewish wine salesman called Ludwig Müller. They claimed to be outraged about the relationship since the beginning of 1933 when they began to watch Müller's comings and goings from Mengerst's flat. None of the neighbours who informed were Nazi Party members. Herr Voll told police that because Müller and Mengerst flaunted their extramarital relationship, he was 'repeatedly' forced to listen to neighbours' stories about the two. On the Sunday afternoon of 20 August 1933 he finally ordered the SS to arrest Müller, and they also paraded him through town with a large cardboard sign around his neck on which was printed in large red letters: 'I have lived in concubinage with a German woman.'

This arrest and search was completely illegal, because at that time there was no law against sexual relations between Jews and non-Jews, and the SS had no police powers. As it turned out, the love affair had gone on for years, and seemed to have stopped at least six months before. In spite of the fact that Müller broke no laws, he was put in 'protective custody' until 2 September and released to leave the country. Today we are left to imagine the ripple effects of his parade

Table 1. Enforcing the social isolation of the Jews in Gestapo case files in Lower Franconia, 1933–1945

Sources of information	Number of cases	%
1. Reports from the population	123	59
2. Information from other control organizations	8	4
3. Observations by Gestapo and Agents	1	0
4. Information via communal or state authorities	0	0
5. Statements at interrogations	26	12
6. Information from businesses	1	0
7. Information via Nazi Party, Nazi organizations, or Party Members	27	13
8. Source not known	24	12
TOTAL	210	100

Source: StA W: Gestapo Case Files.

through the streets on a quiet afternoon when many good citizens, dressed in their Sunday best, were out for a walk. As far as we can tell, the two lovers, who had hoped to marry as soon as Müller's prospects improved, never saw each other again.[115]

The scope of Nazi antisemitism becomes evident in the study of Gestapo case files, a large number of which pertain to the persecution of the Jews.[116] Here I want to deal with what the files reveal about how Nazi policies were enforced in order to break social, friendly, and especially sexual relationships between Jews and non-Jews. I want to focus on three categories of case files, namely, those that deal with accusations or suspicions of 'race defilement', which is how the Nazis termed sexual relations between Jews and non-Jews. I also deal with the ill-defined behaviour deemed by Nazis to be 'friendly to the Jews'.[117]

In the Würzburg archive there are 175 Gestapo case files dealing with charges of 'race defilement' or of being 'friendly to the Jews'. In addition, I analysed a sample of 35 cases of expressions of opinion that were thought at the time to be negative or condemnatory of official policies about the Jews.

These three categories of behaviour break with the letter or spirit of Nazi antisemitic 'law', and how the Gestapo caught those involved tells us a lot about how the dictatorship worked at the ground level. I have reported on some but not all of this sample of 210 cases elsewhere.[118]

I indicate how the Gestapo discovered the allegations of this 'criminal' behaviour in Table 1. Nearly sixty per cent of all these cases began with a denunciation 'from the population'. Simply, this means ordinary people informed the police of their accusations or suspicions, they tipped off the police about what they saw or heard. Without such collaboration the Gestapo would certainly have been hampered. The number of tips from the general population would look much higher still if we included cases that began when members of the Nazi Party passed on the information. As Table 1 shows, the active involvement of members of the Party in this side of the terror was significant, accounting for as many as 27 cases (about 13 per cent of them all). Some of these cases came from neighbourhood or local area Party leaders, but ordinary members also denounced 'crimes'. I have not included tips from the Party as 'from the population' because it is more appropriate to count the contribution of Party members separately. An argument can be made that the Party, including its members, were part of the enforcement apparatus. The same point holds for why I count civil servants as part of the 'state' system. The upshot is that what I have labelled 'information from the population' is a minimal figure, and that the information came from ordinary Germans in the sense that they were not in the police, the Nazi Party, the civil service, and so on.

We would be more justified to include among the cases that began with 'information from the population' the 24 cases (12 per cent of the total) where the police do not say who provided the tip. If such information came from an official source, that would have been mentioned, as such informers would have wanted to take credit. In all likelihood, therefore, when no source of information was given in the files about the origin of the tip, the informer was a civilian whose identity was not known or could not be established. If we were to add such cases with no source of information to those where there are identifiable informers, that would mean that 147 cases (70 per cent of the total) began through the direct involvement of 'ordinary' citizens.

Table 1 also shows that the Gestapo itself was primarily reactive when it came to tracking down these three categories of 'criminal' behaviour. Out of 210 cases in this sample, the Gestapo discovered exactly one on its own. However, once they had someone in their grasp they were able to wrest information from them and Table 1 shows that they began 26 cases (12 per cent of them all) on the basis of information obtained during interrogations. Under pressure, people confessed or at least gave the Gestapo more information. The Gestapo's vaunted network of agents was remarkable by its complete absence as providers of information in this sample of cases. Other control organizations like the Kripo and SD accounted for only 8 cases.

The conclusion is inescapable—without the active collaboration of the general population it would have been next to impossible for the Gestapo to enforce these kinds of racial policies. This social involvement was very pronounced, even in Lower Franconia, an area not known for its support of either Nazism or antisemitism up to 1933. We could guess that this was even the minimal level of support the Nazis obtained, and that the situation was more unfavourable for the Jews and/or those who disagreed with antisemitism nearly everywhere else.

Sarah Gordon studied the same kinds of Gestapo case files from the region in and around Düsseldorf. She analysed 452 case files, but instead of dealing with enforcement issues and how the authorities were put on the track of the 'crimes', she focused on the social identities of the men and women who were accused of maintaining social relationships with Jews. Nevertheless, in passing she noted the same pattern of denunciations we have just seen in Lower Franconia.[119] My own examination of the files she used confirms her general impression, and it is highly probable that a full-scale study of these files in Düsseldorf would turn up a pattern similar to the one I discerned in the Würzburg files, including also the use of the most serious kinds of charges between spouses.[120]

In fairness we have to keep in mind, that we cannot know the full scope of the acts of help, kindness, and assistance offered to individual Jews. What shows up in any police file are the few who are caught, not those who break the law and get away with it. From the diaries of Jews who lived through the era, most notably the massive chronicle of Victor Klemperer, we know that great kindness and help was shown to him in and around Dresden. Klemperer remained immune from deportation as he lived in a 'mixed marriage'. He was forced to wear the yellow star, to live in a 'Jews' house', and was subjected to the everyday terror of the increasingly brutal Gestapo. In spite of the hatred that was occasionally rained down on him by passers-by in the street and by those at work, he could hardly have survived without the help shown to him, but none of it was recorded by the police, as it went undetected.

Denouncers and their Motives

Why did Germans inform the Gestapo when they suspected someone of breaking the regime's anti-Jewish measures? Would it not have been easier to turn the other way? In fact it is possible that many people did look the other way, but clearly many did not, even when they knew that their allegations could have serious, even deadly, consequences. The historian Reinhard Mann attempted to quantify the motives of all the denouncers he found in a systematic study of 825 case files in Düsseldorf. Unfortunately, he excluded from his sample virtually all the files pertaining to the enforcement of racial policies against the Jews and foreign workers, and thus overlooked those who were most vulnerable to the informers, namely, the victims of racial persecution and their sympathizers. Of the 825 Gestapo files he studied, Mann found that 213 (or 26 per cent) began with a denunciation.[121] From the 213 cases opened by an identifiable denunciation, Mann found that only 50 (or 24 per cent) appeared to be motivated by what he called 'system loyal' considerations. Most files either contained no evidence of any motive at all (83 files or 39 per cent), while the largest number of files had primarily selfish motives.[122] It is interesting to note that Mann concluded that only around 25 per cent of all denunciations were motivated by affective motives—such as love of Nazism, patriotism, or hatred of enemies—and far more often, the motives were instrumental or selfish. However, we should not overdraw the distinctions between affective and instrumental motives, because in many files the motives were clearly mixed. Moreover, caution is advised in attributing motives to the men and women who came forward with information to the Gestapo, because the Gestapo, otherwise deeply concerned with the most minute details of their investigations, did not always note the motivations of the denouncers.

From my research into the involvement of German citizens as informants, I have concluded that for the police system, anxious to get information it needed to act, the motives of the denouncers were almost always secondary questions. They are not unimportant for us, because we want to understand not only how the system worked, but also why people denounced, that is, why so many people cooperated with Nazi evil and betrayed their ethical and social commitments to fellow human beings. What can we say about their motives on the basis of the evidence in the Gestapo files?

First of all, Gestapo operating procedures were such that the evidence recorded in the files on the motives of the denouncers is often incomplete and frequently there is no evidence at all. The police responded to denunciations and investigated, no matter how dubious the source or far-fetched the accusation. They grew more concerned about motives when they got bad information, were sent on a wild-goose chase, or when they were drowning in too much information and denunciations became counter-productive. Even if the files are more often than not silent on motives, it is precisely this silence we need to interpret.

In the files that begin with a denunciation, the evidence of affective motivation, especially overt antisemitism, is rare. The motives of the denouncers in Mann's study, in so far as these were recorded, tended overwhelmingly to be instrumental ones, such as informing on a rival or someone involved in a social dispute.[123] The same pattern can be seen in Bernward Dörner's recent study of 'malicious gossip'. Out of a total of 481 denunciations, he found that only 155 of them (or less than one-third) had a predominantly political motive. Most of the remainder (212 cases) were based mainly on personal considerations, but a surprising number (114 cases) in his sample made no mention of the motives of the informer at all.[124]

What was going on? First of all, denouncers took advantage of the state's means of coercion for selfish purposes, and in that respect citizens in Nazi Germany were not entirely unlike those in other 'totalitarian' regimes. They rendered a service to the state, by providing information, and the state rendered a service to them, by settling a conflict or removing one of the parties involved. In all of these systems, citizens lost many of the 'traditional' means for resolving conflicts, but they soon adopted and came to rely on direct access to the means of coercion.[125] We can find an abundance of instrumental denunciations in twentieth-century European history.[126] In Nazi Germany, not only did the denouncers go to the police with information, but civilians offered to work for the Gestapo as agents for all kinds of reasons. That the terror system was not simply feared and avoided, but used and manipulated, was part and parcel of the life-world of denouncers and the agents in Hitler's dictatorship. Denunciations took place within families, among friends and colleagues, and certainly inside the army, so that no social enclave appears to have been entirely immune.

We cannot let the matter rest there, because it is the antisemitic, racist, and pro-Nazi dimensions of denunciations that differentiate informing in Nazi Germany, from Fascist Italy. The problem is that we have little firm evidence on the precise linkages between the life-world in general, steeped as it was in racism, and specific acts as recorded and unrecorded in Gestapo files. What kinds of minimum statements can we make that will help us at least delimit the main parameters, the broad contours of the denouncers' life-world and the social knowledge of the persecutions that was available at the time? What could citizens have known about the Gestapo and expect to happen to the person they denounced? Well, thanks to the never-ending press reports about what was happening to the Jews, we can say that denouncers must have known their information would help to enforce Nazi ideology, because what it stood for was well known. For most denouncers, their act of collaboration implied a degree of agreement with and support for these beliefs, even if they did not accept everything, and even if they merely wanted to take advantage of the system for selfish purposes. Put the other way round, few people would have been disingenuous enough to think they were destroying or undermining the dictatorship by actively collaborating with the Gestapo. We have already seen that citizens in Germany knew much about what happened to the Jews, if not all the details. They could read endless stories about what could and did happen to 'enemies' turned over to the Gestapo. Indeed, it was important to the terror that social knowledge of it should spread, because it was thought by leaders from Hitler on down that heavy punishments should act as deterrents. Even though the stories were usually 'cleaned up' versions of what really happened, no one could be in much doubt that turning over information to the Gestapo was going to lead to a very unpleasant experience for someone. They could hardly fail to be aware that the rule of law as understood in liberal democracies was over in Germany and that 'police justice' replaced it. When it came to denouncing the Jews the immediacy of the terror was made even clearer, as in the case we saw above, when the SS humiliated a Jew by parading him through the streets with a sign around his neck. When all is said and done, we would have to conclude that anyone who denounced someone for breaking with antisemitic measures implicitly accepted that their informing helped to enforce the doctrine and supported the dictatorship.

What was the general social attitude to informing the police at the time? There was a civic tradition in Germany that accepted and even promoted contacts between the people and the police. In this respect German tradition contrasted with modern Italy, with its distrust of the state, and even with France and Britain.[127] However, in Germany informing the police, at least in theory, was supposed to be accompanied by the 'right' motives—upholding law and order for example, by turning in a known criminal.

In the Third Reich, the official stance and attitude towards denunciations was ambivalent. On the one hand, if informing was sincere, came from the heart, and especially if it was based on Nazi convictions and was aimed selflessly at those who were defined as Germany's enemies, then it was welcomed. However, as was all too obvious even to Hitler, many denouncers were prone to act for wholly selfish aims, and he complained at the beginning of May 1933, that some merely capitalized on the fact that they knew some competitor or rival had done something under the table in the past. In running to the police as a way of benefiting from that knowledge, the denouncers were causing concern and disruption and Hitler wanted them stopped.[128] And yet such practices continued and there was a plague of false charges, so much so that in 1934 Minister of the Interior Frick ordered police authorities to do what they could at least to stop the 'frivolous laying of unjustified charges'. He ordered a 'struggle against denunciation' which he said was 'unbecoming of the German people and National Socialist state'.[129] On the other hand, Rudolf Hess, Hitler's right-hand man in the Party told the faithful that the door would always be open to those who were driven to inform by 'honest concerns' about the movement and the people.[130] His promise that no one need worry about being held to account for informing, merely gave a kind of seal of approval for what was happening.

At the beginning of 1939 Minister of the Interior Frick informed police officials about the concerns of Hermann Göring with regard to the 'Jewish question and denunciations'. The issue was not disagreement about the goal of removing the Jews from German economic life, but that some citizens were denouncing others on frivolous grounds, such as having once shopped in a Jewish store. These charges, he said, were disrupting the economy.[131] Shortly after the beginning of war, Heydrich issued orders to the Gestapo to take all necessary steps against 'denouncers, who out of personal motives lay unjustified or exaggerated charges' against other citizens. Solving the problem was easier said than done, however, as indicated by yet another order from on high on 24 February 1941 signed by the head of the Gestapo Heinrich Müller. Apparently, Himmler himself worried that people were denouncing spouses to get better divorce settlements, and he ordered that an exact check be made in the future of the motives of anyone who laid charges against relatives.[132]

That these social practices did not go away, and were condemned, was indicated in Justice Minister Thierack's 'letter of guidance to judges' on 1 August 1943. He used the well-known German motto that 'the denouncer [i.e. in this case an informant with the 'wrong' motives] is the biggest scoundrel in the whole country'.[133] This motto was repeated on more than one occasion by Nazi officials over the years, but usually in the context of condemnations of those who falsely accused.

What changed during the war? From day one, many press reports stated that every effort would be made to uphold the home front and that penalties for minor offences would be severe. In spite of brandishing draconian punishments, the Gestapo continued to have no difficulty in obtaining denunciations even when 'ordinary Germans' were the offenders. The American newspaper reporter William L. Shirer recorded three denunciations in his diary on 4 February 1940. He was particularly baffled at one mother who denounced eight friends and relatives who told her that her son, missing in action when shot down over England, had not been killed. Evidently the BBC reported that he was safe and imprisoned. The mother denounced those who passed on this news, because she knew that by that time it was illegal to listen to foreign radio.[134]

If we look at the motives behind specific denunciations, we find at one end of the scale, people who informed on what seem to have been almost entirely affective motives. Upstanding members of society, some in the name of fulfilling their patriotic duty, during 1940 and 1941 repeatedly denounced one young woman in Würzburg on flimsy grounds because she did not fit in; because she was unconventional; and because among other things she was seen with another woman who 'looked Jewish'.[135] The Gestapo concluded that some denunciations were 'knowingly false' and given to the police in hopes of gaining some personal advantage. Occasionally, such as when an obviously false accusation had serious results (like death through suicide), the Gestapo itself laid charges, as it did in Düsseldorf in late 1935, when a man anxious to get rid of his wife accused her of having illegal sexual relations with a Jew.[136] Indeed, false charges were a continuing problem for the Nazi regime, and one it never solved.[137] Nevertheless, as Sarah Gordon suggests from her study of 452 Gestapo cases involving attempts to isolate the Jews in the Düsseldorf region, even patently selfish and instrumental denunciations promoted and spread hostility and hatred of the Jews.[138] That point holds even for those who used or even 'misused' the system for their own purposes. The widespread incidence of all this behaviour reflected an emerging social consensus and acceptance of the system.[139]

It was against this backdrop, one steeped in antisemitic words and deeds, and further reinforced during the war, that we need to return to the Gestapo's apparent lack of concern about the motives of the denouncers who came forward to inform about someone for allegedly breaking official codes. The Gestapo were zealous sticklers for detail; why not here? One answer pertains to unspoken assumptions and taken-for-granteds. In face-to-face communications between an informer and an official of the Gestapo, many unspoken assumptions, accepted values and axiomatic prejudices, would have gone unmentioned, and would have appeared as 'natural' and not in need of formal (explicit) recognition. It is also reasonable to assume that in the situation at the time, not all verbal utterances and exchanges, nor even explicit expressions of motives, were recorded. The meeting of minds, the social 'givens' might well have been too obvious. It is possible, therefore, to interpret the silences in the dossiers on why denouncers came forward as also signifying affective support for the 'system'.

The End of Jewish Community

Soon after the invasion of the Soviet Union began, 'realistic' newsreels of the situation behind the lines, and stories of alleged Communist atrocities left a great impression on German audiences. According to the Nazis' own survey of public opinion, many Germans took the next step in keeping with official propaganda, and blamed the Jews for being 'the real wirepullers', and that in turn led to demands in some quarters for 'a radical handling of the Jews in the Reich'.[140] When newsreels showed the evacuation of the Jews behind the lines, instead of awakening pity, the scenes aroused feelings of disgust among moviegoers, some of whom raised a question about what ought to happen to such 'hoards' in the future.[141] These were precisely the kinds of reactions that Hitler and other leading Nazis hoped for.

It was certainly known in Germany that soon after the invasion of Poland, Jews between 14 and 60 years of age were conscripted for two years' compulsory labour to clean up the mess made by the German war machine. The police reported in the press that if this work failed in its alleged 'educative aim' with the Polish Jews, then their forced labour would be extended. It was known in Germany by early 1940 that Jews were being deported both from western Poland and from other parts of the Nazi empire to Lublin and eastern Poland.[142]

Stories in the leading Nazi newspaper at this time described the ghettos in the east in terms that were meant to justify what was being done to the Jews and to foster antisemitism in Germany. The Jews in ghettos like Lublin were identified as unclean spreaders of disease, greedy hoarders of goods, and profiteers. Forcing them to work for no pay was said only to mean they would have to live from supplies they already had hidden away. The Head of the Police in the area, the notorious Odilo Globocnik, was praised for exploiting Jewish artisans and skilled workers, who allegedly toiled only four hours per day, after which they could work at their private businesses. Plans were mentioned in the press that in the summer of 1940, very large numbers of Jews would be used on land reclamation projects and other such tasks. The justification offered for what Germans were doing was a kind of 'defensive' antisemitism that was supposedly needed to deal with the Jews in the area. However, these ghettos were said to be the 'breeding grounds' of the Jews in the world, so that Nazi occupation policies were by extension cutting off the power of the Jews everywhere.[143] Even though no hints were given about mass murder in these articles, it would have been difficult not to imagine that the persecution of the Jews in Poland was underway and worse was to come.

A direct result of the terrorization of German Jews was that by May 1939 only 3,461 remained in Lower Franconia, so that about 60 per cent of the pre-Nazi era's community was gone.[144] In neighbouring areas with a more pronounced antisemitic tradition, the decline was even greater.[145] By 1939 the German Jewish community was reduced by more than half through a combination of forced deportations and 'voluntary' emigration.[146] Shortly after the outbreak of the war in 1939, the number of Jews in Germany fell to 190,000, and in three waves of deportations, more than 100,000 German Jews were sent to the ghetto in Lodz, to Riga and Minsk, and to the death camps like Belzec and Auschwitz.[147] In cities like Würzburg in Lower Franconia, through which the Jews were marched on their way to the trains, anyone who showed signs of sympathy or who dared to shed a tear, was denounced, brought to the police, and punished by the Special Courts.[148] The Jews who somehow were exempted, were humiliated by being forced to work at demeaning jobs, and to live in special camps and/or houses.

The public humiliation of the Jews who remained in Germany did not satisfy the more radical Nazis like Goebbels, so that in May 1942 he pressed to have the last Jews deported.[149] The Gestapo and other Nazi institutions put enormous pressure on the spouses in what the Nazis called 'mixed marriages' between Jews and non-Jews, but at the end of 1942, there were still 16,760 of them in 'old Germany'. The RSHA wanted to deport all the Jews, but there were legal complications, and the Justice Ministry objected to some kind of automatic divorce procedure.[150] In the deadlock that ensued, the RSHA decided to take steps of its own, ordering the Gestapo in early 1943 to use measures already on the books to 'frame' Jews in mixed marriages, and then to arrest and deport them. From the post-war trial of the Gestapo in Offenbach am Main, we can see how the police used trumped-up charges, such as accusing someone of writing a letter of complaint to the Nazi Party; listening to foreign radio; failing to use the obligatory 'Sara' or 'Israel' on their personal papers; or having forbidden sexual relations.[151] The Gestapo in Darmstadt used similar tactics, as they did elsewhere in Germany, and in this way deported many people to their deaths.[152]

13. During a demonstration in Berlin on 1 April 1933, Joseph Goebbels calls for a boycott of Jewish businesses

14. The call for the boycott of the Jews went into many localities. This sign in front of a store in Glowitz, in the Stolp district, reads: 'Contribute to the emancipation of Germany from Jewish capital. Don't buy in Jewish shops'

15. The 'populist' side of the early terror is shown by the police seal on a grocery store in Munich in May 1933. The seal reads: 'Business closed by police because of price usury. Business owner in protective custody in Dachau. Signed: Himmler'

16. This boycott of a Jewish business in Berlin warns in German and English to avoid shopping in the store

17. The deportations of the Jews began in late 1941. The police photo (15th in a series of 18) shows the deportation from Kitzingen in 1942. The Jews march between two rows of curious onlookers, some of whom do not look displeased and are smiling

18. After the pogrom in November 1938, which caused enormous damage across Germany, thousands of Jews were arrested and sent to concentration camps. The picture shows the mass arrest of Jews at that time in Baden-Baden

19. A crowd gathered in Hanau in 1942 for an auction of goods from a Jewish household

20. Jews were deprived of making a living, but before they were deported, they were often forced to work. Others like Victor Klemperer were exempt from the deportations because they were married to 'Aryans'. He was forced to work, like this group of elderly men, with their yellow stars showing, and to clear snow from the streets. The picture is after a snowstorm in February or March 1942 in Hanau

21. The 'scientific' investigation by the race experts of the Sinti and Roma can be seen in pictures 21 and 22. The first shows an almost surreal profile of Dr Eva Justin, one of the co-workers of Dr Robert Ritter, the 'Gypsy' expert. She is shown measuring the head shape of a woman in the Palatinate in 1938

22. This picture shows (on the right) Dr Robert Ritter with another assistant and a troubled 'Gypsy' woman, as he investigates her family background in 1938

23. Polish men in Bromberg wait for their transport to Germany in 1939. Women and children in this picture wait behind

24. This somewhat idyllic picture (August 1943) shows Polish workers with a police-prescribed 'P' on their clothing. The picture comes from a farm in Reselkow, Pomerania

25. The picture shows Polish adolescents (male and female) doing road work in 1941 (likely in the summer). Many of them are wearing nothing on their feet

26. Poles in a camp for forced workers in Germany

Erkennungsdienst
Geh. Staatspolizei Duisburg 86/1941

27. This is one page from a Duisburg Gestapo dossier of a 22-year-old woman accused of having sexual relations with a Polish worker. In cases like this the woman usually ended up in a concentration camp and the Polish worker was executed, as here when the 26-year-old Pole was sent to Neuengamme where he was hanged on 18 June 1942

Goebbels and Hitler found it intolerable that any Jews should remain in Germany and especially that so many were clustered in the capital city. Although Hitler was deeply concerned about the annihilation of his army at Stalingrad in early 1943, he took time to order the recruitment of foreign workers from France and Holland so that even the Jews then working in armaments industries could finally be dispensed with. In the light of the Stalingrad catastrophe Goebbels went to Rastenburg on 22 January 1943 and got Hitler's blessing for the final push against the Jews in Germany.[153]

Hitler shared the Propaganda Minister's view that the Jews should be forced out of Berlin, and his determination was reinforced with news that Germany was about to lose what Goebbels estimated as 22 divisions and 220,000 men at Stalingrad. Germany was faced with a major disaster and forced to introduce some of the 'total war' measures Goebbels had long demanded. In the midst of hectic meetings, Hitler and Goebbels agreed that there would be 'no internal security' without getting rid of the remaining Jews in Berlin and Vienna 'as quickly as possible'.[154]

On 20 February 1943, the RSHA issued guidelines for the deportations, but still exempted Jews in mixed marriages and a number of others, such as those over 65 years of age.[155] A special 'factory action' took place a week later, organized by the Gestapo to pick up Jews (male and female) at their work-places, and/or to issue a summons for them to appear where they could be taken into custody. In Berlin alone some 11,000 Jews were taken from war industries, with similar results elsewhere. Many were deported within a few days, and 7,000 were sent to the east from Berlin within a six-day period. Goebbels noted that thanks to the 'short-sighted behaviour' by some factory owners who warned of the impending round-up, 4,000 Jews escaped the dragnet and went underground.[156]

Because the regime still had not made up its mind about what to do with Jews in 'mixed marriages', such special cases were sent home, but not allowed to return to their place of work. There does not seem to have been any intention of deporting these particular Jews, and even those who were picked up were kept apart from the rest, with some even released the next day.[157] Nevertheless, in Berlin and elsewhere Jews in 'mixed marriages' who were taken into custody, brought their spouses enormous anxieties, and led to one of the only protests against the deportations. Two thousand or so Berlin Jews who lived in these mixed marriages were arrested, and no doubt their 'Aryan' (mostly female) spouses concluded these partners were about to be sent to their deaths. To stop that, these 'Aryans' protested over several days on the very doorsteps of the Berlin Gestapo headquarters, and by 6 March most of their Jewish spouses were released, perhaps because the Gestapo really had never intended to deport them. However, the protest almost certainly contributed to the decision to release these Jews, as the regime did not need another public relations disaster on the heels of the defeat at Stalingrad. We need to underline the courage of those who took to the street in Berlin. They had no way of knowing what the Gestapo's plans were, and in fact, regardless of why the police picked up their spouses, the arbitrariness of the situation was such that all the Jews could just as easily have been sent to their deaths as be released.[158] The Gestapo was not in the habit of admitting mistakes.

Even after no more Jews remained in many parts of the country, rumours circulated about what might have happened to those sent to the east. An indication that concerns were in the air, and also of how instrumental denunciations were often barely clothed by paying lip-service to affective considerations, can be seen in the letter of 25 August 1943 written to the Gestapo by August Seufert. The letter stated that a full year earlier, Michael Nusser told Seufert in his home that 'our Jews who were sent to Poland by the government, had to dig their own graves and were executed by a Stalin shot to the back of the neck'. The Gestapo instructed the local gendarme in Winkels, a small town near Bad Kissingen, to investigate. The 51-year-old denouncer Seufert was not a member of the Nazi Party. He had both a poor reputation and lengthy police record (with 11 convictions going back to 1910). Seufert said that Michael Nusser made the remarks during the summer of 1942. In response to the obvious question by the investigating gendarme as to why he waited a year to denounce Nusser, Seufert answered that recently they had had an argument, and it turned out that Nusser owned the laundry business that Seufert had rented. When the lease ran out, Seufert offered to buy the business but Nusser did not want to sell, and the moment the owner turned down the offer, Seufert wrote a high-sounding letter of denunciation to the Gestapo. Michael Nusser admitted to the police under interrogation that a policeman who served in Poland had told him the original story about the execution of the Jews, and that he had passed it on to Seufert. During Seufert's own interrogation he added a new and potentially fatal accusation, namely that Nusser had said recently that Germany was going to lose the war. Such a remark in mid-1943 might well have cost Michael Nusser his life, but the Gestapo decided merely to warn him. The police file shows that they doubted Seufert's credibility from start to finish. But in spite of his base motives, poor reputation, and criminal past, they investigated his accusations because it concerned the Jews. No doubt word that they did so circulated in the small town, and such events reinforced the point that even implied criticism of the government's actions against the Jews would not be tolerated.[159]

However, it was not just the police, but individual citizens who continued to participate in official antisemitism, and some did so for typically personal reasons. For example, in March 1944 a 63-year-old man, along with his sister, denounced his Jewish wife Amalie (62 years of age) to whom he had been married since 1908. He now also filed for divorce, but had contemplated doing so for years because of marital conflicts. When his sister moved into their

Hamburg apartment in 1943, the strain on the relationship reached a breaking point, so that soon brother and sister decided to pounce on some remarks Amalie made, including that the revenge of the Jews was at hand and that Hitler murdered children. At a minimum brother and sister wanted to get this woman out of the house, and for reasons of their own. They were not pressured by the police, but hand-delivered their denunciation, which came at a particularly grave time. Amalie was arrested immediately, the divorce granted in a matter of days, and unprotected by her marriage, the Gestapo sent her to Auschwitz in July 1944. She died there at the end of October, but the precise cause of her death remains unknown.[160]

Denunciations cut several ways at the same time. They made it possible to detect the slightest signs of criticism, discord, or dissent in the broad area of the 'Jewish question'. They helped the Gestapo to proceed against the Jews, even inside the private sphere of home and hearth, but also pointed out anyone not in step with official policies on the Jews. The responsiveness and racism of the police almost ensured that many people would capitalize on racism for reasons of their own. Such informing had additional effects, including fostering rumours about the vigilance of the police, and thus helped to create the impression that no one was entirely beyond the reach of the eyes and ears of 'the Gestapo'. The widespread knowledge or exaggerations about the 'all-knowing' Gestapo created obstacles in the way of those who might have wished to express kindness towards or solidarity with the Jews. As Victor Klemperer's diary shows, even greeting a Jew in the street became a dangerous, almost a foolhardy custom. Citizens knew only too well that the patently innocent could be charged, with complete legal immunity for the accuser, especially if the accusation was aimed at the Jews (or Communists) and their sympathizers. Under all these circumstances, most people in Germany decided to avoid problems, to eschew all contact with Jews, and to avoid discussions of stories that began to filter back to Germany about the mass murders in the east.[161]

Germans and the 'Final Solution'

The Nazis raised the issue of the fate of the Jews for the public to consider on many occasions. Whether or not the Germans wanted or would support the genocide, the Nazis themselves seem to have concluded the people as a whole at least did not want to have it shoved down their throats. By the war years, most stories about the Jews in the newspapers concerned what was happening outside the Reich, with emphasis on the links of the Jews to major decisions taken by the Allies. Jews were invariably accused of being responsible for the war and for keeping up the pressure behind the scenes to defeat Hitler.[162] Newspapers and speeches illustrated the allegation of an international Jewish conspiracy by repeating endlessly how the Jews supposedly convinced the countries at war with Germany to take up arms.[163] Hundreds of press stories tried to show the influence of the Jews in enemy countries.[164] That approach was obviously meant to give weight to Hitler's theory that this was a war of the Jews against Germany, not the other way round.[165]

Another approach was to publish articles about the antisemitic policies and actions of foreign states as indirect testimonials that Germany's approach was catching on.[166] For example, in a story from 15 June 1941 announcing a series of sharper measures against the Jews in France, the French politician Xavier Vallant was quoted as using the ominous phrase that a 'final solution of the Jewish question' would come only after the war.[167]

The social conditions and defeated peoples that Germans found in their march eastward were seen through ideologically tinted glasses, so newspapers eagerly reported that the Jews and the Poles had deplorable living conditions.[168] In mid-October 1940 it was proudly announced that the newly created district (Gau) of Danzig-West Prussia was the first of four new districts in the east to have no more Jews, but nothing was said about how many had lived there, or what might have happened to them.[169] That such stories were printed suggests that press and propaganda officers considered that German readers would accept and even approve such a development.

In the propaganda build-up to the war against the Soviet Union and thereafter, the theme developed in the press was that Jews were linked with the Bolshevism of the Russian Revolution and with Stalin's Communist regime, and especially with Stalin's terror.[170] At the same time, numerous accounts continued of the alleged influence of the Jews on President Roosevelt, before and after Hitler declared war on the United States.[171] In fact the Jews were blamed for almost everything that went wrong for the Germans or their allies, even the overthrow of Mussolini in July 1943 and the attempt to take Italy out of the war.[172] They were blamed for bombing Germany and leading resistance activities in the occupied areas of Europe.[173]

One of the only times the concept of mass murder was mentioned, occurred in the context of stories about the murders of 12,000 or so Polish officers whose graves were discovered at Katyn. When this news was published in April 1943, not just the Russians in general, but the Jews in particular were accused of being the murderers.[174] The Nazis' own opinion surveys of German reactions to the stories about Katyn mentioned popular anxieties that the Germans captured at Stalingrad could expect the same (being shot in the back of the neck), and that the German people were in for horrific treatment should they lose the war. The Nazi opinion surveyors said that many people found it 'hypocritical' that German propagandists now found a heart for the (dead) Poles. Germans felt that their country had done far worse to the Poles and Jews, and so should not be outraged about what the Soviets did.[175]

This is not the place to reconstruct the decision-making behind the 'Final Solution', but historian Christian Gerlach recently has argued that Hitler took the 'fundamental decision' to implement the 'Final Solution' on 12 December 1941, notably just after he declared war on the United States and so fulfilled his own precondition for making all Jews pay. The Holocaust was of course already well under way at that point, but Gerlach shows that another stage in the persecution was reached at that time.[176] When Hitler spoke to his closest Party comrades in December 1941, he reminded them of his 'prophecy', and sounded even more bloodthirsty than usual.[177] The original threat was issued on 30 January 1939, when he said that if the 'Jews of international finance' succeeded in bringing about war again, as they allegedly did in the First World War, then this time 'the result will not be the Bolshevisation of the earth and thereby the victory of Jewry, but the destruction of the Jewish race in Europe.'[178]

Hitler as politician remained as reluctant as ever to spell out precise details of the 'Final Solution'. He certainly knew that, in spite of reservations, by the beginning of the war at the latest, most Germans agreed with Nazi antisemitism and the exclusion of the Jews from national life, and pushing that policy had gained support for the dictatorship.[179] The Nazis fostered a new antisemitic consensus in the war, one that would tolerate, if not support, and at least acquiesce in a radical solution that went far beyond 'mere' legal discrimination. Hitler and other leaders dared not articulate fully their murderous schemes. They did, however, unmistakably keep hitting the same notes, making the same threats, and letting the evidence pile up.

Hitler gave so many hints, that any thinking person would have found it hard not to conclude there might be something behind the habitually bombastic threats. He gave a speech on 30 January 1941, as he usually did on the anniversary of his appointment as Chancellor, yet again reminded the audience of his 'prophecy', and said he hoped that Germany's enemies would recognize that the Jews were the 'greater' enemy of all the warring nations. These nations, he said, should join in a common front, instead of fighting each other.[180] 'The Jew will be exterminated', so ran the headline story in reaction to this speech, and it said the prophecy would be fulfilled 'at the end of this war'.[181] On 8 November 1941 when he spoke to the Party faithful in Munich, he again accused the Jews of starting the fires of war.[182] The reaction to this speech in the Nazi press highlighted his attack on the Jews. One news story carried the headline, 'The Jewish Enemy', and concluded that 'the war against the Jewish international is a life and death struggle that must be ruthlessly fought to the end'.[183] Goebbels referred to Hitler's prophecy in newspaper stories on several occasions, the first time on 16 November 1941, as he tried to justify the decree that Jews must wear a yellow star. He mentioned that Hitler's prophecy was coming true. Many people in Germany apparently agreed that the Jews started the war, at least if official surveys from that period can be believed.[184] Goebbels repeated his message in early

December 1941 and, at the end of an address before distinguished guests at Berlin University, he calmly spoke of 'the historical guilt of the Jews', this at a time when trainloads of helpless German Jews were being sent to the east. He recalled for the audience what was by then Hitler's well-known prediction of early 1939 about the dire consequences for the 'Jewish race in Europe' if, as Hitler would have it, a conspiracy of Jewish financiers were to succeed in plunging the world 'yet again' into war. He added, apparently without needing to be more specific, that 'we are just now experiencing the realization of this prophecy'.[185]

In March 1942, a report alleged that Jews were trying to win public sympathy in Germany by saying that they 'were threatened by the worst of fates in being sent to a secretive swamp area', which sounded like Auschwitz. This rumour was denied. 'Such a danger does not threaten the Jews', the story said, adding the misinformation that 'they would [merely] have to work'.[186] Some pictures were occasionally published of Jews 'as leaders of the Partisans' and of alleged 'Jewish criminal types' who were said to be the 'instigators of a war of shooting people in the back' behind the lines.[187]

Throughout 1942, Hitler repeated in public on three major occasions and several minor ones, his prophecy of what would happen to the Jews.[188] The threats were invariably phrased in terms of future events. On 30 January 1942, for example, he stated that 'the war can only end when either the Aryan peoples are exterminated or the Jews disappear from Europe'.[189] Official surveys of popular reaction to the speech showed there was more concern about other issues raised in it, and in fact how Germans reacted to the prophecy was not mentioned at all. Nevertheless, the opinion survey said candidly, that the people apparently interpreted the threat 'to mean that the Führer's battle against the Jews would be followed through to the end with merciless consistency, and that very soon the last Jew would be driven from European soil'.[190]

Hitler's bombastic threat was uttered briefly in public on 24 February 1943. The prophecy was described as a possible response to the war, and the speech, delivered on Hitler's behalf to a Nazi Party audience, typically avoided specifics.[191] At that moment, Hitler had time to sign what was called a 'decree for the systematic intellectual battle against the Jews, Freemasons, and other enemies of National Socialism allied with them'. This struggle was now termed an 'essential war task'.[192] In the meantime, the deportation of the German Jews moved to its inexorable conclusion. The so-called 'privileged' Jews, who were allowed to stay in Germany because of their marriage ties, were forced to work. In many localities, public institutions, private firms, Nazi Party officials, and even small businesses were involved in the exploitation of these Jews. Historian Wolf Gruner notes dryly that few signs of the solidarity of 'Aryans' with the Jews have come to light.[193]

Victor Klemperer learned about Auschwitz only in March 1942 and that its reputation was as 'the most dreadful' of the concentration camps.[194] He heard rumours of a mass murder near Kiev by April 1942, although the massacre of over 33,000 Jews at Babi Yar (near Kiev) took place at the end of September the year before.[195] He certainly knew what was meant by terms like 'shot while trying to escape' when he heard about deaths at camps like Mauthausen in Austria.[196] He recorded the rumour in November 1942, that vacationers back from Poland reported with disgust that 'hundreds' were being shot each day. By that time, such practices had long since become the standard operating procedure.[197] In the summer and early autumn of 1942, the courageous 'White Rose' resistance students in Munich made specific mention of the murders of the Jews in one of the leaflets they distributed to the public. In it they said, but greatly underestimated, that as many as 300,000 Jews had been murdered in Poland since its conquest. The leaflet called this 'the most frightful crime against human dignity, a crime that is unparalleled in the whole of history'.[198]

Knowledge of what was happening, therefore, got through in bits and pieces. Klemperer was fully aware that German Jews deported to the east were as good as dead, even if the news that gas vans were used to kill reached him only in early 1943, by which time they had been carrying out their murderous tasks for two years.[199] When word reached him of Germany's defeat at Stalingrad, he somewhat unrealistically expected a pogrom, but none came because by then the deportation of German Jews was nearly over and had taken place without causing the slightest ripple in public.[200] Germans who listened to foreign radio, especially the BBC, could hear reports about the mass murder of the Jews from at least mid-1942, and Klemperer heard them repeated on the BBC even after the Allied landings in 1944.[201] These broadcasts provided some details about the persecution and the camps, but, as a thorough examination of them has shown, the unprecedented nature of the Holocaust was such that stories of it on the airwaves were incomplete, and encountered silence, incomprehension, and scepticism in Britain, even in the Jewish community there.[202]

Hitler's 'prophecy' speeches, repeated on numerous occasions by Goebbels, about the imminent fate of the Jews, continued to be short on details, even when in February 1943 almost 4,000 Jews were deported, and in March more than 12,000 followed, the latter being one of the highest monthly rates attained during the persecutions.[203] Goebbels's oft-cited article from May 1943 made the obvious clear, namely, that the war had become a race war, supposedly because Germany had to take up arms against an international conspiracy led by the Jews. The article ended by pointing to the (future) outcome of the war that would see, as Hitler predicted, the destruction of the Jews.[204]

Public concern was riveted on the war itself, whether that was the bombing of German targets, or more distant events like what Goebbels called the 'second Stalingrad', that is, the defeat in North Africa in mid-May 1943, and the resulting capture of 130,000 German and 120,000 Italian soldiers.[205] The mood improved when Germans were momentarily convinced that the war could still be won, for example, when Minister of Armaments and War Production Albert Speer told them in a speech at the Berlin Sport Palace on 5 June 1943, that in spite of the Allied bombing, war production continued to grow. Speer was on the same podium that evening with Goebbels, whose own speech was full of antisemitism and pride in the boast that the Jews were gone. He did not hint at what happened to them, but said that the international power of the Jews, now pressing for an invasion, could be defeated.[206] He noted in his own diary that he adopted a 'realistic approach' in the speech.[207]

As the Jews were deported, a page in Hitler's dictatorship was turned as new 'racially foreign' people, literally millions of foreign workers, were brought into Germany to labour for the Reich. The racist regime regarded Poles and other peoples from the east as racially inferior. They had to be used to win the war, but at all costs they had to be prevented from mixing with German blood. The authorities decided on nothing short of an 'apartheid' system, to keep these 'race enemies' in their place. As we shall now see, this massive exploitative effort unleashed new social dynamics.

7

Special 'Justice' for Foreign Workers

Hitler's dictatorship encroached on the daily lives of citizens on a routine basis, especially during the war years. Germans were constantly reminded of the kind of social and political system that came with Nazism, not only by the persecution of the Jews, but also by the presence in their country of thousands, and then millions, of foreign workers, men and women, and even children who were marked and treated as 'sub-human'. No doubt many Germans were grateful to get cheap help on the farm, or around the house, and for some, having people in their midst who were widely regarded as inferior, reinforced their sense of being part of the 'master race'. Nevertheless, for the Nazis it was a bitter pill to have to bring Polish workers and others into the heart of the Fatherland. They viewed Slavic workers as 'racially foreign', and, therefore a threat to the racially pure 'community of the people' that Hitler and others were then busily creating. By the autumn of 1939, they had already driven many Jews from the country; they had carried out a broad sterilization programme; and they had just begun killing off 'defective' individuals in chronic care who were considered 'life unworthy of living'.

Forcefully recruiting foreign workers made it possible to avoid the compulsory recruitment of German women to cope with the massive labour shortages in the country. The issues surrounding the employment of more single and married German women for the war turned out to be complex, and have been intensely debated by historians. On the one hand, Hitler did not want to use compulsory state measures to get more women to work, but in keeping with the image of a populist dictatorship, he preferred that they volunteer to do so.[1] The fact of the matter was that by the war years very large numbers of women were already working in Germany, in percentage terms, far more than in Britain or the United States.[2] Although historians have highlighted the 'failure' of the Nazi effort to mobilize additional women to work during the war (in comparison to the relatively greater increases achieved by the Allies), they have not paid enough attention to how many were already working before the war began. Indeed, every year from May 1939 to May 1944, a much larger percentage of German women were working in comparison to Britain or the United States. If there was anything like a female labour pool left to be tapped in Germany, then it would be married women.[3] Employed women often resented others they thought of as avoiding their duty, and on occasion it was the working women themselves who demanded full-scale conscription in the name of 'social justice'.[4] Although

Hitler was pressed on this issue from many sides as the war dragged on, he declined to go beyond asking for more volunteers, partly because he was 'fearful of popular objections', and also worried about the health of married women in their child-bearing years.[5] As it was, many German women went to work and put in very long hours under harsh conditions. Richard Overy shows that on balance, and in spite of some idle and privileged women, for working-class and peasant women in Germany, 'the idea of an "easy war" has a hollow ring about it'.[6]

The German war effort needed both more of their own women in the workforce and a lot more foreign workers. In order to limit the damage that Slavic workers could do to the 'body politic', Hitler and Himmler drew up plans for an apartheid system to deal with them, and put the Gestapo in charge of enforcing it. Inside Germany during the war, most of what the Gestapo did was directed at keeping foreign workers on the job, and controlling their contacts with Germans, lest forbidden sexual, or even friendly, relations develop that might corrupt German blood.[7]

Particular attention is devoted in what follows to the Polish workers, because they were the first Slavs, and were subjected to terror unlike anything experienced by most other Europeans, with the exception of the Jews.

Nazi Plans and Policies for the Poles

Hitler began the subjugation of the conquered Polish state as soon as the war started. On 7 September 1939 he told Commander-in-Chief of the army (Brauchitsch) of his wish for the 'ethnic cleansing' of Poland, a wish—transmitted by Heydrich the same day—that was full of deadly implications for Jews and Poles.[8] A month later, he used less murderous sounding (and ambiguous) language for public consumption, but did not hide the fact that Germany was going to remake the area in its own image.[9] Reports out of Poland told of the murder of 'tens of thousands' of civilian Jews and Poles during the first two months of the war.[10] Although the genocide of the Jews really began to deepen after mid-1941, already during late 1939 in Poland, mass murders, including women and children, were common.[11]

By 12 October 1939 Hitler ordered that the western section of Poland was to be 'Germanized', cleansed of Poles and 'returned' to Germany, while for the time being its eastern part was to go to the Soviet Union. The central section was soon turned into the General Government under Hans Frank.[12] At a meeting with the head of the armed forces on 17 October 1939, Hitler said he did not want to turn this General Government into a 'model state along the lines of German order', but to make it a kind of dumping-ground that would allow the Nazis 'to cleanse the Reich of Jews and Poles'.[13]

The Poles were the first of many nationalities 'recruited' by the Nazi regime and many of the measures adopted to deal with them were applied to others, especially those from the Ukraine and Soviet Union after 1941, the so-called 'East' workers. By August 1944, there were no less than 5,721,883 foreign workers employed in Germany, of whom 1,659,764 were Poles—about two-thirds of them working in agriculture.[14] Their exploitation made it possible to avoid the potentially unpopular move of conscripting non-employed German women into factory labour.[15]

The preferred method of dealing with foreign workers was to confine them in special camps.[16] Thousands of such camps were built across the country, and for example, a list from Düsseldorf, undated but most likely from the first half of 1944, shows 155 camps, each of which contained more than 100 foreign workers.[17] Some of the area's best known firms had the largest camps. In Duisburg the Mannesmann operation had a camp with 1,243 foreign workers; Krupp had one with just over 1,000 workers; and August Thyssen had one with some 1,440. In Essen, Krupp alone had 3,154 foreign workers in four different camps; and there were another 1,803 workers in a camp on the premises of the Gute Hoffnungshütte cement works in Oberhausen. The German landscape was dotted with all kinds of camps. Munich's 80,000 or so foreigners in February 1944 were kept in no less than 407 camps (13 of which could hold several thousand).[18] Historians have found evidence of at least 666 foreign worker camps in Berlin, but estimate there were even more.[19] The difficulty with policing the Poles was that so many of them were sent to work on farms where setting up even a rudimentary camp was not always feasible.

Anti-Polish sentiments were reflected in the German citizenship law of 1913, which was drawn up in such a way as to keep German citizenship from the Poles and the Jews coming from the east. The law was based on lineage or blood, so that no matter how long someone lived in Germany, their citizenship claims could be denied. That law was still on the books in the Nazi era, and remained unchanged until recently.[20]

German planners in November 1939 called for nothing less than 'the complete destruction' of the Polish people.[21] The 'General Plan East' formulated on Himmler's inspiration in 1940 and later revised, advocated a 'solution to the Polish question' that would see 80 to 85 per cent of the Poles removed from the German settlement area, and 20 million or so 'racial undesirables' pushed farther east over a 30-year period. The Plan followed Hitler who made clear on many occasions that he wanted Polish workers kept in a permanent condition of inferiority. As he put it on 2 October 1940, the Poles would work at 'lowly tasks, so that they can earn a living; their residence remains Poland, because we certainly do not want them in Germany, nor do we want any blood mixing with our German racial comrades'.[22]

Several factors complicated the issues, however. Polish workers had been used for generations in some parts of the country, as seasonal labourers in agriculture, or in certain sectors of industry, most notably in mining. They were long used to make up for labour shortfalls, as happened during World War I.[23]

The Poles were Catholic, and when they arrived, the Nazis blamed priests for asking parishioners to behave decently towards them.[24] Finally, most Poles went to the countryside, where as Nazi authorities noted with chagrin in late December 1939, the 'simple people had still to find the stance that was necessary for the future attitude of the German people to the Poles'.[25]

For Nazi planners, the genocide of the Poles, though some of them may have desired it almost as much as the annihilation of the Jews, could not proceed in the short run, because 'such a solution to the Polish question would represent a burden to the German people into the distant future, and everywhere rob us of all understanding, not least in that neighbouring peoples would have to reckon, at some appropriate time, with a similar fate'.[26] Later versions of the 'General Plan East' grew more expansive, and envisioned serial genocides and the death or deportation of 30 to 40 million 'racially undesirable' peoples like the Poles and Jews from the area to be colonized in the east. A second group of about 14 million, mainly Slavs, would stay to be used as slaves. Germans and others from 'Germanic nations', like the Norwegians and the Dutch, would settle the new territory.[27] Racist calculations also influenced the thinking of security authorities about the west Europeans enticed or forced to work in Germany. Indeed, the fine distinctions reached a point of absurdity in one attempt from the RSHA (14 January 1941) to classify and differentiate between 'workers of Germanic ethnicity' (those from the Netherlands, Denmark, Norway, the Flemish), and the 'racially foreign' people, among whom were the French, Walloons, Italians, Czechs, Slovaks, Yugoslavians, all of whom were lumped together with the Poles.[28] Different forms of exploitation and persecution would be applied to 'Germanic people' than to those branded as 'racially foreign'. Even if workers from the occupied areas of western and south-eastern Europe were not expressly forbidden from having sexual relations with Germans, as one later Gestapo report put it, 'in order to preserve the racial substance of the German people', such behaviour was definitely 'not desired'.[29]

As of 26 October 1939, all Poles between the ages of 18 (soon reduced to 14) and 60 were 'subject to compulsory public labour'.[30] There were already some 300,000 Polish prisoners of war and 110,000 civilians in Germany.[31] By early 1940, when too few came on their own, force was used.[32] Historian Jan Gross estimates that 'no more than 15 per cent' of all the Poles who went to Germany did so voluntarily.[33] By 30 September 1944, there were 1,701,412 Polish workers there, just over one-third of whom were women, about three-quarters of them in agriculture, while just over two-thirds of the Polish men were so employed.[34] The exploitation of so many Poles condemned what was left of their nation to economic ruin, social disintegration, and in time would have led to genocide.

Himmler sent formal guidelines on the treatment of Poles to the Gestapo on 8 March 1940. The inevitable fate of those who would not adjust was the dreadful Mauthausen camp.[35] Follow-up orders made Poles vulnerable to the arbitrary acts of the police, and even endangered Germans who might wish to socialize or be friendly towards the foreigners.[36] In order to underline these points, Poles were given a set of nine rules about the 'duties of male and female civilian workers of Polish nationality during their stay in Germany'. They were confined to their workplace and to their billets after curfew, and excluded from using public transport except with special permission. The Poles were the first in Germany to be forced to wear a badge—a purple 'P'—sewn to all their clothing. In addition, 'all social contact with the German people' was expressly prohibited, including visits to theatres, cinemas, dances, bars, and churches in their company. Regulations stipulated that any Pole 'who has sexual relations with a German man or woman, or approaches them in any other improper manner, will be punished by death'.[37]

Himmler evidently took a personal interest in pushing judicial officials to take a hard line on the Polish workers whose cases in the early part of the war were sent to court. He even reviewed at least some of the files of Polish workers caught for having 'forbidden relations' with Germans. The arbitrariness and brutality was made clear in February 1941, when Himmler told Max Frauendorfer, head of the labour department in what used to be Poland, that he had ordered the photographs of 180 Polish workers who were accused of 'forbidden relations' to be sent to him, and on that basis he had determined that 'execution was justified in each case from a racial point of view'.[38]

The Poles in Lower Franconia

How did the Gestapo function on an everyday basis in enforcing the apartheid system against Polish foreign workers? I decided to study case files of 'crimes' similar to the ones studied in the last chapter on the enforcement of Nazi anti-semitism. There is a total of 81 cases in the Würzburg collection that deal with banned 'personal, intimate/friendly relations' between Germans and Poles.[39] In addition, two other categories of dossiers are virtually indistinguishable from this first set. There are 36 files that cover forbidden 'friendly or sociable behaviour towards Poles', and 28 more that deal with disallowed or over-generous 'giving to Poles'. Taken together, these files provide evidence of the official effort, led by the Gestapo, to enforce the apartheid system in all of Lower Franconia.

From these 146 case files, I adopted a sampling procedure to make the research tasks feasible. After beginning with a 'chance' selection, I chose every second case for in-depth analysis. The results are summarized in Table 2.

Not a single case began when the local Gestapo itself discovered the 'crime'. One file was started when an inquiry came from another part of the country.

Table 2. Enforcing the social isolation of the Poles in Gestapo case files in Lower Franconia, 1933–1945

Sources of information	Number of cases	%
1. Reports from the population	35	48
2. Information from other control organizations	15	21
3. Observations by Gestapo and Agents	0	0
4. Information via communal or state authorities	4	6
5. Statements at interrogations	0	0
6. Information from businesses	1	0
7. Information via Nazi Party, Nazi organizations, or Party Members	4	6
8. Source not known	14	19
TOTAL	73	100

Source: StA W: Gestapo Case Files.

Other control organizations in the region gave information that originated 15 cases or 21 per cent of them all. In this rural area it should not surprise us that most such cases were brought to the Gestapo by gendarmes, the uniformed rural police. There are hints in these dossiers that the country policemen were tipped off by persons unknown or unnamed.[40] In Table 2, however, all such cases are 'credited' to the police. In reading the table, care should be taken not to infer that other police simply did the surveillance or investigative work in place of the Gestapo, because it was rare for a gendarme to discover crime on his own.[41] The gendarmes were informed if Polish workers tried to flee the area for some reason.[42] New terms were used to describe this criminal behaviour, like 'flight from work', or 'refusal to work'. Indeed, local gendarmes were eventually authorized (4 August 1942) to use corporal punishment by giving such workers 'an appropriate number of blows'.[43]

Communal and state authorities provided tips that led to only four cases, and it seems that they were not very involved in policing these workers once they were 'recruited', brought to Germany, and assigned a place of work. State surveillance of the foreigners persisted at the post office, and clear instructions were issued to keep track of their mail.[44]

The Nazi Party and/or its members were also not that involved, and provided information that led to only four cases.[45] Not all Nazi 'Party comrades' accepted the regime's hatred and hostility aimed at Polish workers, but those who broke the strict rules about socializing were taken to task when their behaviour was brought to the attention of the Gestapo.[46] On one occasion (August 1942) a local branch of the Nazi Party, denounced two German families to the Gestapo for sending wreaths to the funeral of a Pole who had worked for one of them for nearly three years, a gesture termed by the Gestapo as 'base and insidious'.[47] On 17 November 1942, regional Gestapo offices were told that the Nazi Party should become more involved in 'the surveillance of racially foreign workers so as to counteract racial dangers'.[48] However, this order was not easily translated into reality.

Denunciations or 'reports from the population', as indicated in Table 2 were responsible for 35 cases in the sample or nearly half of them all. The extent of this popular involvement is surprising in that the Poles were Catholic and Lower Franconia was a predominantly Catholic region. It should be added that these are identifiable denunciations. If remarks in the files suggest that the local police or other authority had been informed but do not give anything more specific, I did not 'credit' the case to the denouncers, even when there are grounds for concluding that the tip really came from a person outside the police who is not mentioned in the file. Cases that began with tips from members of Nazi organizations, such as the Hitler Youth, were not counted as 'information from the population'. We can see, therefore, that informing from the general population was the most important source for the police.

Denunciations were not only used by Germans, but in eight of these cases (or 25 per cent of all denunciations) they were lodged by the foreign workers, six by Polish women; one by two Polish men; and one by a Soviet worker.[49] The sexual exploitation of these workers is clear in these files, like one from July 1940 near Würzburg. The incident involved a 57-year-old farmer and his son who took advantage of a domestic servant, a Polish girl (aged 16). The farmer's son, a soldier on leave, was charged with rape, but allowed to return to his troop. His father got off with a warning and was barred from employing foreign workers again.[50] More reports of such sexual abuse led Himmler on 3 September 1940 to revise the March guidelines when it came to Polish women.[51] They were not to be executed, but arrested for up to three weeks, forced to change their place of work, and especially if they 'tempted' young men, sent to a concentration camp. The German male involved could suffer a similar fate, but in none of the cases I have examined did that come to pass.

The new regulations did nothing to stop the sexual exploitation of young Polish women or lead to a crackdown on German offenders, especially if they had political connections. Thus, a Nazi Party member and wholesale baker from the Aschaffenburg area repeatedly forced his attentions on his 15-year-old Polish apprentice. Because these were serious charges and the man already had a criminal record, the Gestapo wanted to send him to Dachau. The mayor and magistrate, however, thought otherwise, shifted the guilt to the Pole, and their 'party comrade' was released.[52]

Another case began with an anonymous letter (3 June 1944) to the Gestapo in Würzburg alleging that a prominent Nazi, Karl Kaiser, had 'intimate relations' and gave gifts to Maria Stepien, a Polish servant in his employ. The transgressions had taken place at least two years earlier. Under interrogation, Stepien claimed Kaiser had pressed his attentions on her. The local Nazi Party tried to cover up the misdeeds, and Kaiser himself 'volunteered' 500 Marks to a charitable association. The Polish woman, however, was kept in custody for three weeks and then sent somewhere else to work.[53] Even when Polish women were victims of serious crimes, they were reluctant to bring charges. This anxiety was fully justified, as is shown by a number of cases, including one from early April 1943, that concerned 20-year-old Polish worker Katharina Bocholt. It appears she was repeatedly harassed into sexual relations by her employer, a 69-year-old farmer Philipp Kemp. Bocholt got word to the mayor (8 April 1943), who passed the information to police. All she wanted was to leave because of Kemp's brutalities. After investigation, the gendarme found there was substance to her complaints and sent the case to the Gestapo. Kemp denied everything, but Bocholt offered telling details and they believed her. Although the Gestapo only gave Kemp a warning and soon released him from custody on 6 May 1943, they asked Berlin headquarters (the RSHA) to send the Pole to a concentration camp, a request denied (on 17 June 1943) because of her 'dependency relationship' with Kemp. She was finally released at that time, having been in custody since 10 April, far longer than her attacker.[54]

Denunciations were also used by Polish women to protect themselves from threatening Polish men. For example, a gendarme reported (28 April 1941) that Wanda Adamczyk, Polish civilian worker, told him about Peter Legut, a Pole who was having an affair with the daughter of his employer. When Adamczyk stumbled across them in the stable, Legut warned her to hold her tongue or he would 'cut off her head'. Adamczyk went to the police with the damning information.[55]

Although some Poles, like these women, used the power of denunciations, most of the denouncers were ordinary Germans. Prominent locals were not reluctant to denounce people, even on frivolous grounds, such as not getting the service to which they felt entitled in a restaurant.[56]

In this sample, like those dealing with the Jews, denunciations and false accusations were used for instrumental or selfish purposes that often had nothing explicitly to do with supporting Nazi racism. Denunciations were used to settle all kinds of grievances, including family conflicts. One example concerns 74-year-old Johann Schmidt, who charged his son-in-law with having sexual relations with Polish women. This allegation was considered baseless from the moment it was brought to the police in December 1941. The Gestapo eventually concluded the 'obviously false accusation' came from a desire for revenge. Schmidt had been at odds with his son-in-law for years. The Gestapo noted with some astonishment, that 'even though Schmidt is already a very frail old man, he remains capable of spreading these kinds of untrue rumours and thereby making others look bad'.[57] Anonymous letters of denunciation are also in evidence in this sample.[58] The outcome of one such case was fateful. It was received by the Kripo in Würzburg on 20 June 1943 and concerned farm worker Franziska Rosswirt. She denied everything until her pregnancy became impossible to ignore, at which point attention turned to Kazimierz Kubjak (born 1913) one of the Poles with whom she worked. Under questioning, Rosswirt finally admitted the 'crime'. Kubjak was arrested on 25 August and, perhaps because he was mistreated or frightened by the police, or because he recognized the hopelessness of his situation, he committed suicide during the night in his cell. The case was then forwarded to the Gestapo in Würzburg, who sent Rosswirt to Ravensbrück for two years. There is no word in the file on her fate.[59]

Women who became pregnant like Rosswirt were easy to spot in rural parts, and their excuses that the father was a soldier or some German chance acquaintance, often did not stand up when a healthy Polish man was identified by rumours as the likely sinner.[60] More than one desperate German woman went so far as to insist (falsely) that she had been raped, as one did in March 1941. She later admitted the truth, and after giving birth to the child, was sent to Ravensbrück, and the Polish male was sent to Stutthof.[61]

Maria Neuhof (born 1908), whose husband was absent from home, went in early November 1943 to the police to report that she was raped by a 'foreigner', but they found out she just had a medical examination, and was five months pregnant. The man responsible was Jochaim Osetck, a Pole (born 1907) with whom Neuhof worked on her husband's family farm. The file makes no mention of what happened to Osetck. After Neuhof gave birth to a girl (her fifth child) on 21 January 1944, she was sent to Ravensbrück, in spite of her large family and need to care for the farm. The RSHA made a decision that reveals the Nazi thinking on this issue: 'If the husband forgives, six months concentration camp, of which one week harder ordeal, otherwise one and a half years concentration camp.'[62]

Medical doctors did not always respect the confidentiality of their calling and informed on patients. We can deduce that a doctor was probably the informant in several cases, but we can be certain about one that began in August 1941. Ottilie Klotz, a woman from Miltenberg, made the trip to Külsheim (Baden) to be examined in what she thought was relative security. When the doctor asked about the father, Klotz blurted out that it was a Polish worker, and even gave her correct address. In his letter of denunciation to the Heidelberg Gestapo, Dr Braun said that after he told her she was expecting, she threatened suicide unless he aborted her pregnancy. By 25 September 1941 she was interrogated back home by the Würzburg Gestapo and so was the Polish worker Piotr Wlodarczyk. She was taken into custody, and let out to have the child, which was born on 23 April 1942. In spite of the fact that Ottilie Klotz was found medically 'unfit for a concentration camp', she was rearrested and just over 14 months after the birth of her child (after it was weaned), she was sent to Ravensbrück, where she arrived on 2 July 1943. Efforts of acquaintances to get her released failed, and her death was reported on 22 December 1944. There is no word at all in this file about what happened to the Polish worker, but he was certainly sent to a concentration camp as well.[63]

The head doctor in Schweinfurt wrote to the magistrate in mid-August 1941 to tell of the pregnancy of a young girl (aged 15) brought in by her father. The doctor said he felt 'duty-bound to make this report in order to protect the remaining youth of the village'. His letter led to the brief arrest of the girl and a friend, as well as the Poles with whom they struck up a relationship, Kasimer Jankovski (aged 26) and Eduard Woncik (aged 25).The Gestapo did not want a local execution, but one out of sight in a camp because 'otherwise there can be no doubt that great agitation would have resulted among the Catholic population'. So the Poles were sent to a concentration camp and executed there. [64]

The Apartheid System in the Rhine-Ruhr

The Gestapo's file system in Düsseldorf comprised 52 categories by war's end, according to 'enemy', 'crime', or 'racial' group involved. The closest case file category there, to the ones just examined from Würzburg, deals with 'forbidden contact' between civilian Polish workers and Germans, and could apply to anything from sexual relations to passing on a letter. In the Düsseldorf jurisdiction of the Gestapo, there are 165 dossiers of such 'forbidden contact', and I adopted the same sampling technique as I used in Würzburg, and studied 86 cases, or half of them all. The results are summarized in Table 3.

Once again, not a single case resulted from the observations of the Gestapo and its spy network. Even if one includes four cases based on information obtained in 'statements at interrogations', it is clear that the Gestapo was reactive, and not active, when it came to enforcing the racial policies aimed at the Poles.

In Table 3 we can see that other control organizations, such as the city police or rural gendarmerie, provided information that led to 12 cases.[65] Guards in the camps on the premises of some factories reported a few cases to the Gestapo. Homosexual relations with Poles were also criminalized and a guard was informed upon in early 1944 on that count. Four Polish men were apprehended at the same time in that case, from München-Gladbach. The German was a guard at the factory where the Poles worked, and although the Gestapo concluded he was the main culprit because he bribed the Poles with extra rations,

Table 3. Enforcing the social isolation of the Poles in Gestapo case files in the Rhine-Ruhr, 1933–1945

Sources of information	Number of cases	%
1. Reports from the population	40	46
2. Information from other control organizations	12	14
3. Observations by Gestapo and Agents	0	0
4. Information via communal or state authorities	7	8
5. Statements at interrogations	4	5
6. Information from businesses	6	7
7. Information via Nazi Party, Nazi organizations, or Party Members	4	5
8. Source not known	13	15
TOTAL	86	100

Source: HStA D: Gestapo Case Files.

all were sent to concentration camps, the Poles to the infamous one at Mauthausen and almost certain death.[66]

Although local police helped to enforce the apartheid system, there are hints in the cases they brought to the Gestapo that the information actually came from an 'ordinary citizen', who witnessed the 'criminal deeds'. There were instances when routine police patrol work turned up infractions.[67] For the most part, however, the role even of the uniformed police was reactive, such as when a Pole went to the gendarmerie to register a bicycle his employer ought never have allowed him to use in the first place.[68]

The uniformed police mostly responded to reports from citizens. This point is brought home in a dossier that opens with a typed report of 9 May 1940 on the married couple, Herr and Frau Gehling and the Polish worker Czelaw Burchert. The local gendarme claimed that the Gehlings and Burchert, who worked for the same farmer Alex Jager, not only tolerated the Pole Burchert in their home, but he downed tools when they told him he was being underpaid. His employer (Jager) was almost certainly the one who called the police, and they in turn informed the Gestapo. Gehling lost his job and Burchert was told to avoid socializing with Germans, or he could expect the absolute worst.[69]

If we take these and all other cases that began when 'control organizations' came up with information that led to a Gestapo case, and add the four that the Gestapo itself began when it found information 'from interrogations', then the vaunted Gestapo and police network in the Düsseldorf district was responsible for 19 per cent of these kinds of cases. These figures are similar to the ones for Lower Franconia shown in Table 2.

Communal and state authorities provided information which initiated another 7 cases, but nearly all resulted from mail checks at the post office.[70] One commenced when a German Labour Front (DAF) official in mid-April 1943 spotted several Polish women carrying *wurst* packages, from which he deduced that a German shopkeeper must not be following regulations.[71]

Nazi organizations, or a member of a Party organization such as the Hitler Youth, provided tips that opened four files, one of which begins: 'Members of the Marine Hitler Youth observed while on an outing on 25 May 1941 around 1800 hours, how an approximately 45-year-old man from Dormagen was taking the picture of several Polish civilian female workers and later went walking with them and sat down with them on the bank of the Rhine. It should be noted that the man was a Party member.' He was picked up and kept in custody for eight days.[72]

A cell leader of the NSDAP was told on 13 July 1941 that Polish worker Stanislaus Kaminsky, appeared in public without wearing the required 'P' attached to his clothing. Even more seriously, 'it has been observed' that late in the evening he often got on the tram with 28-year-old Maria Sanders (a divorced seamstress), and they bought tickets for the next town. It was likely that Sanders's neighbours, the three women 'witnesses' named in the dossier, were the ones who noticed she was meeting Kaminsky and alerted the Nazi Party. The damning information was passed up the chain of command in the local Party and found its way to the Gestapo. Sanders insisted that sexual intercourse did not happen, and was kept in the police prison until 9 September. The neighbours added more damning information about Kaminsky when they were questioned, and he was most likely sent to a concentration camp, but his fate cannot be determined from this dossier.[73] (In Table 3 this case is 'credited' to the Cell Leader of the Nazi Party because there is no written proof of who the civilian informers were.)

Denunciations or 'reports from the population' were responsible for 40 cases, or 46 per cent of this sample. The extent of this collaboration suggests considerable social involvement in the terror system. Historian Ulrich Herbert's study of German workers' complicity in the racism aimed at foreigners at the workplace and in the camps, rightly suggests that this behaviour emerged as Germans were put in positions of authority.[74] However, social collaboration extended well beyond the workplace.

Citizens used denunciations to gain redress for supposed slights at the hands of shopkeepers, and especially pronounced were complaints about publicans. Given wartime shortages of goods such as food, cigarettes, and alcohol, retailers were vulnerable if customers felt unjustly treated.[75] It has to be remembered that Germans themselves were subject to rationing and reacted bitterly to cutbacks when more of them were introduced.[76] Complaints were given a special urgency if they could be linked, however vaguely, to 'race questions', such as those surrounding the Jews and Poles. One police report from 26 November 1941 stated that: 'among other things, it has been reported to me, that an old man' from a nearby town 'received no schnapps and then it is said that schnapps was poured for Poles'.[77] A publican got into trouble (March 1941) for allowing Poles in his establishment. Alone among publicans there, he applied for permission to serve Poles, but when he was turned down, he let them in anyway. The gendarme soon heard, and the publican ended up in prison for 21 days.[78] Although such (often baseless) charges might appear from hindsight to be petty, one only has to look through the lengthy files on some of them, put together over several weeks, along with the numerous interrogations that were carried out, to understand how serious they were and that all could have deadly consequences.

Some people were denounced by neighbours, colleagues, or officials because they were eccentric, made sympathetic statements about the Poles, treated them as they would others, and thus seemed not to be holding to Nazi racist imperatives.[79] When a policeman went to the farm of Heinrich Deck on 11 April 1941 at midday, he saw a Polish worker seated between Deck's two sons. No reason is given for the surprise visit, but Deck, a Catholic, born 1881, later said the police were tipped off as an act of revenge by someone. When the policeman entered Deck's home, the Pole tried to hide. This was a sure sign, went the police report, that the Pole knew he and Deck were breaking the rules. Damning testimony was soon collected from Deck's neighbour, the local Nazi peasant leader, who said the family was unloved and related how 'it was said among the people, that the Poles were treated to coffee and cake by the Deck family'. The local magistrate (19 April 1941) concluded that the family head was 'unloved in the whole neighbourhood. The reason for this is, on the one hand, because of his self-righteousness and arrogant style and, on the other hand because of his divergent political views. Finally, it is also suggested that he sets other farm workers against their employers.' Deck was fortunate to escape with several days in custody and a stern warning.[80]

The Gestapo reacted with alacrity if someone informed on former 'opponents', like Communist sympathizer and worker Hans Possi. In September 1940 he allegedly said he was scandalized about the poor food and clothing given Poles where he worked. Possi was vulnerable because of his past politics, and a lengthy arrest record before 1933. He also failed to demonstrate the necessary 'honour and dignity of the German people in relation to the Poles', and was placed in custody for six weeks. By 16 November he ended up in Sachsenhausen concentration camp.[81] Bruno Stemkowski (born 1896), also stood out because of his ties to the Communist Party before 1933. He was officially 'stateless' even though he had lived in Germany since 1912. He was denounced on three different occasions, but got into the most serious trouble in the summer of 1940 supposedly for 'inciting' Polish workers and was sent to the 'work education camp' (AEL) in Recklinghausen.[82]

Priests were known to be sympathetic to the Catholic Poles, and were easy targets for the denouncers. A farmer denounced a priest to a gendarme on 27 September 1940. The priest from Marienhof greeted Poles in the street and asked them to come to Sunday service, which they did.[83] Another priest from Marienhof was denounced by a farmer on 8 June 1942 for asking farmers to let their Polish farm workers know the time of a special service. We can speculate that these farmers reported the priests because they did not want the Poles to leave work to attend services.[84]

There are hints of some resistance to racism in these files, such as a medical doctor who reported a farmer on 30 September 1942 for mistreating a Polish man. (The employer agreed to pay a fine to charity as punishment.)[85] Another case involved Anton Markowiak, a (skilled) and veteran mine-worker who objected when a foreman ordered two Poles to work harder and faster. The denounced man, a Catholic of Polish ancestry (born 1888), was a German citizen. He told the Poles during the night of 16 July 1941, in their native tongue that the foreman was 'crazy', with the implication to ignore him. On the following night when someone reported this to the pit boss, the denounced man was taken to task, and made things worse by saying the informer 'could go to hell'. This behaviour was given a dangerous twist by the trade union, which said that it amounted to turning Polish workers against their superiors, and the matter was turned over to the Gestapo. The foreman demanded only an apology from Markowiak, who had worked in this mine for 30 years. One sees here that denunciations extended down the mine shafts and that they occurred between people long acquainted with each other.[86]

Many of the cases in this sample show how 'ordinary citizens' kept up vigilance over long periods of time, as if determined, without any instructions from the police or the Nazi Party, to stop 'illegal' behaviour. One woman (34 years old) noticed that in front of her home on each Sunday at about 12:30 a Polish woman spoke to a man, and she wanted to know with whom. She finally got close enough to identify Eberhard Schröder (born 1902), a foreman at a nearby factory. Schröder was heard making improper suggestions and allegedly using coarse language and was denounced to the police. Even though there was no proof that anything sexual came to pass with the Polish woman, the woman's report cost Schröder his job and 21 days in 'protective custody'. There is no word in the dossier of what happened to the Polish woman, or what the motive of the denouncer might have been, but she kept up her surveillance over a four-week period.[87]

There is much evidence in this sample (as elsewhere) that denunciations were used for instrumental reasons that had little to do with consciously supporting Nazi racism.[88] Sometimes the Gestapo drew the conclusion that the denouncers acted merely out of 'a certain hatred'.[89] There were also instances of denunciations between spouses in this sample, like one from a small town near

Düsseldorf that began with two letters from a disgruntled wife in early 1941. What turned out to be her baseless complaint was summarized (after investigation) by the Gestapo, as having 'originated out of petty and revenge-seeking emotions'.[90]

Anonymous letters, some of them excruciatingly involved, were investigated by the Gestapo, only to find that essentially they were written for selfish interests. Some of these letters cast suspicion not just over one person, but entire families whose every member was accused of one grievous crime or another. At the end of one case in which a family was accused of everything from breaking the race laws (in dealing with Poles and Jews), the Gestapo wrote that 'all in all it has to be said that the nameless denunciation represents only an act of revenge against this family'.[91]

War exacerbated hardships on the home front and these in turn fuelled resentment and led to accusations. One originated with a complaint from 49-year-old farmer Wilhelm Pinsdorf from Binselberg in distant Württemberg. On 22 September 1943 he reported Gertrud Wunder, a married woman, who with her two children, was quartered on his farm since mid-July. Wunder was sent by Nazi Welfare (NSV), as were many city dwellers, to the relative safety of the rural south. According to Pinsdorf, backed up by his wife, almost upon her arrival Frau Wunder began having 'forbidden contact' with Polish agricultural worker Alexander Frankiewicz, a man who worked for the Pinsdorfs for more than three years and lived in their house. The Pinsdorfs, like many rural dwellers, were unhappy to billet people sent from the city, and by the autumn of 1943, they housed a dozen people. Their home was so crowded that when family members visited, one of the Pinsdorf adults had to sleep on the living room sofa. In the meantime, Frau Wunder had a room to herself and two beds. Resentment spilled over when this city woman struck up a relationship with the Polish worker. By 24 April 1944, having admitted her guilt under interrogation, Wunder was sent to Ravensbrück and an uncertain fate. What became of Alexander Frankiewicz, who was labelled as 'unsuitable for Germanization', cannot be determined, but in all probability he was also sent to a camp.[92]

A few Polish women in the Rhine-Ruhr used denunciations to obtain redress from sexual harassment and physical mistreatment by bosses or employers (or had other people do so on their behalf). In spite of what these women undoubtedly suffered on some farms, as one of them said, she was reluctant to appeal for help because she 'wanted to have nothing to do with the police and nothing to do with the courts'. These were the words of Maria Barczak, a Polish farm worker (born 1917), who claimed to have been raped on two occasions by her employer, the farmer Robert Nöckel. Instead of going to the police, Barczak tried to find another way out, and claimed at the labour exchange that she was too weak for the heavy work she had to do. After a physical examination, she was sent to work for a butcher in another town. Matters did not end there because Nöckel refused to pay her back wages and, though she remained reluctant to inform on him herself, she mentioned what happened to one of Nöckel's tenants (a German male), who went to the police. Nöckel was arrested and placed in 'protective custody' for three months because the Gestapo believed Barczak's story. However, in accordance with a decree of the RSHA issued on 3 September 1940, Barczak was also arrested and kept in custody for three weeks.[93]

There were farmers who did not go as far as Nöckel, but there was little doubt from some of their files that their behaviour towards Polish women in their employ amounted to what was variously termed in the files as 'molestation', or 'immoral advances'. One Polish woman told the farmer's wife what was happening and, not believed, she went to the Gestapo on 28 June 1944. Another woman (from the Ukraine) gave evidence in this case of her own harassment.[94] Still another woman went to the Kripo (13 January 1941) to make a similar complaint. The police language in these dossiers indicates anything but a sympathetic response.[95]

The Poles in the Palatinate and the National Pattern

It is not necessary here to examine at length and in detail how the Gestapo system worked in the Palatinate. However, I want to note the results of my research in the Gestapo materials from that area because they confirm that there was a national pattern in the interaction between the Nazi police system and the German people. The Palatinate, part of Bavaria since 1816, had a total population of just under one million in 1933. It is located along the Rhine river in western Germany between Baden to the south and the Rhine-Ruhr district to the north. It was an economically mixed region, with more Protestants (about 55 per cent) than Catholics.[96] It had more large cities than Lower Franconia to the east, but was less urbanized and industrialized than the Rhine-Ruhr area around Düsseldorf to the north. The Palatinate had three cities with over 100,000 inhabitants, and six more with populations in excess of 50,000. Neustadt an der Weinstraße (with a population of 97,483), was the seat of the regional Gestapo headquarters. Something of the political culture of the area can be gathered from the fact that in the March 1933 national elections, 46.5 per cent of the voters in the Palatinate decided in favour of the Nazis, which made it the 'brownest' of the three regions we are examining here and put it slightly above the German average.[97]

The files of the Gestapo in Neustadt are now in the archive in Speyer and have recently been opened to study. From the 150 files dealing with 'forbidden contact' between Polish foreign workers and Germans, I adopted the same random sampling technique I used for the other two regions, and studied 75 of

Table 4. Enforcing the social isolation of the Poles in Gestapo case files in the Palatinate, 1933–1945

Sources of information	Number of cases	%
1. Reports from the population	41	55
2. Information from other control organizations	10	14
3. Observations by Gestapo and Agents	0	0
4. Information via communal or state authorities	5	7
5. Statements at interrogations	0	0
6. Information from businesses	1	0
7. Information via Nazi Party, Nazi organizations, or Party Members	9	12
8. Source not known	9	12
TOTAL	75	100

Source: LA Speyer: Gestapo Case Files.

them in detail. The results in Table 4 show remarkable consistency with the other two regions.

The Gestapo in the Palatinate discovered no cases on their own. Indeed, out of a total sample of 234 cases from the three regions, the Gestapo did not detect a single case, and only wrested incriminating information from someone already in their grasp in 4 of all these cases. The conclusion is inescapable, that the Gestapo was overwhelmingly reactive when it came to discovering breaches of the apartheid system, and waited on information to flow from outside its own ranks.

In all three districts a significant number of cases opened by the Gestapo gave no indication as to who provided the tip. In the Palatinate 12 per cent of the cases, in the Rhine-Ruhr 15 per cent, and in Lower Franconia, nearly 20 per cent of all the cases, contain no indication as to the original source of the information. It is a fair guess that an 'ordinary citizen' provided these tip-offs, but for some reason the person went unmentioned in the Gestapo file. Given the attention to detail in the files, if the tips came from the regular police and/or other official or Party channels, that definitely would have been acknowledged, and would have been necessary to follow up any subsequent investigation. If we were to add these cases to the ones that began with an identifiable denunciation, then we would conclude that about two-thirds of all these cases (152 of the 234) came to the attention of the Gestapo by way of information from outside official circles.

State and communal authorities had surprisingly little involvement in the enforcement of the apartheid system in the three regions. As Table 4 shows, the

Gestapo in Neustadt received information from such sources in five cases, most from the post office, as elsewhere. Additional information was offered by the gendarmerie in the countryside or the uniformed police in the city.[98] One gendarme in May 1941 put his finger on the key problem that undoubtedly was true for most parts of the country. He noted with resignation on finding Poles in a restaurant drinking coffee with their employer's family, that 'all warnings to most farmers are fruitless. As soon as a Pole works even reasonably satisfactorily, everything is forgotten and a peaceful home community is made for them.'[99] In any event, the rural and city police did not carry out the tasks of the Gestapo, or cover the country like a blanket.

The 'regular SS' ('Allgemeine SS') played little or no role in any of these samples. The SD turned over some information to the Gestapo, but not very much.[100] In the Rhine-Ruhr area, the SD reported only one case in October 1941, when it told the Gestapo of the rumour that a priest was considering entering some Polish workers on the Church tax list.[101]

Table 4 shows that the Nazi Party was slightly more active in enforcing the apartheid system in the Palatinate, perhaps a reflection that the region had more Nazis and fewer Catholics than the other two areas. Party members informed when they saw members of the Hitler Youth going to the movies with Polish girls.[102] Party members or those in other Nazi organizations in this sample tended to take their tips to Party headquarters. In one of the few cases in which such a person contacted the police, a Nazi nurse reported that, while on a house call in June 1943, she was told of a sexual relationship between a Polish worker and a German woman (aged 40). The woman was eventually sent to a concentration camp, and the Pole ended up in the SS camp at Hinzert and an unknown fate.[103]

Some non-Party members brought their information to the Nazi Party first and only later went to the Gestapo, as did a 27-year-old married woman who 'appeared voluntarily' at the Gestapo's office in Ludwigshafen on 16 April 1943 to inform on her neighbour, a Catholic woman who had been lauded by the Nazi regime for having many children. The denouncer said she was offended by her neighbour's lifestyle and that she 'utterly neglected her motherly duties'. The last straw was that she was having an open affair with a Polish worker. The denouncer said that her attempts to get the Nazi Party local group to straighten out the mess, produced no results, so she concluded, 'I see myself pressed to make the Gestapo aware of the actions of the woman, so that they can instruct her as to the reprehensibleness of her behaviour.' Alas, the ultimate 'instruction' the Gestapo provided was to send the woman to the Ravensbrück concentration camp where she remained until the end of 1944. Because the Pole did not pass the race tests, he was shipped to the Natzweiler camp for 25 years and may well have died there.[104]

When German women became pregnant, they presented the racist regime with a dilemma, especially if the Pole appeared 'suitable for Germanization'. The issue was discussed in a note from Gestapo Chief Heinrich Müller to all Gestapo posts on 10 March 1942. If, in an initial judgement, both parties were deemed 'racially acceptable', and if the 'racially foreign person' wanted to marry the woman, no further proceedings would be taken against her. The Pole would be arrested and assessed for his 'potential for Germanization'. If there was a 'positive' result, pictures were to be sent to the RSHA in Berlin, both persons were to be set free, and the case dismissed. If the result was negative, the 'usual special handling request' was to be made for the Polish worker, that is to say, steps taken to liquidate him or send him for life to a camp.[105] We need to recall that such examinations and proceedings would have been unthinkable if the man involved was Jewish, so that the Jews were definitely singled out.

Party members informed the Party watchdogs in their blocks, neighbourhoods, or at local district headquarters, and the Party often resolved the problems on its own. When it could not or the matter was too serious, the case went to the Gestapo, as did one of the very first cases dealing with infringements of the apartheid system in the Palatinate. It began with a complaint of 26 February 1940 from Party headquarters in Kaiserslautern, and asserted that a Catholic priest said from the pulpit that parents should restrain their children from throwing stones and snowballs at Polish workers. Rumour was that the priest also offered the Poles coffee and wine. The only way the Party or the police could have found out about these 'crimes' was if someone, here it was probably a Party member, talked about them. The priest managed to find an excuse by claiming he was told the Poles were in fact, not Poles at all, but returning ethnic Germans. One of the Poles who supposedly told him that (as it turned out, false) story was not so lucky and was sent to Dachau 'to set an example'. The file shows that he was transferred to Sachsenhausen in September and his death was reported there on 15 November 1940.[106]

Pregnancy when the woman was unmarried or the husband was away, was also a source of rumour and suspicion in all these regions. Party headquarters was informed in late 1942 after a pregnancy came to light. Roman Walkiewicz was arrested as the likely father at 13:30 (3 December) and he was found dead in his cell at 8:30 next morning after having committed suicide. The Protestant woman involved was the daughter of the local farmers' leader, and she soon had a miscarriage. The police suggested she needed re-education.[107]

In February 1943 the word in a small village in the area was that a 36-year-old single Protestant woman was pregnant and that the father was likely to be the Pole who worked for neighbours. It was also said that she went to the Saarbrücken area to try to get an abortion. All the information was verified. Eventually, mother and child died of natural causes, but the Gestapo's pressure may have been a contributing factor. The Pole was sent to Hinzert, not a concentration camp, as he was considered 'worthy of Germanization'. He was still there on 21 July 1944 and his fate is unknown.[108] In another such case, the pregnancy of a married woman was mentioned to a policeman on his rounds by a Nazi Party cell leader in mid-September 1942. Once she had the child, the extent of her punishment was put in the usual form to her husband, who was in the Wehrmacht. If he forgave her she would be sent to Ravensbrück for three months, if not it would be for three years. As they had divorced, it was a moot point and she was sent for the longer period and may well have died in the camp. The Polish worker earlier had slipped away to the General Government, and could not be found.[109]

Table 4 makes clear that information from the population provided the greatest single source of all the files in the Palatinate, as in the other two regions. It is reasonable to conclude that the national pattern was that about half the Gestapo cases dealing with the social isolation of the Poles originated from identifiable denunciations.

The extent of this social collaboration in the enforcement of anti-Polish policies was nearly the same as we saw in the last chapter in the enforcement of Nazi antisemitism. The differences were not as great as might be expected, and as often asserted in the literature. A study of all the cases involving racial discrimination and persecution leaves no doubt that ordinary (non-official) Germans were heavily involved.

Anonymous letters of denunciation are found in all the samples, including the one from the Palatinate. In spite of orders from Berlin to ignore such letters, and even to track down the writers and punish them, the Gestapo checked out the tips relentlessly. One writer sent letters to the accused German woman, as well as to the police in a case that took place in March 1943 in Bebenheim. It turned out that a Catholic married woman was having an affair with a Polish worker and was three months pregnant. Faced with the standard choice of what he wanted done to his wife, her husband forgave her and appealed for her release. She was lucky to be set free in July to have the baby. The Pole, who admitted his guilt, was sent to a concentration camp for 30 years.[110]

The police occasionally managed to find the writers of false accusations, like one 63-year-old man who sent a letter to the police in May 1941 charging all kinds of 'forbidden contacts' between Poles and local women. After lengthy investigations, nothing was found to support the charges, and the denouncer was asked to pay a fine of 50 Marks.[111] As is clear from such cases, the police did not want to be too hard lest they discourage others from offering information, and they continued to follow up anonymous letters.[112]

Personal squabbles and neighbourhood strife often motivated denunciations. One long series of charges and counter-charges in the Palatinate, ended with the remark by the investigating gendarme, that the real issue had nothing to do with 'forbidden contact', but was a 'quarrel among families and private matters'. The families were said to be 'enemies and inform on each other at every opportunity'.[113]

Such deep-seated personal conflicts could be given a deadly twist if one of those involved ignored the guidelines about fraternization with the Poles. Rumours in one village began to circulate in late 1941 that a 26-year-old Protestant, Paula Braun was having an affair with a Polish farm worker of the same age. To put a stop to the rumour, Braun physically attacked the neighbour she thought started it. However, it turned out that there was substance to the story, Braun was arrested, and she was eventually sent to Ravensbrück. She returned only on 7 August 1944 after years of ordeal. Once the Pole failed the race tests, the local Gestapo wanted to execute him in the forest near the scene of his 'crimes', but decided instead to send him to Natzweiler for 30 years.[114]

Five of the 75 cases in the sample from the Palatinate began when foreign workers were the informers, at times with tragic consequences as when two Poles were denounced by another whose motives are not clear in the file. One of the men was sent to Mauthausen, where he died.[115] A conflict among foreign workers in May 1944, led one Soviet worker to denounce a Polish colleague who was eventually sent to Buchenwald.[116] Such cases from the other regions suggest that foreign workers used the Gestapo and Party apparatus for instrumental purposes, if to a far lesser extent than did Germans.[117]

One case whose tragic consequences were fully documented began in Kaiserslautern on 30 September 1941, when 26-year-old Amalie Benkel went to the Kripo to report that in May she had a sexual encounter 'against her will' with Polish worker Stephan Kroll and was five months pregnant. She was arrested immediately and, especially because of the charge of rape, so was Kroll. Both worked for Benkel's mother. On 16 October he was interrogated by the Gestapo, denied the charges, but confessed to a sexual relationship over many months. She kept insisting it was a one-time event and that he used force. The Gestapo did not believe her, and that was what mattered, as there was not even a thought of sending cases like this to court. As the woman was pregnant Kroll was given the perfunctory 'race test'. The Gestapo's evaluation of Kroll was totally damning, in that he was described in language laced with personal distaste, racial prejudice, and sexual anxieties.

Their negative report produced the result (8 January 1942) that Kroll failed the test, and the RSHA in Berlin asked local authorities to check whether he had been told about the death penalty for such crimes, to which they responded (10 February) that they even had his signature on the document to prove he had been informed. The RSHA then ordered his execution for 20 April— Hitler's birthday! To avoid taking up the time of officials on such a momentous day, the execution was moved up to 17 April. It took place near the scene of the 'crime', and the 'execution protocol' noted that three members of the Gestapo and an SS doctor were present, as was a translator who informed Kroll that 'by order of the Reichsführer-SS' Himmler, he was 'to be executed by hanging because of the crimes he had committed'. As per routine, the execution itself was carried out by two Polish workers; the 155 Poles who witnessed the execution were led past the body. The German woman involved was released from custody in time to have her baby, after which she was sent to Ravensbrück. Her fate is unknown. The brief public opinion report on local reaction to the execution, written by the gendarme from the area, noted only that the population thought the execution was 'justified'. The policeman concluded that 'generally the view is that the woman ought to have experienced the same thing, because it was a case of a German woman and she had, through her actions, severely damaged the image of the German woman'.[118]

This was the kind of case that judges and others at the time often called 'lynch justice'. This description is not quite apt. The difference between the Nazi form of 'lynch justice' and the kinds of events we usually associate with the term was that the lynching was not carried out by a mob in a moment of inflamed passions. In Nazi Germany, 'lynch justice' was premeditated killing designed for maximum terroristic effect on both the downtrodden Polish workers and on any German who contemplated sleeping with or comforting the enemy.

Not everyone who informed about some misdeed of a Polish worker wanted the full measure of the terror used. There are hints in some files of misguided 'idealism' and expectation that the 'good' Gestapo would straighten out a mess. Other denouncers simply wanted to replace one of their own workers who misbehaved or was no longer worth keeping around. Such a simple intention cost Stanislaus Smyl his life. By all accounts, Smyl was small of stature and at least his Gestapo file states that he was 'not fully responsible mentally'. From early in 1940, he worked for a farmer in the Gestapo jurisdiction of Paderborn. In late May he approached a married woman in the street and, while 'emitting strange sounds' displayed his naked penis. The woman, who was already upset because of the recent death of her husband in the war, asked her relatives to contact Smyl's employer, who agreed that Smyl should not be allowed to stay in the village any longer. The Labour Office was informed and asked to send Smyl somewhere else. However, once word got out that he might have committed a crime, local police were called and soon the case was on the desk of the Gestapo in Paderborn. The medical doctor asked to examine Smyl concluded the man was both unfit to work and 'mentally incompetent', and the Paderborn Gestapo recommended that he be sent back to Poland. For the authorities in the RSHA in Berlin, however, such a move was not in keeping with Himmler's guidelines and they insisted on his arrest. In July 1940, the RSHA reached the decision that Smyl should be hanged in public, and they also ordered that the execution be publicized in the area; that the Poles be brought to witness it; and that Nazi Party organizations send representatives. On 26 July 1940, Smyl was executed in the presence of between 100 and 150 people. A priest who was allowed to give Smyl comfort recalled that the man did not understand what was about to happen.[119]

'People's Justice' and 'Police Justice'

As the executions of Stanislaus Smyl and Stephan Kroll demonstrate, the most brutal sides of the enforcement process did not always take place behind closed doors and in secret. Persecution turned to open terror in the war years, also inside Germany, and some of the cruel realities were brought home to the public in ways that would have been unthinkable before 1939. As Kroll's case and others mentioned in this chapter show, Poles were dealt with directly by 'police justice', they rarely went to court, and usually the German involved (like Amalie Benkel) was dealt with the same way. 'People's justice' against foreign workers and the Germans they became involved with could be cruel, as in the case of farm labourer August Keidel (born 1894) and a Polish farm worker Rosalie Walktor (born 1914). She arrived in Lower Franconia in March 1940 and by July their employer (he later said) began to notice that she and Keidel had become friendly. Whether he denounced them is uncertain, but action was swift once the Nazi peasant leader got wind of it in early August 1940. Local Nazis arranged a public demonstration on 12 August 1940 and Keidel was led through the streets with a sign around his neck that read: 'This lad defiles the German honour. He slept with a Polish wench.' When the Gestapo arrived to make the arrest, they were not unhappy to find what they described as a scene of 'people's justice'. Keidel was on display at the market place where he was surrounded by a jeering mob of 500 people and humiliated. Later he was sent to Dachau for three months and released, with a further warning, on 14 January 1941. Neither he nor the Polish woman were tried in court, but she was sent to Ravensbrück for three months. What became of her is not mentioned in the dossier.[120]

Fraternization of this kind with Poles, led the Würzburg SD in November 1940 to report from its headquarters that German men, especially farm workers, 'did not have the slightest sensitivity' about having sex with female Polish workmates. Rural employers were to be instructed in no uncertain terms that they must impress on Germans that such behaviour was not acceptable. The SD wanted all offenders 'dealt with by Draconian measures, because only thus will the necessary deterrent be achieved. Often more effective than a sentence [for the German] are the measures of popular justice, with heads shaved and a marching about with placards in the village.'[121] There were similar kinds of reports from elsewhere in the country at this time. The Attorney General in Jena noted in March 1940 that the practice in Thuringia, even before a woman was charged, was to parade her with shaved head and placards through the village.[122] Such exhibitions of 'people's justice' and 'police justice' became more prominent in the German countryside.[123]

Another example from Lower Franconia opened on 19 August 1940 with the typed statement of the Würzburg Gestapo that a certain Walter Freitag (born 1920) and the Pole Josefa Kurasz (born 1922), both employed on a farm, had sexual relations 'at the beginning of June in the barn'. It is uncertain whether the Gestapo was at the scene of the subsequent public demonstration that took place in the village, but they questioned Freitag as early as 17 July. The dossier notes laconically that shortly before the arrest of Freitag and Kurasz on 18 August, Freitag was led through the village by about 80 men of the Storm Troopers and Hitler Youth to the accompaniment of trumpets. The demonstration, led by Nazis who came from nearby Kitzingen, ended at the Rathausplatz. There, in the presence of the entire village, the deputy Party boss issued words of warning about 'forbidden relations'. An indication of the unequal justice meted out was that for all of his harrowing experiences Freitag was promptly released. Josefa Kurasz, on the other hand, was sent to Ravensbrück for three months.[124]

August Keidel and Walter Freitag were two of the German males who were paraded in public in this way. It was far more common for German females to be so defamed.[125] The practice went so far that even two young women from a village near Würzburg, one of whom (aged 16) was raped, and the other (aged 17), who was sexually assaulted by Polish prisoners of war in May 1940, had their heads shaved by the Storm Troopers and, with the permission of the magistrate and Party boss, then marched through the streets with signs round their necks that stated they were 'without honour'. The reaction of Catholic townsfolk, was 'complete rejection' of such measures. The injustice became doubly clear when a court later ruled that both women were innocent.[126] Far from that giving pause to the Nazis, the Security Service (SD) that tracked public opinion noted that because of the deep shock of parents and family, these public defamation practices (unjust or not) showed the greater social impact of 'people's justice' over sending cases to court. The SD noted that the public relations effects lasted 'for weeks' as word of the events circulated. 'The most salutary effect' was the fear that such a thing could happen again, so that 'at least for the indefinite future' women would consider it prudent to avoid the Poles.[127]

Himmler learned about such examples of 'people's justice', and agreed with the 'educative' practices as long as they did not get out of hand.[128] There were many Germans, grateful for help on the farm, who were slow to adopt racist attitudes towards the Poles, and there were numerous reports of forbidden socializing.[129] From the Nazi point of view, this behaviour, perhaps fuelled by Christian charity, left much to be desired and was one reason Himmler did not oppose public punishments.[130]

Hitler's direct influence on events, right down to the local level, can be found on occasion, as in the autumn of 1941, when 'people's justice' began to be used more widely, including on persons from nations allied with Germany. Hitler ordered a halt to further public defamations on 16 October 1941 out of concern for the feelings of Germany's allies and friends.[131] On the other hand, he also intervened when he heard of instances when courts showed the slightest sign of being soft on Polish workers, as in one case from 1941. Judges in Lüneburg said there were mitigating factors when a Polish worker sexually assaulted a German girl.[132] Thanks to Hitler's intervention, the judges were removed from the bench.

The Gestapo continued to carry out public executions (by hanging) of Polish men, but did so away from spectators, still to the dismay of judicial authorities. In July 1941 a mildly phrased letter of complaint by the Nuremberg Higher Court President to the Minister of Justice in Berlin noted that the Gestapo hanged Julian Majlca for having an affair with a German who became pregnant (she was later given ten months in jail). After the execution all the Poles in the vicinity were marched past the body. 'The fact that this execution took place without previous judicial hearing, was the subject of lively discussion.' Apparently even the local Nazi Party boss was opposed. The same letter mentioned a case where the Gestapo in Regensburg went to the court jail, picked up another Pole being held for having forbidden relations and executed him. In November the same thing happened in the forest near Eschelbach, where the Pole Jarek was hanged for having relations with a 20-year-old woman. Again, 100 or so Poles from the area were led past.[133] As a judicial report from mid-1942 makes clear, justice authorities were often left in the dark, knowing neither the charges nor even the number of such executions.[134]

The issue of what should become of the German woman was much discussed among police authorities and the people. A popular response, as we have already seen, was that she should not be allowed to get off lightly. In a case from the Düsseldorf area (in June–July 1941), the minimum demand was that the woman have to witness the execution.[135] A judicial report of 4 September 1942 said that 'some Polish civilian workers' were hanged by the Gestapo, but, the writer added, 'one heard nothing about what might have happened to the German girl or the German woman, apart from perhaps a warning being given. Among the people, that is often not understood. It even causes a certain shock, that the dishonourable and worthless behaviour of the German girl or the German woman is not sensibly punished.'[136]

How the Poles were treated elsewhere is suggested by correspondence from other areas in Germany. Thus, a report from the Attorney General in Jena on 31 May 1940 noted that two courts were supposed to deal with a Polish man who was accused of having sexual relations with a German woman; she was given seven years by the court, but before he could be tried, 'an official of the

Secret State Police appeared, took the files, and declared that the RSHA in Berlin had issued orders to hang the Pole'.[137] In another case from the same area on 24 August 1940 the Gestapo took a man from the court prison in Gotha and hanged him in the presence of 50 Poles on the side of the road; the body remained there for 24 hours.[138] More complaints came from Jena in the following months, one of which pointed out that, while 'popular justice' might have a deterrent effect, it gave rise to uncivilized behaviour, and also undermined the existing justice system.[139]

Letters of complaint about high-handed police methods continued to flow from those in charge of the administration of justice all over Germany. Illustrative was one from the Hessian Higher Court President in March 1942. He wrote that on 24 January, a Polish woman near Fulda killed her employer's child with a cleaver and injured another. She was hanged by the Gestapo on its own authority, and in the presence of 200 Poles who were brought to see the spectacle. The Court President did not doubt the Pole deserved what she got, or that the courts would have delivered the same verdict, but lamented that the Gestapo, with its 'lynch justice' was undermining what was left of the justice system. He was particularly disturbed that the Gestapo permitted 500 or so Germans to witness the hanging, along with the 200 Poles brought to see it as a deterrent.[140]

Himmler reacted to the case in a note of 22 April 1942 to Minister of Justice Thierack. He remarked that the woman would probably have been declared by the courts to be deranged, not responsible for her actions, and therefore not subject to the death penalty. For Himmler, that was totally unacceptable. He continued:

As Reichsführer-SS and Chief of the German Police, however, I am responsible to see that such deeds find their just penalty. The community of the people demands the destruction of such parasites, regardless of whether, according to juristic considerations, a subjective guilt exists or not. I cannot accept that a Polish sub-human escapes their punishment through some legal regulation or other.[141]

These remarks show what was at the heart of Himmler's notion of a 'police system of justice', as does the remainder of his letter. He turned to another case in which a Pole attacked and killed his employer in a small town near Rudolstadt. The deed (committed on 24 November 1941) allegedly caused a local uproar. The Pole, who tried to commit suicide, was turned over to the justice authorities, but could not be tried before 8 January 1942. In fact, he died before that date from his self-inflicted wounds. Himmler decided that the murder of the German could not possibly be atoned for by the execution of a single Pole, so opted for a public execution of 11 Poles, to be carried out near the scene of the crime. He noted to the Minister of Justice, that 'the population had accepted the execution I ordered with satisfaction, but was quite rightly irate that absolutely nothing happened to the real culprit'. (Indeed, a later report of the court responsible for this area verified this contention, and that the people there regretted only that the culprit himself—although already dead—had not been hanged alongside the rest.[142]) Himmler continued, that 'it would have been better also in this case, if a transferral to the justice authorities had been avoided, and my decision had been immediately sought. I regard it as my duty, therefore, now as in the past, to decide myself upon such cases immediately after the deed.'[143]

As we saw earlier, after Justice Minister Gürtner's death in early 1941, the Ministry was (from 1 February 1941) put under the leadership of Franz Schlegelberger, who, however, proved not to be radical enough for Hitler's taste and was replaced (from 20 August 1942) by Georg Thierack. He intensified the 'guidance' of the regular court system and systematized it by issuing regular instructions to judges. He also unequivocally demanded in a meeting with higher justice authorities on 29 September 1942, that they work for still harder verdicts and more death sentences.[144] Ten days earlier, at Bormann's suggestion, Thierack met with Himmler. They reached agreement that those in custody who were 'Jews, Gypsies, Russians, Ukrainians, Poles sentenced to over three years, Czechs, or Germans sentenced to over eight years' were to be handed over to Himmler, as also was the vaguely defined group of 'asocial elements'.[145] This agreement (with no basis in law whatsoever), routinized the implicit division of labour by which the Gestapo would henceforth have the blessing of Justice, to deal with all 'racial' problems. In a note to Bormann of 13 October 1942, Thierack outlined the basis of his own thinking on the subject:

With a view to freeing the German body politic of Poles, Russians, Jews and Gypsies, under the concept of freeing up the eastern areas that have accrued to the Reich for the German people, I intend to pass over to the Reichsführer-SS, the criminal prosecution of Poles, Russians, Jews and Gypsies. My point of departure here is that the justice system can only contribute in minor ways to the extermination of these peoples. No doubt, the courts are handing down very hard sentences against such people, but that is insufficient to contribute importantly to the implementation of the above-mentioned concept. It makes no sense to conserve such peoples for years on end in German jails and prisons. . . . Instead of that, I believe that by handing such people over to the police, who can then act free of legal constraints, far better results will be obtained.[146]

On 5 November 1942 Himmler informed the Gestapo across the country of the agreement with Thierack, and of its authorization by Hitler, and he spelled out the implications. These foreigners were 'racially inferior people', and it followed that like 'Jews and Gypsies' they should be subject to a different penal code. Whereas up until then, judges evaluated the personality and motives of men and women before them, henceforth such considerations were to be ignored. Thus, the net effect of the Himmler–Thierack agreement was to put an end to what remained of the flimsy judicial protection of the rule of law for the Poles and the others mentioned above.[147]

At another meeting with Himmler on 13 December 1942, Thierack confirmed and reiterated his intentions about this division of labour, by agreeing
that henceforth Himmler's decrees, would constitute 'the basis for the penal
proceedings against the racially foreign peoples'. As we have seen, most of
these cases were dealt with outside the courts. If French civilians or prisoners
of war were involved it was rare that they were executed, but that happened
on occasion, as when one was shot in Weisingen, near Dilligen/Donau in
December 1942.[148] Usually, however, the cases of west Europeans were sent
either to the regular courts or, if more serious, to the Special Courts. However,
when it came to the Poles or 'east' workers, 'police justice', not bringing the case
to court, was the preferred approach. That few of their cases apparently went to
court in a city like Munich should not, therefore, lead us to conclude that crimes
like 'forbidden contact' were marginal phenomena in the cities.[149]

According to the Himmler–Thierack agreements in 1942, the justice system
was in the future mainly for Germans only.[150] Their agreements went a long
way in recognizing the validity of 'police justice'. Execution orders for Poles,
usually carried out as soon as possible and beyond appeal, were formulated in
such a way as to make clear that the decision was made by the police, not the
courts. As one case from late 1942 put it, 'The Head of the Security Police and SD
has decided,' that the person in question 'is to be hanged'.[151]

The RSHA issued orders to the Gestapo on 30 June 1943, about formally
removing Polish and Soviet civilian workers from the German penal code and
making them subject to the police. The next day, the few remaining Jews in
Germany were also declared to be outside the jurisdiction of the courts.[152]
Removal of all 'racially foreign people' to the sphere of the police was reinforced
by a Himmler directive on 10 February 1944. It pertained to 'serious crimes and
sexual relations of the foreign workers'. The instructions end with the chilling
phrase that 'carrying out of special handling [i.e. executions] aims above all to
be a deterrent to the foreign workers inside Germany'.[153]

The administration of justice ('Rechtsprechung') also concerned how to
publicize court decisions. In the Thierack–Himmler view, the method in rural
areas and villages with fewer than 20,000 inhabitants was for verdicts to be
carried out as quickly as possible and presented to the public to obtain the
maximum social effect. In the cities, where the 'administration of justice' was
more difficult, reports of crimes and punishments of Poles and the other groups
named above were published in carefully worded articles in newspapers or
distributed on posters in the workplace. The city press offered numerous
exemplary stories, not only of the 'heavy penalties for unruly Poles', but also of
what happened to Germans.[154] The public was given instructive stories of the
'false pity' of passing on the letters of Poles to their families.[155] People could read
of a young woman's 'disgraceful behaviour': speaking with a Pole (for which
she was given six weeks in jail). At the head of the newspaper story was the

imperative 'Keep Your Distance'.[156] Even a 54-year-old man (a war veteran and father of nine children) was given a month in jail for his 'disgraceful behaviour': accepting the gift of a raincoat from a French prisoner of war.[157] Thierack favoured what he called the 'administration of justice through the people itself'.[158]

Public Reactions

We do not know how many Poles were executed in Nazi Germany. One post-war German investigation of leaders of the RSHA determined that there was surviving documentation on 270 executions of Poles in western areas of Germany alone, most of them carried out in public.[159] There are indications in the literature that the number of executions greatly exceeded that number.[160]

Although local reports on reactions to the executions were collected, most were destroyed at war's end. We get an indication of what such reports looked like from one by the Security Service (SD) that survives from 17 August 1942 in Bayreuth. It noted that fraternization between Germans and Poles grew in spite of heavy punishments. As for the reactions of local residents to the executions 'in virtually all parts of the district', the report stated that opinions varied greatly.[161] The SD felt that Germans should be kept from witnessing executions, which they believed might lead to disquiet or be unsettling, and condemned what took place in Hildburghausen (Thuringia). When '20 Poles were executed, numerous German national comrades, soldiers and civilians, were present at the site. The figure of between 800 and 1,000 spectators has been mentioned. Besides that, the police kept back an additional 600 to 700 women and children in the forest.' SD reporters felt such a 'mass execution' should not be allowed to turn into a public spectacle.

The SD found, however, that few Germans objected to executions if a policeman was killed and that they agreed with the ratio of ten Poles for one German. Nazis and non-Nazis were said to think it 'self-evident' that executions were appropriate to punish sexual assaults on German women, but religious Germans were inclined to reject sharp measures and execution on humanitarian grounds and because of the absence of a court hearing. As for German women who willingly engaged in illicit sexual relationships with Polish men, Party members insisted that the women were every bit as guilty, and should be hanged as well. Such opinions were said to be common and in Regensburg some even thought that the 'superior' German woman, from whom more ought to be expected, was more guilty than the hapless Pole. Germans felt pity when the Poles were very young and even some Nazis had doubts when the Poles looked 'racially suitable'. According to regulations from Berlin, the Polish workers in the area were to witness executions, and one or several of them had to carry out the hanging. The SD said that 'the impression created by the spectators is on the whole best characterized as "indifference." The Poles accept the event with stoic quiet.'[162]

Executions of the Poles, and the general reactions from mid-war Bavaria, appear to have been similar elsewhere, at least if one can judge from scattered materials that survive from the Gestapo in the Palatinate. There are four separate cases that took place in 1942 and 1943, for which the reports of popular reactions have survived. (More than 100 Poles were forced to witness each of these executions.) In the files, German reactions to the executions varied from what was described as 'justified', 'correct', 'supported', or 'thoroughly appropriate'.[163] In a case witnessed by the gendarme from Bad Dürkheim, he noted in his report, the (standard) demand for the execution of the German woman, even though he suggested that this clamour was based on little knowledge of the case, which involved a mentally 'restricted' woman. The people thought she should be executed along with the Pole, and the same demand was heard elsewhere in Bavaria, such as after the execution of Thomas Wolak in the forest near Landshut. The population reportedly favoured the German woman's execution, and at the very least that she should be forced to watch his hanging. There was said to be popular 'agreement' with what happened to the Pole, but beyond dampening the spirits of the other Poles who were marched past the body, the matter soon was little discussed and 'had no particular influence on the [general public's] mood'.[164]

In another execution case, from December 1942, the population continued to blame the woman (a war widow) even after she committed suicide, because according to the report of the gendarme, they felt she seduced the Pole. In this case Germans enthusiastically gave their strong support to the regime's efforts to punish 'sex crimes'. Nonetheless, the gendarme recommended that future executions be carried out away from public view 'because it is believed in that way a certain disquiet and upset among the people caused by such an execution will be avoided'.[165]

To judge by another execution in the jurisdiction of the Gestapo in Düsseldorf, Catholics continued to make little secret of their displeasure. According to a report from 1 October 1942 of the mayor of Kempen-Niederrhein, the recent 'hanging of a Pole was regarded by the local population with little understanding, because the great majority of them stand on the side of the Roman Catholic Church, which rejects these kinds of measures. Only a few people judge these executions from the standpoint of maintaining the purity of the German blood.'[166]

The national survey of the SD continued to report Germans' failures to keep away from the foreign workers, and, as one report from mid-1944 put it, even 'particularly heavy punishments have, unfortunately, not achieved an overwhelmingly successful result' in terms of deterring disobedience.[167]

The 'Working Group on Foreign Worker's Security Questions' in Berlin recommended, in addition to trying to uphold the system by enforcing regulations, and tying workers to their job more than ever, that less serious (German) offenders be taken aside and given special instruction courses as to the racial and other dangers involved in socializing with Poles and other foreigners.[168] All kinds of other police crackdowns were recommended to keep workers in their place, but many of these (unspecified) measures and suggestions 'quickly were recognized as unenforceable'. Ultimately, more emphasis was put on publicizing deviations from regulations and what happened to delinquents. The Attorney-General's office in Munich continued to complain in June 1944 about the 'sad chapter' that German women did not cease having intimate relations with foreigners of all kinds, and that the illicit acts had increased in volume.[169]

It hardly needs to be said, but the Gestapo system, thanks to the involvement of ordinary citizens in it as denouncers, discouraged even the slightest forms of disobedience and resistance. It was virtually impossible for the Poles to find the kinds of secure enclaves where they could meet and discuss what to do. There was one rare occasion when more than 100 Polish women dared to refuse to work—at Rheinzabern in mid-1943. The protest over poor clothing and other conditions also stopped 300 more workers and brought production at the brickworks to a halt. The event collapsed within two hours when the translator told them of the threat that many would be sent to a concentration camp. It was not long before a denouncer came forward and the female ring-leader was taken into 'protective custody'. She was sent to Auschwitz in September 1943 and her death was reported on 5 January 1944.[170] Poles who dared raise their hand to their employer, as one did in Ebernburg in August 1941, paid with their lives when the matter was reported, not by the employer in this event, but by his family.[171]

Few if any of the Gestapo officials who participated in these executions without trial were taken to task after 1945. One official who was tried specifically for his involvement in the death of Miroslav Wojczakowski near Memmingen, Bavaria on 30 September 1943, was the Head of the Gestapo in Augsburg, who read the verdict. His defence claimed that he believed in the 'legality of the execution', and pointed to the agreement between Himmler and Minister of Justice Thierack about which he was informed on 5 November 1942. The Gestapo official was found not guilty.[172] The same result followed the post-war trial of Franz Sprinz, head of the Gestapo in Cologne during part of the war. He was found not guilty, and for the same reasons, for his part in the executions of four Polish workers.[173]

Many Gestapo cases studied here reflect the development of a kind of therapeutic system in Hitler's dictatorship. The state and/or the Party was called upon to intervene, to solve problems, and to regulate some aspect of social life. One 42-year-old (unmarried) farmer from Dielkirchen in May 1943 informed on himself to the Nazi Party district office. He said that a Polish woman who worked for him was two months pregnant and he was willing to marry her if she passed the race tests. However, the Gestapo, which was informed by the Party of the matter, would not hear of such a thing and, after she gave birth to the child, she was sent elsewhere to work.[174]

Another side of the therapeutic system was the way in which employers, farmers in the countryside, or business owners in the city, called in the police to discipline unruly workers. Industries like IG Farben wanted the Gestapo to take steps when foreign workers would not do as they were told or came up with lame excuses. One such case from late 1942 in Ludwigshafen led to a Pole being sent first to Hinzert, then to Natzweiler, where his death was reported on 19 February 1943.[175] Polish workers who were difficult, and kept wanting to change their place of work, might only be kept in the local jail for a week or two.[176] They might also be subject to Gestapo investigation, and sent to a concentration camp.[177] Poles and other foreign workers who were reported even for minor discipline infractions ended up in concentration camps where many died.[178]

Many German women disregarded the official ban on relations with Polish workers. Women in Germany continued to have sexual and friendly relations with many other foreigners in the country, and the regime found it impossible to demand a general ban, for fear of upsetting allies (like Italy) and for other reasons. It is impossible to estimate the extent of fraternization—forbidden, 'undesired', and otherwise—but as early as January 1942, the Nazis estimated that 'at least 20,000' illegitimate children had been fathered by foreigners.[179] Therefore, in spite of the racist propaganda, harsh laws, observant denouncers, and keen police, some people broke the law and/or rejected the spirit of this side of official racism. How Germans responded to other measures of the dictatorship that had little or nothing to do with race represents another side of the picture, and we take that up in the next chapter.

8

Enemies in the Ranks

Germans were subject to war measures acts that were introduced at the outset of the war to regulate social, economic, cultural, and political life. Some of the most important changes were announced in late August and early September 1939, and many more followed. A 'special war penal code' came into effect on the day of Germany's mobilization and dealt with both military and civilian behaviour. One section of this code specified the death penalty for anyone who sought to 'undermine the will to fight'. Like many other crimes in the Nazi era, this one was broadly defined and elastic. It covered not only obvious cases in which someone encouraged disloyalty or desertion among the troops, but could be extended to deal with those who voiced doubts about the quality of Germany's military leaders, or criticized some aspect of the war effort.[1]

As well, a 'war economy order' of 4 September 1939 promised citizens that their basic needs would be cared for and that the cost of living would not be allowed to get out of hand. Civilians were asked to work without pay on Sundays, to pay more taxes, and to accept a freeze on incomes. Even if these latter stipulations were subsequently relaxed or loosened, the patriotic appeal asked Germans at home to share the burden with the soldiers in the field. The package for consumers was based on fairness, so there was price regulation and rationing of essentials, to ensure that good citizens would not be victimized. Shortages would not lead to price gouging, and hardships would be equal for all, regardless of their situation in life.[2] One account suggests that Germans were already living a Spartan existence before the war broke out, so it was difficult to cut more, and by 1944 they had to make do with two-thirds of the consumer goods they had in 1938 and, moreover, there was a notable decline in quality.[3] Nevertheless, at least according to one comparative study, Germans received a higher level of rations than any of the European belligerents until the last months of the war.[4]

Another measure designed to maintain the home front was the 'ordinance against parasites on the body politic' of 5 September 1939. The concept of 'parasites' had been used long before, but at the beginning of the war an attempt was made to specify this social 'type'. The 'parasites' singled out in the new measure included anyone who took advantage of wartime emergencies to 'plunder', or to commit other crimes, and all could be subjected to the death penalty.[5] A sign of the times, just over a month into the war, was an ordinance by which juveniles over 16 years of age could be tried as adults, and given the same penalties.[6]

Besides sharpening old laws and increasing the punishments, the dictatorship at war launched domestic offensives to invade and control novel areas of social life. Historians have not generally studied ordinary Germans at the grass-roots level who came into conflict with the police during the war. However, their story tells us a great deal about the changing interrelationships between coercion and consent in Hitler's dictatorship, and sheds light on the social history of the German home front.

Ordinary Citizens and the Private Sphere

The 'extraordinary radio measures' of 1 September 1939, which forbad listening to foreign radio stations, deserve special attention here, because they pertained to the effort to police the private sphere. Until that point in time, the dictatorship had relied on cooperation between the police and the people. As we have seen, the new system produced a radical version of surveillance and control. However, the new radio measures represented something new, because the object of the exercise was not only to control public behaviour, but to determine what people heard, even in the privacy of their homes.

The idea of forbidding Germans from listening to foreign radio was initially floated by the staff of Hitler's deputy, Rudolf Hess, in mid-August 1939. Hitler was promptly convinced and ordered the responsible Minister Joseph Goebbels to work out the details. Although insiders, including some in the Justice Ministry and even the police had reservations about the wisdom of such a move, when Goebbels presented the finished product to Hitler on 1 September 1939, the Führer signed it immediately because it addressed his deep concerns about the negative effects of enemy (radio) propaganda on the home front. The Nazi police continued to have reservations for the obvious reason that it would be extremely difficult to enforce such a law.[7]

The 'extraordinary radio measures' decree stated that 'in modern war the enemy fights not only with military weapons, but also with methods intended to influence and undermine the morale of the people. One of these methods is the radio.' Clearly, the preamble went on, 'every word that the enemy sends our way is obviously untrue and is designed to hurt the German people'. It followed that every conscientious citizen would not wish to listen to foreign broadcasts. But for those who lacked that sense of responsibility, the new measure made listening into a serious crime, and even threatened the death penalty.[8] There had been thoughts about making it illegal to listen to Communist radio broadcasts from Moscow as far back as 1937.[9] Although nothing came of that plan, in fact any time someone was so accused, especially if they had a Communist past, the Gestapo treated it as a crime.[10]

Minister of Justice Gürtner raised an important objection to the radio measures, by saying they would open the door to a flood of denunciations.[11] Rudolf Hess discussed such reservations with Hitler, and both knew the measure might well foster the 'undesired and abhorrent' growth of snoopers and denouncers.[12] This gave Hitler pause, but he attached such importance to policing the images of war on the airwaves, that he signed the measure into law. Thereafter, it was difficult even for Ministers and senior civil servants to get permission to listen to foreign radio, even in the line of duty.[13]

The justification in the German press that was offered for the decree, as always, harked back to the 'lessons' of 1918:

At a time in which the German people stand unanimously behind their Führer, only one thing is valid for Germany: the word of the Führer. In the [last] World War, the enemies of Germany worked with the base weapon of incitement, with the poison of the lie and with the seditious provocation—with methods that led to 9 November 1918. The speeches of enemy statesmen, without being censored or commented upon, appeared —even in the year 1918—in the German press . . . Questions only began to be raised when it was already too late.[14]

In trying to control what Germans heard from abroad, there were major problems because from 1933 radios had been widely distributed, so that even low-income groups could buy the 'people's radio', the world's cheapest. The new motto had become, 'the Führer's voice into every home and factory!'[15] By 1939 three million of these sets had been sold, and there was a total of twelve million radios in the country. The official count of radio listeners grew from just over four million in 1933, to nearly four times that number by the mid-war years.[16]

Hitler's Germany became a modern mass media society, in which there were not only millions of newspaper readers and regular consumers of the news at the movies, but radio itself became enormously popular. Once radio overcame the mistake of spending too much time on obvious political messages, its attractions proved almost irresistible. Radio was listened to at home as well as in public places like restaurants and even at work. German broadcasters recognized that they had to provide the right mix of entertainment, news, and specials such as a Hitler speech.

During the war there developed another kind of war on the airwaves for listeners. Germany broadcast in English to Great Britain, to influence morale and win public opinion there, and the BBC retaliated in kind. The BBC (later also, Radio Moscow) made special efforts to attract and keep a German audience by broadcasting in German and by giving out important news from the war front, including, for example, the names of captured German soldiers and sailors. It is difficult to know either how many Germans listened in secretly, and impossible to guess how much they believed of what they heard. By all accounts,

Germans were frequent listeners to foreign radio, including the forbidden BBC. Typical is the somewhat frustrated report of the Nazi Secret Service (SD) from April 1943, which stated that it was 'an open secret' that many listened to the BBC, as many men and women who were busily working in their gardens suddenly all went inside about five minutes before the regular BBC broadcast. Another sign was that people were overheard talking about the exact number of bombers that were shot down and the number and kinds of bombs, but before that information was reported on German radio.[17]

Gestapo Practices and 'Ordinary Germans'

Although nearly everyone who lived through the Nazi era reports of listening to foreign radio, when they did so, they were at risk. The Gestapo was ordered by Berlin headquarters on 7 September to enforce the radio measure to the full and to ensure that genuine 'parasites' were sent to the Special Courts for trial.[18] In the first four months the new measure was on the books, the Gestapo arrested more than 1,100 persons, and over the next six months the number grew to 2,197.[19] We are left to speculate about the number of reports that did not lead to an arrest, but in all likelihood there were many more. The examples of the crimes and punishments that were regularly paraded in the press, carried headlines such as 'Listened to foreign radio: heavy prison sentence—warning to slow learners'.[20] Another stated flatly 'no moderation for radio criminals'.[21] By September 1941, in keeping with the further radicalization of the terror that set in after the beginning of the war against the USSR, there was a first newspaper report of two death penalties for listening to foreign radio. One of these was a man, a former Communist, sentenced by the Special Court in Nuremberg-Fürth. Hardly less vulnerable was the other victim, a Polish woman, the housekeeper of a German doctor, who was sentenced to death by the Special Court in Graudenz. She had the temerity to invite Polish acquaintances to the doctor's house on Saturday evenings to listen to the radio when he was away.[22]

How did the Gestapo discover such delinquents? Table 5 shows the results of my investigation of the Gestapo case files in the three regions of Lower Franconia and Würzburg, the Rhine-Ruhr area around Düsseldorf and the Palatinate and the Gestapo in Neustadt. Using a similar sampling technique to the one I employed in the last two chapters, I selected 62 cases from the Würzburg files, 81 from those in Düsseldorf, and 83 from Neustadt.

The results show that 164 cases out of the total of 226, or 73 per cent of them all, originated with reports from the population. Another 10 per cent provide no hints as to the original source of information, and, as I have already suggested, many of these were probably tip-offs from the population. Even if we exclude these files, however, it turns out that across the three regions, nearly

Table 5. Reports of listening to forbidden radio broadcasts in Düsseldorf, Würzburg, and Neustadt Gestapo case files, 1939–1944

Sources of information	Number of cases	%
1. Reports from the population		
Düsseldorf	55	
Würzburg	45	
Neustadt	64	
TOTAL	164	73
2. Information from other control organizations		
Düsseldorf	2	
Würzburg	—	
Neustadt	6	
TOTAL	8	4
3. Observations by the Gestapo and/or V-persons		
Düsseldorf	4	
Würzburg	—	
Neustadt	2	
TOTAL	6	3
4. Information via communal or state authorities	0	0
5. Statements at interrogations		
Düsseldorf	2	
Würzburg	4	
Neustadt	1	
TOTAL	7	3
6. Information from businesses (in Neustadt only)	1	0
7. Information via Nazi Party, Nazi organizations, or Party Members		
Düsseldorf	6	
Würzburg	3	
Neustadt	8	
TOTAL	17	7
8. Source Not known		
Düsseldorf	12	
Würzburg	10	
Neustadt	1	
TOTAL	23	10
GRAND TOTALS	226	100

Source: Gestapo Case Files in HStA D; StA W; LAS.

three-quarters of all these Gestapo cases began when one 'ordinary German' de-nounced another. The extent of the denunciations was highest in the Palatinate, the area that had supported Nazism before 1933 more than the other two re-gions. In the Palatinate 77 per cent of these cases began with a denunciation. In Lower Franconia the figure was 73 per cent, and in the Rhine-Ruhr it was 68 per cent. Thus, there were regional differences, but the spread was within the range of 10 per cent, so the differences were not as pronounced as we might expect.

Confirmation of what appears to be a national pattern can be found in northern Germany, as can be seen in historian Gerhard Paul's study of Gestapo cases sent to the Special Court in Kiel. He shows that 81 per cent of the 121 accusations of listening to foreign radio came from denunciations and another 3 per cent began from anonymous letters. The Gestapo itself in that region, discovered only 5 cases on its own, and then from men and women already in custody.[23] In the three samples I studied, the Gestapo discovered only 6 cases out of 226. As Table 5 shows, they obtained little help from the rest of the police network or other control organizations, like the SD.

The national pattern in this 'German-on-German' terror, at least if these three regions may be taken as representative, was that the great majority of the cases began with a denunciation. Germans not only watched out for 'crimes' and other deviations committed by social outsiders and ethnic minorities, but they watched each other.

The study of police practices shows that especially by the war years, the Gestapo side of Hitler's dictatorship was driven forward by ordinary citizens who reported their suspicions and allegations. If we add to this picture the important role of denunciations in the enforcement of measures aimed to isolate both the Jews and the Poles, as studied in the last two chapters, then there are grounds to call into question many of the images of how the Gestapo operated. In fact, the Gestapo tended to be reactive and waited for information to come from the outside. Most of it came from 'ordinary' Germans, that is, civilians who were not even members of the Nazi Party.

It is often assumed that antisemitism or some other form of racism lay behind citizen collaboration with the Nazi regime. In fact, the rate of denunci-ation in the sphere of non-racial 'crimes' was proportionally greater than that obtained when it came to enforcing racial policies aimed at the Jews and the Poles. This finding is confirmed by other studies now underway or nearing completion on the role of denunciations in Gestapo enforcement of political 'crimes' that had little or nothing to do with race issues. Gerhard Paul and Klaus-Michael Mallmann's account of the Saarland shows a similar pattern there.[24] Another analysis, which deals with Gestapo enforcement of the so-called 'malicious gossip law' in the Rhine-Ruhr, indicates that nearly 60 per cent of the 261 Gestapo cases studied began on the basis of a named denouncer.[25] Historian Eric Johnson's analysis of the Special Court in Cologne (511 cases) and

of the Gestapo in Krefeld (122 cases) shows that just over 60 per cent of those
dealing with matters other than the 'Jewish question', began with denunciations
and, if one were to add also the anonymous denunciations he found, then the
figure would be closer to 70 per cent.[26]

The assumption we might have that the Gestapo would likely have a more
difficult time obtaining denunciations in policing non-racial aspects of social
life does not hold up. Denunciations that were sent to the Nazi Party, at least to
judge by one recent local study, show a similar preponderance of non-racial
over race-oriented concerns. Gisela Diewald-Kerkmann shows in her analysis
of 292 letters of denunciation sent to the Nazi Party in Lippe, that while the
largest single 'offence' (just over one-quarter of them all) pointed to forbidden
or undesired contact with Jews, virtually all the rest dealt with non-racial
issues.[27]

Just why the rate of denunciations was not lower, but in fact proportionally
higher in the non-racial sphere than it was with regard to racial issues, is
an important question.[28] Although further research is called for, at least six
interrelated factors influenced the varying rates of denunciations elicited with
regard to non-racial crimes and those which offended against antisemitic
'laws'. We can take these in order, beginning with the most obvious. (1) There
is the question of opportunity: Jews only lived in clusters in Germany and the
general population did not have a chance to inform about possible breaches of
racist measures they could claim to have witnessed directly. As the German Jews
emigrated and/or were forcefully deported, such claims and even the pretexts
to inform on Jews and people who offered them help or sympathy diminished
further. Of course, as is only too well known, antisemitism without Jews is
entirely possible, but if there are no Jews, it is difficult to inform on them or on
people who might be sympathetic towards them. (2) The other side of the coin
was that the degree of direct Gestapo involvement was greater when the 'Jewish
question' was at issue. For Hitler's dictatorship, antisemitism was given the
highest priority in racial, and to a great extent, also in political matters, so the
Gestapo itself was more actively involved in cases dealing with Jews. There was
almost certainly more direct Gestapo involvement also against 'hard-nosed'
political opponents like the Communists, and in cases involving open opposition, such as the July 1944 plot to assassinate Hitler. (3) There is the question of
timing. The official drive to isolate Jews in Germany took place mainly before
the war and, by September 1939 many had left, been forced to the large cities
or out of the country, and most of those who remained were deported two
years later. Beginning almost at the same time, the terror system, of which
denunciations constituted a vital ingredient, went into high gear. With the
steady criminalization of various aspects of German social life, the opportunities to lay information about transgressions of all kinds against 'ordinary
Germans' also increased proportionally. (4) One might also mention the circle

of vulnerability. While not everyone could be held suspect in giving sympathy to the Jews or rejecting some aspect of Nazi antisemitism, for example, virtually everyone had access to a radio or was open to a charge of 'malicious gossip'. (5) What about denunciations and the Polish workers? Certainly the arrival of the Poles coincided with the deepening terror. However, many Poles were confined in camps of one kind or another, and/or lived on the farm out in the countryside, and therefore were to some extent out of sight of many potential denouncers. There was also more official involvement in policing foreign workers. And there was even a brake on denunciations of the foreign workers, who arrived at a time of desperate labour shortage. Turning them in might mean the loss of an irreplaceable worker. (6) Denunciations aimed at the main race 'enemies' of the regime inside Germany (in this book, Jews and Poles are the two examples that were studied) pertained to very serious crimes that could easily lead to the death of some or all of the accused. Although initially at least, heavy penalties did not by any means deter denouncers, they may have served as something of a restraint for some. The publicity of what happened to the guilty began to have the effect, unwanted by the authorities, of discouraging people from reporting, at least according to the analysis of the Higher Court President in Cologne during the latter part of 1943. He remarked that 'many citizens are now distressed about making reports to the police, because they do not want to accept the responsibility for the likely heavy punishment that would follow for the denounced person'.[29]

My study of the radio measures shows that the entire police network accounted for only about 10 per cent of these cases. This type of case began most frequently when uniformed police saw windows not darkened enough at night. During inquiries they would then overhear a telling phrase or two that could have come from a foreign radio broadcast. The Gestapo and its mythical 'spy network' were responsible for detecting only 13 cases, over half of them during interrogations. Some of these were inquiries from other Gestapo jurisdictions or all-points bulletins. The only time the Gestapo discovered a case on its own outside police headquarters in this sample was more or less by chance in the course of a police 'round-up' and once when an official overheard a conversation on the bus on his way to work.[30] Such relatively meagre 'active' police work in tracking non-racial crimes of ordinary citizens can be seen clearly in an extensive study of 'malicious gossip' handled by the Gestapo in the Palatinate. It shows that they came up with only 6 out of 660 cases, whereas denunciations accounted for 92 per cent of them.[31]

If we take all the samples together that we have studied in the last three chapters, we have a total of 670 cases. In these samples, the Gestapo on its own detected only 44 of the cases, which is only 7 per cent of the total. In 37 of the 44 cases, the Gestapo wrested the incriminating evidence from men and women already in custody. This relatively low rate of 'active' police detection on the ground would support the hypothesis I have put forward elsewhere, that the Nazi police were by and large reactive rather than active.[32] But even if the Gestapo was mainly reactive, we should not conclude that it was somehow unimportant to the dictatorship. The Gestapo gained a reputation for operating as men who came in the night, who operated secretively, and who were completely beyond the law. In the face of the Gestapo, the rights of citizens, no matter who they were, were completely meaningless. The police could hold suspects as long as they saw fit, beat them with complete legal impunity, and ship them off to a concentration camp. There was no such thing as appealing against anything the Gestapo did, and the existence of this new police undoubtedly set the tone for the dictatorship's approach to all 'law and order' issues. Although much of what the Gestapo did was kept secret, a great deal was publicized, and the publicity undoubtedly terrorized many people, even as it won the Gestapo support.

Although the Gestapo as an institution was generally reactive or even passive, we should not forget that at times it was very active. For example, the Gestapo pulled out all the stops in the wake of the July 1944 plot to assassinate Hitler, and it brought to bear the full measure of all the police expertise it could muster to track down suspects.[33] Without underestimating the importance of this police activity, however, it is evident that at least for the routine operation of the Gestapo, such actions were more the exception than the rule. Although the Gestapo spent a great deal of energy, time, and resources in trying to infiltrate the underground Communist movement, several studies show that even then the police relied on denouncers.[34] Even most of the Communists who were caught listening to Radio Moscow before the outbreak of war in 1939 were brought to the police by attentive citizens.

The findings about the role of denunciations in the everyday operation of the police, and my characterization of the Nazi police as generally being reactive and greatly reliant upon help from the outside, does put into further question at least some of our understandings of the notion of a 'police state' and the usefulness of that concept in helping to explain what Hitler's dictatorship was all about.

Micro-Politics

The social side of the Gestapo's persecution and its terror aimed at Germans during the war can be studied systematically if we look at the content of the denunciations of suspected breaches of the radio measures. We could choose other war measures, but the advantage of studying this particular one is that it was as far removed as we can get from racial issues (such as antisemitism) and from past politics (like Communism or Socialism). By studying the enforcement of the radio measures, we can see the kinds of considerations that seemed to move citizens to denounce one another when racism or other related factors were clearly not involved. We start to notice other aspects of life in the dictatorship. Germans became conscious and self-conscious about language. In conversations about the war, not only did they have to guard against incautious remarks (to police themselves) as to its cause, course, and likely outcome, but they had to watch what they said lest it betray that their source of information might be foreign radio. Again and again in the files, denouncers refer to the 'way people spoke' from which they deduced, and not always correctly, that the speaker must have listened to forbidden broadcasts.[35]

What kinds of motives drove these denouncers? The Socialist underground was inclined to see the provision of tips from the people as a sign of the growing consensus behind the regime.[36] That conclusion was at least partly correct, but we do have to remember that the flood of denunciations in general contradicted one of Hitler's major goals, to create a conflict-free 'community of the people'. We rarely find cases in which the motive behind the informing is unambiguous. When pressed by the Gestapo because of denials by an accused, some denouncers gave even more damning information for reasons that are impossible to explain on the basis of the evidence in the dossier.

One such ordeal led an accused man to commit suicide because he could not carry on in the face of mounting denunciations from neighbours. Briefly, on 12 November 1941, Helene Heinecke, a seamstress wrote to her local Nazi Party headquarters to report that Peter Struckmeyer, a 66-year-old invalid who occupied the small apartment adjoining hers, had listened to enemy radio. She named witnesses and said her room was at the disposal of the Gestapo 'in order to put an end to this nonsense'. She claimed his behaviour was 'dangerous to the state' because he said he would tell people what he heard on the radio. She told police she wanted to stop him from saying things, such as that the policies towards the Jews were improper and that Germany would lose the war. Irmgard Beck (a 36-year-old artist) was drawn into the case when asked by the original snooper to come to her room to overhear Struckmeyer's treasonous remarks. She later told the Gestapo in the presence of the accused, that she had said 'only what I have heard and I am prepared to answer to my conscience and what I can maintain on my oath in court'. By 10 December 1941, the old man was in custody. After face-to-face encounters with his accusers, and hopeless denials, he took his own life and was found dead in his cell at 3 o'clock on 11 December.[37]

Apart from the many files that contain no evidence on motives one way or the other, where there is some evidence, it can be divided into affective and instrumental. This distinction does not always hold up because motives were often mixed.[38] There is substantial agreement in the literature that affective, 'system-loyal' and/or Nazi 'convictions' played a decisive role in around one-quarter of all denunciations to the Gestapo or letters to the Nazi Party.[39] Put the other way round, this means that about 75 per cent of all denunciations were provided for reasons that had little or nothing to do with obviously or expressly supporting the Nazis. Even so, they brought Nazi ideology to life and supported the encroachments of the dictatorship into everyday life.

In the sample of cases dealing with the 'radio measures', expressions of affect-ive motives, such as belief in National Socialism or worship of Hitler were extremely rare. There are instances when such emotions were mentioned or when the citizen's duty to support the system was stated, but as often as not, personal factors soon came to light. For example, a woman in charge of the neighbourhood branch of the Nazi Women's League told the Gestapo that she felt it was her duty to inform (on a 50-year-old widow). The police later concluded the case by saying the allegation was baseless and 'a result of irresponsible nonsense arising out of hatred'.[40]

Denunciations were not simply the expression of rabid Nazism, nor, as we have seen with regard to the enforcement of Nazi antisemitism, was overt or obvious racism always the decisive factor. In these materials, in fact, relatively few people even bothered to make explicit reference to the 'right kinds' of motives, such as hatred of a stigmatized enemy or commitment to an endorsed or privileged 'official' value. One woman who was asked why she denounced her long-time neighbour (on 3 September 1939), merely stated that her first duty was to tell the truth.[41]

But whether or not affective motivation and/or attitudes of civic virtue as defined under Nazism may have lurked behind the acts of some informers on occasion, there is far more evidence of overt and obvious selfish or instru-mental motives. Indeed, it would be safe to conclude that in spite of the newly proclaimed social ideals of the solidarity of a 'community of the people', self-interest seems to have fuelled denunciations to a considerable extent.

In the last two chapters I suggested that many informers on matters dealing with race were motivated by the thought of personal advantages of one kind or another. This instrumental utilization of the Gestapo was at least as pro-nounced in the sample dealing with 'ordinary' Germans and the non-racial crime of listening to foreign radio. Denouncers offered tips in order to get rid of enemies, rivals, competitors, and to have others removed by the Gestapo. No social group and few social enclaves were entirely immune. Social inferiors certainly used denunciations against those up the social scale, like their bosses at work.[42] In theory denunciations offered the less powerful and the disadvant-aged an opportunity to take out their spite against those who stood over them, or those they resented, like the better-off social classes. But social classes did not mix that much, so that informing tended to occur within social classes, neigh-bourhoods, (apartment) houses, even within families.

Extensive private and personal uses were made of informing in order to gain personal advantages, such as when husbands and wives informed on each other, sometimes out of animosity.[43] In one case, the Gestapo said the motive of one spouse was hatred.[44] There also were instances when husband or wife was contemplating divorce.[45] One woman informed on behalf of her sister, who was an abused wife.[46] Such conflicts played themselves out when one or the other spouse went to the Gestapo with damning information to win the conflict, or to tip the scales in their favour when divorce proceedings were under way, or recently granted.[47] Although the alleged cause for running to the authorities was to inform about law-breaking, in fact, the obvious personal aims behind the actions ran from seeking material advantage to gaining emotional revenge.[48] In spite of official guidelines and continuing warnings from the Gestapo and the Minister of Justice to do everything possible to stop precisely these kinds of denunciations, the flood could not be held back.[49]

Informing of this kind occurred within families, such as when a father repeatedly denounced his son to the police, not only for listening to foreign radio but for seeking to avoid military service. Although the allegations were investigated, there was nothing to the charges, but the motive, at least according to the gendarme was that 'the father simply wants very much to have the son out of the house in order to establish a better existence for himself'.[50]

There were sisters who turned in siblings with whom they had never got along, and, in a moment of anger they used the new radio measures decree as a convenient basis to take out their spite.[51] One young girl turned in her brother for being a know-it-all. She tried to convince him that a certain station was really forbidden, but he ignored her. Her motive may have combined some kind of idealism or political faith with the more personal one of putting him in his place. As she explained to the police, 'I only lodged the complaint against my brother in order to show him that he's not always right. My brother is always pig-headed and thinks that what he says is right.'[52] Other relatives informed on each other, like one nephew who turned in a widowed aunt, for no apparent reason. She was nevertheless forced to spend time in custody until the matter was cleared up.[53] Numerous other relatives used the weapon of denunciation for personal motives, like trying to get revenge for some slight.[54]

The new laws on the books and the willingness of police to act on the most outrageous allegations proved irresistible to in-laws who did not particularly like each other or who had other kinds of conflicts. Thus, one man was denounced by his father-in-law for allegedly listening to foreign radio, but this was an attempt to punish him for his part in domestic conflicts. Once the investigative process went into action, however, as often happened, the case took on a momentum of its own and grew beyond the control of the original informer. Perhaps sensing the appalling situation into which he had dragged his son-in-law, the denouncer committed suicide. The police closed the file with the dry comment that the man made 'untrue allegations'.[55] There was another case in which a woman informed on her son-in-law in what the Gestapo tersely called 'nothing else but an instrumental denunciation'.[56] The wife of the denouncer noted with regard to the motives of her husband for turning in her own father, that she felt the 'complaint to police was not lodged out of hatred. It is true of course that in our family from time to time there have been conflicts.'[57]

Denunciations were often used to resolve frictions with neighbours.[58] One person or another tried to win a conflict that might have begun over the rent, by bringing up a 'political crime' and therefore involving the Gestapo. One landlord went on his own to the Gestapo headquarters in Neustadt in April 1943, that is, at a time when word about the enormous losses suffered by the Germans at Stalingrad was known, and after which the terror was stepped up inside Germany. He stated at the outset that he had differences with these tenants, but alleged they also listened to foreign radio. His wife added to the seriousness of the charges. After a considerable investigation, the Gestapo decided there was insufficient evidence to proceed to court and merely scrawled at the end of their report, 'conflicts in the house'.[59]

The landlord in another case, denounced for personal rather than political reasons, was a member of the Nazi Party and the SS, but in spite of being well connected, he had no immunity.[60] One landlady denounced her tenants for listening to the radio, but only after they complained they were not getting enough coal to keep warm.[61] Evidence in one case suggests people in the house denounced a neighbour when they grew afraid they would all end up in jail because he was 'crazy enough' to be listening to the radio which the whole neighbourhood could hear.[62] Other files merely conclude that in spite of the allegations about one person or another committing a political crime, there was little or nothing to the charges, but the individuals involved were simply 'at odds' and were trying to use the new police system to gain an advantage.[63]

A case from Essen illustrates the tangled webs that were woven in this new denunciatory atmosphere. It began on 22 July 1941 with a letter to the Gestapo in which a man, an employee in the court system, 'denounced himself'. He felt it was inevitable that the Gestapo would be at his door. The problem began with a dispute with his wife, who was also embroiled in numerous conflicts with neighbours—so much so that she is referred to by all in the file (including her spouse), as 'not quite right' in the head. During one argument with her husband she called out that he was listening to forbidden news, a point overheard by a male neighbour. The latter only decided to act on this news when he himself subsequently had an argument with the woman. 'In order to get some peace and quiet', as this man explained when later called in for questioning by the Gestapo, he had said to the woman: 'You better be careful, otherwise I shall turn the tables on you and make you a witness against your own husband.' The implication was that the latter would be reported to the authorities and his wife might have to testify against him. That threat was not meant to be serious, because the man insisted later he would never have denounced the husband whom he and everyone else held for a 'fine and upstanding person'. However, once the husband heard of this threat he denounced himself, as he told the Gestapo, because of his vulnerable and public position at the local court and because he had 'no neutral witnesses' who could support his innocence. The wife soon admitted to the Gestapo that she deliberately yelled out and spread rumours in order to damage his reputation and in the hope of getting rid of him. In spite of his excellent reputation, the case was sent to the Special Court. Even though it was soon dropped, we can see in the file the chilling effect of such an experience.[64]

This kind of denunciatory atmosphere covered the country. It was the product of citizen collaboration, but was not always the result of zealous racism or even faith in Nazism and Hitler. Denunciations invaded the conflicts and disputes between workmates in factories.[65] Farm workers who became involved in personal strife on occasion did not shrink from bringing the most serious political allegations against comrades. One example is instructive of the swiftness of the terror 'system' in action. A man was denounced on 3 October 1939 for listening to Radio Moscow, as well as for making unflattering comments about life in Nazi Germany. Soon interrogated, his case was sent to the Special Court, but on 20 November the court said there was too little evidence to proceed to trial and pointed out that even if the man could be found guilty, because his 'crime' fell under a Führer amnesty, the matter should be dropped. The Gestapo was not content with this decision, and, in an example of 'police justice' in action, they not only 'corrected' the court's verdict by placing the accused in 'protective custody', but they quietly ignored Hitler's amnesty as well. Just over a week later the accused was sent by the police 'for the duration of the war' to a concentration camp, initially to Sachsenhausen. His death was noted in his file on 6 November 1940.[66]

Informing the Gestapo was a temptation for fired employees seeking revenge,[67] such as for one young woman who was dismissed as a servant because of petty theft. She tried to retaliate by alleging that her employers listened to forbidden radio broadcasts.[68] In another such case from late 1944, which was fully investigated even though the Allied armies were virtually at the city gates and the war was nearing its end, a fired man denounced his employer and his wife. The credibility of the denouncer should have been obvious from the fact that he was mentally troubled and had been dismissed from the Wehrmacht 'as mentally ill'.[69]

Some people tried to get the boss in trouble when they wanted to cover up their own crimes or just to leave his or her service, which was not always a simple matter.[70] In spite of the often transparent instrumental use of so many of these charges, the police took them very seriously, and pursued them at great length and over a considerable period of time. Being certifiably deranged or mentally incompetent did not seem to cast doubt on the credibility of the allegations, as far as the police were concerned. Even informers who were called psychopathic liars by the Gestapo still got attention, even when their motives were obviously self-serving.[71]

German-on-German denunciations took place among friends and acquaintances, and did not cease in the face of the mythical solidarity of the regular social gathering in a local pub, the so-called *Stammtisch*. One man, a court bailiff, was denounced after he 'made it evident to the five or six acquaintances by how he spoke' of events on the war front, that he must have been listening to foreign news. Moreover, the informer, who took it upon himself to go to the Gestapo, added that the accused often complained about the concentration camps and the SS and that he dared to say it would be better if the people could listen to foreign radio and learn of the lies they were being told about what was happening in Germany. The court official was lucky to get off with a warning.[72]

Was there such a thing as the denouncer as 'social type'? If one looks at the social profile of the denouncers in Nazi Germany, it is safe to say that they tended to originate from the same social milieu as the denounced. Most who appear in the Gestapo files come from the lower end of the social scale. It has to be recalled, however, that the police acted with more restraint when complaints came in about the 'better' classes, who also had other avenues through which they could exercise social power. And as Eric Johnson has suggested, men tended to be more prominent as denouncers than women.[73] In Gisela Diewald-Kerkmann's study, 80 per cent of the people who wrote letters of denunciation to the Nazi Party were male.[74] In the 'radio measures' sample I analysed, there was a more even split, but men still outdid women as denouncers.[75]

What about the impact on the people against whom allegations were launched? Of course, the psychological impact of having a brush with the Gestapo, especially during the war years, when the terror was increasingly radicalized and its arbitrariness well known, can easily be imagined in general terms. The mere mention of the word 'Gestapo', especially for those defined as the regime's race enemies, has been well documented. Less research has been carried out on how the everyday activities of the Gestapo affected 'ordinary citizens', but the files show how Germans, such as shopkeepers or publicans, modified their behaviour to avoid the neighbours' chatter. One merchant even launched counter-charges. The first denunciation against his daughter was given by telephone on 21 July 1941 by a person using a false name. The Gestapo felt the motive was 'probably' some sort of 'jealousy'. The second charge was made by a married woman (born 1903), who appeared personally at the Krefeld Gestapo on 10 December 1941 (indeed, she delivered yet another denunciation by hand on 24 February 1942), and repeated the charges. There simply was nothing to any of them, and the Gestapo observed that the denouncer was a 'numbskull' who had some minor conflicts with the family and was looking for revenge. When the merchant and father of the woman who was repeatedly denounced for having 'forbidden contact' with the Polish workers was told how the case ended, he stated immediately that 'absolutely nothing more would be sold from his food store to the Poles working in the neighbourhood, in order, once and for all, to put an end to the nonsense'. The denouncer went on offering the Gestapo more tips well into 1942. She was subsequently charged with laying 'knowingly false charges', but the case was dropped on 20 August 1942. The baseless charges had been held over the shop-keeper and his family for more than a year.[76]

From other studies we are beginning to see that denunciations also found their way inside the German army, long thought of as one of the social enclaves more or less resistant to this kind of mutual informing.[77] The impression gained by historians who studied many cases of the (vaguely defined) crime of 'under-mining the will to win' (*Wehrkraftzersetzung*)—a total of between 30,000 to 40,000 soldiers who were found guilty by military courts of the crime—was that these soldiers were caught mainly because of investigations that began with a denunciation from one of their comrades in arms.[78]

Soldiers enjoyed no special immunity with the population when they returned to the 'home front'. A study of the Saarland in fact shows that *all* of the cases of 'undermining the will to win' involving members of the Armed Forces there began with denunciations. Their 'crimes' were discovered only with the help of volunteered tips from the population, including neighbours, friends, and even wives and mothers. The motives remain mostly in the dark, but they appear to have ranged from the usual instrumental ones (revenge-seeking, envy, personal conflict), to fear of impending defeat, but there was some polit-ical fanaticism as well.[79]

Time and again we see people informing, even in the latter part of the war, when the terror really was in high gear, and when the charges could have very serious consequences. In September 1944, a member of the Nazi Girls' League (BDM) informed the Security Service (SD) in Würzburg that a family listened to foreign radio. Although we cannot say for certain which of several girls did the informing, it was one of several family friends (all around 15 years of age). Under questioning by the Gestapo, they said the mother and two neighbours listened to foreign radio. All were arrested and interrogated by the Gestapo, and eventually all three cases were sent to court, the mother to the notorious People's Court in Berlin. From the files we do not know what happened to any of them. At the very least they were imprisoned for many months, and some may have been executed. They all could just as easily have been shot out of hand, and certainly the informers had to know that also. When they gave their testi-mony to the Gestapo, however, none of these girls seemed to blink an eye at the prospect, but calmly gave damning details. They never said why they did so.[80] Although these young informers were ordinary Germans, because they were members of a Nazi organization, I did not count them among the 'civilian' denouncers in Table 5.

Another example of how the terror could strike was set in motion in Würzburg in the summer of 1943. A colleague heard Railway Inspector Max Heinrich (born 1896) and his colleague Hans Vogel (born 1891) make negative remarks about the situation in which Germany found itself. Word of the treasonous remarks was reported to local Nazi Party headquarters by a Party member and another railway employee, Friedrich Henning (born 1909). The latter was asked by the Party to listen attentively to the remarks of Heinrich and Vogel, to take exact note of times and places, and thus help build a case against them. Over almost a three-month period, Henning kept track of what was said, much of it 'defeatist' remarks based on listening to foreign radio. All the while he engaged the two in conversation but did not object to anything, lest he alert the suspects of his real opinion. By mid-September he had enough evidence and passed it over to the Gestapo, and they sent the case to the People's Court in Berlin, which sentenced Heinrich to death. The execution took place on 26 September 1944. Vogel's crimes were considered somewhat less serious, and he escaped with a heavy prison sentence, and survived the war.[81]

In this last case, we do know something about the motives of the informant Henning, who as a member of the Nazi Party is not counted as a civilian denouncer in Table 5, but as someone who acted in some kind of semi-legal role. He claimed it was 'difficult for him' to inform on colleagues with whom, at least so he said, he had nothing but the best personal and professional relations. Henning does not say why he did not take the two men aside and warn them to stop, but he did say he felt duty-bound as a National Socialist to inform, particularly at a time when the nation was in danger. The case is one of the many examples of German-on-German terror that in some ways are more difficult to explain than ones in which 'obvious' prejudice like antisemitism was involved.

Manipulating the System 'from below'

We used to think that dictators like Hitler or Mussolini were so powerful that they manipulated the people almost at will. Without underestimating the cunning of these leaders in any way, we can also see how ordinary Germans and Italians manipulated the system for purposes of their own. In Hitler's dictatorship, the German state and Nazi Party were repressive and highly invasive, but even so citizens made the necessary adjustments. Far from spending their every waking moment worrying about the Gestapo and being torn by anxieties over the surveillance and terror system, many people came to terms with it.

From our perspective it is easy enough to overlook the many ways in which the population began to count on, to solicit, and even to expect the interventionism of the system in their daily lives and to calculate how, by offering information or appealing to certain official values, even if they did not mention them explicitly, the 'authorities' could be enticed or manipulated 'from below' into acting on their behalf. Many German citizens began to accept the interventionism of the system as 'normal' and demanded it work on their behalf. This point was brought out in a lengthy report of 20 July 1942 about 'unnecessary demands on the authorities by the population'.[82] From all over the country requests, supplications, and complaints were made to the authorities. Even when such entreaties to Party and state proved fruitless they were repeated endlessly or sent elsewhere. Business competitors, such as one in Breslau who accused another of 'incorrect' practices, brought the most serious possible charges before ten different authorities, from the city administration, magistrate, local (and regional) Nazi Party headquarters, attorney general, and the Gestapo, as well as to three different professional bodies and a branch of the Wehrmacht. This example highlights just some of the ways in which citizens acted in the new opportunities that opened up and were not merely passive, dependent, or powerless.

Indeed, letter-writing to the 'authorities' became a much-favoured form of citizen activity in Nazi Germany as it evidently also did in other dictatorships of the twentieth century.[83] Some people adjusted very quickly to the dictatorship and in early 1933 began writing Hitler countless letters either offering information or seeking favours, so much so that special announcements were made in the press for them to send the letters elsewhere.[84] The letter-writers persisted, however, and at one stage Hitler's Chancellery, was receiving more than 1,000 letters and petitions per working day. According to the post-war testimony of one official, there might have been twice that many.[85] Citizens used such opportunities, freed from bureaucratic and other constraints 'to speak to the Führer' in order to demonstrate their loyalty, to express some wish or to seek some favour. Of the many power struggles that ranged around Hitler, one was about which of the competing leaders in the Chancellery would control the voluminous post he received each day. People also sent letters to many other Nazi leaders, including Himmler and Goebbels. In May 1933, it was reported in the press that Hermann Göring alone received about 2,000 letters a day from those seeking favours or wishing to make complaints, and he asked that in the future such letters be sent to the relevant local authorities.[86] Letters to the editors of national, regional, and local newspapers were frequent, and, like those to the more notorious Nazi rags, like *Der Stürmer*, had specific denunciatory content. They might highlight how some merchant sold goods to Jews or how an ordinary citizen failed to accept the spirit of Nazi antisemitism.[87]

A further indication of citizen activity in the form of letter-writing can be seen in memoranda of the High Command of the Armed Forces (OKW) to regional headquarters. On 5 February 1942 the OKW wrote about the 'numerous' letters, signed and anonymous to the army and even to Hitler, complaining about who was or was not being drafted. Some people pointed to younger men, others to older ones, who could and should be sent to the front. The OKW was concerned that there were many citizens who regarded any able-bodied male not in uniform as a shirker and denounced them for one reason or another. However, such men might very well be essential workers, such as in a munitions factory. The OKW ordered that such denunciations, including anonymous ones, had to be investigated if for no other reason than to halt social discord in its tracks.[88]

The Gestapo acted on the flimsiest of evidence, even when many denunciations were never substantiated enough to merit sending them on to the courts. One new study of a small sample of denunciations in Würzburg suggests that only about 20 per cent of the Gestapo cases went before Nazified courts. And of these nearly 75 per cent were dropped by the courts because they were considered either trivial or without sufficient evidence.[89] Such findings might lead us to suggest the Gestapo was 'inefficient', because so many of its cases did not result in convictions. However, care needs to be taken here, because any evaluation about the efficiency of the Gestapo would have to take into account not only 'successes' in obtaining judicial verdicts, but also political or publicity successes in terms of winning over or influencing popular opinion and/or terrorizing at least sections of the population. A study of the Gestapo's 'efficiency' also would have to deal with the multiplicity of social effects, such as the rumours and gossip which caused anxiety in people faced by the prospect of having to appear at Gestapo headquarters.

The evidence suggests that in Hitler's dictatorship the police thrived not only on what happened to victims before the courts, but as much and even more on the stories and myths that spread about what happened or could happen to anyone who had a brush with the police. So we should not too readily conclude that the Gestapo was somehow 'inefficient' because it did not always get judicial convictions.[90]

The sparse direct contribution to police detection by either the Gestapo or the rest of the police network (mentioned above), and the consequent reliance on sources outside police ranks, and especially on civilian denouncers, may help to account for the fact that many allegations in Gestapo files proved either groundless, or at least dubious, and why a good number were dropped. False accusations and anonymous letters of denunciations were prevalent and, notwithstanding all kinds of efforts to stop them, the problem was never solved. The country's leaders (including Hitler) continued to express consternation about denunciations, because this behaviour contradicted the oft-espoused ideal of the 'community of the people'.[91]

Signs of the denunciatory atmosphere that was part of the new spirit of the times was also in evidence within private business concerns. As Harold James has pointed out, denunciations began to arise inside the Deutsche Bank and were offered not only on racial or even political grounds, nor against 'obvious enemies', but as in German society more generally, for entirely instrumental reasons.[92] It is also true that we can find examples of denunciations for 'idealistic' reasons inside the Deutsche Bank. In the summer of 1943, the branch manager in Hindenburg, Upper Silesia was denounced by one of his staff for remarks such as the following: 'The Führer understands best how to trick our people'; 'Our air force fails against the English'; and, after the fall of the Italian dictator, 'When will it be finished here?' The motivation for the denunciation was apparently political, as the manager was even a family friend of the informant. After a trial on 14 September 1943 before Roland Freisler at the People's Court, the manager was sentenced to death, and he was executed a week later.[93]

Policing and self-policing activities also took place under the auspices of the Nazi Party and its numerous affiliates, such as the Hitler Youth, which assumed some police-like functions most obviously and publicly by way of uniformed patrols through city, town, and countryside.[94] The Nazi Party's major function until 1933 had been mobilizing the voters at elections, but thereafter, as this role became redundant, it took on tasks that bordered on policing.[95] Even if the Party was formally barred from police work, local leaders in city and countryside exercised discretionary, informal, police-like powers. There was some blurring of offices in that some local Nazi Party leaders were granted, or took over, the office of mayor which in German cities carried important police powers. Although it may be an exaggeration to suggest that such Party leaders were the 'real' repressive power over the people, at least out in the countryside, it is certainly clear that such leaders could and did exercise all kinds of pressure (if rarely open police terror) over the population. They did this not merely by turning people over to, or by working closely with the Gestapo, that is, by acting as the extensions of the Gestapo when and where the police were nowhere in sight, but also in other ways, such as by applying direct or indirect social (and economic) pressure and coercion.[96]

If we look even at the wartime activities of Nazi Party organizations in policing the 'radio measures', they were not as involved in this side of the terror as often assumed. Most cases in this sample began when a member of some Nazi organization denounced the crime. Only rarely did the neighbourhood Party hacks overhear someone listening to the radio. To judge by this sample, these officials were less omnipresent than contemporaries believed.[97] Citizens in a dictatorship often project onto such men in uniform, even the lowly block leader, far more power and influence than they actually possess or exercise. The Gestapo files show that citizens themselves were the ones who usually tipped off these officials, who then served as conduits, funnelling information from the population to the Gestapo.

Out of a total of 670 cases I studied closely over the last chapters, the Nazi Party and its affiliations and all their members provided the telling information in 61 cases or just under 10 per cent of them all. The contribution of the Party and its members to the terror was not unimportant, but should not be over-stated. The Gestapo was far more indebted to ordinary citizens for its information, than it was to card-carrying Nazis.

It is true that the Party in rural and urban centres alike received more denunciations than it actually turned over to police. The Party operated as an institution of patronage and it was invariably asked, by state and Party institutions, even private persons, about the political 'reputation' of persons applying for a state job, or a promotion, and this consultative function gave the local Party considerable leverage. From June 1935 this role as local information dispenser was formally conferred on the Party's leaders, but in practice all kinds of officials in the Party continued to be consulted about issues such as the political 'reliability' of candidates for jobs, promotions, or contracts.[98] In order to fulfil those functions by rummaging around behind peoples' back, the Party virtually invited denunciations from the population, whether from well-meaning citizens, rivals for jobs, 'true believers', or just malcontents.

During the war, the people, the police, and the Party cooperated and produced a system of coercion from which it was increasingly difficult to hide. Also during the war, the concentration camps expanded and, by 1944, established a social presence in Germany that became impossible to overlook. We examine that story next.

9

Concentration Camps in Public Spaces

Concentration Camps were firmly established in the public mind in the first years of the dictatorship, but stories slowed to a trickle in the war years. Occasional mention of the camps was made, such as when escaped prisoners were caught and hanged without trial.[1] There were also reports when particularly egregious 'criminals' were sent to, or executed in a camp.[2] Given that the regime did not want to publish anything that would disturb the home front, press officials must have felt that these stories were worth publishing and would be accepted and welcomed by good citizens. When they read stories like one entitled 'Into the Concentration Camp', they knew what it was all about.[3] The press was ordered to be silent about 'euthanasia', and especially the 'Final Solution' in the east, but enough information came through for many Jews to regard being sent to a camp as the equivalent of a death sentence.[4]

If the concentration camps faded in media reports, camp prisoners and slave workers soon appeared in public spaces all over Germany, from factories to city streets, and became impossible to overlook. As the war dragged on, the camp world invaded everyday life as never before, and confronted citizens with the cruellest sides of the dictatorship. By and large, Germans regarded the prisoners in their telltale camp garb and often in wooden shoes in terms they had come to accept from pre-war propaganda. Although we hear from survivors of help and comfort they received, the overwhelming impression is that Germans were at best indifferent and fearful, and at worst they shared the guards' scorn, hostility, and hatred.

We have many indications of how the concentration camp system was affected by the war. Theodor Eicke, who was in charge of the camps, gave a speech on the first day of the war and mentioned Himmler's new policies. Delivered at the Sachsenhausen concentration camp to (incoming and older) members of the SS who were taking over in place of the Death's Head units, the speech was recalled by Rudolf Höss, later commandant of Auschwitz.[5] Eicke said much was expected of guards and that they would have to carry out 'tough orders'. They must keep in mind that the 'main task of the SS in this war is to protect the state of Adolf Hitler from every danger, above all on the home front. A revolution like the one in 1918, [or] an ammunition factory workers' strike [such as occurred at the time] cannot be allowed to happen again. Every enemy of state who surfaces and anyone who sabotages the war effort is to be annihilated.' The Führer supposedly expected the SS to protect the Fatherland, and

Eicke translated these wishes to camp guards and exhorted them to 'unrestrained hardness' towards prisoners they were supposed to 'educate'. Höss recalled that the new tone of the camp was set with an execution of a man, a Communist, sent there by the Gestapo.[6]

The Gestapo itself used what it called 'whisper propaganda' to spread terror-filled rumours to friends and relatives of those they sent to the camps. On 26 October 1939, the head of the Gestapo ordered local officials no longer to inform prisoners how long they were going to be kept in the camp, but merely to say they would be confined 'until further notice'. Local Gestapo officials would be told, if and when Himmler ordered that prisoners be beaten in the camp, and they could then leak that information to heighten the 'deterrent effect'. As per instructions from Berlin, this 'whisper propaganda' was to be passed only to 'especially well-suited and reliable persons'.[7]

An illustration of how the camps were rationalized to the public, held up for their approval, and how they fitted into the war effort, can be seen in an instructive story that appeared in a widely read SS journal at the end of 1939.

The x-thousands of prisoners who are guarded in the concentration camps, are in part by way of personality and in part by their nature, the same enemies of state who undermined Germany's domestic front during the Great War, and did so whether through connections to the external enemy and active high treason and betrayal of their country or through sabotage, by giving a bad example and consciously undermining morale. They showed themselves during the war to be stronger than the external enemy. While the soldier was victorious on all fronts, the internal enemy successfully worked on Germany's defeat behind the back of the soldier. The National Socialist state would not be a state of front soldiers if it had not already ensured, that the front against the internal enemy was erected. It has shown itself to be useful, with those creatures recognized as the enemies of the people, to take them into secure custody and to watch them, before a crisis arises and they can become dangerous. In that sense the concentration camps represent island-like battlegrounds of the home front, battlefields on which respectively a handful of men protect Germany's inner front.[8]

The images of concentration camps that had been widely used in pre-war Germany also were propagated about new camps, like the one at Groß-Rosen in Silesia, which began as a subcamp of Sachsenhausen on 2 August 1940. It quickly grew to be much too big and obvious to be ignored, not least because it was on a hill and fully lit up at night. The camp was linked to the town in many ways, and there were daily contacts with the outside to get provisions. The prisoners were exploited by local farmers, who 'applied' for and 'borrowed' them as cheap labour. The camp was so effectively integrated into the town that, as historian Isabell Sprenger remarks, 'apparently also private citizens did not find it embarrassing to have imprisoned persons forced to work for them; the stigma constructed of the prisoners by the regime of their being "sub-humans", enemies of state and criminals, stuck to them'.[9]

The camp system in the war years was organized around a series of main camps, located at strategic points and covering the entire Third Reich like a blanket. The SS created a series of subcamp networks centred around each main camp. A sense of the public presence of the camps can be seen merely by listing the main camps and the number of subcamps associated with each by the latter part of the war. Dachau, for example, eventually founded 197 subcamps located in or near towns and cities across southern Germany. Sachsenhausen, north-east of Berlin in Oranienburg, came to administer 74 subcamps, as widely scattered as were those under Dachau's control. The pattern was followed by Buchenwald in central Germany, which had had 129 subcamps by the end of the war, dispersed in cities as separated geographically as Braunschweig, Dessau, Düsseldorf, Essen, Leipzig, and Weimar. In the same way, Flossenbürg, north-east of Nuremberg, controlled 97 subcamps. Mauthausen, located in Austria not far from Linz, eventually stood at the head of 62 subcamps, and Ravensbrück, north of Berlin in time had 45 subcamps in its domain. Neuengamme, south of Hamburg, at one point controlled 90 outer camps. At its height, Groß-Rosen (near Breslau), had a total of 118 subcamps, and the main camp at Mittelbau-Dora (just to the north of Buchenwald, also in the neighbourhood of Weimar) eventually had 32 subcamps. Additional main camps were founded inside Germany during the war, most notably Bergen-Belsen, which attained infamy because of the deplorable conditions of the prisoners found there at war's end.

The camps near German borders, including Auschwitz, were founded with the dual function of terrorizing subject nationalities, and dealing with the influx of prisoners who were considered potential opponents.[10] Auschwitz-Birkenau became not only the largest concentration camp, but the biggest death camp. Even excluding Birkenau, Auschwitz established a network of 50 subcamps, and prisoners worked far afield for industry, agriculture, and at clearing up after bombing attacks. Such camps also were conceived as an opportunity to exploit cheap labour, as at Mauthausen in Austria and Natzweiler (near Strasbourg). More main camps and subcamps were founded across eastern Europe, including less known ones in Latvia and Estonia. Majdanek had 14 subcamps; it was partly a death camp and shares that infamy with others like those at Auschwitz-Birkenau, Belzec, Chelmno, Sobibor, and Treblinka. These camps, founded in or near new territories conquered by the Wehrmacht, are outside the scope of this book, but they certainly had an enormously important role to play in the Third Reich, with ramifications also for what happened inside 'old' Germany.

By early 1942, changes in the administration of the camps was signalled with the creation on 1 February of a new SS Economic and Administrative Main Office or WVHA under the leadership of Oswald Pohl. By mid-March the old Inspectorate of Concentration Camps was added, and Pohl was given the task

28. Reich Justice Minister Otto Thierack (with the scar on his cheek) assumed office on 26 August 1942. With him in the picture, from left to right, is the new President of the People's Court, Roland Freisler, State Secretary of Justice Schlegelberger, then Thierack, and then the new State Secretary in the Justice Ministry, Rothenberger

29. Propaganda Minister Goebbels on a tour (31 August 1943) of Berlin after a bombing attack. His popularity with the people comes through in the picture

30. The 2nd SS Construction Brigade made up of concentration camp inmates, clear up a street called Contrescarpe 13 after the bombing raid in Bremen on 13 June 1943

31. The same SS Construction Brigade, clear up the Obernstrasse in Bremen after the bombing raid of 20 December 1943

32. A typical sign of defiant propaganda at the end of the war. The sign in the rubble of Mannheim (22 December 1944), reads, '. . . and even so. Mannheim remains the lively city'

33. The picture (21 October 1944) shows the Volkssturm, the dads' army of older men and young boys that was called into being to defend Germany from the invaders in late 1944

Bekanntmachung

In Kahlberg wurden standgerichtlich erschossen
am 21. Febr. 1945
der Gren. G. und der Obergefr. der Lw. G.
und am 26. Febr. 1945
der Gefr. B. und der Pionier H.
Die Hingerichteten sind als Fahnenflüchtige
und Drükeberger über das Haff gekommen
Sie scheuten den Heldentod vor dem Feinde
und starben den Tod in Schimpf und Schande

Das Standgericht

34. A sign of the times inside Germany as the battlefront approached the home front. This is an announcement of the execution of four German soldiers, allegedly for desertion. The sign ends with the phrase, 'They shied away from heroic death in the face of the enemy and died ignominiously'

35. The following pictures belong to a series taken at the public execution of 11 foreign workers in Cologne-Ehrenfeld between 3:00 and 3:30 p.m. on 25 October 1944. A total of 35 foreign workers (aged between 18 and 20) from Eastern Europe were arrested and murdered at that time on the basis of a denunciation. Six of those who were hanged were from the Soviet Union, others may have been from Poland, but the exact nationality of them all cannot be established. The first picture (the 2nd of 16) shows the men being led to the place of execution

36. The next (the 6th of 16) shows them, each with a Gestapo official on either side, standing before the gallows erected at the Ehrenfeld rail station

37. The 12th picture shows the execution. Because the rope was too long for one poor soul, he survived briefly until a police official held his feet off the ground. The bodies remained on the ropes until 7:00 p.m.

38. Picture 15 of 16 shows only some of the many people who gathered for the public execution

39. The massacre of concentration camp prisoners in April 1945 on a 'death march' that ended in the mass murder of more than 1,000 people in Gardelegen (described in Chapter 10) was discovered by American troops (seen standing in the background). The prisoners had been driven into this barn, which was then set afire, and anyone who tried to flee was shot

40. This picture shows some of the bodies removed from the barn at Gardelegen, with American troops standing in the background

41. On the liberation of Osnabrück in April 1945, British troops and civilians can be seen helping Russian forced workers who had suffered smoke inhalation. A German policeman had barred the women in a basement and set it aflame

42. The death and destruction inside many camps is reported in the text. This picture hints at what happened in this camp in Landsberg. All that remains of the buildings on the right are the chimneys. The caption on the picture explains that the dead were put in these buildings, which were then set on fire before the Americans arrived to liberate the camp

by Himmler of coordinating the labour of concentration camp prisoners and using them in the economic enterprises of the SS.[11]

Within days (7 February) Hitler appointed Albert Speer as Minister of Armaments and War Production, and shortly thereafter (21 March) he named Fritz Sauckel to take charge of procuring more foreign labourers. All three appointments marked a turning point in mobilizing labour to continue the war and in the concentration camps. In a memorandum to Himmler about the camps on 30 April 1942, Pohl reported that there were 21,400 prisoners in Germany's six main camps at the outbreak of the war in 1939, and that those same camps alone had 44,700 at the time of his report. He indicated that the function of the camps as places for 'the custody of prisoners for security, rehabilitation or preventive reasons' was no longer in the foreground. 'The emphasis', he said, 'shifted to the economic side. Mobilization of all prisoner labour, initially for war purposes (increase of arms production) and later for peacetime building work' was now the top priority.[12]

Despite this call for the 'rational' exploitation of prisoners, Pohl attached to his memorandum to camp commandants a note in which he made clear that they were responsible for 'exhaustively' extracting work from prisoners, 'in the literal sense of the word exhaustive'.[13] Thus, even with an awareness that inmate labour was important to the war effort, the Nazis could not bring themselves to preserve life, and conditions in the camps actually deteriorated. Mortality rates continued to climb and until September 1942, the prisoners in the camps died or were murdered faster than they could be replaced, so that in spite of the massive influx of prisoners of war and foreign nationals, the overall camp population declined.[14]

The invasion of the Soviet Union initially had led to the capture of hundreds of thousands of prisoners, and provided what the Nazis saw as an apparently bottomless pool of slave labour. A side-effect of the surplus was that they could murder the Jews without worrying about the loss of their labour.[15] But the murder and mistreatment of the Jews continued long after the tide in the war turned, and Germany grew desperate for labour, so that economics was inevitably secondary when it came to the Jews. Nazi economic experts noted even in December 1941 that killing skilled Jewish workers in the occupied areas of the Ukraine would have an adverse effect on Germany's ability to exploit the area, but these caveats were brushed aside.[16]

There was continuing tension between the hope of exploiting prisoners, and the drive to exterminate them all.[17] Albert Speer, the classic Nazi exploiter, attained a victory of sorts over the SS in meetings with Hitler on 20 to 22 September 1942. Himmler wanted to locate more armaments production and build larger facilities inside the concentration camps, but Speer and others argued in favour of private enterprise and for bringing the prisoners to the factories.[18] Specialists and engineers were on hand in them who were better trained than the

SS to utilize labour resources. This approach was considered by the industrial-ists, by Speer, and by Hitler to be more efficient, and decentralized production facilities offered more protection from never-ending air raids.[19] Prisoners were soon lent to industry at sordidly low rates, and lived in or near factories.

Himmler began to cast the net wider to pick up more prisoners, and it was partly for that reason that he sought an agreement from Minister of Justice Thierack in September 1942 to transfer prisoners from regular prisons to the concentration camps. Thierack handed over the 'preventive detainees', as well as all Jewish, Russian, Ukrainian, and Czech prisoners, all Poles serving more than three-year terms, and all Germans serving longer than eight years.[20] All were subjected to 'destruction through labour', a new phrase of the moment that clearly showed the mix of ideology and economics in Nazi thinking about the camps. By 1 April 1943, of the 12,658 detainees who went to the camps, almost half (5,935) were already dead, and that process continued.[21] So in spite of Speer's rational economic theory, a combination of Nazi ideology and the brutal practices it inspired meant that in fact destruction continued to take precedence over exploitation.

The importance Himmler attached to antisemitism can be seen at this time when he searched for scarce labourers. On 5 November 1942 he deported the last 2,000 Jews from concentration camps inside Germany, rather than use them in German industry. His priority was to make the camps 'free of the Jews', and he sent them to Auschwitz or Lublin and to certain death.[22] More steps were taken to increase the labour pool of the camps. Himmler ordered Heinrich Müller (head of the Gestapo) on 17 December 1942 to have the Gestapo pick up and send to the camps at least 35,000 men from among foreign workers in Germany. The most vulnerable foreign workers were the Soviets and the Poles, and any considered by police to be guilty of small infractions, were now sent straight to a concentration camp.[23] According to a report of 31 December 1942, other sources of supply included Poles who were imprisoned in parts of Poland called the General Government. As well, youthful offenders (over age 16) were picked up from still farther east, those who caused problems, and who had not learned their lesson from time in an 'educative work camp' (AEL).[24]

The situation in which Speer and the industrialists got the upper hand over the SS in the use of camp prisoners, changed slightly at the end of 1943 and into 1944, because of decisions to conceal key munitions factories in underground caves in hope of avoiding the unrelenting bombing attacks.[25] Some not very effective efforts were made to reduce mortality rates in the camps and in the winter of 1943–4 they fell somewhat. However, the massive numbers of people delivered to the camps in 1944 and 1945, partly because of the decision to send larger groups of foreign workers like the Poles and 'Eastern Workers' directly to them rather than to distribute them across the country through labour exchanges, soon led to a deterioration of conditions again.[26]

Other Camps

The *Catalogue of Camps and Prisons*, prepared by the International Tracing Service in 1949, looks like a good-sized city's telephone book. It lists many thousands of villages, towns, and cities in which one or more camps existed during the war, and touches on some of the businesses (factories, mines, and so on) that became involved in the exploitation system.[27] In fact, there were so many different kinds of camps in wartime Germany that at times citizens could hardly keep them straight.[28]

I want to draw attention to several new kinds of camps and how prisoners invaded public spaces in the war years. The Gestapo was authorized to create so-called 'educative work camps' (Arbeitserziehungslager or AEL) on 28 May 1941, but they were operating in many localities beginning in mid-1940.[29] The police had encroached on the workplace from the beginning of the Third Reich, and problem workers, whether in industry or agriculture, were prosecuted.[30] At least some employers did not shy away from using the Gestapo to help them deal with poor work-discipline and tardiness.[31] Into the war years, 'employers frequently turned to the Gestapo with the request to set an example' by sending individual workers to a concentration camp for 'educative purposes'.[32] By the spring of 1940 the police were flooded with so many cases that Himmler attempted, without lasting success, to disentangle the Gestapo from disciplining workers. In the summer of 1940, problems arose with the first Polish foreign workers, and to make matters worse, up to 1,000 miners per day were staying home from work in the Ruhr. There were crisis meetings held on 6 and 16 August 1940 in Münster, with representatives from government agencies and employers, as well as the army and the Gestapo. Friedrich Jeckeln, the Higher SS and Police Leader, suggested a new type of camp be introduced for the 'educative' purpose of bringing unruly or unproductive workers to their senses.[33] He mentioned the 'very successful' effect on work-discipline of a 'punitive camp' on the grounds of the Hermann Göring Works near Salzgitter.[34]

What may have been the first AEL was created in April 1940 in Wuhlheide (Berlin), when representatives of the Gestapo offered the railway some of its 'idle' prisoners for use, supposedly in the hope that work would cure them.[35] That camp and a similar one in Großbeeren existed throughout the war, and according to survivors, conditions in them approached those in concentration camps. They recalled being put to work in Berlin and environs for the railway, but also repaired war-damaged houses in the city. One man from the Netherlands remembered how Germans who saw them in the railway stations reviled and cursed them.[36]

The AEL at Hunswinkel was considered by employers and officials in the Rhine-Ruhr as so successful, that already on 3 January 1941 the mayor of

Recklinghausen suggested to police that a second such camp be opened at nearby Schützenhof. Other mayors in the area mentioned they had a strong interest in having such a camp, presumably to take advantage of the cheap labour they could use for various municipal projects, including help to clean up after bombing attacks. Early in the New Year, branches of the Hunswinkel facility opened nearby, with prisoners put to work by private companies.[37]

Far from being secret, the existence of these camps was widely publicized for the obvious reason that the threat of being sent to such a place was supposed to provide an incentive to hard work for anyone who could be accused of being lazy, tardy, or unreliable. Moreover, prisoners usually worked outside the camps in public view. Inside some factories, the fact that a worker was sent to an AEL was posted in public. One newspaper story from February 1941 described the AEL in no uncertain terms, under the headline, 'A light word, a serious matter'. The camp was described in order to appeal to the public: 'Particularly hard-nosed slackers, who are not to be improved by protective custody [i.e. a concentration camp] or prison sentence, will be sent to a Work Education Camp, in order to make clear to them more forcefully, that in war everyone has to use their labour power to the full.'[38]

On 28 May 1941, in order to discipline German and foreign workers who were employed in important branches of the economy, Himmler instructed that more AELs be established to protect the 'will to win'. Anyone who refused to work or who otherwise endangered morale at the workplace was to be arrested. These 'lazy elements' would be put in camps and given regularized work with an 'educative purpose' in mind.[39]

The flood of foreign workers in Germany and the desire to discipline the slightest signs of resistance meant that these camps, like concentration camps as well, came to be used primarily but by no means exclusively for them.[40] Those who refused to work, showed insufficient enthusiasm, or merely were accused of undermining morale at the workplace were disciplined in such places.[41] Minister of Justice Thierack and Propaganda Minister Goebbels agreed in June 1942, that where appropriate, death sentences of those found guilty of what was called 'work sabotage' should be posted in the factory where the worker was employed.[42] Whereas running the concentration camps was the responsibility of the SS, the AEL were directly under the control of the Gestapo, so much so that they came to serve as a kind of 'private' concentration camp for the use of local Gestapo chiefs.[43] Prisoners worked outside the camps during the day, very much as did those held in many of the concentration camps, on projects like city sanitation works or for industries, always as cheap labour. Scattered evidence suggests that the health and welfare of prisoners was hardly better in the AEL than in the other camps.[44] Their detention could last up to eight weeks, and while conditions might not have been as bad as in a concentration camp, a stay in the AEL, with long hours of work and devoid of rudimentary pleasures like reading, sending or receiving mail, or smoking, was meant to be anything but a pleasant experience. There were the usual, never-ending roll-calls, there was mistreatment, and there were executions.[45] Those who did not gain from the 'educative' experience could be placed in 'protective custody' and sent to a concentration camp. A recent survey has uncovered 106 AELs, with another 18 subcamps. Twenty-three of these camps were for women, 80 for men, and the remainder for both sexes.[46]

There were also SS Special Camps, such as the one at Hinzert near Trier. It was established on 1 October 1939, and in time it was linked to an additional 33 camps, 27 subcamps, and six police jails which themselves had an additional 13 branches.[47] Dealing with unruly workers and discipline problems among those who worked on the West Wall, a line of defences along Germany's western border that was being built (since 1936) against a French attack, began to pose problems shortly after the war broke out, when local prisons soon filled to overflowing with problem cases of the army. In order to confine the West Wall workers who were causing problems for relatively short periods, the police created emergency prisons in which conditions deteriorated quickly.[48] The new and larger camp at Hinzert was meant to replace these camps and to hold up to 1,000 males, for whom the name 'pupils' was introduced as they were said by the camp commandant to be neither 'inmates' nor 'prisoners serving a term'. The 'pupils' supposedly exhibited certain 'failings' and were regarded as 'sinners' who lacked a 'healthy instinct'. They were kept in Hinzert for a minimum of three months, but an SS report of 26 December 1940 suggested that their 'failings' were so deeply ingrained that they would have to be kept there for a lot longer than that.[49]

Some of the prisoners of Hinzert's subcamps were political prisoners and resistance fighters from other parts of Europe. A small group of about 100 was used in Wiesbaden to clean up after bombing attacks in the latter part of the war. The camp was situated on the fair grounds in Wiesbaden, and most prisoners were from Luxembourg, with others from the Netherlands, Belgium, and France.[50]

Indeed, as the Allied bombing of German cities increased over 1940 and grew still worse in 1941, it caused enormous damage to many cities. It was Hitler's 'wish' that the population directly affected be relieved of the stress and strain caused by these raids as quickly as possible. In order to fulfil this wish, Fritz Todt, as the Minister responsible, gave new powers to those carrying out the clean-up, namely the mayors or their deputies who were now made into 'Leaders of Immediate Measures'. The cities most exposed, like Cologne, began using prisoners of war (mostly French) who were fed on an emergency basis and put in buildings at the Cologne fairgrounds. These buildings were directly across the river from the city's famous cathedral, and had been used in May 1940, when Gypsies were interned there in preparation for their deportation.[51]

On 2 September 1941, the first prisoners of war arrived at what became a concentration camp in the centre of Cologne.[52]

The situation in west German cities grew worse in early 1942, when the emphasis of Allied bombing shifted to civilian targets. The campaign was designed to inflict maximum damage, especially by using incendiary bombs. The first major city to be targeted was Lübeck at the end of March, with devastating effects. On the night of 30–1 May, the first 1,000-bomber raid struck Germany and left unprecedented death and destruction in its wake, along with a need for still more help with the clean-up, including dealing with bombs that failed to explode. Since at least January 1941, concentration camp prisoners were used in isolated cases in bomb disposal units, a practice much favoured by Himmler.[53]

Himmler toured heavily bombed areas in the Rhine-Ruhr and in the Hansa cities on 9 September 1942, and recommended to Chief of the Order Police Kurt Daluege that instead of 'our hoodlums sitting safe and sound in a prison or concentration camp', better use could be made of them in cleaning up after the raids, which would avoid endangering the lives of German firemen. Hitler definitely agreed with this approach.[54]

At almost the same time, 'SS-Construction Brigades', which had been mentioned since the beginning of 1942, began to use 1,000 prisoners from three concentration camps—Neuengamme, Sachsenhausen, and Buchenwald. The first city to get these prisoners was Cologne (on 18 September), with others sent within the month to Düsseldorf, Duisburg, Bremen, and so on. The mayors of these cities were desperate for help and, once they got the SS-brigades, they argued strenuously to keep them as long as possible. Prisoners were marched out to backbreaking work by day in commandos watched by guards, and they spent their nights in makeshift 'camps' like the one at the Cologne fairgrounds, where, by the end of 1942, about 1,000 prisoners brought from Buchenwald were housed. They were subject to mistreatment and undernourishment, and by the winter of 1943/4 when some refused to work harder, or simply could not because they were already exhausted, they were executed in the streets.[55] Eventually an estimated 6,000 prisoners went through that tiny camp, apparently most of them non-Germans.

The sight of concentration camp prisoners working in the streets of big cities like Cologne, often without proper footwear, dressed in the pathetic striped garb of the camps, right down to the well-known badges signifying nationality and 'crime', became a new fact of everyday life in Germany. All over Germany, camp prisoners of one kind or another shuffled to and from their camps in full view of citizens who certainly could not fail to notice their mistreatment and deplorable condition.[56]

At the beginning of 1945 there were 13 SS-Construction Brigades across the country, by then on trains and mostly used to clean up the railway lines. Like the ones in Offenburg, there were around 500 prisoners on each train. They were kept in the (unheated) freight cars, and sent up and down the line for repair work.[57] Those who guarded such prisoners, and not just those in Offenburg, tried to make sure that direct contact with the population was kept to a minimum, but prisoners recorded both negative attitudes and helpful gestures. Although on occasion food or cigarettes were tossed to, or left for, these prisoners, the population was overwhelmingly in tune with Nazi propaganda and generally turned against all camp prisoners and all foreigners.

Private Sector

Private companies turned out to be the largest exploiters of concentration camp prisoners, and the process began by using them mainly in construction work. This idea was clearly in the air in late 1940 and into 1941 as can be seen from any number of examples.[58] The aircraft industry apparently led the way, beginning with Heinkel's use of prisoners in Oranienburg in late autumn 1941; by early 1943 it was putting as many as 4,000 to use there, and the company (among others) pointed to that example as reason for doing the same thing, first in construction work, then in assembly-line production of the 'A4' rockets at Peenemünde.[59] Arthur Rudolf, one of the engineers in charge of Germany's rocket programme, accepted an invitation from the SS to tour the rent-a-slave operations of the Heinkel aircraft plant in Oranienburg in mid-April 1943. Far from having these prisoners imposed by Himmler, as Rudolf later said, he convinced himself of the feasibility of using prisoners and became an advocate of doing so. Like other engineers involved in the Nazi rocket programme, Rudolf ended up working for NASA and helped to develop the US space programme.[60]

In 1943 well-known aircraft firms, like Junkers and Messerschmitt followed Heinkel's lead. The uses to which most of the prisoners were put changed at the turn of the year 1943–4, with the decision to transfer production facilities underground, and thousands were worked to death in what was a futile endeavour.[61] At Mittelbau-Dora, prisoners lived underground during the construction phase that began in the autumn of 1943, when mostly Russian, Polish, French, and German prisoners from Buchenwald worked underground in terrible conditions. As many as 8,000 were there by the end of the year. Hans Kammler, Himmler's man on the spot, told those in charge to ignore the costs in terms of the lives of prisoners and to press on. From December 1943 to March 1944 between 20 and 25 prisoners perished on the site every day, and the number would have been greater, had not the SS 'selected' the weakest and sent them to camps like Majdanek and Bergen-Belsen, where many subsequently died or were killed. A sign of the desperate need for workers was that Jews were brought to Dora in the summer of 1944. Mittelbau-Dora had 26,000 prisoners in November 1944, and grew to more than 40,000 by March 1945. In this period there were more than 5,000 deaths, and in March alone there were 162 executions. It is a fact that more people died in the production of the German rocket programme than were killed by the rockets when they hit distant English or continental targets.[62]

IG Farben, the largest corporation in Europe and fourth largest in the world at the time, was also involved in the exploitation of concentration camp prisoners. It was a chemical giant, and among other things, manufacturer of synthetic rubber and fuel. War was good for business and, especially in 1940 when peace with Great Britain seemed remote, and the difficulties of obtaining rubber and fuel were likely to persist, the government and the corporation became convinced that the production of synthetics was needed. The corporation briefly considered the idea of a site in Upper Silesia and at the end of 1940, its experts pointed to Auschwitz as one of several places for a new factory.[63]

By early 1941, Himmler and others involved in the ethnic and social planning for Upper Silesia got wind of IG Farben's interests and, keen to secure the investment, money, and skilled Germans for the area, Himmler even visited the camp on 1 March 1941 and met with IG Farben officials. He decided to do everything possible to convince the corporation to choose Auschwitz. Company managers and construction experts were informed of SS plans to make Auschwitz an attractive option, and they were told that most of the city's population of Jews and Poles would be expelled to make room for Germans. That a concentration camp already existed there (with 7,000 prisoners), who could be made available for construction work on the new plant, obviously at extremely low rates, had been conveyed to IG Farben visitors already on 10 February 1941. In the meeting with Himmler on 1 March, it was announced that the camp would expand to up to 30,000 prisoners, thereby turning Auschwitz, which began less than a year earlier merely as a place to terrorize the local population, into Germany's biggest concentration camp. While the corporation may not have envisaged the full scope of the mass murder that was to follow at Auschwitz, no one in Germany at the time, least of all the senior managers and the planners at Farben, could have been uncertain about what generally happened to people in concentration camps. Farben was fully cognizant that it would be using large numbers of men and women as virtual slaves and had no moral qualms. A sunny future was confidently predicted by the corporation and the SS at a meeting in Kattowitz on 7 April 1941. The corporation, in the words of one its experts at the meeting, Otto Ambros, said that 'with the Auschwitz project' it had 'designed a plan for a new enterprise of giant proportions', one that would influence the environment as positively as did such modern enterprises in the west of Germany. In that way, he continued, the corporation 'fulfils a high moral duty to ensure with a mobilization of all its resources that this industrial foundation becomes a firm cornerstone for a powerful and healthy Germanism in the east'. A spokesman for Himmler at the meeting stated simply that for the Reichsführer-SS, the aim was 'to create on this spot an exemplary eastern settlement—particular attention being paid to settling here German men and women who are particularly qualified'.[64]

For a variety of reasons, not least the relentless mistreatment and outright murder of the prisoners, making an economic success of the IG Farben enterprise at Auschwitz proved more difficult than originally expected. The mortality rates of all those sent to work in one or another of the company's operations in the area rose to catastrophic proportions, and late in the war life expectancy in some of their mines there stood at four to six weeks.[65] Notwithstanding the massive numbers who died or were murdered out of hand in setting up the Buna (rubber) factory at Auschwitz-Monowitz, no synthetic rubber was ever produced.[66]

In the spring of 1941 when the deal was struck between IG Farben and the SS, however, it accelerated the trend by which many of Germany's most renowned companies such as Siemens collaborated in the enslavement and murder of concentration camp prisoners. Siemens was by the Nazi era Europe's largest and most powerful electrical corporation, and although it did not initiate the idea of using prisoners in early 1940 when the possibility was presented in the first place, the company was quick to respond and soon integrated German-Jewish women from the Ravensbrück camp into the production process. This experimental use of slave labour proved profitable because (from September 1941), managers and foremen learned to use the threat of dismissal, which would then have been followed by deportation, as a prod to get prisoners to work harder. After relatively modest beginnings, using less than 2,000 camp prisoners at Siemens in Berlin in 1940, the numbers more than doubled the next year. By 1944, when more subcamps were constructed and the company's production facilities were decentralized, it exploited some 15,200 (Jewish and non-Jewish) prisoners, and had dealings with virtually all the main concentration camps. According to the testimony of survivors, the use of threats and terror to increase productivity was standard practice.[67]

Other companies with international reputations used concentration camp prisoners, among them was Daimler-Benz, a company that also produced for the war, and whose massive operation spread across the Reich. Daimler-Benz used prisoners, including so-called 'work Jews' for the first time at the end of 1941 in the General Government (that is, part of the former Poland). In the years that followed not only Jews (male and female), but other nationalities were used in camps created on company premises inside Germany.[68] Although the total number of prisoners used by Daimler-Benz at one time or another remains unknown, a recent investigation shows more than 10,000 of them worked at various times and camps in the late war years.[69]

In early 1942 the famous entrepreneur Ferdinand Porsche was just as anxious to make deals with the SS as the other leaders of German industry. He suggested to Hitler that prisoners be used to build a foundry, and obtained the Führer's support.[70] Porsche was not shy in meetings with the SS and pushed to get his way.[71] The Volkswagen Works under Porsche's direction established a concentration camp with the revealing name of 'Arbeitsdorf', or Work Village. It was opened in April 1942 when 500 prisoners arrived from Neuengamme to build a light-metal foundry. They seem to have been relatively well treated and clothed, and when their job was finished in mid-September 1942, they were sent back to Neuengamme. From the point of view of the developing plans of the SS, the 'Arbeitsdorf' experiment was regarded as quite successful.[72]

Volkswagen was anxious to become the main producer of the 'flying bomb' (Flugbombe) in the spring of 1943, and keen to take advantage of cheap labour and to build a concentration camp at Laagberg, just over three kilometres from the main VW plant in Wolfsburg.[73] The first 800 or so prisoners were French, Dutch, Russian, Polish, and Spanish, many of whom had been involved in resistance activities, and they were treated every bit as badly at VW as they had been in Neuengamme, where most of them had been.[74] In March 1944, Ferdinand Porsche was quite insistent that in addition to the 3,500 concentration camp prisoners already employed by VW at that point, still more were needed.[75] This time the main recruits were Hungarian Jews from Auschwitz, many of them the very kind of metal-working specialists desperately needed by the company. According to survivors, they were not ill-treated at the VW main works, at least in comparison with what they had seen in their short time in Auschwitz, but were badly undernourished. A bomb attack on the main VW works on 29 July 1944, brought an end to their 'normal' treatment when they were sent off to a branch plant in Tiercelet where, in spite of being prized specialists who had been hand-picked in Auschwitz because of their skills, they were used merely for crude construction and quarry work.[76]

The Bayerische Motoren Werke (BMW) had profited from the beginning of the Third Reich by the expansion of the automobile industry and because it became involved in the production of motors for aircraft. From 1940–1, with the call-up of many German workers to the Wehrmacht and the expansion of BMW, the number of employees grew, many of them made up by prisoners of war from Russia, France, Holland, and concentration camp prisoners. Whether it was the company or the SS who took the initiative remains unknown. By 1939 BMW gained what would become a lucrative monopoly on air-cooled motors which were manufactured at three sites, including one in Allach near Munich.[77]

In August 1941, BMW tried to interest the SS in making concentration camp prisoners available, but that did not work out.[78] By the latter part of 1942 they came to an accord, and the first prisoners arrived at BMW's Allach location from Dachau to carry out construction work. By 22 February 1943 a camp opened there, and quickly expanded. By the beginning of 1944 some 3,434 prisoners working for BMW lived in that camp, while over 2,000 others worked at six other sites.[79] The Allach factory grew enormously from around 1,000 employees in 1939–40, to 5,572 in 1941 and over 17,000 by 1944. This last workforce was cobbled together from roughly 3,000 foreign workers; the same number of prisoners of war (mostly Russian); and as many or more concentration camp prisoners. The several thousand German workers still working for BMW were easily outnumbered.[80] Reports are mixed from survivors as to the behaviour of German civilians in Allach, as in other such camps located on the grounds of private companies. Germans gave them some help, but most were 'all too often willing and eager helpers of the SS'.[81] Prisoners working for private companies seem to have been treated better than they would have been in regular concentration camps, but the SS guards were usually still in charge and continued their mistreatment; work was long and arduous; food, shelter, and sanitation were dreadful. Terror was always a moment away, and there is plenty of evidence of on-the-spot executions.[82]

Late War Camps

The growth of the camps was dramatic in 1944–5, as we can see by what happened to the Dachau network. At the end of 1941 Dachau had eight subcamps; in 1942, some 23 new subcamps were founded, 13 of which were dissolved before the end of the year. Nineteen subcamps were founded in 1943, and in 1944–5, another 120 of them. As recent studies of some of these camps have shown, many were located in the middle of towns and villages and impossible for citizens to miss. Germans showed some kindness towards prisoners in small towns like Saulgau and Friedrichshafen (Bavaria) but negative attitudes were also in evidence.[83] If there was some uniformity in the behaviour of the German population towards the prisoners now in their midst, it was one of distance and uncertainty, especially because the end of the regime was in sight and everyone knew the camps were bound to be liberated. Strict behaviour was enforced by guards and local Nazi enthusiasts, also by vigilant neighbours who threatened those offering even minimal sympathy, much less some food. The usual warning was that the sympathetic Germans would themselves be sent to the camp.[84] Survivors of other Dachau subcamps at Kaufering, Mühldorf, and Überlingen, report that some help was given them, but also recall the indifference and rejection. Historian Edith Raim, who has written about the responses of the prisoners in Dachau subcamps to the life around them, notes that

the civil population of the area symbolized for [many survivors] the normality of life in the middle of the madness of the camp. With wonder and pain the prisoners registered the ordinariness of everyday life—from which they themselves often had been isolated already for years—in villages and small towns hardly affected by the war. Often the inhabitants of the area were repelled by the prisoners and attempted to ignore their existence.[85]

Some subcamps were constructed in desperate circumstances, many not 'camps' at all except in name, set up amidst ruins, like one created in March 1945 in Regensburg's Colosseum theatre, right in the middle of town.[86] We have little information about such places, but from what historians have uncovered in the last several years, it seems as though behind each camp there is another waiting to be discovered. Local historians have played an important part in finding these often obscure camps, like two created in Essen in 1943 and 1944. The first of them, established in late 1943, was composed of up to 150 men who spent their nights in rooms of partly bombed-out buildings with the address, 'Schwarze Poth 13'. According to a Gestapo report of 10 July 1944, the prisoners were mainly Russians (of whom there were 90) and Poles (40), as well as people from France, Belgium, Denmark, Luxembourg, and three Germans. There were no Jews.[87] The camp prisoners worked for an SS company, the German Economic Operations (DWB), and were used on behalf of the city to clean up after bombing attacks. They wore striped clothing and wooden shoes. Apparently not everyone who saw them in Essen recognized the significance of this garb; some thought it was issued by a prison, while the men, who were guarded by policemen in green uniforms rather than by the SS, were believed to be serious criminals. By 21 March 1945, as the Allied armies approached from the west, most of the men still alive in the camp were sent back to the Buchenwald concentration camp. We do not know if any survived.[88]

More is known about the other Buchenwald subcamp in Essen thanks to the research of Ernst Schmidt and Ulrich Herbert. Whereas the Schwarze Poth 'camp' was made up entirely of non-Jewish males used in public works, the camp that was built in the Humboldt Straße in 1944 was composed of Jewish females who were there to work for Krupp, one of Germany's legendary armaments makers. Major industries like Krupp grew dependent on foreign workers to meet greatly increased demand.[89] By early summer 1944, when it became clear that the vast reserves of foreign labourers were gone and could not be replenished, Krupp appealed to the SS for camp prisoners. The SS office in charge (the WVHA) in turn instructed companies to contact the 'relevant' main concentration camp in their area. Krupp sent their Deputy Personnel Manager to Buchenwald where he 'ordered' 2,000 skilled men. It became common to send company representatives into the camps like Buchenwald or Ravensbrück to carry out their own 'selections' of prisoners, including females, who had to stand naked in public for the inspection.[90]

At any rate, late in the war the demand for prisoners was so great and their mortality rates through starvation and mistreatment in the camps so high, that the demand for able-bodied men was impossible to meet. As a stop-gap, Krupp was given the opportunity to select 500 or so workers from a Buchenwald subcamp holding young Hungarian Jewish women. The subcamp was located not far from Essen in Gelsenkirchen. At the end of August 1944 they were brought by streetcar or came on foot to a new Buchenwald subcamp in the Humboldt Straße in Essen. According to one survivor, 'hundreds' of citizens witnessed the daily march of the prisoners, who were in wretched condition, on their way to and from work at Krupp.[91] As Ulrich Herbert shows, far from having such prisoners thrust upon them by the SS, Krupp was persistent in demands for them. The SS itself suggested from the outset that the women were not up to the heavy tasks they would have to perform for the company and within a few weeks the unfortunates were so weakened as to be incapable of any real work. There was no mass murder of the Jewish women in Essen itself, but apart from six who got away, the rest were evacuated to Bergen-Belsen in March 1945, only to arrive in the midst of a typhus epidemic and a complete breakdown of what order remained in the camp. In the end, the only six to have survived for certain did so when they managed to flee before they were shipped out of Essen. They obtained the help of Germans to remain hidden and fed, and thus lived to tell the tale.[92]

The number of prisoners in all the concentration camps, estimated at 25,000 at the beginning of the war, grew dramatically over time. The coming of the war was used as an opportunity to arrest not only those who were on specially prepared lists of those suspected of being security risks, but also groups of social outsiders. In the first war years, as one country after another fell to the Wehrmacht, arrests of variously defined suspicious persons took place, some of whom were sent to camps in Germany, so that increasing numbers of foreign nationals—Poles, Czechs, Norwegians, Frenchmen, Belgians, Dutchmen, and Serbs—were added to the camp population. The Gestapo also began arresting greater numbers of people than ever.[93] By March 1942, the numbers of prisoners in the concentration camps had already increased to roughly four times what it was at the start of the war, up to at least 100,000; by August 1943 (in spite of astoundingly high death rates in the camps) that number more than doubled again to 224,000, and in August 1944, the prisoners numbered 524,268. An official survey of 15 January 1945, put the total population in the concentration camps at 714,211 of whom 511,537 were men and 202,674 were women.[94] When the war ended, there were at least 700,000 prisoners in the camps, but the figure has been put as high as 750,000.[95]

The death toll in the camps in Germany was shocking. The figures for the death camps are even more staggering; of the five main ones, the lowest total was Chelmo, with an estimated 225,000 victims. Another 250,000 were murdered at Sobibor. Larger camps like the one at Treblinka killed nearly one million, and at the Auschwitz complex, the death toll was well over a million.[96]

Prisoners at the Garden Gate

The new and obvious presence of the camps during 1943 and later in cities, towns, and villages in Germany certainly created an atmosphere unlike anything felt before 1939. Just in Munich during the war years there were about 40 subcamps and there were 10 more in communities nearby, like Allach, Schleißheim, Ottobrun, and Neuaubing in which at one time or another there were between 15,000 and 17,000 prisoners.[97] In Berlin there were also around 30 such camps, more than half of them filled with women, as the camp world invaded the capital city. In addition it has been estimated there were about 700 camps of various kinds for foreign workers in Berlin.[98] Many of the latter, mostly established in 1943 and 1944 were large, especially those on the premises of some of Germany's major firms like the one at Siemens in Haselhorst-Nord, with over 2,000 prisoners, 700 of them women.[99] Not unlike elsewhere, prisoners were said to be criminals.[100]

The terror inside Germany was no longer only in the hands of the Gestapo, but for the first time it was also embodied in the SS men and others in charge of the many new camps. The murderous and brutal ways to which they had grown accustomed, especially the SS recruits from eastern Europe who made up some of the guards at these camps in Germany, were used in public view both in factories and in the streets. Virtually all the oral history interviews with Germans about the subcamps built in their area towards the latter part of the war make mention of at least one graphic, cruel, and even murderous incident they witnessed personally between a guard and an inmate, in which the latter was brutally beaten or shot merely for stepping out of line or refusing to work when their last reserves of strength were gone.[101]

In the last analysis it was impossible to keep the prisoners out of sight and out of mind from the population, as there were just too many points of contact. One inmate who worked in a Hamburg camp (the Alt-Garge electrical works) remembered that when 'citizens saw us march by, they stood motionless as stones and just looked at us. The same thing repeated itself every time with our march to and from the camp. We believe today, that everything that the citizens of Alt-Garge saw of our work details did not let them sleep peacefully for many nights.'[102]

One German man recalled the impression made on him (as a 14-year-old at the time) when a camp was built in his small Bavarian home town late in the war: 'I believe that the people in the village first understood what the words "concentration camp" meant, when they actually came face to face with prisoners.'[103] In the desperate drive to make up for labour shortages and to keep the munitions factories going, even if that meant burying them in caves hollowed out of solid rock, workers from across Europe were pressed into service, whether they volunteered or were forced to come to Germany.

It is hard to say what citizens really thought about the camp prisoners. Given the sheer force of the numbers involved, and the mounting rumours of Nazi murderousness, it is difficult to believe that Germans had no inkling at all of what was happening in the camps and that they totally swallowed the propaganda about the increasing numbers of 'dangerous criminals' who had to be locked up and guarded. Of course, there were some people who were convinced that there was some basis to the propaganda. According to one survivor from France, a guard at a subcamp near Bremen, who was not a member of the SS, and who actually helped the prisoners, was nevertheless convinced they were criminals or Communists.[104] In many cases, however, Germans were either unresponsive or indifferent, so that Nazi propaganda was a convenient way out. This seems to have been the case at a small camp (usually holding about 500 prisoners) at Kaltenkirchen in northern Germany, which was created in mid-1944 as a branch of Neuengamme. It contained three main groups, especially Soviet prisoners of war, some political prisoners, and some criminals. The people of the area were told, and many of them apparently chose to believe that the prisoners were all criminals, mostly either homosexuals or others guilty of morals charges. The starving prisoners marching to and from their work seemed to provide visual confirmation of the images conjured up by Nazi propaganda.[105] Not everyone believed the propaganda, however. At least German youngsters who were old enough to know the difference, realized that these prisoners were 'not real criminals', but thought there was something vaguely wrong with them all.[106] 'Those people in the camp are criminals', Baron von Neurath told his young daughter of the prisoners in a camp that was created practically in their own backyard; 'it's a good thing they're so well guarded.'[107]

Camp prisoners forced to work in Germany during 1944–5 also included 'politicals', like those involved in resistance activities. In 1944 some of them worked on a tunnel near the village of Treis, located not far from the picturesque town of Cochem in the Mosel valley. In Treis the SS began looking for a place to set up a 'camp' in the winter of 1943 and opted for the dance hall of a local hotel, much to the chagrin of its owner who hoped instead that well-paying SS guests were merely looking for rooms for themselves. The hotel was soon made over into a miniature concentration 'camp', with other barracks added later that were closer to the work site. Prisoners were mostly political prisoners from France, Belgium, Poland, Russia, and other parts of Europe, but apparently there were no Jews. One Belgian political prisoner recalled that local citizens were told that the prisoners were all 'dangerous criminals', and not infrequently townsfolk shouted expressions of hatred as the prisoners passed on their way to and from work. Survivors recall that some Germans knew they were political prisoners and not criminals, and a few even risked trouble by offering some food.[108]

The largest single transport with 850 men arrived in Treis from Auschwitz on 3 May 1944. It brought mostly Russians and Poles, but it seems no Jews.[109] These and other prisoners (whose total remains unknown), slaved in dreadful conditions to construct a tunnel that was to run between Treis and the next village at Bruttig; it was to house a factory producing light metal for aeroplanes. The many deaths of prisoners are recalled in the area, as are the conditions of work and the atrocious treatment by the guards. Another study of camp labour on the Hamburg docks at the same time, shows that similar kinds of prisoners suffered similar death rates.[110]

In the Mosel area, the SS did not concern itself with the effects on the prisoners of working in impossible conditions. Any sympathy from the local population prompted guards to reinforce the message that the prisoners were 'dangerous criminals'. Rewards were offered to anyone who turned in escapees. Executions took place in the camps at Treis and Bruttig, with the bodies of the hanged victims reportedly open to public view. On at least some occasions, local people were invited to see the executions at first hand.[111]

These and other such stories, often incomplete, are finally emerging as a result of the work of local historians in many parts of Germany. They illustrate the revolutionary developments in the concentration camp system in the latter part of the war and in particular how the camps became part of the social landscape.

Major industrial concerns like VW, converted to war work, were desperate for labourers by the autumn of 1943, all the more as the hitherto apparently unlimited reservoir of Soviet prisoners of war ran dry and it grew next to impossible to recruit workers from Western European countries like France or to fill demands for slave labourers from Eastern Europe. The massive number of prisoners in the concentration camps was an obvious source. By 1943 Himmler and Hitler were more enthusiastic than ever that prisoners should be used to build facilities like underground bunkers for war production. Located in tunnels like the one between Treis and Bruttig, it was thought that such factories would be safe from bombing attacks. Private companies like the well-known Blohm & Voss on the Hamburg docks, involved in building submarines, were no less anxious to acquire concentration camp labour and, once the possibility was opened in the autumn of 1944, tried to get the best-qualified workers from the camp at Neuengamme before their competitors did.[112]

By 1944 at the latest, most Nazi leaders, including Albert Speer and Hermann Göring, were pushing for an increase in the use of these last reserves of labour. By the turn of the year 1944/5 the number of concentration camp prisoners employed in one aspect or another of war industry work rose to nearly one-half million.[113]

Hitler decided on 6–7 April 1944, evidently in response to a suggestion made by the construction Organization Todt (OT), to order that Jews be transported to Germany to work.[114] He personally contacted Himmler to ask that 100,000 Jewish men (from Hungary) be brought to Germany, thus reversing his long-held views. Soon authorization was granted to bring in more Hungarian Jews, to work under SS supervision on OT and other construction projects.[115] German organizations, institutions, and businesses whose emergency needs for labour were becoming critical, 'literally lined up' to plead for Jewish labourers from Hungary.[116] Although a total of 200,000 may have been approved, it seems unlikely that quite that many avoided the gas chambers in Auschwitz and made it to Germany. Many more Jews were available, but were killed instead.

When Hungary was occupied by Germany in March 1944, nearly 800,000 Jews came under their control; instead of conscripting as many as possible for work in Germany, trains shipped them to Auschwitz and by July 1944 approximately 438,000 arrived there, of whom only about 10 per cent were considered fit to work.[117] Most were killed, while the others were sent to Germany; instead of being the healthy men of working age as hoped for by employers, many of the Hungarian Jews who arrived were women.[118]

By war's end, Germany proved unable to exploit camp labour effectively. At a time of desperate need, the country mobilized only 'several hundred thousand' camp prisoners, of whom only a small fraction was involved in production work.[119] These numbers would certainly have been higher if the SS or private industry had done more to preserve the lives of the prisoners by ensuring better treatment. As it was, private firms did too little and even took the deaths of many into account as a matter of course. Exactly how many men and women lost their lives while working for German industries has never been established. As one writer put it recently about Daimler-Benz, the only thought was that 'the larger the concern could become in the war, the better would be the starting basis for the period after the war'.[120]

A sense of what it was like to be used as a slave in the latter days of the war is conveyed by Alexander Donat, one of the Jews brought into Germany at that time. He records both the mistreatment and the help he received at a subcamp in Hessenthal, near Vaihingen. He recalls the daily march of three and a half miles to work, right down the main street of town and 'the civilian faces which peered out at us from behind their curtains with horror and with sympathy'.[121] He observed that 'there were thousands of small camps like ours all over Germany where prisoners worked in factories, on construction sites, military projects, and so on. The big death camps used assembly-line methods of extermination; the little ones were less spectacular and noisy but just as dedicated to killing off their prisoners.'[122]

In many parts of the Third Reich, camp prisoners of all nationalities were walked, trucked, or shipped back and forth across the shrinking territory of what remained of the area under German control in late 1944 and into 1945. That story belongs to the apocalyptic end of Hitler's dictatorship and is discussed in the next chapter.

10

Dictatorship and People at the End of the Third Reich

The war initially had positive effects for Hitler's dictatorship, and many people who vacillated until then, soon fell into line because of their patriotism, or were won over by the first victories. One historian concluded that 'the war strengthened still more the basic acceptance of the regime, until shortly before the end, also as the tides of war changed and the Allied air attacks actually bombed the German "community of the people" into a real "community of fate".'[1]

Even as the situation on the battlefront deteriorated, there was nothing close to a rebellion, and according to Peter Hoffmann's and Joachim Fest's recent studies of the German resistance, on the whole the general population did not favour resistance, but continued to support the government.[2] Nazi opinion surveyers found no more than 'defeatist' statements in the rubble of cities like Berlin or Hamburg in late 1944 and early 1945, and they noted how support continued for the war effort. A common pose was to take a wait-and-see attitude.[3] One report from eastern Germany in March 1945 mentioned that workers not only continued to trust Hitler, but some suggested he adopt Stalinist methods to 'purge' the civil service, army, and Nazi Party.[4] In Hamburg in early April 1945, in spite of everything the city had endured, opinion surveys picked up confident remarks. There were no indications anywhere that a strike, much less surrender, was contemplated by anyone, and into March 1945 hope persisted for a 'good end to the war'.[5] Another report that month from Baden showed some last-minute attitudinal changes as enemy ground troops grew close, and the same happened in eastern Germany.[6] In general, the social consensus persisted that made the dictatorship possible, even if more citizens gave only grudging support.

Hitler's Bloody Visions

As the tide of war went against Germany, Hitler's utopian dreams were gradually displaced by bitter determination to do whatever it took to keep the German home front from faltering. Even when he was still winning, he boasted to a foreign dignitary on 21 July 1941, that if a crisis arose, blood would flow, and he would annihilate all 'dead beats'. He mentioned one of his favourite parables about what should happen at home if things went badly: 'If on the one hand the valuable people put their lives on the line at the front, it is criminal to spare the scoundrels. They have to be destroyed or, if not dangerous to society, barred in concentration camps from which they will never again be permitted to leave.'[7]

The most murderous phase of the war began with the invasion of the Soviet Union in June 1941. Hitler issued a secret decree on 13 May 1941 in which he laid down what was to happen in the east, and called for an even more arbitrary system of 'police justice'. That was followed on 6 June 1941 by the notorious 'commissar order', based on instructions from Hitler. It authorized the execution of all captured Soviet prisoners who were suspected of being Communist Party functionaries or 'commissars'. This order resulted in the deaths of countless thousands. The German army took on the Nazi ethos, became Hitler's army, and it 'not only tolerated mass murder of a totally new quality, but also to a large extent supported it'.[8] The treatment of Soviet prisoners was particularly abominable. An estimated 3.3 million Soviet prisoners died in captivity; many thousands were shot out of hand to avoid taking prisoners; and still more were brought back to Germany to be worked to death or executed by the Gestapo.[9]

Hitler's direct involvement in the brutalization process also can be seen in his attitude towards sabotage. With the German advance into Russia stalled in December 1941, coupled with resistance activities in France and other occupied areas in the West, Hitler told military leaders that attacks on Germans must be dealt with differently than before, as he had concluded that even lifelong prison sentences were being regarded by enemies as a 'sign of weakness'. He suggested that suspects in occupied countries simply disappear without news of their whereabouts, as if they had vanished in 'night and fog'. In practice anyone arrested was tried and often executed within a week, or they were sent to Germany with no information to family or anyone else concerned about what had happened to them.[10] The policy was to keep relatives in the dark about the fate of those suspected of resistance, even when they had died or were executed.[11] Beginning in February 1942 in Cologne, Dortmund, Kiel, and Berlin, new 'night and fog' courts tried foreign nationals sent from France, Belgium, Norway, and the Netherlands. The decree from the head of the Armed Forces (OKW) Keitel, after being 'verified and approved' by Hitler, resulted in an unknown number of deaths, but certainly more than several thousand. Anyone found not guilty was turned over to the Gestapo and in September 1944, that happened to 24,000 'night and fog' prisoners. With the agreement of the Ministry of Justice, and as Hitler wished, all these people ended up in concentration camps.[12]

German defeat at Stalingrad at the end of January 1943, led Nazi opinion surveyors to conclude that 'generally' citizens saw it as a 'turning point'. What made it seem worse was the promise conveyed by press and radio that victory had been just round the corner. Stalingrad was followed by the capture of German and Italian forces in North Africa. The reversals on all fronts, according to the Nazis' own analysis, led some people to conclude that it was the 'beginning of the end'.[13]

The dictatorship grew more vicious towards enemies on the home front, as in 'Operation Thunderstorm' (22 August 1944), in the wake of the attempt on Hitler's life on 20 July. The police picked up an estimated 5,000 people in a pre-emptive strike, one of the largest round-ups ever of non-Jewish Germans.[14] The arrests were partly in response to the assassination attempt on Hitler, and included ex-parliamentary deputies, officials of the old parties, ex-mayors and some ex-civil servants. There were negative reactions in some places to the arrests of these mostly older and politically non-threatening people, with the suggestion that if the state really was worried about them, then the unity of the nation must be in bad shape. Not surprisingly, therefore, to judge by what happened in Bremen, most were quickly released.[15]

Propaganda began to reach its limits when bombs rained from the skies and enemy troops broke through at the front. As one Berlin opinion report for March 1945 put it, 'our propaganda is like the orchestra on a sinking ship that keeps on playing enthusiastically'.[16] The reports we have on public opinion from those times suggest that, even though many citizens were still prepared to support Hitler's dictatorship, some had had enough. An expression that made the rounds in Hamburg stated simply, 'Better an end with horror than horror without end.'[17]

The People and the Police to the End

Despite impending defeat, many people continued to denounce colleagues, neighbours, friends, and relatives to the police. By late 1944 and early 1945, the police dispensed with written records; these tend to fall off after the Normandy invasion. In what follows, I draw on some Gestapo files that survived and supplement them with materials collected for post-1945 trials.

Denunciations persisted, even though the consequences of accusations were often fatal, as happened in a small town near Cologne in mid-1943. A worker denounced his colleague to the Nazi Party for expressing doubts about leadership and telling political jokes. The real motive of the informer, who recently had lost his job, was revenge. He insisted that Party officials press on with his complaint, even though they asked him to reconsider, because the allegations were so serious. At his insistence the case went forward, and by year's end it was sent to the People's Court. The accused was sentenced to death (10 March 1944) for 'undermining the will to win', and the verdict was promptly carried out.[18]

It is less certain why several people turned in Fritz Markart, a 54-year-old locomotive engineer from Wuppertal. From January to May 1943, not long after the battle of Stalingrad, the Gestapo was informed that anonymous letters were being received by families of soldiers missing in action. These notes could only have been written by someone with 'illegal' information obtained by listening to foreign radio. In May and June 1943, perhaps even earlier, the letter-writer Markart began signing his own name and giving his correct address. One woman who turned over the letters received more than a dozen from all parts of Germany giving her news that her husband was captured at Stalingrad. Neither she nor a man who turned the letters over to the police, said why they did so. Once the Gestapo had the incriminating evidence, it was easy to find Markart, who admitted sending letters to 46 different families, whose addresses were found. As far as possible, each of these was investigated, and many almost got into serious trouble for not informing about the treasonous letters. Markart's case went to the Special Court in Wuppertal and on 16 October 1943 (having been in custody since 28 July), he was sentenced to two years in prison. Whether he survived the war remains unknown.[19]

Denunciations were still used to settle neighbourhood disputes, and even 'petty' ones increasingly ended disastrously. Gertrud Schulz, a 48-year-old married woman, denounced her landlord on 16 November 1943. She was his tenant since 1938, but conflict arose because of the chickens she and her husband raised against the landlord's wishes. Although she really only wanted to settle the quarrel with the landlord, Schulz embellished the negative remarks he made about Hitler. By February 1944 the man was handed over to the Gestapo, sent to Berlin where he was tried, found guilty by the People's Court, sentenced to death and executed on 17 July 1944.[20]

False charges continued in these dangerous times. For example, Hugo Bauer had his wife go to the Gestapo on 20 May 1943. Hedwig Bauer claimed she heard radio broadcasts in foreign languages when she walked past the landlord's door. Hugo Bauer himself had a long criminal record and was about to be charged by the landlord with another offence. The Gestapo saw through the allegations, charged the Bauers with laying false charges, and sent the case to court. The police grew annoyed when Bauer was found not guilty by the courts 'because of some kind of legal deficiency'. They corrected that decision, declared him a 'parasite on the body politic', and sent him to Sachsenhausen for the duration of the war. What became of his wife is unknown.[21]

Another late war denunciation concerned a woman who informed on her brother-in-law, a pub owner in a small town. In a letter to the Kripo on 29 June 1944, she said he listened to foreign radio. In spite of a long investigation, the charge could not be substantiated, but it showed she was in the process of getting a divorce and, apparently, had long hated her brother-in-law and wanted to do him harm.[22] In another late case dealt with by the Gestapo in the same area, a woman wrote to the Ministry of Justice in Berlin in November 1944 to inform on her husband for listening to foreign radio broadcasts. She claimed to take this unusual step because (she alleged) she could not get local police to take her accusations seriously. After investigation, however, the matter was dropped. Her motives became clear and had more to do with revenge and conflict with her husband, than any faith in Nazism.[23]

The writer of an anonymous letter of 7 September 1944 to Nazi Party headquarters in Würzburg objected to the political criticisms of Andreas Bender, a 47-year-old city worker and veteran of the First World War. The writer thought Bender should be sent to the front 'as quickly as possible to shut his big mouth'. Even though the letter-writer took pains to hide her identity, police discovered it was Bender's sister-in-law Rosa Kühnreich. At his interrogation by the Gestapo on 14 December, Bender admitted he made critical remarks and listened to foreign radio which had, in words attributed to him and recorded in the protocol, 'thereby poisoned my inner opinions and point of view'. The Gestapo got Bender to admit making many other critical remarks, any one of which could easily have cost him his life. Bender's wife had her brother, Anton Heim write to the Gestapo on her husband's behalf. Heim was a soldier on leave and a Nazi Party member, and in his plea for mercy, explained the motives behind his older sister's denunciation. Heim said Rosa resented her brother-in-law, who was exempted from military service, while her own husband was missing in action. In addition, rumour had it that Bender was cheating on his wife. What became of him is not recorded in his file, but the case dragged into January 1945, when he was still in prison.[24]

The same kind of personal motives can be seen in a case about whose tragic consequences we can be more certain. The events unfolded in mid-September 1944, when a 73-year-old retired major was denounced by his son-in-law, a soldier on leave. The old man was charged with making defeatist remarks and listening to foreign radio. Stalingrad had turned him into a pessimist, and he made no secret of his feelings to his married daughter and to her husband, who lived with him. Arguments heated up when his son-in-law came home on furlough, until the young man made a report to the Kripo. They warned the accuser to reconsider as, obviously, family members were involved and these were serious charges. That advice was ignored, whereupon the accusation was forwarded to the Gestapo, who arrested the old man. During questioning, he inadvertently dragged neighbours into the mess by mentioning how they all listened to foreign radio. All these cases were sent to the Special Court in Braunschweig, which found everyone guilty and sent them to the harshest kind of prison. The retired major died there on 11 March 1945.[25]

The local offices of the Nazi Party became more involved in terroristic activities aimed at ordinary citizens, and continued to play a social role by helping to resolve personal conflicts. People could find advice and assistance at the Party's local offices, and they could also launch accusations there, as did Hilde Berthold. In October 1944 she went to the local SA leader, and then to the town's Party leader to report the potentially serious remarks made by her husband Michael, who was then at the front. These allegedly included the statement, that 'if Hitler had perished on 20 July [1944, as a result of the attempt on his life], then this pigsty would be at an end'. Party officials saw the serious-ness of the charge, so they quietly let the matter drop. At the beginning of 1945, Michael Berthold returned from the front to find another man with his wife. He grew violent and his wife soon went to the police. Michael was arrested, and his case, including the charge of making the anti-Hitler statements, was sent to the military court. Hilde Berthold was determined to testify against her husband, and initially she was persuaded by the judge of the gravity of her charges, and of her right to remain silent. However, once the court found her husband innocent for lack of evidence, she angrily arose, and shouted that she was prepared to swear under oath what she had heard. Her husband was then found guilty of 'undermining the will to win' and sentenced to death. For reasons that are impossible to determine, the verdict was never carried out. At her own post-1945 trial, she was found guilty of attempted murder and for causing his imprisonment, but that verdict was successfully appealed.[26]

Perverted conscientiousness and 'idealism' also led to denunciations. Perhaps the classic example from many such cases in the archives took place in Berlin back in 1942. Max Reiche, a worker, joined the Nazi Party in 1937, became 'block leader' immediately, and soon the 'cell leader'. In the summer of 1942, 37-year-old Reiche noticed that someone had chalked graffiti on the wall of the public toilet he used on his way home from work. The message read: 'Hitler [the] mass murderer has to be murdered to end the war.' When Reiche returned to the toilet over the months that followed, he occasionally found such graffiti again. On 28 October 1942, as he was using the facilities, he heard someone chalking on the wall, and caught Wilhelm Lehmann in the act. Lehmann was a 73-year-old pensioner and an invalid, who was tried, sentenced to death by the People's Court on 8 March 1943, and executed on 10 May. Reiche was given a reward of 100 Marks for his diligence.[27]

Local notables were not immune from denunciation if they dared say the war was lost. Georg Knar a small-town publican in Lower Franconia, informed the gendarme on his Saturday night rounds on 2 September 1944 about an event that evening in the pub. Knar alleged that Baron von Connemann, who lived in the family castle just outside town, asked a non-commissioned air force officer on leave what he thought about the war. When von Connemann got the stock response that Germany would be victorious and the war was as good as won, the Baron allegedly answered 'in a treasonous way' as follows:

The war was lost right from the beginning, it's just a shame that 20 July 1944 [the plot to kill Hitler] did not succeed, and these eight [members of the July conspiracy], who were hanged were honourable people and not criminals, who wanted to do the right thing for the German people, [but] they now had to give their lives in order to keep a few govern-ment scoundrels in their ministerial chairs.

This accusation was backed by other witnesses and led to the interrogation of the Baron on 4 September in Würzburg. Von Connemann, a 52-year-old wounded and decorated veteran of the First World War, a Protestant, and married with two children, described himself as nationalistic and right-wing. According to notes at his interrogation, he was '100 per cent in agreement' with the Führer's 'main, essential idea, the destruction of the Jews and of Communism'. He had been a Party member, but, having been a late joiner in 1937, left in 1943. He denied the accusations, and another that he was 'an England-listener', which is to say, that he tuned in to the forbidden BBC. His wife Klara and her secretary Auguste Schmudt were also questioned as were his sister Amalie and his sister-in-law Elisabeth, all titled nobles who lived at the castle in Neuhaus. The women's cases were sent to the Special Court in Würzburg, but the Baron's found its way to the People's Court in Berlin on 15 February 1945. Thanks to the chaos into which Berlin had fallen at that time, including the destruction of the court and the death of Roland Freisler, its most infamous judge, no report of what happened is contained in the Baron's file. All but one of the women were sentenced to prison terms between one and three years. The local Gestapo wanted to execute the lot. Although the files contain no firm information on what happened, Elisabeth's dossier ends with a communication (23 February 1945) from the Gestapo in Würzburg to head-quarters in Nuremberg, which struck an ominous note. Gestapo official Herbst stated, that 'As matters stand, I consider that the preconditions are met for carrying out the special handling [i.e. execution] of Baron Joachim von Connemann and the rest of the accused and, therefore, request the relevant decision.'[28]

Drum-Head Justice

New drum-head courts were created on Hitler's orders on 15 February 1945. They were tribunals with a judge, a Nazi Party functionary, and an officer from either the Wehrmacht, Waffen-SS or the police, and could try anyone thought to endanger Germany's ability or determination to fight on.[29] The military had been given similar courts on 20 January 1943, and by 1945 all these new courts were operating behind the lines inside Germany.[30] The mentality of judges and other perpetrators became infused with emotions towards the end of the war, including revenge-seeking, bitterness, disappointment, and fear. Even local leaders who dared issue calls to the troops or to the population for a village, town, or city to surrender were not immune, as happened in a small town on the western side of the Rhine near Mainz. Hermann Berndes wanted to spare the town. He was the town's battle-leader and head of its 'Volkssturm', the latter a rag-tag army that Hitler ordered created across Germany on 25 September 1944, following Martin Bormann's suggestions. Over the next months, in four levies, millions of old men and young boys between the ages of 16 and 60 were drafted or volunteered to serve.[31] Herman Berndes, as local Battle Commander and leader of the Volkssturm in Ingelheim, however, wanted to surrender. He was quickly overcome, and then, on orders of the regional Party boss, hanged (without even a semblance of a trial) in the town square on 17 March. Earlier that day he issued orders to stop the shooting to spare the town. His last words were: 'I die, because I love my home.' Nazi diehards saw things differently, and the chief of staff of the district Nazi Party sent to carry out the execution, draped around the victim's neck an ignominious sign that read: 'So die all who betray their Fatherland.'[32]

The same state of mind was summed up in the September 1944 orders from the Higher SS- and Police Leader West, Karl Gutenberger to the head of the Gestapo in Aachen. This was the area in western Germany first evacuated on the approach of the Allies. Gutenberger wanted the Gestapo, uniformed police, and other organizations under his command to keep 'law and order' in the nearly deserted cities of the area. On 20 September 1944, the head of the Aachen Gestapo met with him, and recalled being given the following order: 'Tell your people, that from now on the approach to plunderers, deserters, and assorted riffraff, will be with a gun in the hand.' Such a shoot-to-kill order towards German civilians was unprecedented, so much so that the head of the Aachen Gestapo was reluctant to pass it to his subordinates. Gutenberger insisted: 'From now on, order will rule. Also among our own police officials. Lead the offenders into the forest, if they disobey. Of course you know how that's done.' The Gestapo officials, perhaps sensing they might soon be called to account by the Allies, asked for these orders in writing. Gutenberger would not hear of it: 'Nothing will be written down', he said, adding the delusional phrase as justification, 'We can do that. We are the victors.' Many executions followed even though Allied victory was at hand.[33]

The scope of defeat on the western front at the beginning of 1945 was such, that alone in the month from the end of February to the end of March, the Allies took 300,000 prisoners.[34] On 23–4 March the Allies crossed the Rhine in strength and, as the Germans by that time already had expended most of what resources they had to defend the country, thereafter the effort to hold the line was spotty, strenuous in some places, but hardly worthy of note elsewhere.[35] The Rhine-Ruhr region was encircled by 1 April in a pincer movement that trapped 21 divisions, or 320,000 German troops, which was a greater loss than the Russians inflicted at Stalingrad. Attempts to break out of the 'Ruhr pocket' were fruitless.[36] In cities inside the southern part of this 'pocket' like Düsseldorf and Solingen, as well as in the northern part of it, in Essen, Bochum, Dortmund, Duisburg, and Oberhausen, the German-on-German terror was particularly vicious.

The western section of Düsseldorf on the left-bank of the Rhine was occupied already on 2 March 1945, but, because the bridge over the river was knocked out and because of determined German resistance, the city held on until 17 April. In the last days of the war, the Gestapo in the area dropped most of what remained of their bureaucratic routine and at times executed their victims on the spot as they saw fit. On 17 January 1945 in Cologne, the only record of the 30 executions carried out that day alone was a cryptic note about the delivery of bodies to the cemetery.[37]

Social life in bombed-out cities ended, as did regular supplies of water, gas, and electricity. The stragglers in the rubble lived a hand-to-mouth existence.[38] Yet even there, the terror did not relent. In one of the last editions of the Düsseldorf newspaper, a front-page story on 24 March carried news of two death penalties handed down by a drum-head court and already carried out.[39]

Although on 15 April Field Marshal Walter Model ceased trying to defend Düsseldorf, Nazi Party Gauleiter Karl Florian wanted to carry on to the last bullet. In response, a small group of concerned citizens approached Franz Jürgens, Commander of the uniformed police, but known to be less enthusiastic about continuing. They met with him on 15 April and next day at 1:00 p.m. gathered at police headquarters, from where one group went to make contact with the Americans, while Jürgens led the other to arrest Police President August Korreng. Police still true to the Nazi cause, however, soon put an end to the revolt, and Jürgens, along with four civilians were tried by a drum-head court, and executed late on 16 April or early in the morning of 17 April. Americans took the city only hours later.[40]

Although the decree establishing drum-head courts mentioned that they could reach two verdicts, guilty (with an automatic death penalty), innocent, or decide to send a case to some regular court, in their post-war testimony, those who served on these courts claimed they had to choose between guilty (and death) or innocence. The full scope of these courts needs to be investigated, but we get a glimpse of what happened by looking at Lower Franconia. Würzburg itself suffered a massive bombing on 16 March during which the entire city went up in flames and as many as 5,000 people were killed.[41] Numerous other cities in the area also were bombed, such as Aschaffenburg, which experienced a major bombing on 21 March.

Hard-core Nazis clung to the promise of a 'miracle weapon' that would reverse the tide. Albert Speer, Hitler's Minister of Armaments, who happened to be in Würzburg on 28 March, was asked in all seriousness by the local Party leader Otto Hellmuth: Just when was Hitler going to use the magical weapon? Speer had to tell Hellmuth, as he had so often told others, that there was no such thing.[42] What makes the story of interest is that it indicates the underlying mentality of German-on-German terror at war's end. They tied their fate to a miracle, and grew more ruthless.

A kind of punitive will also developed on the ground, as we can see from the example of the military drum-head court in Aschaffenburg. The court was set up on Palm Sunday (25 March) in the middle of chaos, with only two members, a Major Robert Jung and Lieutenant Wolfgang Bonfils. On 28 March 1945 they tried and convicted 26-year-old Lieutenant Friedel Heymann on the charge of 'desertion and cowardice in the face of the enemy'. He was executed almost immediately, less than a week before the Americans liberated the city on 3 April. The court could easily have found a way to spare the man's life. The verdict itself was at best dubious, in that Heymann had not deserted, but was recovering from wounds in hospital and, in the confusion had lost his papers.[43]

Major Erwin Helm headed another drum-head court in the Aschaffenburg-Würzburg area during the last days of the war. Helm's activities and his 'flying court' against German soldiers and civilians, began to the north in Hessen, stretched to the south across Lower Franconia, and extended into the present-day Czech Republic to the south-east. The bloody deeds of this court were partly reconstructed during post-war trials, at which Helm freely admitted to being involved in between 20 and 30 death sentences. In fact, the (19-year-old) corporal who had served as Helm's executioner testified that there were 56 executions, and that he was paid 50 Marks in money or kind for each.[44]

One case handled by Helm began in the church square of Zellingen, a village not far from Karlstadt, on Palm Sunday. When Helm showed up in Karlstadt on 28 March, he was briefed by the Volkssturm's commander (and physician) Dr Kühner, about what had happened when he addressed his men three days earlier in Zellingen. Kühner had told them that because the war was getting closer, regulations would get stiffer, and anyone who did not obey would be shot. Such threats caused anger among the rag-tag 'army' of men and boys, and several shouted the derisive remark, 'Oho!' The shout was taken by commander Kühner as criticism, but he did nothing. Two days later, when the bridge over the river Main was blown up to halt the American advance, it damaged Karl Weiglein's home. He was a 60-year-old farmer who made the 'Oho!' remark, and who also yelled at two Volkssturm leaders in the street (including the local commander) that 'those who blew up the bridge should be hanged'. Next day (28 March) when Helm arrived in the evening, he heard about Weiglein, exclaimed that the man had undermined the will to win, and sent someone to find a rope. By the next day, Helm and his 'flying court' had tried Weiglein. Helm would stop at nothing short of immediate execution, and for special effect, decided to hang Weiglein in front of his own home. As per routine, his body was left hanging for three days under guard. As Helm drove off, the bitterness of the townsfolk was such that shots rang out after him, but, unfazed he moved on to his next victims down the road.[45] His was not the only drum-head court in the area by any means, or the only one to use the death penalty to punish Germans who dared show their doubts. A local medical doctor in Lohr was executed even as the position was under fire by American troops.[46]

Hints of Resistance

The women who demonstrated in a village near Würzburg on 1 April apparently got away with shouting in front of the headquarters of the Wehrmacht, that the officers should 'take off, or we'll burn the house over your heads'.[47] Only days later, in another village not far away, villagers grew restless as the army prepared defences. A delegation of women implored the commander to move on. One of the better-off women was to speak in the evening to a large group in the town hall, but the commander managed to diffuse what he derisively called a 'storm of women', by pretending that an air raid was imminent. The Gestapo in Nuremberg were informed and sent officer Karl Schmid to investigate. He found and shot the main 'offender' at the front door of her home, arrested others, and put an end to the 'revolt'.[48]

According to orders issued from Berlin, military leaders were to execute anyone who showed the white flag, and burn their home to the ground. One 55-year-old miller (married with three children), living south-east of Würzburg, was searched by American troops on 11 April. They spared his house because he showed a white cloth. Unfortunately, when two Wehrmacht officers drove up next day, this sign of surrender was still there. Major Erich Stentzel would hear no excuses, shot the miller on the spot, and torched the house. We only know of this event because Stentzel was captured by the Americans who returned when they saw smoke, and had him arrested and tried. We can only speculate how often such events played out elsewhere.[49]

When the Americans took Ansbach itself shortly afterwards, they found the body of 20-year-old Robert Limpert still hanging from a tree near the town hall. In his youth Limpert had been ill-disposed towards Nazism, and not allowed to finish school in town. A heart condition put military service out of the question and in the winter of 1944–5 he attended courses at the university in Würzburg, until in March it was destroyed in a massive bombing raid, and Limpert returned to Ansbach. He then joined others to produce leaflets to encourage citizens to stand up against 'Nazi executioners', and to raise the white flag. He approached the mayor on 18 April and convinced him to give over the city. The battle commander wanted to fight to the finish, however, so Limpert decided that next day (19 April) he would cut the radio cable linking army headquarters in town to the troops. Two members of the Hitler Youth witnessed what he did, and denounced him to the police, who found and arrested him. By 1:00 p.m. that day the battle commander, a learned doctor from Freiburg and formerly an assistant for physics at Leipzig University, went to the town hall to see the prisoner. A drum-head court was convened and a speedily carried out trial found Limpert guilty. He was hanged within no more than 15 minutes from the time the 'trial' began, and a little more than two hours after his 'crime'. Orders were to let the body hang from a tree for at least three days or until it began 'to stink'. Americans found it when they took the town only hours later.[50]

Although we do not know how many such executions took place, there is some testimony from Victor Klemperer. He and his wife survived and fled Dresden after the massive bombing raid there on 13 February 1945, which killed an estimated 50,000 people. They went west to avoid the Russians and south in hopes of being able to fade into the countryside of southern Bavaria. At the end of April they found shelter in a tiny village between Regensburg and Landshut, just north of Munich. Klemperer reports several women saying at the time: 'Now we fear *only* the *German* soldiers.' He noted also the sense in which other refugees and those around him began to distance themselves from the worst excesses of the regime, including what happened to the Jews. Even so, Hitler continued to speak of the approaching Soviet army as 'the Jewish-Bolshevik deadly enemy'.[51]

Close to where the Klemperers found refuge, they heard on 29 April how a farmer was hanged by the SS for daring to throw an anti-tank weapon into the Danube. When two local notables, the mayor and local farmers' leader, objected, the SS hanged them. That same day, Klemperer recorded rumours that Bavaria's Nazi Party boss, Franz Ritter von Epp, either was deposed or ordered fighting to halt.[52] These were false rumours spread from a radio station in Munich early on the morning of 28 April by a group calling itself the 'Bavarian Liberation Action' (or FAB). As word from FAB reached some villages, local leaders like teachers or priests wrongly concluded that the war must be over and, like village priest Josef Grimm, they lowered the Nazi flag and raised Bavaria's colours. Unfortunately, the attempted revolt by FAB failed within hours, and Grimm, who was caught by the SS, was executed at the side of the road after a perfunctory hearing.[53]

There were positive responses to the call from FAB elsewhere. In Landshut, the uniformed police even joined the call to resist; they barred entry to the town hall and arrested some Gestapo officials who worked there. That was soon halted by the Gestapo and Kripo who came from Regensburg and saw to it that the local notable who raised the Bavarian flag was executed, also without trial.[54] In another village in the region, local magistrate Dr Kehrer played a role in the attempted revolt and, among other things, ordered the arrest of several key officials, including the mayor, who promptly shot himself. It soon became obvious also there, however, that the announcement from Munich was premature, and Kehrer either committed suicide or was shot in his office. Immediately, a list of 10 or so others in Landshut who were thought to have collaborated with

Kehrer was drawn up and local Nazi Party boss Schwägerl ordered the executions of all who could be found.[55] The FAB, whose radio announcement had inspired these attempts at resistance, was led by Captain Rupprecht Gerngroß, Major Alois Braun, and Lieutenant Ottoheinz Leiling, officers of the Wehrmacht stationed in and around Munich. Among other things they called for the civil population to carry out a 'pheasant hunt' for Nazis, that is, to get rid of their Nazi leaders and raise white flags. The FAB's ten-point proclamation included long-cherished demands for peace and the end of militarism. The radio announcement falsely claimed that Ritter von Epp had joined them and was already negotiating an armistice with the Allies, but in fact the FAB revolt did not get off the ground.[56]

Apart from the individuals already mentioned, the main group to suffer the consequences were those who once had sympathies for the working-class movement in towns like Burghausen and Penzberg located in the vicinity of Munich. A sympathy strike for FAB broke out at a factory in Burghausen, and Nazi Party boss Schwägerl ordered members of the SS to travel there to shoot the three ring-leaders.[57] The revolt in Penzberg, a mining town known for its working-class movement and hostility to Nazism prior to 1933, cost the lives of 16 men and women on 28 April. Socialists and Communists joined together to try to save the mines from the rumoured demolition that was planned as part of the scorched-earth policy. The hope of the resisters was at least to safeguard miners underground and to stop further killing. The Penzberg revolt, however, was quickly put down by the army. On the orders of Nazi Party Gauleiter Paul Gießler, those involved were executed, at least three of them in Munich by members of the Volkssturm.[58] Gießler also sent a unit of 'Werwolves' under Hans Zöberlein, a well-known Nazi fanatic, to Penzberg to put things 'in order'. The Werwolves were Nazis determined to carry on, if necessary behind the lines after the war was over. Besides the men shot by the Wehrmacht, eight more people (two of them women) were hanged by the Werwolves. As so often, the senselessness of the murders was underlined when the Americans found the bodies next day and took the town without a struggle.[59]

The Final Effort to Deal with Nazism's 'Enemies'

We have only hints, and few reliable documents on Nazi policies for dealing with inmates in Germany's prisons and concentration camps as the Allies approached. On the one hand, the regime wanted to retain the only major pools of labour that were left, and on the other hand, they did not want their worst 'enemies' to run free behind the lines, or to fall into the hands of the Allies. The determination to keep prisoners under control can be seen in a document from 16 March 1945, when the head of a prison near Bristly reported to the regional

Attorney General that 574 prisoners were moved from Görlitz to Zeitz, a fairly short train journey that still took 13 days. We have no idea how many died during this evacuation, but the object of the exercise was not to murder, but to utilize these prisoners in cleaning up war debris.[60] Similar orders were issued to other prisons, like one in Bochum on 29 March 1945 to move all prisoners. They were in such bad shape already that 560 marched out in the direction of Celle, but almost as many were left behind because they were too weak to move. It is not known how many died over the next few days, but we know about the evacuation because one man survived who was shot and left for dead.[61]

Apparently, the other side of the coin, was that 'dangerous' prison inmates who could not be moved were to be killed. When the town of Bensheim (just to the north-east of Mannheim, across the Rhine) was on the verge of being overrun by American troops in mid-March 1945, the Gestapo herded together about 200 inmates of a 'police prisoner camp' and others in preparation for their evacuation further east. Most were foreign workers, but perhaps one-quarter were German. The Gestapo evacuated all prisoners fit to march, and executed 14 of 25 prisoners too weak to travel, presumably because they were considered potentially dangerous and/or for political reasons.[62] Between 26 and 30 March, the Gestapo in Frankfurt murdered 87 prisoners, including Germans and foreigners from various camps, among them at least 44 women.[63]

The Gestapo in Hanover decided to move the prisoners (mostly foreign workers) in the AEL at Lahde-Weser (near Hanover), but before the evacuation began the SS hanged or shot those too weak to move. The remaining 800 or so marched in the direction of Hanover, but apparently before they even arrived, head of the Gestapo Johannes Rentsch ordered that 200 of them were to be shot 'in the interests of the civilian population'. The plan could not be carried out because the Americans drew near, however, on 5 April, 154 prisoners were systematically shot. The post-war investigation found it difficult to ascertain the nationalities and identities of the victims, and for a long time the view was that they were all Soviet prisoners of war, when in fact between 20 and 30 were Italians, and others may have been prisoners from the Ahlem jail.[64] Many such events happened all over Germany, like the 71 executions of inmates held near Düsseldorf in the prison at Lüttringhausen on 13 April 1945.[65] In Leipzig, the head of the Gestapo ordered a list of the 'dangerous' political prisoners in the police prison and some nearby camps. Eventually 53 prisoners (including Germans, Czechs, Russians, Poles, and French) were shot on 12 April and thrown into a mass grave. The next day, another 32 people, sentenced by the 'People's Court', and later brought to Leipzig from Dresden, were executed on orders from the RSHA by a squad made up of soldiers. The notion of what constituted a 'dangerous criminal' was arbitrary, as the most common crime committed by these people seems to have been listening to foreign radio.

Hans-Dieter Schmid has studied the background of these murders, including a massacre committed at Abtnaundorf, one of Buchenwald's subcamps northeast of Leipzig. On 17 April orders were issued (exact source unknown) to the Gestapo to shoot 100 or so sick prisoners who had been left behind after the camp was evacuated. Orders to kill were carried out by seven SS guards and some 17 members of the (elderly) Volkssturm who forced the prisoners into one of the barracks and then set it on fire. A minimum of 100 prisoners died in the conflagration that followed.[66]

We have very few details about the mass murders that took place in and near Dresden at the end of 1944 and beginning of 1945, but there are reports that 422 people were shot by the Gestapo.[67] There is also evidence of centrally directed orders to kill specific individuals and certain groups. In mid-April 1945 the RSHA ordered the Gestapo in Württemberg to execute three men guilty of aiding the enemy. The executions were carried out two days before the Allies arrived.[68] Similar orders were most likely sent to the Gestapo in Giessen, who shot at least three people at the end of March 1945. We only know of the latter case because one person managed to escape.[69] In Deggendorf, near Munich, orders were received on 26 April 1945, exact source unknown, but quite probably from the RSHA in Berlin, to execute all political prisoners who had been sentenced to death. Apart from one elderly woman, a teacher, who was killed, it remains uncertain how many others died. The People's Court had sentenced her to death for listening to foreign radio in November 1944. The verdict was carried out at the insistence of a local Nazi Party boss. She was shot by a member of the SS and her body was dumped into the Danube.[70]

During the last days of the war, execution orders were sent either from the RSHA to newly created (local) 'Commanders of the Security Police', or KdS, who were frequently regional heads of the Gestapo, as happened in Kassel in early 1945. The RSHA apparently ordered the liquidation of 28 Gestapo prisoners from France, the Netherlands, and the Soviet Union, and on Good Friday (30 March) the same Gestapo and Kripo officials shot 12 inmates from the prison at Wehlheiden near Kassel. Along with foreigners, they executed Germans with lengthy prison records. A sense of how the killing escalated can be seen in what the same officials did on Easter Saturday (31 March) at Wilhelmshöhe, another small town near Kassel. When word reached the KdS in Duisburg about a crime in progress at a nearby railway station, a Gestapo commando was sent with orders to kill. By the time they arrived, the regular police had the situation in hand. A supply train sitting in the station had been pillaged by hungry German and Italian construction workers. The Gestapo searched all the Italians, found what were considered stolen goods on 78 of them, and marched them in groups to the edge of a bomb-crater, where all were summarily executed. The other Italians had to fill in the bomb-craters used as makeshift graves. It is not clear from the post-war trial what happened to the German 'plunderers'.[71]

Italian workers fell victims to the late-war bloodbath more often than is commonly known. When Italy left the war in the summer of 1943, Hitler and Himmler decided to mobilize for work all those Italian soldiers who did not opt to continue the war on Germany's side, and that turned out to be the vast majority.[72] By the end of September, Italian 'prisoners of war' were given the dubious status of 'military internees', and by April 1944, 515,478 were forced to work inside the Reich.[73] Italian and German historians have estimated that around 45,000 Italian workers died from a variety of causes, including hunger and cold, and the almost complete absence of proper medical care. However, as Gerhard Schreiber has shown, an untold number were murdered in the last months of the war. It seems that the Gestapo, SS, German military, or even the Volkssturm, were perfectly capable of shooting whole groups of Italians on the evacuations. In early April 1945 they shot an estimated 100 or so from the 'punishment camp at Pothoff'.[74] Only a handful of people survived to tell that tale, and Italians were struck down elsewhere, when in separate incidents, hundreds more, along with other foreign workers were murdered.[75]

Italians were executed in Hildesheim at the end of March by the Gestapo and SS in what must rank as one of the most heartless and horrifying massacres in the bloody history of the Third Reich. Hildesheim suffered a series of disastrous bombing attacks culminating on 22 March that left the city in ruins and caused nearly 1,000 deaths. Several days later, Italian and German workers who were trying to clean up the mess came upon a bombed-out food depot and were encouraged by the German guard to help themselves to the largely spoiled food in the ruins. Some of this 'plundered' food was then discovered by police on several hundred of the 500 or so Italian prisoners. The post-war investigation pieced together what happened. It found a mass grave with 208 bodies (17 of them women), of whom an estimated 130 were Italians. In this event, execution was by hanging, and was carried out on an improvised gallows with five nooses. Each victim was forced to stand on a table, had one of the nooses placed around his or her neck, and, when the table was kicked away, each slowly strangled to death. Even as the first person struggled in their death throes, the next victim was led to the table and the noose, and the procedure continued until all five nooses were full. The others awaiting death nearby under SS guard, could see what was in store for them, and after 20 minutes, when the five dead bodies were removed, the first of the next five Italians was led to the gallows. German bystanders, mostly women, apparently watched the executions 'fairly impassively'.[76] In a related, but separate incident, at least one Jewish concentration camp prisoner who had recently arrived in the area was executed by a member of the Volkssturm.[77] The Gestapo also shot three eastern workers, and at least one German for plundering in Hildesheim.[78]

In Dortmund the Gestapo murdered most of the prisoners in their custody, regardless of whether they were Germans or foreigners during Easter week 1945. As contact with the RSHA in Berlin was almost certainly broken by then, it was likely that the KdS in Dortmund made the decision. The post-war trial estimated that between 230 and 240 men and women were shot, but these figures are the bare minimum. The victims included Germans identified with resistance activities, but most were foreign workers.[79]

In mid-March there was a meeting in Dortmund of Gestapo officials, including those from outlying cities under the authority of Dortmund headquarters, to discuss how to deal with serious cases as contact with Berlin was becoming problematical. The head of the Gestapo in Dortmund made it clear that henceforth he would decide on 'special handling' cases, which is to say, he would authorize the executions himself. The Gestapo posts under Dortmund, like the one in Bochum, then drew up lists of candidates for execution and made their recommendations. Between 26 March and 8 April, the Bochum Gestapo liquidated at least 20 Eastern workers and three Germans.[80]

Similar events took place all over the Rhine-Ruhr. The RSHA also authorized the Gestapo in Duisburg to execute 24 members of a 'band' of foreign workers led by the Ukrainian Kovalenko on 7 and 10 February 1945. By March, Duisburg's prison was filled to overflowing with foreign workers and Germans. Instead of running for it, the Gestapo decided to execute those charged with 'serious' offences. On 21 March, between 27 and 29 of them were shot, and later on 8 April, between 6 and 9 additional executions took place, the latter including several women and Germans.[81]

Sometimes local Gestapo officials took the initiative, as when the heads of the Gestapo in Düsseldorf and Essen constituted themselves as a drum-head police court on 11 March and 'sentenced' to death 35 eastern workers who were imprisoned in Essen. Ulrich Herbert points out that the Gestapo and Kripo gave the task of carrying out some of these executions to those of their members who had not been involved in such activities before, to compromise them and assure their later silence. He suggests that in the last weeks of the war in the Rhine-Ruhr area alone, thousands of foreign workers fell victim to the death squads of the Gestapo and we cannot even guess at the figures for Germany as a whole.[82]

There had been worry from at least the autumn of 1944 about how the millions of foreigners would react as order collapsed, and we have evidence of mass executions of some right in the factory grounds.[83] The anxieties deepened into 1945 as we can see from the behaviour of Hans Kammler, a high-ranking member of the SS, a true believer, and a man who had Hitler's confidence.[84] By chance we have evidence of the policy he recommended to keep the foreign workers in line at the end of the war. In concluding a meeting in Langenbachtal (near Warstein, a town in the forests of the Sauerland) in March 1945, Kammler proposed a simple method to the military to deal with foreign workers. He said it was necessary 'substantially to decimate' them, that is, to shoot a significant number out of hand. He was especially concerned about those from the Soviet Union who were thought to be under the influence of Bolshevik propaganda and who, when he arrived in Langenbachtal, had milled around his car and seemed threatening. Kammler considered that such foreigners posed a danger to 'general security and good order'. Officers in charge devised a trick to discover which of these workers were still energetic, and thus likely to be troublemakers, and asked them who would like to be transferred to another camp, to which 14 men and 56 women from Russia and Poland responded positively. On 20 March all were trucked out at night and summarily shot by a squad of soldiers. The next day, in a similar process in nearby Eversberg, 80 more foreign workers were executed by soldiers. From the evidence it would seem the killing continued afterwards.[85]

Hitler as Nero

Hitler often stated, as Albert Speer recalled, that German soldiers would have nothing to fear about the home front breaking down behind the lines, because no mercy would be shown to potential 'back-stabbers'. During the last months Hitler kept emphasizing, as he had for years, that the concentration camps and all their prisoners should be blown up.[86] However, in 1945 Hitler's wishes were not immediately translated into reality by those around him, as they once would have been. The 'moderate' Albert Speer, the Minister of Armaments, remembered an exchange he had with Hitler in mid-March 1945. Speer stated in a note to Hitler for discussion at a meeting on 18 March, that 'it cannot possibly be the purpose of warfare at home to destroy so many bridges that, given the straitened means of the postwar period, it will take years to rebuild this transportation network. . . . Their destruction means eliminating all further possibility for the German people to survive.'[87] After the meeting broke up early in the morning of 19 March, Hitler met privately with Speer. Hitler stated flatly, that 'if the war is lost, the people will be lost also. It is not necessary to worry about what the German people will need for elemental survival. On the contrary, it is best for us to destroy even these things. For the nation has proved to be the weaker, and the future belongs solely to the stronger eastern nation. In any case only those who are inferior will remain after this struggle, for the good have already been killed.'[88]

Hitler immediately issued what historians have dubbed the Nero order. The order, which was resisted by his once faithful paladins, called for the laying to waste of Germany, including 'all military, transport, communication, industrial, and supply installations, as well as anything else of value inside the Reich area'.[89] Hitler wanted a scorched-earth policy to hinder the advance of the Allies and to destroy anyone considered an 'enemy' behind the lines. Hitler's will to destruction, at least if the post-war testimony of Hermann Göring is to be believed, went so far as to consider the extermination of all Allied prisoners of war, including more than 200,000 from the West (American, British, Canadians, and others), as well as some one million Soviet prisoners. At least that particular Hitler wish was subverted by subordinates.[90]

Hitler's will to destruction was in evidence in the forced retreat of the military from the Soviet Union, as well as from France. He had earlier concluded that, before leaving France, all industries should be levelled, but that was another wish not implemented by those in charge. He was furious to learn that by January 1945, after the Germans left, French production was restored, and approached its pre-war levels. When asked about the press report, Speer put Hitler off by saying that such accounts were nothing but enemy propaganda.[91]

There were other Hitler wishes or direct orders for total destruction that were ignored or not implemented fully, as when he made it clear to Arthur Seyss-Inquart, Nazi Commissioner General for Holland, and to others, that he wanted to flood Holland by destroying the dykes. By mid-March 1945 Seyss-Inquart decided not to issue such an order and Himmler reached the same conclusion.[92] In spite of Hitler's growing infirmity, he was still capable of wreaking revenge on sworn enemies who were within reach. Pastor Dietrich Bonhoeffer, one of the conspirators against him, was evacuated from Buchenwald on 3 April, almost certainly on instructions from Berlin. A decision to execute Bonhoeffer and others who had been part of the plot seems to have been taken only on 5 April, during midday discussions with Hitler. There is no way of knowing if Hitler himself gave the final order, as seems likely, given the prominence and political importance of those who had been involved in the conspiracy. At any rate, the revenge against those who had tried to topple Hitler was carried out, first in Sachsenhausen on 6 April, and three days later in Flossenbürg, where after a summary trial before a drum-head court Bonhoeffer, Admiral Canaris, General Oster, and others were hanged. Other prominent political prisoners were assembled in Dachau, and marched off towards the South Tyrol, where they were liberated by American troops.[93]

Back in Berlin on the night of 22–3 April a Gestapo execution detachment picked up 16 people associated with the resistance, of whom one managed to escape. The rest were shot, and the murders continued into 24 April. An unknown number of other prisoners held at what was left of Gestapo headquarters at Prinz Albrecht Strasse were also killed at that time.[94]

Death Marches

As the war drew to a close, one of the most pressing issues for Himmler and those involved was what to do with the hundreds of thousands of prisoners still in Germany's vast camp and prison empire. The story is yet to be written, and considerable mystery is likely to remain because so few documents have survived. Somewhere along the line the Nazis decided not to leave the prisoners behind, but to evacuate them. We have few details of the decision-making behind the evacuations, and in addition, the events on the ground locally became overwhelmed in chaos and confusion, so that apart from orders 'from above', what took place needs to be studied on a camp-by-camp basis.

Several factors help explain in general why the Nazis evacuated the camps, and certainly one initial consideration was a desire to cover up the crimes. In March 1943 Himmler ordered a systematic cover-up operation to destroy the Operation Reinhard death camps. Not only was every trace of the buildings removed, but all the bodies were exhumed and cremated.[95] However, more was involved when it came to all the other camps and the prisoners still in them. Documents from mid-summer 1944 show that Himmler gave orders for 'Case A'—the 'A' standing for 'alarm'—to regional Higher SS and Police Leaders (HSSPF). They were to take control of the camps and, with the approach of the enemy, to evacuate prisoners to the next available camp.[96] These orders applied not only to Jews, but to all inmates in all concentration camps and also to prison inmates.

Some evidence of the thinking behind the evacuations is contained in the 20–1 July 1944 orders from the Commander of the Security Police (KdS) to local authorities for Cracow and Radom. The topic was 'clearing the prisons', and instructions were that if enemy forces drew near, a 'complete evacuation' was to follow. In case of surprise attack, when evacuation was impossible, all prisoners were to be liquidated, and their bodies burnt. These measures were against Jews and non-Jews, and end with the chilling phrase, variations of which soon became all too common: 'Under all circumstances it must be avoided, that prison inmates or Jews be liberated by the enemy, . . . which is to say, should fall into their hands alive.'[97] Similar orders appear to have been communicated to the concentration camps, to the Gestapo across Germany, and other authorities over the next months stretching into the new year. On 25 November 1944, Himmler ordered the dismantling of the last major killing installation at Auschwitz-Birkenau.

According to a document of 15 January 1945, there were 511,537 male and 202,674 female prisoners in all the concentration camps that remained.[98] Plans were to evacuate all inmates who could travel, but these 'evacuations' almost immediately became in fact the 'death marches' they were named by survivors. The strongest prisoners were already weak before the marches began; there was little food, poor clothing, and no shelter. To make matters worse, the marches took place during the depths of the winter of 1944–5, and the guards proved utterly merciless, shooting anyone who could not keep up. Historians need to devote more attention to the story of these death marches. We know that at least some written orders for the evacuations were given by Himmler, and he gave others by telephone or by radio. We can deduce that centrally directed orders were issued, because virtually all the main concentration camps, most of their subcamps, and even many prisons were evacuated at about the same time. According to the post-war testimony of Rudolf Höss, former Commandant of the camp, and since late November 1943 one of the heads of the concentration camp system under Oswald Pohl, Himmler ordered the final evacuation of Auschwitz in mid-January 1945. However, Pohl himself said he saw plans to clear Auschwitz in the autumn of 1944 when he visited there as Chief of the SS Economic and Administrative Branch (WVHA).[99] When the advancing Red Army began to find traces of the crimes in mid-1944 as it entered the territory of the Third Reich, and published stories in the press, Nazis grew alarmed that they would soon have to answer for their crimes in court, and so were interested in destroying as much evidence as possible.[100] The liberation of Majdanek at the end of July 1944, and the stories told of what had occurred there, fuelled the cover-up efforts elsewhere and also played a role in the decision to evacuate the remaining camps and to destroy as much evidence as possible. At the massive Auschwitz-Birkenau complex, from August 1944 until it was almost fully evacuated in January 1945, the Nazis took measures to deal with the fact that the camp would soon be overrun by the Soviets. First of all, far from dismantling the industrialized killing process, they accelerated it until November 1944, when a stop was put to the mass killing. The prisoners who last serviced the gas chambers and crematoria were murdered. The evacuations to the west began already in August 1944 and, until mid-January 1945, the Nazis moved out approximately 65,000 people, about 15,000 of whom included nearly all the remaining Poles, Russians, and Czechs.

On 21 December 1944, Fritz Bracht, the Gauleiter and Commissar for Defence of the Reich in Upper Silesia gave orders for the evacuation of the camp complex at Auschwitz. He wanted all civilians, especially the 'working population', moved to the west in five 'treks'. Each trek was given a secret codename for specific groups: the non-working civilian population; all workers who could possibly be spared; police prisoners (including the Auschwitz camp) and those in jails; prisoners of war; and foreign workers. The Bracht order is one of the few that survives and suggests that the object of the exercise was not to kill all the prisoners, but somehow to preserve them, and keep them within the German sphere of influence.[101]

We can trace the travels of one (non-Jewish) man who was moved from Auschwitz just before the main evacuation. Wieslaw Kielar, a Polish inmate in Auschwitz for years, having been taken from there in early October 1944, worked at one place or another until mid-April 1945. His stopovers included Berlin, then he was sent north to Sachsenhausen, west by train to Minden and to a camp called Porta Westfalica, involved in aircraft production. When Kielar arrived, this camp was already hopelessly overcrowded, and he was soon sent on foot to a work camp at Schandelach, near Braunschweig. On 10 April 1945 he and others were entrained to Magdeburg, but found themselves stranded on a siding alongside many other trains full of prisoners from other camps. After a five days' journey he ended up at a labour camp not far from Wittenberg, where he was found by the Americans. He makes no mention in his memoir of any kindnesses shown to him anywhere he went in Germany, but we can gather from what he says that ordinary citizens reflected the negative attitudes about camp prisoners to be found in Nazi propaganda.[102]

The last roll-call held at Auschwitz (including Birkenau and the subcamps) was on 17 January 1945, and over the next several days 58,000 men and women were evacuated on foot or by train. Much of the killing machinery at what remained of Auschwitz-Birkenau was demolished by the SS before they left, and the last crematorium was blown up on 26 January, the day before the camp was liberated.[103] The roadways and train lines from Auschwitz were soon covered with thousands of bodies, men and women who were shot when they would not or could not continue, or died of exhaustion. Others travelled by trains north-west to Bergen-Belsen, and still more went south to Mauthausen. Many tramped through snow-covered roads in below-freezing temperatures, and the standard operating procedure was to kill anyone who could not keep up. It has been estimated that between 9,000 and 15,000 of the Auschwitz prisoners perished during the evacuations.[104]

The marches were so chaotic and confused that Polish civilians who witnessed them said later that groups of prisoners went first in one direction, and hours later retraced their steps. The surest signs that the marchers had been there were the dead bodies left in their wake. Witnesses also reported that bystanders occasionally offered help in spite of the threats of the guards.[105] The testimonies of survivors at post-war trials strongly suggest that conditions on these marches, in terms of suffering and death, were if anything worse than they had been in the camps.[106]

The evacuation of Auschwitz-Monowitz began on 18 January with an estimated 9,000 to 10,000 prisoners, but was reduced by around 3,000 people when the march reached Gleiwitz only two days later. The prisoners were then jammed into freight cars for the trip to Mauthausen, but as it was impossible to get through, the train had to retrace its course. After 12 days around 2,000 reached the final destination at Oranienburg.[107] Martin Gilbert shows some, but by no means all of these marches in his *Atlas of the Holocaust*. One of the marches from Auschwitz-Birkenau lasted six weeks, and of the 3,000 prisoners who set out in mid-January, only 280 arrived at Geppersdorf, just west of Breslau.[108]

The general pattern was that guards stayed until the last minute and, in the days or even hours before the Soviet armies arrived, they forced the evacuation of all prisoners fit to travel. The treatment of the Jews invariably remained terrible to the end, but clearly all of them were not shot out of hand. At

Auschwitz, many Jews and other prisoners who were too ill and unable to travel were left behind, and contrary to their own expectations, were not killed.[109]

We have already seen isolated examples where all or nearly all non-Jewish camp evacuees in a given march were murdered, but some of the worst cases happened during the evacuation of Mittelbau-Dora. According to Joachim Neander, the camp and its subcamp system contained roughly 40,500 prisoners on the eve of the evacuation in April, of whom a minimum of 11,000 died or were murdered during the 'death marches' to the north in the direction of Bergen-Belsen, to the south towards various camps, and to the north-east, towards Sachsenhausen and Ravensbrück.[110] Some of these latter columns soon found themselves surrounded on all sides by the rapidly advancing Americans in the area around Gardelegen, just to the north of Magdeburg, and many SS guards simply deserted. Apparently hundreds of prisoners escaped, and rumours circulated locally that they were plundering and raping women. In response on 11 or 12 April, the Gauleiter as the 'Reich Defence Commissar', and thus the highest civil authority in the area, ordered Kreisleiter Gerhard Thiele to put down the troubles, and to gather all camp prisoners there in one place. Thiele was assisted by Wehrmacht units, the remaining SS, Hitler Youth, the Volkssturm, Landwacht, and others to capture the escaped prisoners, many of whom were shot on the spot. Apparently the SS, Party, and Wehrmacht agreed among themselves that all prisoners would be killed before the Americans arrived, which they expected in a matter of hours. The prisoners were assembled and guarded by about 30 air force paratroopers, the same number of SS, but they were assisted by others, including 20 or so German 'green' or criminal prisoners, who volunteered to do so. These guards then forced all prisoners into a barn of the Remount School in Gardelegen (carrying in those too sick to make it on their own) and set the whole thing on fire. Anyone who tried to escape or rushed the door was met with a hail of bullets, and the shooting kept up half the night. The fire was still burning next day when the 102nd Infantry Division of the United States Army arrived. Altogether they found just over 1,000 bodies, half as many again were found in other places in the area.[111] The perpetrators went well beyond the SS, and included what Neander calls a 'representative sample' of the male population of the area. His research shows that 'the great majority' of the victims wore red badges, and so were 'political' prisoners.[112]

The massive Stutthof camp near Danzig, along with its subcamps, was evacuated at the end of January 1945, but when it proved impossible to move the prisoners by sea because the necessary ships were not available, Nazi leaders decided that 11 columns of 1,000 prisoners each, would go on foot to a destination estimated to be week's walk away. The first columns set out on 25 January 1945, but the confusion, freezing temperatures, and deep snow soon took such a heavy toll, that the original goal proved totally unrealistic. Many columns made camp to the west until mid-February when, even more unrealistically, orders arrived to use prisoners for the heavy work of building defensive positions for the Wehrmacht.[113]

Although many nationalities were represented at Stutthof and its subcamps, the Jews suffered more than all others, as can be seen in the evacuation of 1,500 Jews from the Stutthof subcamp at Seerappen in East Prussia, which began on 20 January 1945. They were soon joined by prisoners from other camps until there was a total of around 7,000 Jews (6,000 women and 1,000 men). Those who survived the 10-day ordeal that followed (thought to have cost the lives of about 700), were driven into the freezing waters of the Baltic Sea on 31 January near Palmnicken, just north of the city of Königsberg, where they were machine-gunned to death. One recent account suggests that the evacuations of the Stutthof subcamps alone cost of the lives of approximately 12,000 people, the majority of whom were Jewish women.[114]

The 11,000 or so prisoners left behind at Stutthof fared little better than those evacuated. Over several months, thousands were murdered, and as many or more died from disease and malnutrition, so that by the last count on 23 April 1945, only 4,508 prisoners were still alive. A final evacuation of 3,300 Stutthof prisoners began two days later. Even on the first night, 200 weakened Jewish women were executed, while the remainder boarded ships, and the ordeal dragged on into May. More than 2,000 people died or were murdered outright during this totally senseless evacuation. Taken together, therefore, during the last months of the war, a total of more than 25,000 men and women lost their lives either in Stutthof itself or during its evacuations or those of its subcamps.[115]

Rudolf Höss was sent by Oswald Pohl in early 1945 to investigate the evacuation of Auschwitz, but could not get through because of the rapid advance of the Soviet armies. Höss checked the situation at Groß-Rosen, one of the destinations for the evacuees, and found total disorder. He wrote in his memoirs how he was shown a radioed order from Himmler to Higher SS- and Police Leader (HSSPF), to evacuate Groß-Rosen and to leave no healthy prisoners behind.[116] At that time, there were approximately 75,000 prisoners in the Groß-Rosen system, but more trains arrived with new prisoners from other camps. Höss also describes how these scenes were replayed during the evacuations of Sachsenhausen and Ravensbrück.

In March and April the SS drove camp prisoners into areas still under German control, and travelled great distances on foot. For example, two columns set off from the camp at Nordhausen in early April; one headed for Flintsbach am Inn (885 kilometres away), and the other headed for Bergen-Belsen (a trek of 345 kilometres). Numerous such senseless evacuations have been recorded.[117] A transport of 800 prisoners left Flossenbürg for Regensburg to the south on 27 March, but instead of heading south, it went north. By the time the column reached its destination, originally 'only' 80 kilometres away, it had travelled 420 kilometres and, not surprisingly only a handful of people had made it.[118]

Certainly if Hitler's wish and/or orders had been followed, none of these 'enemies' would have survived. Himmler's views vacillated between wanting to kill them all and keeping some alive, particularly the Jews. He even entertained hopes that the Jews and certain other nationalities might be used in negotiations for money or for essential war goods.[119] At one stage in early March 1945, he was repeating to Felix Kersten, his doctor, his own long-held view, that the prisoners all should be killed. Kersten quotes Himmler as saying, that 'if National Socialist Germany is going to be destroyed, then her enemies and the criminals in the concentration camps shall not have the satisfaction of emerging from our ruin as triumphant conquerors. They shall share in the downfall. Those are the Führer's direct orders and I must see to it that they are carried out down to the last detail.' That statement could have been made by Hitler himself, who certainly inspired it. Kersten recorded that on 12 March Himmler changed his mind and decided after all against issuing Hitler's order to kill. He claimed that he wanted no more prisoners to die and for the camps to be handed over intact. In addition, the murder of the Jews was supposed to stop, and they were to be treated as other prisoners.[120] Whether or not Felix Kersten recorded Himmler's change of heart accurately, what happened on the evacuations was decided on the spot, and the murders continued unabated.

From post-war trials we learn how a camp near Hanover at Stöcken was cleared in early April after a telephone call from Neuengamme. The order, no copies of which apparently have survived, was that 'no living inmate shall be allowed to fall into the hands of the enemy'. On 7 April approximately 1,000 prisoners set out for Bergen-Belsen; 500 or so others who were totally unfit to make such a trip were handed over to the police, and not executed. Precisely how many survived the march to Bergen-Belsen remains uncertain, but, as usual, anyone who grew weak and could not keep up was shot.[121]

The Sachsenhausen camp near Berlin was evacuated on 21 April when orders were given for prisoners to be led by foot into the forests of Mecklenburg. It was estimated at post-war trials that a minimum of 15,000 were evacuated. The Camp Commandant supposedly ordered that no prisoner was to be left behind during the march, nor any allowed to fall into the hands of the Russians.[122] Once these marches began, moreover, a deadly dynamic set in. The guards (not all SS) were few and the prisoners many, so that to keep moving forward, guards invariably mixed brutality, murder, and their own prejudices against prisoners, with a perverted sense of duty and a determination to keep order.[123] There is an abundance of evidence that many of them vented their hatreds, especially towards the Jews. In fact, when the Commandant of Sachsenhausen, after protests by members of the Swedish Red Cross about shooting the marchers, reversed his shoot-to-kill order on the march, it remains uncertain if he was obeyed.[124]

Himmler may well have insisted, as he is said to have done around 13 April 1945, that no more Jews were to be killed. By that time, however, these marches, like the military situation, were beyond the control of leaders in Berlin.[125] A recent study of the death march from the camp at Helmbrechts, a short distance north-east of Nuremberg, shows that the killing continued regardless of central orders to cease. The march itself was divided about evenly between the 580 Jewish and 590 non-Jewish prisoners. For whatever reason, on the seventh day of the march, the guards left many non-Jewish prisoners (mainly Russian and Polish women) behind at a stopover camp. Other non-Jewish prisoners, including 25 Germans, and all Jews, continued. The post-war investigation stated that 178 Jews died, 49 of them from beatings and shootings, and the remainder as a result of malnutrition and disease. Even if that was a conservative estimate, the death rate of the Jews at near one-third, shows that, even as the Third Reich entered its final days, the murderous impulses of the guards continued.[126]

Another factor that influenced the decision to evacuate the camps and prisons was that the Nazis refused to give up on victory or at least could not visualize that defeat was so near, so that all prisoners, including the Jews, who could still work, had to be kept alive and brought back to Germany, where they could be exploited. They represented the last reservoir of labour, and somehow would be bludgeoned into a workforce. By 1945, that was a completely unrealistic wish, as hopelessly weak prisoners would have to travel many days by road, rail, or on foot. It was out of the question that they would be productive workers, but by then fantastic aims were commonplace.

On 6 April, less than a week before the liberation of Buchenwald, there was an announcement in the camp that 1,500 men were going to Leitmeritz in Bohemia to work on an earth-moving project. These prisoners left the next day, along with about 3,100 Jews, even as the sounds of battle could be heard in the distance; it is estimated that half these Jews were soon murdered.[127] Over the next three days the SS used the most brutal methods to assemble and evacuate approximately 40,000 prisoners of various nationalities, especially Russians, Poles, and Czechs, and somewhere approaching 13,500 of them were murdered in the course of the march. The Jews continued to suffer disproportionately at the hands of the Nazis, as is indicated by what happened to 4,340 Jews evacuated from the last Buchenwald subcamp at Rehmsdorf on 13 April. Only 500 of them reached the destination at Theresienstadt.[128] The same conclusion emerges from the story told by Adam Schteinbrecher, a Jewish prisoner in Buchenwald since the beginning of 1945. He was evacuated along with other political prisoners of various nationalities on 8 April, but the 'march' was mainly by train, which soon came under aircraft attack. He tells how everyone took cover, after which the guards managed to get all the prisoners together and back on the train, with the exception of the Jews who, as far as possible, were separated and murdered.[129]

At some of the subcamps of Groß-Rosen, prisoners continued into April to be thought of as useful for certain tasks and were employed to dig trenches.[130] Rudolf Höss said that he and others in the SS continued to work with tenacity for victory into April 1945. Even when Berlin was surrounded they insisted on doing everything possible to keep the armaments factories going full blast by using camp prisoners.[131]

Chaos and confusion overwhelmed the entire system, and just moving prisoners from one place to the next cost the lives of thousands and ruined the health of any who made it. In addition, the prejudices and the ingrained brutalities that the guards had cultivated for years towards all prisoners, could not simply be turned off, and the guards' undoubted antisemitism made them particularly eager to kill Jews. There is testimony that the guards' brutalities were nearly limitless towards all prisoners, even bystanders, who could be shot on a whim during the marches.[132]

The rapid advance of the Allies caught some of the camps by surprise, as in April 1945 when the Americans reached Buchenwald. In spite of Himmler's order to halt evacuations, which might have been overruled by Ernst Kaltenbrunner, head of the RSHA, Buchenwald's Camp Commandant decided on wholesale evacuation when it was obvious that the Americans were getting close. According to survivors, on 8 April he told senior block leaders to clear the camp within the hour, and only well-led passive resistance of the prisoners subverted this order. Even so, guards managed to round up another group of 4,800 (recently arrived) prisoners and marched them out of the camp on 8 April. On 10 April Russian, Polish, and Czech prisoners were similarly rounded up and led away. On 11 April the SS gave up the idea of evacuating the camp and took flight, and later that day its 21,400 prisoners were liberated.[133]

Hitler grew enraged upon learning that the liberated Buchenwald prisoners had pillaged the nearby town of Weimar and, on or about 15 April, ordered (yet again) that no concentration camp be surrendered before it was evacuated or all prisoners had been liquidated.[134] Although no written order to this effect from Hitler has been found, several historians have located mid-April orders from Himmler to the camps within the shrinking German sphere of influence. There is evidence that these orders were addressed to Dachau and Flossenbürg, but may have been communicated to all remaining camps. The text of the order runs as follows: 'Surrender is out of the question. The camp must be evacuated immediately. No prisoner may fall into enemy hands alive. The prisoners behaved brutally against the civil population of Buchenwald.'[135]

The diary of Edgar Kupfer-Koberwitz, a survivor from Dachau has recently come to light, and provides a detailed record from the inside. He noted on 20 April 1945, that 1,800 people had died in the camp (excluding the subcamps) during December 1944; in January 1945, the number rose to 2,800; in February, there were 3,000; and during March 4,000.[136] As if malnutrition and disease were not bad enough, the SS grew more vicious, and as well, endless columns of prisoners arrived on foot or by train from other camps. The stories they told of thousands who were shot, terrified Dachau.[137] At one stage rumour in the camp was that orders had been given, supposedly from Himmler, to evacuate everyone, including the 3,000 in the sick bay. Although that did not happen, on 26 April 6,000 'Germans and Russians' left, other nationalities were supposed to follow, and prominent prisoners were taken away.[138] At that late date, the Jews in Dachau were not murdered, but on 24 April, 1,700 of them boarded trains. The events that followed are uncertain, but many Jews doubtlessly had died by 29 April, when the Americans arrived.[139]

As Gordon Horwitz shows with regard to the Mauthausen camp, citizens on the outside did not rush to help the camp prisoners during their evacuations.[140] There were occasional offers of food and water, there were gestures of sympathy, and even the odd protest about the brutality of the SS or other guards. For the most part, however, good citizens did nothing, either out of fear for their own lives, or because they had grown apathetic or indifferent. Survivors remembered the inhumane attitudes of bystanders, some of whom clearly shared the view that the prisoners should not be freed. In fact on marches to or from Mauthausen, not just the SS guards got involved in killing stragglers, but so did soldiers, members of the Nazi Party, and ordinary citizens as well. Some locals took part in the massacres of Jews, and others shot Jews who happened to survive when they were left behind.[141]

The women's camp at Ravensbrück was one of the last major camps to be evacuated. On 15 January 1945, the census registered 46,070 women, and 7,848 men for the camp and its subcamps. In the months preceding evacuation, the scenes behind the barbed-wire fences were worse than anything in the camp's horrific history.[142] Before the end, the SS introduced systematic mass murder in its own gas chamber, built in the autumn of 1944 and put into operation in December at the nearby Uckermark Youth Camp. Germaine Tillion, a French camp survivor, was in a position to learn that SS officials in Berlin informed the camp on 1 October that they were displeased with the 'low' mortality rate, presumably as the new inmates were causing overcrowding, so a gas facility and mass executions were introduced in the camp to speed up the killing of the weak and infirm.[143] Until the camp was finally evacuated, an estimated 6,000 women, children, and men, were murdered in the gas chamber there.[144] Death by 'natural causes' and disease, especially typhus, additionally led in the main camp to more than 1,000 deaths in each of the first three months of 1945.[145] Some evacuations went ahead, such as one to Mauthausen in early March, of 2,000 French, Belgian, and Sinti and Roma women (with no more than 740 of them ever reaching their destination). By the end of March, there were still officially 37,699 prisoners in Ravensbrück, and the SS accelerated murder, using the gas facility or shooting. The Swedish Red Cross managed to rescue a total of about 7,500 women, including women from France, Sweden, and Poland, a large group of whom left by train on 21 April. In fact, on that day Himmler, who had been negotiating for weeks with Count Folke Bernadotte, deputy head of the Swedish Red Cross, agreed to release all the prisoners in Ravensbrück, but nothing really came of it.[146] Even with representatives of the Red Cross in the camp, guards were still executing prisoners (by shooting), and 'selections' continued. Finally on 27 April the evacuation of the remaining prisoners went ahead, but within two days the marchers were left to fend for themselves as the guards took flight and the war came to an end.[147]

If we take the death marches as a whole, it is impossible to say how many people were evacuated, let alone how many died or were murdered in the process. We simply do not have sufficient documentation. Martin Broszat does not give a total of those forced onto the death marches, but suggests that 'at least' one-third of the 700,000 or so prisoners who were in the camps at the beginning of 1945, died either as a direct result of the marches, in the transport trains, or perished in the overcrowded reception camps in the weeks and months before liberation.[148] In all likelihood these numbers do not include additional thousands of concentration camp prisoners, many of them Jews, who were working as forced labourers, and one estimate puts those numbers at 200,000 people.[149] And if that is the case, and we accept that around one-third of all concentration camp prisoners died, then the final figure would be well in excess of the 70,000 deaths usually mentioned in the literature.

Yehuda Bauer concludes that in the final analysis 'it is impossible to estimate the number of victims' who died on the marches. We have no accurate figures of the survivors found in the camps, and how many were liberated during the marches.[150] Nor is it possible to establish the national identities of the marchers. Shmuel Krakowski shows that on some of the evacuations, particularly the one that ended in the massacre at Palmnicken, nearly all the marchers were Jews. He does not put a final figure to the number of men and women of all nationalities who died or were murdered, but suggests that during the most hectic period, between March and April 1945 alone, at least 250,000 prisoners were evacuated, about one-third of whom may have been Jews.[151]

Israeli historian Daniel Blatman concludes his investigation of the marches by suggesting that there is no evidence in the evacuation orders, nor in the oral testimony, that Nazi leaders had given orders to kill all the Jews. However, the earlier planned and methodical annihilation, and the conditions themselves at war's end in which these marches took place, coupled with the brutalized, antisemitic, racist guards—by no means all of them in the SS, as we have seen—led almost inevitably to murder on a vast scale.[152]

The Consensus Holds

Social support for Hitler and for National Socialism steadily eroded as the war encroached more and more into Germany, and many people were certainly fed up. What is remarkable, however, was how resilient public opinion was, and, in spite of one defeat or major setback after the next, the surveyors of opinion found innumerable statements to indicate that morale held, in the sense that many people from all ranks of life were willing to continue the fight, even in the face of great hardship. Thus, after the Normandy invasion in June 1944, there were widespread signs of a positively exuberant optimism and some people yearned to get their hands on Allied troops. An even greater show of support for Hitler, virulent hatred of the conspirators, and expressed willingness to shoulder more burdens followed the attempt on his life on 20 July 1944. His explanation of the attempted coup, along with the use of the V-1 flying bombs and V-2 rockets—retaliatory 'miracle weapons'—served only to renew the public's faith in his ability to see them through. Opinion reports stated that 'almost everywhere the bonding to the Führer is deepened and the trust in the leadership strengthened'.[153]

Historian Marlis Steinert, who notes these trends, adds that there was nothing less than 'an astonishingly positive reception' to Hitler's New Year's proclamation for 1945 and his confidence in victory.[154] She and several others who have studied public opinion closely, have tended to magnify the 'negatives', like signs of dissolution, loss of faith, and the collapse of morale. However, while the mood and attitude of the people certainly shifted with the military or political situation, many people, and not just the died-in-the-wool Nazis, showed themselves anxious to interpret events in the most optimistic way possible.

The last Nazi opinion reports from Berlin in March 1945 contain evidence that many citizens finally began to question propaganda stories and the more outlandish claims, but that many still showed 'a good and confident attitude'. If the pessimists and defeatists were in the majority, the Nazi reporters were of the view that the balance would shift back if only the Wehrmacht could show an important victory. Certainly these last glimpses of popular opinion showed signs that people were losing faith, like three women who scoffed at a sign with the words of inspiration that Berlin 'works, fights, and stands', placed in the windows of Berlin's famous department store, the Kaufhaus des Westens.[155]

We also find remarks scattered in these last reports that suggest what Germans were saying among themselves. Two workers in Spandau-West were overheard by the opinion surveyors as saying 'that we have only ourselves to blame for this war because we treated the Jews so badly. We shouldn't be too surprised, if they now do the same thing to us.' These workers acknowledged Germany's persecution of the Jews, but there are no indications they felt any remorse. They were prepared for the inevitable outcome and believed, as Hitler had prophesied, that they were experiencing the retaliation of the Jews and their influential friends around the world. The Nazi reporter who overheard this exchange noted that 'similar observations now are often heard'.[156]

Such fragmentary evidence suggests that Nazi allegations over the years that the Jews and some sort of conspiracy caused the war had taken root. In fact during the last two years of the war, letters (including some from academics) were sent to the Ministry of Propaganda suggesting that the Jews remaining in Germany be collected at likely bombing targets. The number killed would be publicized after each raid. One letter said that even if this did not work to stop the Allied flyers, at least many Jews would be exterminated. Another suggestion was to threaten the Americans and British that tenfold the number of Jews would be shot for civilians killed in a given bombing raid.[157]

At any rate, the last reports reflected widespread knowledge of German atrocities in the east. The report of 23 March mentioned reactions to stories about the 'terrifying sentences' used by the occupation forces in the western part of Germany. These stories were put in the Nazi press to scare Germans into fighting on. Two Berlin men were overheard saying that newspapers should not make such a fuss, because 'everyone of course knows that our SS in the occupied areas also did not exactly use kid gloves, which was also fully understandable. That the enemies now act that way ought to surprise no one.'[158] The overall assessment of the 31 March 1945 report out of Berlin concluded, 'the mood [of the public] is not very good, but one of wait and see and essentially still prepared for anything!'[159] In Hamburg, where the Nazi opinion surveyors found evidence that many still hoped for a satisfactory end to the war as late as March 1945, negative attitudes spread and there were some objections to carrying on to the final bullet.[160]

A report of the situation (from 7 April 1945) for the area around Munich reflected the conditions elsewhere. It stated that there was little organized resistance by foreign workers, who were more concerned about getting home or just finding food. Plenty of information existed, it said, about the regrettable acts of the Germans with respect to the foreigners. 'The instances of unbefitting, defeatist, insurrectionary, and treasonous behaviour of German citizens, also of those in official positions, with regard to foreign workers and prisoners of war, gather daily to such an extent, that coping with their full scope in a report is completely impossible any further.' The report offered evidence that 'in wide circles of the German public sphere, particularly of the rural population whose unbefitting behaviour with regard to the foreigners, resulted from a general morale decline, [there was] outright defeatism and open anxiety'. The report ended with a call for still tougher 'measures of a state-police kind' that should be aimed 'with a strong hand and absolutely without mercy' at both foreigners and Germans who endangered Germany's will to resist.[161] Nazi propaganda played upon German fears about what would happen if or when the Soviets arrived on German territory, in order to try to strengthen the determination to resist. The warning of retribution to come for Nazi barbarities committed in the Soviet Union led many Germans to flee to the west. Those who could not or would not go were overrun by the Soviet advance. Some stayed behind in the mistaken view that the treks to the west would be more dangerous, because some people thought that after all 'the Russians could not murder everyone, and better times would come soon enough'. No doubt such people were shocked at what took place, because the treatment of the civilian population by Soviet troops was far worse than they had anticipated. Soviet leaders such as Marshal Zhukov in January 1945, fanned soldiers' lust for revenge with orders that read in part: 'Woe to the land of the murderers. We will get our terrible revenge for everything!'[162]

On the eve of crossing into German territory in East Prussia, the Main Political Administration of the Soviet Army declared that 'on German soil there is only one master—the Soviet soldier, that he is both the judge and the punisher for the torments of his fathers and mothers, for the destroyed cities and villages . . .'[163] Wartime Soviet propaganda publicized Nazi crimes, stories of what the Nazis did circulated widely, and Soviet soldiers were now indirectly and sometimes directly encouraged to pillage and plunder; they raped German women, at times virtually all of them, in the rampages through some towns and villages, from the very young to the very old, and with no worry that they would be held accountable by anyone. The only way out for some German women was suicide, and in some localities that happened a lot.

Hitler's political testament, written up on 29 April in the bunker, stated that he would rather die than be taken prisoner and deposed, and he asked his successors to do what they could to strengthen the spirit of resistance and continue the war. Before he committed suicide, he appointed a new government and stripped Himmler and Göring of their offices for opening negotiations with the Allies. He could not end without rehashing his favourite antisemitic allegations, most notably that an international Jewish conspiracy had started the war. He referred again to his notorious 'prophecy' about what would happen to the Jews should 'they' involve the world in another war. In the end, Hitler held grimly to his own propaganda and allegations.[164]

Conclusion

The process by which the German people came to support Hitler and the Nazi dictatorship can be divided into three phases: the first from his appointment in 1933 to 1938–9; the second ran from the outbreak of the war to the beginning of the invasion in 1944; and the final phase went from there to the end.

In the months after Hitler's appointment in January 1933 Germans began to experience something like a return of 'normalcy'. For people whose sense of social equilibrium had been shaken by years of crisis, this mythical 'normalcy' meant a steady job again, some security, and hope for a better future. The Socialists (SPD), the Party that backed the Weimar Republic through thick and thin, waited for the Nazis to make revolutionary moves, perhaps do something clearly illegal, and imagined that, in response, they and the trade unions would organize some kind of general strike, as they had done in earlier days.[1] The Nazis studiously avoided such 'mistakes' and instead presented what they did as necessary pre-emptive strikes to protect the people from a Communist revolution of some kind. The police and Nazi Storm Troopers went into action in the early months of 1933, and a mini-wave of terror followed. The coordination, or Nazification of the country took place in stages, and all non-Nazi organizations, especially political parties, were eliminated. The approach taken was calculated and shrewd, because all the parties were not outlawed at one fell swoop, but one at a time. By and large, however, terror was not needed to end all non-Nazi organizational life in the country, nor was it used to force the majority or even significant minorities into line. Many Germans, wooed by Hitler who appealed over and over to their deepest anxieties and most secret hopes, liked what they heard and became instrumentally and emotionally invested in the Nazi dictatorship. On balance, most people seemed prepared to live with the idea of a surveillance society, to put aside the opportunity to develop the freedoms we usually identify with liberal democracies, in return for crime-free streets, a return to prosperity, and what they regarded as a good government.[2]

There was no organized resistance. Indeed as Dietrich Orlow somewhat harshly puts it, there was 'very little unorganized grumbling'.[3] Hartmut Mehringer has written how the new regime soon 'had far more than the great majority of the population behind it', and they remained steadfast in that support, up to and especially even after the coup attempt in July 1944.[4]

Hitler never set out to confront large segments of his social world and to break them to his will, as did Stalin. Rather, he wanted to establish a uniquely styled dictatorship, and ended up conducting what historian Martin Broszat once called an 'experiment in plebiscitarian dictatorship'.[5] He aimed for an authoritarian and leader-oriented system, but one that had popular backing, and his regime was deeply concerned, one might say, even paranoid, about popular opinion and citizens' reactions to official measures of all kinds. Germans were not expected merely to adjust and accommodate themselves to the new system, but to become 'idealistically' motivated, to reflect back to the Nazis that what the Third Reich stood for was in the 'best' of German traditions, to get involved in displays of affection for Hitler and his vision of 'community', and in practical terms, to help bring about the new order by actively cooperating with the police and the Party.[6]

In their successful cultivation of popular opinion, the Nazis did not need to use widespread terror against the population to establish the regime. They had little need to use terror as had the makers of the great modern revolutions, like those in France, Russia, or China. Many Germans went along, not because they were mindless robots, but because they convinced themselves of Hitler's advantages and of the 'positive' sides of the new dictatorship. There was a tendency to excuse Hitler if things went wrong or not according to plan, and to blame such problems on the 'little Hitlers', that is, the leaders below the Führer.

In writing this book I was constantly reminded of the phrase in the title of one of Fritz Stern's essays on 'National Socialism as Temptation'. He suggests how even the most educated Germans found reasons for supporting the system, and were less regimented, cajoled, or forced than we often assume.[7] Many Germans clearly supported the crackdown on those whom the Nazis branded as political criminals, and were certainly pleased to see such persons sent off to newly established concentration camps. As the camps were created they were widely publicized, and even the local populations living in the vicinity of the camps were generally in favour of them.

Most people in Nazi Germany had no direct confrontation with the Gestapo, Kripo, or the concentration camps. Moreover, while they read many stories about the 'People's Court', rather few people attended its sessions. In other words, for most Germans, the coercive or terroristic side of Hitler's dictatorship was socially constructed by what was passed along by word of mouth, by what they read of it in the press, or heard on the radio. Historians have paid remarkably little attention to these representations, when in fact these played an important role in the dictatorship.

At every level there was much popular support for the expanding missions of the new police and the camps, especially as the latter were presented in the media and elsewhere as boot-camps in which the state would confine both political 'criminals' and variously defined asocials, in order to subject them to 'work therapy'. In the 1930s there were thousands of stories about these camps, and of the more radical 'preventive' approach to criminals who reoffended. Such stories were published to gain support and win approval.

When we talk about the coercive practices of the Third Reich, we usually think about the Gestapo, and what the SS did in the camps, but not the uniformed police and the Kripo. In the book I have also studied the Kripo, whose 'successes' helped to shore up support for the dictatorship because for the most part solid citizens were pleased that the police put away people commonly regarded as criminals and the 'dregs of society'. It is only in the last several years that we have come to see that the ordinary uniformed police and their leaders played a key part in the Holocaust in eastern Europe, but it is no less clear that they played a crucial role in legitimating the dictatorship at home.[8]

A temptation for any citizen living through what is popularly regarded as a crime wave, such as the one thought by many to exist in Germany between 1929 until Hitler's appointment, is to cheer on a campaign against crime and against what is widely believed to be immoral behaviour. Without deeply rooted democratic traditions, and in the context of the sorry Weimar experiment, the German people under Hitler showed they were prepared to go to extraordinary lengths, to give their support to this mission. Moreover, as readers of the newspapers of the day could see, the new police encroached into ever more areas of social and intimate life, and the entire thrust of the new system was to expel or exclude ever wider categories of people who would not, or could not, fit in. The point was reached where some officials wanted to do something about anyone considered merely socially 'inadequate'. A proposed law on 'aliens of the community' targeted men and women who demonstrated (among other things) 'abnormal defects of intellect or character', and who thereby would always be 'incapable of fulfilling the minimum requirements of the community of the people'.[9] Although versions of this proposed law were discussed for years on end, and even though no such measure made it onto the books, the outlines that survive, suggest the extraordinary measures that could be conceived in the context of the exclusionary dynamics of social racism. At one point in the war, two university doctors estimated that as many as one million German citizens would have to been eliminated—by sending them to camps or killing them— in order to purge all forms of deviance from the body politic.[10] We can only speculate how good citizens would have responded to the growing reach of the state and its normalization efforts with regard to such widely defined 'aliens'.

The coercion and confinement in the 1930s were neither wholesale nor entirely random, but selective and focused. As the rule of law was eliminated, superseded as it was by 'police justice' and special courts, an element of arbitrariness and unpredictability crept into law and order procedures, and in so far as that happened, citizens let the dictatorship know of their displeasure. For the most part, however, this kind of 'terror' was not designed as a ruling strategy to govern and control the entire nation, but aimed at eliminating certain 'obvious enemies' who were already on the margins of society or thought to be threatening in some way. The definition of 'enemy' (or social 'alien') grew over time, but that trend also reflected the wish to gain support and win over the people. The targets of discrimination, persecution, and confinement, therefore, were not chosen by Hitler and his henchmen merely because of their own idiosyncratic prejudices and dislikes. On balance, the coercive practices, the repression, and persecution won far more support for the dictatorship than they lost.

Care needs to be taken to avoid assuming that Germany as a whole was like some kind of military training camp in which the people are subjected to the double strategy of propaganda and terror. Nazi propaganda is poorly understood if we think of it simply as brainwashing or mere emotional manipulation. The idea of brainwashing circulated during the Cold War, and may have been used on certain individuals. However, the very idea of brainwashing a nation of more than 60 million Germans—or treating them as if they all were in a military boot-camp—is so implausible that it should be dismissed out of hand. If it seems to be one of those groundless ideas that keeps recurring, perhaps in the end it represents the fact that it is so hard for us to face up to the difficulty of trying to cope with the full enormity of the many atrocities committed in the name of, and with the support of, so many Germans.

Nazi propaganda was not, and could not, be crudely forced on the German people. On the contrary, it was meant to appeal to them, and to match up with everyday German understandings. Another way of thinking about the content of this propaganda, which was meant to be attractive and convincing, might be to regard it 'as an indicator of what people sincerely hoped to be true'.[11] Thus, far from forcing unwanted or repellent messages down the throats of the population, Hitler and the Nazis carefully tailored what they said, wrote, and especially what they did, in order to win and hold the support of the people.

We need to recall that the 'positive spin' about the Third Reich, which was churned out under the jurisdiction of the Ministry of Popular Enlightenment and Propaganda, was accompanied, very early on, by successful policies like the work-creation programme, building the autobahns, promising a family car and cheap vacations, and holding the Olympics. The regime quickly won converts by what it did and not only by the image it presented of itself. Even though many of these great 'accomplishments' were paid for very dearly later on, in the short run, they made it possible for the dictatorship to become established, to thrive, and to grow more ambitious.

Hitler won acclaim in the 1930s, perhaps first and foremost for beating the Great Depression, and for curing the massive unemployment in the country. Although definitely no economist himself, his regime overcame the Depression more quickly than any of the other advanced industrial nations. We know that some of the methods used to get people back to work, such as compelling them to work at jobs they did not want, would never have been acceptable in a democracy. What seemed to count for most Germans, however, was that millions of people began to find jobs again and earnings grew steadily while the cost of living did not. If we look at German history in the twenty years prior to 1933, replete as they were with economic dislocation and social chaos, we can get a sense of why many people were grateful that Hitler apparently restored some semblance of the 'good old days'.

In Victor Klemperer's diary we can find a graphic illustration of how someone in Germany might respond to the gradual, but clear improvement in the employment opportunities opening up all over the country. In an entry dated 24 November 1936, the ever-observant Klemperer, reflecting on his many experiences during the day, recalled that he had bumped into a stranger in a busy street in Dresden. 'A young man hurries past me in the crowd', he remembered, 'a complete stranger, half turns and says with a beaming face, "I've got work—the first time in three years—and good work—at Renner's—they pay well!—for four weeks!"—and runs on.'[12] Here was a young person who was overjoyed at the thought of having what he took to be a decent job, one that was supposed to last all of four weeks. His happiness seemed almost boundless, and we can surmise that his need to shout his good fortune in the street most likely also translated into thankfulness and support for the changes the new Hitler government had introduced.

After what seemed like years of weak and uncertain government, Hitler was conveying the impression that there was a steady eye and firm hand at the helm again. Hitler's image as strong leader was to a great extent supported by Germany's actions in international affairs. He made no bones about putting his foot down, and forcing the issue. The irony was that Britain and France helped to foster Hitler's stature in the eyes of his own people. During the 1920s those two countries took a very hard line against Germany, and without intending to do so, they made its fledgling democracy seem weak, ineffective, and even spineless. No sooner was Hitler in power, than Britain and France adopted the new strategy of appeasement, as Hitler tore up the Versailles settlement of 1919 one paragraph at a time. In so far as these Allies did nothing, they made him look good, indeed they made him seem like the greatest leader since Bismarck, perhaps since Frederick the Great. In the eyes of the German people, he managed the impossible by restoring Germany's 'rightful' place on the continent, and by doing so without firing a shot. Through war that Hitler inevitably brought about, of course, the nation would eventually pay an enormous price for those first easy victories.

The second stage in the relationship between the German people and the Nazi dictatorship began with the coming of the war in 1939. Once the war came, nationalism became a factor and many who might have had second thoughts and grave reservations about Hitler and Nazism now put their country first. The dictatorship reaped the benefits, while for Hitler the war represented the beginning of a new stage in the realization of his more radical plans and racist visions, and those aims included many sweeping changes inside the Fatherland itself.

The war, therefore, revolutionized the revolution. We saw this most clearly in the vast expansion of the concentration camp system, the persecution of social outsiders, the 'euthanasia' programme, and in the whole sphere of racial policy. The radical tendencies in Nazism that had been latent or only partially articulated until then were now allowed to express themselves, urged on at every turn by Hitler. Countervailing tendencies, like what remained of the liberal 'rule of law', were pushed aside, and the trend was for police prerogatives to take precedence over the courts and the rights of all citizens.

Racism in the war period reached its dreadful climax in Poland and elsewhere in the east. The Jews who had not left Germany by September 1941 were forced to wear a yellow star, to live in isolated 'Jewish houses', and soon they were systematically deported to the east and to horror-filled fates. The Jews who were exempted, like those living in 'mixed marriages', were humiliated at every turn. Alongside them, foreign workers, initially from Poland, were forced to work as virtual slaves. Germans could not fail to see how many thousands of 'racially foreign people' were treated, and forced to live in an apartheid system in their midst. Daily experiences of this everyday racism left side-effects all over the country. Although not all citizens followed the dictates to avoid the foreigners at all costs, there is evidence in this book that the majority more or less accepted the racist teachings, and at the very least showed few signs of being troubled by them.[13]

Until recently historians frequently emphasized the passivity of German citizens in the Third Reich, and wrote about the Nazi 'police state' as if it were so invasive as to leave little room for citizen initiative beyond mere ceremonials and rituals. We now know that even if all citizens did not agree with everything, including certain aspects of the persecution of the Jews and foreign workers inside Germany, the regime had no difficulty in obtaining denunciations from the population about suspected breaches of the racist system. Providing information to the police or the Party was one of the most important contributions of citizen involvement in the Third Reich. After all, it was one thing for the regime to promulgate new laws and ordinances, to shout the regulations from on high, but quite another to enforce them in society at large. It was a characteristic feature of the Third Reich, one that set it apart from Italian Fascism, that the regime found no difficulty in obtaining the collaboration of ordinary citizens. People cooperated when it came to enforcing antisemitism and the racial measures aimed at foreign workers, and they were certainly not reluctant about informing when it came to ordinary crimes.

The Nazis claimed to be dedicated to attaining a 'community of the people'. In attempting to forge that 'community', which was based on a maddening logic of sameness, purity, and homogeneity, they and the German people got caught up in a murderous game of pillorying, excluding, and eventually eliminating unwanted social 'elements' and 'race enemies'. That process began as many ordinary citizens learned how to use (sometimes for selfish purposes) notions about who was in and who was out of the 'community of the people'. No doubt there were true believers and committed zealots, but, as we have seen, it was not necessary for all Germans to become died-in-the-wool Nazis in order for the regime to actualize its ideological aims. When anyone, regardless of their motives, reported infringements of race laws to the police or wrote letters to the Party about politically 'undesired' social behaviour, regardless of whether they were 'sincere' or selfish, they contributed to the realization of Nazi ideology and made the dictatorship work.[14] In that sense, all denunciations were system-supportive, and there never seemed to be a shortage of them.[15]

This kind of citizen involvement and their willingness to inform the police or Nazi Party about their suspicions had devastating effects on resistance. Barrington Moore has pointed out that the 'one prerequisite' for expressions of disobedience to take place is that there be 'social and cultural space' which 'provides more or less protected enclaves within which dissatisfied or oppressed groups have some room', so that they can meet and talk and mobilize for action.[16] Because many ordinary people served as the eyes and ears of the police, those who might have wished to resist could not gather to organize or to form solidarities.[17] Those who still wanted to say 'no' had to swim against the tide, and were driven to individual acts of defiance that were important for them as moral individuals, but in the short run not threatening to the dictatorship.[18]

The invasion of the Soviet Union accelerated the murderousness, and provided the context in which the Holocaust took place. The eastern 'war of annihilation' was used as the occasion for systematic mass murder on a scale that was and remains without precedent. Genocidal practices were aimed at Jews in Eastern Europe, and the war against the Soviet Union soon came to entail the mass murder of untold millions as well. Richard Overy has shown that the war against the Soviet Union was vicious in every respect, with the Soviets losing by his estimate some 25 million people, 17 million of them civilians.[19]

The brutalizing effects of the Holocaust and the war against the Soviet Union made their way back to the Fatherland, as we have seen with regard to the police and concentration camp system. The camps that to some extent had disappeared from the news with the outbreak of war in 1939 began to invade the social landscape of Germany from the mid-war years onward. The presence of camp inmates in everyday life became impossible to overlook. If anything, however, like the millions of slave workers, they seemed to many Germans to confirm Nazi theories and to affirm their own perverted sense of social and racial superiority.

The falsely idyllic and utopian images of the camps in the media, and the rationalizations for their existence left their marks on Germans' imaginations and helped shape their views of what was going on. This is not to say that the representations of the camps and the terror had uniform effects on the population. The social reception of the images that were projected no doubt varied enormously. At one end of the scale these published accounts had a terrorizing or deterrent effect on potential opponents of Nazism and those who were officially stigmatized. Certainly, many people in the country would have seen through the propaganda. However, for 'good citizens' who wanted a return to an idealized version of German 'law and order', these images helped to ease the acceptance of even the terroristic sides of Hitler's regime. They could read in the press that those who suffered at the hands of the new system were 'other' people, Communists and various social outsiders and the Jews. 'Good citizens' were invited to see the camps as educative institutions and as a 'correction and a warning' to those described as 'social rabble', that is, men and women who were habitual criminals, the chronically unemployed, beggars, alcoholics, homosexuals, and repeat sex offenders.

Ulrich Herbert recently suggested that during the Nazi years there was 'a growing lack of moral concern in German society for human rights and the protection of minorities, which grew rapidly during the years of the dictatorship, and which led to a profound moral brutalization in Germany'.[20] I have suggested that part of the explanation for this social desensitization and one of the keys to understanding the origins and growth of this 'moral brutalization' may be sought in studying the representations of the concentration camps and their prisoners in the media of the day. What is at issue is no longer whether or not Germans knew about the camps, but rather what kind of knowledge they had and how it was conveyed. I have argued that we need to investigate not only the secret, but also the public sides of the terror and take seriously what the regime publicized about the camps and their prisoners.

The final, most dramatic and murderous period of the dictatorship in Germany itself took place in the last six months or so, as the home front also became the battlefront. Almost every city, town, and village experienced its own version of the apocalypse in scenes we can construct only incompletely on the basis of post-war trials. As I wrote the last chapters of this book, I became acutely aware of how much remains to tell of that story.

I described some of the late war atrocities, many of which took place in the streets of towns and villages across Germany. We can see that the circle of victims grew in the last months to include any Germans who stepped out of line or who showed the slightest unwillingness to continue. While many people staggered toward the end, there were always others willing to fight on. The brutalities of the police, SS, Wehrmacht, and even the elderly members of the Volkssturm seemed nearly limitless. We cannot explain the urge to continue with reference to a single motive, not even racism, as the killers did not hesitate when the victims were German, Italian, or French.

Why did Germans carry on and for the most part support Hitler to the end? A combination of factors was involved that no doubt varied from person to person. On the one hand there were optimists who were unwilling to accept the fact that the war was really lost. They combined hope with the dream of the 'miracle weapon' that would turn things around. Even pessimists worried, especially about the Soviets and what was expected to be a murderous invasion. Some people looked to a change in fate, and soldiers fought on with grim determination against an enemy that had long since become demonized. No doubt some people hoped that the Western democracies would 'see the light' and join Germany in an anti-Soviet war. Others refused to contemplate defeat and thought only of victory and 'doing their duty', as one 17-year-old boy said as he went to fight the British in early April 1945.[21]

In the closing days of the Third Reich, there were optimists, pessimists, 'idealists', and fatalists. But there was no shortage of Nazi fanatics determined to fight to the end. Many people apparently could not afford to let themselves see the situation, including the brutalities, for what they really were, and could do nothing more than be for Hitler or at least for Germany.

NOTES

Introduction

1. See the notes of General Liebman (3 Feb. 1933), reprinted in *Nazism Docs.*, iii. 628–9.
2. For relevant documents, see *Nazism Docs.*, i. 142 and 161–2.
3. For a recent critical analysis and survey of the literature, see Hartmut Mehringer, *Widerstand und Emigration: Das NS-Regime und seine Gegner* (Munich, 1997). The major survey in English is Peter Hoffmann, *The History of the German Resistance 1933–1945*, trans. R. Barry (Cambridge, Mass., 1977).
4. For useful remarks, see Norbert Frei, *Der Führerstaat: Nationalsozialistische Herrschaft 1933 bis 1945* (Munich, 1987), 120–9.
5. See Richard Bessel, 'Political Violence and the Nazi Seizure of Power', in Richard Bessel (ed.), *Life in the Third Reich* (Oxford, 1987), 1–15, here 15.
6. The more subtle aspects of control can be seen even in spheres of activity such as music and art; see esp. Michael H. Kater, *The Twisted Muse: Musicians and their Music in the Third Reich* (Oxford, 1997); Jonathan Petropoulos, *Art as Politics in the Third Reich* (Chapel Hill, NC, 1996).
7. For an overview, see Peter Fritzsche, *Germans into Nazis* (Cambridge, Mass., 1998).
8. See Jill Stephenson, 'War and Society in Württemberg, 1939–1945: Beating the System', *GSR* (1985), 89–105. For a thorough recent account, see esp. Klaus-Dietmar Henke, *Die amerikanische Besetzung Deutschlands* (Munich, 1995).
9. Ian Kershaw, *The 'Hitler Myth': Image and Reality in the Third Reich* (Oxford, 1987), esp. 247–52; Detlev Peukert, *Volksgenossen und Gemeinschaftsfremde: Anpassung, Ausmerze und Aufbegehren unter dem Nationalsozialismus* (Cologne, 1982), 85.
10. Alf Lüdtke, 'The Appeal of Exterminating "Others": German Workers and the Limits of Resistance', in Michael Geyer and John W. Boyer (eds.), *Resistance against the Third Reich 1933–1990* (Chicago, 1994) 53–74, here 53–4. The same point is made in Peukert, *Volksgenossen*, 82–3.
11. See the testimony of contemporaries in Laurence Rees, *The Nazis: A Warning from History* (London, 1997).
12. See Ute Frevert, *Women in German History: From Bourgeois Emancipation to Sexual Liberation*, trans. S. McKinnon-Evans (New York, 1989), here 250 and 252.
13. See the many examples in Alison Owings, *Frauen: German Women Recall the Third Reich* (New Brunswick, NJ, 1993), here 8, 9, 13. The emphasis is in the original.
14. Daniel Jonah Goldhagen, *Hitler's Willing Executioners: Ordinary Germans and the Holocaust* (New York, 1996), 443. For detailed reviews of this book, see Robert Gellately in *JMH* (1997), 187–91; and Richard J. Evans, *Rereading German History, 1800–1996* (London, 1997), 149–81.
15. See esp. Ulrich Herbert (ed.), *Nationalsozialistische Vernichtungspolitik 1939–1945: Neue Forschungen und Kontroversen* (Frankfurt am Main, 1998). A useful collection

of specific critiques is Robert R. Shandley (ed.), *Unwilling Germans? The Goldhagen Debate* (Minneapolis, 1998). The most trenchant reviews are Norman G. Finkelstein and Ruth Bettina Birn, *A Nation on Trial: The Goldhagen Thesis and Historical Truth* (New York, 1998).

16. For a convincing account based especially on the contemporary writings and memories of German Jews, see Marion A. Kaplan, *Between Dignity and Despair: Jewish Life in Nazi Germany* (New York, 1998).

17. See the testimony of two exiles, who became prominent historians, and also about the changes in Werner T. Angress, *Generation zwischen Furcht und Hoffnung: Jüdische Jugend im Dritten Reich* (Hamburg, 1985), 9–15; Peter Gay, *My German Question: Growing up in Nazi Berlin* (New Haven, 1998), esp. 57–83.

18. See Ulrich Herbert, 'Vernichtungspolitik: Neue Antworten und Fragen zur Geschichte des "Holocausts"', in Herbert (ed.), *Vernichtungspolitik*, 9–66, here 65.

19. Christa Wolf, *Patterns of Childhood*, trans. U. Molinaro and H. Rappolt (German edn., 1976) (New York, 1980).

20. See Norbert Frei, *Nationalsozialistische Eroberung der Provinzpresse: Gleichschaltung, Selbstanpassung und Resistenz in Bayern* (Stuttgart, 1980), esp. 251–321.

21. See Norbert Frei and Johannes Schmitz, *Journalismus im Dritten Reich* (Munich, 1989), 9–19, here 12–13. See also Hitler cited in Oron J. Hale, *The Captive Press in the Third Reich* (Princeton, 1964), 78; and Joseph Wulf, *Presse und Funk im Dritten Reich: Eine Dokumentation* (Hamburg, 1983), 52.

22. Jürgen Hagemann, *Die Presselenkung im Dritten Reich* (Bonn, 1970), 123–4.

23. See David Stout, 'U.S. Knew Early of Nazi Killings in Asylums, Official Documents Show', *New York Times* (29 July 1999). The death notices appeared in the autumn of 1940 of those killed in Grafeneck, and word of them was relayed to Washington.

24. Newspaper readership fell off in 1933 and declined slowly thereafter, partly because the Nazis shut down about 150 Communist and Socialist newspapers, and an estimated 1,300 'Jewish and Marxist' journalists were purged from the profession. The religious-oriented press was suppressed later on as well. Newspaper readership recovered and climbed again once the war began. For details, see Frei and Schmitz, *Journalismus*, esp. 36–7.

25. See the theoretical explorations of Niklaus Luhmann, *Die Realität der Massenmedien*, 2nd edn. (Opladen, 1996).

26. For a recent overview and study of the literature, see David Welch, *The Third Reich: Politics and Propaganda* (London, 1993).

27. Lisa Pine, *Nazi Family Policy, 1933–1945* (Oxford, 1997), 117.

28. For further exploration, see Eberhard Jäckel, *Hitler in History* (Hanover and London, 1984).

29. Ian Kershaw, *Hitler 1889–1936: Hubris* (London, 1998).

30. Victor Klemperer, *Ich will Zeugnis ablegen bis zum letzten: Tagebücher 1933–1945*, 2 vols. (Berlin, 1995).

31. Klemperer, *Zeugnis*, i. 185 (21 Feb. 1935).

Chapter 1

1. In 1932 President Hindenburg issued 66 emergency decrees to carry on the business of governing. By contrast, the Reichstag, whose sessions were reduced to a few days, managed to pass a mere 5 laws.

2. For an analysis of the behind-the-scenes scheming and the errors of those involved in the decision to appoint Hitler, see Henry Ashby Turner, Jr, *Hitler's Thirty Days to Power* (Reading, Mass., 1996), esp. 163–83.

3. For the general background, see Hans Mommsen, *Die verspielte Freiheit: Der Weg der Republik von Weimar in den Untergang 1918–1933* (Frankfurt am Main, 1990), 361–547; for last-minute negotiations, see Turner, *Thirty Days to Power*, esp. 135–61.

4. On the reserved stance of business until 1933, see Henry Ashby Turner, Jr, *German Big Business and the Rise of Hitler* (New York, 1985), 272–339, here 322.

5. This is the thesis of the classic local history of William Sheridan Allen, *The Nazi Seizure of Power: The Experience of a Single German Town, 1922–1945*, rev. edn. (New York, 1984).

6. See Detlev Peukert, *Die Weimarer Republik: Krisenjahre der Klassischen Moderne* (Frankfurt am Main, 1987), 246, 271.

7. For a general discussion, see Paul Weindling, *Health, Race and German Politics between National Unification and Nazism 1870–1945* (Cambridge, 1989), 441–87, here 457–62; Atina Grossmann, *Reforming Sex: The German Movement for Birth Control and Abortion Reform 1920–1950* (New York, 1995), 79–135.

8. Cornelie Usborne, 'The New Woman and Generational Conflict: Perceptions of Young Women's Sexual Mores in the Weimar Republic', in Mark Roseman (ed.), *Generations in Conflict: Youth Revolt and Generation Formation in Germany 1770–1968* (Cambridge, 1995), 137–63.

9. See Renate Bridenthal, ' "Professional" Housewives: Stepsisters of the Women's Movement', in Renate Bridenthal, Atina Grossmann, and Marion Kaplan (eds.), *When Biology Became Destiny: Women in Weimar and Nazi Germany* (New York, 1984), 153–73, here 164.

10. Ute Frevert, *Women in German History: From Bourgeois Emancipation to Sexual Liberation*, trans. S. McKinnon-Evans (New York, 1989), 209.

11. See Jürgen W. Falter, *Hitlers Wähler* (Munich, 1991), 136–46.

12. For an overview, see Richard Bessel, 'Germany from War to Dictatorship', in Mary Fulbrook (ed.), *German History since 1800* (London, 1997), 235–57.

13. See the excellent discussion in Falter, *Hitlers Wähler*, 292–3. See also Peter Fritzsche, *Germans into Nazis* (Cambridge, Mass., 1998), here 155.

14. See Anthony McElligott, *Contested City: Municipal Politics and the Rise of Nazism in Altona, 1917–1937* (Ann Arbor, 1998), 182.

15. By Jan. 1933, the Nazi Storm Troopers grew to well over half a million and as a united force was much the largest and most fearsome of the right-wing combat leagues. The Socialists' uniformed corps (the Reichsbanner), at least on paper, was far larger at around 3.5 million, of whom an estimated 1 million were active. The Communists' paramilitary group (the Rote Frontkämpferbund) made up in activism what it lacked in numerical strength, but even so, if we include the

youth corps, there were around 100,000 uniformed members in Communist organizations. See James M. Diehl, *Para-Military Politics in Weimar Germany* (Bloomington, Ind., 1977), 293–7.

16. See McElligott, *Contested City*, 194.

17. See Turner, *Thirty Days to Power*, 109–10.

18. The three leading parties in the last four federal elections were the NSDAP, the SPD, and the KPD. See the convenient table in Holger H. Herwig, *Hammer or Anvil? Modern Germany 1648–Present* (Lexington, Mass., 1994), 247. For a social analysis of voting, see Thomas Childers, *The Nazi Voter: The Social Foundations of Fascism in Germany, 1919–1933* (Chapel Hill, NC, 1983), 192–261; for the Party itself, see Michael H. Kater, *The Nazi Party: A Social Profile of Members and Leaders, 1919–1945* (Cambridge, Mass., 1983), 51–71.

19. For an extensive examination of this topic, see Richard F. Hamilton, *Who Voted for Hitler?* (Princeton, 1982), here 98.

20. See Falter, *Hitlers Wähler*, here 327–39.

21. For the voting behaviour of the unemployed, see ibid., here 310.

22. Fritzsche, *Germans into Nazis*, 204.

23. M. Rainer Lepsius, 'From Fragmented Party Democracy to Government by Emergency Decree and National Socialist Takeover: Germany', in Juan L. Linz and Alfred Stepan (eds.), *The Breakdown of Democratic Regimes* (Baltimore, 1978), 34–79, here 46–9.

24. See Ian Kershaw, *Hitler 1889–1936: Hubris* (London, 1998), 439.

25. Golo Mann, *Deutsche Geschichte des 19. und 20. Jahrhunderts* (Frankfurt am Main, 1967), 811.

26. See Domarus (ed.), *Hitler Reden*, i. 229–37, here 232–3.

27. For the concept of 'legal revolution', see Karl Dietrich Bracher, *The German Dictatorship: The Origins, Structure, and Effects of National Socialism*, trans. J. Steinberg (Harmondsworth, 1973), 243–52.

28. See e.g. Ulrich Herbert, ' "Die guten und die schlecten Zeiten": Überlegungen zur diachronen Analyse lebensgeschichtlicher Interviews', in Lutz Niethammer (ed.), *'Die Jahre weiß man nicht, wo man die heute hinsetzen soll': Faschismus Erfahrung im Ruhrgebiet* (Berlin, 1983), 67–96.

29. For an analysis, see R. J. Overy, *War and Economy in the Third Reich* (Oxford, 1994), 37–67.

30. See Gabriele Czarnowski, 'The Value of Marriage for the "Volksgemeinschaft": Policies towards Women and Marriage under National Socialism', in Richard Bessel (ed.), *Fascist Italy and Nazi Germany: Comparisons and Contrasts* (Cambridge, 1996), 94–112.

31. Alison Owings, *Frauen: German Women Recall the Third Reich* (New Brunswick, NJ, 1993), here 119. For the other examples, see 36, 59 and 73, 187.

32. See Dan P. Silverman, *Hitler's Economy: Nazi Work Creation Programs, 1933–1936* (Cambridge, Mass., 1998), 69–96.

33. See R. J. Overy, *The Nazi Economic Recovery, 1932–1938*, 2nd edn. (Cambridge, 1996), here 60.

34. For a recent account, see Doris L. Bergen, *Twisted Cross: The German Christian Movement in the Third Reich* (Chapel Hill, NC, 1996), here 7.

35. See Ernst Christian Helmreich, *The German Churches under Hitler: Background, Struggle, and Epilogue* (Detroit, 1979), 142–3.
36. Historians in the former German Democratic Republic stated that of 300,000 members in the KPD up to 1933, around half experienced some form of persecution. These figures are cited by Hartmut Mehringer, *Widerstand und Emigration: Das NS-Regime und seine Gegner* (Munich, 1997), here 84.
37. Mehringer (ibid. 84) suggests that economic recovery from 1935 was at least as important as the arrests of activists and the exhaustion of others in the elimination of the reservoirs of strength to carry on the illegal activities. For the context of this consensus, see Ulrich Herbert, 'Arbeiterschaft im "Dritten Reich" ', in his, *Arbeit, Volkstum, Weltanschauung: Über Fremde und Deutsche im 20. Jahrhundert* (Frankfurt am Main, 1995), 79–119, here 113.
38. See Alf Lüdtke, 'The Appeal of Exterminating "Others": German Workers and the Limits of Resistance', in Michael Geyer and John W. Boyer (eds.), *Resistance against the Third Reich 1933–1990* (Chicago, 1994), 53–74, here 66–7.
39. Koppel S. Pinson, *Modern Germany: Its History and Civilization*, 2nd edn. (New York, 1967), here 604.
40. Kershaw, *Hitler 1889–1936*, 495. The election and plebiscite results are in Domarus (ed.), *Hitler Reden*, i. 331. In the plebiscite, 95.1 per cent voted 'yes' and 4.9 per cent voted 'no'.
41. See the still hopeful July/Aug. report of *Sopade* (1934), 347–56.
42. See e.g. Hitler's 20 Aug. 1934 speech in Domarus (ed.), *Hitler Reden*, i. 445.
43. See the Apr./May report of *Sopade* (1938), here 395.
44. For a detailed analysis, see Kater, *Nazi Party*, here 263.
45. Mathilde Jamin, *Zwischen den Klassen: Zur Sozialstruktur der SA-Führerschaft* (Wuppertal, 1984), here 1–5.
46. For these figures, see Jill Stephenson, *The Nazi Organization of Women* (London, 1981), 139 and 148.
47. Adelheid von Saldern, 'Victims or Perpetrators? Controversies about the Role of Women in the Nazi State', in David F. Crew (ed.), *Nazism and German Society 1933–1945* (London, 1994), 141–65, here 151. See also Gisela Bock, 'Ordinary Women in Nazi Germany: Perpetrators, Victims, Followers, and Bystanders', in Dalia Ofer and Lenore J. Weitzman (eds.), *Women in the Holocaust* (New Haven, 1999), 85–100, esp. 91. For different conclusions, see in general Stephenson, *Nazi Organization of Women*.
48. See esp. Tim Mason, *Nazism, Fascism and the Working Class*, ed. Jane Caplan (Cambridge, 1995), 150.
49. See e.g. *VB* (1, 2, 3 Feb. 1933) for stories of Communists killing Nazis.
50. *RGBL*, i. 35–41 (6 Feb. 1933), 'Verordnung des Reichspräsidenten zum Schutz des deutschen Volkes vom 4. Feb. 1933'.
51. 'Zum Schutz des deutschen Volkes: Die Verordnung gegen Gefährdung der Sicherheit und gegen Landesverrat', in *VB* (7 Feb. 1933).
52. Among the stories in the *VB* (5/6 Feb. 1933) were some under the following headlines: 'Wieder drei SA-Männer ermordet'; 'Maschinengewehr bei Kommunisten beschlagnahmt'; 'Erfolgreiche Aktion der Breslauer Polizei gegen Marxisten'.

53. See the front-page headline, 'Aufsehenerregende Entlaßungen hoher Beamter im Berliner Polizeipräsidium', in *VB* (19–20 Feb. 1933). On the same page was an account of Communists shooting at the SA, in 'Blutiger Terror in Berlin'.

54. 'Veränderungen bei der Preußischen Polizei', in *BM* (5 Feb. 1933).

55. 'Zwangsweise beurlaubt', in *BM* (14 Feb. 1933).

56. For Dortmund, see 'Der neue Geist in der Polizei'; for Berlin, see 'Das Berliner Polizeipräsidium unter nationalsozialistischer Führung', in *VB* (18 Feb. 1933).

57. See the front-page account, 'Rücksichtloser Waffengebrauch gegen den roten Terror!', in *VB* (22 Feb. 1933).

58. 'Umbau der Politischen Polizei', in *VB* (25 Feb. 1933).

59. See e.g. 'Geheime Staatspolizei in Preußen', in *BM* (28 Apr. 1933).

60. See the explanation in 'Hilfspolizei zum Schutze der staatsbewußten Bevölkerung', in *VB* (26–7 Feb. 1933). Note also the front-page story from Berlin, 'Kommunisten beschießen Polizei' and 'Wieder ein Hitlerjunge erstochen', in *VB* (28 Feb. 1933).

61. Georg K. Glaser, *Geheimnis und Gewalt: Ein Bericht* (Frankfurt am Main, 1956), 51–2, as cited in Eve Rosenhaft, *Beating the Fascists? The German Communists and Political Violence* (Cambridge, 1983), 214.

62. Kurt Daluege's report (1 Feb. 1934) is cited in Peter Leßmann, *Die preußische Schutzpolizei in der Weimarer Republik* (Düsseldorf, 1989), 388.

63. See Hans-Dieter Schmid, *Gestapo Leipzig: Politische Abteilung des Polizei-präsidiums und Staatspolizeistelle Leipzig, 1933–1945* (Beucha, 1997), 17–18.

64. See George C. Browder, *Hitler's Enforcers: The Gestapo and the SS Security Service in the Nazi Revolution* (New York, 1996), 85.

65. For an examination of the 'purge' and relevant literature, see Robert Gellately, *The Gestapo and German Society: Enforcing Racial Policy 1933–1945* (Oxford, 1990), 50–7.

66. Rudolf Diels, *Lucifer ante portas . . . es spricht der erste Chef der Gestapo* (Stuttgart, 1950), 194.

67. *RGBL*, i. 83 (28 Feb. 1933), 'Verordnung des Reichspräsidenten zum Schutz von Volk und Staat vom 28 Feb. 1933'.

68. See e.g. 'Reich übernimmt Polizei', in *BM* (9 Mar. 1933).

69. See 'Polizeiaktionen im Reich', in *VB* (1 Mar. 1933); 'Die Polizeiaktionen werden erfolgreich fortgesetzt: Über 2000 Verhaftungen'; and for a report from Berlin, 'Blutiger Kommunisten-Terror', in *VB* (3 Mar. 1933).

70. See Detlev Peukert, *Die KPD im Widerstand: Verfolgung und Untergrundarbeit an Rhein und Ruhr 1933 bis 1945* (Wuppertal, 1980), 83–9; Allan Merson, *Communist Resistance in Nazi Germany* (London, 1985), 45–61.

71. See e.g. 'Schwer bewaffnete Kommunisten' and 'Die Ausrottung des Kommun-ismus', in *VB* (8 Mar. 1933); 'Erfolgreiche Polizeiaktionen gegen den Marxismus', in *VB* (15 Mar. 1933); 'Erfolgreiche Polizeiaktionen gegen Marxisten', in *VB* (25 Mar. 1933). This last story was one of the first to mention concentration camps and 'protective custody'—although this last term was used as early as 10 Mar. 1933 in the *VB*. These stories often contained many shorter ones from various cities across Germany.

72. 'Konzentrationslager', in *BM* (21 Mar. 1933).

73. See e.g. the reaction of a liberal newspaper, 'Der Brandstifter van der Lubbe', in *BM* (2 Mar. 1933).
74. See Kershaw, *Hitler 1889–1936*, 456, 460.
75. See Richard J. Evans, *Rituals of Retribution: Capital Punishment in Germany 1600–1987* (Oxford, 1996), 619–20, 665–9.
76. 'Rückgang der Todesfälle bei politischen Gewalttaten', in *BM* (6 May 1933).
77. See 'Rotmord wird ausgerottet', in *VB* (8 Sept. 1933); and 'Vier Todesstrafen beantragt', in *VB* (17–18 Sept. 1933). For a description of the events in Altona and Cologne, including the news coverage, see Evans, *Rituals of Retribution*, 644–6.
78. See Victor Klemperer, *Ich will Zeugnis ablegen bis zum letzten: Tagebücher 1933–1945* (Berlin, 1995), i. 43 (entry 28 July 1933).
79. See e.g. 'Viele Richter versetzt', in *BM* (21 Mar. 1933).
80. 'Der Wortlaut der Notverordnungen über Amnestie und Sondergerichte', in *VB* (24 Mar. 1933). The instructive term used in the 'Presidential amnesty decree' was '*Straffreiheit*', that is, impunity from criminal proceedings.
81. See *RGBL*, i. 135–8 (22 Mar. 1933), 'Verordnung des Reichspräsidenten zur Abwehr heimtückischer Angriffe gegen die Regierung der nationalen Erhebung vom 21 März 1933', 'Verordnung der Reichsregierung über die Bildung von Sondergerichten vom 21 März 1933'. See also '13 Sondergerichte in Preußen', in *VB* (28 Mar. 1933).
82. Lothar Gruchmann, *Justiz im Dritten Reich 1933–1945: Anpassung und Unterwerfung in der Ära Gürtner* (Munich, 1988), 946.
83. 'Neue Notverordnungen', in *BM* (22 Mar. 1933).
84. See 'Kabinettsberatung über Todesstrafen für politische Verbrecher', in *VB* (25 Mar. 1933); and *RGBL*, i. 151 (31 Mar. 1933), 'Gesetz über Verhängung und Vollzug der Todesstrafe vom 29. März 1933'.
85. *RGBL*, i. 341–8 (30 Apr. 1934), 'Gesetz zur Änderung von Vorschriften des Strafrechts und des Strafverfahrens vom 24. Apr. 1934'.
86. This concept was first used in 1941 by Ernst Fraenkel, *The Dual State*, trans. E. A. Shils (New York, 1969), 3.
87. 'Schaffung eines Geheimen Staatspolizeiamtes', in *VB* (28 Apr. 1933).
88. For a study of Gestapo personnel, including their local distribution and organization, see Gellately, *Gestapo and German Society*, 44–76.
89. See *IMT*, xxix. 250–2, Dokument 2104-PS and 2105-PS.
90. 'Der neue Geist im Münchener Polizeipräsidium', in *VB* (15 Mar. 1933).
91. Shlomo Aronson, *Reinhard Heydrich und die Frühgeschichte von Gestapo und SD* (Stuttgart, 1971), 104.
92. This point is convincingly argued by Karl Schleunes, *The Twisted Road to Auschwitz: Nazi Policy Toward German Jews 1933–1939* (Urbana, Ill., 1970), 62–91, here 71.
93. See Christoph Graf, *Politische Polizei zwischen Demokratie und Diktatur* (Berlin, 1983), 233–42.
94. 'Der neue Geist im Münchener Polizeipräsidium', in *VB* (15 Mar. 1933).
95. See Anlage 2, 'Verordnung des Staatsministeriums des Innern vom 1. Apr. 1933', in Martin Faatz, *Vom Staatsschutz zum Gestapo-Terror: Politische Polizei in Bayern in*

der Endphase der Weimarer Republik und der Anfangsphase der nationalsozialistischen Diktatur (Würzburg, 1995), 570; see also 396–7.

96. See Andreas Seeger, 'Gestapo Müller': *Die Karriere eines Schreibtischtäters* (Berlin 1996), 32–41.
97. Graf, *Politische Polizei*, 232.
98. Browder, *Hitler's Enforcers*, 78; see also Peukert, *KPD im Widerstand*, 92.
99. 'Um die Entlassung politischer Schutzhäftlinge', in *DD* (9 May 1933).
100. For a detailed examination of these events, see Gellately, *Gestapo and German Society*, 36–40. For a local case study and relevant literature, see 94–104.
101. 'Warnung an Hetzer und Drahtzieher', in *FZ* (16 June 1933); 'Festnahme im Reich', in *VZ* (28 June 1933); 'Ebert und Heilmann im Konzentrationslager', in *HN* (9 Aug. 1933).
102. See George C. Browder, *Foundations of the Nazi Police State: The Formation of Sipo and SD* (Lexington, Ky., 1990), 239.
103. See e.g. 'Auf dem Wege zum einheitlichen Staatsschutzkorps: Weitere Aufnahme von Polizeiangehörigen in die SS', in *BBZ* (6 Jan. 1938).
104. Robert Koehl, *The Black Corps: The Structure and Power Struggles of the Nazi SS* (Madison, 1983), 159–60.
105. 'Polizei und SS wachsen zusammen', in *VB* (8 May 1937).
106. Cited in Ulrich Herbert, *Best: Biographische Studien über Radikalismus, Weltanschauung und Vernunft 1903–1989* (Bonn, 1996), 170.
107. Reinhard Heydrich, 'Die Bekämpfung der Staatsfeinde', in *DR* (15 Apr. 1936).
108. See Edward B. Westermann, ' "Ordinary Men" or "Ideological Soldiers"? Police Battalion 310 in Russia, 1942', *GSR* (1998), 41–68, here 45.
109. The notion of 'schooling' the police into becoming Nazis is mentioned by Kurt Daluege, *Tag der deutschen Polizei 1934* (Munich, 1935), 9; it was already underway by 1934. For later examples, see e.g. IfZ, Dc15.16, *Schulungs-Leitheft für SS-Führeranwärter der Sicherheitspolizei und des SD* (n.d. [1940]); also in IfZ, Dc01.07: RFSS Rund Erl. (2 June 1940): 'Richtlinien für die Durchführung der weltanschaulichen Schulung der Ordnungspolizei während der Kriegszeit'. See also *Befehlsblatt des Chefs der Sipo und SD* (20 Mar. 1945), 58–60.
110. See e.g. *Schriftenreihe für die weltanschauliche Schulung der Ordnungspolizei* (1941 ff.), which included special issues on race and 'blood questions'.
111. See Peter Longerich, *Die braunen Bataillone: Geschichte der SA* (Munich, 1989), 176.
112. Klemperer, *Zeugnis*, i. 9 (entry 10 Mar. 1933).
113. Bay HStA: Abt. I, MF 19/67403: Kabinettssitzung (7 Apr. 1933).
114. See Saul Friedländer, *Nazi Germany and the Jews, i. The Years of Persecution 1933–1939* (New York, 1997), 15. For additional details, see Ino Arndt and Heinz Boberach, 'Deutsches Reich', in Wolfgang Benz (ed.), *Dimension des Völkermords: Die Zahl der jüdischen Opfer des Nationalsozialismus* (Munich, 1991), 23–65.
115. See Bergen, *Twisted Cross*, 83–4.
116. See Jeremy Noakes, 'The Development of Nazi Policy towards the German–Jewish "Mischlinge" 1933–1945', in *Leo Baeck Institute Year Book* (1989), 291–354, here 293.
117. For a useful reminder of this fact, see Friedländer, *Nazi Germany and the Jews*, here 157. For a story of one person of 'mixed race', see Owings, *Frauen*, 32–53.

118. For a detailed recent analysis, see Beate Meyer, '*Jüdische Mischlinge*': *Rassenpolitik und Verfolgungserfahrung 1933–1945* (Hamburg, 1999), 162–259.

119. See table 4, Gerhard Paul, *Aufstand der Bilder: Die NS-Propaganda vor 1933* (Bonn, 1992), 220.

120. The poster is reprinted in Hagen Schulze, *Germany: A New History*, trans. D. L. Schneider (Cambridge, Mass., 1998), 240.

121. See Anthony Kauders, *German Politics and the Jews: Düsseldorf and Nuremberg 1910–1933* (Oxford, 1996), 182–3.

122. Ian Kershaw, *The 'Hitler Myth': Image and Reality in the Third Reich* (Oxford, 1987), 232–4.

123. For example, in Berlin on 9 Mar. numerous East European Jews living in the Jewish quarter (Scheuenviertel) were picked up and taken to SA 'camps'. See Longerich, *Die braunen Bataillone*, 170.

124. For a general survey, see Peter Longerich, *Politik der Vernichtung: Eine Gesamtdarstellung der nationalsozialistichen Judenverfolgung* (Munich, 1998), 25–30.

125. For a copy of the law and others applying to the civil service, see Ingo von Münch (ed.), *Gesetze des NS-Staates*, 3rd edn. (Paderborn, 1994), 26–8.

126. 'Nur deutschblütige Beamte dürfen die Staatsautorität verkörpern', in *VB* (4 Apr. 1933); 'Säuberung des Beamtentums', in *VB* (13 Apr. 1933).

127. Jane Caplan, *Government without Administration: State and Civil Society in Weimar and Nazi Germany* (Oxford, 1988), 143–6. For a local examination, see Karl Teppe, *Provinz, Partei, Staat* (Münster, 1977), 36–68.

128. The phrases are from government officials as cited in Horst Göppinger, *Juristen jüdischer Abstammung im 'Dritten Reich'*, 2nd edn. (Munich, 1990), 59; see also 'Aufbruch zum Recht', in *VB* (6 Apr. 1933).

129. 'Gegen jüdische Richter und Anwälte', in *BM* (1 Apr. 1933).

130. See Kershaw, *Hitler 1889–1936*, 472–3.

131. See 'Überall Boykott-Komitees gegen das Judentum', in *VB* (29 Mar. 1933); and 'Aufruf an die Partei', in *VB* (30 Mar. 1933).

132. See the front-page story 'Gegenschlag gegen die jüdische Greul-Propaganda', in *VB* (28 Mar. 1933). From the endless articles, see e.g. 'Jüdischer "Kriegsrat" in Amerika verkündete Vernichtung der deutschen Wirtschaft durch Weltboykott', in *VB* (4 Apr. 1933); 'Die jüdisch-kommunistische Hetze: Boykott in England, Rumänien und Polen', in *VB* (9–10 Apr. 1933); 'Enthüllungen über die jüdisch-marxistische Hetzzentrale in Prag', in *VB* (10 Aug. 1933).

133. See Claudia Koonz, *Mothers in the Fatherland: Women, the Family and Nazi Politics* (New York, 1987), 190.

134. 'Aufruf an die Partei', in *VB* (30 Mar. 1933).

135. 'Der Reichskanzler rechtfertigt den Lügen-Abwehrkampf vor dem Kabinett', in *VB* (30 Mar. 1933).

136. See 'Erste Boykottanordnungen' and 'So sehen die Abwehr-Plakate aus', in *VB* (31 Mar. 1933).

137. 'Stuttgart im Abwehrkampf voran!', in *NS-Kurier* (1 Apr. 1933), reprinted in Paul Sauer (ed.), *Dokumente über die Verfolgung der jüdischen Bürger in*

Baden-Württemberg durch das nationalsozialistische Regime 1933–1945 (Stuttgart, 1966), i. 9–10.

138. 'Boykott-Posten: Abwehrkampf in Württemberg', in *NS-Kurier* (3 Apr. 1933), reprinted in Sauer (ed.), *Dokumente*, i. 10–12.

139. Johannes Ludwig, *Boykott, Enteignung, Mord: Die 'Entjudung' der deutschen Wirtschaft* (Hamburg, 1989), 113–14.

140. See the account of Kurt Schatzky, in Monika Richarz (ed.), *Jüdisches Leben in Deutschland: Selbstzeugnisse zur Sozialgeschichte 1918–1945* (Stuttgart, 1982), 292–300, here 293.

141. *FZ* (2 Apr. 1933), reprinted in *Dokumente zur Geschichte der Frankfurter Juden 1933–1945* (Frankfurt am Main, 1963), 22–3.

142. See Schleunes, *Twisted Road*, 88; also Michael Burleigh and Wolfgang Wippermann, *The Racial State: Germany 1933–1945* (Cambridge, 1991), 77–8; Ian Kershaw, *Popular Opinion and Political Dissent in the Third Reich: Bavaria 1933–1945* (Oxford, 1983), 232.

143. 'Boykottpause bis Mittwoch', in *VB* (2–3 Mar. 1933).

144. 'Vorbereitung des Dauerboykotts', in *VB* (4 Apr. 1933).

145. 'Warum der Einfluß des Judentum gebrochen werden muß', in *VB* (19 July 1933).

146. See Klemperer, *Zeugnis*, i. 15 (30 Mar. 1933).

147. Edwin Landau's account is in Richarz (ed.), *Jüdisches Leben*, 99–108; for an example of sympathy offered to the Jews (in Bingen), see the story of Marta Appel, 231–43.

148. 'Der Zionismus erobert die deutsche Judenschaft', in *VB* (21 July 1933).

149. See Max Reiner's report in Richarz (ed.), *Jüdisches Leben*, 109–19.

150. Klemperer, *Zeugnis*, i. 25 (25 Apr. 1933).

151. Richard Bessel, *Political Violence and the Rise of Nazism: The Storm Troopers in Eastern Germany 1925–1934* (New Haven, 1984), 108.

152. See e.g. Kershaw, *Popular Opinion*, here 239.

153. For a full account, see Göppinger, *Juristen*, 49–111, here 51. On the purges of the professions, see Konrad H. Jarausch, *The Unfree Professions: German Lawyers, Teachers, and Engineers, 1900–1950* (New York, 1990), 115–227.

154. See 'Aktion gegen jüdische Richter in Frankfurt a.M.', in *VB* (1 Apr. 1933); also Göppinger, *Juristen*, 54–5; 'Berliner Strafgerichte judenrein', in *VB* (21 Mar. 1933).

155. See Geoffrey J. Giles, *Students and National Socialism in Germany* (Princeton, 1985), 14–72; for background, see Michael H. Kater, *Studentenschaft und Rechtsradikalismus in Deutschland 1918–1933* (Hamburg, 1975).

156. Giles, *Students*, 121.

157. 'Entfernung von Marxisten und Juden aus Lehrämtern und Anstalten', in *VB* (14–15 Apr. 1933).

158. 'Der Reichskanzler umreißt die rasse-hygenischen Aufgaben der Ärzte', in *VB* (7 Apr. 1933).

159. See Michael H. Kater, *Doctors under Hitler* (Chapel Hill, NC, 1989), 177–221, here 183–5.

160. See *Nazism Docs.*, ii. 458.

161. Kater, *Doctors*, 38.

162. On the reshaping of doctors' professional organizations, see Kater, *Doctors*, 19–25.
163. Gisela Bock, *Zwangssterilisation im Nationalsozialismus: Studien zur Rassenpolitik und Frauenpolitik* (Opladen, 1986), 232, 238.
164. Czarnowski, 'Women and Marriage', 98.
165. See the autobiographical accounts reprinted in Geert Platner (ed.), *Schule im Dritten Reich: Erziehung zum Tod? Eine Dokumentation* (Munich, 1983), 129–83.
166. For a large collection of newspaper clippings from 1933, see *Das Schwarzbuch, Tatsachen und Dokumente: Die Lage der Juden in Deutschland 1933*, ed. Comité des délégations juives (Paris, 1934; repr. Frankfurt am Main, 1983).
167. Bessel, *Political Violence*, 113.
168. Kershaw, *Popular Opinion*, 236–7. In fact, far from being sent to prison, in July Bär returned to the pub where the pogrom began, and shot dead the Jewish publican as well as severely wounded his son. He was again tried and found guilty, but merely put on probation.
169. Marion A. Kaplan, *Between Dignity and Despair: Jewish Life in Nazi Germany* (New York, 1998), 63.
170. Peter Gay, *My German Question: Growing up in Nazi Berlin* (New Haven, 1998), 75–83.
171. 'Die erfolgreiche Arbeit des Geheimen Staatspolizeiamtes', in *DAZ* (24 Nov. 1933); 'Das Geheime Staatspolizeiamt an der Arbeit', in *VB* (25 Nov. 1933); 'Neuorganisierung der Geheimen Staatspolizei', in *VB* (3–4 Dec. 1933).
172. See *IMT*, xlii. 300–2, Dokument Gestapo-31, reprint of an article from the *Berliner Lokalanzeiger* (10 Mar. 1934) further indicating that the need for concentration camps was diminishing 'because of domestic political tranquillity'. This point was made by Göring also in 'Die Stellung der Geheimen Staatspolizei in der Verwaltung', in *VB* (18–19 Mar. 1934).
173. 'Die Stellung der Geheimen Staatspolizei in der Verwaltung', in *VB* (18–19 Mar. 1934).
174. 'Die Aufgaben der Politischen Polizei', in *VB* (23 Jan. 1934).
175. See e.g. 'Reichsführer SS Kommandeur der Politischen Polizei in Hamburg, Mecklenburg und Lübeck', in *VB* (28 Nov. 1933 and 12 Dec. 1933; 22 Dec.1933).
176. Göring decree 20 Nov. 1934, cited in full in Hans Buchheim, 'Die SS—Das Herrschaftsinstrument', in Hans Buchheim et al., *Anatomie des SS-Staates*, 5ᵗʰ edn. (Munich, 1989), i. 43.
177. For a detailed account and citation of the literature, see Browder, *Foundations*, 50–90.
178. 'Die Geheimen Staatspolizeiämter aller deutschen Länder in einer Hand vereinigt', in *VB* (21 Apr. 1934).
179. 'Gesetz über den Neuaufbau des Reiches vom 30 Januar 1934', reprinted in Martin Hirsch, Diemut Majer, and Jürgen Meinck (eds.), *Recht, Verwaltung und Justiz im Nationalsozialismus* (Cologne, 1984), 132.
180. See Hans-Ulrich Thamer, *Verführung und Gewalt: Deutschland 1933–1945*, 2ⁿᵈ edn. (Berlin, 1986), 307.
181. See 'Vorläufiges Gesetz zur Gleichschaltung der Länder mit dem Reich vom 31 März 1933' and 'Zweites Gesetz zur Gleichschaltung der Länder mit dem Reich

vom 7. Apr. 1933', in Hirsch, Majer, and Meinck (eds.), *Recht, Verwaltung und Justiz*, 127–32.

182. The process was covered extensively in the press: see e.g. 'Die Vereinheitlichung der Justiz', in *VB* (24 Oct. 1934); 'Das Reichsjustizministerium und das Preußische Justizministerium vereinigt', in *VB* (30 Oct. 1934); 'Der Weg zur Reichsjustiz', in *VB* (16–17 Dec. 1934); 'Ab 1. January 1935 einheitliche Reichsjustizverwaltung', in *VB* (22 Dec. 1934).

183. Klemperer, *Zeugnis*, i. 69 (entry 14 Nov. 1933).

Chapter 2

1. There were 121,252 reports of theft and 48,477 of armed robbery to the Prussian police in such large cities in 1927; these figures grew in each of the following years and by 1932 nearly doubled to 214,696 cases of theft and 99,095 of armed robbery. See the tables in Patrick Wagner, *Volksgemeinschaft ohne Verbrecher: Konzeptionen und Praxis der Kriminalpolizei in der Zeit der Weimarer Republik und des Nationalsozialismus* (Hamburg, 1996), 31–5. Youth also had problems, even while their convictions for crime did not change that much. For the period as a whole, see Detlev Peukert, *Jugend zwischen Krieg und Krise: Lebenswelten von Arbeiterjungen in der Weimarer Republik* (Cologne, 1987), here 273–7.

2. A colourful introduction is Otto Friedrich, *Before the Deluge: A Portrait of Berlin in the 1920s* (New York, 1972).

3. See the contemporary literature reprinted in Anton Kaes et al. (eds.), *The Weimar Republic Sourcebook* (Berkeley, 1994), 721–41.

4. For a synthesis, see Ute Frevert, *Women in German Society: From Bourgeois Emancipation to Sexual Liberation*, trans. S. McKinnon-Evans (New York, 1989), 168–216.

5. He kept a diary and published his stories based on them in 1935. See Christopher Isherwood, 'Goodbye to Berlin', in his *Berlin Stories* (New York, 1954), 203.

6. For the interview, see Alison Owings, *Frauen: German Women Recall the Third Reich* (New Brunswick, NJ, 1993), 83–98, here 88.

7. 'Todesstrafe und Zuchthaus für Anschläge und Verrat', in *VB* (2 Mar. 1933).

8. 'Der neue Geist in der Polizei', in *VB* (18 Feb. 1933).

9. See 'Berlins Polizeipräsident über seine Aufgaben', in *VB* (24 Feb. 1933); 'Für Ruhe und Ordnung, Zucht und Sitte', in *DA* (17 Feb. 1933); 'Neue Männer in Preußen', in *BT* (16 Feb. 1933).

10. 'Wechsel in den Polizeipräsidien', 'Die neuen Männer', in *VB* (28 Mar. 1933).

11. See e.g. 'Strafverschärfung für Verrat militärischer Geheimnisse—Straffreiheit für Mensuren', in *VB* (21–2 May 1933); 'Schwere Strafen für Kapital und Steuerflucht', in *VB* (10 June 1933).

12. 'Der Strafvollzug wird verschärft: Verbrecher sollen es in Zukunft nicht noch besser haben als Erwerbslose', in *VB* (14 July 1933).

13. Johannes Tuchel shows Hitler's key role in the creation of the terror in several studies; see e.g. his collection of documents, *Die Inspektion der Konzentrationslager 1938–1945* (Berlin, 1994), esp. 40 ff.

14. Christoph Graf, *Politische Polizei zwischen Demokratie und Diktatur* (Berlin, 1983), 282. See also Edward N.

Peterson, *The Limits of Hitler's Power* (Princeton, 1969), 166–79; Peter Diehl-Thiele, *Partei und Staat im Dritten Reich* (Munich, 1971), 75–85.

15. See Günter Neliba, *Wilhelm Frick: Der Legalist des Unrechtsstaates: Eine politische Biographie* (Paderborn, 1992), 253.

16. In the early months of 1934 the Reich Ministry of the Interior tried on at least three separate occasions to curtail abuses, to insist on proper police procedures, and to limit the involvement of the Party and the SA. The Ministry did not want 'protective custody' over-used, but reserved only for those who 'directly' endangered 'public security and order'. Police measures were not supposed to be used as punishment for indictable offences, nor applied to those whose behaviour was considered by police (or others) as reprehensible, but was not politically suspect (or criminal). Martin Broszat, 'Konzentrationslager', in Hans Buchheim et al., *Anatomie des SS-Staates*, 5th edn. (Munich, 1989), ii. 33; Hans Tesmer, 'Die Schutzhaft und ihre rechtlichen Grundlagen', *Deutsches Recht* (1937), in Martin Hirsch, Diemut Majer, and Jürgen Meinck (eds.), *Recht, Verwaltung und Justiz im Nationalsozialismus* (Cologne, 1984), 332.

17. See e.g. 'Konzentrationslager für Steuerverweigerer', in *VB* (10 Jan. 1934); 'Unsozialer Betriebsführer in Schutzhaft', in *DA* (28 Oct. 1934); 'Neue Schutzhäftlinge', in *DD* (27 Feb. 1934); 'Verlagsdirektor Bitter-Recklinghausen in Schutzhaft', in *DAZ* (17 Mar. 1934); 'Schutzhaft gegen einen Bergwerksdirektor', in *DD* (17 Apr. 1934); 'Ein Mieter in Schutzhaft', in *BT* (18 Dec. 1934).

18. 'Gegen gewissenlose Ausbeuter', in *VB* (7 July 1933).

19. Wolfgang Ayaß, *'Asoziale' im Nationalsozialismus* (Stuttgart, 1995), 24, estimates 'several tens of thousands'. Michael Burleigh and Wolfgang Wippermann, *The Racial State: Germany 1933–1945* (Cambridge, 1991), 170, put the number taken into custody as high as 100,000.

20. The first story is from the *DZ*, the second from the *VZ*, as cited in Ayaß, *'Asoziale'*, 39.

21. In *VB* (29 Dec. 1933).

22. See the case study in Justizbehörde Hamburg (ed.), *'Von Gewohnheitsverbrechern, Volksschädlingen und Asozialen . . .': Hamburger Strafurteile im Nationalsozialismus* (Hamburg, 1995), 78–83.

23. *RGBL*, i. 995–9, here 998 (27 Nov. 1933), 'Gesetz gegen gefährliche Gewohnheitsverbrecher und über Maßregeln der Sicherung und Besserung vom 24. Nov. 1933'.

24. See e.g. 'Schnelle Strafvollstreckung—Gnadenerweise nur in Ausnahmefällen', in *VB* (19 Aug. 1933).

25. 'Zum Schutz von Volk und Staat: Verfügung der Landesjustizverwaltung Hamburg', in *VB* (2 Aug. 1933).

26. After a great deal of discussion, on 14 Oct. 1936, Hitler himself decided in favour of the 'falling axe' machine, or *Fallbeil*. They used this curious term to avoid the word 'guillotine', not just a foreign word, but one that invited invidious comparisons between Nazi Germany and the French Revolution. For the background, see

Richard J. Evans, *Rituals of Retribution: Capital Punishment in Germany 1600–1987* (Oxford, 1996), 651–9.

27. 'Nationalsozialistisches Strafrecht', in *VB* (30 Sept. 1933).

28. See e.g. 'Das kommende deutsche Strafrecht', in *VB* (31 Aug. 1934); Hans Frank, 'Recht—eine Angelegenheit der Volksgemeinschaft', in *VB* (2 July 1935); Roland Freisler, 'Volksverrat—das schwerste Verbrechen', in *VB* (3 Aug. 1935); and the essays in Franz Gürtner and Roland Freisler, *Das neue Strafbuch: Grundsätzliche Gedanken zum Geleit*, 2nd edn. (Berlin, 1936).

29. See Hans Frank, 'Revolution im Strafrecht', in *VB* (5 July 1935).

30. 'Wichtige Änderung des Strafgesetzbuches', in *VB* (6 July 1935).

31. See 'Mahnmarken auf Straf- und Streitakten in Thüringen', in *VB* (10 July 1934). For the larger issues, Martin Broszat, 'Zur Perversion der Strafjustiz im Dritten Reich', *VfZ* (1958), 390–443, here 394.

32. Full text of this speech is in *VB* (31 Jan. 1937).

33. 'Stabchef Röhm und mehrere SA-Führer erschossen', in *VB* (3 July 1934).

34. Victor Klemperer, *Ich will Zeugnis ablegen bis zum letzten: Tagebücher 1933–1945* (Berlin, 1995), i. 121 (entry 14 July 1934).

35. See Richard Bessel, *Political Violence and the Rise of Nazism: The Storm Troopers in Eastern Germany 1925–1934* (New Haven, 1984), 139–40; Peter Longerich, *Die braunen Bataillone: Geschichte der SA* (Munich, 1989), 227–30; Hans-Ulrich Thamer, *Verführung und Gewalt: Deutschland 1933–1945*, 2nd edn. (Berlin, 1986), 333; and Gunter d'Alquen, 'Unsere Pflicht', in *VB* (24/25 June 1934).

36. Lagebericht des Regierungspräsidenten von Osnabrück (10 Aug. 1934) and Lagebericht der Staatspolizeistelle an das Geheime Staatspolizeiamt (Juli 1934) of 2 Aug. 1934, in Gerd Steinwascher (ed.), *Gestapo Osnabrück meldet . . .* (Osnabrück, 1995), 77, 80.

37. See e.g. Lagebericht des Hildesheimer Regierungspräsidenten, for July 1934 (8 Aug. 1934), in Klaus Mlynek (ed.), *Gestapo Hannover meldet . . .* (Hildesheim, 1986), 198.

38. 'Straffreiheitsgesetz zur Übernahme der Amtsbefugnis des Reichspräsidenten durch Adolf Hitler', in *VB* (10 Aug. 1934).

39. See 'Entlassung von Schutzhäftlingen', in *VB* (17 Aug. 1934) and 'Weitere 742 Schutzhäftlinge entlassen', *VB* (2/3 Sept. 1934).

40. For a study of these developments, see Johannes Tuchel, *Konzentrationslager: Organisationsgeschichte und Funktion der 'Inspektion der Konzentrationslager' 1934–1938* (Boppard, 1991), 203, 307 ff.

41. In *VB* (12 Sept. 1935), reprinted in Domarus (ed.), *Hitler Reden*, ii. 525–6.

42. See Ulrich Herbert, *Best: Biographische Studien über Radikalismus, Weltanschauung und Vernunft 1903–1989* (Bonn, 1996), 168–70; Tuchel, *Konzentrationslager*, 312–13.

43. Herbert, *Best*, 151–3.

44. See the extensive explanation of Werner Spohr, 'Schutzhaft und ordentliches Gericht', in *Der Deutsche Justizbeamte* (11 Apr. 1937).

45. 'Gesetz über die Geheime Staatspolizei vom 10. Feb. 1936', in Hirsch, Majer, and Meinck (eds.), *Recht, Verwaltung und Justiz*, 329–30. See also Diemut Majer, *Grundlagen des nationalsozialistischen Rechtssystems: Führerprinzip, Sonderrecht, Einheitspartei* (Stuttgart, 1987), 110.

46. See e.g. the President of Prussian Higher Administrative Court on 'Polizei, Gesetz und Rechtskontrolle', in *FZ* (5 May 1936).

47. AES, Rund Erl. des Gestapa: Betr. 'Schutzhaft' (17 Dec. 1936).

48. 'Keine Verwaltungsklage gegen Akte der Staatspolizei', in *FZ* (23 May 1937).

49. See e.g. 'Gestapo ohne Agenten und Spitzel', in *PZ* (8 Jan. 1937); 'Aufgaben und Organe der Staatssicherung', in *RLZ* (19 Jan. 1938).

50. Werner Best, 'Die Geheime Staatspolizei' (1936), reprinted in Hirsch, Majer, and Meinck (eds.), *Recht, Verwaltung und Justiz*, 328–9.

51. 'Die präventive Aufgabe der Geheimen Staatspolizei', in *FZ* (5 Mar. 1938). 'Aufgaben und Organe der Staatssicherung: Sondervortrag der Verwaltungsakademie', in *RLZ* (19 Jan. 1938).

52. Heinrich Himmler, 'Aufgaben der Polizei des Dritten Reiches', in *HF* (12 Mar. 1937).

53. Hans Frank, 'Die rechtlichen Grundlagen der heutigen Polizeiarbeit', in *VB* (20 Jan. 1937).

54. 'Neben der siegreichen Waffe das neue Recht', in *RLZ* (5 Dec. 1939); see also his speech, 'Recht ist mehr als Justiz', in *VB* (26 Mar. 1939).

55. Werner Best, 'Volksordnung und Polizei', in *Deutsche Verwaltung* (20 Apr. 1939).

56. BA: R58/242: Gestapa an Stapo(leit)stellen (8 May 1937). For background, see Lothar Gruchmann, *Justiz im Dritten Reich 1933–1945: Anpassung und Unterwerfung in der Ära Gürtner* (Munich, 1988), 600.

57. See AES, Rund Erl. RMI: Betr. Schutzhaft, 25 Jan. 1938; and Rund Erl. des Chefs Sipo (21 Feb. 1938).

58. See Gerhard Werle, *Justiz-Strafrecht und polizeiliche Verbrechensbekämpfung im Dritten Reich* (Berlin, 1989), 564.

59. For post-war trials in which members of the Gestapo admitted they knew some of the people they charged were innocent, see Klaus Moritz and Ernst Noam (eds.), *NS-Verbrechen vor Gericht 1945–1955: Dokumente aus hessischen Justizakten* (Wiesbaden, 1978), here 286.

60. See Werle, *Justiz*, 576.

61. See Hans Mommsen, 'The Political Legacy of the Resistance: A Historiographical Critique', in David Clay Large (ed.), *Contending with Hitler* (Cambridge, 1991), 151–62, here 161.

62. See Klaus Oldenhage, 'Justizverwaltung und Lenkung der Rechtsprechung im Zweiten Weltkrieg: Die Lageberichte der Oberlandesgerichtspräsidenten und Generalstaatsanwälte (1940–1945)', in Dieter Rebentisch and Karl Teppe (eds.), *Verwaltung contra Menschenführung im Staat Hitlers* (Göttingen, 1986), 100–20, here 108.

63. See e.g. Johnpeter Horst Grill, *The Nazi Movement in Baden, 1920–1945* (Chapel Hill, NC, 1983), 377–80.

64. 'Polizei als Freund und Helfer', in *VB* (18 Dec. 1934). See also 'Ein Jahr nationalsozialistische Polizei', in *VB* (31 Jan. 1935).

65. 'Der Tag der Deutschen Polizei', in *VB* (9 Dec. 1936).

66. Reinhard Heydrich, 'Zum Tag der deutschen Polizei', in *VB* (15 Jan. 1937); 'Kamerad und Helfer', in *VB* (16 Jan. 1937).

67. 'Polizei—Träger der Staatsgewalt', in *VB* (16 Jan. 1937).

68. 'Die Aufgaben der deutschen nationalsozialistischen Polizei: Die Rundfunk-ansprache des Reichsführers SS. und Chef der deutschen Polizei', in *VB* (16 Jan. 1937).
69. Heinrich Himmler, 'Aufgaben der Polizei des Dritten Reiches', in *HF* (12 Mar. 1937).
70. 'Polizei und SS wachsen zusammen: Der Reichsführer SS vor dem Polizei-offizierkorps', in *VB* (8 May 1937); 'Rechtstellung des Reichsführers SS und Chefs der Deutschen Polizei', in *VB* (3 June 1937).
71. 'Die Abwehr der Staatsfeinde', in *VB* (26 Jan. 1938).
72. 'Kripo und Gestapo: Die Aufgaben und die Arbeit der deutschen Sicherheits-polizei', in *DN* (29 Jan. 1939).
73. 'Die deutsche Polizei im Osten', in *VB* (18 Feb. 1940).
74. 'Polizei und SS im Osten: Eindrucksvolle Hörberichte im Rundfunk', in *VB* (19 Feb. 1940).
75. 'Fasten und Dunkelzelle hörten auf', in *VB* (27 June 1940), refers to the Sudetenland; 'Deutsche Polizei schafft wider Ordnung', *VB* (11 Aug. 1940), deals with Alsace-Lorraine.
76. 'Deutsche Ordnung durchgesetzt: Polnischen Verbrechertum ein Ende bereitet— die Leistungen der Polizei', in *VB* (29 Nov. 1940).
77. See 'Kampf der SS und Polizei im Osten: Erlebnisberichte im Deutschen Rundfunk', in *VB* (30 Dec. 1939).
78. '"Standgerichte der Heimat": Sondergericht—erste und letzte Instanz für Volksschädlinge und Gewaltverbrecher', in *VB* (23 Dec. 1939).
79. Arthur Nebe, 'Aufbau der deutschen Kriminalpolizei', in *Kriminalistik* (1 Jan. 1938).
80. See 'Die einheitliche Polizeiexekutive: Garde des Staates', in *DAZ* (19 June 1936); 'Die Einheitsorganisation der deutschen Polizei', in *VB* (1 July 1936). For background and much useful information, see George C. Browder, *Foundations of the Nazi Police State: The Formation of Sipo and SD* (Lexington, Ky., 1990), 231 ff.
81. 'Die Polizei im Reichsaufbau', in *BT* (1 July 1937), reported that a fully nationalized German police, replacing all provincial (*Land*) police formally began to function from 1 Apr. 1937 and police officials were covered by a single civil service law from 1 July 1937. See also 'Die Einheitsorganisation der deutschen Polizei', in *VB* (1 July 1936); Herbert, *Best*, 170; and for an insider's view, see Bernd Wehner, *Dem Täter auf der Spur: Die Geschichte der deutschen Kriminalpolizei* (Bergisch Gladbach, 1983), 161.
82. See e.g. the testimony of Karl Heinz Hoffmann, in *IMT*, xx. 176.
83. Cited in Wagner, *Volksgemeinschaft ohne Verbrecher*, 264.
84. For an introduction to the set-up of the police in general, see Gellately, *Gestapo and German Society*, 68–72.
85. Broszat, 'Zur Perversion der Strafjustiz im Dritten Reich', 395–6.
86. 'Hochschule gegen Verbrechen', in *VB* (16 Jan. 1937).
87. 'Deutsche Sicherheitspolizei vorbildlich', in *VB* (8 Jan. 1938).
88. See e.g. 'Wissenschaftszentrale gegen Verbrecher: Aufgaben des Kriminal-technischen Instituts der Sicherheitspolizei', in *BBZ* (6 July 1939).

89. 'Die neue Reichskriminalpolizei', in *BT* (21 July 1937).
90. 'Aus der Verwaltung: Aufbau und Aufgaben der deutschen Reichskriminalpolizei', in *DRA* (21 July 1937).
91. 'Spezialisierung der Polizei', in *FZ* (26 Aug. 1937).
92. Wagner, *Volksgemeinschaft ohne Verbrecher*, 243–53.
93. *RGBL*, i. 135–8 (22 Mar. 1933), 'Verordnung der Reichspräsidenten zur Abwehr heimtückischer Angriffe gegen die Regierung des nationalen Erhebung vom 21. März 1933'; 'Verordnung der Reichsregierung über die Bildung von Sondergerichten vom 21. März 1933'.
94. *RGBL*, i. 1269–71 (29 Dec. 1934), 'Gesetz gegen heimtückische Angriffe auf Staat und Partei und Gesetz der Parteiuniformen vom 20. Dez. 1934'.
95. See e.g. Walter Wagner, *Der Volksgerichtshof im nationalsozialistischen Staat* (Stuttgart, 1974), 393, 415, 665.
96. *RGBL*, i. 340–8 (30 Apr. 1934), 'Gesetz zur Änderung von Vorschriften des Strafrechts und des Strafverfahrens vom 24. Apr. 1934'.
97. The three judges (*Berufsrichter*) dispensed with civilian involvement of three judges (*Volksrichter*) who participated before regular courts. The Special Courts used only a chief justice (*Vorsitzender*) and two additional junior judges (*Landgerichtsräte als Beisitzer*), all of whom were called to serve by the president of each district court (*Landgericht*).
98. Martin Broszat, 'Nationalsozialistische Konzentrationslager 1933–1945', in Hans Buchheim et al., *Anatomie des SS-Staates*, 5ᵗʰ edn. (Munich, 1989), ii. 87.
99. See *RGBL*, i. 1632 (21 Nov. 1938), 'Verordnung über die Erweiterung der Zuständigkeit der Sondergerichte vom 20. Nov. 1938'. For other changes to the courts, see *RGBL*, i. 405–11 (26 Feb. 1940): 'Verordnung über die Zuständigkeit der Strafgerichte, die Sondergerichte und sonstige strafverfahrensrechtliche Vorschriften vom 21. Februar 1940'.
100. *VB* (23 Dec. 1939), 'Standgerichte der Heimat'. The story picked up the phrase used by an attorney general in regard to a Berlin case in early Nov. 1939.
101. Cited in Werner Johe, *Die gleichgeschaltete Justiz* (Frankfurt am Main, 1967), 91.
102. See Robert Gellately, 'Die Gestapo und die "öffentliche Sicherheit und Ordnung"', in Herbert Reinke (ed.), '... *nur für die Sicherheit da ...? Zur Geschichte der Polizei im 19. und 20. Jahrhundert* (Frankfurt am Main, 1993), 94–115.
103. Johe, *Justiz*, 92.
104. See 'Todesstrafe für Volksschädling', in *HannZ* (26 Aug. 1943). An early example was 'Der Vernichtungskampf der Geheimen Staatspolizei gegen die Volksschädlinge', in *VB* (30 Aug. 1933).
105. This point is made by Klaus Marxen, 'Strafjustiz im Nationalsozialismus: Vorschläge für eine Erweiterung der historischen Perspektive', in Bernhard Diestelkamp and Michael Stolleis (eds.), *Justizalltag im Dritten Reich* (Frankfurt am Main, 1988), 101–11, esp. 106.
106. For a study of this topic, esp. of the press officers, see Edmund Lauf, *Der Volksgerichtshof und sein Beobachter* (Opladen, 1994), 59–110.
107. HStA D: RW 18/d3, 19: Gestapa an Staatspolizeistellen (20 Sept. 1935): Betr.: Presseveröffentlichungen über staatspol. Massnahmen.

108. See USHMM, RG 11: Moscow State Archives: 501–1–261, E. H. Schulz, 'Judentum und Kriminalität', *Ziel und Weg* (1934), 1–19.

109. See e.g. 'Der Jude als Verbrecher', with the subtitle, 'Ungeheurer Anteil der Juden an der Kriminalität', a front-page story in the *VB* (21 July 1935); or 'Der Jude als Verbrecher' with the same subtitle in *VB* (11 Dec. 1936).

110. From many examples, see 'Hohe Zuchthausstrafen gegen den jüdischen Schieber Falk beantragt', in *VB* (3 Oct. 1934); 'Jüdischer Großschieber vor Gericht', in *VB* (31 Aug. 1935); 'Viehschiebungen unter jüdischer Leitung', in *VB* (17 Sept. 1937)— deals with a 'discovery' about the years 1927 to 1930.

111. See e.g. 'Zuchthaus für Devisenjuden', in *VB* (12 Nov. 1934); 'Jüdischer Großschwindler zu Zuchthaus verurteilt', in *VB* (8 May 1935); 'Kölner Geschäftsjude mit 25000 Mark geflüchtet', in *VB* (10 July 1935); 'Jüdischer Devisenschmuggler geflüchtet', in *VB* (15 Nov. 1935); 'Festnahme eines jüdischen Wucherers', in *VB* (23 Jan. 1936); 'Jude als "König der Rauschgifthändler"', in *VB* (19 June 1938).

112. USHMM, RG 11: Moscow State Archives: 501–1–261, Gestapa an Stapo (24 Apr. 1937).

113. For similar conclusions, see Ulrich Herbert, 'Von der Gegnerbekämpfung zur "rassischen Generalprävention": "Schutzhaft" und Konzentrationslager in der Konzeption der Gestapo-Führung 1933–1939', in Ulrich Herbert, Karin Orth, and Christoph Dieckmann (eds.), *Die nationalsozialistischen Konzentrationslager: Entwicklung und Struktur* (Göttingen, 1998), i. 60–86, here 81.

Chapter 3

1. Johannes Tuchel, *Konzentrationslager: Organisationsgeschichte und Funktion der Inspektion der Konzentrationslager 1934–1938* (Boppard, 1991), 38.

2. For all of the above, see Tuchel, *Konzentrationslager*, 42–3. Although Oranienburg was initially founded by the SA, and was one of the few to last beyond a few months and to attain infamy, it survived because it came under regional state control.

3. See Tuchel, *Konzentrationslager*, 38–40. For inside the camps, see esp. Wolfgang Sofsky, *Die Ordnung des Terrors: Das Konzentrationslager* (Frankfurt am Main, 1993).

4. See Kurt Schilde and Johannes Tuchel, *Columbia-Haus: Berliner Konzentrationslager 1933–1936* (Berlin, 1990), 22–8.

5. The press clippings are reprinted in Günter Kimmel, 'Das Konzentrationslager Dachau: Eine Studie zu den Nationalsozialistischen Gewaltverbrechen', in Martin Broszat et al. (eds.), *Bayern in der NS-Zeit* (Munich, 1979), ii. 349–413, here 355–7.

6. See 'Ein Konzentrationslager für politische Gefangene', in *MNN* (21 Mar. 1933), reprinted in full in Hans-Günter Richardi, *Schule der Gewalt: Das Konzentrationslager Dachau* (Munich, 1983), 37; and 'Konzentrationslager für Schutzhäftlinge in Bayern', in *VB* (21 Mar. 1933).

7. See e.g. from the far north of Germany, *Anzeiger für das Fürstentum Lübeck* (22 Mar. 1933) and Lawrence D. Stokes, 'Das Eutiner Schutzhaftlager 1933/34: Zur Geschichte eines "wilden" Konzentrationslagers', in *VfZ* (1979), 570–625.

8. See e.g. 'Wieder kommunistische Mordlisten', in *VB* (31 Mar. 1933); 'Die Polizeiaktionen werden erfolgreich fortgesetzt: Über 2000 Verhaftungen', in *VB* (3 Mar. 1933); 'Die Ausrottung des Kommunismus', in *VB* (8 Mar. 1933); 'Erfolgreiche Polizeiaktionen gegen den Marxismus', in *VB* (15 Mar. 1933).

9. For a brief account of early newspaper reports from many parts of Germany, see Klaus Drobisch and Günther Wieland, *System der NS-Konzentrationslager 1933–1939* (Berlin, 1993), 88–94. More recently, see Sybil Milton, 'Die Konzentrationslager der dreißiger Jahre im Bild der in- und ausländischen Presse', in Ulrich Herbert, Karin Orth, and Christoph Dieckmann (eds.), *Die nationalsozialistischen Konzentrationslager: Entwicklung und Struktur* (Göttingen, 1998), i. 135–47.

10. 'Ausländer besichtigen Gefängnis Sonnenburg', in *BM* (25 May 1933).

11. 'Bayern entläßt 1000 Verhaftete', in *BM* (16 Apr. 1933).

12. 'Der Vernichtungskampf der Geheimen Staatspolizei gegen die Völksschädlinge', in *VB* (30 Aug. 1933).

13. *Dachauer Zeitung* (28 Mar. 1933), cited in Sybille Steinbacher, *Dachau—Die Stadt und das Konzentrationslager in der NS-Zeit: Die Untersuchung einer Nachbarschaft* (Frankfurt am Main, 1993), 93.

14. *Dachauer Zeitung* (22 Mar. 1933), cited in Steinbacher, *Dachau*, 94.

15. Steinbacher, *Dachau*, 137–44.

16. See *Dachauer Zeitung* (23 May 1933) in Steinbacher, *Dachau*, 151.

17. 'Gang durch das Konzentrationslager Dachau', in *BH* (22 June 1933), cited in Richardi, *Schule der Gewalt*, 59–61.

18. Eugen Mondt as cited in Steinbacher, *Dachau*, 187.

19. Ibid. 184.

20. See articles from the *NS-Kurier* (14 Mar. and 27 Mar. 1933), reprinted in Markus Kienle, *Das Konzentrationslager Heuberg bei Stetten am kalten Markt* (Ulm, 1998), 127, 130.

21. Cited in Kienle, *Heuberg*, 137.

22. Full texts of selected newspaper articles are reprinted in Kienle, *Heuberg*, here esp. 150.

23. Dietfried Krause-Vilmar, 'Das Konzentrationslager Breitenau in der zeitgenössischen Presse', *DH* 12 (1996), 215–29, here 217–18.

24. Cited in ibid. 222–3.

25. Cited in ibid. 224–5.

26. See Bernd Sösemann and Jürgen Michael Schulz, 'Nationalsozialismus und Propaganda: Das Konzentrationslager Oranienburg in der Anfangsphase totalitärer Herrschaft', in Günter Morsch (ed.), *Konzentrationslager Oranienburg* (Berlin, 1994), 78–94, here 84–6.

27. 'Eine Stunde im Konzentrationslager', in *DA* (29 Mar. 1933).

28. 'Im Konzentrationslager Oranienburg', in *BM* (7 Apr. 1933).

29. 'Der Staat erzieht marxistische Funktionäre: Ein Rundgang durch das Konzentrationslager in Oranienburg', in *DT* (9 Apr. 1933).

30. 'Um die Entlassung politischer Schutzhäftlinge', in *DD* (9 May 1933).

31. For a brief description of Gestapo interrogations in the camps, see *The Buchenwald Report*, trans. and ed. David A. Hackett (Boulder, Colo., 1995), 34–5.

32. 'Bilder aus dem Konzentrationslager Wittmoor', in *HF* (8 June 1933).
33. See *GE* (28 May 1933), in Sösemann and Schulz, 'Nationalsozialismus und Propaganda', 92–3.
34. See Sybil Milton, 'Die Bedeutung von Photodokumenten als Quelle zur Erforschung der NS-Konzentrationslager', *Revue d'Allemagne* (Apr.–June 1995), 175–86. She generously supplied me with a copy of pictures taken of Dachau and published in *BH* (22 June 1933), 172–3.
35. *Braunbuch über Reichstagsbrand und Hitler-Terror* (Basel, 1933).
36. Werner Schäfer, *Konzentrationslager Oranienburg: Das Anti-Braunbuch über das erste deutsche Konzentrationslager* (Berlin, 1934).
37. Ibid. 25, 31.
38. For the lengthy reports of the *Anhalter Anzeiger* (25 July 1933) and *Deutsche Postzeitung* (17 Aug. 1933), see Schäfer, *Konzentrationslager*, 88–107.
39. For example, the *HF* reprinted some of Schäfer's story and pictures. See Ulrich Bauche et al. (eds.), *Arbeit und Vernichtung: Das Konzentrationslager Neuengamme 1938–1945*, 2ⁿᵈ edn. (Hamburg, 1991), 31.
40. For an account of one such visit to Dachau, said to include foreign journalists, see 'Konzentrationslager Dachau', in *Der Jungdeutsche* (28 May 1933).
41. Additional pictures were published in *VB* (10 Aug. 1933) and others in *VB* (5/6 Nov. 1933).
42. The pictures and text of a photo-essay from the *Münchner Illustrierte Presse* (16 July 1933), are reprinted in Sybil Milton, 'Argument oder Illustration: Die Bedeutung von Fotodokumenten als Quelle', in *Fotogeschichte: Beiträge zur Geschichte und Ästhetik der Fotografie* (1988), 61–90, here 63–8.
43. 'Das neue Konzentrationslager im Emsland', in *Der Ems-Zeitung* (the story was carried in two other locals (28 June 1933); reprinted in Erich Kosthorst and Bernd Walter, *Konzentrations- und Strafgefangenenlager im Emsland 1933–1945: Zum Verhältnis von NS-Regime und Justiz* (Düsseldorf, 1985), 22.
44. See the local newspaper reports in Elke Suhr, 'Konzentrationslager—Justizgefangenenlager—Kriegsgefangenenlager im Emsland 1933–1945', in Ludwig Eiber (ed.), *Verfolgung, Ausbeutung, Vernichtung* (Hanover, 1985), 66–89.
45. Cited in Elke Suhr, *Die Emslandlager: Die politische und wirtschaftliche Bedeutung der emsländischen Konzentrations- und Strafgefangenenlager 1933–1945* (Bremen, 1985), 208. The lengthy article is also reprinted in Kosthorst and Walter, *Emsland*, 345–9.
46. See Memorandum (4 June 1936), reprinted in Arthur C. Cochrane, *The Church's Confession under Hitler* (Philadelphia, 1962), 268–79, here 277.
47. Sven Hedin, *Germany and World Peace*, trans. G. Griffen (London, 1937), 284–9.
48. See table 12, in Drobisch and Wieland, *NS-Konzentrationslager*, 73–5.
49. Martin Broszat, 'Nationalsozialistische Konzentrationslager', in Hans Buchheim et al., *Anatomie des SS-Staates*, 5ᵗʰ edn. (Munich, 1989), ii. 20. For an analysis of this figure which concludes by upholding the final count—as a maximum figure for the period from 28 Feb. to 30 June 1933—but on the basis of better and more detailed research, see Tuchel, *Konzentrationslager*, 96–103.
50. The figures of all those in 'protective custody' that survive for 31 July 1933, show that 54 per cent lived in various parts of Prussia. It seems likely that also during Mar.

and Apr. a similar percentage of people were in non-Prussian camps in the rest of Germany.

51. See Drobisch and Wieland, *NS-Konzentrationslager*, 71 and 100. See also Monika Herzog and Bernhard Strebel, 'Das Frauenkonzentrationslager Ravensbrück', in Claus Füllberg-Stolberg et al. (eds.), *Frauen in Konzentrationslagern: Bergen-Belsen Ravensbrück* (Bremen, 1994), 13.

52. See e.g. 'Entlassungen aus der Schutzhaft', in *BM* (21 Apr. 1933).

53. Broszat, 'Konzentrationslager', 24.

54. 'Nur 18000 Schutzhäftlinge in Deutschland', in *VB* (12 July 1933), which also stated that false reports from abroad put the number at 100,000.

55. See 'Alfred Braun und Genossen im Konzentrationslager Oranienburg', in *VB* (10 Aug. 1933); 'Ebert und Hellmann im Konzentrationslager', in *HN* (9 Aug. 1933); 'Aus dem Konzentrationslager entlassen', in *VB* (16 Nov. 1933); 'Hamburg entläßt 150 Schutzhäftlinge', in *VB* (18 Nov. 1933); '5000 Schutzhäflinge in Preußen amnestiert', in *VB* (9 Dec. 1933); 'Entlaßung von Schutzhäftlingen in Oranienburg und Brandenburg', in *VB* (20 Dec. 1933).

56. The exact monthly number of prisoners in Dachau between June 1933 and Nov. 1934 is reconstructed in Tuchel, *Konzentrationslager*, 155.

57. See Johannes Tuchel and Reinold Schattenfroh, *Zentrale des Terrors: Prinz-Albrecht-Straße 8: Hauptquartier der Gestapo* (Berlin, 1987), 114; and Martin Broszat et al. (eds.), *Ploetz: Das Dritte Reich* (Freiburg, 1983), 93; Kimmel, 'Das Konzentrationslager Dachau', 360.

58. Drobisch and Wieland, *NS-Konzentrationslager*, 40.

59. Tuchel, *Konzentrationslager*, 100, suggests that the number in Prussia alone reached into five-figure digits.

60. For the full list, see Tuchel, *Konzentrationslager*, 155–6.

61. 'Das Ende eines der gefährlichsten Kommunisten', in *MNN* (24 Aug. 1933) in which he was shot while trying to escape even though allegedly he was warned repeatedly to stop; cited in Richardi, *Schule der Gewalt*, 189.

62. Cited in Steinbacher, *Dachau*, 186.

63. David Bankier, *The Germans and the Final Solution: Public Opinion under Nazism* (Oxford, 1992), 24

64. 'Konzentrationslager für Berufsverbrecher', in *VB* (26/27 Nov. 1933); 'Das Konzentrationslager als Erziehungsstätte für Gesindel: Beispiele zur Belehrung und Warnung', in *VB* (4 Apr. 1936).

65. See the still hopeful July/Aug. report of *Sopade* (1934), 347–56.

66. The official announcement was on 7 Dec. and was published in the press later, for example, as '5000 Schutzhäflinge in Preußen amnestiert' and 'Entlassung von 500 Schutzhäflinge in Bayern', in *VB* (9 Dec. 1933).

67. 'Neuorganisierung der Geheimen Staatspolizei', in *VB* (3/4 Dec. 1933).

68. 'Weihnachtsamnestie Görings', in *HF* (8 Dec. 1933); 'Den Schutzhäftlingen wird der Weg zur Volksgemeinschaft geebnet', in *DD* (20 Dec. 1933); 'Gnadenerweise zu Weihnachten: Entlassungen aus den Konzentrationslagern', in *VB* (25/26 Dec. 1933).

69. 'Neuorganisierung der Geheimen Staatspolizei', in *VB* (3–4 Dec. 1933); Hitler's speech in *VB* (5–6 Dec. 1933).

70. In *VB* (19 Feb. 1934), reprinted in Domarus (ed.) *Hitler Reden*, i. 364–5.
71. See e.g. dissolution of Sonnenburg announced in *VB* (8 Mar. 1934) and the reduction of facilities in Baden in *VB* (27 Mar. 1933). Some '600 Schutzhäftlinge' were released in Bavaria according to *VB* (20 Mar. 1934) and another 200 in *VB* (4 May 1934); one-third of those in Bad Sulza (Thüringen) were set free, see *VB* (17 Aug. 1934); some 742 Schutzhäflinge were released from Oranienburg and its dissolution was announced in *VB* (2/3 Sept. 1934).
72. 'Ein Interview Ministerpräsident Görings über die Sicherheit in Deutschland', in *VB* (22/23 Apr. 1934).
73. 'Das Konzentrationslager in Oranienburg aufgelöst', in *VB* (2/3 Sept. 1934).
74. Tuchel, *Konzentrationslager*, 308.
75. These statistics are from Tuchel, *Konzentrationslager*, 161 and 308.
76. Himmler, still Inspekteur of the Gestapo, and his efforts to secure funding (from 18 Aug. 1934) are discussed in Shlomo Aronson, *Reinhard Heydrich und die Frühgeschichte von Gestapo und SD* (Stuttgart, 1971), 221–2; George C. Browder, *Foundations of the Nazi Police State: The Formation of Sipo and SD* (Lexington, Ky., 1990), 159.
77. Tuchel, *Konzentrationslager*, 309, 312.
78. See Herbert, *Best*, 168–9; Tuchel, *Konzentrationslager*, 312.
79. BA: Sammlung Schumacher/271: Himmler an RJM (6 Nov. 1935).
80. Tuchel, *Konzentrationslager*, 203. See also Broszat, 'Konzentrationslager', 61, who estimates that there were between 7,000 and 9,000 in Mar. 1935.
81. For a general introduction, see Charles W. Sydnor, *Soldiers of Destruction: The SS Death's Head Division, 1933–1945* (Princeton, 1977), 3–36.
82. A sign of the importance Himmler attached to Eicke's assignment was that soon after his appointment as inspector of the camps, he was (on 11 July 1934) promoted to the rank of SS-Gruppenführer—roughly a Lieutenant-General in the British and American armies—which was the same rank Himmler's close collaborator Reinhard Heydrich held in the SS at the time. The seven camps were at Dachau, Esterwegen, Lichtenburg, Sachsenburg, Columbia-Haus, Oranienburg, and Fuhlsbüttel. When reduced to four in Aug. 1937, the camps were still at Dachau and Lichtenburg, and there were two new camps at Sachsenhausen and Buchenwald.
83. Issued 1 Oct. 1933, the complete regulations, from a document (1 Oct. 1943), are reprinted in *IMT*, xxvi. 291–7, 'Aufzählung der Strafgründe und der Strafarten, einschließlich der Todesstrafe, für Häftlinge des Konzentrationslagers Dachau'.
84. See Eugen Kogon, *The Theory and Practice of Hell* (New York, 1950). It is a translation of his *Der SS-Staat*, originally published in 1946.
85. The schema is reprinted in Broszat, 'Konzentrationslager', 58.
86. From the end of 1934 Eicke was 'Inspekteur der Konzentrationslager', and also 'Führer der SS-Wachverbände'. From 1938–9 he used the title 'Führer der SS-Totenkopfverbände und Konzentrationslager'. Broszat, 'Konzentrationslager', 62–3.
87. Tuchel, *Konzentrationslager*, 315–17.
88. For an early example, see the picture and story on 'Das erste Konzentrationslager für Bettler in Deutschland', in *VB* (4 Oct. 1933); also 'Das Konzentrationslager als Erziehungsstätte für Gesindel', in *VB* (4 Apr. 1936).

89. See e.g. 'Rechtsprechung und Judentum', in *VB* (12 June 1935); and Kurt Daluege's address to the press in a feature story called the 'Ungeheurer Anteil der Juden an der Kriminalität', in *VB* (21 July 1935). During the summer of 1935, several feature articles discussed the alleged criminal proclivities of Jews and there were a number of reports on 'race defilement', that is, extramarital sexual relations involving a Jewish and non-Jewish citizen, curious because this was not made into a 'crime' until Sept. See e.g. in *VB* (16 July 1935, 19 July 1935, 20 July 1935).
90. 'K.Z. und seine Insassen', in *DSK* (13 Feb. 1936).
91. Tuchel, *Konzentrationslager*, 203 n. 222.
92. See e.g. 'Erbliche Minderwertigkeit fördert das Verbrechertum', in *VB* (23 May 1937).
93. 'Konzentrationslager Dachau', in *Illustrierter Beobachter* (3 Dec. 1936).
94. Full text of this speech is in *VB* (31 Jan. 1937).
95. Himmler's address to the Wehrmacht was published in the *BBZ*. See *IMT*, xxix. 206–34, Dokumente 1992 (A)-PS.
96. 'Polizei erhält Fahnen aus der Hand des Führers', in *VB* (11 Sept. 1937).
97. BA, Sammlung Schumacher 329: Pressestelle RFSS an PersStab RFSS (1 Mar. 1938), suggested the names for Himmler's approval of the journalists who were to be invited.
98. No stories on the visit appeared in the *VB* during Mar. or Apr., when most reports dealing with the police and SS lauded what they did in Austria.
99. 'Die SS-Totenkopfverbände', in *VB* (26 Jan. 1939).
100. Reinhard Heydrich, 'Die deutsche Sicherheitspolizei', in *VB* (28 Jan. 1939).
101. ' "Die Polizei, dein Freund, dein Helfer." Rundfunkansprache Himmlers zum "Tag der Deutschen Polizei" ', in *VB* (30 Jan. 1939). The speech also is partly reprinted in *Nazism Docs.*, ii. 505.
102. Toni Siegert, *30,000 Tote mahnen! Die Geschichte des Konzentrationslagers Flossenbürg und seiner 100 Außenlager von 1938 bis 1945* (Weiden, 1984), 9.
103. See Wolfgang Ayaß, *'Asoziale' im Nationalsozialismus* (Stuttgart, 1995), 162.
104. Siegert, *30,000 Tote*, 12.
105. Toni Siegert, 'Das Konzentrationslager Flossenbürg: Gegründet für sogenannte Asoziale und Kriminelle', in Broszat et al. (eds.), *Bayern in der NS-Zeit*, ii. 429–92, here 446.
106. Siegert, *30,000 Tote*, 20.
107. See Siegert, 'Flossenbürg', 446, 461, 469.
108. Ibid. 450.
109. Siegert, *30,000 Tote*, 6; Siegert, 'Flossenbürg', 452.
110. Ibid. 452.
111. Ibid. 470.
112. Siegert, *30,000 Tote*, 6; Siegert, 'Flossenbürg', 477.
113. For the exact figures, see ibid. 490–2.
114. This is the number cited by a recent textbook. See John Merriman, *A History of Modern Europe* (New York, 1996), ii. 536.
115. Gordon J. Horwitz, *In the Shadow of Death: Living Outside the Gates of Mauthausen* (New York, 1990), 28–9.
116. The speech was reported in *The Times* of London and is partly reprinted in Horwitz, *In the Shadow of Death*, 28.

117. For a brief account of the mentality of the SS, see Hans Marsalek, *Die Geschichte des Konzentrationslagers Mauthausen: Dokumentation*, 2nd edn. (Vienna, 1980), 201–7.
118. Horwitz, *In the Shadow of Death*, 35–9.
119. Sofsky, *Ordnung des Terrors*, 57.

Chapter 4

1. The classic account is Tim Mason, 'The Legacy of 1918 for National Socialism', in his *Social Policy in the Third Reich: The Working Class and the 'National Community'*, trans. J. Broadwin (Oxford, 1993), 19–40. The theme is also skilfully traced in Philippe Burrin, *Hitler and the Jews: The Genesis of the Holocaust*, trans. P. Southgate (London, 1994).
2. See e.g. Hitler's remarks in Werner Jochmann (ed.), *Adolf Hitler Monologe im Führerhauptquartier 1941–1944: Die Aufzeichnungen Heinrich Heims* (Hamburg, 1980), 59 (talk on the night of 14–15 Sept. 1941).
3. Ibid. 126 (talk at midday on 5 Nov. 1941).
4. Briefly, army leaders like Erich Ludendorff recognized defeat in Aug. and Sept. 1918, and engineered a new government led by Prince Max of Baden on 3 Oct. In early Nov. with defeat already in the air, mutinies in the North Sea ports put the torch to social discontent, led to the overthrow of the government, abdication of the Kaiser, proclamation of the new Republic on 9 Nov., and armistice on 11 Nov. The sequence of events was, thus: defeat, revolution, armistice, and peace. In the climate of confusion at the time, right-wing Germans distorted the sequence— or preferred to see it—as revolution, armistice, defeat, and peace. For a recent analysis and further literature, see Roger Chickering, *Imperial Germany and the Great War, 1914–1918* (Cambridge, 1998), esp. 189–91; and Richard Bessel, *Germany after the First World War* (Oxford, 1993), 254–84.
5. For a brief overview, see Andrew Thorpe, 'Britain', in Jeremy Noakes (ed.), *The Civilian in War: The Home Front in Europe, Japan and the USA in World War II* (Exeter, 1992), esp. 14–34, here 21.
6. William L. Shirer, *Berlin Diary: The Journal of a Foreign Correspondent* (New York, 1940), 150 (entry for 3 Sept. 1939).
7. See Thorpe, 'Britain', here 21–2.
8. Shirer, *Berlin Diary*, 164 (entry for 20 Sept. 1939).
9. See Wolfram Wette, 'Ideologien, Propaganda und Innenpolitik als Voraussetzungen der Kriegspolitik des Dritten Reiches', in Wilhelm Deist et al., *Das Deutsche Reich und der Zweite Weltkrieg* (Stuttgart, 1979), i. 137–42.
10. For an excellent discussion of the issues, including the role of women, see Richard J. Overy, 'Guns or Butter? Living Standards, Finance, and Labour in Germany, 1939–1942', in his *War and Economy in the Third Reich* (Oxford, 1994), 259–314.
11. See Table 7.1 in Overy, 'Germany, "Domestic Crisis," and War in 1939', in his *War and Economy*, 205–32, here 216.
12. Alf Lüdtke, 'The Appeal of Exterminating "Others": German Workers and the Limits of Resistance', in Michael Geyer and John W. Boyer (eds.), *Resistance against the Third Reich 1933–1990* (Chicago, 1994), 53–74, here 54.

13. BA: R58/243, 276. Chef Sipo, Schreiben an Stapostellen (31 Aug. 1939), Betr.: 'Entlastung der Geheimen Staatspolizei'.
14. In 1937 there was a total of about 7,000 employees of all kinds in the entire Gestapo, and even by 1 Aug. 1941, the total was only 7,700 for all of the *alt Reich*—that is, pre-war Germany. See Elisabeth Kohlhaas, 'Die Mitarbeiter der regionalen Staatspolizeistellen: Quantitative und qualitative Befunde zur Personalausstattung der Gestapo', in Gerhard Paul and Klaus-Michael Mallmann (eds.), *Die Gestapo: Mythos und Realität* (Darmstadt, 1995), 219–35, here 223, 225. The newest and most complete quantitative analysis is Jens Banach, *Heydrichs Elite: Das Führerkorps der Sicherheitspolizei und des SD 1936–1945* (Paderborn, 1998), 20, table 1, for Gestapo, Kripo, and SD 'office holders'.
15. Martin Broszat, 'Nationalsozialistische Konzentrationslager', in *Anatomie des SS-Staates*, 5th edn. (Munich, 1989), ii. 93.
16. Ibid. 86–7.
17. Victor Klemperer, *Ich will Zeugnis ablegen bis zum letzten: Tagebücher 1933–1945* (Berlin, 1996), i. 483, 487.
18. See table 48 in Klaus Drobisch and Günther Wieland, *System der NS-Konzentrationslager 1933–1939* (Berlin, 1993). 339.
19. The Oberbürgermeister of Recklinghausen suggested the police open a second such camp in Schützenhof on 3 Jan. 1941. See HStA D: RW 37/15, 1 and RW 37/17, 1. A camp at Hunswinkel opened in Aug. 1940. For Berlin's authorization, 28 May 1941, to open the camps, see BA: R58/1027, 142 ff.
20. Drobisch and Wieland, *Konzentrationslager*, n. 10, 339.
21. HStA D: RW35/7, 1 ff. and RW34/26, 39 ff.
22. Lothar Gruchmann, *Justiz im Dritten Reich 1933–1945: Anpassung und Unterwerfung in der Ära Gürtner* (Munich, 1988), 676.
23. For a discussion, see Robert Gellately, 'Allwissend und allgegenwärtig? Entstehung, Funktion und Wandel des Gestapo-Mythos', in Paul and Mallmann (eds.), *Die Gestapo*, 47–70, here 63.
24. BA: R58/243, 202–4: Chef der Sipo Runderl.: Grundsätze der inneren Staatssicherung während des Krieges (3 Sept. 1939).
25. BA: R58/243, 215: Chef der Sipo: Betr.: Grundsätze der inneren Staatssicherheit während des Krieges (20 Sept. 1939).
26. AES, Rund Erl.: RMI (4 Oct. 1939) Betr. Verlängerung der Frist für vorläufige Festnahmen im Schutzhaftverfahren.
27. AES, Rund Erl.: Chef Sipo (24 Oct. 1939).
28. BA: R58/1027, 114: RSHA an Stapo usw.
29. BA: R58/1027, Rund Erl. Chefs Sipo: Betr. 'Grundsätzliche Anordnung des Reichsführers-SS und Chefs der Deutschen Polizei über Festnahme staatsfeindlicher Elemente nach Beginn des Feldzuges gegen die Sowjetunion' (27 Aug. 1941).
30. BA: R58/1027, Rund Erl. des Chefs Sipo: Betr.: 'Vereinfachung im Schutzhaftverfahren' (4 May 1943). See the follow-up instructions that make this point in BA: R58/1027, Rund Erl. des Chefs Sipo: Betr.: 'Vereinfachung im Schutzhaftverfahren' (6 Aug. 1943).

31. See *RGBL*, i. 372 (2 July 1943), 'Dreizehnte Verordnung zum Reichsbürgergesetz vom 1. Juli 1943', according to which criminal acts of the Jews—who were now set below the status of Poles—were to be dealt with exclusively by the police ('Strafbare Handlungen von Juden werden durch die Polizei geahndet').

32. For an outline of the organization and its many tasks and addresses in Berlin, see Reinhard Rürup (ed.), *Topographie des Terrors* (Berlin, 1987), 70–81.

33. *RLZ*, 8 Sept. 1939.

34. Gruchmann, *Justiz*, 677–8.

35. See esp. Detlev Garbe, *Zwischen Widerstand und Martyrium: Die Zeugen Jehovas im 'Dritten Reich'* (Munich, 1994), 78, 411–15.

36. See Hans Hesse (ed.), *'Am mutigsten waren immer wieder die Zeugen Jehovas': Verfolgung und Widerstand der Zeugen Jehovas im Nationalsozialismus* (Bremen, 1998), 426–30.

37. See e.g. Victor Klemperer, *Ich will Zeugnis ablegen bis zum letzten: Tagebücher 1933–1945* (Berlin, 1995), ii. 498 (entry for 15 Mar. 1944).

38. On Hitler's decision, see Ulrich Herbert, *Best: Biographische Studien über Radikalismus, Weltanschauung und Vernunft 1903–1989* (Bonn, 1996), 240–9, here 241; and Helmut Krausnick and Hans-Heinrich Wilhelm, *Die Truppe des Weltanschauungskrieges: Die Einsatzgruppen der Sicherheitspolizei und des SD 1938–1942* (Stuttgart, 1981), 63–5.

39. See *Die Tagebücher von Joseph Goebbels*, T. 1, Bd. 7 (entry 30 Sept. 1939), 130.

40. Domarus (ed.), *Hitler Reden*, iii. 1383.

41. The phrase is from a Feb. 1940 list of complaints presented to Commander-in-Chief of the army, and is cited in Raul Hilberg, *The Destruction of the European Jews*, rev. edn. (New York, 1985), i. 190–1.

42. *Die Tagebücher von Joseph Goebbels*, T. 1, Bd. 7 (entry 31 Oct. 1939), 176.

43. Ibid. (entry 2 Nov. 1939), 177. For Hitler's agreement (3 Nov. 1939), 180.

44. Ibid. (entry 19 Dec. 1939), 237.

45. For this and other excesses, Krausnick and Wilhelm, *Die Truppe*, 63–106, here 93.

46. *Meldungen aus dem Reich* (20 Oct. 1939), 376.

47. Gruchmann, *Justiz*, 682.

48. See Dokument 3 (NG-190), reprinted in Martin Broszat, 'Zur Perversion der Strafjustiz im Dritten Reich', *VfZ* (1958), 408–9.

49. See Dokument 4 (PS-3813), reprinted in Broszat, 'Zur Perversion der Strafjustiz', 409–10.

50. Dokument 5 (NG-190), reprinted in Broszat, 'Zur Perversion der Strafjustiz', 411: Handschriftliche Notiz von Reichsjustizminister Dr. Gürtner, (14 Oct. 1939) on the basis of a visit from Hans Heinrich Lammers on Hitler's behalf.

51. For Gürtner's reaction, see Gruchmann, *Justiz*, 680.

52. Ibid. 681–2.

53. Much remains to be written on Hitler's uses of amnesties and also of his desire to hold the power to issue pardons and grace to those sentenced to death.

54. See Richard J. Evans, *Rituals of Retribution: Capital Punishment in Germany 1600–1987* (Oxford, 1996), 698; and Ralph Angermund, *Deutsche Richterschaft 1919–1945* (Frankfurt am Main, 1990), 194.

55. See e.g. 'Zwei Volksschädlinge', in *RLZ* (8 Nov. 1939), one of whom was a Jew.
56. 'Sondergericht verhängt Todesstrafe für Straßenräuber', in *VB* (5 Nov. 1939).
57. For examples of verdicts Hitler was said to have found unacceptable (*völlig unverständlich*) on the basis of press reports and for evidence of his ordering of executions as 'corrections', see Dokument 7 (23 Sept. 1940); Dokument 9 (25 May 1941); Dokument 11 (29 Oct. 1941), reprinted in Broszat, 'Zur Perversion der Strafjustiz', 416 ff.
58. See Schlegelberger an Hitler (10 Mar. 1941), reprinted in Broszat, 'Zur Perversion der Strafjustiz', 417–18.
59. See BA: R43 II, 1542 (a), Bormann an Lammers (26 Mar. 1941) and the correspondence that followed, 103–8.
60. Generalstaatsanwalt bei dem Kammergericht, report (30 Jan. 1941), reprinted in Bernd Schimmler (ed.), *Stimmung der Bevölkerung und politische Lage: Die Lageberichte der Berliner Justiz 1940–1945* (Berlin, 1986), 53.
61. The guess was 13 or so executions in the two-week period ending on 31 Mar. Generalstaatsanwalt bei dem Kammergericht, report (31 Mar. 1942), reprinted in Schimmler (ed.), *Stimmung*, 68.
62. See documents in Broszat, 'Zur Perversion der Strafjustiz', 417 ff.
63. 'Todesurteil sechs Tage nach der Tat', in *RLZ* (7 Sept. 1940). For a case from Essen, see 'Todesstrafe für Kleinviehdieb', in *RLZ* (13 Apr. 1941).
64. 'Zwei Volksschädlinge hingerichtet', in *RLZ* (8 Dec. 1940).
65. Nuremberg trial document NG-4697, 'Bestellungen aus der Pressekonferenz vom 15. Sept. 1939'.
66. 'In Deutschland ist kein Platz für Verbrecher', in *RLZ* (5 Jan. 1940); and 'Volksschädlinge zum Tode verurteilt', in *RLZ* (6 Jan. 1940).
67. 'Todesstrafe für Landesverräter', in *RLZ* (7 Jan. 1940).
68. See e.g. *RLZ* (3 June 1940, 7 July 1940, and 5 Dec. 1940).
69. See Edmund Lauf, *Der Volksgerichtshof und sein Beobachter* (Opladen, 1994), 198.
70. 'Vollstreckung von Todesstrafen', in *RLZ* (5 Jan. 1942).
71. *Meldungen aus dem Reich* (5 Mar. 1942), 3417–22.
72. Ibid. (24 June 1943), 5398.
73. Ibid. (16 Sept. 1943), 5775.
74. From many such cases, see e.g. '75 jähriger Schwarzschlächter hingerichtet', in *RLZ* (6 May 1943).
75. 'Zuchthaus für Volksverräterin', in *RLZ* (4 Jan. 1940).
76. 'Volksschädlinge wegen ihrer Tat', in *RLZ* (7 Oct. 1943).
77. For just such a case from around Hamburg, to be sure, involving more serious fraud, see 'Todesstrafe für Vertrauensbruch', in *RLZ* (9 Jan. 1944); for another in Düsseldorf, see 'Todesstrafe für Hochstapler', in *RLZ* (11 Mar. 1944).
78. BA: R22/3355, Generalstaatsanwalt bei dem Oberlandesgerichte Bamberg an Reichsminister (30 Apr. 1940). For a repeat of this complaint, see also the report of 4 Feb. 1941. See also BA: R22/3387: Oberlandesgerichtspräsident in Stuttgart an Reichsminister (6 Nov. 1940).
79. See e.g. *Meldungen aus dem Reich* (13 Nov. 1941), 2982–4.
80. See the cases cited in ibid. (17 Sept. 1944), 6711–20.

81. 'Tod und harte Strafen für Pflichtvergessene', in *RLZ* (8 Feb. 1945).
82. 'Die Waffe des Rechts', in *VB* (7 Dec. 1940).
83. 'Die Aufgabe der Justiz im Kriege', in *VB* (26 Mar. 1944).
84. Jochmann (ed.), *Monologe im Führerhauptquartier*, 271–2 (entry for 8 Feb. 1942).
85. *RGBL*, i. 139–40 (26 Mar. 1942): 'Erlaß des Führers über die Vereinfachung der Rechtspflege vom 21. März 1942'. Hitler wanted only judges who were deeply convinced that 'the law existed not for the security of the individual from the state, but primarily ought to ensure that Germany does not go to ruin'. See Henry Picker, *Hitlers Tischgespräche im Führerhauptquartier*, 3ʳᵈ edn. (Stuttgart, 1976), 158 (entry for 29 Mar. 1942).
86. 'Erlaß über die Strafvollstreckung im Kriege' is reprinted in Domarus (ed.), *Hitler Reden*, iv. 1860–1.
87. See 'Aussetzung der Strafvollstreckung zum Zwecke der Bewährung', 18 Sept. 1940, reprinted in Hans-Peter Klausch, *Die Bewährungstruppe 500* (Bremen, 1995), 361–8. Klausch maintains that being sent to serve was not meant to be a death sentence—even though the casualty rate was enormous—because the Nazis really believed that 'through blood even great guilt can be atoned'. The precise figures of all those who served and were killed in these battalions has not been established.
88. See the earlier articles making Hitler's supreme legal powers clear in Hermann Göring's speech, 'Oberster Richter ist der Führer', in *VB* (28 Mar. 1938); and Hans Frank's speech before the Academy of German Law, 'Die geistesgeschichtliche Lage der Rechtswissenschaft', in *VB* (19 June 1938).
89. The speech was published—and was almost certainly broadcast on radio—and is reprinted in Domarus (ed.), *Hitler Reden*, iv. 1865–76.
90. The case, tried before the Oldenburg Landgericht in Mar. 1942, concerned Ewald Schlitt. To satisfy Hitler's expressed outrage, justice officials convened a special court hearing which sentenced Schlitt to death and he was executed already by 2 Apr. See Domarus (ed.), *Hitler Reden*, iv. 1856–7; for the newspaper notice of the execution, see 1860.
91. Insiders also saw it that way. Goebbels reported that Hitler 'is now determined to proceed very radically against a judiciary that was out of tune with the people'. *Die Tagebücher von Joseph Goebbels*, T. 2, Bd. 4 (27 Apr. 1942), 188.
92. See *Meldungen aus dem Reich* (27 Apr. 1942), 3671–4.
93. The speech was published and is reprinted in Domarus (ed.), *Hitler Reden*, iv. 1913–24; for the 8 Nov. 1942 speech, see 1933–4.
94. For the statistics, see table 1 in Evans, *Rituals of Retribution*, 916.
95. Jochmann (ed.), *Monologe im Führerhauptquartier*, 347–54.
96. This estimate (which puts the death sentences at 'around 16,000' (etwa) is from a volume edited by the present Federal Ministry of Justice, *Im Namen des Deutschen Volkes: Justiz und Nationalsozialismus* (Cologne, 1989), 206.
97. Andreas Seeger, 'Hinrichtungen in Hamburg und Altona 1933 bis 1944', in Angelika Eppinghaus and Karsten Linne (eds.), *Kein abgeschlossenes Kapitel: Hamburg im 'Dritten Reich'* (Hamburg, 1997), 319–48, here 331 shows that 140 (29.5 per cent) of the 475 executed from northern Germany in Hamburg were foreigners; 3 of them were Jews, 25 were women, and thus most of the victims were German citizens.

98. Martin Hirsch, Diemut Majer, and Jürgen Meinck (eds.), *Recht, Verwaltung und Justiz im Nationalsozialismus* (Cologne, 1984), 479.
99. For a list of 18 police executions between 6 Sept. 1939 and 20 Jan. 1940, see *Im Namen des Deutschen Volkes*, 258–9.
100. For these figures, see Omer Bartov, *Hitler's Army: Soldiers, Nazis, and War in the Third Reich* (New York, 1991), 95–6.
101. Angermund, *Deutsche Richterschaft*, 158–79, esp. 177.
102. See Horst Göppinger, *Juristen jüdischer Abstammung im 'Dritten Reich'* (Munich, 1990), 45–83.
103. Ingo Müller, *Hitler's Justice: The Courts of the Third Reich*, trans. D. L. Schneider (Cambridge, Mass., 1991), 176–7.
104. See Helge Grabitz, 'In vorauseilendem Gehorsam . . . Die Hamburger Justiz im "Führer-Staat" ', in Justizbehörde Hamburg (ed.) , *'Für Führer, Volk und Vaterland . . .': Hamburger Justiz im Nationalsozialismus* (Hamburg, 1992), 21–73; and Hubert Rottleuthner, 'Rechtsphilosophie und Rechtssoziologie im Nationalsozialismus', in Ralf Dreier and Wolfgang Sellert (eds.), *Recht und Justiz im 'Dritten Reich'* (Frankfurt am Main, 1989), 295–322.
105. For this and numerous other relevant citations, see Hans Michelberger, *Berichte aus der Justiz des Dritten Reiches* (Pfaffenweiler, 1989), 367–74, here 373.
106. 'Nationalsozialistischer Kampf gegen das Verbrechertum: Ein Rechenschafts-bericht deutscher Polizeiarbeit', in *VB* (3 Apr. 1936).
107. 'Politisches Soldatentum in der Polizei', in *VB* (17 Feb. 1941). See also in the same issue 'Polizei—beliebt wie noch nie'.
108. For a summary of the crimes brought to the regular courts between 1930 and 1940, see *Statistisches Jahrbuch für das Deutsche Reich*, lix (Berlin, 1941–2), 649.
109. See e.g. Generalstaatsanwalt bei dem Kammergericht, report 30 Jan. 1941, in Schimmler (ed.), *Stimmung*, 53.
110. See BA: R22/1221, 296–301: 'Die Amnestien im letzten 6 Jahren'.
111. See e.g. Generalstaatsanwalt bei dem Kammergericht, report 31 May 1940, in Schimmler (ed.), *Stimmung*, 43.
112. See *Statistisches Jahrbuch für das Deutsche Reich* (Berlin, 1935–).
113. See BA: R22/1160, 'Die Entwicklung der Kriminalität im Deutschen Reich vom Kriegsbeginn bis Mitte 1943' (Berlin, 1944), 26–66.
114. See BA: R22/4003, 86–9: Informationsdienst des Reichsministers der Justiz, 'Die Erwachsenenkriminalität im Kriege' and 'Die Jugendkriminalität im Kriege' (Oct. 1944).
115. There were 82,184 reports of such cases in 1938 and the figure rose every year until it almost doubled in 1943 to 160,900.
116. These statistics are from table 11, in Patrick Wagner, *Volksgemeinschaft ohne Verbrecher: Konzeptionen und Praxis der Kriminalpolizei in der Zeit der Weimarer Republik und des Nationalsozialismus* (Hamburg, 1996), 317. There were an estimated 14,358 crimes committed by youths in 1938 and 22,702 in 1942 (see p. 319).
117. For further analysis of the impact of the Gestapo on crime, see Robert Gellately, 'Die Gestapo und die "öffentliche Sicherheit und Ordnung" ', in Herbert Reinke (ed.), *'. . . nur für die Sicherheit da? . . .': Zur Geschichte der Polizei im 19. und 20. Jahrhundert* (Frankfurt am Main, 1993), 94–115.

Chapter 5

1. For an excellent introduction, see Jeremy Noakes, 'Social Outcasts in the Third Reich', in Richard Bessel (ed.), *Life in the Third Reich*, (Oxford, 1987), 83–96.
2. For an interesting overview, see Uli Linke, *German Bodies: Race and Representation after Hitler* (London, 1999), esp. 37–54.
3. For the pre-1914 background, see Brigitte Hamann, *Hitler's Vienna: A Dictator's Apprenticeship*, trans. T. Thornton (Oxford, 1999), 78–85.
4. *IMT*, xxix. 220: Dokument 1992(A)-PS, 'Vortrag Himmlers über Wesen und Aufgabe der SS und der Polizei', from Nationalpolitischer Lehrgang der Wehrmacht vom Januar 1937.
5. Daniel Pick, *Faces of Degeneration: A European Disorder, c.1848–1918* (Cambridge, 1989), 128.
6. Lombroso had a considerable influence on Nazi criminological thinking, which went unacknowledged because of his Jewish ancestry.
7. The passage from Hitler's *Mein Kampf* is cited by Oberregierungsrat Dr Albrecht Böhme, 'Die Vorbeugungsaufgaben der Polizei', in *Deutsches Recht* (15 Apr. 1936), 142.
8. Lothar Gruchmann, *Justiz im Dritten Reich 1933–1945: Anpassung und Unterwerfung in der Ära Gürtner* (Munich, 1988), 719–21.
9. In *RGBL*, i. 995–9 (27 Nov. 1933), the concept is 'gefährliche Gewohnheitsverbrecher'. In the Prussian decree the concept is 'Berufsverbrecher'. For the background, see Karl-Leo Terhorst, *Polizeiliche planmäßige Überwachung und polizeiliche Vorbeugungshaft im Dritten Reich* (Heidelberg, 1985), 75 ff. The extension (Erweiterung) of the Prussian decree was 10 Feb. 1934.
10. 'Neues Strafrecht Anfang 1934', in *VB* (3 Oct. 1933).
11. 'Bekämpfung des gemeinschädlichen Verbrechertums', in *VB* (18 Nov. 1933).
12. 'Konzentrationslager für Berufsverbrecher', in *VB* (26/27 Nov. 1933).
13. 'Fühlbarer Rückgang der Kriminalität', in *DT* (27 Nov. 1933).
14. 'Unsicherheit läßt nach: Heute kann man wieder ruhig in der Nacht nach Hause gehen', in *VB* (29 Dec. 1933).
15. 'Der Vollzug der Sicherungsverwahrung', in *VB* (29 Dec. 1933).
16. See 'Neue Reichsgrundsätze für den Vollzug von Freiheitsstrafen und von sichernden Maßnahmen', in *VB* (19 May 1934); also 'Strafvollzug, der Werte schafft: Blick in Zuchthäuser und Sicherungsanstalten', in *BBZ* (31 May 1942).
17. 'Vorbeugen ist besser als Einschreiten', in *VB* (18 Dec. 1934).
18. 'Erfolge der Verbrecher-Bekämpfung', in *VB* (13 Feb. 1934).
19. *RGBL*, i. 995–9 (27 Nov. 1933), 'Gesetz gegen gefährliche Gewohnheitsverbrecher und über Maßregeln der Sicherung und Besserung vom 24. Nov. 1933'.
20. See e.g. Adolf Hitler, *Mein Kampf*, trans. R. Manheim (Boston, 1971), 254–5.
21. *RGBL*, i. 529–31 (14 July 1933), 'Gesetz zur Verhütung erbkranken Nachwuches vom 14. Juli 1933'.
22. For an excellent study, see Henry Friedlander, *The Origins of Nazi Genocide: From Euthanasia to the Final Solution* (Chapel Hill, NC, 1995), here 23.
23. Ibid. 27.

24. See esp. Gisela Bock, *Zwangssterilisation im Nationalsozialismus: Studien zur Rassenpolitik und Frauenpolitik* (Opladen, 1986), 230–8.
25. Christine Charlotte Makowski, *Eugenik, Sterilisationspolitik, 'Euthanasie' und Bevölkerungspolitik in der nationalsozialistischen Parteipresse* (Husum, 1996), 151–2.
26. Cited in Stefan Kühl, *The Nazi Connection: Eugenics, American Racism, and German National Socialism* (New York, 1994), 46.
27. Cited in Claudia Koonz, 'Eugenics, Gender, and Ethics in Nazi Germany: The Debate about Involuntary Sterilization 1933–1936', in Thomas Childers and Jane Caplan (eds.), *Reevaluating the Third Reich* (New York, 1993), 66–85, here 68.
28. Kühl, *Nazi Connection*, 24. For support for the argument that Germans were probably more in favour of such a law, see Kurt Nowak, *'Euthanasie' und Sterilisierung im 'Dritten Reich': Die Konfrontation der evangelischen und katholischen Kirche mit dem 'Gesetz zur Verhütung erbkranken Nachwuchses' und der 'Euthanasie'-Aktion* (Göttingen, 1980), 71.
29. They fell to 1,464 (in 1935); 946 (in 1936); and 765 (in 1937); thereafter there was an increase to 964 (in 1938); 1,827 (in 1939); 1,916 (in 1940); and 1,651 (in 1941), the last year for which we have complete statistics. For the statistics, see Christian Müller, *Das Gewohnheitsverbrechergesetz vom 24. November 1933: Kriminalpolitik als Rassenpolitik* (Baden-Baden, 1997), 54. For slightly different figures, see Gruchmann, *Justiz*, 727–8.
30. Between 1934 and 1939, the courts sent 5,142 people to state hospitals; 885 alcoholics to rehabilitation institutes; 7,503 individuals to workhouses; and 1,808 people to be sterilized. Müller, *Gewohnheitsverbrecher*, 53.
31. Gruchmann, *Justiz*, 729.
32. ' "Vorbeugen ist besser als Einschreiten": Der Grundsatz der neuen volksverbundenen Polizei', in *VB* (18 Dec. 1934); 'Polizeirecht zum Schutz der Volksgemeinschaft: Nicht Paragraphen sondern der Geist entscheidet!', in *VB* (3 Dec. 1935).
33. 'Rückgang der Verbrechen bis zu 50%', in *VB* (25 May 1935); 'Erfolgreiche Arbeit der Kriminalpolizei im neuen Reich: Rückgang bis zu 50 vom Hundert', in *VB* (26 May 1935).
34. 'Vorbeugungshaft—das hilft!', in *DA* (24 Aug. 1935).
35. 'Aufklärungswoche der Polizei', in *VB* (5 Mar. 1936).
36. Oberregierungsrat Dr Albrecht Böhme, 'Die Vorbeugungsaufgaben der Polizei', in *DR* (15 Apr. 1936), 142–5.
37. See Gruchmann, *Justiz*, 729 n. 42, for the communications from the Ministry of Justice (21 May 1935 and 25 Mar. 1941).
38. See 'Bekämpfung Asozialer' in Thierack's 'Richterbrief' (1 Jan. 1943), in Heinz Boberach (ed.), *Richterbriefe: Dokumente zur Beeinflussung der deutschen Rechtsprechung 1942–1944* (Boppard, 1975), 51–67.
39. See Boberach (ed.), *Richterbriefe*, xi; and Hans Peter Bleuel, *Sex and Society in Nazi Germany*, trans. J. M. Brownjohn (Philadelphia, 1973), 211.
40. The phrase is from a Bremen law (11 Aug. 1933), reprinted in Wolfgang Ayaß (ed.), *'Gemeinschaftsfremde': Quellen zur Verfolgung von 'Asozialen' 1933–1945* (Koblenz, 1998), 33.

41. The *VB* (Munich) printed the call of the Bavarian government (18 Sept. 1933), reprinted in Ayaß (ed.), *Gemeinschaftsfremde*, 42–3.
42. See Schriftenreihe des Reichskriminalpolizeiamtes, Nr. 45, *Vorbeugende Verbrechensbekämpfung, Erlaßsammlung*, communications of 27 Jan. 1937; 23 and 27 Feb. 1937. Henceforth cited as RKPA VE
43. Terhorst, *Polizeiliche planmäßige Überwachung*, 109.
44. Ibid. 113.
45. RKPA VE: Rund Erl. RFSS (19 Nov. 1937).
46. Gruchmann, *Justiz*, 725.
47. The professional criminal (*Berufsverbrecher*) was defined as someone who made crime their business and who lived in part or whole from the gains of their crimes; they were sentenced at least three times for a minimum of three months. The repeat offender (*Gewohnheitsverbrecher*) was not a professional, but, driven by a criminal drive and predisposition (*Treiben oder Neigungen*) had a similar record.
48. RKPA VE: Erlaß RMI, 'Grundlegender Erlaß über die vorbeugende Verbrechensbekämpfung durch die Polizei' (14 Dec. 1937).
49. RKPA VE: Rund Erl. RKPA, 'Vorbeugende Verbrechensbekämpfung durch die Polizei' (8 Feb. 1938).
50. 'Vorbeugende Verbrechensbekämpfung', in *VB* (16 Jan. 1938).
51. Kripo Gleiwitz an Oberstaatsanwalt in Neisse (15 June 1938), reprinted in Ayaß (ed.), *Gemeinschaftsfremde*, 135–6.
52. Gerhard Werle, *Justiz-Strafrecht und polizeiliche Verbrechensbekämpfung im Dritten Reich* (Berlin, 1989), 507. See also Wolfgang Ayaß, *Das Arbeitshaus Breitenau* (Kassel, 1992), 319–27.
53. RKPA VE: Rund Erl. Reichskriminalpolizeiamt: 'Richtlinien des Reichskriminalpolizeiamtes über die Durchführung der vorbeugenden Verbrechensbekämpfung' (4 Apr. 1938).
54. RKPA VE: Himmler an Gestapa, RKPA, 'Schutzhaft gegen Arbeitsscheue' (26 Jan. 1938).
55. See e.g. correspondence of the Gestapo in Düsseldorf to the Landrat in Kleve in HStA D: RW 18/d23.
56. Wolfgang Ayaß, *'Asoziale' im Nationalsozialismus* (Stuttgart, 1995), 143.
57. See e.g. the later communication on this point in RKPA VE: RKPA an Kripostellen, 'Vorbeugende Verbrechensbekämpfung' (1 Sept. 1938).
58. SS-Oberführer Ulrich Greifelt, Chef der Dienststelle Vierjahrplan im Persönlichen Stab des Reichsführers SS (Jan. 1939): Nürnberg Dokument NO-5591, reprinted in Hans Buchheim, 'Aktion "Arbeitsscheu Reich"', *Gutachten des Instituts für Zeitgeschichte* (Stuttgart, 1966), ii. 189–95, here 192–3.
59. See the reminder in RKPA VE, RKPA an Kripostellen, 'Vorbeugende Verbrechensbekämpfung durch die Polizei' (23 June 1938).
60. See e.g. his remarks at a Nov. 1936 meeting of Attorneys General (Staatsanwälten) as cited in Gruchmann, *Justiz*, 728.
61. 'Sicherungsverwahrung in Deutschland und Italien', in *VB* (23 June 1938).
62. RKPA VE (25 May 1939).
63. Johannes Tuchel, *Konzentrationslager: Organisationsgeschichte und Funktion der 'Inspektion der Konzentrationslager' 1934–1938* (Boppard, 1991), 361.

64. Ulrich Greifelt as stated in IfZ, Nürnberg Dokument NO-5591.

65. See RKPA VE, 'Erfassung arbeitsscheue Personen' (18 Oct. 1939).

66. Tuchel, *Konzentrationslager*, 361. These figures, from 28 Oct., were before the mass arrests of the Jews that followed in the wake of the 'night of broken glass' in Nov. 1938.

67. See the table in Michael Zimmermann, *Rassenutopie und Genozid: Die national-sozialistische 'Lösung der Zigeunerfrage'* (Hamburg, 1996), 120.

68. See Terhorst, *Polizeiliche planmäßige Überwachung*, 153.

69. RKPA VE, RSHA an Kripo 'Vorbeugende Verbrechensbekämpfung durch die Polizei' (20 Mar. 1940).

70. RKPA VE: RMJ an Generalstaatsanwälte, 'Entlassung aus der Sicherungs-verwahrung' (4 May 1940).

71. RKPA VE: RSHA an Kripo, 'Haftprüfung der gemäß Erlaß vom 1. Juni 1938 festgenommenen Personen' (18 June 1940).

72. See BA: NS3/19: RMI an Kripo, 'Vorbeugende Verbrechensbekämpfung durch die Polizei' (23 Jan. 1941).

73. See Victor Klemperer, *Ich will Zeugnis ablegen bis zum letzten: Tagebücher 1933–1945* (Berlin, 1995), ii. 272 (entry for 6 Nov. 1942).

74. See Michael Burleigh, *Death and Deliverance: 'Euthanasia' in Germany 1900–1945* (Cambridge, 1994), 97.

75. For the background, see Götz Aly, 'Medicine against the Useless', in Götz Aly, Peter Chroust, and Christian Pross, *Cleansing the Fatherland: Nazi Medicine and Racial Hygiene*, trans. B. Cooper (Baltimore, 1994), 22–98, here 29–31.

76. Morell told Hitler of a 1920 survey of 200 parents by Ewald Meltzer (an opponent of 'euthanasia'), of whom only 20 answered 'no' to all four questions put to them. See Aly, 'Medicine', 29–31.

77. For a copy, *Nazism Docs.*, iii. 1006–7.

78. Robert N. Proctor, *Racial Hygiene: Medicine under the Nazis* (Cambridge, Mass., 1988), 188.

79. See Burleigh, *Death and Deliverance*, 99–100.

80. See Friedlander, *Origins of Nazi Genocide*, 136–40; also Ernst Klee, *'Euthanasie' im NS-Staat: Die Vernichtung 'lebensunwerten Lebens'* (Frankfurt am Main, 1983), 95–100.

81. For minutes of the meeting (with misprint in the target figure, which is 70,000, not 75,000) see *Nazism Docs.*, iii. 1010–11.

82. Correspondence is reprinted *IMT*, here xxxv. 689.

83. See the extensive report in William L. Shirer, *Berlin Diary* (New York, 1941), 423–7 (entry for 25 Nov. 1941).

84. Marlis G. Steinert, *Hitler's War and the Germans: Public Mood and Attitude during the Second World War*, trans. T. E. J. de Witt (Athens, Ohio, 1977), 80–1. See also the reports from late 1939 reprinted in Alexander Mitscherlich and Fred Mielke (eds.), *Medizin ohne Menschlichkeit: Dokumente des Nürnberger Ärzteprozesses* (Frankfurt am Main, 1960), 197.

85. For a discussion, see Burleigh, *Death and Deliverance*, 171–2.

86. See the internal T-4 statistics (1 Sept. 1941) in Ernst Klee (ed.), *Dokumente zur 'Euthanasie'* (Frankfurt am Main, 1985), 232.

87. For letters of concern from local officials, see Klee (ed.), *Dokumente*, 221–32.
88. *Die Tagebücher von Joseph Goebbels*, T. 2, Bd. 1 (23 Aug. 1941), 299. He wondered about the recent radical scale of the programme, and also thought it unwise to challenge von Galen at such a time in the war.
89. See Burleigh, *Death and Deliverance*, 180.
90. See e.g. what happened at Hadamar as reflected in the extensive post-war trial in *Justiz und NS-Verbrechen*, i. 304–79.
91. For this and other examples, see Aly, 'Medicine', 55–6.
92. Klee, '*Euthanasie*', 345.
93. See Götz Aly, '*Endlösung*': *Völkerverschiebung und der Mord and den europäischen Juden* (Frankfurt am Main, 1995), 330.
94. See Hans-Walter Schmuhl, *Rassenhygiene, Nationalsozialismus, Euthanasie: Von der Verhütung zur Vernichtung 'lebensunwertes Lebens', 1890–1945* (Göttingen, 1987), 218.
95. For these and other cases, see Friedlander, *Origins of Nazi Genocide*, 148.
96. See Burleigh, *Death and Deliverance*, 221.
97. For details, see Burleigh, *Death and Deliverance*, 220–9; Schmuhl, *Rassenhygiene*, 218; and Friedlander, *Origins of Nazi Genocide*, 142–50.
98. See Ian Kershaw, *Popular Opinion and Political Dissent in the Third Reich: Bavaria 1933–1945* (Oxford, 1983), 340. For silence or indifference, combined with support for antisemitism among some Christians, see Doris L. Bergen, *Twisted Cross: The German Christian Movement in the Third Reich* (Chapel Hill, NC, 1996), 38–43.
99. Proctor, *Racial Hygiene*, 194.
100. This is also the conclusion, after an extensive re-examination of the evidence, of Kurt Nowak, 'Widerstand, Zustimmung, Hinnahme: Das Verhalten der Bevölkerung zur "Euthanasie"', in Norbert Frei (ed.), *Medizin und Gesundheitspolitik in der NS-Zeit* (Munich, 1991), 235–51.
101. Michael Burleigh and Wolfgang Wippermann, *The Racial State: Germany 1933–1945* (Cambridge, 1991), 153.
102. For a detailed analysis of how the nurses involved continued their work, sometimes in spite of their moral reservations, see Bronwyn Rebekah McFarland-Icke, *Nurses in Nazi Germany: Moral Choice in History* (Princeton, 1999), esp. 257–64.
103. See Guenther Lewy, *The Catholic Church and Nazi Germany* (London, 1964), 224–67.
104. See e.g. Martin Schmidt, Robert Kuhlmann, and Michael von Cranach, 'Heil- und Pflegeanstalt Kaufbeuren', in Michael von Cranach and Hans-Ludwig Siemen (eds.), *Psychiatrie im Nationalsozialismus: Die Bayerischen Heil- und Pflegeanstalten zwischen 1933 und 1945* (Munich, 1999), 265–325, here 286.
105. Notes of the meeting (23 Apr. 1941) are reprinted in Klee (ed.), *Dokumente*, 219–20.
106. See ibid. 227–8. For a general account, see Hans-Ludwig Siemen, 'Die bayerischen Heil- und Pflegeanstalten während des Nationalsozialismus', in von Cranach and Siemen (eds.), *Psychiatrie*, 417–74.
107. See BA R22/3355, Generalstaatsanwalt Bamberg an RJM (4 Feb. 1941).
108. For an excellent analysis of this and other killing films, see Burleigh, *Death and Deliverance*, 183–219.

109. *Meldungen aus dem Reich* (15 Jan. 1942), 3177–8. For a detailed analysis of this report, see Burleigh, *Death and Deliverance*, 218–19.
110. Aly, *Endlösung*, 372.
111. Aly, 'Medicine', 93.
112. For a similar interpretation and excellent overview also of asocials, see Richard J. Evans, *Rituals of Retribution: Capital Punishment in Germany 1600–1987* (Oxford, 1996), here 683–4.
113. See Zimmermann, *Rassenutopie*, 93–4.
114. Sybil Milton, 'Vorstufe der Vernichtung: Die Zigeunerlager nach 1933', *VfZ* (1995), 115–30.
115. For isolated statistics, see Zimmermann, *Rassenutopie*, 115–16.
116. See Ludwig Eiber, *'Ich wußte, es wird schlimm': Die Verfolgung der Sinti und Roma in München 1933–1945* (Munich, 1993), 41.
117. RKPA VE: Rund Erl. RFSS, 'Bekämpfung der Zigeunerplage' (8 Dec. 1938).
118. Zimmermann, *Rassenutopie*, 127.
119. RKPA VE: RKPA, 'Ausführungsanweisung' (1 Mar. 1939).
120. RKPA VE: RKPA an Kripo, 'Erfassung aller wehrunwürdigen Personen' (7 July 1939).
121. Proctor, *Racial Hygiene*, 203.
122. For critical evaluation of Ritter's background and research, see Zimmermann, *Rassenutopie*, 125–38.
123. Robert Ritter, 'Kriminalität und Primitivität' (1940), as cited in Proctor, *Racial Hygiene*, 202.
124. Ibid. 203.
125. RKPA VE: RKPA an Kripo Wien (5 June 1939).
126. Document 3363–PS in *Nazi Conspiracy and Aggression*, vi. 97–101; reprinted in Isaiah Trunk, *Judenrat: The Jewish Councils in Eastern Europe under Nazi Occupation* (New York, 1972), 2–4.
127. See Zimmermann, *Rassenutopie*, 167.
128. See Friedlander, *Origins of Nazi Genocide*, 260–1.
129. See Aly, *Endlösung*, 62.
130. RKPA VE: RSHA Schnellbrief an Kripo, 'Zigeunererfassung' (17 Oct. 1939).
131. Ritter as cited in Eiber, *'Ich wußte, es wird schlimm'*, 59–62.
132. BA R18/5644, 229, RMI an Sipo, RKPA, usw. (24 Jan. 1940). The telling phrase in this communication, showing that genocide was the intent, runs as follows: 'daß eine endgültige Lösung des Zigeunerproblems nur durch Unfruchtbarmachung der Zigeuner bezw. Zigeunermischlinge erfolgen kann.'
133. RKPA VE: RFSS Schnellbrief an Kripo, 'Umsiedlung von Zigeunern' (27 Apr. 1940).
134. RKPA VE: RFSS 'Richtlinien für die Umsiedlung von Zigeunern' (27 Apr. 1940).
135. Michael Zimmermann, *Verfolgt, vertrieben, vernichtet: Die nationalsozialistische Vernichtungspolitik gegen Sinti und Roma* (Essen, 1989), 46.
136. RKPA VE: RSHA an Kripo, 'Abschiebung der ostpreußischen Zigeuner' (22 July 1941).
137. Zimmermann, *Verfolgt*, 53–4.

138. See e.g. RKPA VE: RSHA an Kripo, 'Auswertung der rassenbiologischen Gutachten über zigeunerische Personen' (7 Aug. 1941 and 20 Sept. 1941).
139. This investigation was in Mar. 1944. See Hans Hesse (ed.), *'Am mutigsten waren immer wieder die Zeugen Jehovas': Verfolgung und Widerstand der Zeugen Jehovas im Nationalsozialismus* (Bremen, 1998), 430.
140. See Zimmermann, *Rassenutopie*, 160–1, 297–304.
141. See Michael Zimmermann, 'Die nationalsozialistische "Lösung der Zigeunerfrage" ', in Ulrich Herbert (ed.), *Nationalsozialistische Vernichtungspolitik: Neue Forschungen und Kontroversen* (Frankfurt am Main, 1998), 235–62, here 255.
142. See RKPA VE: RSHA an Kripo usw., 'Einweisung von Zigeunermischlingen, Rom-Zigeuner und balkanischen Zigeunern in ein Konzentrationslager' (29 Jan. 1943). For details see Zimmermann, *Rassenutopie*, esp. 295–6, 316–17.
143. For this, and the reactions from elsewhere in Europe, see Zimmermann, *Rassenutopie*, here 308.
144. Ibid. 372. See also Hans-Joachim Döring, *Die Zigeuner im NS-Staat* (Hamburg, 1964), esp. 112–39.
145. Zimmermann, *Rassenutopie*, 381.
146. We have no accurate figures on the total in all of Europe, but one provisional estimate set the death toll at 219,700; see Donald Kenrick and Grattan Puxon, *The Destiny of Europe's Gypsies* (New York, 1972), 184. Another estimate puts the number murdered between 220,000 and 500,000; see *Enzyklopädie des Holocaust* (Munich, 1995), iii. 1633.
147. See Sybil H. Milton, ' "Gypsies" as Social Outsiders in Nazi Germany', in Robert Gellately and Nathan Stoltzfus (eds.), *Social Outsiders in Nazi Germany* (Princeton, forthcoming).
148. See e.g. Hitler, *Mein Kampf*, 246–8.
149. For a useful collection of documents, see Ayaß (ed.), *Gemeinschaftsfremde*, here, 3–5: Erlaß Göring an Polizei (22 Feb. 1933); Gesetz zur Abänderung strafrechtlicher Vorschriften (26 May 1933).
150. Ayaß, *Asoziale*, 187.
151. Bock, *Zwangssterilisation*, 417–18, suggests that 'tens of thousands' were rounded up in 1933 and sent to concentration camps or workhouses.
152. For this case, see David F. Crew, *Germans on Welfare from Weimar to Hitler* (New York, 1998), 150–1.
153. The term is 'Personen mit häufig wechselndem Geschlectsverkehr'. See Ayaß, *Asoziale*, 187.
154. RKPA VE RMI an Landesregierungen usw. (9 Sept. 1939).
155. RKPA VE RMI an Landesregierungen usw. (18 Sept. 1939).
156. She was not Jewish; her Kripo Essen files (and others as well), are reprinted in Ayaß (ed.), *Gemeinschaftsfremde*, 286–7.
157. For this case and similar ones from Duisburg, see Patrick Wagner, *Volksgemeinschaft ohne Verbrecher: Konzeptionen und Praxis der Kriminalpolizei in der Zeit der Weimarer Republik und des Nationalsozialismus* (Hamburg, 1996), 367–73, here 368 and 371.
158. See Anette F. Timm, 'The Ambivalent Outsider: Prostitution, Promiscuity and VD Control in Nazi Berlin', in Gellately and Stoltzfus (eds.), *Social Outsiders*.

159. *Meldungen aus dem Reich*, 6069–71 (29 Nov. 1943).
160. For evidence of Hitler's early aversion to homosexuality, see Hamann, *Hitler's Vienna*, 362.
161. 'Minister Göring säubert Preußen von Schund und Schmutz', in *VB* (2 Mar. 1933); 'Große Polizeiaktion in Breslau', in *VB* (14 Oct. 1933).
162. 'Bekämpfung von Schund und Schmutz', in *BM* (30 Mar. 1933).
163. See the 1937 speech of Dr Josef Meisinger in *Nazism Docs.*, iv. 391. For an analysis, see Claudia Schoppmann, 'National Socialist Policies towards Female Homosexuality', in Lynn Abrams and Elizabeth Harvey (eds.), *Gender Relations in German History: Power, Agency and Experience from the Sixteenth to the Twentieth Century* (Durham, NC, 1997), 177–87.
164. See ' "Säuberungsaktion" gegen Homosexuelle in Hamburg', in *NZ* (28 Aug. 1936), in the documentary collection, Günter Grau (ed.), *Homosexualität in der NS-Zeit: Dokumente einer Diskriminierung und Verfolgung* (Frankfurt am Main, 1993), 173.
165. From numerous examples from 1936, see: '276 Ordensgeistliche angeklagt', in *VB* (27 May 1936); 'Sodom und Gomora in den rheinischen Franziskanerklöstern', in *VB* (20 June 1936); 'Perverse Entartungen auf dem Wege zum Gebet', in *VB* (25 June 1936). There were even more stories in 1937, such as 'Die Öffentlichkeit zu den Prozessen gegen Sittlichkeitsverbrecher im Priesterrock zugelassen', in *VB* (8 May 1937).
166. A spectacular trial (as reported in the *VB*) in Schwerin opened on 22 Jan. 1936 against a man accused of murdering 12 boys; he was eventually found guilty and his execution was reported.
167. Statistics are reprinted in Grau (ed.), *Homosexualität*, 197.
168. See table 3, Burkhard Jellonnek, *Homosexuelle unter dem Hakenkreuz: Die Verfolgung von Homosexuellen im Dritten Reich* (Paderborn, 1990), 285.
169. See table 2, in ibid. 283.
170. See Jürgen Müller, 'Die alltägliche Angst: Denunziation als Instrument zur Ausschaltung Mißliebiger' and Cornellia Limpricht, ' "Homosexuelle Verfehlungen": Der Fall Bartels', in Cornellia Limpricht, Jürgen Müller, and Nina Oxenius (eds.), *'Verführte' Männer: Das Leben der Kölner Homosexuellen im Dritten Reich* (Cologne, 1991), 96–103 and 82–94.
171. See table 2, in Jellonnek, *Homosexuelle*, 283.
172. For isolated Kripo arrest statistics for homosexuals, see Wagner, *Volksgemeinschaft ohne Verbrecher*, 249.
173. See Elke Fröhlich, 'Die Herausforderung des Einzelnen', in Martin Broszat and Elke Fröhlich (eds.), *Bayern in der NS-Zeit* (Munich, 1983), vi. 76–114.
174. See the examples in Prosper Schücking and Martin Sölle, 'Para. 175 StGB—Strafrechtliche Verfolgung homosexueller Männer in Köln', in Limpricht, Müller, and Oxenius (eds.), *'Verführte' Männer*, 104–19.
175. See e.g. RKPA VE, 'Richtlinien des Reichskriminalpolizeiamtes über die Durchführung der vorbeugende Verbrechensbekämpfung' (4 Apr. 1938).
176. RKPA VE, RFSS an RKPA: 'Freiwillige Entmannung von Vorbeugungshäftlingen' (20 May 1939).
177. RKPA VE, RSHA an Kripo: 'Vorbeugende Verbrechensbekämpfung durch die Polizei' (12 July 1940); the last condition was added on 23 August 1940.

178. See RKPA VE, RSHA an Kripo: 'Polizeiliche Vorbeugungsmaßnahmen gegen Entmannte' (2 Jan. 1942); and note Appendix from RMI, 'Untersuchung Entmannter' (13 Nov. 1941).
179. This finding will be published in John C. Fout, *Nazis and Homosexuals: Police State Repression of Male Homosexuality and the Gay Subculture in Nazi Germany 1933–1945* (Columbia University Press, forthcoming), ch. 12.
180. 'Erlaß des Führers zur Reinhaltung von SS und Polizei' (15 Nov. 1941), reprinted in Grau (ed.), *Homosexualität in der NS-Zeit*, 244.
181. 'Befehl Reichsführer-SS und Chef der Deutschen Polizei' (7 Mar. 1942), reprinted in ibid. 248–51.
182. Jellonnek, *Homosexuelle*, 328. He deals with the persecution by the Gestapo on the basis of case files in Düsseldorf, Würzburg, and Speyer. He shows (p. 308) that on average the Gestapo sent around 50 per cent of the cases they began to the courts.
183. Burleigh and Wippermann, *Racial State*, 196, say that the 'usual figure' is 10,000, but believe that as many as 15,000 homosexuals may have died in the camps. Jellonnek, *Homosexuelle*, 328, puts the limits at between 5,000 and 15,000.
184. See the oral history report of Alexander von Plato, 'The Hitler Youth Generation and its Role in the two Post-War German States', in Mark Roseman (ed.), *Generations in Conflict: Youth Revolt and Generation Formation in Germany 1770–1968* (Cambridge, 1995), 210–26.
185. See Melita Maschmann, *Fazit: Mein Weg in der Hitler-Jugend* (Munich, 1981; orig. edn. 1963), 225–9.
186. See BA: R22/4089, 86–7, Informationsdienst des Reichsministers der Justiz (Oct. 1944); Jörg Wolff, *Jugendliche vor Gericht im Dritten Reich: Nationalsozialistische Jugendstrafrechtspolitik und Justizalltag* (Munich, 1992), 270–4.
187. See BA: R22/1221, 296–301: 'Die Amnestien im letzten 6 Jahren' (14 Feb. 1939); also Ulrike Jureit, *Erziehen, Strafen, Vernichten: Jugendkriminalität im Nationalsozialismus* (Münster, 1995), 57–60.
188. For the exact dates, see *Nazism Docs.*, ii. 420. See table 1.3 in Gerhard Rempel, *Hitler's Children: The Hitler Youth and the SS* (Chapel Hill, NC, 1989), 54–5; and Arno Klönne, *Jugend im Dritten Reich: Die Hitler-Jugend und ihre Gegner* (Düsseldorf, 1982), 258.
189. For an overview, including detailed local case studies, see 'Cliquen- und Bandenbildung unter Jugendlichen', from the Reichjugendführung (Sept. 1942), reprinted in full in Detlev Peukert, *Die Edelweißpiraten: Protestbewegungen jugendlicher Arbeiter im 'Dritten Reich'* (Cologne, 1980), 160–229.
190. See Alfons Kenkmann, *Wilde Jugend: Lebenswelt großstädtischer Jugendlicher zwischen Weltwirtschaftskrise, Nationalsozialismus und Währungsreform* (Essen, 1996), esp. 342–54.
191. RKPA VE, Rund Erl. RMI, 'Bekämpfung der Jugendkriminalität' (24 May 1939).
192. RKPA VE, RSHA an Kripo, 'Bekämpfung der Jugendkriminalität' (1 Dec. 1939).
193. RKPA VE, RSHA an Kripo, 'Polizeiliche Unterbringung krimineller und asozialer Minderjähriger' (1 Apr. 1940).
194. Uckermark began operations on 1 June 1942.
195. See RKPA VE.: RSHA an Kripo, 'Anträge auf Unterbringung krimineller und asozialer Minderjähriger in Jugendschutzlager' (26 June and 16 Aug. 1940).

Notes to pages 118–120 303

196. See Heinrich Muth, 'Das "Jugendschutzlager" Moringen', *DH* (1989), 223–52, here 246–7.
197. *Kölnische Zeitung* (16 Nov. 1940), reprinted in Muth, 'Moringen', 248–9.
198. It was the third camp to use the facilities of the old provincial workhouse located there. A concentration camp existed there until late autumn 1933, and a special camp for women used the buildings between 1935 and 1938. For background see Ino Arndt, 'Das Frauenkonzentrationslager Ravensbrück', *DH* (1987), 125–57, here 129–30; the maximum number of women in the camp (Dec. 1937) was 200.
199. A contemporary's description is cited in Muth, 'Moringen', 245.
200. RKPA VE: RSHA an Kripo, 'Anträge auf Unterbringung krimineller und asozialer Minderjähriger in Jugendschutzlager' (8 July 1940).
201. RKPA VE: 'Einweisung in das Jugendschutzlager Moringen' (3 Oct. 1941).
202. Muth, 'Moringen', 250.
203. Bericht Essener Landgerichtspräsidenten an das Reichsjustizministerium (31 July 1944), reprinted in Peukert, *Edelweißpiraten*, 137–45, here 144.
204. The statistics on the male and female prisoners for 1940–3 are from Rempel, *Hitler's Children*, 98–9.
205. 'Wichtige Verordnung zum Schutze der deutsche Jugend', in *VB* (21 Mar. 1940).
206. 'Die Kriminalpolizei greift ein', in *VB* (29 July 1940).
207. 'Jugendarrest statt Gefängnisstrafe', in *VB* (17 Oct. 1940).
208. Muth, 'Moringen', 229–30.
209. The resistance thesis is refuted by Bernd-A. Rusinek, *Gesellschaft in der Katastrophe: Terror, Illegalität, Widerstand, Köln 1944–45* (Essen, 1989); for more on the debate, see Wilfried Breyvogel (ed.), *Piraten, Swings und Junge Garde: Jugendwiderstand im Nationalsozialismus* (Bonn, 1991).
210. See Werner Präg and Wolfgang Jacobmeyer (eds.), *Das Diensttagebuch des deutschen Generalgouverneurs in Polen 1939–1945* (Stuttgart, 1975), 552–60 (entry for 29–31 Aug. 1942).
211. See IfZ, Nürnberg Dokument NO-1285, for the correspondence, including information on the mortalities from 'Chef SS-WVHA an Himmler' (16 Mar. 1943).
212. For a full discussion, see Nikolaus Wachsmann, ' "Annihilation through Labor": The Killing of State Prisoners in the Third Reich', *JMH* (1999), 624–59, here 649–50.
213. Wachsmann, 'Annihilation', 656.
214. Broszat, 'Konzentrationslager', 125.
215. See IfZ, Nürnberg Dokument PS-682 for Goebbels's mention of this concept (14 Sept. 1942). See also *Die Tagebücher von Joseph Goebbels*, T. 2, Bd. 5 (15 Sept. 1942), 504–5.
216. Detlev Peukert, *Volksgenossen und Gemeinschaftsfremde: Anpassung, Ausmerze und Aufbegehren unter dem Nationalsozialismus* (Cologne, 1982), 260–1.
217. For the first example, see *Meldungen aus dem Reich* (23 Apr. 1942), 3666; for the latter example, see (2 Oct. 1941), 2828.
218. *Meldungen aus dem Reich* (26 Mar. 1942), 3526–9.
219. Ibid. (13 Nov. 1941), 2983.
220. Ibid. (5 Mar. 1942), 3417.
221. Ibid. (29 Nov. 1943), 6078.

Chapter 6

1. For additional evidence, see David Bankier, *The Germans and the Final Solution: Public Opinion under Nazism* (Oxford, 1992), 35–6.
2. GSA: HA/Rep.90P: Gestapo Osnabrück (4 Sept. 1935). See also the collection, Thomas Klein (ed.), *Die Lageberichte der Geheimen Staatspolizei über die Provinz Hessen-Nassau 1933–1936*, 2 vols. (Cologne, 1986).
3. See e.g. 'Kauft nicht beim Juden!', in *VB* (15 Sept. 1935).
4. See e.g. 'Lagebericht der Staatspolizeistelle Stettin an das Geheime Staatspolizeiamt über den Monat August 1935' (4 Sept. 1935), in Robert Thévoz et al. (eds.), *Pommern 1934–35 im Spiegel von Gestapo-Lageberichten und Sachakten (Quellen)* (Cologne, 1974), 129.
5. See Lagebericht der Staatspolizeistelle für den Regierungsbezirk Münster für Juni 1935, in Joachim Kuropka (ed.), *Meldungen aus Münster 1924–1945* (Münster, 1992), 286.
6. See Lagebericht der Staatspolizeistelle Hannover an das Geheime Staatspolizeiamt Berlin für den Monat September 1935 (1 Oct. 1935), in Klaus Mlynek (ed.), *Gestapo Hannover meldet . . . Polizei- und Regierungsberichte für das mittlere und südliche Niedersachsen zwischen 1933 und 1937* (Hildesheim, 1986), 423.
7. See ibid. 374, Regierungspräsident Bericht (Apr./May 1935); and (416) Lagebericht der Staatspolizeistelle Hannover (Aug. 1935).
8. Lagebericht Staatspolizeistelle Hannover (Sept. 1935), in ibid., here 423.
9. Bankier, *Germans*, 38–40. For a recent analysis, see Peter Longerich, *Politik der Vernichtung: Eine Gesamtdarstellung der nationalsozialistischen Judenverfolgung* (Munich, 1998), 70–101.
10. See the detailed reports (July and Aug.) *Sopade* (1935), 800–14; and 920–37, for the remark, 922.
11. For an analysis of the social background to these Laws, see Robert Gellately, *The Gestapo and German Society: Enforcing Racial Policy 1933–1945* (Oxford, 1990), 102–10.
12. For the decision-making process and Hitler's stance, see esp. Ian Kershaw, *Hitler 1889–1936: Hubris* (London, 1998), 559–71.
13. On this point, see Saul Friedländer, *Nazi Germany and the Jews*, i. *The Years of Persecution, 1933–1939* (New York, 1997), 148.
14. 'Wer ist Jude im Sinne des neuen Gesetzes?' in *VB* (17 Sept. 1935); 'Der Führer über die Bedeutung der neuen Gesetze', in *VB* (17 Sept. 1935).
15. See Friedländer, *Nazi Germany and the Jews*, 146–51.
16. See Kershaw, *Hitler 1889–1936*, 572.
17. Lagebericht Staatspolizeistelle Hannover (Feb. 1936), in Mlynek, *Gestapo Hannover*, here 512.
18. *The Times* (8 Nov. 1935).
19. 'Die Verordnung zum Reichsbürger- und zum Blutschutzgesetz, 15 Nov. 1935', in *VB* (16 Nov. 1935).
20. See Bankier, *Germans*, 80.
21. Otto Dov Kulka, 'Die Nürnberger Rassengesetze und die deutsche Bevölkerung im Lichte geheimer NS-Lage- und Stimmungsberichte', *VfZ* (1984), 582–624.

22. Longerich, *Politik*, 108–9.
23. Victor Klemperer, *Ich will Zeugnis ablegen bis zum letzten: Tagebücher 1933–1945* (Berlin, 1995), i. 215 (16 Sept. 1935).
24. Ibid., i. 224 (19 Oct. 1935).
25. Marion A. Kaplan, *Between Dignity and Despair: Jewish Life in Nazi Germany* (New York, 1998), 44.
26. Bankier, *Germans*, 73–4.
27. See the Dec. report *Sopade* (1936), 1648–64.
28. From many examples, see Dec. report *Sopade* (1936), 1660–3; and for Nov. (1937), 1568.
29. RKPA, VE, Chef Sipo an Kripo und Gestapo: 'Schutzhaft für jüdische Rassenschänder' (12 June 1937).
30. Erlaß reprinted in Hans Buchheim, 'Die Aktion "Arbeitsscheu Reich"', in *Gutachten des Instituts für Zeitgeschichte* (Stuttgart, 1966), ii. 192.
31. See Michael Wildt (ed.), *Die Judenpolitik des SD 1935 bis 1938: Eine Dokumentation* (Munich, 1995), 56.
32. See RKPA VE, Chef Sipo an RKPA: 'Vertraulich' (19 Oct. 1938); and 'Entlassung jüdischer Vorbeugungshäftlinge' (3 Nov. 1938).
33. Peter Gay, *My German Question: Growing up in Nazi Berlin* (New Haven, 1998), 112.
34. Ibid. 71. The *VB*, 'Sensationskomplexe' (19 July 1935) played down the antisemitic excesses and suggested that foreign journalists who reported the stories had exaggerated.
35. See Michael Wildt, 'Gewalt gegen Juden in Deutschland 1933 bis 1939', *Werkstattgeschichte*, 18 (1997), 59–80, here 65.
36. See Avraham Barkai, '*Volksgemeinschaft*, "Aryanization" and the Holocaust', in David Cesarani (ed.), *The Final Solution: Origins and Implementation* (London, 1994), 33–50.
37. Ibid. 41. See also Gerhard Kratzsch, *Der Gauwirtschaftsapparat der NSDAP: Menschenführung, 'Arisierung,' und Wehrwirtschaft im Gau Westfalen-Süd* (Münster, 1989), 115–27.
38. See these and other examples in Frank Bajohr, *'Arisierung' in Hamburg: Die Verdrängung der jüdischen Unternehmer 1933–1945* (Hamburg, 1997), here 137 and 141.
39. 'VO über die Anmeldung des Vermögens von Juden', reprinted in Joseph Walk (ed.), *Das Sonderrecht für die Juden im NS-Staat*, 2nd edn. (Heidelberg, 1996), 223.
40. Helmut Genschel, *Die Verdrängung der Juden aus der Wirtschaft im Dritten Reich* (Berlin, 1966), 175.
41. 'Jüdisches Vermögen bis 30. Juni meldepflichtig', in *VB* (28 Apr. 1938); 'Jüdische Betriebe werden gekennzeichnet', in *VB* (17 June 1938).
42. 'Gesetzliche Maßnahmen zur Ausschaltung des jüdischen Einflusses in der Wirtschaft', in *VB* (23 June 1938).
43. See e.g. the July report *Sopade* (1938), 732–71, esp. 750; for the quotation see 758.
44. See e.g. 'Erstes Berliner Urteil gegen einen rassenschänderischen Juden', in *VB* (18 Dec. 1935); 'Festnahme eines jüdischen Wucherers', in *VB* (23 Jan. 1936); 'Jüdischer Großbetrüger entlarvt', in *VB* (5 Nov. 1936).

45. There were stories from countries such as France, Poland, England, Hungary, Romania, Paraguay, various African countries, the United States, and Italy. See e.g. from the USA, 'Kampf gegen Kommunisten, Katholiken, Juden und Neger', in *VB* (17 June 1936); 'Die Trennung der Rassen in den Schulen Deutschlands und der Vereinigten Staaten', in *VB* (22 Sept. 1936).
46. 'Der Führer über die deutschen Judengesetze und den Aufbau der Wehrmacht', in *VB* (28 Nov. 1935). From many other articles, see e.g. 'Das jüdische Gesicht des Bolschewismus', in *VB* (10 Feb. 1937).
47. See e.g. Goebbels's speech, 'Der Bolschewismus muß vernichtet werden, wenn Europa wieder gesunden soll!' in *VB* (11 Sept. 1936).
48. See *VB* (20 Oct. 1937).
49. See Dan Diner, *America in the Eyes of the Germans: An Essay on Anti-Americanism*, trans. A. Brown (Princeton, 1996), 79–103.
50. See e.g. 'USA unter jüdischer Diktatur', in *VB* (6 Jan. 1939).
51. See the excellent analysis in Philipp Gassert, *Amerika im Dritten Reich: Ideologie, Propaganda und Volksmeinung 1933–1945* (Stuttgart, 1997), esp. 183 ff.
52. See *Meldungen aus dem Reich* (20 Jan. 1941), 1917–19.
53. For an analysis, see Eric Rentschler, *The Ministry of Illusion: Nazi Cinema and its Afterlife* (Cambridge, Mass., 1996), here 149–69.
54. The film was 'Ich klage an'. For a report, see *Meldungen aus dem Reich* (15 Jan. 1942), 3175–8.
55. For this conclusion, see Ian Kershaw, *Popular Opinion and Political Dissent in the Third Reich: Bavaria 1933–1945* (Oxford, 1983), 272.
56. See the Nov. report *Sopade* (1938), 1177–1211, here 1177.
57. See BA: R58/276, 'Aufenthaltsverbot für Juden polnischer Staatsangehörigkeit' (26 and 27 Oct. 1938); also Trude Maurer, 'Abschiebung und Attentat: Die Ausweisung der polnischen Juden und der Vorward für die "Kristallnacht"', in Walter H. Pehle (ed.), *Der Judenpogrom 1938: Von der 'Reichskristallnacht' zum Völkermord* (Frankfurt am Main, 1988), 52–73.
58. For an account of the directed press coverage, see Wolfgang Benz, 'Der Novemberpogrom 1938', in Wolfgang Benz (ed.), *Die Juden in Deutschland 1933–1945: Leben unter nationalsozialistischer Herrschaft* (Munich, 1988), 499–544, here 505–12.
59. *Die Tagebücher von Joseph Goebbels*, T. 1, B. 6 (10 Nov. 1938), 180.
60. BA: R58/276, 124: Fernschreiben an Stapo (9 Nov. 1938), 'Geheim'.
61. BA: R58/276, 125–6: Fernschreiben an Stapo (10 Nov. 1938): Betr.: 'Maßnahmen gegen Juden in der heutigen Nacht'.
62. BA: R58/276: 136–7: Funkspruch, Daluege an Orpo (10 Nov.1938).
63. *Die Tagebücher von Joseph Goebbels*, T. 1, B. 6 (11 Nov. 1938), 182.
64. BA: R58/276, 129, Chef Sipo an Stapo (10 Nov. 1938): Betr.: 'Maßnahmen gegen Juden'.
65. See Gellately, *Gestapo and German Society*, 112 ff.
66. See e.g. the Nov. report *Sopade* (1938), 1186–1211.
67. Excerpts from the press are reprinted in Heinz Lauber, *Judenpogrom 'Reichskristallnacht' November 1938 in Großdeutschland* (Gerlingen, 1981), 125–47.

68. 'Aufruf des Reichsministers Dr. Goebbels an die Bevölkerung: Neue gesetzlich Regelung der Judenfrage angekündigt', in *VB* (11 Nov. 1938).
69. 'Waffenbesitz für Juden verboten', in *VB* (11 Nov. 1938). In fact, since 16 Dec. 1935, Jews could no longer obtain a shooting licence (*Waffenscheine*). See Walk (ed.), *Das Sonderrecht für die Juden*, 146, allegedly because this would 'endanger the German population'.
70. *IMT*, xxxii. 1–2, Dokument 3058-PS, 'Schnellbrief an Göring'. The Nazi Party's high court, later estimated that 91 Jews were killed, and this must be taken as a minimum figure.
71. Konrad Kwiet and Helmut Eschwege, *Selbstbehauptung und Widerstand: Deutsche Juden im Kampf um Existenz und Menschenwürde 1933–1945* (Hamburg, 1984), 202–5. See table 'Selbstmordkurve der Juden in Deutschland 1933–1945', 199.
72. Figures cited in Lauber, *Judenpogrom*, 124, suggest that 10,911 were sent to Dachau, 9,815 to Buchenwald, and 5,000 to 10,000 to Sachsenhausen. The large figure for Buchenwald, based on a closer study, is given by Rudi Goguel, 'Vom großen Pogrom bis zur Entfesselung des Krieges (1938/39)', in Klaus Drobisch et al., *Juden unterm Hakenkreuz* (Frankfurt am Main, 1973), 194. See also Benz, 'Novemberpogrom', 528.
73. See the statistics in Goguel, 'Vom großen Pogrom bis zur Entfesselung des Krieges',194.
74. See accounts from Dec. reports *Sopade* (1938), 1332–50.
75. See e.g. stories of the mistreatment of the Jews in Dachau in Hans-Günter Richardi, *Schule der Gewalt: Das Konzentrationslager Dachau* (Munich, 1995), 202 ff.
76. See Leni Yahil, 'Jews in Concentration Camps in Germany Prior to World War II', in *The Nazi Concentration Camps* (Jerusalem, 1984), 69–100.
77. These figures are from a report prepared by camp prisoners shortly after its liberation. See *The Buchenwald Report*, trans. and ed. David A. Hackett (Boulder, Colo., 1995), 34.
78. 'Empörte Volksseele schafft sich Luft', in *VB* (11 Nov. 1938).
79. See Karl Dürkefälden, *'Schreiben wie es wirklich war'! Aufzeichnungen Karl Dürkefälden aus den Jahren 1933–1945* (Hanover, 1985), 89.
80. Walter Tausk, *Breslauer Tagebuch 1933–1940* (Berlin, 1988), 200.
81. 'Abrechnung des Reiches mit den jüdischen Verbrechern', in *VB* (13 Nov. 1938).
82. See Daniel Jonah Goldhagen, *Hitler's Willing Executioners: Ordinary Germans and the Holocaust* (New York, 1996), 103.
83. See Ruth Andreas-Friedrich, *Der Schattenmann: Tagebuchaufzeichnungen 1938–1945* (Frankfurt am Main, 1983), 25–35; Dürkefälden, *Schreiben wie es wirklich war!* 85–102.
84. Bankier, *Germans*, 86–7, emphasis is in the original.
85. See Dec. report *Sopade* (1938), 1352–3.
86. 'Die Sühneleistung der Juden', in *VB* (24 Nov. 1938).
87. See Hans Safrian, *Eichmann und seine Gehilfen* (Frankfurt am Main, 1995), 23–56.
88. See *IMT*, xxviii. 499–540, 1816-PS, 'Stenographische Niederschrift der Besprechung über die Judenfrage bei Göring am 12. Nov. 1938', here 534.

89. 'Dr Goebbels über die endgültige Lösung der Judenfrage', in *VB* (14 Nov. 1938).

90. 'Reinliche Scheidung zwischen Deutschen und Juden', in *VB* (16 Nov. 1938).

91. See e.g. USHMM: RG 11, 500-1-160, SD-Hauptamt, 'Vortrag: Die Judengesetzung seit 1933' (n.d., most likely early Jan. 1939).

92. *Die Tagebücher von Joseph Goebbels*, T. 1, B. 6 (14 Nov. 1938), 186; (22 Nov. 1938), 195.

93. See the Feb. report *Sopade* (1939), 201–2; and for Apr. *Sopade* (1940), 256–68.

94. For a brief account, see Alan Bullock, *Hitler and Stalin: Parallel Lives* (Toronto, 1991), 642.

95. 'England und Juda die geistigen Urheber des Münchner Verbrechens', in *VB* (11 Nov. 1939).

96. For the SS perpetrators' post-war trial, see *Justiz und NS-Verbrechen*, iv. 678–98.

97. See e.g. Peter Brommer (ed.), *Die Partei hört mit: Lageberichte und andere Meldungen des Sicherheitsdienstes der SS aus dem Großraum Koblenz 1937–1941* (Koblenz, 1988), 155–7 (25 Nov. 1938).

98. See e.g. H. G. Adler, *Der verwaltete Mensch: Studien zur Deportation der Juden aus Deutschland* (Tübingen, 1974), 819–23, and what happened to Robert Fuchs (born 1871).

99. See Bajohr, *Arisierung*, here 334.

100. See e.g. 'Jüdisches Umzugsgut unter dem Hammer', in *HF* (29 Mar. 1941), cited in Bajohr, *Arisierung*, 332 n. 28.

101. For a description of one such auction, see the American newspaper reporter's story in Howard K. Smith, *Last Train from Berlin* (New York, 1942), 191.

102. See esp. Wolf Gruner, *Der Geschlossene Arbeitseinsatz deutscher Juden: Zur Zwangsarbeit als Element der Verfolgung 1938–1943* (Berlin, 1997), 271.

103. Ibid. 313.

104. See Raul Hilberg, *The Destruction of the European Jews*, rev. edn. (New York, 1985), ii. 614. An indication that the police acted on their own also in Western Europe can be seen in an event from 8 Aug. 1940, when Police Major Walter Krüger in Bordeaux, deported 1,400 of these deported Jews in his jurisdiction to the unoccupied part of France across the demarcation line. See Michael R. Marrus and Robert O. Paxton, *Vichy France and the Jews* (New York, 1981), 10.

105. For a detailed study based on Gestapo materials, see Adler, *Der verwaltete Mensch*, 91 ff.

106. BA: R58/276, 300: RSHA an Stapo, 'Verhalten Deutschblütiger gegenüber Juden' (24 Oct. 1941).

107. *Meldungen aus dem Reich* (9 Oct. 1941), 2849.

108. Ibid. (24 Nov. 1941), 3020–3.

109. Ibid. (2 Feb. 1942), 3233–48.

110. Herbert Schultheis, *Juden in Mainfranken 1933–1945* (Bad Neustadt a. d. Saale, 1980), 34.

111. Kershaw, *Popular Opinion*, 27–8.

112. Peter Spitznagel, *Wähler und Wahlen in Unterfranken 1919–1969* (Würzburg, 1979).

113. Roland Flade, *Juden in Würzburg 1918–1933* (Würzburg, 1985), 352–5.

114. StA W: NSDAP/GL/XII/2 (13 Oct. 1933).

115. StA W: Polizeidirektion Würzburg, G 274. Apparently there is no Gestapo file on this case.

116. See esp. Adler, *Der verwaltete Mensch.*

117. Klemperer, *Zeugnis*, i. 440 (3 Dec. 1938).

118. See Gellately, *Gestapo and German Society*, 129–214.

119. Sarah Gordon, *Hitler, Germans, and the 'Jewish Question'* (Princeton, 1984), 241.

120. HStA D: Gestapo 65053. For illustrative denunciations, see 1798; 17922; 45101; and 45031.

121. Another 103 cases (or 13 per cent) contained no information about why the Gestapo began a case, but probably many of these also commenced when a tip was passed along by a civilian.

122. Reinhard Mann, *Protest und Kontrolle im Dritten Reich: Nationalsozialistische Herrschaft im Alltag einer rheinischen Großstadt* (Frankfurt am Main, 1987), 295.

123. Mann, *Protest und Kontrolle*, 287–312.

124. Berward Dörner, *'Heimtücke': Das Gesetz als Waffe: Kontrolle, Abschreckung und Verfolgung in Deutschland 1933–1945* (Paderborn, 1998), 102.

125. There are a series of relevant studies in Sheila Fitzpatrick and Robert Gellately (eds.), *Accusatory Practices: Denunciation in Modern European History, 1789–1989* (Chicago, 1997).

126. See e.g. Jan T. Gross, *Revolution from Abroad: The Soviet Conquest of Poland's Western Ukraine and Western Belorussia* (Princeton, 1988), 119–20.

127. See Tim Mason, 'Whatever happened to Fascism?' in his *Nazism, Fascism, and the Working Class*, 329. Note also the detailed study of Jonathan Steinberg, *All or Nothing: The Axis and the Holocaust 1941–1943* (London, 1990).

128. Cited in Lothar Gruchmann, *Justiz im Dritten Reich 1933–1945: Anpassung und Unterwerfung in der Ära Gürtner* (Munich, 1988), 835.

129. StA L: LRA Öhringen, FL 20/14/4750: RMI, Runderl. an die Landesregierungen vom 28. 4. 1934, betr. 'Bekämpfung des Denunziantentum'.

130. Cited in Richard Grunberger, *Das zwölfjährige Reich: Der Deutschen Alltag unter Hitler* (Munich, 1972), 116.

131. BA: R 58/264, 192: Frick an Reichsstatthalter, betr. 'Judenfrage und Denunziantentum' (10 Jan. 1939).

132. BA: R 58/243, 317: Chef Sipo an Stapo, betr. 'Anzeigeerstattung von Verwandten untereinander, insbesondere bei Ehegatten' (24 Feb. 1941).

133. See Heinz Boberach (ed.), *Richterbriefe: Dokumente zur Beeinflußung der deutschen Rechtsprechung* (Boppard, 1975), 171.

134. William L. Shirer, *Berlin Diary* (New York, 1941), 214–15.

135. StA W: Gestapo 16015.

136. HStA D: Gestapo 65053.

137. For an analysis of the relevant sources and further examples of denunciations, see Gellately, *Gestapo and German Society*, 138–43.

138. Gordon, *Hitler*, 241.

139. See Bernd Stöver, *Volksgemeinschaft im Dritten Reich: Die Konsensbereitschaft der Deutschen aus der Sicht sozialistischer Exilberichte* (Düsseldorf, 1993).

140. *Meldungen aus dem Reich* (10 July 1941), 2505.

141. Ibid. (14 Aug. 1941), 2650.

142. See Apr. report *Sopade* (1940), 265–8.

143. See 'Brutstätte des Weltjudentums', in *VB* (21 Mar. 1940).

144. Baruch Z. Ophir and Falk Wiesemann (eds.), *Die jüdischen Gemeinden in Bayern 1918–1945* (Munich, 1979), 24.

145. Ophir and Wiesemann (eds.), *Die jüdischen Gemeinden*, 24.

146. Also for what follows, see Ino Arndt and Heinz Boberach, 'Deutsches Reich', in Wolfgang Benz (ed.), *Dimension des Völkermords: Die Zahl der jüdischen Opfer des Nationalsozialismus* (Munich, 1991), 23–65, here 34 and 36.

147. For a detailed account of the deportations, see Schultheis, *Juden in Mainfranken*, 534–616.

148. See StA W: Gestapo 10810, also in Dörner, *Heimtücke*, 234.

149. *Die Tagebücher von Joseph Goebbels*, T. 2, Bd. 7, 305 (entry for 17 May 1942).

150. For a brief account of the mixed marriages, see Hilberg, *Destruction of the European Jews*, ii. 427–30.

151. For the post-war trial of the Gestapo, see *Justiz und NS-Verbrechen*, xi. 256–73.

152. See *Justiz und NS-Verbrechen*, xxii. 658–82.

153. Gruner, *Arbeitseinsatz*, 314.

154. *Die Tagebücher von Joseph Goebbels*, T. 2, Bd. 7 (23 Jan. 1943), 177.

155. Guidelines are reprinted in Adler, *Der verwaltete Mensch*, 199–200.

156. *Die Tagebücher von Joseph Goebbels*, T. 2, Bd. 7 (11 Mar. 1943), 528.

157. Gruner, *Arbeitseinsatz*, 316.

158. The full story is recounted in Nathan Stoltzfus, *Resistance of the Heart: Inter-marriage and the Rosenstrasse Protest in Nazi Germany* (New York, 1996), 243 for Goebbels's order.

159. StA W: Polizeidirektion Würzburg, G 8846.

160. See *Justiz und NS-Verbrechen*, ii. 490–9.

161. See e.g. StA W: Gestapo 2635, for a case from July 1944 in which a woman was accused of saying that an SS man told her that he once 'bathed up to his knees in blood' during the murder of 40,000 Jews. She was warned not to repeat such stories.

162. See e.g. 'Judas Krieg!' in *VB* (19 Sept. 1939); and 'Judas Krieg (II)', in *VB* (28 Sept. 1939); 'Förmliche Allianz zwischen England und Weltjudentum', in *VB* (25 Oct. 1939).

163. 'Judenhörigkeit der britischen Regierung', in *VB* (5 Dec. 1939); 'Das judenhörige Kabinett Daladier', in *VB* (7 Jan. 1940).

164. See e.g. 'So machen Juden Frankreichs öffentliche Meinung', in *VB* (29 Jan. 1940): 'Norwegens jüdische Verführer', in *VB* (23 Apr. 1940); 'Neu Yorker Juden hetzen zur Fortsetzung des Krieges', in *VB* (23 July 1940); 'Wer hetzt Amerika auf? Die Juden!' in *VB* (7 Feb. 1940); 'Weltjuda fordert von England "Kampf bis zum Ende"', in *VB* (30 Apr. 1941).

165. 'Rund um Roosevelt—Juden', in *VB* (23 Mar. 1941).

166. 'Solidarisch mit Deutschland: Europas Stellungnahme zur Judenfrage', in *VB* (29 Mar. 1941).

167. 'Vichy erläßt schärfere Judengesetze', in *VB* (15 June 1941).
168. See e.g. 'Begegung mit Juden in Polen', in *VB* (28 Nov. 1939); 'Südostpreußen vom polnischen Schmutz befreit', in *VB* (7 Sept. 1940).
169. 'Ein Jahr Aufbauarbeit im Reichsgau Danzig-Westpreußen', in *VB* (14 Oct. 1940).
170. 'Der Bolschewismus enthüllt sein jüdisches Gesicht', in *VB* (10 July 1941); 'Bolschewistische Weltrevolution Werk der Juden und Freimauer', in *VB* (9 May 1944).
171. 'Hebräer um Roosevelt', in *VB* (25 Sept. 1941); 'Ein waschechter Jude auf dem Thron der Vereinigten Staaten', in *VB* (16 Jan. 1943).
172. 'Juda und Freimaurerei standen hinter Badoglios Verrat', in *VB* (3 Mar. 1944).
173. See e.g. 'Jüdischer Luftterror', in *VB* (3 Mar. 1943); 'Jude leitet Frankreichs Mordbanden', in *VB* (17 Mar. 1944).
174. 'Der Massenmord von Katyn das Werk jüdischer Schlächter', in *VB* (15 Apr. 1943); 'Wie lange schweigt England zum Massenmord von Katyn?' in *VB* (16 Apr. 1943).
175. See *Meldungen aus dem Reich*, 5144–5 (19 Apr. 1943).
176. Christian Gerlach, 'Die Wannsee-Konferenz, das Schicksal der deutschen Juden und Hitlers politische Grundsatzentscheidung, alle Juden Europas zu ermorden', *Werkstattgeschichte*, 18 (1997), 7–44.
177. *Die Tagebücher von Joseph Goebbels*, T. 2, Bd. 2 (13 Dec. 1941), 498–9.
178. Full text is reprinted in Domarus (ed.), *Hitler Reden*, iii. 1047–67. For the brief threat about the Jews, 1058.
179. Bankier, *Germans*, 139–40.
180. The text is reprinted in Domarus (ed.), *Hitler Reden*, iv. 1657–64, here 1663–4.
181. ' "Der Jude wird ausgerottet werden" ', in *VB* (27 Feb. 1942).
182. 'Der Führer zerstört die Wunschträume des Feindes', in *VB* (10 Nov. 1941).
183. 'Der jüdische Feind', in *VB* (12 Nov. 1941).
184. 'Die Juden sind Schuld!' in *Das Reich* (16 Nov. 1941), 1–2. For public reaction, see *Meldungen aus dem Reich* (20 Nov. 1941), 3007.
185. 'Wir können siegen, wir müssen siegen und wir werden siegen!' in *VB* (3 Dec. 1941).
186. 'Arbeit—für die Juden ein "schreckliches Schicksal" ', in *VB* (27 Mar. 1942); 'Salonikis Juden müssen nunmehr arbeiten', in *VB* (13 July 1942).
187. 'Juden als Partisanenanführer', in *VB* (9 Oct. 1941).
188. In 1942 the prophecy was mentioned in speeches he gave on 30 Jan., 30 Sept., and 8 Nov. All these speeches were published at the time and are reprinted in Domarus (ed.), *Hitler Reden*, vol. iv. For an analysis, see Ian Kershaw, *The 'Hitler Myth': Image and Reality in the Third Reich* (Oxford, 1987), 241 ff.
189. The text is reprinted in Domarus (ed.), *Hitler Reden*, iv. 1826–34, here, 1828–9.
190. See *Meldungen aus dem Reich*, ix. 3235 (2 Feb. 1942).
191. 'Wir zerbrechen die Macht der jüdischen Weltkoalition', in *VB* (25 Feb. 1943). The prophecy was alluded to briefly in his message at the beginning of the New Year. In 1943 he mentioned the prophecy also on 21 Mar. and, finally, on 26 May 1944.
192. Reprinted in Domarus (ed.), *Hitler Reden*, iv. 1845.
193. Gruner, *Arbeitseinsatz*, 226.
194. See Klemperer, *Zeugnis*, ii. 47 (16 Mar. 1942).

312 *Notes to pages 149–152*

195. Ibid., ii. 68 (19 Apr. 1942). For a remarkable account by a Russian who lived near the site and later wrote of it, see Anatoli Kuznetsov, *Babi Yar*, trans. D. Floyd (Harmondsworth, 1982). For the death toll, see *Enzyklopädie des Holocaust*, i. 145.
196. Klemperer, *Zeugnis*, ii. 252 (4 Oct. 1942).
197. Ibid., ii. 270 (2 Nov. 1942).
198. Inge Scholl, *Die weisse Rose* (Frankfurt am Main, 1955), 102.
199. Klemperer, *Zeugnis*, ii. 284 (29 Nov. 1942).
200. Ibid., ii. 335 (27 Feb. 1943).
201. Ibid., ii. 565 (20 Aug. 1944).
202. See Jeremy D. Harris, 'Broadcasting the Massacres: An Analysis of the BBC's Contemporary Coverage of the Holocaust', in *Yad Vashem Studies* (1996), 65–98.
203. For the statistics, see the table in Gruner, *Arbeitseinsatz*, 351.
204. 'Der Krieg und die Juden', in *Das Reich* (9 May 1943).
205. *Die Tagebücher von Joseph Goebbels*, T. 2, Bd. 8 (9 May 1943), 242.
206. Helmut Heiber (ed.), *Goebbels Reden* (Munich, 1972), ii. 218–39.
207. *Die Tagebücher von Joseph Goebbels*, T. 2, Bd. 8 (6 June 1943) 430.

Chapter 7

1. For the key documents, see *Nazism Docs.*, iv. 302–66.
2. See Richard J. Overy, 'Guns or Butter? Living Standards, Finance, and Labour in Germany, 1939–1942', in his *War and Economy in the Third Reich* (Oxford, 1994), 259–314, here 305.
3. The German Labour Ministry was apparently convinced by the end of 1941 that female employment was already close to the ceiling. See Overy, 'Guns or Butter?', 310 n. 157.
4. *Meldungen aus dem Reich* (26 Feb. 1942), 3386–7.
5. See Elizabeth D. Heineman, *What Difference Does a Husband Make? Women and Marital Status in Nazi and Postwar Germany* (Berkeley, 1999), 60.
6. Overy, 'Guns or Butter?' 310.
7. See Wolfgang Schumann et al., *Deutschland im Zweiten Weltkrieg* (Berlin (East), 1975), ii. 412 and (1985), iv. 407.
8. On Hitler's decision, see Ulrich Herbert, *Best: Biographische Studien über Radikalismus, Weltanschauung und Vernunft 1903–1989* (Bonn, 1996), 240–9, here 241; and Helmut Krausnick and Hans-Heinrich Wilhelm, *Die Truppe des Weltanschauungskrieges: Die Einsatzgruppen der Sicherheitspolizei und des SD 1938–1942* (Stuttgart, 1981), 64–5.
9. Hitler's speech is reprinted in Domarus (ed.), *Hitler Reden*, iii. 1383.
10. The phrase is from a Feb. 1940 list of complaints presented to Commander-in-Chief of the army, and is cited in Raul Hilberg, *The Destruction of the European Jews*, rev. edn. (New York, 1985), i. 190–1.
11. For this and other excesses, Krausnick and Wilhelm, *Die Truppe*, 63–106, here 93.
12. Horst Rohde, 'Hitlers erster "Blitzkrieg" und seine Auswirkungen auf Nordosteuropa', in *Das Deutsche Reich und der Zweite Weltkrieg* (Stuttgart, 1979), ii. 139 ff.
13. *IMT*, xxvi. 864–PS, 377 ff.

14. There were in addition, 28,316 Polish prisoners of war. After a late start, there were 2,758,312 Soviet workers in Germany, including 631,559 prisoners of war, the largest group in that year. There were nearly two million prisoners of war in the country at that time. See 31 Oct. 1944: 'Der Arbeitseinsatz im Großdeutschen Reich', Nr. 10, reprinted in Ulrich Herbert, *Geschichte der Ausländerbeschäftigung in Deutschland 1880 bis 1980* (Berlin, 1986), table 12, 145.

15. Tim Mason, *Social Policy in the Third Reich: The Working Class and the 'National Community'*, trans. J. Broadwin (Providence, RI, 1993), 348–9.

16. See e.g. Walter Struve, *Aufstieg und Herrschaft des Nationalsozialismus in einer industriellen Kleinstadt: Osterode am Harz 1918–1945* (Essen, 1992), 427 ff.

17. See HStA D: RW36/10, 102–14, also for what follows.

18. Andreas Heusler, *Ausländereinsatz: Zwangsarbeit für die Münchner Kriegswirtschaft 1939–1945* (Munich, 1996), 175.

19. Reinhard Rürup (ed.), *Der Krieg gegen die Sowjetunion 1941–1945* (Berlin, 1991), 213.

20. Rogers Brubaker, *Citizenship and Nationhood in France and Germany* (Cambridge, Mass., 1992), 114 ff.

21. BA: R 49/75; 16 ff.: Dr E. Wetzel and Dr G. Hecht, 'Denkschrift des Rassenpolitischen Amtes der NSDAP' (Nov. 1939).

22. This was how Martin Bormann recorded Hitler's stance. *IMT*, xxxix, doc. 172-USSR, 425 ff. 'Aktenvermerk'.

23. Herbert, *Ausländerbeschäftigung*, 100. See also Martin Broszat, *Nationalsozialistische Polenpolitik 1939–1945* (Stuttgart, 1961), 9 ff.

24. *Meldungen aus dem Reich* (4 Dec. 1939), 528.

25. Ibid. (4 Dec. 1939), 528.

26. Helmut Heiber, 'Der Generalplan Ost', *VfZ* 6 (1958), 306–9.

27. See Czeslaw Madajzyk, 'Vom "Generalplan Ost" zum "Generalsielungsplan"' and Karl Heinz Roth, '"Generalplan Ost"—"Gesamtplan Ost." Forschungsstand, Quellenprobleme, neue Ergebnisse', in Mechtild Rössler and Sabine Schleiermacher (eds.), *Der 'Generalplan Ost': Hauptlinien der nationalsozialistischen Planungs- und Vernichtungspolitik* (Berlin, 1993), 12–24; 25–117.

28. BA: R58/1030, 95 ff. Schnellbrief Himmler an Stapostellen.

29. HStA D: RW36/d42, 89, Stapo Düsseldorf an Aussendienststellen (17 Nov. 1942).

30. Alfred Konieczny and Herbert Szurgacz, *Praca przymusowa polakow pod panowaniew hitlerowskim 1939–1945* (Poznan, 1976), 319 ff.

31. Edward L. Homze, *Foreign Labor in Nazi Germany* (Princeton, 1967), 23.

32. See Werner Präg and Wolfgang Jocobmeyer (eds.), *Das Diensttagebuch des deutschen Generalgouverneurs in Polen 1939–1945* (Stuttgart, 1975), 96 ff. (19 Jan. 1940); Jochen August, 'Die Entwicklung des Arbeitsmarkts in Deutschland in den 30er Jahren und der Masseneinsatz ausländischer Arbeitskräfte während des Zweiten Weltkrieges', *Archiv für Sozialgeschichte*, 24 (1984), 342 ff.

33. Jan Tomasz Gross, *Polish Society under German Occupation: The Generalgouvernement* (Princeton, 1979), 79.

34. See Ulrich Herbert, *Fremdarbeiter: Politik und Praxis des 'Ausländer-Einsatzes' in der Kriegswirtschaft des Dritten Reiches* (Berlin, 1986), 272; Czeslaw Luczak, *Polozenie polskich robotnikow przymusowych w Rzeszy 1939–1945* (Poznan, 1975), 201; Eva Seeber, *Zwangsarbeiter in der faschistischen Kriegswirschaft* (Berlin (East),

1964), 152; Ingrid Schupetta, *Frauen- und Ausländererwerbstätigkeit in Deutschland von 1939 bis 1945* (Cologne, 1983), 97.

35. BA: R58/1030, 28 ff.

36. See Christoph U. Schminck-Gustavus, 'Zwangsarbeitsrecht und Faschismus: Zur "Polenpolitik" im "Dritten Reich" ', *Kritische Justiz*, 13 (1980), 1–27, 184–206.

37. BA: R58/1030, 42 ff.

38. See Peter Witte et al. (eds.), *Der Dienstkalender Heinrich Himmlers 1941/42* (Hamburg, 1999), n. 24, 121 (entry for 22 Feb. 1941). Frauendorfer told Ulrich von Hassell this story later (18 May 1941).

39. At war's end the Gestapo's case files were destroyed everywhere with the exception of 70,000 in Düsseldorf, 19,000 or so in Würzburg, and about 12,000 in Speyer. The files pertain respectively to the Gestapo's jurisdictions of the Rhine-Ruhr, Lower Franconia, and the Palatinate.

40. See StA W: Gestapo 1771 and Gestapo 13788 for such a case from Amorbach (4 Oct. 1941) and another from Kitzingen (24 Aug. 1944).

41. See StA W: Gestapo 15235 from Mömbris (1 Dec. 1941).

42. See StA W: Gestapo 12733.

43. HStA D: RW36/d25, 2 ff. Chef Sipo an Stapo: 'Verschärfte Behandlung arbeitsunwilliger polnischer Zivilarbeiter'.

44. See e.g. StA W: Gestapo 15243, from Würzburg (Jan. 1945).

45. The Party was involved in two related cases from Ochsenfurt in mid-Sept. 1941. See StA W: Gestapo 5711 and 16374. See Gestapo 6523, for a case in Bergrheinfeld (Jan. 1941), when an HJ leader denounced an HJ member to the local gendarme.

46. See StA W: Gestapo 8271, for a case against a Nazi peasant leader in Pfändhausen (mid-June 1940). He took a Pole who worked for him to a film, only to be denounced by the Party 'cell leader'. For a similar example from Westheim, Mar. 1941, see Gestapo 2762.

47. StA W: Gestapo 5361; 16397. The case is from Ochsenfurt. If not prosecuted for sending the wreath, the farm woman was interrogated by the gendarme.

48. See HStA D: RW36/d42, 88 ff.

49. See StA W: Gestapo 4322: in Castell a German worker assaulted a Polish female co-worker (Oct. 1940). See e.g. Gestapo 1469: near Gerolzhofen, a German employer pressed his attentions on a female employee (May 1943).

50. StA W: Gestapo 5645.

51. BA: R58/1030, 88 ff.

52. StA W: Gestapo 17008. See also Gestapo 4280; 9631 from Rieneck (May 1940).

53. The case is from Unterwestern. StA W: Gestapo 3026.

54. StA W: Gestapo 3685.

55. The case is from Aub. StA W: Gestapo 14349.

56. StA W: Gestapo 6963.

57. The case is from Rottendorf. StA W: Gestapo 12867. For another such case, see Gestapo 4929.

58. StA W: Gestapo 14819: A letter was sent to the SD in Aschaffenburg about a pub owner who allowed Poles on the premises (Jan. 1940).

59. The case is from Aub. StA W: Gestapo 5050.

60. See e.g. StA W: Gestapo 7991, from Aub (Dec. 1943), the woman was later sent to Ravensbrück; the Pole was subjected to 'special handling'. See Gestapo 12948, from Prosselsheim (Mar. 1942). Rumours were investigated that a pregnant young woman may have had a relationship with a Pole. For a Polish woman, see e.g. Gestapo 13788.

61. The case is from Dettelbach. StA W: Gestapo 18117.

62. The case is from Poppenhausen. StA W: Gestapo 8414.

63. StA W: Gestapo 17068.

64. StA W: Gestapo 6962; 8548. The woman later had a miscarriage.

65. See HStA D: Gestapo 5719, from Königsberg (a suspicion was raised about a woman who was five months pregnant) and Gestapo 70150 from Karlsruhe. In Gestapo 53496, from Köslin, policemen found a suspicious photo album during another investigation.

66. HStA D: Gestapo 58364.

67. HStA D: Gestapo 2111. The suspect here (in Apr. 1942) was sterilized (1935) because of mental incompetence ('wegen geistiger Minderwertigkeit').

68. HStA D: Gestapo 68176.

69. The case is from Metzkausen. HStA D: Gestapo 4082.

70. HStA D: RW36/d25, Chef Sipo an Stapo (12 Nov. 1940).

71. The case is from Krefeld. HStA D: Gestapo 58730.

72. HStA D: Gestapo 41327.

73. The case began in Krefeld-Kempen and was handled by the Krefeld Gestapo. HStA D: Gestapo 40144; 41754.

74. Herbert, *Fremdarbeiter*, 100–1.

75. See e.g. HStA D: Gestapo 1826, from Nievenheim (20 July 1941); a coal dealer (44 years of age) falsely reported that Poles were served in a pub.

76. *Meldungen aus dem Reich*, 1873–4 (Dec. 1940); 2148 (Mar. 1941); 3496 ff. (Mar. 1942).

77. The case is from Opladen. HStA D: Gestapo 41817.

78. The case is from Winnekendonk. HStA D: Gestapo 11619. For an example (10 June 1941), of a similar denunciation from a woman, see HStA D: Gestapo 8662.

79. A 28-year-old worker, who denounced a family, said he 'would guess that the Poles enjoy speaking with the woman as she speaks Polish well'. He worried that the Poles were getting goods in short supply. HStA D: Gestapo 11084.

80. The case is from Kervendonk. HStA D: Gestapo 10001.

81. The case is from Duisburg-Hamborn. HStA D: Gestapo 15618.

82. The case is from Essen-Schuir. HStA D: Gestapo 42350.

83. HStA D: Gestapo 56051.

84. HStA D: Gestapo 61063.

85. HStA D: Gestapo 32416.

86. The case is from Homberg. HStA D: Gestapo 50537.

87. HStA D: Gestapo 36288.

88. HStA D: Gestapo 19117.

89. HStA D: Gestapo 66185.

90. The case is from Kettwig. HStA D: Gestapo 11730 and 32719.

91. The letter was sent to the Gestapo in Krefeld (19 Dec. 1942). See HStA D: Gestapo 65970.

92. HStA D: Gestapo 50618.

93. The case is from Burscheid. HStA D: Gestapo 15630.

94. The case is from Emmerich. HStA D: Gestapo 20687.

95. The case is from Wuppertal. HStA D: 1199.

96. See Helmut Prantl (ed.), *Die kirchliche Lage in Bayern nach den Regierungspräsidentenberichten 1933–1943*, v. *Regierungsbezirk Pfalz 1933–1940* (Mainz, 1978), xxvii–lxviii.

97. See Hans-Joachim Heinz, '"... die Reihen fest geschlossen": Organisations-geschichtliche Aspekte der pfälzischen NSDAP und ihrer Gliederungen', in Gerhard Nestler and Hannes Ziegler (eds.), *Die Pfalz unterm Hakenkreuz: Eine deutsche Provinz während der nationalsozialistischen Terrorherrschaft* (Landau, 1993), 87–117, here, 87.

98. LAS: Gestapo 4628; 574.

99. The case is from Ramstein. LAS: Gestapo 4526.

100. StA W: Gestapo 11267, from SD-Ebern (11 Feb. 1942).

101. HStA D: Gestapo 43815.

102. See e.g. LAS: Gestapo 1775; 1498.

103. The case is from Lauterecken. LAS: Gestapo 4098.

104. LAS: Gestapo 1282.

105. BA: R58/1030, 168 ff.

106. The case is from Schallodenbach. LAS: Gestapo 1764.

107. The case is from Alensborn. LAS: Gestapo 7265.

108. The case is from Oberalben. LAS: Gestapo 6800.

109. The case is from Roth. LAS: Gestapo 6091.

110. LAS: Gestapo 1617.

111. The case is from Dackenheim. LAS: Gestapo 2464.

112. LAS: Gestapo 2746.

113. LAS: Gestapo 2071.

114. The case is from Mechtersheim. LAS: Gestapo 1638.

115. LAS: Gestapo 2836 and 4491.

116. LAS: Gestapo 319.

117. LAS: Gestapo 11.

118. LAS: Gestapo 524.

119. The post-war trial of the responsible Gestapo official—he was sentenced to one year, six months—is in *Justiz und NS-Verbrechen*, xviii. 716–26.

120. The case is from Rimpar. StA W: Gestapo 7292.

121. StA W: SD 9 (22 Nov. 1940).

122. BA: R22/3369, 12, GSA beim OLG Jena (30 Mar. 1940).

123. See e.g. BA: NS 29/4, 103–4, for a German woman in Oschatz (in Saxony, Sept. 1940).

124. The case is from Enheim. StA W: Gestapo 10570.

125. StA W: Gestapo 7292.

126. StA W: SD (7 Sept. 1940).

127. StA W: SD (7 Dec. 1940).
128. BA: R58/1030, 53: Himmler an Hess (8 Mar. 1940).
129. See e.g. *Meldungen aus dem Reich*, 528 (4 Dec. 1939).
130. See e.g. Klaus Wittstadt (ed.), *Die kirchliche Lage in Bayern nach den Regierungspräsidentenberichten 1933–1943*, vi. *Regierungsbezirk Unterfranken 1933–1944* (Mainz, 1981), 163, report Dec. 1939, for acts of Christian charity, also resulting in the intervention of the Gestapo. See also Helmut Witetschek (ed.), *Die kirchliche Lage in Bayern nach den Regierungspräsidentenberichten 1933–1943*, ii. *Regierungsbezirk Ober- und Mittlefranken* (Mainz, 1967), 345–6, report for Mar. 1940.
131. BA: R 43 II, 1542(a), 170, Lammers an Schlegelberger.
132. BA: R 43 II, 1542(a), 103, Bormann an Lammers (26 Mar. 1941).
133. BA: R22/3381, 76 ff., 88 ff.; OLGP Nuremberg.
134. BA: R22/3381 (11 Aug. 1942).
135. See HStA D: Gestapo 23027, from Grünhof.
136. BA: R22/3381, 119.
137. BA: R22/3369, 9 ff.
138. BA: R22/3369, 28.
139. BA: R22/3369, 38–9 (31 Dec. 1940).
140. BA: R22/3371, 71: OLGP Kassel (5 Mar. 1942).
141. BA: R22/851, 1 ff., Himmler an Schlegelberger.
142. See also BA: R22/3369, 77 ff.; OLGP Jena (27 Feb. 1942).
143. BA: R22/821, 31–2, Himmler an Schlegelberger.
144. Thierack's remarks are reprinted in Heinz Boberach (ed.), *Richterbriefe: Dokumente zur Beeinflußung der deutschen Rechtsprechung* (Boppard, 1975), 449–54.
145. BA: R22/4062, 35a. Besprechung Thierack–Himmler (18 Sept. 1942).
146. Schreiben Thierack an Bormann (13 Oct. 1942), cited by the Generalstaatsanwalt bei dem Kammergericht Berlin, Abschlußvermerk (15 Sept. 1970) to 1 Js.1. 64 (RSHA), 66.
147. HStA D: RW36/10, 71 'Strafrechtspflege gegen Polen und Angehörige der Ostvölker'.
148. StA NadD: GL Schwaben 2/27. Even Party members were reported to be shocked about the event.
149. Heusler, *Ausländereinsatz*, 390.
150. BA: R22/4062, 28 ff., Besprechung Thierack–Himmler.
151. LAS: Gestapo 5595; the Polish worker was executed one hour after his arrival in Natzweiler.
152. HStA D: RW 36/10, RSHA an Stapo (30 June 1943), 'Verfolgung der Kriminalität unter den polnischen und sowjetrussischen Zivilarbeitern'.
153. HStA D: RW 36/d43, 95 ff. Himmler an HSSPF.
154. See *RLZ* (6 May 1941).
155. *RLZ* (5 Sept. 1940).
156. *RLZ* (9 Oct. 1940).
157. *RLZ* (3 Sept. 1940).

158. See BA: R22/4062, 28 ff.; 35a ff. Besprechungen Thierack–Himmler (18 Sept. 1942 and 13 Dec. 1942).

159. The investigation was carried out by the Generalstaatsanwalt bei dem Kammergericht in Berlin.

160. See C. U. Schminck-Gustavus, *Das Heimweh des Walerjan Wrobel: Ein Sondergerichtsverfahren 1941/43* (Berlin, 1986), 142.

161. For what follows, see StA B: M30/1049 (17 Aug. 1942).

162. StA B: M30/1049, SD (17 July 1942). For execution protocols, see BA: R58/241, 355–60.

163. LAS: Gestapo 524.

164. StA Landshut: Rep.164/10, Nr. 2331, Gend.-Posten Adlkofen (15 Mar. 1942).

165. The last case is from Eisenberg LAS: Gestapo 2313. The cases pertain to Stefan Krol, Wasyl Pawlyk, Franz Crzesiak, and Leon Dudas.

166. HStA D: Gestapo 74302.

167. BA: R22/3379, 115; GSA beim OLG Munich (10 June 1944).

168. BA: R16/162, recommended (18 July 1943), tried out in Halle-Merseburg and Würzburg (14 Oct. 1943).

169. BA: R16/162, Arbeitskreis meeting (1 Oct. 1943).

170. LAS: Gestapo 1605.

171. LAS: Gestapo 2004. The Pole was sent to Flossenbürg (8 Dec. 1941) and his death reported (26 Mar. 1942).

172. See *Justiz und NS-Verbrechen*, iv. 3–10.

173. See *Justiz und NS-Verbrechen*, xi. 174–203.

174. LAS: Gestapo 6575.

175. LAS: Gestapo 2955.

176. See e.g. StA Landshut: Rep. 164, Nr. 10, 2331, report to the gendarme in Essenach (15 May 1940) and the resultant decision of the Regensburg Gestapo (29 May).

177. LAS: Gestapo 4894.

178. See e.g. LAS: Gestapo 6064, for a businessman from Ludwigshafen (Feb. 1942) who reported a Pole in his employ; the man died in Flossenbürg in Oct. In LAS Gestapo 6535, a farmer from Rülzheim (Aug. 1943) reported a Pole who was then sent to Natzweiler and on to Buchenwald where he died in Oct.

179. *Meldungen aus dem Reich*, 3200 (report for 22 Jan. 1942).

Chapter 8

1. See *RGBL*, i. 1455–7 (26 Aug. 1939), Verordnung (17 Aug. 1939).

2. *RGBL*, i. 1609–13 (4 Sept. 1939). See also Marie-Luise Recker, *Nationalsozialistische Sozialpolitik im Zweiten Weltkrieg* (Munich, 1985), 37.

3. Norbert Frei, *Der Führerstaat: Nationalsozialistische Herrschaft 1933 bis 1945* (Munich, 1987), 134.

4. Gerhard L. Weinberg, *A World at Arms: A Global History of World War II* (Cambridge, 1994), 471.

5. *RGBL*, i. 1697 (5 Sept. 1939), 'Verordung gegen Volksschädlinge'.

6. *RGBL*, i. 2000 (4 Oct. 1939), 'Verordnung gegen jugendliche Schwerverbrecher'.

7. See BA: 50.01, 630, 'Entstehung der Rundfunkverordnung'.
8. *RGBL*, i. 1683 (1 Sept. 1939), 'Verordnung über außerordentliche Rundfunkmaßnahmen'.
9. BA: R43 II, 386, 56 Goebbels an Lammers (26 Jan. 1937).
10. See e.g. StA W: Gestapo 12650 (from 1937).
11. BA: R43 II/639, 116–17, Gürtner an Goebbels (1 Sept. 1939).
12. BA: R43 II/639, 131–3, Hess an Ministerrat für die Reichsverteidigung (3 Sept. 1939).
13. For a selection of documents, see C. F. Latour, 'Goebbels "Ausserordentliche Rundfunkmassnahmen" 1939–1942', *VfZ* (1963), 418–35.
14. *VB* (3 Sept. 1939).
15. Kate Lacey, *Feminine Frequencies: Gender, German Radio, and the Public Sphere, 1923–1945* (Ann Arbor, 1996), 102.
16. See appendix 1, in ibid. 247.
17. BA:R58/626, 135–6, SD-Hauptaußenstelle Münster an RSHA (9 Apr. 1943).
18. BA: R58/626, 2 Chef Sipo an Stapo.
19. BA: R58/626, 13 RSHA (10 Jan. 1940); and 58 (19 July 1940).
20. 'Äusländische Sender abgehört: Zuchthausstrafen verhängt—Warnung an Unbelehrbare', in *VB* (20 Dec. 1939).
21. 'Keine Milde für Rundfunkverbrecher', in *VB* (5 Oct. 1940); see also in *VB*: 'Ausländischen Sender abgehört: Zuchthaus' (22 Dec. 1939) and 'Keine Nachsicht für diese Volksfeinde' (30 June 1940).
22. 'Todesurteil für Rundfunkverbrecher', in *VB* (29 Sept. 1941). See also 'Das Hören ausländischer Sender', in *Göttinger Tageblatt* (30 Jan. 1940); 'Feindsender abgehört: Todesurteil', in *Hann Z* (7 Mar. 1945).
23. See table 5, in Gerhard Paul, *Staatlicher Terror und gesellschaftliche Verrohung: Die Gestapo in Schleswig-Holstein* (Hamburg, 1996), 125.
24. See Klaus-Michael Mallmann and Gerhard Paul, *Herrschaft und Alltag: Ein Industrierevier im Dritten Reich* (Bonn, 1991), 238–41; and their 'Gestapo—Mythos und Realität', in Bernd Florath, Armin Mitter, and Stefan Wolle (eds.), *Die Ohnmacht der Allmächtigen* (Berlin, 1992), 100–10, here 105.
25. Bernward Dörner, 'Nationalsozialistische Herrschaft und "Heimtücke": Untersuchungen zu den Auswirkungen des "Heimtücke-Gesetzes" vom 20.12.1934 am Beispiel der Stadt Krefeld', Wissenschaftliche Hausarbeit (Berlin, 1987), 90.
26. Eric A. Johnson, 'Gender, Race and the Gestapo', paper to a conference on 'Gender and Crime in Britain and Europe' (London, 3 Apr. 1995), table 3.
27. See Gisela Diewald-Kerkmann, *Politische Denunziation im NS-Regime, oder die kleine Macht der 'Volksgenossen'* (Bonn, 1995), 62–122, table 1 (63) and table 2 (91).
28. Johnson, 'Gender', also found this variation; in another sample (of 73 Krefeld Gestapo cases) he found that 47 per cent began with denunciations and a further 7 per cent from anonymous tips. Johnson excludes cases from his analysis where no source of information can be established. Of a total of 90 Gestapo cases on the 'Jewish question', 17 (or almost 20 per cent of them) were of this type.
29. BA: R22/3374, 117: OLGP (30 Nov. 1943).
30. LAS: Gestapo 2613; HStA D: Gestapo 42516 and 55490.

31. Eginhard Scharf, 'Justiz und Politische Polizei', in *Justiz im Dritten Reich während der Jahre nationalsozialistischer Herrschaft im Gebiet des heutigen Landes Rheinland-Pfalz* (forthcoming), 611–711, esp. 685.

32. Dr Werner Best, one of the key Gestapo leaders behind the scenes, claimed it was mainly reactive. See Nachlaß Werner Best, in BA: NL 23, iv. 60.

33. For useful reminders of this aspect of the Gestapo, see the contributions in Brigitte Berlekamp and Werner Röhr (eds.), *Terror, Herrschaft und Alltag im National-sozialismus* (Münster, 1995).

34. See esp. Detlev Peukert, *Die KPD im Widerstand: Verfolgung und Untergrundarbeit an Rhein und Ruhr 1933 bis 1945* (Wuppertal, 1980).

35. See HStA D: Gestapo 58426; Gestapo 38569; Gestapo 58336.

36. Bernd Stöver, *Volksgemeinschaft im Dritten Reich: Die Konsensbereitschaft der Deutschen aus der Sicht sozialistischer Exilberichte* (Düsseldorf, 1993), 327.

37. She went to the police in Essen Centre. See HStA D: Gestapo 16584 and 61077.

38. See Reinhard Mann, *Protest und Kontrolle im Dritten Reich: Nationalsozialistische Herrschaft im Alltag einer rheinischen Großstadt* (Frankfurt am Main, 1987), 295, who shows that of 213 denunciations he analysed, only 50 (24 per cent) were motivated by what he terms 'system-loyal views (political motives)'; on the other hand, more people (80 of them or 37 per cent of the 213) informed for 'private motives, resolving private conflicts'; and in 83 instances (39 per cent of these cases) there was no evidence he could discern as to why information was offered.

39. See Diewald-Kerkmann, *Denunziation*, 136, 150, who shows that only 30 per cent of the 292 letters of denunciation to the NSDAP she analysed were 'system-loyal', while 38 per cent had a 'private' or personal motive, and 4 per cent were anonymous. Presumably the rest had no discernible motive. For a revealing analysis, drawn from surviving letters to another local Party, see John Connelly, 'The Uses of *Volksgemeinschaft*: Letters to the NSDAP Kreisleitung Eisenach, 1939–1940', in Sheila Fitzpatrick and Robert Gellately (eds.), *Accusatory Practices: Denunciation in Modern European History, 1789–1989* (Chicago, 1997), 153–84.

40. The case is from Hassloch. LAS: Gestapo 5043.

41. HStA D: Gestapo 25088.

42. See Diewald-Kerkmann, *Denunziation*, 136 ff.

43. HStA D: Gestapo 53387; StA W: Gestapo 13900; LAS: Gestapo 2907.

44. HStA D: Gestapo 64749,

45. For denunciations grounded also in such claims see HStA D: Gestapo 57013; LAS: Gestapo 1341; and LAS: Gestapo 1925.

46. StA W: Gestapo 9395.

47. HStA D: Gestapo 42295; and LAS: Gestapo 2240.

48. HStA D: Gestapo 68352; 64749; 42407; 45907; LAS: Gestapo 1872.

49. BA: R58/243, 317 f., Chef Sipo an Stapo (24 Feb. 1941). See also 'Richterbrief' (1 Nov. 1944), in Heinz Boberach (ed.), *Richterbriefe: Dokumente zur Beeinflussung der deutschen Rechtsprechung 1942–1944* (Boppard am Rhein, 1975), 363–76.

50. LAS: Gestapo 2570.

51. See HStA D: Gestapo 60365. The denouncer here said she lived in conflict with her sister (who had 9 children).

52. HStA D: Gestapo 16582.
53. StA W: Gestapo 2607. The 49-year-old woman was kept in jail from 5 Dec. 1941 until early in the new year.
54. LAS: Gestapo 1517.
55. StA W: Gestapo 2260.
56. StA W: Gestapo 11250.
57. HStA D: Gestapo 6524.
58. See e.g. HStA D: Gestapo 58102; Gestapo 5574; Gestapo 38794; Gestapo 52146; StA W: Gestapo 8071.
59. LAS: Gestapo 5317.
60. LAS: Gestapo 5317.
61. LAS: Gestapo 6594.
62. HStA D: Gestapo 58889.
63. LAS: Gestapo 6223. The Gestapo concluded the two women here were 'verfeindet'.
64. HStA D: Gestapo 63380.
65. HStA D: Gestapo 9755. See also Gestapo 58353 where 'hatred' between workmates was said by the Gestapo to have caused the denunciation.
66. HStA D: Gestapo 67565.
67. HStA D: Gestapo 47042.
68. LAS: Gestapo 6939.
69. LAS: Gestapo 5249.
70. LAS: Gestapo 5745 and Gestapo 4035.
71. See e.g. the allegations of a 26-year-old woman, whose denunciation of her landlady, was almost certainly to avoid paying the rent. StA W: Gestapo 13226.
72. LAS: Gestapo 6142. The phrase was 'ließ . . . durchblicken'.
73. Eric A. Johnson, 'German Women and Nazi Terror: Their Role in the Process from Denunciation to Death', paper given at the IAHCCJ, Paris, June, 1993. He identifies about 20 per cent of the denouncers as civilian females, about 60 per cent as males, with the rest coming from officials or anonymous sources. For an opposite point of view, see Helga Schubert, *Judasfrauen* (Frankfurt am Main, 1990). For a critical analysis see Inge Marßolek, *Die Denunziantin* (Bremen, n.d. [1993]).
74. Diewald-Kerkmann, *Denunziation*, 131.
75. There were 86 male, 77 female informers, and 10 anonymous tips.
76. HStA D: Gestapo 62689. See also 31565 from Flandersbach (8 Apr. 1941), where the denouncer was later charged and tried ('wegen wissentlich falscher Anschuldigung'), and given one month in jail.
77. See Manfred Messerschmidt, 'Der "Zersetzer" und sein Denunziant: Urteile des Zentralgerichts des Heeres—Außenstelle Wien—1944', in Wolfram Wette (ed.), *Der Krieg des kleinen Mannes: Eine Militärgeschichte von unten* (Munich, 1992), 255–78.
78. Manfred Messerschmidt and Fritz Wüllner, *Die Wehrmachtjustiz im Dienste des Nationalsozialismus* (Baden-Baden, 1987), 143; Norbert Haase, 'Aus der Praxis des Reichskriegsgerichts: Neue Dokumente zur Militärgerichtsbarkeit im Zweiten Weltkrieg', *VfZ* (1991), 379–411; Bernward Dörner, ' "Der Krieg ist verloren!" "Wehrkraftzersetzung" und Denunziation in der Truppe', in Norbert

Haase and Gerhard Paul (eds.), *Die anderen Soldaten* (Frankfurt am Main, 1995), 105–22.

79. See the study of the Saarland, Gerhard Paul, *Ungehorsame Soldaten: Dissens, Verweigerung und Widerstand deutscher Soldaten (1939–1945)* (St. Ingert, 1994), 106.
80. StA W: Gestapo 11899; 12938; 14919.
81. See StA W: Gestapo 6715.
82. The phrase is 'unnötige Beanspruchung der Behörden durch die Bevölkerung'. See *Meldungen aus dem Reich*, 3968–79.
83. See Sheila Fitzpatrick, 'Suppliants and Citizens: Public Letter-Writing in Soviet Russia in the 1930s', *Slavic Review* (1996), 78–105.
84. 'Es wird dringend empfolen', in *BM* (26 Mar. 1933).
85. See Jeremy Noakes, 'Philipp Bouhler und die Kanzlei des Führers der NSDAP: Beispiel einer Sonderverwaltung im Dritten Reich', in Dieter Rebentisch and Karl Teppe (eds.), *Verwaltung contra Menschenführung im Staat Hitlers* (Göttingen, 1986), 208–36, esp. 221. From 1937 to 1940, between 229,101 and 294,568 letters per year were sent in by citizens. For the larger figure, see the evidence cited in Michael Burleigh, *Death and Deliverance: 'Euthanasia' in Germany 1900–1945* (Cambridge, 1994), 93.
86. See *BM* (6 May 1933).
87. See e.g. Fred Hahn, *Lieber Stürmer: Leserbriefe an das NS-Kampfblatt 1924 bis 1945* (Stuttgart, 1978).
88. BA/MA: RW 21-65/13 (a).
89. See Gerhard Paul, 'Kontinuität und Radikalisierung: Die Staatspolizeistelle Würzburg', in Gerhard Paul and Klaus-Michael Mallmann (eds.), *Die Gestapo: Mythos und Realität* (Darmstadt, 1995), 161–77.
90. See Burkhard Jellonnek, *Homosexuelle unter dem Hakenkreuz: Die Verfolgung von Homosexuellen im Dritten Reich* (Paderborn, 1990), 308–9 and Hans Robinsohn, *Justiz als politische Verfolgung* (Stuttgart, 1977), 78.
91. See e.g. Heydrich in Dieter Rebentisch, *Führerstaat und Verwaltung im Zweiten Weltkrieg: Verfasssungsentwicklung und Verwaltungspolitik 1939–1945* (Stuttgart, 1989), 126.
92. Harold James, 'Die Deutsche Bank und die Diktatur 1933–1945', in L. Gall, G. D. Feldman, H. James, C. L. Holtfrerich, and H. H. Büschgen, *Die Deutsche Bank 1870–1995* (Munich, 1995), 342–3.
93. Her trial is in *Justiz und NS-Verbrechen*, xiv. 442–57.
94. See Gerhard Rempel, *Hitler's Children: The Hitler Youth and the SS* (Chapel Hill, NC, 1989), 47 ff.
95. For useful information on all these developments, see George C. Browder, *Foundations of the Nazi Police State: The Formation of Sipo and SD* (Lexington, Ky., 1990).
96. See e.g. Zdenek Zofka, *Die Ausbreitung des Nationalsozialismus auf dem Lande* (Munich, 1979), 300 ff.
97. See e.g. Aryeh L. Unger, *The Totalitarian Party: Party and People in Nazi Germany and Soviet Russia* (Cambridge, 1974), 99–104.
98. See e.g. Gerhard Kratzsch, *Der Gauwirtschaftsapparat der NSDAP: Menschenführung, 'Arisierung', Wehrwirtschaft im Gau Westfalen-Süd* (Münster, 1989), 91 ff.

Chapter 9

1. See e.g. 'Durch Erhängen gesühnt', in *DAZ* (12 Dec. 1939).
2. 'Erpresser kommen ins Konzentrationslager', in *RLZ* (8 Feb. 1941).
3. See e.g. 'Ins Konzentrationslager', in *VB* (1 Apr. 1942).
4. See Marlis G. Steinert, *Hitler's War and the Germans: Public Mood and Attitude during the Second World War*, trans. T. E. J. de Witt (Athens, Ohio, 1977), 55. See also Victor Klemperer, *Ich will Zeugnis ablegen bis zum letzten: Tagebücher 1933–1945* (Berlin, 1995), i. 481–2 (3 Sept. 1939) and 555–6 (14 Oct. 1940).
5. See BA: R2/12164: Himmler an Reichsminister der Finanzen (8 Oct. 1938), for an outline of earlier personnel changes and pay for the SS substitutes.
6. The speech is recorded in Rudolf Höß, *Kommandant in Auschwitz* (Munich, 1963), 71.
7. See *IMT* xxvii. 325–6, RSHA, Amt IV (Gestapo) an Stapo etc. 'Schutzhaft-vollstreckung' (26 Oct. 1939).
8. The article is reprinted in Hans Marsalek, *Die Geschichte des Konzentrationslagers Mauthausen: Dokumentation*, 2nd edn. (Vienna, 1980), n. 13, 207.
9. Isabell Sprenger, *Groß-Rosen: Ein Konzentrationslager in Schlesien* (Cologne, 1996), 159–60.
10. See e.g. Sprenger, *Groß-Rosen*, 16–32.
11. Hermann Kaienburg, 'KZ-Haft und Wirtschaftsinteresse: Das Wirtschafts-verwaltungshauptamt und der SS-Wirtschaft', in Hermann Kaienburg (ed.), *Konzentrationslager und deutsche Wirtschaft 1939–1945* (Opladen, 1996), 29–60, here 50.
12. *IMT*, xxxviii. 362–5, Dokument 129-R, Pohl an Himmler (30 Apr. 1942). He mentioned that there were nine additional main camps, but gave no figures on the number of prisoners.
13. *IMT*, xxxviii. 365–7 Dokument 129-R: Anlage, Pohl an Lagerkommandanten ua (30 Apr. 1942).
14. Kaienburg, 'KZ-Haft und Wirtschaftsinteresse', 57.
15. See Ulrich Herbert, 'Arbeit und Vernichtung: Ökonomisches Interesse und Primat der "Weltanschauung" im Nationalsozialismus', in Dan Diner (ed.), *Ist der Nationalsozialismus Geschichte?* (Frankfurt am Main, 1987), 198–236, here 213 and 234.
16. *IMT*, xxxii. 71–5, Dokument 3257-PS, Bericht eines Rüstungs-Inspekteurs in der Ukraine an General Thomas (2 Dec. 1941).
17. See e.g. Reinhard Otto, *Wehrmacht, Gestapo und sowjetische Kriegsgefangene im deutschen Reichsgebiet 1941–42* (Munich, 1998), here 268.
18. See Albert Speer, *Infiltration: How Heinrich Himmler Schemed to Build an SS Industrial Empire*, trans. J. Neugroschel (New York, 1981), 22–4.
19. See Speer, *Infiltration*, 22–5, and also appendix 1, 307–10, for more details on the impact of those meetings.
20. See *IMT*, xxvi. 200–3, Dokument 654-PS, Besprechung Thierack–Himmler (18 Sept. 1942). The first known mention of the phrase (14 Sept. 1942) was in a conversation with Goebbels (Dokument 682-PS), cited in Hermann Kaienburg, *'Vernichtung durch Arbeit': Der Fall Neuengamme* (Bonn, 1991), note 2, 13.

Notes to pages 208–209

21. See Kaienburg, *Vernichtung*, note 3, 13.
22. See Raul Hilberg, *The Destruction of the European Jews*, rev. edn. (New York, 1985), ii. 453–4.
23. *IMT*, xxvi. 701–5, Dokument 1063(d)-PS, Chef Sipo und SD an alle Befehlshaber der Sipo ua (17 Dec. 1942).
24. See BA: NS 19/1829: Chef Sipo an Chef WVHA, 'Einsatz von Häftlingen in Rüstungsbetrieben' (31 Dec. 1942) and 'Behandlung jugendlicher Ostarbeiter' (29 Jan. 1943).
25. Rainer Fröbe, 'Der Arbeitseinsatz von KZ-Häftlingen und die Perspektive der Industrie, 1943–1945', in Ulrich Herbert (ed.), *Europa und der 'Reichseinsatz': Ausländische Zivilarbeiter, Kriegsgefangene und KZ-Häftlinge in Deutschland 1938–1945* (Essen, 1991), 351–83, here 357.
26. Martin Broszat, 'Konzentrationslager', in Hans Buchheim et al., *Anatomie des SS-Staates*, 5th edn. (Munich, 1989), ii. 111; Kaienburg, 'KZ-Haft und Wirtschafts-interesse', 57–60.
27. Republished as Martin Weinmann (ed.), *Das nationalsozialistische Lagersystem* (Frankfurt am Main, 1990).
28. Broszat, 'Konzentrationslager', 102.
29. HStA D: RW 37/17, 1 ff., contains evidence that other such camps were already operating in the Rhine-Ruhr area well before May 1941, like one at Hunswinkel that opened in Aug. 1940.
30. See Tim Mason, *Arbeiterklasse und Volksgemeinschaft: Dokumente und Materialien zur deutschen Arbeiterpolitik 1936–1939* (Opladen, 1975), 801, Dokument 138 (15 Aug. 1939), for a case from Brandenburg; and Tilla Siegel, *Leistung und Lohn in der nationalsozialistischen 'Ordnung der Arbeit'* (Opladen, 1989), 50, for a list of 20 such sentences from Saxony (30 July 1940). All these cases involved breaking the wage contract of 25 June 1938 and other such agreements worked out later.
31. The massive collection of documents by Tim Mason shows at many points how private employers called on the Gestapo to deal with labour problems. See e.g. Dokument 123, a report of the Dresden Gestapo (29 June 1939) in his *Arbeiterklasse und Volksgemeinschaft*, 722–5.
32. Stephen Salter, 'Structures of Consensus and Coercion: Worker's Morale and the Maintenance of Work Discipline, 1939–1945', in David Welch (ed.), *Nazi Propaganda: The Power and Limitations* (Beckenham, 1983), 88–116, here 104–5. Between Jan. and Aug. 1940, while the Gestapo retreated from the workplace in some parts of the country, in others such as the Ruhr, 767 workers were arrested under 'protective custody' orders.
33. See Ruth Bettina Birn, *Die Höheren SS- und Polizeiführer: Himmlers Vertreter im Reich und in den besetzten Gebieten* (Düsseldorf, 1986), 316–19.
34. Gabriele Lofti, 'Der Einsatz der Ordnungspolizei in Arbeitserziehungslagern der rheinisch-westfälischen Gestapo', in Alfons Kenkmann (ed.), *Villa ten Hompel: Sitz der Ordnungspolizei im Dritten Reich* (Münster 1996), 11–27.
35. For the most recent work, and for useful references, see Wolfgang Wipper-mann, 'Ein Denkmal im Tierpark—Zur Geschichte und Nachgeschichte des "Arbeitserziehungslagers" Berlin-Wuhlheide', in Rimco Spanjer, Diete

Oudesluijs, and Johan Meijer (eds.), *Zur Arbeit gezwungen: Zwangsarbeit in Deutschland 1940–1945* (Bremen, 1999), 57–62.

36. See e.g. Rinus van Galen, 'Erinnerungen an das AEL Großbeeren', in Spanjer et al. (eds.), *Zwangsarbeit*, 70–1. This volume contains other useful survivor testimony.

37. See HStA D: RW 37/15, 1 ff. for relevant correspondence, and 51 ff. for new camps.

38. The article appeared in *DAZ* (11 Feb.) and is cited in Wolfgang Franz Werner, '*Bleib übrig': Deutsche Arbeiter in der nationalsozialistischen Kriegswirtschaft* (Düsseldorf, 1983), 178.

39. BA: R58/1027, 142 ff.: Himmler an die Befehlshaber und Inspekteure der Sipo, usw.: Betr.: 'Errichtung von Arbeitserziehungslagern' (28 May 1941).

40. See HStA D: RW 37/17, 33, Lagebericht for Hunswinkel (12 Dec. 1940). Of the 517 'Erziehungshäftlinge' who lived in the camp up to that point, 457 of them were Germans, 39 were Poles and assorted other foreigners. For further exploration of another area, also of the most recent local literature Walter Struve, *Aufstieg und Herrschaft des Nationalsozialismus in einer industriellen Kleinstadt: Osterode am Harz 1918–1945* (Essen, 1992), 452 ff.

41. See HStA D: RW 37/d14, 2–4. Creating the camps was discussed by local officials and others from Berlin at a meeting in Münster (8 Aug. 1940). The complaint about the Poles was that at best their productivity was 30–5 per cent of German workers.

42. BA: R22/4089, Führerinformation, Nr. 32 and Nr. 38 (5 and 12 June 1942).

43. This point is made clear in *IMT*, xxvi. 695–700, Dokument 1063 (a-b)-PS, here 699–700: RSHA an die Höheren SS- und Polizeiführer ua. (26 July 1943). See also Detlef Korte, '*Erziehung*' *ins Massengrab: Die Geschichte des 'Arbeitserziehungslagers Nordmark' Kiel Russee 1944–1945* (Kiel, 1991), 32 ff.; for the AEL Farge, see Inge Marßolek and René Ott, *Bremen im 3. Reich: Anpassung, Widerstand, Verfolgung* (Bremen, 1986), 425–48.

44. See e.g. correspondence from Hunswinkel listing the various maladies prisoners suffered over the years in HStA D: RW 37/17.

45. See e.g. Marcel Ménage, 'Franzosen in Großbeeren und Wuhlheide', in Spanjer et al. (eds.), *Zwangsarbeit*, 72–5.

46. Gudrun Schwarz, *Die nationalsozialistischen Lager* (Frankfurt am Main, 1990), 83.

47. Schwarz, *Die ns. Lager*, 86–7.

48. BA: NS4/Hi./vorl. 2, 'Bericht über Aufbau und Führung der Polizeihaftlager am Westwall, sowie das SS Sonderlager Hinzert' (25 July 1940).

49. BA: NS4/Hi./vorl. 2, 'SS-Sonderlager Hinzert'.

50. See Bärbel Maul and Axel Ulrich, *Das KZ-Außenkommando 'Unter den Eichen'* (Wiesbaden, 1995), 22–8.

51. See Michael Zimmermann, *Rassenutopie und Genozid: Die nationalsozialistische 'Lösung der Zigeunerfrage'* (Hamburg, 1996), 173.

52. See Karola Fings, *Messelager Köln: Ein KZ-Außenlager im Zentrum der Stadt* (Cologne, 1996), 33–43.

53. RKPA VE: 'Entlassung von Häftlinge, die zur Beseitigung von feindlichen Blindgängern eingesetzt waren' (31 Jan. 1941).

54. Cited in Fings, *Messelager Köln*, 44–5.
55. The case is cited in ibid. 134.
56. Ibid. 43–58. For information on such commandos in the area, see Hans Müller, '*Wir haben verzeihen aber nicht vergessen . . .*' *Das KZ-Außenlager Buchenwald in Dortmund* (Dortmund, 1994), 14–15. See also Korte, *Erziehung*, 217–23.
57. Bernd Boll, '*Das wird man nie mehr los . . .*': *Ausländische Zwangsarbeiter in Offenburg 1939 bis 1945* (Pfaffenweiler, 1994), 314–15.
58. Herbert Obenaus, 'Die Außenkommandos des Konzentrationslagers Neuengamme in Hannover', in Kaienburg (ed.), *Konzentrationslager*, 212–26, here 214.
59. See Florian Freund, 'Die Entscheidung zum Einsatz von KZ-Häftlingen in der Raketenrüstung', in Kaienburg (ed.), *Konzentrationslager*, 61–74, here 66.
60. Michael J. Neufeld, *The Rocket and the Reich: Peenemünde and the Coming of the Ballistic Missile Era* (New York, 1995), 186–7.
61. See Fröbe, 'KZ-Häftlingen', 356.
62. Neufeld, *The Rocket and the Reich*, 210; for the mortality rates during construction (211); for 1945 (261–2); for his cost-benefit analysis, 267–79. He estimates (264), that about 5,000 people were killed by the 'miracle weapons' that many Germans expected to snatch victory from the jaws of defeat. A minimum of twice that number lost their lives in the production of the rockets. Additional thousands died at other camps in the production system, including those at Zement, Lehesten, Rebstock, Zeppelin, and elsewhere.
63. Also for what follows, see Debórah Dwork and Robert Jan van Pelt, *Auschwitz: 1270 to the Present* (New York, 1996), 197–235.
64. Cited in Dwork and van Pelt, *Auschwitz*, 209–11.
65. See Peter Hayes, *Industry and Ideology: IG Farben in the Nazi Era* (Cambridge, 1987), 350–61, for the death toll, 360.
66. See Dwork and van Pelt, *Auschwitz*, 235.
67. For an introduction, see Karl Heinz Roth, 'Zwangsarbeit im Siemens-Konzern (1938–1945): Fakten—Kontroversen—Probleme', in Kaienburg (ed.), *Konzentrationslager*, 149–68.
68. Birgit Weitz, 'KZ-Häftlinge', in Barbara Hopmann et al., *Zwangsarbeit bei Daimler-Benz* (Stuttgart, 1994), 345–442, here 356.
69. For the camp-by-camp story, see Weitz, 'KZ-Häftlinge', for the table, 439–40.
70. A copy of Hitler's order (11 Jan. 1942) is reprinted in Klaus-Jörg Siegfried (ed.), *Rüstungsproduktion und Zwangsarbeit im Volkswagenwerk 1939–1945: Eine Dokumentation* (Frankfurt am Main, 1986), 61–2.
71. Aktenvermerk, meetings (29 Jan. and 3 Feb. 1942) of Porsche with Oswald Pohl and others to iron out details for 'Arbeitsdorf', now reprinted in Siegfried (ed.), *Rüstungsproduktion*, 63–4.
72. Hans Mommsen and Manfred Grieger, *Das Volkswagenwerk und seine Arbeiter im Dritten Reich* (Düsseldorf, 1996) 496–515.
73. Ibid. 766–8.
74. Ibid. 772–99.
75. Ibid. 861.

76. For a detailed account of prisoners from various concentration camps sent to VW and its branches, see ibid. 862–75.

77. Harold James, 'Die Deutsche Bank und die Diktatur 1933–1945', in L. Gall, G. D. Feldman, H. James, C. L. Holtfrerich, and H. H. Büschgen, *Die Deutsche Bank 1870–1995* (Munich, 1995), 396–7.

78. See ibid. 498.

79. Apart from the number of prisoners, little information exists on the six camps mentioned by Ludwig Eiber, 'KZ-Außenlager in München', *DH* (1996), 58–80, here 61 n. 15.

80. See Zdenek Zofka, 'Allach—Sklaven für BMW: Zur Geschichte eines Außenlagers des KZ Dachau', *DH* (1986), 68–78, here 70.

81. For the remark from a survivor, see ibid. 76; for the rescue of six Jewish women, see Ulrich Herbert, 'Von Auschwitz nach Essen: Die Geschichte des KZ-Außenlagers Humboldtstraße', *DH* (1986), 13–34, here 31–2—the number of others who spent time in the Essen camp and survived is unknown.

82. For a general account, Neil Gregor, *Daimler-Benz in the Third Reich* (New Haven, 1998); and Bernard P. Bellon, *Mercedes in Peace and War: German Automobile Workers, 1903–1945* (New York, 1990).

83. See e.g. Georg Metzler, *'Geheime Kommandosache.' Raketenrüstung in Oberschwaben: Das Außenlager Saulgau und die V2 (1943–1945)* (Bergatreute, 1996), 160–4.

84. Edith Raim, 'Die Dachauer KZ-Außenkommandos Kaufering und Mühldorf. Rüstungsbauten und Zwangsarbeit im letzten Kriegsjahr 1944–45', Phil. Diss. (Munich, 1991), 268–70; Adam Puntschart, *Die Heimat ist weit: Erlebnisse im Spanischen Bürgerkrieg, im KZ, auf der Flucht*, trans. O. Burger (Weingarten, 1983), 124–6.

85. Raim, 'Kaufering und Mühldorf', 269.

86. See Hans Simon-Pelanda, 'Im Herzen der Stadt: Das Außenlager Colosseum in Regensburg', *DH* (1996), 159–68.

87. See Ernst Schmidt, *Lichter in der Finsternis: Widerstand und Verfolgung in Essen 1933–1945* (Essen, 1988), ii. 188–9.

88. For an account of this camp, based in part on interviews, see Schmidt, *Lichter*, 187–98.

89. See Hayes, *Industry*, 346–7.

90. Weitz, 'KZ-Häftlinge', 436.

91. Schmidt, *Lichter*, 217.

92. Herbert, 'Humboldtstraße', 13–34. Their story is also told in Schmidt, *Lichter*, 198–220.

93. For example, in Oct. 1941, some 10,776 people were arrested in (newly expanded) Germany, but excluding the eastern territories. In that month most arrests were for discipline problems at work (7,729), followed by those charged with opposition (1,518) and for Communist activities (544); a total of 162 Jews were taken into custody. See Broszat, 'Konzentrationslager', 95.

94. The statistics are from Broszat, 'Konzentrationslager', 132. For a series of detailed studies of women, see Claus Füllberg-Stolberg et al. (eds.), *Frauen in Konzentrationslagern: Bergen-Belsen und Ravensbrück* (Bremen, 1994).

95. See Wolfgang Sofsky, *Die Ordnung des Terrors: Das Konzentrationslager* (Frankfurt am Main, 1993), 52; Gerhard Werle, *Justiz-Strafrecht und polizeiliche Verbrechensbekämpfung im Dritten Reich* (Berlin, 1989), 533.

96. The figures (some of them conservative estimates) for the totals of those who died of mistreatment or were killed include the following: 31,591 (of a total of 206,206 prisoners) at Dachau; 56,545 (of 238,979) for Buchenwald; 28,374 (of 96,217) in Flossenbürg; 55,000 (of a total of 106,000) at Neuengamme; 20,000 of the total of 60,000 at Mittelbau; 40,000 of the 120,000 prisoners who spent time in Groß-Rosen; 50,000 of the 125,000 who experienced the horrors of Bergen-Belsen, a camp that only operated from 1943 to 1945, and so on. A complete list is provided in Sofsky, *Ordnung des Terrors*, 57. There are variations in the figures of some of the camps because of incomplete or destroyed data. For analysis of Auschwitz, see Franciszek Piper, 'The Number of Victims', in Yisrael Gutman and Michael Berenbaum (eds.), *Anatomy of the Auschwitz Death Camp* (Bloomington, Ind., 1994), 61–76. He concludes (72) that as many as 1.5 million were killed at Auschwitz, of whom 1.35 million were Jews. The minimum total of all Jews killed has been set recently at 5.29 million by Wolfgang Benz, 'Die Dimension des Völkermords', in Wolfgang Benz (ed.), *Dimension des Völkermords: Die Zahl der jüdischen Opfer des Nationalsozialismus* (Munich, 1991), 1–20, here 17.

97. Eiber, 'München', 58.

98. For an overview, see Stefanie Endlich and Wolf Kaiser, 'KZ-Häftlinge in der Reichshauptstadt: Außenlager in Berlin', *DH* (1996), 230–54, here 230.

99. Ibid. 246.

100. See Ruth Zantow, *'Das sind doch Verbrecher . . .': Konzentrationslager Sachsenhausen Außenlager Lichterfelde* (Berlin, 1990), as cited in Endlich and Kaiser, 'Berlin', 248 n. 46. See also the memoir about the camp at Vaihingen of Alexander Donat, *The Holocaust Kingdom* (New York, 1963), 252; and Stefan Romey, *Ein KZ in Wandsbek: Zwangsarbeit im Hamburger Drägerwerk* (Hamburg, 1994), 49.

101. See e.g. a case of an SS guard, who brought a 17-year-old Russian worker in 1944 to be tended by a medical doctor for an ugly wound he received for disobedience. The SS guard told the doctor not to take too much trouble, as the Russian was to be hanged in the morning. The guard then said: 'Until then I'm taking him to my room and play my little games with him', that is, he made no secret that he was going to torture this person for the fun of it. ('Vorher nehme ich ihn mit auf mein Zimmer und spiele mein kleines Spielchen mit ihm.') When asked what the unfortunate had done, the guard said he had stepped out of line and begged for bread. See Elmer Luchterhand, 'Das KZ in der Kleinstadt: Erinnerungen einer Gemeinde an den unsystematischen Völkermord', in Detlev Peukert and Jürgen Reulecke (eds.), *Die Reihen fast geschlossen: Beiträge zur Geschichte des Alltags unterm Nationalsozialismus* (Wuppertal, 1981), 435–54, here 453. For another example, see Struve, *Aufstieg und Herrschaft*, 459.

102. Hermann Kaienburg, ' "... sie nächtelang nicht ruhig schlafen ließ." Das KZ Neuengamme und seine Nachbarn', *DH* (1996), 34–57, here 49.

103. Cited in the oral history account of Luchterhand, 'KZ in der Kleinstadt', 441.

104. Cited in Kaienburg, 'Nachbarn', 39–40.

105. See Gerhard Hoch, *Hauptort der Verbannung: Das KZ-Aussenkommando Kaltenkirchen* (Bad Segeberg, 1979), 22.
106. Luchterhand, 'KZ in der Kleinstadt', 442.
107. Wendelgard von Staden, *Nacht über dem Tal: Eine Jugend in Deutschland*, 2nd edn. (Munich, 1983), 51.
108. Ernst Heimes, *Ich habe immer nur den Zaun gesehen: Suche nach dem KZ Außenlager Cochem*, 2nd edn. (Koblenz, 1993), 55–6, 68.
109. Heimes, *Cochem*, 86, 111. The total number of prisoners to work at these camps is not clear. The chronicle of Treis parish for 1944 notes that 1,500 prisoners were at work on the tunnel in the summer.
110. See Ludwig Eiber, 'Außenlager des KZ Neuengamme auf den Hamburger Werften', *1999: Zeitschrift für Sozialgeschichte des 20. und 21. Jahrhunderts*, 2 (1995), 57–73, here 64–5.
111. Heimes, *Cochem*, 117, 125–7.
112. See Eiber, 'Hamburger Werften', 61, who cites a note from Rudolf Blohm.
113. Mommsen and Grieger, *Volkswagenwerk*, 859–61.
114. 'Organization Todt' or OT, which was dedicated to various war-related construction and defence projects. By the end of 1944, OT inside Germany had a strength of 1.4 million, mostly foreigners, including an unknown number of prisoners of various kinds and some Jews. The records show few prisoners from concentration camps worked in OT, but might have been employed on the same site. The figures are as follows: of the total of 1.4 million, only 336,000 were Germans. There were more than a million foreigners—including 165,000 prisoners of war and another 140,000 made up of assorted prisoners (*sonstige Häftlinge, Strafgefangene*) and Jews. OT had worked also on many projects outside Germany at one time, but withdrew when the tide of war changed. See Franz W. Seidler, *Die Organisation Todt: Bauen für Staat und Wehrmacht 1938–1945* (Koblenz, 1987), 145–7.
115. Herbert, 'Arbeit und Vernichtung', 231.
116. Dietrich Eichholtz, *Geschichte der deutschen Kriegswirtschaft 1939–1945* (Berlin, 1996), iii. 238.
117. For an overview, see Randolph L. Braham, 'Hungarian Jews', in Gutman and Berenbaum (eds.), *Auschwitz*, 456–68.
118. Eichholtz, *Kriegswirtschaft*, iii. 241.
119. Fröbe, 'KZ-Häftlingen', 361–2.
120. Birgit Weitz, 'Der Einsatz von KZ-Häftlingen und jüdischen Zwangsarbeitern bei Daimler-Benz AG (1941–1945): Ein Überblick', in Kaienburg (ed.), *Konzentrationslager*, 169–95, here 190.
121. Donat, *The Holocaust Kingdom*, 260.
122. Ibid. 279. Exemplary studies of Hessental and six other subcamps in Württemberg can be found in Herwart Vorländer (ed.), *Nationalsozialistische Konzentrationslager im Dienst der totalen Kriegsführung* (Stuttgart, 1978).

Chapter 10

1. Hartmut Mehringer, *Widerstand und Emigration: Das NS-Regime und seine Gegner* (Munich, 1997), 233.

2. See Peter Hoffmann, *German Resistance to Hitler* (Cambridge, Mass., 1988), 51; and Joachim Fest, *Plotting Hitler's Death: The Story of the German Resistance*, trans. B. Little (New York, 1996), 335.

3. Berlin reports for Nov. 1944–Mar. 1945 are reprinted in Volker R. Berghahn, 'Meinungsforschung im "Dritten Reich": Die Mundpropaganda-Aktion der Wehrmacht im letzten Kriegshalbjahr', *Militärgeschichtliches Mitteilungen*, 1 (1967), 83–119.

4. Bericht an das Reichsministerium f. Volksaufklärung u. Propaganda (19 Mar. 1945), in *Meldungen aus dem Reich*, 6732.

5. Hamburg reports for Mar.–Apr. 1945 are reprinted in Volker R. Berghahn, 'Hamburg im Frühjahr 1945: Stimmungsberichte aus den letzten Wochen des zweiten Weltkriegs', *Hamburgische Geschichts- und Heimatstblätter* (Dec. 1969), 194–211, here 196 (report for 8–14 Mar.).

6. Bericht an das Reichsministerium f. Volksaufklärung u. Propaganda (28 Mar. 1945), in *Meldungen aus dem Reich*, 6732–4.

7. The visitor was Croatian deputy leader (*stellvertretender Staatschef*) Marshal Sladko Kvaternik. The most complete notes are reprinted in Andreas Hillgruber (ed.), *Staatsmänner und Diplomaten bei Hitler* (Frankfurt am Main, 1967), i. 609–15; see more cryptic notes on the Jews, 614–15.

8. Christian Streit, 'The German Army and the Policies of Genocide', in Gerhard Hirschfeld (ed.), *The Politics of Genocide: Jews and Soviet Prisoners of War in Nazi Germany* (London, 1986), 1–14, here 7. On the general theme, see esp. Omer Bartov, *Hitler's Army: Soldiers, Nazis, and War in the Third Reich* (New York, 1991).

9. For example, in Nov. 1942 the total in the country declined from 713,325 to 636,219, which meant that a minimum of 77,106 had died that month alone. The extent of the mass murder of the Soviets fluctuated over the next months, and the death rates for 1944 can no longer be reconstructed because at that stage no statistics were kept. See Christian Streit, *Keine Kameraden: Die Wehrmacht und die sowjetischen Kriegsgefangenen 1941–1945* (Stuttgart, 1978), 244, 247.

10. See *IMT*, xxvi. 245–9, Dokument 669-PS Verordnung Chef des OKW, 'Verfolgung von Straftaten gegen das Reich oder die Besatzungsmacht in den besetzten Gebieten' (12 Dec. 1941).

11. See *IMT*, xxvi. 242–5, Dokument 668-PS, Chef Sipo an Chef OKW, 'Verfolgung von Straftaten gegen das Reich oder die Besatzungsmacht in den besetzten Gebieten' (24 June 1942).

12. See e.g. (on the basis of incomplete data) that up to the end of Apr. 1944, the Kiel court tried 2,014 cases, involving 6,639 accused, of whom 1,793 were sentenced to death. For additional details on this and the other courts, see 'Nacht und Nebel', in *Enzyklopädie des Holocaust*, ii. 984–6.

13. See *Meldungen aus dem Reich* (4 Feb. 1943), 4750–1.

14. The notion that the arrest sweep was long planned is in Peter Hoffmann, *The History of the German Resistance*, trans. R. Barry (Cambridge, 1977), 516–17.

15. For the Bremen file, see BA: R58/775, esp. 19–20.

16. Berlin reports are reprinted in Berghahn, 'Meinungsforschung', here the report (31 Mar.), 114.

17. Berghahn, 'Hamburg' (5 Apr. 1945), 206.
18. The case is from Olpe. See *Justiz und NS-Verbrechen*, i. 662−77.
19. She lived in Wetzlar, he lived in Berlin. HStA D: Gestapo 41892.
20. The case is from Satrup (Schleswig-Holstein). See *Justiz und NS-Verbrechen*, ii. 396−407.
21. The case is from Wuppertal. See HStA D: Gestapo 358.
22. The case is from a town near Ludwigshafen. LAS: Gestapo 4272.
23. She was from Kaiserslautern. See LAS: Gestapo 5710.
24. StA W: Gestapo 4598.
25. The case is from Goslar. See *Justiz und NS-Verbrechen*, vi. 630−49. For a similar case from Lower Franconia, see StA W: Gestapo 2222.
26. The case is from Gmünden. See *Justiz und NS-Verbrechen*, xii. 62−89.
27. See *Justiz und NS-Verbrechen*, ii. 419−21.
28. The case began in Altenschönbach near Gerolshofen. See StA W: Gestapo 122, 124, 125, 13761.
29. *RGBL*, i. 30 (20 Feb. 1945), 'Verordnung über die Errichtung von Standgerichten vom 15. Februar 1945'.
30. A copy of the guidelines (Merkblatt) is reprinted in *Justiz und NS-Verbrechen*, x. 208−9.
31. The name 'Volkssturm', or 'storm of the people', harked back to the Napoleonic era and the idea that the German nation as a whole rose up and lashed out at the invader. In 1944/5, however, it was easier to sign up such an army than it was to train and supply it with arms. The Volkssturm has been rightly called a military paper tiger, but it was effective in disciplining the people in the face of the advancing armies. See Franz W. Siedler, *'Deutscher Volkssturm': Das letzte Aufgebot 1944−45* (Munich, 1989), esp. 372−3.
32. The case is from Ingelheim. See *Justiz und NS-Verbrechen*, xv. 798−839.
33. *Justiz und NS-Verbrechen*, vii. 764−810.
34. For a masterful account of the American conquest, that combines extensive examination of what happened behind the German lines, see Klaus-Dietmar Henke, *Die amerikanische Besetzung Deutschlands* (Munich, 1995), 343−77.
35. Gerhard L. Weinberg, *A World in Arms: A Global History of World War II* (Cambridge, 1994), 812−13.
36. Henke, *Besetzung*, 400.
37. See Bernd-A. Rusinek, *Gesellschaft in der Katastrophe: Terror, Illegalität, Widerstand Köln 1944−45* (Essen, 1989), 446.
38. See the report in *RLZ* (7 Mar. 1945).
39. *RLZ* (24 Mar. 1945).
40. See Volker Zimmermann, *In Schutt und Asche: Das Ende des Zweiten Weltkriegs in Düsseldorf* (Düsseldorf, 1995), 76−93; and *Justiz und NS-Verbrechen*, iv. 192−257.
41. For a detailed account, see Heinrich Dunkase, 'Würzburg, 16. März 1945 21.25 Uhr −21.42 Uhr: Hintergründe, Verlauf und Folgen des Luftangriffs der No. 5 Bomber Group', in *Mainfränkisches Jahrbuch* (1980), 1−31. For an overview, see Max Domarus, *Der Untergang des alten Würzburgs im Luftkrieg gegen die deutschen Großstädte* (Würzburg, 1985).

42. See Albert Speer, *Inside the Third Reich*, trans. R. Winston and C. Winston (London, 1970), 599–600.
43. See Alois Stadtmüller, *Aschaffenburg im Zweiten Weltkrieg*, 3rd edn. (Aschaffenburg, 1987), 247–51.
44. For what follows, including the lengthy post-war investigations, see StA W: Polizeidirektion Würzburg, 348 'Standgericht Helm'. For other deaths, see 289.
45. See StA W: Polizeidirektion Würzburg, 348 for later examples.
46. See Alois Stadtmüller, *Maingebiet und Spessart im Zweiten Weltkrieg*, 3rd edn. (Aschaffenburg, 1987), 551–9.
47. The case is from Aub. See *Justiz und NS-Verbrechen*, v. 570–600.
48. The case is from Bad Windsheim. See *Justiz und NS-Verbrechen*, iii. 172–86.
49. The post-war trial is in *Justiz und NS-Verbrechen*, xv. 372–97.
50. See *Justiz und NS-Verbrechen*, i. 114–29; 644–59.
51. Victor Klemperer, *Ich will Zeugnis ablegen bis zum letzten: Tagebücher 1933–1945* (Berlin, 1995), ii. 751–5 (22 to 25 Apr. 1945).
52. Ibid., ii. 759.
53. He lived in Götting, a small town near Rosenheim (south-east of Munich). For details, see *Justiz und NS-Verbrechen*, ii. 284–317.
54. See ibid., iii. 762–94.
55. The case is from Altötting. See ibid., iii. 680–92; for another, even more senseless killing in this town on 1 May, see x. 545–63.
56. See e.g. the father of one suspect shot by local Nazi functionaries in Berg am Laim, in ibid., ii. 752–66.
57. Details are in ibid., xiii. 772–90.
58. For events in Munich, see ibid., ii. 48–74.
59. The post-war trials are in ibid., iii. 66–128, but there were many follow-up trials as well, most also reprinted in this collection. The story is retold in detail in Klaus Tenfelde, 'Proletarische Provinz: Radikalisierung und Widerstand in Penzberg/ Oberbayern 1900–1945', in *Bayern in der NS-Zeit*, iv. 1–382.
60. NA: T 178/Roll 9 (16 Mar. 1945).
61. See *Justiz und NS-Verbrechen*, iv. 619–30.
62. See ibid., v. 268–84.
63. See Adolf Diamant, *Gestapo Frankfurt am Main* (Frankfurt am Main, 1988), 295.
64. For a detailed account and the relevant literature, see Gerhard Schreiber, *Die italienischen Militärinternierten im deutschen Machtbereich 1943–1945: Verraten, Verachtet, Vergessen* (Munich, 1990), 553–9. See also Daniel Blatman, 'Die Todesmärsche—Entscheidungsträger, Mörder und Opfer', in Ulrich Herbert, Karin Orth, and Christoph Dieckmann (eds.), *Die nationalsozialistischen Konzentrationslager: Entwicklung und Struktur* (Göttingen, 1998), ii. 1064–92, here 1085.
65. Zimmer, *Schutt und Asche*, 64.
66. Hans-Dieter Schmid, *Gestapo-Leipzig: Politische Abteilung des Polizeipräsidiums und Staatspolizeistelle Leipzig 1933–1945* (Beucha, 1997), 61–4. There are only hints of the identities of the victims, but most were East Europeans, though none apparently were Jewish.
67. See Adolf Diamant, *Gestapo Leipzig* (Frankfurt am Main, 1990), 203–5.

68. The executions were in a forest near Riedlingen. See *Justiz und NS-Verbrechen*, ii. 520–35; and iv. 34–44.

69. See ibid., ix. 131–6.

70. See ibid., i. 751–81.

71. Ibid., ix. 210–33.

72. See Luigi Cajani, 'Die italienischen Militärinternierten im nationalsozialistischen Deutschland', in Ulrich Herbert (ed.), *Europa und der 'Reichseinsatz': Ausländische Zivilarbeiter, Kriegsgefangene und KZ-Häftlinge in Deutschland 1938–1945* (Essen, 1991), 295–316.

73. For the geographical distribution of the prisoners, see table 19 in Schreiber, *Militärinternierten*, 312.

74. See ibid. 549.

75. See e.g. Unterlüß (also in the Hanover-Osnabrück area), and Treuenbrietzen (south-west of Berlin), in ibid. 549–52.

76. See *Justiz und NS-Verbrechen*, ix. 118–28. The full story is reconstructed in Schreiber, *Militärinternierten*, 563–72.

77. The Jewish victim was a young man of 17, who was executed long after the tins of peas he tried to steal had been returned. See *Justiz und NS-Verbrechen*, ix. 105–15.

78. For additional details on events in Hildesheim, see ibid., x. 775–93.

79. For details, see ibid., ix. 390–556.

80. Ibid., xii. 420–94.

81. Ibid., xv. 662–91.

82. Ulrich Herbert, *Fremdarbeiter: Politik und Praxis des 'Ausländer-Einsatzes' in der Kriegswirtschaft des Dritten Reiches* (Berlin, 1985), 337.

83. For the story of the execution of 9 Soviet males on 3 Sept. 1944, see Gerhard Wysocki, *Die Geheime Staatspolizei im Land Braunschweig: Polizeirecht und Polizeipraxis im Nationalsozialismus* (Frankfurt am Main, 1997), 182–6.

84. On 27 Mar. 1945 Hitler put Kammler in charge of air armaments, and on 3 Apr. gave him the even more grand-sounding, but utterly unrealistic task of rebuilding the air force. See Albert Speer, *Infiltration: How Heinrich Himmler Schemed to Build an SS Industrial Empire*, trans. J. Neugroschel (New York, 1981), 235–44.

85. See *Justiz und NS-Verbrechen*, xvii. 280–310.

86. Speer, *Infiltration*, 238.

87. See *IMT*, xli. 420–5, Speer-23 (15 Mar. 1945); also Speer, *Inside the Third Reich*, 583–4.

88. Cited in Speer, *Inside the Third Reich*, 588.

89. See *IMT*, xli. 430–1, Speer-25.

90. See the account of Göring's recently discovered interrogation from May 1945, in *Globe and Mail* (21 Aug. 1997).

91. See Speer, *Inside the Third Reich*, 579.

92. See Felix Kersten, *The Kersten Memoirs 1940–1945*, trans. C. Fitzgibbon and J. Oliver (London, 1956), 264–70; and Speer, *Inside the Third Reich*, 610–11.

93. For a succinct account, see Hoffmann, *German Resistance*, 529–30.

94. See ibid. 530–3; and Eberhard Bethge, *Dietrich Bonhoeffer: Theologian, Christian, Contemporary*, trans. E. Mosbacher, P. Ross, B. Ross, F. Clarke, and W. Glen-Doepel (London, 1970), 796–836.

95. Yitzhak Arad, *Belzec, Sobibor, Treblinka: The Operation Reinhard Death Camps* (Bloomington, Ind., 1987), 370.
96. Isabell Sprenger, *Groß-Rosen: Ein Konzentrationslager in Schlesien* (Cologne, 1996), 292–3.
97. See *IMT*, xxxvii. 486–7, Dokument 053-L, for a copy of the order.
98. The document is reprinted in Johannes Tuchel (ed.), *Die Inspektion der Konzentrationslager 1938–1945* (Berlin, 1994), 212–13.
99. Rudolf Höß, *Kommandant in Auschwitz* (Munich, 1963), 145.
100. Hilberg, *Destruction*, iii. 980.
101. Reichsverteidigungskommissar f.d. Reichsverteidigungsbezirk Oberschlesien (Kattowitz) 21 Dec. 1944 an s. Verteiler, betr. Räumung, reprinted in Andrzej Strzelecki, 'Evacuation, Liquidation and Liberation of the Camp', in Danuta Czech et al., *Auschwitz: Nazi Death Camp* (Oswiecim, 1996), 269–89, here following 272.
102. Wieslaw Kielar, *Anus Mundi: 1500 Days in Auschwitz-Birkenau*, trans. S. Flatauer (New York, 1980), 260–300.
103. For details, see Danuta Czech, *Auschwitz Chronicle 1939–1945* (New York, 1990), 781–805.
104. See Strzelecki, 'Evacuation', 269–89.
105. See the testimonies in Strzelecki, 'Evacuation', 275–6.
106. For Auschwitz-Birkenau, see *Justiz und NS-Verbrechen*, xv, esp. 320–30.
107. For detailed testimony, see ibid., xvi. 62–76.
108. Martin Gilbert, *Atlas of the Holocaust* (Toronto, 1993), 216–17.
109. See the classic account of camp survivor Primo Levi, *Survival in Auschwitz: The Nazi Assault on Humanity*, trans. S. Woolf (London, 1959).
110. Joachim Neander, *Das Konzentrationslager 'Mittelbau' in der Endphase der nationalsozialistischen Diktatur* (Bremen, Uni. Dissertation, 1996), 335–6.
111. The American report (which is citied as US Microfilm M 1079, Roll 11, 270–3) is partly reprinted in Neander, *Mittelbau*, 474–7.
112. Ibid., 466–73, here esp. 473. See also Daniel Jonah Goldhagen, *Hitler's Willing Executioners: Ordinary Germans and the Holocaust* (New York, 1996), 367–8, who offers Gardelegen as an example to support his thesis that the death marches showed 'the fidelity of the Germans to their genocidal enterprise'.
113. Janina Grabowska, 'K. L. Stutthof: Ein historischer Abriß', in Hermann Kuhn (ed.), *Stutthof: Ein Konzentrationslager vor den Toren Danzigs* (Bremen, 1995), 8–94, here 73–81.
114. Ibid. 83.
115. Ibid. 90.
116. Höss, *Kommandant in Auschwitz*, 147.
117. For an overview, see 'Todesmärche', in *Enzyklopädie des Holocaust*, iii. 1412–16.
118. Yehuda Bauer, 'The Death-Marches, January–May, 1945', in Michael R. Marrus (ed.), *The Nazi Holocaust: Historical Articles on the Destruction of the European Jews* (Westport, Conn., 1989), ix. 491–511, here 499.
119. For a detailed account of Himmler's negotiations to 'sell' the Jews, see Yehuda Bauer, *Jews for Sale: Nazi-Jewish Negotiations, 1933–1945* (New Haven, 1994), 239–51.

120. Kersten, *Memoirs*, 277.

121. See *Justiz und NS-Verbrechen*, xix. 74–94. For this and other death marches from the Hanover area, see Herbert Obenaus, 'Die Räumung der hannoverschen Konzentrationslager im April 1945', in Rainer Fröbe et al, *Konzentrationslager in Hannover: KZ-Arbeit und Rüstungsindustrie in der Spätphase des Zweiten Weltkriegs* (Hildesheim, 1985), Teil 2, 493–544.

122. See *Justiz und NS-Verbrechen*, xviii. 764–77.

123. Bernhard Schlink's recent best-selling novel focuses on a female guard who watched as a church burnt to the ground after it was hit by a bomb. Jews were held in the church overnight, and in spite of their screams as the fire engulfed it, guards would not open the doors. See his *The Reader*, trans. C. B. Janeway (New York, 1998), here 127–8.

124. See *Justiz und NS-Verbrechen*, xviii. 768.

125. The Himmler order is mentioned, without an exact date, in Goldhagen, *Hitler's Willing Executioners*, 356.

126. If murder was the ultimate aim, as suggested by Daniel Goldhagen, why bother to drag out the process over many days and nearly 200 miles? Goldhagen, *Hitler's Willing Executioners*, 345–54.

127. See *The Buchenwald Report*, trans. and ed. David A. Hackett (Boulder, Colo., 1995), 327.

128. For this story and general account, see *Enzyklopädie des Holocaust*, iii. 1412–16, here 1415.

129. See Blatman, 'Todesmärsche', 1082.

130. Sprenger, *Groß-Rosen*, 299.

131. Höß, *Kommandant in Auschwitz*, 145.

132. For a recent collection of 732 survivors' accounts, see Martin Gilbert, *The Boys: Triumph over Adversity* (Toronto, 1996), esp. 213–35. See also Eugène Aroneanu (ed.), *Inside the Concentration Camps: Eyewitness Accounts of Life in Hitler's Death Camps*, trans. T. Whiessen (Westport, Conn., 1996), esp. 137–42.

133. See *The Buchenwald Report*, 328–31.

134. Peter Black, *Ernst Kaltenbrunner: Ideological Soldier of the Third Reich* (Princeton, 1984), 250.

135. See esp. Stanislav Zamecnik, 'Kein Häftling darf lebend in die Hände des Feindes fallen: Zur Existenz des Himmler-Befehls vom 14.–18. April 1945', *DH* (1985), 219–31, here 219.

136. Edgar Kupfer-Koberwitz, *Dachauer Tagebücher: Die Aufzeichnungen des Häftlings 24814* (Munich, 1997), 429 (entry 20 Apr. 1945).

137. Ibid. 425 (12 Apr. 1945).

138. Ibid. 435 (26 Apr. 1945); 439 (27 Apr. 1945).

139. Ibid. 433 (24 Apr. 1945); 435–6 (26 Apr. 1945).

140. See Gordon J. Horwitz, *In the Shadow of Death: Living Outside the Gates of Mauthausen* (New York, 1990), 144–63.

141. See *Justiz und NS-Verbrechen*, xviii. 406–25.

142. See Monika Herzog and Bernhard Strebel, 'Das Frauenkonzentrationslager Ravensbrück', in Claus Füllberg-Stolberg et al. (eds.), *Frauen im Konzentrationslager: Bergen-Belsen, Ravensbrück* (Bremen, 1994), 13–26, 22–3.

143. Germaine Tillion, *Ravensbrück*, trans. G. Satterwhite (Garden City, NJ, 1975), 93.

144. See Sigrid Jacobeit (ed.), *'Ich grüße Euch als freier Mensch': Quellenedition zur Befreiung des Frauen-Konzentrationslagers Ravensbrück im April 1945* (Berlin, 1995), 13.

145. Tillion, *Ravensbrück*, 98.

146. See Bauer, *Jews for Sale*, 246.

147. Jacobeit (ed.), *Quellenedition*, 19–20.

148. Broszat, 'Konzentrationslager', 132.

149. The estimate is by Polish historian Zygmunt Zonik, as cited in Blatman, 'Todesmärsche', 1067.

150. Bauer, 'Death Marches', 492–3.

151. Shmuel Krakowski, 'The Death Marches in the Period of the Evacuation of the Camps', in Marrus (ed.), *Nazi Holocaust*, ix. 476–90, here 483.

152. Blatman, 'Todesmärsche', 1087.

153. *Meldungen aus dem Reich* (28 July 1944), 6684.

154. Marlis G. Steinert, *Hitler's War and the Germans: Public Mood and Attitude during the Second World War*, trans. T. E. J. de Witt (Athens, Ohio, 1977), esp. 293.

155. Berghahn, 'Meinungsforschung', 117, 118.

156. Ibid. 117–19 (reports for 19–22 Mar. 1945), here 119.

157. Many of these letters have since found their way to the Wiener Library. See the collection No. 3040. Such letters are also studied in Steinert, *Hitler's War*, 145.

158. Berghahn, 'Meinungsforschung', 118.

159. Ibid. 116.

160. See also Jill Stephenson, ' "Resistance" to "No Surrender": Popular Disobedience in Württemberg in 1945', in Francis R. Nicosia and Lawrence D. Stokes, *Germans Against Nazism: Nonconformity, Opposition and Resistance in the Third Reich* (New York, 1990), 351–67.

161. BA: RSHA St.3/915, 1 ff., SD an RSHA (7 Apr. 1945). See also Christoph U. Schminck-Gustavus (ed.), *Hungern für Hitler: Erinnerungen polnischer Zwangsarbeiter im Deutschen Reich 1940–1945* (Reinbek bei Hamburg, 1984), 120 ff.

162. See Norman M. Naimark, *The Russians in Germany: A History of the Soviet Zone of Occupation, 1945–1949* (Cambridge, Mass., 1995), 72.

163. Naimark, *Russians in Germany*, 72.

164. Nuremberg Dokument 3369-PS, reprinted in Domarus (ed.), *Hitler Reden*, iv. 2236–9, here, 2237.

Conclusion

1. The Kapp Putsch of 1920 was stopped by a general strike. The classic account of the wait-and-see attitude of the SPD in 1933 at the local level is William Sheridan Allen, *The Nazi Seizure of Power: The Experience of a Single German Town 1922–1945*, rev. edn. (New York, 1984).

2. See Bernd Stöver, *Volksgemeinschaft im Dritten Reich: Die Konsensbereitschaft der Deutschen aus der Sicht sozialistischer Exilberichte* (Düsseldorf, 1993), 171–2.

3. Dietrich Orlow, *The History of the Nazi Party: 1933–1945* (Pittsburgh, 1973), 24.

4. Harmut Mehringer, *Widerstand und Emigration: Das NS-Regime und seine Gegner* (Munich, 1997), 233.

5. Martin Broszat, *Hitler and the Collapse of Weimar Germany*, trans. V. R. Berghahn (New York, 1987), 149.

6. For studies that shift the focus away from the machinations of leaders, to investigate new forms of citizen involvement, see e.g. Robert Gellately, *The Gestapo and German Society: Enforcing Racial Policy, 1933–1945* (Oxford, 1990); and Sheila Fitzpatrick and Robert Gellately (eds.), *Accusatory Practices: Denunciation in Modern European History, 1789–1989* (Chicago, 1997). A similar and related point is made about the army, most recently by Omer Bartov, 'Soldiers, Nazis and War in the Third Reich', in Christian Leitz (ed.), *The Third Reich: The Essential Readings* (Oxford, 1999), 133–50. For specific studies that have followed this approach, see esp. Klaus-Michael Mallmann and Gerhard Paul, *Herrschaft und Alltag: Ein Industrierevier im Dritten Reich* (Berlin, 1991); Gerhard Paul and Klaus-Michael Mallmann (eds.), *Die Gestapo: Mythos und Realität* (Darmstadt, 1995); Gisela Diewald-Kerkmann, *Politische Denunziation im NS-Regime oder die kleine Macht der 'Volksgenossen'* (Bonn, 1995); and Katrin Dördelmann, *Die Macht der Worte: Denunziationen im nationalsozialistischen Köln* (Cologne, 1997).

7. See Fritz Stern, *Dreams and Delusions: The Drama of German History* (New York, 1987), 147–91.

8. The pioneering study is Christopher R. Browning, *Ordinary Men: Reserve Police Battalion 101 and the Final Solution in Poland* (New York, 1992).

9. For comments and copy of the law, ready to be signed on 9 Aug. 1944, but prevented from promulgation because of the war, see *Nazism Docs.*, iv. 134–5.

10. See Norbert Frei, *Der Führerstaat: Nationalsozialistische Herrschaft 1933 bis 1945* (Munich, 1987), 148.

11. Lothar Kettenacker, 'Sozialpsychologische Aspekte der Führer-Herrschaft', in Gerhard Hirschfeld and Lothar Kettenacker (eds.), *Der 'Führerstaat': Mythos und Realität. Studien zur Struktur und Politik des Dritten Reiches* (Stuttgart, 1981), 98–132, here 131.

12. Victor Klemperer, *Ich will Zeugnis ablegen bis zum letzten: Tagebücher 1933–1945* (Berlin, 1995), i. 323 (24 Nov. 1936).

13. See the remarkable testimony of 'Nelly' in the famous novel based on childhood experiences in Christa Wolf, *Patterns of Childhood*, trans. U. Molinaro and H. Rappolt (New York, 1980), 248–9. She writes of how when she picked potatoes with Ukranian women in the fall of 1943, she was not allowed to put them in the same basket with theirs.

14. For exploration of some of these issues, see John Connelly, 'The Uses of *Volksgemeinschaft*: Letters to the NSDAP Kreisleitung Eisenach, 1939–1940', in Fitzpatrick and Gellately (eds.), *Accusatory Practices*, 153–84.

15. See Robert Gellately, 'Denunciations and Nazi Germany: New Insights and Methodological Problems', *Historical Social Research* (1997), 228–39.

16. Barrington Moore, Jr, *Injustice: The Social Bases of Obedience and Revolt* (White Plains, NY, 1978), 482–3.

17. For discussion of the problems of resistance in such a society, see Robert Gellately, 'Surveillance and Disobedience: Aspects of the Political Policing of Nazi Germany', in Leitz (ed.), *The Third Reich*, 183–203.

18. See the thoughtful remarks in Michael Geyer, 'Resistance as Ongoing Project: Visions of Order, Obligations to Strangers, and Struggles for Civil Society 1933–1990', in Michael Geyer and John W. Boyer (eds.), *Resistance Against the Third Reich 1933–1990* (Chicago, 1994), 325–50.

19. Richard Overy, *Russia's War: A History of the Soviet War Effort, 1941–1945* (New York, 1998), 288.

20. Ulrich Herbert, 'Vernichtungspolitik: Neue Antworten und Fragen zur Geschichte des "Holocaust"', in Ulrich Herbert (ed.), *Nationalsozialistische Vernichtungspolitik: Neue Forschungen und Kontroversen* (Frankfurt am Main, 1998), 9–66, here 64.

21. See Jurgen Herbst, *Requiem for a German Past: A Boyhood among the Nazis* (Madison, 1999), 180.

A NOTE ON SOURCES

Federal Archives

Primary 'Reich' materials are located in the new federal archives (Bundesarchiv) in Berlin (cited as BA). I used most of these sources either when they were in Koblenz, or in the (East) German Democratic Republic's archives at Potsdam. Since reunification, all 'Reich' collections have been moved to Berlin. There are also useful sources in the Bundesarchiv-Militärarchiv-Freiburg (BA-MA). Captured German materials have been opened for study in the Osoby Archive in Moscow, and I used copies in the United States Holocaust Research Institute Archive at the United States Holocaust Memorial Museum (USHMM) in Washington. The files provided additional information, but they do not fill the considerable gaps that remain in the documentation. Invaluable materials are located in Munich's Institut für Zeitgeschichte (IfZ), including primary documents. The IfZ has copies of Gestapo decrees in the Allgemeine-Erlaß-Sammlung (AES), and similar ones of the Kripo, the Vorbeugende Verbrechensbekämpfung, Erlaßsammlung (RKPA VE).

Regional and Local Archives

Sources for the study of the social dimensions of consent and coercion include original Gestapo case files. These kinds of files were destroyed nearly everywhere in Germany with the notable exception of the 70,000 in Düsseldorf (the Nordrhein-Westfälisches Hauptstaatsarchiv-Düsseldorf—cited as HStA D); approximately 19,000 in Würzburg (the Staatsarchiv-Würzburg, cited as StA W); and about 12,000 in Speyer (Landesarchiv-Speyer, cited as LAS). The files pertain respectively to the Gestapo's jurisdictions of the Rhine-Ruhr, Lower Franconia, and the Palatinate. More Gestapo files, pertaining mainly to Polish foreign workers, have recently turned up in the materials of what was the Berlin Document Center, and copies of them are now located at the National Archives in Washington, DC.

In addition to the Gestapo files and the documentary collections in Düsseldorf, Würzburg, and Speyer, I have drawn on other local archives, such as those located in Bamberg, Berlin, Koblenz, Landshut, Ludwigsburg, Marburg, Munich, Neuburg an der Donau, and Stuttgart. The quantity and quality of the documentation varies enormously. I was also given access to the materials collected for the post-war trials of leading RSHA officials by the Generalstaatsanwaltschaft bei dem Kammergericht Berlin.

Published Documentary Collections

For this study the most important published documents were the trials of the major war criminals. I used the German edition: *Der Prozess gegen die Hauptkriegsverbrecher vor dem internationalen Militärgerichtshof*, 42 vols. (Nuremberg, 1949), cited as *IMT*. An invaluable source, especially for the latter part of the war, when the Gestapo and all other authorities gradually ceased keeping detailed records, is *Justiz und NS-Verbrechen: Sammlung deutscher Strafurteile wegen nationalsozialistischer Tötungsverbrechen 1945– 1966*, currently 22 vols., with more to come (Amsterdam, 1968–), cited as *Justiz und NS-Verbrechen*. The latter trials, mainly in western Germany, generated an enormous amount of information, which must be studied critically.

For the war years, an invaluable collection is Heinz Boberach (ed.), *Meldungen aus dem Reich: Die geheimen Lageberichte des Sicherheitsdienstes der SS 1938–1945*, 17 vols. (Herrsching, 1984). (These are cited as *Meldungen aus dem Reich*.) These surveys of public opinion have some curious silences, including what people knew about such developments as the 'Final Solution' and the death camps. For what Nazi leaders and especially Hitler, revealed in public, an essential source is Max Domarus (ed.), *Hitler Reden und Proklamationen 1932–1945*, 4 vols. (Leonberg, 1973). Also important are the diaries of Joseph Goebbels, now enlarged with new material from Moscow, and critically edited by Elke Fröhlich and her colleagues at Munich's IfZ. See Elke Fröhlich et al. (eds.), *Die Tagebücher von Joseph Goebbels*, 24 vols. (Munich, 1993–)

A most useful documentary collection for English readers, and a good place to begin any study of the Third Reich, is J. Noakes and G. Pridham (eds.), *Nazism 1919–1945: A Documentary Reader*, 3 vols. (Exeter, 1983–8). Especially important is a fourth volume by Jeremy Noakes (ed.), *The Home Front in World War II* (Exeter, 1998). These have been cited as *Nazism Docs*. An important 'alternative' account of the Nazi years, based on countless thousands of underground reports penned by the Socialists, is published in the collection *Deutschland-Berichte der Sozialdemokratischen Partei Deutschlands (Sopade) 1934–1940*, 7 vols. (Nördlingen, 1980). These were cited as *Sopade*. The reports contain long excerpts of local accounts of what was happening on the ground, but reflect the hopes of the men and women in the underground, that the German people would not be deceived for long and would cast out the Nazi oppressors. The most important diary to appear recently is Victor Klemperer, *Ich will Zeugnis ablegen bis zum letzten: Tagebücher 1933–1945*, 2 vols. (Berlin, 1995). These diaries are now being translated into English.

Newspapers

The key newspaper for this study was the main paper in the Nazi era, namely the *Völkischer Beobachter* (the *VB*). It began as the Nazi Party's own paper, but in the Third Reich became the main German newspaper and semi-official publication from which many other newspapers took their cue. Also important is the newspaper of the SS, the *Schwarze Korps* (*DSK*). I studied how German newspapers gradually were Nazified by focusing on one major newspaper, the *Berliner Morgenpost* (*BM*). The regional angle was covered by looking at the significant *Rheinische Landeszeitung* (*RLZ*). There are many newspaper collections in Germany, the most useful one I found was put together by the German Labour Front (DAF). I used those materials when they were still in the Deutsches Zentralarchiv in Potsdam (62 DAF), but they have since been moved to Berlin.

Secondary Sources, Reference Works

Precise references to the extensive published secondary sources used can be found in the endnotes. The best guide in English to the vast literature is still Ian Kershaw, *The Nazi Dictatorship*, 3rd edn. (London, 1993). Very useful on many points is Israel Gutman (ed.), with Eberhard Jäckel, Peter Longerich, and Julius H. Schoeps, *Enzyklopädie des Holocaust*, 4 vols. (Munich, 1995). An English edition is also available. I began my own exploration of Nazi Germany in *The Gestapo and German Society: Enforcing Racial Policy 1933–1945* (Oxford, 1990), in which I also detail the creation of the Gestapo and discuss its local operations. There have been many studies of the Nazi police since then. Particularly useful is Gerhard Paul and Klaus-Michael Mallmann (eds.), *Die Gestapo: Mythos und Realität* (Darmstadt, 1995). A new local study by Eric A. Johnson, *Nazi Terror: The Gestapo, Jews, and Ordinary Germans* (New York, 1999) was published too late to be included in the body of this book. His quantitative analysis confirms what I and several others have written since 1989, but the book says little about the terror inflicted on foreign workers, and little about the massive brutalities in the last year of the war. The role of the Kripo in Nazi Germany has been generally neglected, but a well-balanced study is Patrick Wagner, *Volksgemeinschaft ohne Verbrecher: Konzeptionen und Praxis der Kriminalpolizei in der Zeit der Weimarer Republik und des Nationalsozialismus* (Hamburg, 1996).

For Hitler's role, we now have the first part of the new Hitler biography by Ian Kershaw, *Hitler 1889–1936: Hubris* (London, 1998). The best source for reliable information on virtually any aspect of the Holocaust, including the Nazi terror inside 'old Germany' and in the expanded reaches of the Third Reich, is Raul Hilberg, *The Destruction of the European Jews*, 3 vols., revised edn. (New York, 1985). Peter Longerich, *Politik der Vernichtung: Eine Gesamtdarstellung der nationalsozialistischen Judenverfolgung* (Munich, 1998) is a fine one-volume analysis of the persecution of the Jews from 1933 to the Holocaust years. Daniel Jonah Goldhagen, *Hitler's Willing Executioners: Ordinary Germans and the Holocaust* (New York, 1996), is a more controversial account. It was a popular success, but assailed by many historians. He spends much of the book dealing with the death squads and death marches in the eastern occupied areas of the Third Reich. For the original account of ordinary policemen in the Holocaust, see Christopher R. Browning, *Ordinary Men: Reserve Police Battalion 101 and the Final Solution in Poland* (New York, 1992).

The best guide to date on the origins and growth of the concentration camp system can be found in Hans Buchheim, Martin Broszat, Hans-Adolf Jacobson, and Helmut Krausnick, *Anatomie des SS-Staates*, 2 vols., 5th edn. (Munich, 1989), of which there is an abbreviated English translation. Valuable studies are also contained in Ulrich Herbert, Karin Orth, and Christoph Dieckmann (eds.), *Die nationalsozialistischen Konzentrationslager: Entwicklung und Struktur*, 2 vols. (Göttingen, 1998). An essential source is Johannes Tuchel, *Konzentrationslager: Organisationsgeschichte und Funktion der 'Inspektion der Konzentrationslager' 1934–1938* (Boppard, 1991), and also useful is Klaus Drobisch and Günther Wieland, *System der NS-Konzentrationslager 1933–1939* (Berlin, 1993). For the justice system, a mine of information is the massive study by Lothar Gruchmann, *Justiz im Dritten Reich 1933–1940: Anpassung und Unterwerfung in der Ära Gürtner* (Munich, 1988). A remarkable study of 'justice' in action, which in fact deals with more than capital punishment, is Richard J. Evans, *Rituals of Retribution: Capital Punishment in Germany 1600–1987* (Oxford, 1996). A suggestive analysis of the 'People's Court' with emphasis on its public or media side is Edmund Lauf, *Der Volksgerichtshof und sein Beobachter: Bedingungen und Funktionen der Gerichtsberichterstattung im Nationalsozialismus* (Opladen, 1994).

There is now a considerable literature on what happened to specific social groups in Nazi Germany. For a collection that deals with the whole range of those who were pilloried, see Robert Gellately and Nathan Stoltzfus (eds.), *Social Outsiders in Nazi Germany* (Princeton, forthcoming). For a good general interpretation, see Detlev Peukert, *Volksgenossen und Gemeinschaftsfremde: Anpassung, Ausmerze und Aufbegehren unter dem Nationalsozialismus* (Cologne, 1982), of which there is an English translation. On women, an instructive oral history is Alison Owings, *Frauen: German Women Recall the Third Reich* (New Brunswick, NJ, 1993). For the organizational side, see Jill Stephenson, *The Nazi Organization of Women* (London, 1981); and for a controversial account, see Claudia Koonz, *Mothers in the Fatherland: Women, the Family and Nazi Politics* (New York, 1987). There are a number of relevant essays in Dalia Ofer and Lenore J. Weitzman (eds.), *Women in the Holocaust* (New Haven, 1998). On the persecution of the Jews (apart from the works already mentioned), see Marion A. Kaplan, *Between Dignity and Despair: Jewish Life in Nazi Germany* (New York, 1998) and Saul Friedländer, *Nazi Germany and the Jews*, i. *The Years of Persecution, 1933–1939* (New York, 1997). One of the long-neglected social groups is now covered by Beate Meyer, *'Jüdische Mischlinge': Rassenpolitik und Verfolgungserfahrung* (Hamburg, 1999).

There are a number of excellent studies of sterilization and 'euthanasia', and for one that traces developments from the turn of the century to the murder sites, and deals also with the attempts to 'sell' the programme, see Michael Burleigh, *Death and Deliverance: 'Euthanasia' in Germany 1900–1945* (Cambridge, 1994). Also important is Henry Friedlander, *The Origins of Nazi Genocide: From Euthanasia to the Final Solution* (Chapel Hill, NC, 1995). For the policies aimed at foreign workers, the study to consult is Ulrich Herbert, *Fremdarbeiter: Politik und Praxis des 'Ausländer-Einsatzes' in der Kriegswirtschaft des Dritten Reiches* (Berlin, 1985); an English translation is now available. On Sinti and Roma, the best study now is Michael Zimmermann, *Rassenutopie und Genozid: Die nationalsozialistische 'Lösung der Zigeunerfrage'* (Hamburg, 1996). An account of the 'asocials' is provided by Wolfgang Ayaß, *'Asoziale' im Nationalsozialismus* (Stuttgart, 1995). On the persecution of homosexuals, the best work to date is Burkhard Jellonnek, *Homosexuelle unter dem Hakenkreuz: Die Verfolgung von Homosexuellen im Dritten Reich* (Paderborn, 1990).

For the economy, see R. J. Overy, *War and Economy in the Third Reich* (Oxford, 1994). I recommend his study of the war in Russia, a topic beyond the scope of this book: see his *Russia's War* (Harmondsworth, 1998). On more general themes, see Omer Bartov, *Murder in our Midst: The Holocaust, Industrial Killing, and Representation* (New York, 1996). For studies of propaganda, see studies by David Welch, including especially the volume he edited, *Nazi Propaganda, the Power and the Limitations* (London, 1983). On public opinion, there is David Bankier, *The Germans and the Final Solution: Public Opinion under Nazism* (Oxford, 1992) and Marlis G. Steinert, *Hitler's War and the Germans*, trans. T. E. J. de Witt (Athens, Ohio, 1977).

A key source on the home front, is Jeremy Noakes's book already mentioned. Omer Bartov, *Hitler's Army: Soldiers, Nazis, and War in the Third Reich* (Oxford, 1991), provides a challenging account of how the German Army was transformed in the Third Reich. For the resistance, a convenient overview with citations of the relevant literature is Hartmut Mehringer, *Widerstand und Emigration: Das NS-Regime und seine Gegner* (Munich, 1997). A detailed account is Peter Hoffmann, *The History of the German Resistance 1933–1945*, trans. R. Barry (Cambridge, Mass., 1977). The essays in Michael Geyer and John W. Boyer (eds.), *Resistance Against the Third Reich 1933–1990* (Chicago, 1994), can be supplemented with those in the equally good David Clay Large (ed.), *Contending with Hitler: Varieties of German Resistance in the Third Reich* (Cambridge, 1991). The end of the regime in western Germany is covered in detail by Klaus-Dietmar Henke, *Die amerikanische Besetzung Deutschlands* (Munich, 1995), and what happened in the east is described dramatically by Norman M. Naimark, *The Russians in Germany: A History of the Soviet Zone of Occupation, 1945–1949* (Cambridge, Mass., 1995).

ABBREVIATIONS

AEL	Arbeitserziehungslager, Educative Work Camps of the Gestapo
AES	Allgemeine-Erlaß-Sammlung, the important collection of Gestapo documents on protective custody (for details, see the note on sources)
BA	Bundesarchiv, Berlin
BA/MA	Bundesarchiv-Militärarchiv, Freiburg
Bay HStA	Bayerisches Hauptstaatsarchiv, Munich
BBZ	*Berliner Börsen Zeitung*
BH	*Bayerischer Heimgarten*
BM	*Berliner Morgenpost*
BPP	Bayerische Politische Polizei (Bavarian Political Police, after 1936 part of the Gestapo)
BT	*Berliner Tageblatt*
DA	*Der Angriff*
DAF	Deutsche Arbeitsfront (German Labour Front)
DAZ	*Deutsche Allgemeine Zeitung*
DD	*Der Deutsche*
DH	*Dachauer Hefte*
Die Tagebücher von Joseph Goebbels	The Goebbels diaries, edited by Elke Fröhlich (see the note on sources)
DN	*Düsseldorfer Nachrichten*
DNVP	Deutschnationale Volkspartei (German National People's Party)
Domarus (ed.), *Hitler Reden*	Hitler's speeches and proclamations, edited by Max Domarus (for details, see the note on sources)
DR	*Deutsches Recht*
DRA	*Deutscher Reichsanzeiger*
DSK	*Das Schwarze Korps*
DT	*Der Tag*
DZ	*Deutsche Zeitung*
FZ	*Frankfurter Zeitung*
GE	*Gruenewald Echo*
Gendarmerie	Rural and small town uniformed police

Gestapa	Geheimes Staatspolizeiamt (Central offices of the Gestapo in Berlin)
Gestapo	Geheime Staatspolizei (Secret State Police, also called Staatspolizei or Stapo)
GL	Gauleitung (Regional headquarters of the Nazi Party)
GSA	Geheimes Staatsarchiv Preußischer Kulturbesitz, Berlin-Dahlem
GSR	*German Studies Review*
HannZ	*Hannoversche Zeitung*
HF	*Hamburger Fremdenblatt*
HN	*Hamburger Nachrichten*
HSSPF	Höhere SS- und Polizeiführer (Higher SS and Police Leader)
HStA D	Hauptstaatsarchiv Düsseldorf
IAHCCJ	International Association for the History of Crime and Criminal Justice
IfZ	Institut für Zeitgeschichte
IMT	*Trials of the Major War Criminals before the International Military Tribunal*, 42 vols. (German edition)
JMH	*Journal of Modern History*
Justiz und NS-Verbrechen	Justice and National Socialist Crimes, post-war trial proceedings (for details, see the note on sources)
KPD	Communist Party of Germany
Kripo	Kriminalpolizei (Criminal Police)
KZ	Konzentrationslager (Concentration Camp), sometimes also KL
LAS	Landesarchiv Speyer
LRA	Landratsamt
Meldungen aus dem Reich	Regular SD Reports from the Reich (for details, see the note on sources)
MNN	*Münchner Neueste Nachrichten*
NA	National Archives, Washington, DC
Nazism Docs.	Collection of documents edited by J. Noakes and G. Pridham (for references, see the note on sources)
NSDAP	National Socialist German Workers' Party (Nazi Party)
NZ	*National Zeitung*
Orpo	Ordnungspolizei (Order Police, or the regular uniformed police, which also included the Schutzpolizei—in towns and cities—and the Gendarmerie in the countryside)
PZ	*Pommersche Zeitung*

RFSS	Reichsführer-SS, Himmler's title as head of the SS
RGBL	*Reichsgesetzblatt*
RJM	Reichsjustizministerium (Ministry of Justice)
RKPA	Reichskriminalpolizeiamt (Berlin headquarters of the Criminal Police)
RKPA VE	Reichskriminalpolizeiamt, Vorbeugende Verbrechensbekämpfung, Erlaßsammlung, an important collection of Kripo documents on preventive arrests
RLZ	*Rheinische Landeszeitung*
RMI	Reichsministerium des Innern (Ministry of the Interior)
RSHA	Reichssicherheitshauptamt (Reich Security Headquarters, founded in 1939 to head the Gestapo, Kripo, and so on)
SA	Sturmabteilung (the Nazi 'Brownshirts')
Schupo	Uniformed city police, see also Orpo
SD	Sicherheitsdienst (Security Service of the Party)
Sipo	Sicherheitspolizei (founded in 1936 as the umbrella organization for the Gestapo and Kripo)
Sopade	Sozialdemokratische Partei Deutschlands: Executive of the Exiled SPD with headquarters in Prague (1933–8), Paris (1938–40), London (1940). For their records, see the note on sources
SPD	Social Democratic Party of Germany
SS	Schutzstaffel, Himmler's Black-shirts
StA	Staatsarchiv (state archives)
StA B	Staatsarchiv Bamberg
StA L	Staatsarchiv Ludwigsburg
StA NadD	Staatsarchiv Neuburg a. d. Donau
Stapo	short form for the Staatspolizei (Secret State police) or Gestapo
StA W	Staatsarchiv Würzburg
USHMM	United States Holocaust Memorial Museum, archives
VfZ	*Vierteljahrshefte für Zeitgeschichte*
VB	*Völkischer Beobachter* (main Nazi newspaper)
VZ	*Vossische Zeitung*

INDEX

Index

Index